J. C. Boone

10-14-64 (54-13284)

THE CLASSICAL HERITAGE
AND ITS BENEFICIARIES

THE
CLASSICAL HERITAGE
AND ITS BENEFICIARIES

BY

R. R. BOLGAR

CAMBRIDGE
AT THE UNIVERSITY PRESS
1963

PUBLISHED BY
THE SYNDICS OF THE CAMBRIDGE UNIVERSITY PRESS
Bentley House, 200 Euston Road, London, N.W. 1
American Branch: 32 East 57th Street, New York 22, N.Y.
West African Office: P.O. Box 33, Ibadan, Nigeria

First Edition 1954
Reprinted 1958
1963

First printed in Great Britain at the University Press, Cambridge
Reprinted by offset-lithography by John Dickens & Co. Ltd, Northampton

CONTENTS

CONTENTS

PREFACE

A book of this kind necessarily owes a great deal to the labours of others. I have done my best to indicate in the notes the sources to which I was indebted; but it remains a matter of regret that considerations of space prevent my describing in detail the interest and the admiration which so many of them inspired in me and would certainly inspire in others. I can only hope that the reader who finds himself wearied by the deficiencies of the present narrative will turn to them for satisfaction and enlightenment.

My personal thanks are due in the first place to the Provost and Fellows of King's College, Cambridge, and to the Syndics of the Cambridge University Press, whose generosity made my research easy and the publication of my finished work possible. I should like also to take this opportunity to express my gratitude to Professor R. A. B. Mynors of Balliol College and Mr D. H. Beves and Mr L. P. Wilkinson of King's College for their many valuable suggestions; to Professor J. B. Trend and Mr N. Glendinning for help with the list of Spanish translations in Appendix II; to Mr T. E. Dryer of Dorking Grammar School whose reading of my original draft brought a number of omissions and weaknesses to light; to Mrs Dorothy Chaplin whose care and skill reduced my awkward manuscript to neat typescript; and last but not least to my wife whose help was often demanded and whose patience never failed.

R. R. B.

CAMBRIDGE 1953

INTRODUCTION

Fifty years ago the classical education still enjoyed an exceptional measure of public esteem. That training in taste and accuracy of thought, that lucid if somewhat factitious understanding of human institutions and human nature, which a close acquaintance with the Greek and Roman authors could give, were considered to fit the young supremely for the conduct of life. Those who had undergone the rigours of the traditional Humanist discipline in school and university were accepted by the majority of their contemporaries as an authoritative élite. The classical student of Edwardian times had reason to feel that he, if any man, possessed the magic key which would unlock the kingdoms of this world.

His modern counterpart is less fortunately placed. Not only have a number of other disciplines—historical, literary, scientific and technological—taken their place alongside the classical curriculum as its manifest equals in merit, but the struggles that occurred while they made good their claims have left a sad memorial in the shape of a prejudice against Greek and Latin, which philistinism has been quick to use. For if most people are ready to sing the praises of education when their opinion is formally required, the enthusiasm they so easily express too often represents only one aspect of their inner feelings. A manual worker will sometimes educate his children at a great personal sacrifice—and then mock them for their book-learning. An academic worker will sometimes devote his life to scholarly pursuits and still nourish a barely concealed contempt for all subjects but his own. These are obvious examples of the ambiguity which in some degree characterises the attitude of the majority of human beings towards the acquisition and the advancement of knowledge. A consciously fostered esteem, the product of our liberal traditions, coexists with a latent hostility. Let some particular subject fall out of popular favour, and this hostility, which has its roots in ignorance, finds an immediate release. Its forces are canalised for a frontal attack on the limited sector which is no longer protected by the conventions of public approval.

During recent years it has been the fate of classical studies to suffer from one of these attacks. The original onslaught was launched by the partisans of the subjects whose development had been hindered by the educational monopoly of the Humanities. But the hostility which was aroused rapidly developed an impetus of its own, and like the metaphorical snowball managed to reach surprising proportions, with the result that since the beginning of this century classical scholars have been more and more occupied with the defence of their specialism. Some have taken the line of explaining how the ancient literatures affected their personal experience and have sought to put into words the imponderable values of a spiritual experience. Others have tried to turn to advantage the discoveries and techniques of social science, putting their faith in such concepts as the transfer of training or in the analysis of planned questionnaires. Experiments have been made with new methods of teaching. New aspects of the classical subject-matter have been emphasised in order to subserve modern interests; and the discipline which during the nineteenth century nurtured so many scholars, administrators and statesmen now trembles on the edge of the melting pot.

This book has been written in the hope that it may contribute, within the narrow boundaries of its specialised approach, to the work of revaluation which all these changes have rendered necessary. The classical heritage has played a distinctive part in the shaping of European culture. The long unbroken tale of its quickening influence stretches from Columban to E. M. Forster and Jean Anouilh. In every age, from the first to the last, the categories of European thought and the common institutions of European life have all borne to some degree the imprint of antiquity. In every age, we can find writers and men of action who benefited from their contacts with the Graeco-Roman past. We may expect therefore the history of the last fifteen hundred years to shed some light on the educational potentialities of the Greek and Latin literatures. It is not unreasonable to assume in view of Europe's long affiliation to the ancient world that an historical enquiry may prove as efficacious as psychological experiment or personal reminiscence to illuminate the manifold problems that face the classics teachers of today.

In the pages that follow we shall consider the fortunes of the Graeco-Roman heritage from the beginning of the Dark Ages to the close of the sixteenth century. In some ways admittedly the history of classical studies is a single whole. As Sir John Sandys pointed out, the achievements of scholarship accumulated gradually, each generation building on the foundations left by its predecessor. The instruments of learning multiplied, its techniques improved, in a steady progression from Alcuin to Wilamowitz. But these factors which made for an over-all unity were not in the last analysis the most important at work; and when we consider the detailed movement of events it becomes obvious that the complete story of the classical heritage fails to form an intelligible unit of study. Instead, it divides into two distinct historical parts.

At first, the modern world was vastly inferior to the ancient. Its aesthetic achievements, its political organisation, its mastery of the material environment all fell short of the levels which Greece and Rome had previously attained. In these circumstances, the study of the classics was bound to play a unique role. It became the focus of progress, the principal instrument of the effort the modern world was making to recapture the glories of the past by learning all that the past had to teach. The emphasis was on imitation.

By the end of the Renaissance, however, the steady efforts of centuries had reaped their reward. The new culture was no longer noticeably inferior to its Graeco-Roman model, and it began to develop of its own accord along hitherto unexplored paths. Progress was no longer through imitation but through discovery. Thus, the nature of the influence exercised by the classics changed. Its scope was narrowed. Its effects made themselves felt in a different context. Now, men turned to the ancient literatures not so much to learn a necessary lesson as to enjoy a salutary contrast. The republican virtues of Rome, the good life of the Athenian heyday became myths which served as a rallying point for spiritual discontents, providing glimpses of a culture that was now pictured as essentially different from the pattern of contemporary Europe.

The student curiosity and imitative enthusiasm of earlier ages stand at such a vast remove from the Hellenism of a Goethe, a Matthew Arnold or a Moréas, that the two periods in the history of the classical heritage plainly require separate treatment. One must choose between them, and in making the choice, one must be guided by the fact that the earlier is undoubtedly the more important. For in those remote centuries before the end of the Renaissance, religion and philosophy, law and medicine, language and art, politics and daily behaviour were all equally involved in the educational process. It is true that we can trace some striking differences and discontinuities between one country and another, between one generation and the next. It is true that until the Renaissance, the Western peoples knew only small and isolated portions of the Greek legacy, while the Eastern Empire remained, after the sixth century, completely unfamiliar with anything written in Latin. It is true also that in the West, the amount of Latin literature available for study varied from one generation to the next, as did men's attitudes to antiquity, so that from a certain point of view, the eleventh and twelfth centuries were ages of progress, while the glorious thirteenth was an age of reaction. But these were incidental differences, and they do not affect the main pattern of a gradual but increasing assimilation.

Naturally, the assimilation was never complete. No European of the seventeenth century was more of an antique Roman than he was an Englishman, a Frenchman, a German or a Dane. Even at the height of the Renaissance, the non-classical elements in European culture vastly outnumbered the classical, the more so since anything taken from antiquity was soon altered out of all recognition by the mere process of development in an alien setting, as the opinions of the Roman jurists acquired feudal interpretations, and the Virgilian hexameter ended up as a frame for an elaborate rhyme pattern.

> Hora novissima, tempora pessima sunt, vigilemus.
> Ecce minaciter imminet arbiter ille supremus.

Nevertheless, the debt was there and its steady growth through the period is equally undeniable.

Without the written heritage of Greece and Rome our world would have worn a different face. How that heritage was studied and eventually assimilated ranks therefore as one of the major problems of European history and by that token alone might well take precedence of any alternative field of enquiry.

The story of how our civilisation drew sustenance from its great predecessor is of evident interest; and when one considers its importance, one is bound to be surprised at the disproportionately small number of works which have attempted to give an account of it. 'There is, as far as I know, no single book which gives even in outline a survey of the whole field of Greek and Roman influence on modern literature', writes Professor Highet.* His own recent volume on the classical tradition has done much to fill this gap and provides an invaluable pendant to Sandys' well-known *History of Classical Scholarship*. But neither literature, nor scholarship, is sufficiently wide in its scope to allow a treatment which would cover the whole field; and the same criticism applies with even greater force to the more specialised subjects, such as mythology and literary criticism, on which we find comprehensive surveys.* The influence of the classical heritage includes and transcends them all.

4

The magisterial publications of the Warburg Institute, the excellent American series that bears the title *Our Debt to Greece and Rome* and such books as J. A. K. Thomson's *The Classical Background to English Literature* stand as evidence of a vast amount of detailed work. If this scholarship had been devoted to a reasonably circumscribed topic, it would have been sufficient by now to create an impressive structure of theory and fact. Bestowed upon the fortunes of the classical heritage, it has done little more than explore a number of preliminary problems. The absence of general surveys is to be explained by the fact that the attention of scholars has been focused rather on points of detail, a great many of which still require elucidation. The incidental difficulties of the field have proved unexpectedly numerous.

An example will make the truth of this statement more obvious. A subject which immediately suggests itself for enquiry in connection with the classical heritage is the teaching of the ancient languages and the ancient literatures in the schools. The early training of the educated class must have gone far to determine how much Latin and Greek was known by each generation and precisely which portions of the classical legacy were singled out for attention. Here then is a compact and apparently simple problem which can serve the student as a starting point.

But on closer consideration the appearance of compactness and simplicity vanishes. The effect produced by a school course upon the mind depends on three factors. (It is essential to note that we are concerned here with the general effect, the one which is produced to a greater or less degree in the large majority of cases. The effect on any particular individual is always incalculable.) The three factors in question are the books used, the method of approach and the values to which the teacher and pupil subscribe. The importance of the first is self-evident and requires no proof. One's field of study is limited to the information that is accessible. But within those bounds, learning is a subjective process. The student who reads a book will remember only a small portion of its contents. He will select; and how will his selection be guided? It will be determined partly by the learning techniques he has been taught and partly by his and his teacher's specific interests. If he has been trained to look for a certain type of fact, he will find that almost to the exclusion of everything else. If he has some concern which occupies his mind, his memory will feed that preoccupation and neglect what is irrelevant to it.

Let us now consider what evidence is available on these three points, taking first of all the one which on the face of it appears the simplest namely the question of which books were used. This is information which the historian of a contemporary educational system discovers from printed curricula and bibliographies. But for the period we are investigating, these easy sources are the exception, not the rule. There exist admittedly certain lists of books prescribed for study at the universities from the thirteenth century onwards; and in a very few cases, teachers such as the thirteenth-century John of Garland, or the fifteenth-century Battista Guarino, have left us systematic accounts of the reading necessary for a classics course. But here already we are faced with a difficulty. For it is not always easy to tell whether the writer is describing what was actually read or what he thought ought to be read. We have no means of knowing on which side we are of that monstrous gap which yawns between theory and practice. Moreover, there are whole centuries for which we lack even these fragmentary aids, where the only data provided by contemporary writings are those casual and tantalising hints that poets or men of letters occasionally let drop on the subject of their education. Such hints being necessarily vague and incomplete are quite as likely to confuse as to enlighten, and even where they exist in sufficient numbers, as in the poems of Ausonius, the attempt to weld them into a coherent picture is bound to end in failure.

The evidence drawn from contemporary documents must be supplemented by bibliographical material, from library catalogues and from what can be discovered about the history of manuscripts and later of printed books. In other words, the historian has to depend not incidentally (as is often the case), but primarily, on the results obtained in a field which ranks among the most difficult that scholars have ever tackled. The libraries of Europe and America can tell us a great deal about which classical works were available and which were the most popular at different periods. The publications of scholars like Traube, Manitius, Ruf, Gottlieb, Lehmann, James and Savage on the medieval catalogues and the researches of Müntz, Fabre, Legrand, Omont and Sabbadini on Renaissance manuscripts, to say nothing of divers excellent bibliographies of printed works, have done much to provide a factual outline within which surmise can move with some safety. Much also has been discovered during the past fifty years about medieval translations from the Greek. The projected edition of the medieval Aristotle promises to be of inestimable value. But much remains to be done. This field of learning appears remote, and its importance is appreciated for the most part only by scholars. It does not attract public subsidies. The work involved demands, if it is to be successful, long training and practice and is moreover so arduous, because of the ceaseless attention which must be paid to detail, that experts qualified to carry it out are few and far between. Add to this the circumstance that of recent years such experts have been hampered by restrictions on travel as well as by lack of funds for publication, and it becomes sufficiently evident why progress has been and must continue to be grievously slow. Yet on this progress the completeness of the picture we form of the classical education must ultimately depend.

Leaving aside certain other difficulties concerning the books which provided the material of instruction, let us now turn to the problem of method. Here the most obvious source of information is the educational treatise; but that genre did not come into favour until the fifteenth century and even when it did appear, it tended to discuss general principles and ideals rather than the realities of the class-room. Once again the investigator is in the position of having to collect scattered facts from wherever he may find them. Once again he has to rely on casual indications in books about other subjects to provide him with glimpses of how things may have been. But most of the reminiscences which have survived (and this is certainly true of the period before the Renaissance) are too limited in scope, too unsystematic and biased to be of real value. The famous description of school life at Chartres which John of Salisbury inserted in the haphazard pages of the *Metalogicon* stands alone in its evocative completeness. Consequently, our most reliable information as to method comes from the technical works actually used in teaching.

These class-books were of two kinds. Students had to familiarise themselves with certain general guides, such as grammars and treatises on rhetoric, and they were also expected to study line by line commentaries on the authors selected for their reading. Both the general theory and the specialised comment called attention, however, to the same set of problems. They both emphasised the linguistic and stylistic aspects of literature; and we can trace to them that interest in the mechanics of composition which is the hallmark of medieval learning outside the specialised field of the professional disciplines. But here again if we want to clarify specific issues, we must discover which textbooks and which commentaries were most commonly used, and needing to have recourse as before to the data of bibliographical research are inevitably harnessed to its limitations.

Finally, we come to the question of aims. The emphasis given them should require no excuse. Certain educators have maintained that the personality of a teacher counts for far more than the subject-matter he may try to impart; and the view is almost certainly correct. Whatever he expounds, the vital impression he leaves on his pupils will derive from the quality of his mind, from his tastes, his attitudes and his outlook. At the same time, it is a commonplace of educational thought that the teacher is helpless without co-operation from the parents. The child's response to what a school may have to offer is decided by the values taught to him at home. Both these conclusions have the backing of practical experience, and both point to the same basic fact, that the results of the educational process are enormously influenced by the psychological background of those who take part in it.

Thus, to understand the real nature of the classical education we shall need to study the outlook of both teachers and pupils. But how is this to be done in the case of an epoch which we know imperfectly, and where our knowledge consists of facts about the fate of peoples and cities, unsupported by intimate revelations? As it happens, the difficulties are not insurmountable. Attitudes have their roots in experience; and in every man's life two sorts of experience can be traced, which we may call private and public after their origins. The private kind arises out of the impact of circumstances peculiar to the individual in question. It is the fruit of his specific destiny. The public kind on the other hand belongs not to the individual alone, but to the social group, and much of it is bound up with the cultural tradition. To some extent, all the members of a society think along the same lines; and within certain limits we can always find a common outlook, the central theme of endless private variations.

Both these elements of human experience have their effect upon education. But the private world of each teacher influences only his particular pupils; the private world of each student concerns only himself. The common tradition on the other hand sets its stamp upon everyone, and its effects are reinforced by their very multiplication. Thus, over a wide field—for the education of a country or a period viewed in its entirety—the private variations cancel out, and the common element remains as the essential determinant. That element however—the spirit of the age—is a public fact about which there exists plenty of evidence for every part of the epoch we are considering.

It is possible therefore to discuss the aims of the classical education from century to century. But here again the attempt involves our examining a fresh and very wide field. For to describe the outlook of an epoch or society, it is necessary to take into account the whole range of cultural development as well as the economic and political movements which are its determinants.

We have considered so far only the teaching given in schools, and already we have come across a multitude of difficulties. A complete narrative, which aimed to present the fortunes of the classical heritage in their entirety, would involve even more branches of knowledge and would raise a correspondingly greater number of problems. For the purposes of such a narrative, the history of the schools would require to be supplemented by a fairly exhaustive account of the development of law, philosophy and medicine, which fell outside the normal school course; and the literature of these specialities bristles with highly technical questions which still await solution. Furthermore, the advances made in private study would have to be described. Individuals often attained levels of learning far beyond the average of the schools, and their achievements are therefore of a primary importance. But to be able to describe them we should have to examine what each student read, and how each reacted to his reading. In other words, we should once again have to face the intricacies of bibliography and the subtle task of tracing cultural developments. Nor would that be all. For no enquiry into the classical learning of individuals could properly neglect the study of literary borrowings, the results of that extraordinarily laborious research which elucidates the origins of quotations, references and attempts at imitation.

The works of a number of major writers have been examined from this point of view, and we are in a position to form a clear picture of the classical reading of Alcuin, John of Salisbury, Dante, Chaucer, Rabelais, Ronsard, Spenser, Shakespeare and Ben Jonson, to name only a few. Caution, however, is very necessary. If a man quotes a passage, he has read it; but we must not assume that he has read the work in which it occurs. Quotations were often taken second-hand from grammar books. The researches of C. K. Ullman have revealed that anthologies contributed largely to the classical knowledge of medieval scholars; and everybody has been aware for a long time now that many of the Renaissance pundits, like Rabelais and Ben Jonson, similarly derived the greater part of their erudition from popular handbooks. Nor can we accept without reserve the claims made by individuals that they or others had read certain classical authors, for no medieval or Renaissance writer is altogether free from the minor vice of exaggeration.

Moreover, classical quotations and references plainly represent only a part of the debt, medieval and Renaissance authors owed to antiquity

Such clearly identifiable material is not all that stays in our minds when we read a book. Much of what we remember verges on the imponderable. Sometimes our sensibility is affected or a rhythm continues to haunt our ears. Sometimes our attention is caught by a quality which belongs to a book or poem as a whole, by the categories it uses to interpret experience or by its subtle artistic balance.

A complete account of the classical elements in medieval or Renaissance literature would involve therefore the examination of this general debt. But such an examination, while desirable in theory, is scarcely possible in practice. The difficulties would be overwhelming. First of all, there would be a vast amount of detail to discuss for every work of every author. Secondly, a single work, however extensive, would not constitute an intelligible unit of study. For all the writers concerned borrowed from their contemporaries and immediate predecessors as well as from the classics, so that to assess, for example, the classical borrowings of a twelfth-century poet, we should require to know as a preliminary how much classical material had been taken over during the earlier part of the Middle Ages. Thirdly, the nature of this classical element would be hard to define. How hard and how subtle the task of such a definition would prove can be judged from the fact that the devotional language of the great Victorine Hymns to the Virgin is supposed by certain scholars to have owed a good deal to Ovid's *Ars Amatoria*. The precise character of that debt, if indeed it existed, is likely to baffle the most careful analyst. And that is only one instance among many.

The recital of these varied difficulties—and in a longer account one could add substantially to their number—explains why there have been so few comprehensive accounts describing the fortunes of the classical heritage. The subject lies at the point of intersection of several disciplines. The data it requires must be sought at one and the same time from bibliography, from literary studies, from the history of culture and from the specific histories of education, law, medicine, philosophy and science. It must wait upon their progress which is necessarily slow; and even when that progress has been made, there still remains the problem of combining sets of information which are so different in character into a coherent whole.

During the past thirty years several of the specialities mentioned above have been radically transformed. The long labours of the bibliographers have at last reached a point where systematisation could begin. New conceptions have changed our ideas on the nature and development of culture. The history of philosophy has been enriched, and that of science, medicine and law has been altered out of all recognition, by recent research. Moreover, this many-sided advance is still going on. There is every hope that in another twenty years we shall know a great deal more about the utilisation of the classical heritage than it is possible to discover today.

Plainly then, the moment has not yet arrived for the writing of that authoritative survey which will at long last give the subject a definite pattern, taking all the facts into consideration and assigning its proper weight to each. Nor indeed would the powers of the present writer be equal to that herculean task. The aim of the chapters that follow is of a much lower order. Since the confused actual state and probable rapid growth of our knowledge concerning the fortunes of the classical heritage are likely to preclude the writing of a comprehensive history for some years to come, and since a great interest naturally attaches to the subject, there would seem to be room in the meantime for a brief introductory account; and it is hoped that the present work may do something to satisfy that need.

As the material available in this field consists of relatively disconnected bodies of information deriving from different specialities, the main problem has been to discover some unifying principle which might serve as the basis for a fairly generalised survey; and it became obvious on consideration that for the time being the only feasible way of giving unity to the story was to put the emphasis on men's attitude and approach to the ancient world, that is on the aims and methods of classical studies. For these aims and methods are on the one hand closely linked with the general unified development of European culture, while on the other hand they can be validly regarded as the determining causes of the type of influence which the classics eventually came to exert.

Men's approach to the classics altered in conjunction with their general outlook; and so with this point of reference, it has been possible to present the material to hand in a more or less straightforward chronological order, except that a separate chapter has had to be included on Byzantium which was at all times culturally distinct from the West, and the several Western countries have had to be separately discussed in connection with the Renaissance, for by that time they were sufficiently differentiated to form to some extent independent societies.

But the classical heritage as embodied in Greek and Roman literature was a permanent feature of the European scene; and so the educated public's attitude to it, though always influenced by the conditions of the moment, was not at any point their exclusive product. Tradition played its part in determining the pattern, and what we find in each generation is not a new attitude to the classics, but a complex of inherited attitudes and methods that are progressively modified. Each chapter must be regarded as setting the stage for the one following.

In the first instance, however, at the very beginning of this process, the starting-point was provided by the educational traditions of the collapsing Empire. It has been felt necessary therefore to add two preliminary chapters, one on the pagan, and another on the Christian attitudes to literature and learning during the patristic period; and finally there is a short discussion on the nature of the classical heritage itself, which our point of reference makes unavoidable. The view that at different ages men had different attitudes to the classical heritage, only makes sense if we can regard the aforesaid heritage for all intents and purposes as a cultural unit. But the fact that this was so is not immediately obvious. Thus it has appeared desirable to begin with a brief analysis indicating why and to what extent the literatures of Greece and Rome, composed in two languages over a vast period of time, were nevertheless (if we except certain writings) the product of one underlying culture, so that when we talk of antiquity exercising an influence, we have in mind an organic whole and not a mere accidental assemblage of culturally unconnected patterns.

CHAPTER I

THE BACKGROUND

I. THE CHARACTER OF THE CLASSICAL HERITAGE

No one has ever brought together on the shelves of a single library all
that has been written in Latin and ancient Greek. The collection would
be imposing even by modern standards; and for quality as well as for
quantity. But its most remarkable feature would have nothing to do
with its size or even with the great number of masterpieces it contained.
More has been written in English alone; and the best of English writers
can take their place without question alongside their classical predecessors. No, the noteworthy and indeed unique characteristic of such
a collection would be the space of time it covered, extending from
Homer to the present day. For although ancient Greek has been truly
a dead language for almost two centuries, Latin is still used by scholars
and by the Roman Catholic Church.

The question therefore arises as to how much of this monumental
array we can regard as the proper subject-matter of classical studies.
No one has ever suggested that the latest Papal encyclicals should be
read by classicists alongside Livy and Virgil. But men have wondered
about Psellus, and the superiority of Petrarch to Cicero has been
seriously maintained. There have been teachers prepared to include
Alan of Lille in the curriculum, just as there have been others who
were prepared to exclude Tacitus.

We shall find, however, that in practice modern students of the
classics tend to regard any work written after the close of the sixth
century A.D. as falling outside their proper field of study; and they also
tend to neglect the theologians and other specifically Christian authors
who flourished before that date. There exist, in short, certain conventions governing the classical curriculum which command the tacit
support of the majority of scholars; and they would seem to have their
roots in an intuitive judgement that the pagan writers of the period
before A.D. 600 had some important characteristic in common which
their Christian contemporaries and medieval successors manifestly
lacked. For if there was no common element to distinguish the writings
we call classical, if the literary productions of ancient times had no bond
of union other than their date, there could be no good reason for feeling

that one must exclude St Augustine and St Gregory while including Symmachus and Boethius.

Such a common element would be nothing unusual. It is widely recognised that there have been numerous examples of the literature—and even of the whole artistic output—of a society, possessing at a given period a marked unity of character. For a proof of this we need look no further than eighteenth-century England. Between the verses of Pope, the cynicism of Chesterfield, the embattled periods of Gibbon, the façade of Blenheim, Brown's gardening and the geometrical design of an Adam ceiling, there exists a link whose precise nature is difficult to define, but whose impact remains undeniable. The impossibility of finding an adequate description has given rise to the habit of talking in vague terms about an eighteenth-century spirit.

The same phenomenon can be observed in the case of other periods. Romanticism set a recognisable stamp on literature and art, so did seventeenth-century Classicism, so—we are beginning to discover—did the late nineteenth century. The fact that these broad similarities cannot be described in satisfactorily positive terms need not trouble us. We are not dealing with something altogether intangible. There is a line of approach to the puzzle which does provide a clear-cut answer.

Suppose we abandon all attempts at description and turn our attention instead to the origins of this curious impression of unity which meets us in the classics, in eighteenth-century literature and elsewhere. When we do this, various possibilities present themselves, some of which can be speedily eliminated. Language, or to be precise, the more obvious elements of linguistic usage, would appear to be largely irrelevant. *La Princesse de Clèves* makes use of the same vocabulary and the same classical French syntax as *Les Liaisons Dangereuses*; yet there is a world of difference between the impressions produced by the two books. On the other hand, *Pantagruel* and the *Moriae Encomium*, written the first in French, the second in Latin, belong manifestly together. Form in its broader aspects is similarly unimportant. The sonnets of Mallarmé have more in common with the free verse of Laforgue than they have with the sonnets of Du Bellay or Ronsard. The impression gained by the reader cannot be associated with the utilisation of a particular genre or group of genres. It seems to attach itself, like some pervasive scent, to every kind of writing within a period. It derives not from the literary forms themselves, which we may find elsewhere used with a different impact, not from niceties of construction, metaphors, epithets or tricks of speech, but rather from the kind of choice which is made with regard to each of these separate elements of style. It is the perfume of the personality behind the writing.

A work of art reflects the landscape of its creator's mind. It enshrines some aspects of his sensibility, some of his attitudes to experience. The picture it gives is incomplete. A single poem or even a group of poems never contains more than a sample of the poet's mental world. But at the same time it never adds successfully to the content of that world from alien sources. The personality of the creative artist sets the limits within which his art can move.

What is true of art applies more or less to all forms of writing. The limiting factor is always the mind of the writer. But the human mind bears the stamp of society. It is moulded by the education, the language, the experience which each individual shares with a larger or smaller group of his contemporaries. Man is culturally conditioned; and those indefinable common characteristics, which we note for example in all the productions of the eighteenth century, are nothing else than the reflection at the level of creative activity of the coherent eighteenth-century culture pattern.

This relationship between literature and culture is of primary importance for our purposes; and we shall do well to take a closer look at the concepts involved. Many of them are self-explanatory, but they need to be kept in mind. Each society has its own way of life, its particular apparatus of practical and intellectual techniques. Some of these techniques may be the private endowment of individuals, but most are held in common, either in the sense that they are used simultaneously by a great number, or in the sense that they are handed down from generation to generation for the performance of specific tasks. In a tribe, this common stock of cultural techniques is shared by nearly everybody. Where we have a large society, made up of several distinct social groups, each group has of course its own stock and the several traditions merge more or less successfully into an overall pattern. In the latter instance, the concept of cultural coherence needs a more subtle analysis than we can appropriately discuss in this context. But the essential point is clear enough. Whether we have in mind a social group, or a simple, or a complex society, the common way of life, to which its members subscribe, must be one which they can comfortably follow. Otherwise, there are disruptive conflicts. So except in the case of societies which are undergoing rapid change or stand on the verge of collapse, the common patterns of living will possess what we might call a psychological coherence. The institutions on which they are based, the economic and social activities which they require, the forms of sensibility which they favour and the ideas whose spread they advance, will be in harmony one with another; or at least the oppositions between them will not provoke conflict. In short, there will be a real pattern whose ultimate principle is the spiritual comfort of the individual.

It would appear therefore that we ought to look for an explanation of that similarity, which by general consent marks Greek and Latin literature from Homer to Boethius, in the existence of a common classical culture. But here we come up against an obvious difficulty. The world of Homer was not the world of Demosthenes, Rome was not Greece, the Republic was not the Empire. The semi-tribal societies at the dawn of Greek history were replaced by the city-states which in turn yielded before the megalopolitan civilisation of the Hellenistic Age. These sank into a world empire; and uneasy prosperity was succeeded by a disintegration full of incidental horrors. The history of the period offers us a spectacle of restless social change. How then could there be cultural unity?

We shall find the answer to this question if we consider in detail under what circumstances, and with what aims in view, the various sections of ancient literature came to be written. The conditions of the time did not favour what we have come to regard as the normal relationship between literature and culture. Their intimate connection was disturbed by a series of accidents.

The scene of the Homeric poems is set in the Heroic Age of tribal warfare, when noble birth and prowess in personal combat were the highroads to social eminence, and man moved in a world he did not try to understand, content to see himself as the plaything of supernatural forces beyond his ken. The *Iliad* and the *Odyssey* describe this primitive epoch with considerable accuracy. The space allotted to accounts of hand-to-hand fighting and to the fantasy life of Olympus reflects in the very construction of the poem the overriding importance which these elements had for Achaean culture. Nevertheless, the description for all its faithful detail is not from the inside. We know that these epics were composed originally to amuse the great men of the post-tribal period, and that they were not given their final form until the recension of Peisistratus, by which time the city-state was a social reality. Consequently, they lay an understandable emphasis on those traits which the pictured past shared with the emergent civilisation of the *polis*, on the popular assembly, the interplay of prestige and eloquence, and the reasoned exploitation of practical possibilities. At the same time, specifically primitive themes, such as the struggles in Olympus which have their effects on earth, are depicted with a slightly cynical exuberance in which the absence of belief is manifest. Culturally speaking, the Homeric poems belong rather to the beginnings of the city-state than to the heroic period of Mycenae and Troy. Moreover, throughout Greek history, but in particular during the golden age of Athens, they played the same role as the Authorised Version later did in England. They formed the source-book of the educated imagination; and their intellectual magnetism exerted a constant pull to bring Greek civilisation back through all its changes into nearer contact with its first origins. As a result, the Homeric world picture is much more closely integrated into the later Greek tradition than at first sight appears; and what has been said about Homer applies with almost equal force to the rest of the early epic literature.

The period from the seventh to the fourth century B.C. saw the rise, the glory and the political eclipse of the city-states. Unhampered by the rigours of climatic extremes, sheltered (at least during the critical hundred and twenty years that followed Salamis) from the interference of outside powers, and predisposed to enterprise by the rewards of an expanding economy, their citizens lived in a world whose problems were for once not beyond man's power to solve. They developed as children develop to whom a wise teacher sets tasks within their capacity, learnt to observe and to plan, to make use of facts and reason, to be self-reliant and persevering; for they had no need to be discouraged, as so many have been since the beginning of time, by habitually losing the fruits of their vigour and sagacity through the operation of agencies outside their control.

The city-states provided Europe with its first concept of a reasonable society, as man would run it if nature did not interfere by setting him insoluble problems. Their example, idealised, was to serve future generations as an inspiring myth. But perhaps their finest achievement was to bring into existence the earliest written literature. Other civilisations had discovered the practical value of writing and had employed it to preserve notices of laws, details of ownership or financial transactions and chronicles of events, as well as the songs, legends and rituals of religion, but these early written memorials had been in the main innocent of artistic intention. The Greeks were the first to record compositions intended to give aesthetic pleasure. They seem to have been exceptional among the societies which knew how to write, in possessing a lively poetic tradition. Accustomed to the Homeric recitations of the rhapsodes, the epinicean odes and the dramatic contests, they placed a high value on the songs and verse narratives which their ancestors had handed down verbally from one generation to the next, with the result that they were the people to take the decisive step of entrusting poetic material to those written records which until then had been used for utilitarian purposes.

This practice, which by the middle of the fifth century had gone some way towards the creation of a written literature, then received a violent stimulus from the popularity of rhetoric, a development directly due to the political conditions of the city-state. Gorgias and others worked out rules for public speaking, exact techniques for making an impression. Experts trained in these methods travelled from city to city vending their intellectual wares; and soon no orator dared to trust to spontaneous inspiration. This movement had a double effect. It made men more conscious that composition was an art; and at the same time it led to the increased use of writing. Speeches had to be prepared in advance and then reproduced with great verbal exactitude. Even if you made them up yourself you were grateful for a record to which you could refer; but eventually most plain men did not trust their own skill, they employed professionals to provide them with a brief, and then a written memorial was indispensable. So between 450 and 350 B.C. writing and reading which had been rare accomplishments became the necessary instruments of every-day living.

By the birth of Alexander, Athens had produced a literature in which the principles of artistic composition were applied to tragedy and comedy in addition to several other poetic genres, to the numerous forms of oratory, to history and to the philosophical dialogue. Nothing like it was known at the time; and its uniqueness was to have a most remarkable influence.

In Asia and Africa, Hellenisation was confined to the larger towns, where the inhabitants lived in a way which differed in every essential from the old city-state pattern. They had not even the beginnings of independence and security. Few of them owned land; fewer still possessed any controlling interest in the production of necessary raw materials. They depended for all their requirements on the military dominance of the rulers they served, on the subservience of a peasantry they met only as customers and on the hazards of distant markets. Their physical surroundings emphasised their helplessness. Crowded in their tenements, they were peculiarly susceptible to the ravages of disease, to mass starvation if supplies should fail and to the shocks of mass hysteria, while the heavy monuments of royal and military power were there in the midst of their streets as a daily reminder of the arbitrary will which cut across their destinies. Such people could not have either self-respect or self-reliance. What use had they for observing reality or measuring means to ends? They were the playthings of circumstances; and their only god was Luck.

At the same time, on the mainland of Greece and the islands the old world still survived though without much of its vitality. Men still lived in small and largely self-subsistent cities over which they could feel to have some control. But the national economy was no longer expanding and a general restriction of life was the order of the day. So there were no new advances, but enough remained of the old conditions to make the fifth-century patterns of thought still acceptable. The old values of self-development, rational action and public service still made sense.

That is the background against which we must set the work of the Alexandrian scholars and poets; and then we shall not be tempted to deride them as pedants or to accuse them of living in an ivory tower. They may have been pedants, and they may have been obscure. But they were not remote from the world. If anything, they erred in the opposite direction. They had their practical aims too persistently in view. How else would they have had the patronage of Philadelphus and Euergetes who were not men to be fooled by academic fashions?

Philetas came from Cos, Zenodotus from Ephesus, Lycophron from Calchis, and the polymath Eratosthenes had studied long at Athens. Drawn from these areas where the old culture still lingered, and paid to pass their lives among the products of an imperfect Hellenisation, it would have been strange if they had not regarded themselves as the representatives of the fifth-century tradition; and they were encouraged in this attitude by their masters who had sound political reasons for desiring that tradition to be glorified. The interpretation which Philetas and his successors gave to their task, led them to open several fields of activity which were to prove of the greatest importance for the history of Greek literature and indirectly for the history of the world. They tried to establish and explain the texts of the great Greek authors, starting significantly enough with the ones their contemporaries must have found the most difficult, namely the great epic cycles, the lyric poets, and the tragedians. They prepared to this end recensions, commentaries and lists of difficult words, and to reinforce their academic teachings, filled their own verse with a plethora of mythological allusions. Like the rest of their work this cult of mythology served the ultimate purpose of keeping intact their contemporaries' links with the past, and at the same time, they attacked also from another quarter. Producing lexicons and later grammars of Attic usage, and imitating the established genres, they inaugurated a linguistic, as well as an antiquarian, revival.

Thus, Greek ambitions, Greek patriotism and the natural wish not to lose touch with a unique and glorious past led to the breaking of the links which had existed until then between the language of artistic composition and the spoken idiom; and simultaneously the content of literature was dissociated from everyday interests. The prose writers of the golden age had used the language of their contemporaries, ornamenting it perhaps by occasional phrases from epic poetry which was after all a popular possession, and if the poets had employed a more elevated style, they had similarly drawn upon the familiar Homeric heritage. These writers had produced their works for public occasions, for religious festivals, for the celebration of athletic victories, for drama competitions, for the hustings or the law courts. Unless they aspired to be historians or philosophers, all their masterpieces were composed with reference to some social event. But with the Alexandrians the connection between literature and life came to an end. Literature stopped being the artistic expression of contemporary culture and became instead an instrument of education.

This development was of the greatest importance; and since it has often been attacked on the ground that it distorted the natural growth of Greek culture, certain points might reasonably be made in its defence. We shall do well to remind ourselves first of all that if the Alexandrian scholars had not produced their imitations of existing genres, there would in all probability have been no Hellenistic literature at all. For the Hellenistic societies did not provide their writers with the stimuli that had called into being the odes of Pindar or the drama of Athens. Places like Alexandria and Antioch had little in common with the fifth-century states. They resembled rather the great urban agglomerations of the Orient which through the many centuries of their existence produced no literary work of merit. They were commercial entrepôts, wasteful of human energy, and we should be foolish to regard them as potential breeding grounds for art. Furthermore, if local literatures had managed to arise and if by some strange chance a school of Egyptian or Syriac writers had come to reflect faithfully the outlook and sensibility of Hellenistic man, it is necessary to remember that the emergence of these new literatures written in the new forms which the Greek language was taking, would have led to the neglect and eventually to the loss of the fifth-century heritage. In that case, too, posterity would have suffered.

Thanks to the efforts which had for their centre the library at Alexandria, the Greek writers of the four centuries that followed the death of Alexander remained faithful to the old tradition. Their imitations were admittedly not exact. They did not know enough about style or language. They lacked as yet the necessary apparatus of grammars and lexicons which would have enabled them to reproduce Homer or Demosthenes without a fault; and so their works show traces of the new Hellenistic idioms and of the new Hellenistic sensibility. But these traces are slight. The main pattern of thought, feeling and expression is that of the Golden Age.

These writers (and the educated men who read them) saw their world through the spectacles of the fifth century. Using the language of the past, they thought to a large extent in the categories of the past, neglecting much and distorting even more of the experience that was directly and personally theirs. This ordering of their world within the framework of outmoded perspectives came easily to them because the city-state culture still persisted in a weakened form. Most of them came from regions where a local autonomy still preserved the trappings of the old freedom; and in any case the new ways of life were repellent. The *douceur de vivre* pleaded strongly for a revival of the Periclean Age.

The inordinate sweep of Alexander's conquests was the original cause which first dissociated literature from contemporary culture in the Greek-speaking world. But single upheavals, however notable, are rarely sufficient to achieve long-lasting results, and the survival of the dissociation was due to another influence. During the second century B.C. the cult of the past was given an added sanction through the rise of Roman power. Rome, admittedly, had never been a democratic city-state as Greeks understood the term; and after the Punic Wars it was fast losing even its original oligarchic structure. But although by the time of the Eastern Wars the senate had shed much of its authority, the credit of its members as individuals remained considerable. They were still the most powerful men in the commonwealth. They were the élite whom all admired and they set the tone which was to be reflected in the general orientation of Roman culture. These senators of the decaying republic who were prepared one and all to exploit to the full the opportunities of a dictatorial age, who intrigued unceasingly for personal power, continued at the same time to hitch their waggon to the star of the old republican ideals. They vaunted Cincinnatus going back to his plough and Regulus going back to Carthage. Cicero seems to have believed without any doubt that all his political allies would have preferred to live in those primitive times when a public-spirited self-abnegation was habitual.

It is clear enough of course that this cult of the early republican virtues owed some of its popularity to the fact that the losing party whose ambitions were frustrated could use it with good effect as a weapon against their successful opponents. Nevertheless, its influence must not be underrated. The well-to-do senatorial circles who gave Roman society its pattern did maintain throughout the storms of the late Republic and the Empire a theoretical preference for the past as against the present. For whatever motives, they were in the habit of judging everything they saw around them according to a scale of values based on the much more limited experience of their remote ancestors; as if the improvident Roman mob was still a body of prudent farmers and craftsmen, as if finance was still a matter of driving away a few cows from a neighbouring city.

This preference led them to embrace enthusiastically the Greek city-state tradition and the literature in which it was embodied. Their enthusiasm moreover was reinforced by the usefulness of Greek rhetoric for pleading in the law courts and for the debates which cloaked the intrigues that really decided politics. So captive Greece enjoyed its intellectual triumph; and the works of Cicero, Livy and Virgil were written.

Thus, Roman literature started at the point which Greek literature reached only with the Hellenistic Age. Traditional in spirit and imitative in technique, it was never a direct expression of contemporary experience. Its language was from the first an artistic confection ordered by scholarship and remote from ordinary speech.

By the second century of the Empire, the literary traditions of both Greece and Rome were firmly linked to the past. The writers of the Alexandrian school had not imitated the language or the techniques of their models with an absolute precision. They had not yet been conscious of a need for such exactitude; nor had they yet possessed the means to achieve exact results. The road of plagiarism requires to be paved with more than intentions. The would-be imitator who relies on his memory alone will find that he reproduces little beyond an occasional phrase or turn of thought typical of his model. To do more requires a systematic approach.

When the Alexandrians had tried to write in the established tradition, to assimilate their epics and hymns to Homeric and their prose to Attic models, they had soon become conscious of a need for systematic guides to these various forms of the literary language. So Philetas had produced a glossary of difficult poetic words and Zenodotus a glossary to Homer; a certain Philemon had written on Attic nouns and Aristophanes of Byzantium had collected the Attic and Laconian terms covering all the usual social relationships. Their work had been continued by their successors of the second and first centuries B.C., by Dionysius Thrax, the founder of systematic grammar, by the fantasti cally industrious Didymus who produced vast tomes on metaphors and on comic and tragic diction, and by Tryphon who appears to have written on synonyms, on musical terms and on the names of animals and plants. With the passage of time, more and more aspects of the traditional written language had been explored in greater and greater detail, until by the second century A.D., the scene was set for a final systematisation.

It is important to realise that the Atticists came at the end of this long tradition. In effect, they were no more responsible for their programme than is the soldier for the shot he fires. Aelius Dionysius, Pausanias and Phrynichus merely completed a process when they sorted out the component parts of literary Attic in their huge dictionaries and grammars and enunciated the principle that any usage which differed from those they had noted was a damnable barbarism. Here at last were the necessary instruments for a perfect imitation. Intending writers had merely to study them, to digest them thoroughly; and the great wind of Attic glory would blow again. That the categories of language set limits upon thought, that using only the expressions sanctioned by the past forces one's experience on to a procrustean bed, cutting it down in effect to those elements which the present and the past have in common, did not enter their heads. The final absurdity of the prison they prepared for genius was hidden from them. They were concerned only with imitation.

In the meantime, Latin had undergone a similar development. Its rules had been formulated by a succession of learned grammarians from Stilo to Palaemon; and the techniques of imitation, the habit of reading notebook in hand to collect telling words and phrases, metaphors, parts of speech and arguments and the desirability of memorising this material until it became part of the natural furniture of one's mind were all regularly taught in the rhetorical schools.

Thus, during the last centuries of the Empire, the imitative tendency which had characterised all literature since the death of Alexander was sharply intensified. The well-organised educational system of the Empire had for its main aim to teach the two literary languages and to inculcate in the minds of all its pupils the established methods and desirability of imitation.

Moreover, just as the difficulties of the Diadochi had originally helped to preserve the fifth-century Greek heritage and the thwarted ambitions of the Roman Senate had led its members to idealise the city-state, so once again political considerations intervened to further the spread of what had become the official Graeco-Roman tradition. As the protective might of the legions weakened, so the imperial government came to rely to an ever greater extent on its intangible assets; and the excellence of Graeco-Roman culture was turned into a useful bait for retaining the loyalty of the uncertain provincials. Steel was in short supply. So the provinces were to be grappled to the soul of Rome by hoops of a different make. Literature was taught with great zeal as an introduction to the Roman way of life; but what it introduced men to was in the last analysis the old life of the city-states.

Enough has been said perhaps to indicate why the classical literatures are unified as to their cultural reference in spite of the obvious social changes which occurred during the period of their composition. Among the reasons why the Empire failed we ought probably to number the intellectual failure of its educated class. Hampered by their traditionalism and by the strict linguistic discipline which they imposed upon their minds, the members of that class could not solve their immediate problems. They could not for a start suddenly invent after centuries of neglect the terms in which these problems might have been properly posed. But while they suffered in consequence, we, the recipients of the heritage they preserved, have on our side immeasurably gained.

This traditionalism which we have described did not carry all before it. There were exceptions to the general trend; and now and then in the later authors we catch glimpses of the horrors of megalopolitan culture. Theocritus has left some suggestive pieces; and there are passages of subtle understanding in Polybius. The novelists who wrote without the guidance of traditional models benefited from this liberty to produce some vivid sketches of contemporary life, while Philo and the Neo-platonists went a long way towards giving philosophical form to the longings and beliefs of the contemporary urban population. But in all these cases, the contemporary response was still to some extent clothed in the accepted traditional categories, as in the haunting rhythms of the *Pervigilium Veneris* the longing for a magical rebirth, that external salvation which had always been the comfort of the helpless, finds expression through the etiolated prettiness of the familiar worship of Love. The emotion which sprang from a deep contemporary need and the shop-worn trappings which poets had used for centuries with no background of feeling sit uneasily together. The result is a work of art which leaves the reader with a slight discomfort, as if he were suspended between two worlds.

The life of the great urban populations was characterised, as we have said, by an acute sense of personal helplessness. Crowded conditions and the spread of endemic malaria multiplied the common dangers of death and disease. The supply of food was erratic, dependent on the dubious success of large-scale feats of organisation, while war, lawlessness and the incidental ferocities of arbitrary governments were an ever present threat. Add to this the fact that the great numbers of slaves and freedmen were constantly exposed to suffering from the cruelty or irresponsibility of their masters, and the general picture becomes one that we cannot contemplate without feeling outraged. The idleness, dishonesty and deep-seated corruption which the historians of the time proclaim to have been the characteristics of the urban populace, its avowed preference for living on charity and its delight in the public sufferings of others were but the natural outcome of the appalling conditions under which it was forced to exist.

With this chaos around him, man could not have had any confidence in his power to mould his destiny. The old beliefs in the value of effort and calculation vanished; and the insecure turned for help and solace to the supernatural. In the failure of reason, magic was invoked as a means of controlling events. The idea that everything might be determined by the operation of forces outside of the material universe which the initiate could influence, provided no doubt a certain measure of comfort. At the same time, the Orphic mysteries and the cults of the Magna Mater and Mithras gave in their emotional rites moments of heightened experience with the promise of similar happiness in the future. Placing the goal of life outside of a sordid and insecure reality, they made daily commerce with that reality more tolerable.

These cults and religions, though they satisfied the longings of millions, had not the moral and intellectual content which would have enabled them to leave their mark on literature. That role was reserved for Christianity; and the Christian literature of the patristic age contains the most detailed expression we possess of the human mind during the later phases of ancient culture. The evidence it offers is limited in scope, for every topic is treated from a strictly religious viewpoint; and even the best of its products are not entirely free from the stamp of the traditional Graeco-Roman outlook, for the Fathers made their own the categories in which the Greeks habitually interpreted their experience. But all the same it offers us a concept of man and his fate which differs considerably from earlier formulations.

Thus, we shall find it convenient to divide the writings of antiquity into two groups. All the pagan works, with the possible exception of the novels, have their roots primarily in the culture which grew up in the city states. The Christian literature, on the other hand, in spite of its affinities with this pagan tradition, belongs in its deepest essence to that later world of rabbit-warren towns and monster autocracies, to despair born of chaos.

If we were therefore to make a sharp chronological division and were to set ourselves the task of describing the influence on later ages of all that had been written before A.D. 600, we should have to treat our subject under two heads between which there would be only the arbitrary connection of temporal coincidence. Such a study would lack even the semblance of cohesion. It has appeared more suitable therefore to limit our enquiry to the first or pagan group of writings. They constitute what is normally meant by the classical heritage, whose most perfect expression is found in the masterpieces of Athens and Augustan Rome.

II. THE EDUCATIONAL INHERITANCE

The road to the classical heritage has always lain through the schools. Classical Greek and Latin are not easy languages to master; and the fact that since the Dark Ages they have been learnt for the most part from books has added substantially to the labour involved. To toil through a grammar unsupported demands a degree of will-power, zeal and efficiency which very few possess. Most people perform that arid task best with help and under compulsion. So we find that at all periods the majority of those who came to know something about the classics started young and, even if they later became great scholars through their private efforts, acquired the beginnings of their competence through the daily routine of the class-room: which makes that routine of primary importance.

The first evidence we have about how Latin was taught comes in the writings of the scholars who worked in the Anglo-Saxon and Carolingian schools; and there we meet a reasonably comprehensive curriculum, effective text-books and well-planned techniques of instruction. But neither the curriculum, nor the methods, are original. We have no difficulty in recognising them as borrowed from the educational system which had been in existence during the last centuries of the Roman Empire. They represent a new variation on a traditional theme.

We know next to nothing about the schools of the Dark Ages except that they were very sparse on the ground. Small groups of teachers in the Italian towns probably kept alive to some extent the learning of their ancestors. But they were not sufficiently numerous, nor sufficiently active, to justify our regarding them as the main channel through which Roman pedagogic ideas were transmitted to the ninth century. Books undoubtedly played a much more important part than this uncertain verbal tradition. The grammars of Donatus and Priscian with their references to classical usage, the *ad Herennium* with its analyses of rhetorical technique, the commentaries of Servius which showed how a text should be explained, the *de Nuptiis* of Capella and the *de Doctrina* of St Augustine in which the scope of education was outlined, were the well-springs where Bede and Alcuin went for their pedagogic ideas. They moulded their teaching on the information these records gave them about what had been done in the past. They put into practice what they read, and found that it worked.

We can trace a large number of classical elements in all education previous to the eighteenth century. There is a continuity of tradition in the West from Alcuin to Erasmus, from the school of Chartres to the schools of Port-Royal, because each generation clung conservatively to the methods of its predecessor, and because the ancient text-books exercised a direct influence on each new group of teachers. Nor was the situation any different in the East. Substitute Aphthonius for Donatus, Photius for Alcuin, the era of the Paleologi for the High Renaissance, and the same generalisations about classical influence hold good. Byzantium also had its roots in the past.

The education of our period cannot be understood without some previous reference to Graeco-Roman pedagogy. Here, however, a certain difficulty presents itself. The teachers of ancient times were admittedly conservative. When Alaric sacked Rome, they were still using methods that Cicero would have found familiar. But all the same there had been changes—important changes which we must take into account. Educational theory in particular had undergone a significant trans-formation during the last chaotic ages of collapse, when the demands of new conditions were at last making themselves felt; and this new departure was to leave its mark on the future. Some of the books on which the medieval and renaissance schools principally relied, belonged to what we might call the earlier and more general tradition; but others, the works of Augustine, Capella and Cassiodorus for example, were the very fountain-heads of the later developments in theory. In this field at least Greece and Rome passed to their successors a legacy full of implicit contradictions, whose nature can be comprehended only in an historical setting.

Ancient education was dominated by the schools of grammar and rhetoric. Before the fifth century B.C. the Greeks had given their children a type of training which is common to all semi-primitive societies, and whose aim is to produce good fighting men versed in the usual religious practices and traditions. Since they lived in well-organised communities they did not leave the performance of these tasks to individual parents but arranged them on a group basis. They had schools where children learnt music or recited Homer; they had gymnasia; and they had communal instruction for the performers in the great festivals.

It is likely that these pleasant activities would have represented the high peak of Greek educational achievement, if rhetoric had not sud-denly become popular and if the ability to read had not become an important asset. The emergence of democracy made the winning of votes a vital matter—and placed a premium on the novel skills involved in composing, recording and interpreting a speech. The need to acquire these skills was an educational challenge which no other society had ever yet faced, and the Athenian response to it produced the changes we hear about from Plato and Isocrates and from Aristophanes in the *Clouds*.

After a preliminary period of adjustment, the new needs were met by the appearance of two new classes of teachers, the grammarians and the rhetoricians. The former taught reading. The instruction they offered was grafted on to the established routines of reciting and music so that by a natural transition the schools for the young fell under their care. When the Greeks talked of learning to read, they meant more than just learning to recognise words from the appropriate alphabetic signs. They had in mind always the correct and intelligent spoken rendering of a written passage. As Rutherford pointed out, the grammarians had to teach voice control and expression, thus preparing the ground for the rhetoricians; but above all they had to make sure that the authors they read were understood. They were expected to elucidate problems of syntax and morphology and to explain all difficulties with regard to the subject-matter. In short, they were expected to provide a commentary not unlike the ones we still find nowadays in the notes to classical authors.*

When rhetoric first became popular, the Sophists had travelled from city to city, collecting considerable sums from the pupils of all ages who flocked to their lectures in order to learn the art of producing an impressive argument. The later rhetoricians were the professional descendants of these prodigious salesmen. But since their subject had become less of a novelty, they earned smaller fees and their audiences were drawn from a more limited class. They attracted adolescents who hoped to enter public life. The courses they gave were supposed to cover everything a man might need to know in order to compose good speeches, with the result that potentially their field was very wide. As Isocrates pointed out, successful oratory requires a man versed in all knowledge and possessed of great sagacity. A proper training in rhetoric would therefore be the most complete education that any man could desire. That ideal was not however realised in practice. The best teachers of rhetoric lost themselves in pointless discussions on styles; while the worst were satisfied to teach rule of thumb methods for construction of various types of oration. They had a living to earn and their pupils were not likely to look beyond a cheap success.

These two types of school provided the staple education of the Greek world from the fifth century B.C. onwards and were introduced into Rome after the Punic Wars. The position of the grammarians remained unchallenged throughout our period. The written word had become such an important asset that men's need for skill in reading remained unaffected by the social and cultural changes that occurred. Indeed, the conditions of the Hellenisation period, when the desire to preserve the fifth century legacy was paramount, specifically favoured a form of instruction that did so much to further the understanding of literature. The grammarians were the standard-bearers of Hellenism.

The rhetoricians did not enjoy quite as firm a popularity. For all their success, they never had a monopoly of high education. The forces of convention were never strong enough to still the voice of good sense.

The most intelligent men of every century went to war against the narrowness and insincerity of rhetorical teaching, while the philosophical academies of Athens continued to propagate from the unshakeable fortress of their prestige the idea of an intellectual training that looked beyond the immediate needs of the courtroom or the hustings. Moreover, the political situation during the Alexandrian Age which favoured the grammar schools militated against the rhetoricians since the popular assemblies had lost much of their power. In that respect, however, the rise of Rome had redressed the balance; for under Roman rule the provincial cities had a measure of local autonomy which lent interest to the debates of local bodies while the survival of those republican forms which still cloaked the brutalities of senatorial intrigue provided the art of persuasion with a new, if illusory, importance at the very seat of power.

Indeed, none of the early attacks upon the rhetorical schools and none of the setbacks they suffered had any great consequence. The apparent usefulness of the skills they taught and the lack of any suitable alternative in higher education assured their survival. During the second century A.D. we find them still in almost undisputed control of the field.

By that time, however, conditions were no longer quite so favourable for a continuance of their supremacy. Speech-making had possessed a certain limited value during the period of the Hellenistic states and Republican Rome, so that, in the absence of any obvious alternative, men had not been inspired to look for a substitute to replace the rhetorical schools. But as Rome progressed further and further with its task of imposing an ordered government upon the Mediterranean world, as the need for competent officials well-informed on a wide range of subjects became more and more evident, it was no longer possible to ignore the shortcomings of an education which substituted words for facts. Already Cicero had voiced certain criticisms which were echoed a century or so later by Quintilian. But both these men were successful orators and as such were unwilling to cast any slur upon the activity which had earned them their fame. So their strictures were presented as recommendations for reform. They did not attack the teaching of rhetoric, but merely certain contemporary practices in the schools. Refusing to admit that these practices were unavoidable, they condemned them in the name of an ideal which could never be realised.

Accordingly, the exact import of the *de Oratore* and the *Institutiones Oratoriae* is difficult to assess. They transport us into a cloud-cuckoo-land of unrealisable ideals; and as we study the magnificent array of their arguments, marshalled with so much art to arrive at such impractical conclusions, we cannot help feeling ourselves face to face with some remarkable aberration of the human genius. Yet behind the façade provided by the constructions of a misplaced ingenuity, there is more than a grain of good sense. The motive force which led to the writing of these books was the perception of a genuine contemporary need; and the point clearly emerges that both authors were troubled by the narrowness of the fashionable rhetorical training. They were aware at least that the problems of their time called for something more than a professional skill in persuasion. They wanted to see the curriculum of the schools widened to include a larger range of subjects; and Quintilian moreover had a plan as to how this could be done.

When reading had been first introduced into elementary education, it had taken its place alongside the music, poetry and simple arithmetic already taught to young children, and although it came eventually to play a dominant role, it never displaced these rivals from the time-table. Moreover, reading—or grammar to give it its classical name—was comprehensive rather than exclusive in its interest. Since the grammarians were expected to lecture on all the topics treated by their authors, they were bound within the compass of a reasonably wide course of reading to cover nearly everything that an educated man might need to know. Thus, their schools were centres of a general, if somewhat elementary, education which was recognised as such by the Greeks who coined for it the name *egkuklios paideia*. During the early Empire, however, the grammar schools lost something of their encyclopedic character and were tending to offer little more than just an introductory course to rhetoric, and this was the innovation of which Quintilian most strongly disapproved. What he suggested in its place was the introduction of rather more advanced studies over the whole range of the traditional curriculum including music, mathematics, history and even philosophy.

The subsequent development of education is in harmony with both the strength and the shortcomings of Quintilian's programme. Moved by an intuitive suspicion rather than by any clear understanding of what was required, he had sketched out his remedy within the narrow limits of the traditional system; and since the generations that followed shared his partial vision, it was natural that they too should have striven to solve their problems by the same imperfect means. With the governmental machine increasing from year to year in size and complexity, the

Empire's need for competent civil servants able to handle administrative and financial difficulties was from year to year more urgent. But the situation was new and caught men's minds unprepared. Many centuries were to pass before anyone arrived at a clear conception of the qualities required in an administrator, a bureaucrat or a business chief; and many more before men worked out what training such activities would demand.

Besides, rhetoric still had some uses, and that fact gave the old ways in education a certain credit. The public assemblies had lost most of their powers; and as law grew complicated, forensic speaking was becoming more and more the special province of trained lawyers. But when these fields, where the orators of the past had won their greatest triumphs, grew increasingly restricted, a new opportunity for rhetoric suddenly presented itself. The imperial government was by this time making considerable efforts to win the loyalty of its provincials by persuading them of the benefits of Roman rule and Roman culture; and it was soon realised that good use could be made for this purpose of speeches delivered on public occasions. The resounding paragraphs of a skilled orator, spoken in the midst of some solemn ceremonial and greeted with the enthusiasm appropriate to such celebrations, were in themselves likely to give a favourable impression of the culture to which they owed their excellence; and they could at the same time serve as a means of informing the audience about the reasons for some particular policy, about the achievements of the reigning emperor, or more generally about the traditions, the glories and the history of Greece and Rome. For by the third century the Hellenic legacy also counted among the benefits conferred by the imperial power.

The usefulness of education to the State was first realised by the Flavians who took steps to see that teachers employed by public authorities received sufficient pay, and who endowed a couple of chairs in Rome. From that point onwards, one Emperor after another made provision for an increase in the number of schools and for the payment of teachers, until there was education available in every sizeable town, and salaries were sufficiently regular, as well as sufficiently high to attract capable men.* This officially sponsored education took, under the pressure of the various considerations we have mentioned, a form subtly different from the system which preceded it. An edict published by Diocletian in 301 lists the several classes of instructors in the order of their importance. The lowest rate of all is paid to the ushers who look after the children's personal wants, to the teachers of gymnastic and elementary reading, and to the instructors who trained slaves to copy books. Teachers of writing and arithmetic receive half as much again. Teachers of architecture twice as much. At the top of the scale are the grammarians and geometricians with four times, and the rhetors with five times the minimum pay.

The rhetor is still the most important member of the academic hierarchy; but the gulf which formerly separated him from other teachers had grown much smaller. He stands now only a little way above the grammarian and above the specialist in charge of mathematics, a subject which two centuries before had been merely incidental to the grammar course. And numerically the grammarians preponderated. At Bordeaux in the fourth century they outnumbered the rhetors as six to four, while in Constantinople some eighty years later the proportion was twenty to eight.*

Our knowledge is tantalisingly scanty in the directions that we should like to know most. But we have at least a glimpse of a typical fourth-century school in the verses of the Bordeaux master, Ausonius.* From his accounts of his own career and from the references he makes to his colleagues, there emerge one or two significant facts. It becomes clear for example that the different grades mentioned in Diocletian's edict represented to some extent the steps on an official ladder of promotion. A man could rise from being a teacher of the alphabet to the eventual dignity of rhetor. Moreover, the duties appropriate to each grade were not distinguished by any hard and fast divisions. Sometimes a grammarian would take children at a very early age and teach them even the rudiments. Sometimes, however, he would delegate such elementary and not very pleasant tasks to a less qualified assistant.*

In considering these schools, we must consciously avoid thinking in present-day terms. Modern education is geared to curricula which might almost be described as traditional, and which in many cases command an almost universal acceptance. To take an extreme instance, the amount of mathematics a middle-class boy learns is much the same whatever country he lives in. Our teachers have to keep to courses fixed for them and controlled by examinations. What is more, their courses are connected in groups. Every child is supposed to follow several which dovetail into an education. The teachers specialise and co-operate. One is so familiar with these arrangements that one tends to read them into the history of every sort of school. It takes an effort to remember that they were absent from the Roman scene. A school for the ancients was merely a geographical expression. It was a place where several teachers found it convenient to teach. There is never any suggestion that these teachers co-operated in the way that modern schoolmasters co-operate. They merely co-existed as lecturers in different faculties co-exist in the modern university. Admittedly, there was a certain general agreement about the ground which a rhetorician or grammarian might be expected to cover, but the conception was extremely vague and allowed for an amount of latitude which would amaze any present-day pedagogue.

This dovetailing of the functions of grammarian and rhetor will appear more natural if we remember that their purpose was first of all to teach Latin; for the purity of the written language in official use was becoming increasingly hard to maintain. Correct usage was fixed, with reference to the norms of the Golden Age. But even educated speech was tending to diverge radically from these, while the idiom of the poor, which had always been different, was now becoming unrecognisably so. The situation—bad enough in Italy—was worse in the provinces. There the people talked local dialects based on an admixture of Latin with the vernaculars, and learning the official language was a major task for the educated provincial.* But he had to be encouraged to learn it, if the Empire was not to collapse for lack of local administrators. So the government provided the necessary facilities in the shape of schools.

The traditional techniques of the grammarians were particularly suited for the teaching of comprehension, while the exercises associated with the study of rhetoric could be advantageously adapted for inculcating the active use of the official Latin. But the true division between these two aspects of linguistic instruction is vertical, not horizontal. Passive and active knowledge must grow simultaneously, the former only a little in advance of the latter. Accordingly, the importance that had to be given to the teaching of Latin in a provincial town like Bordeaux led, in so far as there was any division of labour, to a levelling of the positions occupied by the grammarian and the rhetor, a levelling which took place the more easily since the old distinction between their activities was further diminished owing to the emphasis which both were expected to give to literary studies. Since one of the major aims of education was to spread the knowledge of the Graeco-Roman legacy, the rhetor as well as the grammarian had to do his share in explaining and popularising literature. Thus, the two grades differed in the end only with regard to their respective standing in the academic hierarchy and because of the added importance which the rhetor derived from his position as an official publicist.

The school of Bordeaux, as described by Ausonius, belongs to the fourth century; but we can regard its methods as typical of the Roman educational system up to the collapse of the Empire. The reforms they embodied, slight as these were, represent the furthest limits reached in practice by the movement to bring the training of the young in harmony with the needs of a world state. Nor was the East further advanced. It differed from the West only in emphasising Attic Greek rather than Latin. If anything, the Greek system was more backward than the Roman. The grammarian played a humbler role, the cult of a rhetoric based on narrowly interpreted formal principles reigning almost supreme. The grammars of the Atticists determined the language, the text-books of Themistius and Aphthonius the form, of most educated writing, while the school study of literature, still dominated by the wish to teach intelligent reading, had not, as we shall see, progressed far beyond the realm of incidental comment.

The educational innovations of the late Empire were all in theory. The schools went on much as before; but individuals writing on education developed the ideas which had been implicit in the criticisms of Quintilian and worked out on their basis the beginnings of a new curriculum.

Quintilian had claimed that the perfect orator would be capable of holding any office or dealing with any emergency, and within the ambit of his argument he had been indubitably right. For he defined the perfect orator as a man who was familiar with every branch of knowledge and possessed a wide practical experience for good measure. But it is plain to us that in so far as oratory itself is concerned, many of the qualifications which he demands have at best only a marginal value. His ideal could not have been formulated anywhere except in a society where the rhetorical training did duty for a general education but where it was fast losing its practical value; and we have to wait until the fifth century to find his successors. Then with barbarians at the gate, and within sight of that collapse which is finally to stop the imperial machine, three books are written breaking new ground. The attempt to find arguments for general knowledge within the limits of the oratorical ideal is summarily abandoned. Instead, in the treatises of Augustine, Capella and Cassiodorus the seven liberal arts feature as the basis of a new school curriculum. The desirability of a wide erudition is taken for granted. 'I know', says Cassiodorus, 'that secular literature is most keenly studied, for the majority of men believe that such studies bring worldly wisdom.'*

No evidence has been found, however, to suggest that these schemes were fully put into practice. To start with, there was no agreement as to which were the Seven Liberal Arts. Augustine names grammar, logic, rhetoric, music, geometry, arithmetic and philosophy, while Capella and Cassiodorus replace philosophy by astronomy.* Then, we have no traces of any school where the seven arts received individual and equal attention. The Bordeaux professors mentioned by Ausonius were either grammarians or rhetoricians. Sidonius Apollinaris in the next century speaks of eminent astronomers, musicians, geometricians and the like, but one finds on investigation that the same teachers often figure in several roles,* and the only non-vocational subjects listed in the imperial rescripts are again grammar, computation and rhetoric. One is left with the impression that everything else was taught in conjunction with these three, that a grammarian would lecture on philosophy when he came across a philosophical passage in an author, much after the style of Macrobius' commentary on the *Somnium Scipionis.* If he did this well, if he was interested and made full use of his opportunities, he would earn the title of philosopher. Only in the old established schools of the East which seem to have attained a much higher academic level, was philosophy kept more or less distinct; and even there we have Themistius simultaneously a rhetorician and a philosopher, Hypatia a mathematician and philosopher, Proclus a philosopher and a poet.*

We are forced to conclude that Augustine and Capella (and later Cassiodorus) were independent theorists, concerned to improve and not merely to describe current educational practice. But that does not detract from the importance of their treatises as plans for the future. To include logic, which had previously been studied only in the schools of philosophy, as a basic subject for general education was to take a great step forward. It was to recognise the fact that clear thinking in private, rather than eloquence in public, was the activity which the problems of the age required. The recognition accorded to sciences like arithmetic and geometry, not as specialities, but as necessary parts of a normal curriculum, pointed the same way. But the greatest virtue of the new theories was perhaps their providing a reasoned alternative to the system of Quintilian. For the world in which oratory had flourished was dying; and the new civilisation destined to replace it was to have no knowledge of popular assemblies or forensic triumphs. The men of the centuries to come, whose lives were to be centred on the manor and the monastery, would have found it a definitive disadvantage if the educational tradition on which they depended had put before them an ideal whose significance they could not grasp, if Capella and Augustine had not replaced Quintilian. Thanks to these late theoreticians, whose writings probably had next to no influence on their contemporaries, the Middle Ages could set the linguistic discipline which they inherited from the Roman schools within a theoretical framework that had some meaning for their times.

Such briefly were the main developments we can trace in ancient education; and it is against this background of hesitant theory and slow-moving practical change that we must set the works which were to prove a major influence on the schools of the Middle Ages and the Renaissance. Some of these text-books—for that is the name we may most aptly give them—belonged to that early tradition which had reigned supreme before Quintilian. Others, including the *Institutiones Oratoriae*, came from the pens of that tradition's most telling contemporary critics. Others again reflected the teaching methods actually in use at the end of the Empire, while a small, but most important group, the product of the theorists of that chaotic age, pictured innovations far beyond anything that had been accomplished in practice.

It will be convenient to start with rhetoric since the text-books which influenced its teaching were on the whole earlier in date than those used for other subjects. During the Middle Ages, the anonymous *ad Herennium* and the *de Inventione* of Cicero's nonage occupied a dominant position in the schools, both by their own right and through the contemporary works they inspired;* and we must lay to their door the responsibility for that lack of artistic structure, that inexactness and those tasteless amplifications which weary us in so much of medieval writing. Their schematic analyses of style and their interminable lists of figures of speech and forms of argument, considered without any reference to their context, were typical products of the first century B.C. and reflected the aridity and purely technical preoccupations which characterised the rhetorical schools of that period.

The position occupied by the *ad Herennium* and the *de Inventione* in the West fell in Byzantium to a group of treatises dating from the second and fourth centuries A.D. They have the advantage of not being theoretical analyses, but consist of chosen passages in which the theoretical rules are exemplified. They also give evidence of the later rhetorician's growing interest in literary history and criticism. But in spite of these improvements, the cloven hoof of the old rule-of-thumb tradition still shows through.

The ancient science of rhetoric consisted for the most part of an elaborate system of classification based upon the analysis of oratory into its constituent elements and serving in practice as a mnemonic. The purpose of the analysis was largely utilitarian. It was thought that a theoretical knowledge of the different types of demonstration would enable a speaker to choose and present in succession the ones best adapted to his case, while a theoretical knowledge of the rhetorical figures which were known to the grammarians would by a similar process of plagiaristic choice give wings to his invention. The mnemonic value of the classifications was then further increased by the memorising of particular examples, the purpose of the teacher being always to build up a stock of argument and illustration on which his pupil could afterwards draw. Rhetorical training began by careful exercises in certain types of expression, which received the name of *Progymnasmata*. We shall hear of these repeatedly until late in the Byzantine age; but the earliest by Theon, Hermogenes and Aphthonius were the most famous and are probably the best.

They present us with the peculiar debris of an abandoned and virtually forgotten science. Aphthonius divides the art of oratory into several sections, defines each and then illustrates each by passages which his pupils are expected to imitate.

In dealing with narrative, he lists the points one ought to watch if one wants to tell a clear story. What has been done? When? Where? How? and Why? He distinguishes between descriptions which involve merely space and those which bring in time. He lays down the rule that in delineating persons one should proceed from the head to the feet, while scenes should be represented following the movements of the eye from a fixed angle of view. Description of character has a separate section allotted to it. Here we have the famous *ethopoeia* or short character sketch to which Theophrastus, La Bruyère, and indirectly the modern novel, owe so much.

Schoolboys were given a good deal of practice in inventing speeches to be uttered by mythological, historical or altogether imaginary characters. They were told to imagine a person of a known type, a Hercules or an Aristides, or alternatively a soldier, a misanthrope, or a usurer, faced with some obvious and appropriate situation, and they were told to record what he would say. The purpose in all cases was to make the language true to type. Ideally, such an exercise would require fine observation and some degree of the ability which makes it possible for us to identify ourselves with others. But in the hands of schoolmasters and their uninterested pupils it became a mere routine of repeating traditional formulae associated with traditional characters. It was in this uninspired form (which proved popular precisely because it was crude) that the practice came to influence the mental development of the Greeks and Romans. All their ideas on psychology and consequently on ethics were affected by their tendency to divide people into types and to represent these types to themselves in a naive and stereotyped fashion.

Along with the general rules of good narrative and description, the student was given advice on how to ornament his material. The main forms of adornment considered are those which we should class nowadays as anecdotes, quotations, allusions and epigrams.* All these could be practised, and what was even better, collected and learnt by heart for the future. The trained orator had always a number ready for use on all occasions.

Further sections then deal with such problems as how to praise or blame a person, how to refute or confirm a story. The possible grounds for each attitude are listed in detail. A refutation for example can be suitably based, according to Aphthonius, on any of the following: the obscurity or illogicality of the narrative, the unlikelihood, impossibility, impropriety or inexpediency of believing the facts described.

These exercises taught the young an easy method of enlarging on any topic they might wish to discuss, by training them to look for ideas along fruitful lines. They had been designed originally to promote a ready inventiveness. But as language-learning came to play an increasingly large part in education, their secondary function of affording practice in the rules of grammar became more and more emphasised. The ability to use Attic Greek, that is the ability to avoid solecisms in the traditional written idiom, had long been regarded in the Hellenised East as one of the marks of an educated man; and by the fifth century a similar situation had developed with regard to Latin in the West. The contemptuous references of Sidonius to the grammatical errors of his contemporaries and his tendency to identify linguistic rectitude with the maintenance of cultural standards indicate what a dominant position language teaching must have acquired in the schools, and this is further borne out by the fuss which a Cassiodorus or a Venantius makes during the following century when convicted of a grammatical fault.*

So, right through the Middle Ages a partial and misleading conception of the writer's art remained dominant in the West and East alike. The great classical expositions of that art, which took a suitably wide view of its possibilities and its relation to experience, the *Poetics* of Aristotle, the works of Cicero's maturity, the critical treatises of 'Longinus' and Dionysius of Halicarnassus, remained without influence, if not wholly unknown, until the Renaissance and in some cases until the sixteenth century. In no other field was Europe so tardy about taking the best that the past had to offer.

The study of grammar was more straightforward and requires less discussion. Here the principal text-books were the systematic expositions of Donatus and Priscian in Latin and the works of the Atticists in Greek. Based on the best tradition of classical learning in both the normative and the descriptive field, they provided an easy introduction to the uniformities of the ancient languages while keeping well to the fore the anomalies of specific usage. Their habit of citing examples served to recommend afresh the great authors of the Golden Age of Athens and Rome to each new generation and did much to keep alive an interest in antiquity at times when men might otherwise have been content with second-rate summaries.

More important than the grammars in the width and subtlety of their influence were the works of the commentators. They embodied for the medieval world and to a great extent also for the Renaissance the teaching of the ancients on literary history and literary criticism and helped to determine how the classical authors were interpreted.

We have mentioned earlier that the grammarians were in the habit of explaining the texts which they taught their pupils to read; but so far no account has been given of their methods. These are best examined in conjunction with those commentaries which, written down at the time, proved influential in the sequel, and which we shall now have to consider.

The main tradition of ancient scholarship and literary study had its roots in a desire to make easy the correct reading aloud of the authors who were the glory of Greek and Latin culture. Such works as the *Poetics* of Aristotle or the *de Oratore* of Cicero, which treated questions of form and content from a general viewpoint, were exceptional. Based on the data of private experience and the insight of genius, they stood apart from the common current, and if they influenced the schools, did so from the outside and to little effect. But of the multitudinous commentaries and incidental essays which constitute the great bulk of ancient scholarship, the opposite is true. These were written by practising grammarians or by men on whose minds the classroom had left an ineffaceable stamp, and their influence was undoubted since they were the product of the very activities they sought to forward. The subtle Aristarchus, the encyclopedic Philostratus of Lemnos, the soberly erudite Servius were the djinns of the unpretentious, somewhat battered, grammar-school lamp.

The successful reading of an author depended upon three things: the possession of a correct text, the understanding of the language, and the reader's ability to make sense of mythological and historical references. The tradition we are considering had these three aspects. Individually, their usefulness cannot be gainsaid. But it is worth noting that they were all three concerned with matters of detail; and even though they complemented each other, they did not tell the student more than a moiety of what by modern standards we should consider desirable to know.

Perhaps the most influential of the Latin commentaries were the famous notes of Servius on Virgil. These have been shown to depend extensively on earlier commentators; and may be taken therefore as representative. Servius is interested primarily in linguistic problems. He tells us the meaning of difficult words, explains unusual forms and unusual constructions. Well over half his notes are of that order. A further substantial number are devoted to the naming and elucidation of rhetorical figures. The non-linguistic parts of his commentary occupy only about a third of the whole.

What is the content of that third? When we look at the notes of general interest in greater detail, we find that some of them are explanations of historical and literary allusions, some elucidate obsolete customs, and some—to a proportion of about one to three—can be best described as psychological in intention. Their aim is to show that although certain actions described by Virgil may appear puzzling, the people concerned are nevertheless acting in character,* the general conceptions of character being taken over from the type-psychology of the rhetoricians.

One cannot fail to be struck by the almost complete absence from the notes of any discussion on the wider problems of aesthetics and literary form. It was not the case that these problems had received no attention. Servius was a man of wide reading, and he could scarcely have been ignorant of what had been said by Aristotle or of the points raised in the *Treatise on the Sublime*. It is evident, however, that he did not consider that these matters called for his attention. A similar narrowness of approach can be observed in his treatment of historical and cultural material. Though it would be pointless to criticise him for falling short of standards imposed by the mental habits of a later age, a comparison between his interests and those of modern scholarship is nevertheless instructive. Servius does not make the slightest attempt to reconstruct the personal or cultural background of his poet or of the period in which the action of the poem is ostensibly set. His explanations deal exclusively with matters of detail which he discusses in a spirit of antiquarian curiosity.

In this he was typical of his age and profession. The historians of the ancient world had been outstanding. Thucydides and his school had followed scientific principles. Livy and Tacitus had pleaded a special brief. But they had all been aware that the events of history group themselves in wide movements and vast panoramas, that the phenomena of life abound in connections. But those who undertook to relate the history of literature never envisaged their task in any nobler light than the collecting of chance items of information, curiosities and anecdotes to amuse an idle hour. It was not by chance that the late Empire produced the *Deipnosophistae*. That farrago of inconsequential facts which meets us in the pages of Athenaeus was not the creation of an isolated eccentric brain. He, like Aulus Gellius before him, drew on the accumulated scholarship of his age; and his frivolity of mind just brings into sharper relief that dilettantism which is equally observable in the works of the most sober commentators.

Such was the teaching material in rhetoric, grammar, criticism and literary history that posterity was to inherit from the Graeco-Roman schools. Its principal virtues were a serious and constructive preoccupation with language, a striving after linguistic exactitude and the excellent habit of attentive reading. Its main fault, measured by the needs of the imperial period itself, was the narrowness of its scope, which was to result in the neglect of some of the finest features of the classical legacy so long as the schools of Europe did not shake themselves free from the cramping influence of classical teaching methods.

But alongside these works we must place those others, already mentioned, whose theoretical constructions had remained without much practical influence in their own day: namely the treatises on the liberal arts. The earliest, Augustine's projected book, which he began at the end of the fourth century, was never completed and survived only in fragments. Its immediate successor, the *de Nuptiis Mercurii et Philologiae* of Martianus Capella gave, in so far as its fanciful form permitted, a comprehensive and useful account of both the Trivium and the Quadrivium, while the sixth-century *Institutiones* of Cassiodorus had by reason of its Christian authorship, its seriousness and evident sincerity, perhaps the most effective claim upon the attention of the future. No emphasis need be given to the obvious defects of these treatises, which have been heavily criticised by nearly every writer on the culture of the Middle Ages. Their summaries of the various branches of knowledge erred on the side of a jejune brevity; and it has been said that wishing to cover too much, they ran the risk of omitting everything of genuine interest. Certainly, as guides to knowledge they left much to be desired. To their major fault of condensing too much, they added the further sin of not always following the best authorities. What Cassiodorus tells us about rhetoric, for example, has the same arid, penny-wise quality that we have noted in the prescriptions of the *ad Herennium*.

In the event these shortcomings proved to have their advantageous side; for the harassed ignorant world of the Dark Ages would have found it difficult to assimilate a stronger and more sustaining intellectual fare and might well have recoiled from learning altogether if its only choice had been the ambrosia of the best authors. But that circumstance was a mere accident of fortune and should not perhaps be placed to the credit of Capella and Cassiodorus. They had, however, another virtue which is rightfully theirs in that very comprehensiveness that was the cause of their imperfections; and because of it, the history of education must allow them a distinguished eminence. They were not the first to take an encyclopedic view and to name the different branches of human learning. Their debt to Varro in particular is evident. But Varro's *Disciplinae* had been, so far as one can tell, merely an account of existing knowledge. It was left for Augustine and his successors to take the all-important step from the library to the schoolroom, from the compilation of a work of reference to the planning of a compendious curriculum. Therein lay their originality and their proper claim to fame. They provided their contemporaries and the generations to come with an educational ideal that was at once inspiring and practicable, adequate in scope and not too difficult to realise.

Alongside the treatises on the liberal arts, we must note another fourth-century work which occupies a somewhat unique place among the text-books favoured by the Middle Ages. The commentary of Macrobius on the *Somnium Scipionis* of Cicero is startlingly different from the products of that general academic tradition which Servius exemplifies. It makes next to no mention of grammar, antiquities or history, but concerns itself almost exclusively with philosophical or pseudo-philosophical problems. It elucidates at length and with an un-expected air of intelligent charm such topics as the mystical significance of numbers, the after-life of the virtuous and the influence of the spheres. By the time the last page is reached, the reader has come to know a good deal about Neoplatonism. The text has been used as a peg on which to hang a more or less systematic exposition of the one subject which the author considered all important. We cannot identify Macrobius with any particular individual among a number of possible contemporary figures. The circumstances of his life remain unknown to us. His other extant work, the *Saturnalia*, is of a character to suggest if not the pro-fessional grammarian then at least one well acquainted with the profes-sional tradition; but when he came to write on the *Somnium Scipionis*, his Neoplatonist enthusiasms carried him away; and in the effort to communicate his cherished beliefs, he evolved what was in effect a new method of treating texts chosen for study. The popularity of this commentary during the Middle Ages was due primarily to its content. It provided the best available source from which a knowledge of the Neoplatonic philosophy could be gained; and that philosophy, so close in spirit to Christianity and yet so subtly different in its methods and implications, was to have a compulsive fascination for the ages of faith. But influential as his ideas were, the importance of Macrobius derives less from them than from the credit which their influence won for his method. The commentary which combined the elucidation of a text with a systematic exposition of the topics discussed therein was eventually to play a vital part in the development of European thought.

Such were the main pillars of the pedagogic tradition which the Middle Ages inherited and which largely determined their use of the classical heritage. This tradition fell, as has been shown, into two parts. On the one hand, it provided a detailed analysis of two subjects, grammar and rhetoric, together with complete and detailed techniques for teaching them. On the other hand it provided a plan for a more comprehensive curriculum including a number of other subjects such as mathematics and logic whose content was insufficiently analysed and for whose teaching no methods had been evolved. Any educational system which rested on these foundations was bound to run into serious difficulties owing to the discrepancy between its theoretical ideals and its practical endowments; and we shall find that difficulties of this nature were indeed a great bugbear in the medieval schools. Perhaps the finest of the many intellectual triumphs to the credit of the men of the Middle Ages and the Renaissance is that they eventually did manage to make good the deficiencies of the tradition they had inherited by working out an adequate apparatus of learning and instruction for all the subjects of the Trivium and Quadrivium and for such others as they felt desirable to add to the original list. But at the dark moment when St Gregory the Great met the Lombards outside Rome, these achievements were still far distant. For the moment the educational legacy of the imperial schools offered the sole resource on which the architects of Europe's intellectual development could reasonably depend.

III. THE PATRISTIC TRADITION

Among the various factors which decided the fortunes of the classical heritage, the influence of Christianity holds an obvious pride of place. By the end of the sixth century, the Christian religion not only commanded the faith and ultimate hopes of millions. It had set the impress of its principles on all the more important spheres of human activity, in the number of which the acquisition of knowledge was naturally included; and it had come to dominate the field of affairs through an institution which disposed of an authority greater than that of any prince.

For the contemporaries of St Gregory the Great, the literary heritage of the past was already something outside of their own world, which they could accept because of its usefulness, or reject because of the dangers it might bring in its train. The predominance of Christianity had therefore the effect of making the views of the Christian community extremely influential when it came to determining how the classical heritage was to be studied. Was the conscience of the time to sponsor the rebuilding of the ancient world with a wholehearted approval? Or was it to oppose such an effort? There was no unanimous answer.

This uncertainty had good reasons to excuse it. The Christian and classical patterns of life possessed many traits in common; but equally there was much to divide them. The former had developed originally within the culture where the latter was supreme, and was bound to it by the strongest ties of affiliation. The nature of the debt which the dogma, discipline, law and ritual of the patristic Church owed to pagan Greece and Rome cannot be described in detail without impinging on abstruse and controversial issues. But its great extent remains beyond dispute. Equally indisputable, however, is the importance of the differences which sundered that pagan order from its Christian successor, the Rome of the Forum from the Rome of the Popes. The Faith which had built the catacombs and sustained the tortures of the arena had its roots in experiences of which its persecutors were necessarily ignorant; and religion was a lion unlikely in any case to lie down in peaceful concord with the lamb of sweet reason.

The result was that the two traditions presented a strange variety of similarities and discords which now drew them together, now forced them bitterly apart; and of these one example may perhaps be given. Both the Hellenic and the Christian outlook laid a notable stress on personal responsibility. This trait was for each the keystone of its special values, and served to distinguish them both from those creeds and cultures that made man a helpless or a worthless pawn. But the best of the Greeks had sought to be responsible in the wise assessment and control of material circumstances for the purpose of achieving a worldly happiness. The Christians on the contrary were concerned with the choice between the road of salvation and the road of evil. The former had held themselves accountable for rational conduct in the natural sphere. The latter measured all things, responsibility among them, by the yardstick of an eternal law. Compromise between these two attitudes was admittedly possible. The Christian view can without being inconsistent admit worldly happiness as a permissible secondary aim, and it is not difficult to find support for a similar hierarchy of values in the writings of the most eminent Greek philosophers. But a compromise of that nature could not be permanent. Ideological enthusiasm affords such a convenient outlet for human aggressiveness that no complex attitude which depends on accepted principles *not* being carried to their logical extremes, has ever enjoyed a long lease of life; and in this instance the chances of survival were less than usual since the extreme positions, both on the Christian and on the Humanist side, had a strong attraction for certain temperaments. The unconditional service of Heaven was a comfort to those who were inhibited from enjoying the pleasures of this world, while Hedonism had its charms for those compulsively attracted to luxury or lust.

We must keep in mind however that the men of the early Middle Ages did not try to settle these problems of conflict and compromise from first principles. They did not think for themselves to any great extent. Their attitude to the classical heritage was determined by the history of the preceding six centuries; and if we are to understand Gregory I or Alcuin, we must take into account the opinions of the patristic age.

The majority of early Christians entertained ambivalent feelings about the Roman world. Passionately resenting some of its aspects, they were prepared to cling with equal passion to the rest. They hated the immoralities they saw around them. They wanted paganism destroyed; but they would have been horrified by the thought that the civilisation they knew might not be preserved. After the Christian religion had spread to include vast numbers of converts, most of its adherents were normal men and women, busy about everyday things; and their normality prevented them from visualising life independent of society, or society constituted otherwise than its familiar setting of rabbit-warren cities and an undermanned countryside. They wanted to be Christians, but amid the usual appurtenances of Roman life.

Similarly they were in two minds about the pagan literature which, as the basis of grammar and rhetoric, formed the staple subject-matter of the schools. If we can still be moved by the beauty of these works which spring from a world separated from us in some cases by more than two thousand years, and which are written in languages we have never heard spoken, how great must have been the spell they exercised over the minds of those who knew them as their national heritage. In spite of the intense hatred of all pagan practices and beliefs which the persecutions and the social depravity of the age naturally aroused, there were many educated Christians whose devotion to the poets and orators nothing could shake. We shall be discussing the case of Jerome in some detail; but he was not alone in his attitude. Even during the period when the imperial power was doing its best to stamp out Christianity, we find Arnobius and Lactantius upholding as zealously as any pagan rhetor the conventional values of linguistic exactitude and style; and it is evident from the dismay aroused by Julian's edict which forbade Christians to lecture on authors with whom they did not agree, as also from the number of the professors who resigned, that by the middle of the fourth century the representatives of the new religion were well entrenched in the schools and their academic work was sufficiently after the normal pattern to earn the respect of their colleagues. They could not have differed from these colleagues in the value they set upon their common subject-matter.

The ancient literatures, beside their aesthetic charm, embodied the best aspects of the pagan tradition; and so they could not be rejected by anyone who was not at the same time prepared to cut himself off from the whole of existing civilisation. Indeed many who were prepared to reject all else, many who had nothing but contempt for the world around them, still retained in their hearts a liking for Cicero or Virgil which no prejudice could dispel.

This ambivalence which characterised the outlook of the Christian in the street, also affected the most eminent and influential of the Fathers. An Augustine, a Jerome, a Basil of Caesarea had not the kind of outlook which enables its possessors to consider life from a narrow angle as an assemblage of purely personal problems. The difficulties that engaged their attention and could mobilise the vigour of their feelings were present to their consciousness in the wider involvement of a social context. Their temperaments were such that they sought spontaneously for solutions which presupposed the noise and turmoil of men living together, which accordingly accepted civilisation and all its works. They were prepared to assume that in the new Christian society of the future numerous traits of the pagan world would be preserved although paganism itself would need to be purged away. Fundamentally, their attitude, which had the implicit support of the majority of their co-religionists was one of compromise.

But side by side with the tolerant majority there existed also a small and highly articulate minority who contended that the faithful ought to sever all contact with a degraded and degrading paganism. These zealots argued from premises well-grounded in Christian belief that the world in general was evil, and that a world dominated by pagan ideas must in consequence be doubly damned; that life in society was no preparation for the judgement to come; that the satisfaction of bodily needs, the improvement of property and the peaceful production of wealth and children had no real importance in the eyes of a jealous God; and that the prayer and vacant contemplation which are man's right true end, were most effectively practised in the decent untroubled solitude of a desert cell.

The fervour of these extremists, the prevalence of the evils they combated and the ruthless logic of their ideas had the effect of installing them as the keepers of the Christian conscience. Their single-mindedness was a powerful asset. For during these dislocated centuries which preceded the Dark Ages, no man could gauge the extent of the calamities which so plainly threatened. None therefore could feel confidence in his own sober judgement of what action was expedient or good; and the wisest Fathers of the Church had their fearful and uncertain moments. The ways of wisdom appear to us so complicated, so awkward to sum up in formulae, that even in easy times we find it hard to believe their worth. When difficulties threaten, they are quickly relinquished. In crises men are emotionally prepared to grasp at any panacea provided that it is firmly enough offered; and here the panacea had certain merits of its own. For that abandonment of the world, which the zealots were preaching, presented itself, on the one hand, as an escape from formidable moral and practical problems and so appeared desirable to the weary. On the other hand, being a mortification of the flesh it provided simultaneously with rest a welcome relief from anxiety. Its self-inflicted punishment anticipated the dreaded punishments of fortune. Thus, we find the Fathers every so often driven from the citadels of their common sense into a more or less whole-hearted acceptance of a policy of flight, from which, and on calmer occasions, they again withdraw, to put forward with their usual hesitations the balanced views of compromise.

We have talked so far as if patristic literature gave expression to a common outlook, and that is perhaps legitimate. For the opinions of the Fathers do add up to a unified tradition. But all the same they differed as individuals in the degree of their respect for the non-Christian past. The Greek Church supplied distinguished champions of the liberal policy which recommended imitating the best in paganism. Clement of Alexandria, who died early in the third century, had never felt the need to apologise for his wide reading. He had spread the legend that Greek literature went back to Jewish sources* and had then cheerfully drawn on the Greek authors for argument and illustration. He was the first to propound the view, which was to gain considerable currency later, that the pagan literature was a propaedeutic to the Scriptures; and unlike most of those who repeated his remark, he had in mind not the information the Greek writings contained but what he was pleased to describe as their power to dispel prejudice.*

Clement had been prepared to admit that he was influenced by Hellenism. Others had felt the same influence, but failed to make the same admission. Origen, whose theology was expressed in Neo-Platonic terms, scorned the thinkers whose ideas he had borrowed. And there were many who followed Origen's pattern. But the spirit, which lends dignity to the utterances of Clement, inspired, a hundred and fifty years later, a brilliant generation of young men who grew up at the precise point of time when the old traditions were still strong, but Christianity was already respectable. St Basil of Caesarea and his friend St Gregory Nazianzen had studied under Himerius in Athens, Theodore of Mopsuestia had sat at the feet of Diodorus in Antioch, while St John Chrysostom had been the favourite pupil of Libanius. All four possessed an expert knowledge of the ancient classics. Theodore spent his life in ardent controversies in the course of which he tried to persuade his fellow theologians to apply to the Scriptures the interpretative methods traditional in Greek scholarship. The other three were primarily stylists. Trained by the most eminent of contemporary Atticist scholars, they expressed Christian beliefs in the language, and therefore within the system of ideas, which Athens had bequeathed to the world. They were all zealous littérateurs as was also that lesser figure Bishop Synesius.* But Basil and Gregory were also the boldest and most open protagonists of a Christian Humanism who had ever dared to make their voices heard. They went beyond the position taken up by Clement that pagan philosophy had the power of dispelling prejudices meaner than itself, and suggested that it would actually ennoble the minds of its readers.* After their death the learning of the Greek theological schools took a different turn and ran dry in the aridities of sectarian conflict. But their writings had a great influence and the mantle of their sanctity was always there to protect and sanction in the Greek Church a reasoned tolerance of the pagan past.

The literature of ancient Greece was largely philosophic in tone. That of Rome contained a much higher proportion of the merely lascivious. Thus, it was in the West that paganism wore its most immoral, repellent and anti-Christian face; and for that reason, the Latin Fathers, while accepting the dependence of a future Christian society upon the old culture, were more inclined than their Greek compeers to treat that culture with suspicion, to play down its usefulness, and even for moments to condemn it altogether.

So we find Tertullian most reluctant to see Christian children in the pagan schools, but permitting their attendance because he realises that they must master reading and writing with at least a modicum of general knowledge, and realises too that the conventional grammar schools afford the only means to that end. He then straightaway cancels out this concession by forbidding Christians to teach. Pagan education may have been indispensable. All the same it was not to be countenanced.*

Tertullian was a pioneer, theologically suspect, and his influence was therefore never great. Jerome and Augustine were the men who decided the educational future of the West. They were the contemporaries of Basil and Gregory, but they inhabited a different and more alarming world than was visible to the placid East. Their countries were torn by dissension and war; and the impermanence of all civil power was plainly manifest to their eyes. There must have been moments when they thought that civilisation could not survive. Since men's interest in pagan literature derived from their hope for an ordered and civilised future, this greater uncertainty of life in the West will perhaps account for the hectic fluctuations of mood and judgement which can be observed in the writings of the two Latin Fathers.* For sometimes they are as broadly Humanist as Basil himself; but sometimes they turn quite the other way and, victims of some urgent anxiety, take refuge in the emotional extreme of an absolute rejection.

St Jerome had studied under Donatus and adored beauty of language with a passion which it is not easy for our more literate age to imagine. When he was already a mature man and a scholar whose reputation had been safely established, he fell ill during a trip to the East. In a dream at the crisis of his fever he pictured himself before the judgement seat of God and heard a plangent voice accuse him of being no Christian but a Ciceronian.* This experience left him shaken as after a profound shock. He immediately abjured all profane studies. Following the current ascetic custom he fled to the desert; and there he stayed for the full five years of a slow spiritual convalescence, first lying on the sand black with dust and eating uncooked food, then working with his hands, then copying books and finally undertaking the study of Hebrew. By 380 he was back in Constantinople and back too at his old habits, reading Greek books under the benevolent eye of Nazianzen; and it was a little while later that he began his great Latin version of the Bible. His old age was spent in a cloister near Bethlehem, busy with his translating, with his book of biographical sketches after the manner of Suetonius, with lecturing on the pagan authors to a class of boys.* During the Middle Ages his example came to inspire both the partisans and the opponents of the studies he loved. The legend of his dream was used to deter the studious. But the Vulgate was always there to remind the Church of the blessings which accrue when a saint is inconsistent in his contempt for mundane beauty.

St Jerome was an artist. A graceful style filled him with keen delight. He was prepared to read the pagan writers, and to see his fellow Christians read them. He was prepared to tolerate even the morally dubious Comedians and the Satirists because they wrote correctly and rhythmically, because there was beauty in their imagery and aptness in their figures of speech, and because personally he never looked much beyond their literary qualities. Their content did not interest him. To the inattentive all things are pure; and those Christians whose love of pagan literature was based on a genuine failure to see that literature whole, whose interest was focused on its formal elements and who were nearly blind to all else, the writers in short and the connoisseurs, found in his sanctity and in his great service to Christian letters an unshakeably convincing justification of their attitude; and during the long Middle Ages that justification was to be sorely needed.

His example was, however, supplemented for Christendom by the teachings of St Augustine. The Bishop of Hippo was in many ways the antithesis of his aesthetically perceptive contemporary; and that he should have left written precepts where Jerome left a legend, a fact unimportant in itself, is an interesting symbol of the differences which divided the two men. Augustine was an intellectual for whom every sphere of knowledge and experience resolved itself into a collocation of definable details. It has been remarked that he considered the art of writing to be no more than the cunning use of literary devices, and that he treated systems of philosophy as if they had been mathematical theories. He had the scientific approach before the days of science. His intellect moreover was one of exceptional power. It could impose a clear mental pattern on the most complicated and most refractory of subjects. There were no limits to its span, and nothing dismayed its unflagging energy.

This vigour of mind, so far above the normal as to constitute a veritable prodigy of genius, shaped Augustine's outlook in a way which was to have great importance for his treatment of educational problems. Since it cost him no trouble to envisage elaborate and subtle relationships interacting over a wide field, he was not tempted to blind himself to the difficulties which arise because man is a social animal. When he considered the human condition, he thought naturally in terms of communities and not of individuals. Salvation as far as he was concerned presupposed the City of God and not merely the divine vision granted to an artificially isolated anchorite.

Thus, Augustine was admirably fitted to provide a reasoned explanation of that attitude to the pagan heritage which the majority of Christians inarticulately shared. He could understand those social pressures and needs which the ordinary man felt but could not put into words. Convinced that the virtues of the elect ought to find social expression, and that it was the duty of every Christian to facilitate such social improvements as could be achieved, he put forward a single solution to the problem of how to preserve civilisation without preserving paganism. Giving free play to his curious talent for splitting up organic wholes into artificial but easily definable parts, he envisaged the separation of all that was useful in the pagan legacy from its impious, immoral, or merely dispensable accompaniments. Christian culture could then take the first and jettison the second with a clear conscience. The analogy he used to illustrate his principle was the looting of the Egyptians by the people of Israel. Rome was laden with heterogeneous treasures, distinct and quickly recognisable, which the hosts of Christendom might appropriate and employ without prejudice for their own purposes.

Besides formulating this general principle, which was so attractive in its simplicity, and which minds familiar with the procedures of war found easy to comprehend, Augustine also made certain suggestions of a more specific character.

He advised the use of summaries. As a young man, round about the time of his conversion, he had begun a systematic survey of the liberal arts; and though he failed to complete this work a passage in his *Retractationes* shows that he continued to consider it of potential value.* It was evident that such compendia, where Christian teachers brought together the essential facts on a number of important topics, could give the young safe access to information which they would otherwise need to seek from dangerous sources: and within a limited sphere, Augustine had no doubts about their efficacy.

Another suggestion he made was concerned with the teaching of rhetoric. In that all-important subject, text-books had only a limited value. Rules could be systematically stated, but as everyone knew, a bald statement was not sufficient. Pupils required examples. They could remember only what they had seen a hundred times embodied in an actual text: and where except in the established classics could suitable texts be found? The general attitude of Christian teachers on this point was that of Lactantius who had bewailed the supremacy of the pagans but had firmly refused to consider any alternatives to their use. Augustine who was deeply concerned about religious needs and whom the aesthetic beauties of a Virgil or a Cicero did not move as deeply as they moved Jerome, saw an alternative and had no hesitation in putting it forward. The Christian preachers, he pointed out, would find all the rules of rhetoric illustrated in the Scriptures. If they had a technical treatise to tell them what to look for, and a Bible in which to search out their examples, they would be adequately equipped.*

These incidental suggestions are of more considerable import than might at first appear. A pillaging of the classical heritage, whose spoils were then gradually embodied in new technical and literary works to the replacement of their pagan predecessors, was likely to have very different results in the long run from a pillaging which had always to begin afresh so that each generation came into direct contact with the masterpieces of the past. Augustine wrote so much and expressed so great a variety of opinions that one cannot venture on any hard and fast judgement about what he may have thought on a point that he did not specifically develop. But the probability is that he did not envisage the replacing of pagan literature at least for many generations to come. His remark about the Bible occurs in a treatise where he is dealing specifically with the education of the clergy; and even in that context it was only for the study of rhetoric that he had in his own opinion proved the pagan authors redundant: though this is in the very field where according to Jerome they were indispensable. As regards content, he realised that there was material of great value in both poets and prose writers which could not be excerpted and would need to be gathered from the original texts so that Christians would always have to rely on the firmness of their principles to enable them to retain the good and to give the bad no foothold in their memory.*

Augustine represented in this matter the midpoint of the Christian attitude. Those Greek Fathers who were humanistically inclined like Basil and Gregory Nazianzen were prepared to allow pagan literature to be taught in the schools to Christian children because they regarded it—the obviously gross writers apart—as a suitable introduction in both form and subject-matter to the study of theology. Jerome was prepared to allow it to be taught, because of its beauty; and blinkered by his artist's viewpoint he too failed to make any clear distinction as regards subject-matter. These writers stood at one end of the scale. Against them were arrayed men like Ennodius and Claudius Victor who were ready to blame all the misfortunes of the age on the reading of Virgil and Ovid,* and men who like Paulinus of Nola were prepared to flee into solitude. Augustine took up a position half-way between the contending parties. He never considered the possibility of a sudden break with Graeco-Roman culture, but he dismissed the arguments of Jerome and attenuated those of Basil, making it clear that while a limited amount of borrowing from paganism was vitally necessary, the amount could be limited. Bringing to bear on the problem that cut and dried simplifying spirit which was his notable contribution to the development of his age, he worked out a solution which ordinary men could easily accept.

The next theologian whose opinions were to count for much in the future was Gregory the Great. During the two centuries which separate him from Augustine, certain important developments had taken place.

Martianus Capella had composed his playfully pedantic treatise on the Seven Arts, which had proved popular, and had been revised a hundred years or so after its original appearance by the Christian rhetorician, Memor Felix. Cassiodorus had written his *Institutiones* with the avowed purpose of providing an easy and safe equivalent of traditional education for his monks. These works, along with the comprehensive and monumental encyclopedia of Isidore, the brother of Gregory's friend Leander, were to become the favourite text-books of the early Middle Ages; and it is reasonable to assume that they owed their popularity to the circumstance that they did summarise more or less adequately the most basic and most obvious material that the Christian world wanted from the pagan. They implemented to a great extent the first part of that programme which we saw sketched out in the fourth century.

At the same time, Christian literature had grown in volume and dignity. Christian poets used the classical metres with skill. The monk who was interested in verse could study Prudentius, Paulinus or Sidonius instead of Ovid or Virgil, and they would teach him all he might want to know about rhythm and poetic language. In prose, there was the Vulgate and there were the stylists among the early Fathers. Salvian, educated in Gaul during the fifth century, already knew his Lactantius better than his Cicero and was a skilled rhetorician for all that.* The Christian writings of the first four centuries have been studied for the most part as theology and not as literature; and scholarship has not yet revealed how much they owed to their models. But the debt was certainly great enough for them to fulfil one function. They supplied an adequate set of illustrations for the rules contained in the text-books.

To see the relationship in which the Christian culture of the late Empire stood to its predecessors, we need to take another look at the written language. By the fifth century there had developed independently in the East and in the West those variations on the official idioms, which we now call ecclesiastical Greek and Latin. These differed from their classical norms both by omissions and additions. They lacked those subtleties which derive from the involved possibilities of an elaborate and logical syntax, the classical usage having been in many cases replaced by a cruder one drawn from current speech. And what was perhaps more important, their vocabulary was smaller. A good number of the less common words of antiquity appear to have escaped the notice of the patristic writers altogether, while many others retained only the simplest of their several shades of meaning. These losses were to some extent compensated by the addition of numerous theological terms, technical in character and cautiously defined, but nevertheless capable of arousing strong feeling. In their sentimental balance at least the two ecclesiastical idioms differed markedly from their secular counterparts. Less vivid on the whole, they had a great emotive power concentrated in their newly-coined religious terminology.

These were the observable differences; but what really counted was not that the ancient languages had altered, but that men's attitude to them had changed. Your second-century Atticist—and for that matter your second-century Ciceronian—wanted his writings to form an integral part of the literature of an earlier age. He tried therefore to familiarise himself with the language of that age and thus gained through a thousand casual clues a very full picture of its ways of thought, its habits, and its sensitivity. The Christian aims affecting the literary field were simpler and less organic. The faithful of the fifth century were not interested in sharing the literary skill of their earlier brethren, but only in sharing their beliefs. They consulted their authorities for accounts of certain events, for the explanation of certain doctrines and for encouragement to observe the moral standards arising out of these doctrines. To achieve these limited purposes, it was not necessary to maintain an exact correspondence between the idioms they used and those of their most respected texts. A general correspondence was sufficient provided that the technical terms remained fixed. In ecclesiastical Greek and Latin we get a falling away from the strict classical standards, which fluctuates in its extent but never goes beyond a certain point. With linguistic change kept within these bounds, the records of traditional Christianity never lost their value. The main features of the ideology set down in them were never obscured, and the subtleties did not matter. Indeed, there were no subtleties except those of doctrine which were guarded by the careful definition of the theological terms. Christian literature did not mirror the Christian culture pattern. It dealt with the legends and beliefs which formed the focal point of that pattern; but how their influence manifested itself, for different men in different walks of life, does not seem to have been known at this point and certainly passed unrecorded.

Given these circumstances, it is easy to see how a highly intelligent man like Gregory I could regard ancient literature as outmoded and the effort to write correct Latin as pointless. He did not see any good reason why he should avoid solecisms and barbarisms;* and he was right. In his case, no reason existed. For he did not set any value upon that underlying purpose which had prompted men in earlier times to be Atticists or Ciceronians. He wrote to Bishop Desiderius of Vienne calling him to order for instructing boys in the pagan classics. Such activities were scarcely suitable for laymen; and they were shocking in the case of a bishop. Gregory was definite in his opinion that enough had been taken over from pagan sources. He did not believe that the Christian world would benefit from further contact with pagan literature. He had Prudentius. He could do without Ovid.

St Jerome, St Augustine, St Gregory the Great in the West, St Basil of Caesarea and St Gregory Nazianzen in the East, these were the oracles to which the future was to turn for guidance. The opinions they had advanced on pagan studies had been conditioned, as we have seen, by their temperaments and interests, by the specific needs of the societies in which they lived, and sometimes, as with Augustine and Gregory I, by the limited requirements of some particular situation. In reading Jerome it is necessary to keep in mind that he is vividly aware of form in literature almost to the exclusion of content. When Augustine advised the use of the Bible as a source-book for rhetoric, he had no one in mind but the preachers whose education he was planning, and there is no evidence of his wishing to suggest that the Bible rendered all ancient literature redundant from every point of view. Nor can we suppose that Gregory, when he trounced Desiderius, meant his words to apply outside their context. He was concerned primarily with the conduct of bishops, secondarily perhaps with the usefulness of pagan authors in grammar teaching. It is unlikely that he would have denied the value of classical writings as a source of general information, or that he would have looked with anything but favour upon the great enterprise of Isidore's encyclopedia.

Very little attention was paid, however, to these modifying circumstances by the generations that were to govern their conduct by the prescripts of the Fathers. Each saying was elevated into a principle of wide application and indiscriminately applied. The results were somewhat confusing. Patristic authority could be quoted for almost any attitude between a complete rejection and a very generous acceptance of the classical heritage. Every Humanist and every anti-Humanist could find a text to support his case.

In general, however, in spite of the opportunities which Jerome and the Greek Fathers gave to those enthusiasts for ancient letters who wanted to plead their special case, the main influence of the patristic tradition was against the free study of the classical authors. All the

Fathers envisaged some restrictions, and a few, as for example the extremely influential Gregory the Great, could be interpreted to recommend that pagan authors were best avoided. Since Latin was the indispensable official language of the Church, and since the classical heritage contained so much to forward the growth of European civilisation, neither the prohibitions attributed to Gregory I nor the moderate limitations proposed by Augustine could gain general acceptance even in the West. In the East, where the views of Basil and Gregory Nazianzen set the tone, the Hellenists anyway enjoyed a fair modicum of ecclesiastical support.

The study of the ancient literatures could not be stopped. It could not even be restricted within set limits as Augustine had hoped. The suspicion with which they were regarded by certain Christians could not do much to hinder their spread. Yet, although it is clear that the tide of learning flowed with an ever increasing vigour from the sixth century to the sixteenth, we should do wrong to dismiss as unimportant that opposition it aroused and which had its origins in the Fathers' distrust of all things pagan. For if this opposition could not hinder the movement, it nevertheless could and did serve to canalise it into specific channels, so that certain types of study were preferred to others, and the assimilation of classical material proceeded unequally.

CHAPTER II

THE GREEK EAST

Roman education under the Empire used to emulate the god Janus in looking two ways at once; and schoolboys were expected to acquire a simultaneous knowledge of Latin and Greek. A smaller state could not have been so prodigal of human effort. In the ages to which we turn now, which lie between antiquity and the Renaissance, East and West having parted company in politics saw no reason why they should labour to maintain a difficult cultural concord. The West gave its mind to Latin and neglected Greek. It met Greek books only in translation, or in the libraries of the supremely erudite; while in the East the Byzantines, who used Greek currently, knew no Latin at all. The two halves of Europe were thus educationally distinct. They must be studied separately; and for reasons which will appear later, it is convenient to take the East, that is Byzantium, first.

The world whose brightest stars were Photius, Psellus and Anna Comnena inevitably presents a number of strange features: and the causes of its educational pre-eminence and its educational failures must be sought in the action of somewhat unexpected factors.

The wealth of Byzantium made it the target of constant attacks. Its domains were ringed by enemies who fought now singly, now in alliance, but who were never quiet. Generally, they were held at bay; but from time to time, as the movements of peoples drew reinforcements into the battle, the assailants were in a position to outclass the defence; and the Byzantine State had to look for survival to the circumstance that its territories, originally very large, were criss-crossed by natural ramparts. Each province in turn could be individually sacrificed without interfering with the viability of the rest. Retreat was possible even to the walls of the capital where as a last resort the city with its fleet and its stores of treasure could stand a longish siege. These advantages would not have availed against an overwhelmingly powerful enemy; but the enemy's power was never overwhelming. Now and then a bold barbarian commander might score an exceptional triumph, but such victories were never sustained. The intensity of hostile pressure increased on the average very slowly, and the Byzantines were again and again able to achieve a new parity by shortening their lines. Thus, they survived a millenium of conflict, not by heroic effort, not by rising to the challenge of circumstances, but by a gradual and inglorious retrenchment.

War is commonly regarded as the midwife of change; but the warfare which the Byzantines knew had not this usual character. Once they had adjusted their lives to a state of emergency, its continuance tended to preserve rather than to alter the pattern they had adopted. Fears of external danger prevented innovations which might have interfered with the requirements of defence, while the impulse to promote such innovations was itself diminished since men's energies were canalised elsewhere. At the same time, the high level of routine efficiency which war demands made any serious deterioration impossible. Conditions remained static in all those spheres where progress might have had repercussions upon the conduct of hostilities; and those wide social and cultural upheavals which we observe in other countries over similar periods of time, and which interact so remarkably with education, were effectively restrained.

The events recorded in Byzantine history are mostly of one kind. They issue from those endless broils which lend colour to the pages of Gibbon. The activity they indicate is therefore unimportant; for the broils did not affect the structure or the essential safety of the Byzantine state, although they concerned the person of the Emperor and the possession of the throne. Byzantium had inherited a powerful bureaucratic machine from Imperial Rome, and it is a characteristic of bureaucracy that the identity of its leaders should be a matter almost of indifference. Important business nearly always had precedents and could move along accustomed paths. Only the unimportant was habitually left to the judgement of the man at the helm; and even in the case of the unimportant he did not decide between a wise course and a foolish one, but between two alternatives of equal worth presented to him by his subordinates. His capacity was therefore of small consequence. A strong emperor was useful now and again to pull the threads of the administration together and to establish new precedents. But for the greatest part of the time a nonentity did just as well. The need for an emperor derived from the circumstance that even insignificant decisions cannot be indefinitely postponed, and he fulfilled the function of a final court of appeal. The position, however, was infinitely rewarding not only for the man who held it but for his friends and hangers-on. The sweets and sinecures of office, as well as the privileges of exercising the modicum of initiatory power the emperor possessed, became the bone of contention between well-organised pressure groups. The party in power wrought its will within the limits set by certain institutions regarded as essential to the safety of the State.

So we find, as a particular instance of this general tendency, that elementary schooling was always available. It was required by the civil servants, the lawyers, the doctors, and other professional men as a preliminary to their specialised studies. Its lack would have caused severe inconvenience. So it was kept in being. But the same considerations did not apply to higher education of the more general type. Since the training of the professional categories was received by them informally in the course of their duties, the smooth running of the administration was quite independent of the higher schools. The teaching of literature and philosophy, those disciplines which are of special interest to us, were uncontrolled and unprotected. They were so to speak outside that special area of Byzantine life which the bureaucracy was at pains to keep static: and being therefore subject to change, they became involved in the only sort of change that was taking place. They became a weapon in the struggle of the pressure groups round the throne. Higher education was attacked and defended in turn by the bureaucratic court party, by the feudal party and by the Church. In the absence of widely-based social and cultural developments, affecting the whole life of Byzantine society, the alterations which occur in the opportunities, methods and ideals of the Byzantine teachers of Greek above the elementary stage can all, or nearly all, be traced back to the intrigues of those groups for power; and the influence that political conflict can exercise upon the supposedly independent life of the schoolroom is displayed in an experimental isolation which would do credit to a laboratory.

I. THE ATTACK ON HELLENISM

The Roman government had used education for its own political purposes. It had tried to buttress its authority by inculcating the barbarians with a taste for Graeco-Roman culture. Virgil was to replace a legion. But the general acceptance of Christianity had made inexpedient a practice which involved a public homage to pagan authors; the use of the schools as instruments of propaganda had become impossible after the fourth century; and so from that time on, the State both in Rome and Byzantium had gradually lost interest in teachers and teaching.

At the beginning of the seventh century Phocas shut down the University of Constantinople, and the new centre of learning which opened in the following reign was controlled by the Church, the only institution still interested in the spread and control of ideas. Known as the Oecumenical College, it had twelve professors who gave instruction in theology but also in a variety of secular subjects.* It possessed a fine store of books, and the principal was permitted to call himself Oecumenical Teacher, a title formerly reserved for the Fathers of the Church. The emergence of this new foundation had been more or less inevitable from the moment the University had closed. The Church had to move into the educational field. She had no choice but to step in where the State refused to tread; for men's minds were her province, and she had in pagan education an old rival to reform. The study of the past was reorganised on Christian lines which meant less concern for exactitude in the teaching of language, less interest in literature, and a greater attention paid to the strictly useful. But within those bounds Hellenism was tolerated; and so far from arousing hostility, it figured rather in the light of an ally since danger threatened from another quarter.

With the coming of the eighth century, the fury of the iconoclast movement burst like a storm bringing disaster to Christianity and Hellenism alike. The causes of this famous conflict over the veneration of images were numerous and diverse. The protagonists on either side were actuated by the oddest combination of nobler and baser motives, a fact which probably accounted for their inability to compromise. On the practical level, there was the question of the donations made to the shrines. These were most generous. For the superstitious Byzantines were ready to bid high for the support of their saints and provided the monasteries, which were the bastions of Church independence, with an important source of revenue. Not unnaturally, the courtiers greedy for money and the bureaucrats greedy for power resented this diversion of wealth from the realms taxed by the State to the advantage of their bitterest rivals. They wanted the donations at an end, and saw in the campaign against images an easy way of achieving their purpose. For the liberality of the faithful was excited more by the supposed powers of individual statues and pictures than by the virtues of the Blessed in Heaven; and to destroy the visible image was to take away the income of the shrine it adorned. This somewhat sordid dispute, an incident in the struggle between two pressure groups, was the spark which started the conflagration, but the fuel which built up the blaze came from other sources.

Theologically, Iconoclasm represented the resurgence of an old error. On many earlier occasions, the desire to emphasise the spirituality and separateness of God had found expression in ways which had needed to be condemned by the Church. The Incarnation had been denied. The propriety of representing Christ and the Saints had been denied. Heathenish purification rites had been advocated and so had an ethic which, preaching the abnegation of this world, tended to look askance at all human effort beyond what was required for mere subsistence. Tenets of this kind were common in the Persian religions and had figured in the teaching of the Gnostics, in the beliefs of Mani, as well as in the doctrines of the sub-sects which had followed his lead. Recently, that is just before the first moves of the Iconoclasts, the old wine of Manichaeism had been poured into the Paulician new bottles where it still set the teeth of the orthodox on edge. The persecution of the Paulicians had been vicious, and many of them had no doubt abjured their faith unwillingly before the threat of an agonising death while many potential converts must have failed to hear the promptings of their consciences. All of these were glad when they were given the chance by the Iconoclast decrees to attack on one count a religion they hated on several. They joined enthusiastically in the fray, and with them joined a great many others who for their part had no strong interest in the slogans of theological thought, but who were motivated by the same sentiments to which the Paulicians had given a doctrinal form. For the religious discord was not primary but had its roots in another and yet wider field.*

Byzantium lay astride the boundaries of Asia and Europe. In its streets Armenians from remote hill villages jostled immigrants from Hymettus; and its traditions were similarly derived from these two discordant sources. Superficially, the city resembled a Hellenistic megalopolis. The Byzantines were proud of their roots in the past. Their intellectual culture was Greek and so was their language, although its idioms would have outraged Phrynichus. The villas scattered over the country-side which fed the gargantuan capital, housed wealthy families whose ancestors had lived there since Graeco-Roman times, and whose aristocratic conservatism and self-worship passed muster for fidelity to ancient traditions. In the deserted valleys of Asia Minor and Greece, herdsmen and peasants still led the simple and laborious lives which Dion of Prusa so amiably describes. From Athens to Alexandria, from Alexandria to Antioch and Byzantium, the line of succession appeared unbroken. The casual observer had an illusion of continuity. But there was another side to the picture. The priest-politicians and the courtier-soldiers, the imperial rivals who expiated their ambition or eminence in blinded solitude, the long-bearded and flea-bitten monks who wagged their heads over the Bogomil heresy, these colourful characters of Gibbonesque romance, had little in common with the scholars of Ptolemaic Alexandria and even less with the men of Athens. If their spiritual ancestors had fought at Marathon, it must have been in the Persian ranks. Nor did the institutions of the Byzantine state trace their origins from the Greek cities. The centralised autocracy, the provinces ruled through the agency of military governors, the hierarchy of court officials, the endless and endlessly elaborate ceremonials had been the gifts of Persia to Alexander and Diocletian. The Asiatic element which had played a subordinate role in the formation of the Hellenistic world had increased in scope and intensity until, as far as politics are concerned, it dominated the Greek.

Between such disparate elements conflict was bound to arise. The issue of Greece against Asia was never consciously raised. The nature of the struggle remained hidden from its protagonists. But it worked itself out tortuously in connection with the major controversies and under the mask of petty intrigues which on the surface had a merely temporary significance. It was a blind underground war.

Fundamentally, Iconoclasm was an attack on the Hellenic element in the Church, and as such, it extended to Greek studies which were in any case under ecclesiastical control. Christian orthodoxy, like the Byzantine state, rested on a compromise between Greece and Asia. Half its concern was for the intellectual needs of the Greek mind, half for the simpler ethical preoccupations of the masses from the East. There was some substance in the argument that the new Christian icon was but the old pagan idol writ large; but in the last analysis both icon and idol were symbols of that tendency to link God and man which must count as the greatest virtue of the Greek spirit, and the veneration accorded to images must be regarded as a proof of the Church's claim to assert in a pleasing synthesis the Greek respect for humanity and the Jewish respect for God.

The Emperor Leo the Isaurian (717–41), an Asiatic turned autocrat, was influenced both by the practical and the cultural objections to images. He was fortunate in finding morally repellent a practice which was economically to his disadvantage; and his edict of 726 proscribed all religious pictures and statues. This provoked a violent resistance; and the struggle between the parties lasted for over a century.

This period (726–842) is the dark age of Byzantine education. Leo asked the Oecumenical College to support his policy.* On his request being refused, the college was instantly disbanded; or according to a more colourful account, the gates were locked, the buildings set on fire, and the professors burnt along with their books. Public support was then withdrawn from higher education.*

The monks continued with their studies along the traditional Christian lines and produced the only literature of the period in some superb hymns and a triad of histories in ecclesiastical Greek. But we have no evidence that they took much interest in the ancient language or in the ancient writers.

The grammar schools used by the professional classes continued to function, but they taught little beyond the correct use of language. Their time went on grammar, orthography and the simple composition prescribed in the *Progymnasmata*, which was a poor substitute for wide reading.* The dedication to a contemporary treatise on orthography tells us that the author, a certain Theognostus, had laboured long over the study of grammar and had pestered his pupils until they knew the position of the accent on every Greek word.* This recital of his industry is intended to win the favour of the Emperor Leo the Armenian (813–20); but the mere fact of his appeal cannot be taken as proof that Theognostus enjoyed special favour at court. The tone of his compliments suggests rather an obscure man protesting his loyalty as a matter of course. His treatise is accurate though notably unoriginal, and much of it is devoted to indicating the differential spelling of vowel sounds that had come to be pronounced alike. Industrious, mediocre, naively pedantic, and insufficiently rewarded for his pains, we may look upon him as the type of the lay grammar teacher under Iconoclasm; and a very dispiriting type it was.

Successful educators did exist at any rate by the ninth century, but they were men of a very different stamp from Theognostus. To win recognition as a scholar one had to work along the lines which were becoming popular in contemporary Arab circles, and to show interest in a science not untinged by charlatanism and magic. We hear of Charax who after supporting the Iconoclasm of Leo the Armenian, became tutor to the sons of Michael II (820–29), and whom Theophilus (829–42) appointed Patriarch. He was famed as an astrologer. His nephew, Leo the Byzantine, specialised in mathematics. The latter was the only man to hold a publicly paid post as professor under an Iconoclast monarch. He received an appointment to console him for not being allowed to go to Baghdad when the Caliph Al Mamun asked for his services. If Leo's learning had not been of a kind to interest the Arabs, the Caliph's request would never have been made. Certainly, in his choice of subject, and probably in his approach to knowledge, he followed the Eastern tradition although in his youth he had seen something of Greek schools.

Plainly then, if the Iconoclasts had continued in power a new type of learning would have arisen. It would have used material of a scientific and factual character from Greek antiquity but its methods would not have been the traditional ones of grammar and rhetoric. There would have been no linguistic imitation after the Atticist manner, no interest in literary form, no re-living of the past. The lessons of Greek experience would have been lost while the errors of Greek science were carefully preserved.

II. ECCLESIASTICAL HELLENISM

The last Iconoclast emperor died in 842, and the following year a Synod legalised the worship of images. From this event we date a new period in the history of Byzantine education, lasting the best part of two hundred years, during which time the schools and scholarship remained strictly under the control of the Church.

The best schools in the early part of the ninth century were found outside of Constantinople in the areas where the orthodox were strongest. That much is evident from the career of Leo the Byzantine. He was a youth with excellent connections, the nephew of the Patriarch, one to whom every door was open. He was in a position to choose the finest tuition available; and when he wanted to study rhetoric, after leaving his grammar school in Constantinople, he went to Andros. Significantly too it was an Iconodule ecclesiastic, Michael Syncellus, who wrote the best contemporary work on language, a Syntax which remained popular for centuries and could still be read in the Renaissance. One sees traces among the members of the orthodox party of a revival of interest in Greek studies even before 842; and once the burden of Iconoclasm is lifted, this interest increases suddenly by leaps and bounds.

But the revival had a special character. Men's enthusiasm for the past was not unconditional. It was directed to certain specific ecclesiastical ends. Faced with the fury of the Iconoclasts who had been simultaneously anti-Hellenic and anti-Christian, education and the

Church had been driven into a firm alliance. In a manner quite contrary to what was to happen in the West, enthusiasts for antiquity and enthusiasts for religion became aware of the similarities in their two traditions rather than of the differences. Christianity was seen as Hellenism's second pillar, Hellenism as Christianity's propaedeutic; and the more powerful ally imposed its pattern upon the weaker. The Church had emerged from her battles more powerful than before; education on the other hand had been smashed, its institutions destroyed, its tradition lost. Ecclesiastical Hellenism had, however, its moments of achievement which were almost moments of glory. In the years after the death of Theophilus the darkness which shrouds the early part of the ninth century is dispelled and suddenly—for we have little cause to expect it—we catch a glimpse of a circle with a well-developed intellectual life. Among the boys who grew up during the final persecutions to make their careers under a triumphant orthodoxy were the two brothers, Photius and Tarasius. They were rich. They were clever. They belonged to the inmost circle of the victorious Iconodule aristocracy. Their great-uncle had been the Tarasius whom Irene had appointed Patriarch to guide her short-lived revival of image worship. They had every right to expect glittering prizes from the new régime, and their expectations were not disappointed. The prizes came. Tarasius married a sister of the dowager Empress Theodora. Photius became intimate with her brother, Bardas. That ambitious and intelligent prince who acted as Regent for the dissolute Michael III was for a time the real master of Byzantium. He tried out his two friends in diplomatic posts. Photius who held a titular post as Captain of the Guards travelled on a mission to Assyria where, it can be presumed, his work proved competent, for he rose in the bureaucratic hierarchy; and in 857 he was picked to replace Ignatius as Patriarch. The next six years formed the apogee of his life. He rode on the crest of the wave. But Byzantine history records the activities of many other distinguished officials who excelled in the finesses of intrigue; and these honours taken in themselves would not now do much to keep the memory of Photius green. They serve mainly to complete our picture of his character. His fame depends on an incidental interest which he could hardly have regarded as more than a hobby.

The absence of a university—and of any equivalent for it—had made unorganised, private education popular in Byzantium. Young people came together to study. Distinguished old men collected round them the children and grandchildren of their friends. Experienced officials instructed their juniors. Photius was still young when he made himself the leader of a group that was almost a school. A capacious memory and a vast store of clear-cut opinions assured his ascendancy over his contemporaries. They read books, asked questions, listened to his answers, and in the *Myriobiblon* he sends his brother a record of the work done by the group over a period when Tarasius was away on an embassy. This impressive book comprises two hundred and eighty chapters, one for each volume read and reviewed. The notices consist for the most part of brief summaries with quotations and comments, in the normal vein of Greek literary criticism. The whole thing has been regarded as a miracle of encyclopedic learning, which it certainly is not. A conscientious undergraduate will work through that amount of material in a year and make as efficient judgements. The miraculous element, if we are to call it such, is located not in the scholarship but in the educational intention. With Photius and his friends, the intellectual life of Byzantium not only revived, but revived in a novel fashion. The Iconoclasts' recent flirtation with Eastern learning and the encouragement of fact-collecting traditional in the Christian attitude to antiquity, combined to produce a new approach, or rather the vague aims and tentative methods which one day might have developed into a new approach to education. Over half the notices in the *Myriobiblon* discuss theological works. For the rest, history, oratory, science and travel are well represented, though there is no mention of poetry; and the omission of Plato, Aristotle, Thucydides and Xenophon is as glaring as the neglect of the poets. The argument has been put forward that the collection is incomplete; but that plea will not really hold water. Photius must have realised that the book would become the memorial of his teaching activity. If he had felt deeply about poetry, if the poets had all been studied during a period when Tarasius was present, if that absence was indeed the cause of, and not just an excuse for the book, he would have found some means of explaining the situation. He would have been eager to correct any possible misconceptions about the scope of his teaching. The absence of such explanations suggests that he scarcely cared, that in his view the sample was representative.*

So we have three innovations to consider: first, the shift of interest to the patristic age with the result that the Athenian legacy is treated as a not very important part of Greek literature; secondly, the attention paid to informative books; thirdly, the technique of quick reading and brief general comment which is so startlingly different from the line by line discussion usual in the past, and which was extremely well adapted to throw the emphasis on content and not as previously on imitation and style.

Personal predilections must have counted for a great deal in these developments. Unfortunately, we know too little about the principal actors to gauge at all precisely how much each contributed to the general effect. Was Photius responsible for the renaissance of learning commonly associated with his name? Or had the initiative come originally from Bardas? Or perhaps from someone else? A third person can be glimpsed, moving mysteriously in the background, but with a finger in every educational pie. We meet Leo the Byzantine again; but this time it is in the houses of the Iconodule nobility, where he is content to appear a pupil of Photius. Theophilus had promoted him from his professorship into the hierarchy, and he had been Metropolitan of Thessalonica when Theodora started her reforms. He lost his see, but the recognition of his abilities or perhaps some well-timed servility or recantation had preserved him from worse fates. In any case, there he was a few years after the event, back again at the seat of power, learned, polite, and like his uncle prepared to make capital out of a reputation for wizardry. In 863 Bardas decided to supply the crying need there was for higher education by a properly organised college, and he offered the headship to Leo. The choice indicates the tone of the teaching, which continued at an official level the informal classes of Photius. Leo himself lectured on philosophy and mathematics. It is not unreasonable to suppose that his philosophy was that of a mathematician. Two of his former pupils held the chairs of arithmetic and geometry. But we hear of no instruction in rhetoric, though Photius may have treated the subject in some lectures he gave between his resignation of the Patriarchate and his exile; and grammar was entrusted to the cripple Cometas who appears to have been a specialist on Homer.

It is not clear whether the college survived the murder of Bardas in 867. An epigram tells us that Leo the Byzantine was still alive in the reign of Leo the Wise; and Photius who had spent the years 867–77 in exile, but had then returned to favour and to a second spell as Patriarch, might in his moment of success have been expected to support a foundation for which he was partly responsible. But short-lived or not it set its stamp upon contemporary education.

Evidence of that comes from the writings of a monk who lived in the time of Basil I (867–86). He describes secular education as containing the following stages: first, grammar which is limited by his account to morphology and syntax; then the reading of Homer; then rhetoric, for the student to learn the common tropes; then dialectic; and finally arithmetic, geometry and astronomy. He pictures the curriculum of the Seven Arts, really followed out as it never was in the West. The description is incidental to a wish to demonstrate that saints can do without such fripperies, and in consequence does not aim at accuracy. But the order of subjects is nevertheless significant. Science has pride of place.

This trend carried to completion would have led from the indiscriminate collecting of material to its classifying under subjects and to the development of appropriate methodologies for each subject. The educational programme of the Bardas University could have ushered in a reorganisation of knowledge similar in scope and results to the one which transformed Europe in the seventeenth century. It could have, but did not. For there were two obstacles which under the limited incentives of Byzantine life proved insurmountable. Without the impulse provided by the urgencies of a rising capitalism, the zeal of scholars and the curiosity of practical men could not overcome the suspicions of the Church which, finding it difficult to adapt her theology even to the existing state of secular knowledge, tended to discourage all new ideas; and then the scholars themselves who should have been able to move straight to their goal, were hampered by the rhetorical tradition from which they could not yet escape. The moment they were prepared to go beyond superficialities and to delve more deeply, the familiar ways of scholarship stretched invitingly before them. It seemed to them unprofitable to break new ground while there was still so much to be learnt, presumptuous to start thinking while there was still so much they did not know: accordingly they abandoned science and fact and plunged back into the study of language.

Such at least was the fate of Photius. The innovator of the *Myrio-biblon* became the compiler of lexicons. When he switched from the wide interests of his youth to a more intensive study of theology, as was incumbent upon a Patriarch, he learnt the importance of words. The fear of being misinterpreted which at the time carried considerable risks, led him to insist upon a fixed usage as the only guarantee against such errors. His quest for this unchanging language made him a careful student of the meaning and construction of words. It sent him searching into old dictionaries and grammars and then systematically collecting his results so that without favouring the Atticist ideal, he paved the way for a future Atticism.*

This change of heart in Photius did not immediately swing over the balance from the new tradition back to the old. For another hundred years, the study of style and language, and the practice of imitation, remained the hobbies of a minority, and were relegated to form a subsidiary stream of cultural development. When Constantine VII (912–59) pulled the reins of power into his own hands half-way through the tenth century, he had to bring about an educational revival; for in the words of the chronicler, learning had long been dead owing to the ignorance and neglect of the authorities.* Constantine was an impassioned collector of facts in whose eyes the construction of encyclopedias was man's noblest work. He set on foot an extensive scheme to summarise existing knowledge, ostensibly for the benefit of his son and successor, the tennis-playing Romanus, but no doubt with an eye to the general good of the state. To this he contributed from his own pen a treatise on the ceremonies of the court and another on the administration of the Empire while he commissioned scholars to compile encyclopedias of history and political thought, agriculture, medicine and even veterinary surgery. When we compare these works with the *Myriobiblon*, we find a notable advance in method. Photius had been content to make summaries of individual books. Here the information is assembled under subject-headings. The volume on history comprises fifty-three sections with titles like 'Embassies', 'Conspiracies', 'Stratagems'. The classification is unsound. It does not illuminate the significant relationships between the facts; but there is an attempt to classify. From such foundations a proper methodology might eventually have developed.

Constantine and his collaborators had no special interest in the Athenian Age. Most of their sources dated from the fourth century A.D.; and nothing drew them to the study of style. In the hope of being more easily understood, they garnished their pages with colloquialisms which the historians of demotic Greek have learnt to cherish. But if they went to extremes with their linguistic freedoms, they were still in harmony with the majority of their generation. The chroniclers and the historians of the time write in the ecclesiastical idiom which they trick out with quotations from the Septuagint. They almost revel in their solecisms.* Nevertheless, traditional methods continued to attract those who turned to scholarship with no clear aim in view. The *Lexicon* of Photius had drawn upon Aelius Dionysius and Pausanias the Atticist alongside specialised vocabularies for Homer and Plato. It had popularised the fascinating craft of dictionary making and had helped indirectly to promote the reading of authors; for the more conscientious lexico-graphers were eager to add to the examples they found in their sources. They were not yet Atticists any more than Photius had been; but they were philologists. One famous manuscript contains in addition to Phrynichus and Moeris, specialised vocabularies to Homer, Plato and Herodotus; a collection of legal, and two collections of rhetorical terms, scholia to the *Alexandra* of Lycophron, a syntax, numerous lists of Scriptural sayings, and finally a polemical work directed against the Atticists.*

The monumental compendia which we know as the *Etymologicum Magnum* and the *Lexicon* of 'Suidas' are based on a similarly haphazard selection of authorities. 'Suidas' for example is believed to have read over and above his lexicographical sources: Homer, Hesiod, Pindar, Sophocles, Aristophanes, Herodotus, Thucydides, Xenophon, three plays of Aeschylus, as well as a large number of later writers.*

The necessary basis of Atticism was being unwittingly constructed. But for the time being these lexicographical efforts had no measurable influence upon the literature. The Anthology of Cephalas reflects only a contemporary taste for epigrams, which is an advance upon the prose-bound dilettantism of Photius. But as a presage of the future we have at the end of the century the first serious attempt at imitation, a satire in the manner of Lucian.*

III. THE ELEVENTH-CENTURY RENAISSANCE

At this juncture, political change again intervened to alter the normal processes of educational and cultural growth. As the result of certain economic and military developments it had become possible for a powerful group to derive tangible benefits from fostering an admiration for the Greek past; and the cult of antiquity which had been the pre-occupation of remote scholars was given status by a successful revolu-tion. It was popularised and established as a settled feature of the Byzantine way of life. But a specific cult of ancient Greece implied primarily the study of her literature; and that presupposed a return to the traditional methods and the traditional ideals of the Graeco-Roman schools. No one in the eleventh century could have invented an approach to literature which by-passed these hoary canons. Thus, by a strange chain of causes and effects, the shift of the political pendulum brought about the resurgence of a full-blown Atticism.

What had occurred is perhaps best described as a nationalist revival.

Even in the tenth century, the officials who ruled Byzantium were cosmopolitan in their outlook. They inherited their traditions from that senatorial class of mixed origins that had followed Constantine to the banks of the Bosphorus and had regarded the Greeks with a certain contempt as one subject race among many. The possession of Syria and Egypt until the seventh and of Calabria until the eleventh century had helped to foster these illusions of kinship with Rome, and so had the presence of foreign adventurers at the court. These men were the faithful servants of the autocracy, useful to the emperor because no ties of sentiment bound them to the people they governed. They could applaud Theophilus when he constructed a palace on a model brought from Ctesiphon, and they would have been no doubt willing to share the cargoes of luxury goods which Theodora had purchased in the Syrian market. They admired the glamour of the Eastern courts, but Greek learning never won their support. This deracination of the Byzantine ruling class was most marked under the Heraclian and the Iconoclast emperors. After that for a number of reasons it declined. The passage of time weakened the ties with the Roman past. The loss of Ravenna, the separation of the Churches, and the establishment of a rival Carolingian Empire had broken the strongest ties with the West. The dreams of world conquest had grown increasingly faint. Nor did the Arab caliphates long continue to attract men's eyes to the East. With the removal of their seat of government to Baghdad, the Abbasids gradually lost control of Egypt and Syria until with the advent of the Seljuk Turks a morose barbarism eventually replaced the once seductive civilisation of Islam. But the decisive factor in the transformation of the bureaucracy was the rise of a new class more kindly disposed towards the Greek tradition. In spite of laws designed to protect the small cultivator, estates had continued to grow during the Macedonian period; and the simultaneous decline of trade which weakened the merchants had further increased the relative power of the great landowners. These old established feudal families, the Angeli, the Comneni, the Porphyrogeniti, had a stake in the country as it stood. They were the natural leaders of the nation once it became aware of its identity; and what could the nation feel itself but Greek. Moreover, their following was located principally in the rural areas. Many of them had estates in Greece and the islands. Their vassals were Greek-speaking, and the loyalty they commanded could be strengthened by their appearing the champions of the Greek spirit. Had they wished it, their wealth alone would have been sufficient to give them a voice in the control of the army, but as it happened they could add to their economic prestige the further advantages of military skill. Theirs was the property first to be ravaged when enemy forces crossed the frontier. So for their own protection they had mastered the problems of defence, and their leaders stood high in the councils which managed the troops in the field.* The half century between the death of Basil II (976–1025) and the accession of Alexius Comnenus (1081–1118) witnessed a complicated succession of intrigues as a result of which the former leaders of the bureaucracy were displaced from power; and in these intrigues a note-worthy part was played by a group of men who were at the same time responsible for a revival of education focused on antiquity. The leading Hellenist of the century, Michael Psellus, was also a leading politician; and Isaac Comnenus Porphyrogenitus, one of the members of the ruling family, was also the author of two short treatises on the characters in Homer.* That tiny detail symbolises the connection between the social and educational revolutions of the age.

During the successive reigns of the military heroes, Nicephorus, Zimisces, and Basil the Bulgar-Slayer, education had received no public support and had come to depend wholly upon the personal enterprise of individuals.* Psellus, who reached adolescence during the third decade of the eleventh century, studied under two of these private teachers. The first, Nicetas of Byzantium, seems to have been a very ordinary, petty-school grammarian, but the second, John Mauropus, was a remarkable man. His spirit had responded to the growing national consciousness of the time and to the consequent growing interest in ancient Greece. Valuing the past as such implied, under the circum-stances, valuing it for the beauty it had to offer; and Mauropus acted instinctively upon that conclusion. He possessed that charm and simplicity which so often distinguish the precursors of great move-ments, men who walk contentedly between two worlds and teach with-out excitement truths which will later strike a revolutionary note. In his rather pedestrian verses proving that Plato must have been Christian because he was so fine a philosopher, and in his statements to Psellus that ideas gained in value when they were expressed in beautiful language we see the future foreshadowed. We are on the threshold of the Humanist age.*

Psellus himself had been born into that section of society which needs to live by its wits. His parents were short of money but cultured and ambitious; and the boy according to his own later boast knew the *Iliad* by heart while he was still in his teens. He grew up possessed of a retentive memory, a keen intelligence, and that aptitude for pliant time-serving which ambition demands from the indigent. When he had finished studying grammar under Nicetas and rhetoric under Mauropus, he made a compact with a young lawyer, Xiphilinus; and in order to improve his chances of profitable employment, taught the latter oratory in return for instruction in law. The experiment proved successful. It was in fact as a lawyer that Psellus first made his name. He began by practising in the provinces, but by 1042 he had obtained a post at the court where he became a favourite of the new emperor, Constantine Monomachus (1042–54). Legal instruction had sunk to a shockingly low level since there was no responsible law school in Byzantium, and Xiphilinus who had become a lawyer of note was pressing for a reform. Psellus must have used his personal influence to back the arguments of his friend; but when the Emperor gave his consent a bitter dispute arose. Xiphilinus insisted on the primacy of legal studies. But Psellus was eager for an arrangement which would give him a chance to shine personally. Fired by his awareness of a growing interest in his subject, he put forward a plan for a rhetorical curriculum with law as a subsidiary. The calculation that such educational activities could serve the ends of statecraft did not interest Xiphilinus. If the consciousness of a common heritage came to grapple the Byzantine people to their rulers, his party was not likely to benefit. He represented the narrow professional interests of the law, as later he was to represent with an equal bigotry the professional interests of the Church; so the quarrel between him and Psellus waxed furious. Each party had its connections in the grim world of pressure politics, and soon riots ensued, until Monomachus settled the matter by appointing two faculties, one for law, and one for philosophy under Psellus, with Nicetas and Mauropus as his assistants. *

The constitution of the law faculty as drawn up by John Mauropus is still in existence; but the parallel document which dealt with the school of philosophy has been unfortunately lost. We have to reconstruct its provisions from hints in the writings of Psellus. From this somewhat unsatisfactory evidence it emerges that for the first part of the course the curriculum followed the lines traditional in the grammar schools, except that the instruction given in literature and in rhetoric was more thorough and covered a wider field than usual. Nicetas taught orthography presumably to the youngest boys. This was then completed or amplified by the reading of authors. Psellus names Homer, Epicharmus, Archilochus, Nicander, Pindar, and dismisses the rest in a phrase, which makes one suspect that he used an anthology. There does not seem to have been any organic relation between these literature lessons and the teaching of rhetoric. The latter was organised along traditional lines. Its purpose, as always in Byzantine schools, was to train the students in the genres defined by Aphthonius. Psellus mentions delivering a speech of reproof which was to serve as a model for his class. He seems to have composed his examples himself* and they were no doubt richer and more instructive than the current texts. But the form of the curriculum was rigid and the hands of the individual teachers were in consequence more or less tied.

The second half of the course consisted of lectures on general knowledge and the advanced study of philosophy. Metric, astronomy, arithmetic and geometry were included in this part of the curriculum. But there is reason to suspect that the instruction given was neither thorough nor systematic. We hear of no professors specifically appointed for these subjects. Instead Psellus tells us about a type of lecture which he much disliked giving when he was expected to answer extempore any questions his pupils cared to ask. He held what in modern parlance would be described as a one-man Brains Trust; and although the evidence is far from conclusive, one is left with the impression that when Psellus talks of teaching subjects other than philosophy or rhetoric, he is referring to these ingenious displays of learning. It appears that he recognised their inadequacy from the educational point of view and tried to enforce a rule whereby the questions on a particular day would be limited to a set subject. But his students refused to co-operate. They were not prepared to exchange an amusing pastime for serious work. Philosophy on the other hand was seriously taught. Unlike Photius who preferred Aristotle, Psellus was devoted to Plato and the Neo-Platonists. His devotion coloured every theme he touched in his voluminous and many-sided writings; and his lectures did much to popularise the Platonic doctrines. The primacy of the philosophical discipline in the school as well as this orientation of its beliefs is further borne out by the appointment of John Italus as the successor of Psellus. John was a philosopher who never looked beyond philosophy and a Neo-Platonist whom the Church eventually condemned for his opinions.

Thus, the new university had a certain superficial resemblance to its ninth-century predecessor. In both cases the curriculum looks as if it was based on the Seven Arts. But these similarities are deceptive. The differences are far more important. The emphasis was now firmly on the literary side. Rhetoric, so far from being neglected, was taught by the head of the college. The sciences, so far from capturing the majority of the staff, lacked teachers altogether. The character of those general lectures which Psellus gave shows very clearly how absolute the subordination of science to rhetoric had become. For Psellus was a sophist. He could treat so many subjects with such facility because he never sought after the truth but only used such facts as he knew to create an effect. He could talk of mathematics and astronomy, but he was never a mathematician or astronomer; he was never anything but a clever orator. His real interest was for words; his deepest feelings were inspired by the beauty of their combinations. He admired the ancients because they had used words well. He admired the Platonic philosophy because it justified his taste for a perfection residing in form. The range of his general knowledge was extremely wide. It embraced besides literature, history and law, astronomy, physics, physiology, psychology, mathematics and even medicine. But at the same time it was narrow. For he resolved all these subjects into one. He was no systematiser. He had no ambition to produce for posterity the definitive account of any branch of knowledge. He was an artist.

His school made the admiration of antiquity a living force and reintroduced the practice of imitating the ancient writers. These were important changes: for they opened men's eyes to the ideals and the behaviour patterns that had formed the Athenian way of life. Like Petrarch two centuries later, Psellus was a clumsy exponent of the craft of literary imitation. His idioms, his vocabulary were too often drawn from a variety of doubtful sources; and his short rhythmic clauses, linked in a prolonged series of antitheses remind us of the techniques in contemporary hymn-writing. Except in theory, he was no Atticist, just as Petrarch was no Ciceronian. But these defects of his practice did not affect his propagandist ardour. He wanted to turn Byzantium into the spiritual heir of Athens; and he nearly succeeded. In a revolutionary age, an emergent group will tolerate remarkable excesses in its supporters so long as these contribute to its ultimate triumph. Psellus was a most valued supporter of the Comneni and the cause of landed aristocracy. He served them not only as publicist but as a prime minister; and his neo-paganism was therefore tolerated, during those early years when the fate of the Empire still hung in the balance. But once the struggle was over, the attitude of the emperors altered. They became eager to compromise with other pressure groups, and notably with the Church, and the hopes of the Hellenists were duly sacrificed.

In the Macedonian period, the interests of the Church had acted as a check upon the development of science, and had in consequence forwarded the growth of a literary Hellenism. Now the process was repeated, and Hellenism in its turn was checked. Neither in the realm of thought, nor in the realm of feeling could the secular spirit be long tolerated.

IV. THE COUNTER-ATTACK BY THE CHURCH

Psellus escaped unscathed. He was vastly distinguished and vastly tactful. Besides, he had thrown his sop to theology in a dialogue against the Euchitae. He was allowed to die in peace. But his successor, the uncompromising Italus, was almost immediately tried for heresy on account of his Platonism; and after the undistinguished headship of Theodore of Smyrna no one was appointed and the philosophy school was allowed to disappear.

This did not mean, however, that education was allowed to languish. The secular university was still in existence when, in the school attached to the Patriarchal Court, a master of rhetoric was appointed to help the existing teachers of theology; once the hopes of the secular teachers had collapsed, the ecclesiastical curriculum was gradually extended. By the beginning of the twelfth century it covered all the subjects in which Psellus and his colleagues had given instruction.* This Patriarchal School was in a position to command the services of the best teachers since it offered an easy road to ecclesiastical preferment; and it became the most distinguished centre of learning in the Empire under the later Comneni. So great was its success that towards the end of the century we hear of a second important school also under the general direction of the Patriarch. This was located in the Church of the Apostle, and according to its historian, Nicholas Mesarites,* the curriculum included grammar (focused as usual on the distinctions between the written and spoken idiom), rhetoric, dialectic, physics, the theory of medicine, mathematics and music. The Patriarch, Mesarites goes on to tell us, was equally expert in all these fields.

As the ecclesiastically controlled schools came to dominate education, there occurred certain important changes in teaching method. What we know about twelfth-century disciplines comes to us from a variety of insufficient sources; but their scattered evidence adds up to a fairly sufficient picture. The first stage in every boy's training was to acquire an adequate mastery of the official written language. This took him until his sixteenth or seventeenth year.* The normal course included orthography and grammar. In both these subjects the emphasis was laid on those aspects of the classical idiom which demotic speakers found particularly difficult: a practice which the ninth century had already followed. But in place of the Homer or Euripides which earlier grammarians had been accustomed to read with their pupils, using the verses as a peg on which to hang information about morphology and syntax, the twelfth-century teachers had recourse to collections of brief, contemporary texts. These were analysed in great detail, and constituted at the elementary level the staple reading of the class. The technique was known as σχεδογραφία or parsing. Its pedagogic advantages were obvious. A literary work however carefully selected was bound to contain some unmanageable passages, some rare idioms, and perhaps some dangerously pagan ideas. Material composed specifically for schools avoided all these embarrassments. But one observer at least condemns the practice as harmful to serious studies.*

Schedography was followed or perhaps in some cases accompanied by the reading of the usual authors. Psellus tells us that in such a lesson he used to comment on the general form, the choice of words, the rhetorical devices, and finally on the sentence structure. He also criticised each piece in respect of its content. This programme gives one the impression that he taught just like the Graeco-Roman grammarians.

But we possess among his miscellaneous writings certain small essays which betray the real character of this criticism he talks about. It emerges that he regarded, or affected to regard, all poetry as allegory which deserved a serious man's notice only because its fictions hid some commonplace philosophical concept; and he considered that a commentator's most important task was to bring such hidden meanings to light.* In that regrettable belief, he was followed by the most eminent of twelfth-century scholars. Tzetzes, introducing his notes on Hesiod, asserts that the critic's duty consists in expounding the following topics: the origins of the poet, his life, his other writings, his contemporaries, the aim of the work under review, the metre, and finally the allegorical interpretation of the mythology. Tzetzes had a written commentary in mind. But it seems reasonable to assume that the points he thought fit to put in a book were those he discussed with a class. Allegorising was not a Byzantine invention. The game of finding hidden meanings in Homer had been played as far back as Periclean times; but its aim and effect had always been to replace the ideas of the epic age by others more acceptable to the scholar and his audience. The

Pericleans had disliked the immoral stories told about the gods, which did not square with their own rationalist ethics; so they had hit on the idea of saying that to talk of the gods was a picturesque way of talking about the forces of nature. But the Byzantines went further than anyone had before. Their concern was not to justify the pagan gods but to explain them away altogether. The activities of the Pantheon could not be allowed to pass unchallenged in a Christian society. Thus, no sooner is a god mentioned than the commentator hastens forward with some elaborate rationalist or philosophical rigmarole. Psellus has several lines of attack. Sometimes he gives divinity the lie direct and assures us with a positivist aplomb that the tomb of Cronus can be found in Crete, headstone and all, but that the tomb of Zeus has still to be located.* Sometimes, he imitates earlier allegorists and makes his gods into forces of nature. Circe for example becomes a symbolic figure representing pleasure and the manner in which it degrades its devotees; while the Sphinx stands for the multiplicity of man compounded out of the rational and the irrational. But in most cases he relies on the Neo-Platonic cosmogony to furnish him with a convincing argument. Thus Tantalus becomes the aetherial fire which rests upon the damp lower air while its upper surface is threatened by a fixed sphere which appears as the stone over Tantalus' head.* Tzetzes also uses these arguments; but he more commonly relies upon astrology. Aphrodite saving Paris is in his opinion a poetic way of saying that Paris was lucky because he was born under Venus. Occasionally the connection is somewhat complicated. The luck of Achilles is associated with winter. Therefore he is described as the son, that is the favourite, of the sea-mist Thetis which heralds the approach of winter.* These explanations may or may not have convinced. At times one feels that the commentator himself doubts their validity. But one effect they certainly had. They must have killed Homer's poetry for the Byzantine student.

In the allegories of Tzetzes very little survives of Homer except the story itself which is then garnished by twelfth-century rationalist and pseudo-rationalist mumbo-jumbo. Yet patently that is all Tzetzes thought worth preserving. He believed himself to have written a useful popularisation; and as far as one can tell his work was appreciated.* The average Hellenist under the Comneni must have done his reading in blinkers.

Rhetoric was classed among the higher studies which did not begin until after a boy had left the grammar school. The text-books in popular use were still the *Progymnasmata*, and the rules illustrated by their exercises were all the majority of Byzantines ever learnt about the art of writing. The techniques which make real literary imitation possible, which help the student to identify himself with his model, although used by individuals, were not taught in the schools.*

About the other subjects taught we now know next to nothing. The main interest of twelfth-century educators was for literature. After the disgrace of John Italus, students of philosophy seem to have confined themselves to logic. Medicine and natural science appear in the curriculum of the school at the Church of the Apostle, but the only fact that has come down to us about the teaching is that group discussion was preferred to the usual lecture method, which suggests a sophistical rather than a systematic treatment.* The medical students stood around a fountain discussing veins and arteries, the incidence of fevers, the heart, the liver and the pancreas while the philosophers gathered some way off to follow their favourite intellectual exercise. This consisted in taking some plausible generalisation about the natural world and deducing from it by the strictest processes of logic some obviously untrue conclusion. It gave them great satisfaction to demonstrate that reality and dialectic were at cross-purposes.

Looking over the whole field, it becomes obvious that the method of instruction was in every case calculated to diminish the influence of the pagan authors whose works ostensibly formed the subject-matter of the course. The learning of rules illustrated by contemporary examples, the reading of texts whose plain meaning is always twisted to suit the Christian moralist, the uninspired copying of model passages, the getting by heart of formulae for describing a character or praising a friend, the neglect of speculative philosophy for the technicalities of logic, the neglect of serious science for dilettante chatter were not likely to promote a deep understanding of the Greek tradition. Hellenism was tamed, its scope limited, its interests confined to questions of form and language.

It is essential to remember, however, that we are dealing here with tendencies and not with accomplished facts. The Church did not fetter, and did not even wish to fetter the imagination of every Hellenist. We can see from the literature of the period, from the work of a Eustathius or an Anna Comnena, from the collection of rhetorical pieces found in the Escurial Manuscript* that a substantial minority of gifted scholars did devote themselves to ancient literature and conned their grammar and lexicons in order to develop a finer style. But the majority were checked. Not fully, for the techniques of the teachers merely hindered, they did not absolutely prevent, the appreciation of what was taught. Now and then an enthusiast would still emerge. But ninety-nine out of every hundred lost among the trees of a Christian pedagogy failed signally to find the pagan wood.

V. THE LATIN INVASION AND THE FOURTEENTH-CENTURY RENAISSANCE

Then suddenly from one day to the next, Byzantium, which had been a flourishing centre of intellectual life, became a hunted city under the domination of an ignorant overlord. The Latin conquest proved a cultural disaster, and an unproductive century separates the Comnenian and Paleologue periods of the Hellenist revival. In their victory march through the capital the Franks displayed with glee a sheet of paper, an inkhorn and a pen to symbolise the triumph of the sword over a people of scribes and scholars; and one may be tempted to see the event as indeed the triumph of an emergent over a regressive culture. But neither the soldiers, nor their generals represented the best elements in Western life. They admired only the military virtues to which they owed their success, and this made them despise the intellectual techniques of a society more advanced than their own. To the Greek officials who remained at their posts, the Frankish leaders appeared uneducated to the point of illiteracy. Baldwin's plan of founding a school to latinise the Greeks never passed beyond the paper stage, a worthy prelude to the turbulent administration of his successors, which remained to the last unfavourable to learning. Nor could education flourish in the small beleaguered principalities where the Byzantines contrived to hold their own. Their struggle to survive left them with little energy for scholarship and thought. Standards were highest still in Asia Minor. There were schools in Nicaea itself, in Prusa and in Ephesus. The Lascarids did their best to patronise learning and the banished empire was distinguished by the erudition of Blemmydas. But in the splinter kingdoms, the Byzantine culture pattern disintegrated, and the use of the traditional written language was largely lost. At the beginning of the fourteenth century, the courtiers of Epirus were not sufficiently instructed to understand even the simplified Homer of Tzetzes; and a local poet had to be found to translate the latter's *Allegories* into a demotic poem of short trochaic lines with eight accentual feet.*

When Constantinople was recaptured in 1261, Michael VIII allowed Georgius Acropolites to quit his post in the civil service and to devote all his energies to teaching. Acropolites was appointed professor of Aristotelian philosophy, but we find him giving instruction also in mathematics and rhetoric; and the fact that one of his pupils was the twenty-six year old Gregory of Cyprus suggests that the school served pupils of all ages. Everybody was making up for lost time. Six years later the task of Acropolites was made easier by the reconstitution of the Oecumenical College, and by the choice of Maximus Holobolus to take charge of the education of the clergy; but in spite of their joint efforts and in spite of the support given by the emperor, progress was bitterly slow. Sixty years of educational stagnation could not be made good in a day. The general level of attainment was low; and what was worse, the linguistic situation had undergone a vital change. Demotic had made considerable strides, and was now invading the field of literature.* Its claim to be a separate entity from the written Greek of tradition could no longer be denied. On the other hand, it was not yet sufficiently developed for anyone to consider it as a feasible alternative. Bilingualism seemed inevitable; and under the circumstances Attic was the obvious choice for a second language. So the educators had two tasks, both of them tremendous; the first to raise the standard of education over a wide field, the second to reorganise the teaching of the written idiom so that students could master it, not as a variation on their ordinary speech, but as a dead language which was an independent whole.

The best part of a century was to pass before these tasks could be completed. At first, the setting up and running of grammar schools, apart from the Oecumenical College, was left to the private enterprise of individual teachers. The experiment was not a success, for most of these grammarians followed the easy road of ignorance and taught a highly artificial language which had no connection with the speech either of past or present. It had all the disadvantages of Attic without any of its virtues. It was remote and difficult without being, as Attic would have been, euphonious, accurate and culturally inspiring. But in the meantime every scholar of note was engaged on a grammar; and their opinion of these fashions was far from favourable.

I finally set my face [Metochites tells us] against the foolish attitude of my contemporaries, many of whom disdained the ancients and their lofty standards. Such a spirit of revolt is considered fashionable at the present time. Its adherents revel in artificial beauties which although to the taste of a decadent vulgarity, are unfit for serious literature. With these they pollute our language in their idle folly, and fill our dull ears which are ignorant of the true glory of Greek with the thunder of eccentric neologisms calculated to disgust all cultured and intelligent people.*

Erasmus himself could not have stated more clearly the feelings of a humanist educator. Metochites and his friends won their battle. Artificiality declined.* He himself became Grand Logothete, a Minister of Education, and as such, all the schools were put under his charge. The teachers who were maintained from the imperial coffers, could not vacate their posts without permission and had to carry out the orders given them. Atticism became the order of the day.

Elementary grammar at an earlier period had been largely concerned to point out the differences between written and spoken Greek. Orthography in particular had come in for a good deal of attention. Advanced grammar on the other hand had served the needs of interpretative scholarship. It had treated of rare words and dialect usages with the view to helping in the elucidation of the more obscure texts.* But now with this fourteenth-century educational reform both underwent a sharp transformation. Not only were the differences between Attic and Demotic much more fully set out, but in many cases the rules for writing Attic were fully discussed in a schematic form. The grammars of Planudes, Glykys and Moschopoulus were the first to provide in a more or less complete form a course for learning Greek as a dead language.*

Successful imitation does not, however, depend on grammatical accuracy alone. Some way had to be found for storing within the mind, ready for use, the specific vocabulary and idioms employed by the writers whose works are selected for a model; and it is in this field that the Paleologue educators made their most significant contribution. They worked out a number of efficient devices which were to be copied by future generations. If we take these devices in the chronological order of their appearance, so as to trace more clearly the development of what was to become the Renaissance imitation-technique, the first we come across is the word-list.

Moschopoulus and Thomas Magister revived a linguistic aid already familiar to the contemporaries of Phrynichus. They compiled vocabularies of Attic words and usages in a form convenient for reference or even for learning by heart. About the same time a Thessalian monk called Lecapenus wrote two text-books which proved popular and which now serve to show us what techniques were used in the classroom. He collected in a volume some letters by Libanius, and then later in a second volume some of his own, with a commentary to explain the exact meaning and use of the words.* The importance of these two works derives from the fact that they were intended to replace existing

Progymnasmata such as the one by Pachymeres. They offered passages
for imitation which were wider in scope than usual; for Lecapenus did
not keep to the time-worn list of topics. They were also more classical
in their language and laid the emphasis on accuracy of usage and not on
rhetorical form. These two techniques—the use of the word-list and
the classroom practice of commentary and reproduction—were then
combined towards the end of the century into a single system by a
teacher of remarkable genius, Manuel Chrysoloras.

The hard work of the Paleologue scholars during the first half of the
century was crowned by intellectual revival in its middle decades. The
Church had supported their activity more or less uncritically, regarding
it as a battle against ignorance waged on a level where secular knowledge could do no harm; and when it turned out that the pupils of the
new schools were after all more eminent and more pagan in spirit than
any Byzantines for centuries, the only alternatives before the ecclesiastical authorities were acceptance or persecution. Accordingly, some
scholars were persecuted, notably Gregoras and Plethon; but for the
moment the educational system could not be brought under control.
Moreover, owing to the methods they used, the degree to which these
men's minds had been influenced by antiquity was not immediately
obvious. The wide reading and the attention to detail required by their
Atticism made them aware of how the ancient world lived, and how it
thought about its experience. But often their intellectual assimilation to
their pagan models was most marked in those fields in which the Church
had least interest and least control; and they found it easy to reconcile
a pagan attitude to art or even a pagan view of human psychology with
the observances of a pious Christian life.

It is true that the schools of this late period have come in for a good
deal of criticism. In particular they have been severely censured by two
contemporary writers, the Patriarch Gennadius and the Italian Filelfo,
whose opinion modern scholarship has tended to accept. But in point
of fact, neither the Patriarch nor the Humanist can be regarded as an
unprejudiced witness. Gennadius condemned his fellow-countrymen
as ignorant compared with the Italians or the French, but he was a
devotee of Aristotle and as such had a boundless admiration for the
achievements of scholastic philosophy. An enthusiastic specialist, he
judged the world in terms of his speciality, and because Byzantium was
inferior to the West in Aristotelian philosophy, concluded it must be
inferior in everything. As for Filelfo, he never had a good word to say
for anyone. He had fifteen children to feed, and it was a matter of some

importance for him to set his own value high by implying that his father-in-law had been the only efficient scholar in Constantinople.* There is plenty to be said on the other side. Many of these fourteenth-century teachers were men whose ability and personal character won the admiration of their contemporaries. Many too have solid achievements to their credit. Melitoniotes, who was head of the Oecumenical College soon after 1350, wrote the most learned and extensive treatise on astronomy composed during the Middle Ages, and he also produced a lengthy commentary on the Gospels. Plethon was incontrovertibly the most influential Platonist of his day. He had originality, great personal charm, and a quite remarkable honesty of purpose. Manuel Chrysoloras proved his worth in Italy as an inspiring teacher and tactful diplomatist. Gennadius himself was an efficient philosopher who tackled with courage the unpleasant task of being the first Patriarch under Turkish rule, while Argyropoulos, the last to hold the position of teacher to the Imperial Court, showed himself during the second half of his career as in every way equal, if not superior, to the Italian Humanists among whom he worked. Would these men have had so many and such enthusiastic pupils if they had been without ability? Would their pupils have turned out such eminent men?*

For us, the most important of the group is Manuel Chrysoloras who united in his work the various strands of Byzantine scholarship to form a whole which was then handed over to the West. He stands thus at the end of one epoch and the beginning of the next. But before we can appreciate the full significance of his teaching, there is still some more background to cover, still another aspect of Byzantine pedagogy to examine. The middle years of the fourteenth century had seen a change in men's attitude to the ancient world, which at the time had no obvious connection with the contemporary developments of Atticism. This change had been foreshadowed in the composition of the Planudean Anthology and in the writings of Metochites, but it was not until much later that it found a decisive exponent in Gemistus Plethon. This man whom we meet in his old age at the Council of Florence as an eccentric who charmed everybody by the force of his intellectualism and his devotion to the simple life, used to teach in Constantinople until the middle of the century when he was exiled for his heretical opinions. His pupils included the best of the younger generation. He lectured on the writers of antiquity, first on the poets, then on the philosophers; but he did not study them for style only, as had been the Christian habit. His aim was to bring his own ideas in communion with theirs.* In other words, he was the pioneer of an attitude which was to become very common during the Renaissance. He wished to extend imitation from manner to matter, from the way of writing to the way of living. It was not possible for the Church to tolerate the open avowal of such a programme, although the influence of linguistic imitation working in an unobtrusive way towards the same ends was passing unnoticed. Plethon was exiled; but the notions he had championed survived his disgrace, and what was more, received support from an unexpected quarter. The doctors and scientists were becoming increasingly conscious again of the value of classical sources in their disciplines, and a renewed interest in ancient knowledge as well as a resumption of ancient techniques in these specialised fields aroused a certain sympathy for those who wished to revive the philosophical ideas and tastes of the past.*

Plethon's Humanism was therefore kept alive after his exile by other and more discreet scholars who wanted to smooth over rather than to emphasise the eventual contradictions between the trend of their scholarship and the sincerity of their religion. Chief among these was Chrysoloras.

He was personally instrumental in shaping the future of the Renaissance because of that visit he paid to Italy in 1397 in the train of the Emperor Manuel; and a letter by his Italian admirer Guarino, who followed him back to Constantinople and spent five years in his household, gives the best account we have of his system of instruction. According to Guarino, Chrysoloras laid the strongest possible stress upon reading. It was to be wide, attentive and analytical. The student was to note every expression which struck him as apt or colourful; and he was to impress them upon his memory by a constant repetition until their use became second nature to him. But he was not to confine his attention to language alone. The same techniques were to be applied to the subject-matter; and anecdotes which described noteworthy actions or pointed remarks were to be learnt by heart whenever possible; by this process, not only the ways of thought, but the experiences on which ancient writers based their work could be securely assimilated, and the student's mind transformed until it came to resemble in its content and operations the mind of a fifth-century Greek. A colossal effort of memory was plainly required before this end could be achieved, and to facilitate it Chrysoloras suggested two methods. The first was that the student should repeat every evening what he had learnt during the day, and that he should set aside a definite time each month for a general repetition of all his knowledge. The second was the keeping of a note-book in which phrases and passages could be written down prior to being learnt and where they would be ready if ever memory failed to do its work.*

The intellectual consequences of literary imitation depend upon the character and scope of the intellectual differences between the imitator and his model. When Quintilian in the first century A.D. suggested to his pupils that they should read, dissect and remember the writers he chose for their models, the processes he recommended, though similar in type to the pedagogics of Chrysoloras, were bound to have more restricted results. For the students of rhetoric in the Flavian Age still had the same cultural background as Cicero or Hortensius, with the result that imitation was in fact limited to tricks of style and the niceties of rhetorical argument. But a Byzantine of the late fourteenth century lived in a world which had very little in common with the world of Demosthenes. In imitating the latter meticulously he would therefore make his own not only rhetorical techniques but a whole new cultural background; and the effects upon his manner of thought and behaviour were likely to be proportionately greater.

With Chrysoloras the development of Byzantine education came to an end. His system was its gift to the future. The last agonised years brought no change. Polite and efficient, Joannes Argyropoulus enjoyed the Emperor's favour and taught at the Petra Hospital lecturing on medicine while a few miles away the Turkish generals piled up their armaments. When the blow fell, he escaped to Italy where he continued to teach for over thirty years and was much esteemed as a translator of Aristotle, still polite, still efficient, if a little homesick and regretful. An Earl of Worcester came to hear him lecture; and he numbered among his pupils Reuchlin and Politian. Melanchthon has preserved the story that one day the young Reuchlin read a passage of Thucydides in class, and Argyropoulos was struck by the excellence of his pronunciation. 'Greece has flown over the Alps', he exclaimed, 'thanks to our exile.'

We are now better placed to answer the puzzling question as to why the Byzantines did not do better with all the resources at their disposal. It has long been accepted even by the most zealous partisans of ancient learning that in Byzantium the classical education had failed lamentably.

The peculiar indispensable service of Byzantine literature was the preservation of the language, philology and archaeology of Greece. It is impossible to see how our knowledge of ancient literature and civilisation could have been recovered, if Constantinople had not nursed through the early Middle

Ages the vast accumulations of Greek learning in the schools of Alexandria, Athens and Asia Minor; if Photius, Suidas, Eustathius, Tzetzes and the Scholiasts had not poured out their lexicons, anecdotes and commentaries; if the *Corpus scriptorum historiae Byzantinae* had not been compiled; if indefatigable copyists had not toiled in multiplying the texts of ancient Greece. Pedantic, dull, and blundering as they are too often, they are indispensable. We pick precious truths and knowledge out of their generalities and stupidities, for they preserve what otherwise would have been lost for ever. It is no paradox that their very merit to us is that they were neither original nor brilliant. Their genius indeed would have been our loss. Dunces and pedants as they were, they servilely repeated the words of the immortals.*

No one would try to explain these stupidities and pedantries by blaming them on a natural incapacity. One cannot assume the incapacity of a population of several millions over a period of more than a thousand years; but in the field of education which we have been considering one can find an answer to the puzzle: or more correctly two answers.

We have seen how, in Byzantium, war left only a small section of the community life free to develop or change. Thus neither literature nor science benefited from those strong impulsions which they normally derive from the human energies that are released in the seasonal transformations of society. For all progress, all movement was blanketed by the requirements of defence. Nor on the other hand could literature and scientific advancement exercise their potentially great influence; for the developments which they might have set in motion were at every turn stopped by the same obstacle.

Then, there was a second hindrance which acted as a further check on progress even within the limited sphere that war left open. The Church was there to circumscribe the action of secular studies which, properly followed, were bound to fill men's heads with pagan ideas. After the shock of the Iconoclast controversy the religious authorities realised that pagan studies were inevitable, that they could not be stopped without destroying the culture from which the Church itself benefited. But efforts were made, sometimes consciously, sometimes unconsciously, to keep Hellenism under control. In the ninth century, when the main secular interest was for science, the Church preferred to encourage the formal study of language. In the eleventh century when a secular revolution with a nationalist bias had made the pagan past momentarily popular, the Church took over education on a large scale and introduced techniques of study which left the shell of Atticism without its substance. In the fourteenth century some of the more

89

daring Hellenists were persecuted, and had it not been for the general collapse, the Church would no doubt have tried again to get control of the educational system.

These were the conditions under which Byzantine scholars had to work. When one considers them in detail, one is no longer surprised that they did not achieve more. Indeed, it is surprising that they achieved so much.

CHAPTER III

THE CAROLINGIAN AGE

Having arrived at the very threshold of the Renaissance, we must now return to the beginning of the Dark Ages and consider the development of the West during those same seven hundred years whose course we have just surveyed in the East. For conditions in the two halves of Europe were vastly different. In Byzantium we saw the shrinking nucleus of a superior civilisation, fearful of loss, constantly on the defensive, stereotyped in its institutions and culture. In the West we shall see by contrast evidences not of atrophy but of growth. The Western peoples were more anxious to acquire new blessings than to preserve the few they could already command. Their world had touched rock bottom, had been plunged into chaos and was now in mid-passage out. Unafraid of change, they were not desirous of barring its effects from any sector of their lives. The period of the Roman past glittered in their traditions as a golden age which having existed once could no doubt be restored; and that conviction in the midst of their ever-present discontents made them eager to throw as much as possible into the melting-pot.

Our proper starting-point is in time the sixth century and in space a remote island to which Roman power had never extended its latinising sway. The Ireland of St Patrick was the first place to which the literary heritage of the classics came, as it was to come eventually to the whole of Western Europe, from the outside, a gift of the gods to be won through judicious learning, a gift possibly of forbidden fruit.

The ancient literatures could not become the principal avenue of approach to Graeco-Roman culture until the passage of time and the introduction of alien influences had brought about a clear break with the Graeco-Roman world. In the East that break had occurred when Islam had engulfed half the seminal area of Greek civilisation and the Iconoclast controversies had thrown the rest in turmoil. In the West, its incidence cannot be linked with such specific and spectacular events. The collapse of the Western Empire was due to a gradual disorganisation that followed the repeated barbarian inroads: and so occurred first in the areas furthest removed from the centre of Roman power. The forces of destruction worked inwards from the periphery. The Danube and Rhine frontiers were breached, Britain was abandoned, Spain became a Visigothic kingdom. But Gaul and Italy even when nominally conquered, still retained much of their old civilisation. Only with the passage of time, through the continual wars between the Frankish kingdoms and after the Lombard invasions, did they too sink reluctantly into barbarism. The new order which was to replace the Empire took shape first in localities far distant from Italy, and then worked inwards, through Britain and Gaul, to join hands in the end with the last faint survivals of Roman life that had managed to hold their own in what had once been the seat and nerve-centre of Roman power.

I. CLASSICAL STUDIES IN IRELAND AND BRITAIN
450–650

The notion that St Patrick brought classical learning to Ireland, or that such learning might have existed there prior to his arrival, rests on the flimsiest of evidence. The reproaches which the Saint addresses in his *Confessio* to those he calls 'rhetoricians unacquainted with God' have been taken to indicate that the townships of Ireland sheltered some of the professional colleagues of that fifth-century Lampridius who is recorded as having declaimed in Greek and Latin before his pupils at Bordeaux. Since there were Christians in Ulster and Leinster from about the middle of the fourth century, it is admittedly possible that schoolmasters from Britain or Gaul could have been found among them. But it is well to remember that Latin by this time hung on to life primarily as the language of administration and the organised Church. In a country where the usages of Roman government could not have survived, and where the Church had not yet penetrated, such an official idiom would have had little value and rhetoricians would have found very few pupils. It seems more likely therefore that St Patrick, whom his style shows to have been no scholar, was attacking the intellectuals among his own collaborators. He would not have been alone among his contemporaries to see in the pursuit of learning the abandonment of that single-minded fervour which religion required.

The next two hundred years saw, however, the foundation of the great monasteries at Clonard, Movilla, Kells and Durrow. The Irish, who had a highly developed culture of their own with a rich verbal literature and a relatively advanced system of law, seem to have looked favourably upon the contemplative life and the practices of learning. Thus once Ireland had been converted, its Christian communities flourished remarkably; and the story that John Bull resorted to his other island in search of enlightenment can be attested from the pages of Bede.

Many of the nobility and lower ranks of the English nation were there at the time (664). They had forsaken their native island and retired thither, either for the sake of divine learning or through desire of a more continent existence. Some of these had speedily devoted themselves to a monastical life; while others had chosen to apply themselves to study, going about from one monk's cell to another. The Scots (i.e. the Irish) received them all with equal willingness and took care to supply them with food, as also to furnish them with books to read and free instruction.

Divine learning was the great glory of the Irish monks as Bede remarks. They were the eager students of the Scripture, the superb illuminators of the Book of Kells, the composers of the first Latin hymns in which we catch a hint of rhyme. As such, they deserve and have received an unstinted admiration from posterity. But the full extent of their achievements went beyond the bounds of Church or Bible, and the scope of their popular reputation fails to indicate every aspect of their importance. Their learning made a dual impact. It was of some account outside the strictly religious sphere; and we must look upon them not only as the exponents of an artistic and con-templative monasticism, but also as the pioneers who were the first to study the classical heritage as it was to be studied from that point on-wards against the background of a world that had lost all other contact with the classical past.

Necessarily, they learnt Latin without which the Psalter and the Bible itself would have been meaningless; and in doing so they made use of the traditional instruments of secular education, copying gram-mars and compiling elaborate and somewhat obscure word-lists. Having access in part at least to bilingual Bibles, they extended the field of their researches to Greek and even at times to Hebrew. We need lay no emphasis on the well-known failure of their achievements to equal their ambitions. The Latin they wrote was, at its best, poor, thin in vocabu-lary and incorrect in idiom. At its worst, it was a linguist's nightmare, an unwitting reconstruction of the confusions of Babel.* With the solitary exception of Columban, there is no Irish scholar known to us prior to the end of the seventh century who quotes any pagan author; and the letters and poems in which Columban shows his knowledge were all written long after he had left his homeland.*

We may in another context legitimately doubt the competence of those fifth-century Gaulish Hellenists whose names meet us in the pages of Sidonius; but even they must have known infinitely more Greek than any Irishman during those two hundred years when Ireland is supposed to have been the sole Western repository of Greek culture. The contemporaries of Cummian, Tirechan and Muirchu Maccu Machtheni could not have read a page of Demosthenes. The structure of the language, the linguistic relationships that determined its usage, were unfamiliar to them. What they studied were isolated words, culled from lists or extracted from bilingual texts, nouns whose declension remained a mystery, verbs to whose conjugations they had no clue. They knew Greek as an apprentice magician might know a supposed language of sorcery.

Yet, poor though their scholarship was, its importance and interest are beyond question. Its value derived not from its quality, but from the circumstances which attended its development. Here for the first time men were reduced to approach the classical heritage by the means which all future generations would be compelled to use, the limited and unsatisfactory medium of book-learning. The Irish were the first to build the castles of their classical knowledge on the exclusive basis of dictionaries, word-lists and such help as the ancient texts themselves could supply. If they built unwisely, if they relied too much on the lath and plaster of fancy to fill the gaps between the bricks of fact, their error was one common to all pioneers; and the strictures piled on their heads by critics like Roger are in the last analysis quite undeserved.

Allied to the Irish schools and similar to them in many respects were the centres of learning in western Britain; but the foundations of Llan-Carvan and Llan-Iltud did not enjoy the prosperity that distinguished their fellow monasteries over the water; and the British contribution to classical studies was less weighty than the Irish. During the fifth and early sixth centuries, the dwindling remnants of what had been the province of Britain still retained certain vestiges of Roman culture. Latin was still spoken, not indeed by everybody, but in sufficient measure to give men like Gildas, Iltud or Paul Aurelian a dim kinship with their contemporaries in Gaul for whom the tongue of Cicero remained a living language. These ultimate representatives of an etiolated Rome may have provided their Irish contemporaries with some of the material from which the latter constructed their education; and in that sense they may be viewed as bridging the gap between the old order and the new. But soon the flame of that Roman life which the British had managed to cherish burnt too low to be of any account. The old order came definitely to a close; and by the second half of the sixth century, the monasteries of Wales were facing the same problem that the Irish had come upon earlier and were now ready to solve. Like Clonard and Movilla, Llan Iltud had now to keep alive the spark of Latin learning in its schools without the aid of an external supporting culture: and this could only be done by taking Irish experience as a guide.

Thus, the first epoch in the history of the classical education is associated primarily with Ireland, and the credit for having taken the first steps in that educational labyrinth where the classical writings were man's only guide belongs without question to the Irish. That epoch came to an end however with the seventh century. The torch of educational advance passed into other hands; and the work which the Irish had attempted, the training of Latin scholars in the monasteries of a barbarian people, was repeated more successfully among the Anglo-Saxons. The new learning was moving inwards from the periphery, one stage nearer to the old centre of Rome. After 668, the future lay with Canterbury and York. It is true that some of the most brilliant triumphs of Irish learning were still to come. But those triumphs— though they added to Western knowledge—did not contribute vitally to pedagogic technique; and they were to some extent dependent upon the work done by the Anglo-Saxons. History repeated itself. Ireland became educationally subordinate to England, as earlier Celtic Britain had fallen under the Irish spell. It is true that the extent of Anglo-Saxon influence on the Irish scholars from 668 onwards cannot be accurately estimated; and we cannot be sure of its impact in any particular case. But when we find that Muirchu's Life of St Patrick contains a reminiscence of Virgil and another of Valerius Flaccus, when Adamnan of Iona refers to the *Aeneid* in his life of St Columba and is mentioned as a commentator in a manuscript of the *Georgics*,* we can no longer feel certain that their scholarship was the unaided product of the Irish tradition. The Anglo-Saxon scholars were already at work, and the future of the classical education was in their hands.

II. THE ANGLO-SAXON SCHOOLS
650–800

As soon as the conversion of the previously unromanised and wholly unlettered Anglo-Saxons was well on its way, the Irish situation of the sixth century repeated itself in the England of the seventh. The priests who served the churches, the monks who filled the monasteries, had for obvious reasons to be drawn from among the people whose spiritual needs they sought to satisfy. Brought up to speak a vernacular which had no relation to Latin, they had to be taught the language of the Church. Every word, every form, every idiom was strange to them and would become familiar only after patient effort. Under these circumstances, schools were essential if Christianity was to survive.

This was a novel situation, and before we pass on to consider the history of the Anglo-Saxon schools, it will be convenient to examine in greater detail where its novelty lay. For this purpose, we can do no better than return once again to St Gregory's rebuking of Bishop Desiderius.

The numerous good reports which we had received concerning your studies, gave us so much pleasure that we had every inclination to grant your request. But more recently a circumstance came to our notice, which cannot be mentioned without shame, namely that you, our brother, give lessons in grammar. This news caused us such annoyance and disgust that all our joy at the good we had heard earlier was turned to sorrow and distress, since the same lips cannot sing the praises of Jove and the praises of Christ. Consider yourself how serious and shocking it is that a bishop should pursue an activity unsuitable even for a pious layman. Our beloved son, the presbyter Candidus, who arrived after we received this information, has on being closely questioned denied its authenticity, and being a relation of yours has been at pains to clear you. Nevertheless, we have not yet put the matter out of our mind since the execrable nature of this charge, when made against a priest, renders it essential that we should have clear and detailed proof of its truth or falsehood. Thus (you may take it) that we give thanks to God, Who has not allowed your heart to be sullied by blasphemously praising the wicked, and that we have already in hand the granting of your request, easy in mind and untroubled by doubts, provided that this information which has come to us shall have been proved manifestly untrue, and you will not be shown to spend your time on the follies of secular literature.*

If we are to interpret this letter correctly, we must remember that Gregory was in Italy while Desiderius worked in Gaul. Italy had not known—and indeed never was to know—that complete destruction of civilised life which had followed the breakdown of Roman power in most other areas. She had been exceptionally fortunate. Of her invaders, the Vandals had shown no desire to stay, the Ostrogoths comparatively few in number, had been under a ruler who encouraged them to take their place peacefully alongside the Roman population, while the Lombards, although more numerous and disorderly than the Ostrogoths, were less destructive than a tribe like the Franks. When Gregory wrote, much of the peninsula was still free from all barbarian control. Rome maintained its precarious independence; and in the south the old Graeco-Roman culture survived almost unimpaired. The Church existed in the midst of a Latin-speaking society whose upper classes at least were prepared for the tasks of administration and trained to the literary use of the classical tongue by private and municipal schools. Gregory himself had grown up at a time when according to Cassiodorus such schools still abounded,* and he had come to take their existence for granted. In his view general education was a service which the secular world automatically supplied so that the task of the clergy was limited to the provision of specifically religious teaching. His censure of Desiderius must be set against this background.

It originated in a misconception, in a perhaps pardonable failure to distinguish between the Italy he saw and the Gaul he knew only through reports. Gaul had been a prey to disorder ever since 405 when the northern tribes first broke the military barrier on the Rhine. The successive invasions of the Visigoths, the Burgundians and the Franks, the wars between them and the internecine conflicts of the Frankish kingdom which followed the deaths of Clovis and Clothair I had caused a vast amount of local damage; and the gradual accumulation of that damage had resulted in the total ruin of Gallo-Roman civilisation, a disaster for which the experience of Italy furnished no parallel. The secular schools had been the first victims of this mounting chaos. Few survived the fifth century; and the vigour with which the Council of Vaison emphasised the desirability of each parish priest instructing boys in the psalms and pious reading, may have been prompted by its awareness of the difficulties which were arising since the educated class from which the clergy had been recruited in the past, the men who could be trusted to read the Bible for themselves, had now virtually disappeared. But the fathers of Vaison, though aware that something was amiss, did not yet see the situation clearly enough to analyse its causes. Time was needed to show the effects of their loss. A generation had to grow up without its customary intellectual sustenance; and in 529 that had not yet happened. Fifty years later there was no room for doubt. Pope Gregory's contemporary, Gregory of Tours, bewailed the disastrous condition of the country where Romanisation had seen its greatest success. 'Humane learning is on the decline or rather is perishing altogether in the cities of Gaul where no distinction is made between good and evil, no bounds are set on the ferocity of peoples or the madness of princes....'* The disappearance of the secular schools had resulted in a situation which imperilled the existence of the Church; and a conscientious bishop like Desiderius had every reason to know that only on a firm foundation of secular learning, only on the basis of those grammatical studies which the Church had hitherto regarded as outside its province, could the religious life of the future safely be built. We do not possess the answer in which he set forth his defence; but the strength of his case is evident. Given the conditions prevailing in Gaul, the teaching he undertook was undoubtedly needed; and what was true of Gaul applied with even greater force to England. A radical change had come over those parts of Europe which lay north of the Alps, as a result of which the old relations between pagan learning and the Christian Church had been radically transformed. The building of the City of God now necessitated the rebuilding of Rome on barbarian soil. Latin had to be taught to Franks and Saxons to help them understand their Faith.

The reorganisation which brought fame to the Anglo-Saxon schools and made them into models for the whole of Europe to follow, derived its first impetus from an ecclesiastical controversy. As so often happens, we find a wide and apparently inevitable movement—in this case the spread of education under the aegis of the Church—hastened into a specific channel by some temporary development irrelevant to the main tenor of its growth. During the seventh century, the Irish made England their principal mission field, and in the course of that pious endeavour, they clashed with the successors of Augustine who had been working outwards from Kent since 597. The differences between the Celtic and the Roman Church concerned matters of observance and jurisdiction. No major philosophical or moral issue was at stake; but the passions aroused were nevertheless so intense that at times we find them overcoming the charity of even the Venerable Bede; and when Bede composed his history he was viewing the dispute in retrospect. By about the year 650 since the number of conversions had been large, the spheres of influence of the rival missionaries were beginning to overlap, and the relations between them became increasingly strained, until the danger point was reached when each side made efforts to attract the adherents of the other.

Benefiting by their experience in their own island, the Irish monks organised the training of their clergy. Soon the schools of Lindisfarne and Streaneshalch were turning out large numbers of young Englishmen who could talk to the people in their own language and were yet familiar enough with Latin to make effective priests. This move put the

Roman party at a serious disadvantage, since in Kent there were no large-scale schemes for teaching English-born novices. Such informal instruction as the Bishops could make available either in song-schools or in their households was plainly insufficient to do more than provide a handful of young barbarians with an elementary understanding of Latin. Nor could the lack of local talent be made good by recruits from abroad; for the latter faced a language difficulty of their own. They were sound Latinists perhaps, but they could not talk to their flocks, and in any case they were not available in sufficient numbers. It was plain that schools under Roman control were needed if the struggle against Iona was to be effectively won. Even the Synod of Whitby (664), which looked like a Roman triumph since it involved the submission of their opponents, did not solve the problem, for the personnel of the Celtic party were so much superior in numbers and talent that following the amalgamation of the Churches they threatened to acquire a controlling position in the hierarchy.* The situation bristled with pitfalls, and its dangers provided the argument which finally led the Church of Rome to enter the educational field in a systematic fashion.

It must not be supposed that someone surveyed the situation and thought out a bold plan for using the methods of the secular schools to teach Latin under the auspices of the Church. This development came about in small stages and as it were by accident. When Pope Vitalian appointed Theodore of Tarsus in 668 to the See of Canterbury, left vacant by the death of Archbishop Deusdedit, there is no evidence that he had a definite policy in mind. It may be that he was guided by no more than an obscure feeling that a scholar was perhaps the best person to deal with a situation created by the learning of the Celtic monks; and Theodore in his turn did only what the circumstances obviously indicated. When he and his friend Hadrian arrived in England, they gathered round them a band of pupils to whom they gave instruction. In that they followed a common practice; and if they had been a couple of ordinary ecclesiastics with the sort of background which was common in the contemporary Anglo-Saxon Church, their teaching would have had no startling results. But they had more to give than a Deusdedit or even a Benedict Biscop. They came from the Mediterranean lands from among the vestiges of the old classical culture. They had both been educated in secular schools, Theodore actually in Athens. They both knew Greek well; and a greater sympathy for the pagan past, which was the product of their Greek training, distinguished them from even their Italian contemporaries.

Bede speaks of their work in terms of unreserved enthusiasm.

Since they were both deeply learned in sacred and profane letters alike, they gathered round them a band of disciples whose hearts they daily refreshed with the waters of healthful knowledge, teaching their hearers the rules of metric, astronomy and the computus as well as the works of the saints. The proof of this is that we can find pupils of theirs even to-day who know Latin and Greek as accurately as their own mother tongue....*

Later in his narrative Bede tells us the names of some of these young Anglo-Saxons who benefited from the new teaching. There was Albinus, later Abbot of St Peter's, Canterbury, who had much Greek and more Latin; and there was Tobias who spoke both languages as he did his mother tongue.* Unfortunately, their writings, if they left any, have not survived. The real extent of that learning which brought them so much honour in their own day cannot now be checked; and the credit it should reflect upon their teachers must remain in some degree open to question. But this lack of evidence is not absolute. One at least of Hadrian's pupils put pen to paper with startling effect, leaving us ample memorials from which to judge his gifts and erudition.

As so often happens, the spirit of the age was exemplified in an individual, and the career of Aldhelm is an index to the common experience of his generation. Here was a boy of royal blood, born in the remote west country, who received his initiation into knowledge, as had the successors of St Patrick, at the feet of a learned anchorite. The story of his youth possesses that pastoral and almost heroic character which makes the heyday of the Celtic culture the nearest Britain ever knew to a Homeric epoch. Aldhelm, a relative of King Ini, went to the monk Maidulf as Achilles to Chiron. But then the pattern changes; and in the bishop, that the Wessex prince became, we can trace the familiar lineaments of a great medieval churchman. Moving freely on the wide stage of European learning, expounding the technicalities of rhetoric and science, encouraging hopeful neophytes and rebuking unchristian monarchs, he appears the prototype of a Gerbert or a Lanfranc: so much so that one is tempted to think of him as having managed by some miracle to comprise two aeons of human existence within the span of a single lifetime.

It is true that the sharpness of this general impression grows blurred on a closer study of the facts. Aldhelm, even at the height of his powers was no Gerbert. He remained to the end of his days clumsy and somewhat naïve in the handling of his knowledge; and his turgid style, which trapped Taine into some rash generalisations on the Anglo-

Saxon genius, had marked affinities to Celtic latinity. But these short-comings cannot in the last analysis be regarded as of more than minor importance. They serve to make the proportions of his achievement credible. They do not alter its character. The fact remains that he was brought up in a tradition which (in so far as secular studies were concerned) had taken strange and not altogether desirable forms owing to its limited command of the necessary sources of knowledge; and having imbibed from that tradition the fiery reverence for learning which was its noblest feature, and having come at last to Canterbury he attained under the tuition of Hadrian to a very thorough mastery of Latin grammar, read the Christian and many of the pagan authors, and progressed so far even as to gain some familiarity with the sciences of the Quadrivium.

The evidence at our disposal suggests therefore that Theodore and Hadrian did for Anglo-Saxon education what Iltud and Gildas had done for the Irish. Acting as a link between the present and the past, they provided that essential basis of information and that guidance as to standards of attainment without which the new traditions could hardly have come into being.

Much, however, still remained to do. The Irish schools owed their importance to the fact that Comgall and his contemporaries had worked out methods by which the knowledge they had gained from teachers who had been in personal contact with the Roman scholastic tradition in a more or less Roman community, could be preserved in a world of barbarians. These methods the Anglo-Saxons had still to master.

To teach Latin to boys when your mother tongue and theirs has no affinities with any classical language, requires special techniques; and we have no reason to think that Theodore and Hadrian had made a study of the problems involved. The number of their successful pupils was not so great as to preclude the hypothesis that it was the brilliant who benefited from their instruction. Aldhelm certainly had a richly endowed intellect which did not require that its path to learning should be carefully smoothed.

Great importance must therefore be given to the work of Aldhelm's own generation and their immediate successors. Theodore and Hadrian had been responsible for a significant addition to the common stock of Anglo-Saxon knowledge; and in this they had received valuable help from Benedict Biscop, who deserves to figure as the patron and exemplar of all British librarians, having made one at least of his five voyages to Rome for the specific purpose of collecting books, a seventh-century Aurispa visiting the seventh-century Constantinople. But the final step of organising this knowledge for use under existing circumstances was in all probability not taken until after Hadrian's death. It was the work of Aldhelm, but more especially of men like Tatwine and Bede who applied the teaching methods of the Celtic tradition to the new material from Italy. The central purpose of these new educators was still the comprehension of the Scriptures just as it had been in the days of the Irish schools. But to this main ideal they now added two secondary aims. They wanted to give their pupils a good grounding in the generality of Christian literature; and what was even more revolutionary, they wanted to teach them the art of fluent expression in both verse and prose.

To be viable, a system of educational training must possess a certain internal harmony. The student must not be troubled by being taught contradictory notions of the world, mutually exclusive values, or incompatible tastes. That type of harmony the Anglo-Saxon schools certainly achieved. The three ends they followed were mutually illustrative. The three bodies of information they drew upon were neatly dovetailed. In the writings of the time, the champions of grammatical studies liked to advance the argument that their speciality helped in the understanding of Scripture. It was a valid defence. The Bible was a foreign text. So long as the exact meaning and construction of the words used was not known, it could not be safely interpreted; and without skilled interpretation there could be no theology. Furthermore, certain parts of the New Testament and in particular the writings of St Paul contained an excessive number of rhetorical figures and were bound to be obscure to anyone ignorant of rhetoric. In that connection, there was an obvious need for some familiarity with tropes, another branch of grammar. A moderate degree of grammatical knowledge would, however, have been sufficient to satisfy these moderate requirements; and on these grounds alone scholarship would not have obtained much support from the theologians. But as it happened theology now had other and wider needs. The medieval interpreters of Scripture were not usually content with extracting a plain meaning from the words. In the first place, it was necessary, since the Bible was the Book of God, that the real sense of every passage should be acceptable to the contemporary Christian conscience. There were occasions where the surface meaning had to be explained away; and even where that was not the case, a single meaning, a single excuse for piety was not considered enough. The devout leisure of the monks was not content until the last drop of edification had been squeezed from every phrase; and four exegetical methods were employed to that end. Everything had its historical, allegorical, anagogical and tropological purport; and in the elaboration of these subtleties a familiarity with grammar and rhetoric was to prove most helpful.

Then if the pursuit of literary excellence was sometimes carried further than the strict needs of Biblical exegesis immediately warranted, the scholars had yet another line of defence. They could put forward the argument that Christians ought to be able to express their ideas with the greatest possible force and ought therefore to have all the tricks of the trade, all the techniques of composition at their finger tips. Thus championed, the position of grammar in the Christian curriculum was inassailable.

Somewhat similar claims were made for metric—the other secular subject to receive considerable attention. Text-books on metric dealt largely with rules for determining quantity and stress,* and such information was held to be essential if the ritual of the Church was to be properly carried out. That seemingly innocent argument has its own peculiar interest. The spontaneous assumption that mispronouncing a few Latin words would impair the dignity of a psalm, betrays to what extent these early scholars regarded Latin as a fixed language with unalterable rules and usages, to what extent too they regarded it as sacred, a language especially dedicated to the service of God;* and it is easy to see how such beliefs could prepare men's minds for studying Latin as an end in itself irrespective of its ecclesiastical uses: but that was to be a later development.

As we have seen, Aldhelm's contemporaries, the personal pupils of Theodore and Hadrian, were enthusiasts and in some cases remarkable scholars; but the task of turning scholarship into education fell rather to their immediate juniors. The Graeco-Roman schools had been so tradition-ridden that these men were really the first to solve a clear-cut pedagogic problem since the days of Isocrates. The novelty of their achievement was therefore remarkable; but its scope should not be overrated. They did not cover an enormous field. What they did was to simplify the teaching of grammar and versification so as to bring these subjects within the grasp of students who had needed to start Latin from the beginning. The Roman schoolmasters had taught boys whose normal speech was akin to written Latin, or who spoke a variety of Latin as a second language. So the ancient authorities on grammar were accustomed to take a good deal for granted. They set up to be philosophers, revelled in definitions and argued about the logical distinctions between the parts of speech; but never distinguished at all clearly between the study of language in general and the study of a single language, Latin, in particular. The great monasteries and cathedrals of eighth-century England possessed some at least of the Roman books about grammar, and it must have been obvious to every competent teacher that the material they contained was under the circumstances pedagogically useless. A man who sits down to learn a foreign language because it is the official idiom of his Church wants paradigms, not philosophy. So Bede and his contemporaries compiled their own grammars. Three of these have come down to us: one by Bede himself which was presumably used in his school at Jarrow, one by Boniface* used by him at Nursling near Exeter, and one by Tatwine. They are none of them original. The statements they make and the examples they quote are copied from obvious sources. Tatwine's effort is in any case a failure. It reproduces many of the worst faults of its models. But the other two are more successful. They are free of irrelevant discussion. They present the material to be learnt in a clear and compendious form, making use of such aids to learning as paradigms and word lists. The same is true about the other text-books of the time: the works of Bede on orthography, on metre and on the various figures of speech. They are all practical and they are all simple.*

The two best-known schools of the time were at Jarrow and York. The former had grown up casually in an ordinary monastery, thanks to the pedagogic genius of Bede. The latter was created by Bishop Egbert of York who extended and institutionalised the domestic, informal instruction which his predecessors gave to the members of their households. The man who had been Bishop of York at the beginning of the century used to take boys around with him and teach them to write and sing in the intervals of episcopal business.* Egbert by contrast set up a proper school under a full-time master, his kinsman and eventual successor Elbert. Bede died soon after 731; and Egbert, who was actually one of his pupils, did not become Bishop until 732 so that the two great schools were successive rather than contemporary; but between them they gave Anglo-Saxon education its final form.

Bede during his teaching career, which covered the first third of the eighth century, made certain additions to the programme we have outlined. Since Easter played such a vital part in current religious controversy, the lessons given by Theodore and Hadrian had certainly included some account of the procedures required for its computation and also some elementary arithmetic and astronomy by way of a propaedeutic. Bede with his usual compendiousness brought this material into order in a little book which he wrote in 703 and which contains all he taught his pupils about calculating the divisions of time. Three decades later, in response to their requests for more information, he wrote a second and longer work which is still just a summary of Roman sources, but usefully and lucidly arranged. It remained the authoritative account of the subject throughout the Middle Ages and popularised the technique of reckoning years from the birth of Christ rather than from the hypothetical beginning of the world.

Born into a generation whose intellectual curiosity had just been fired by a new teaching and having himself a taste for omniscience, it would have been odd if Bede had not become interested in natural history. That subject had not figured in the curriculum of Hadrian, but among the books which he and his friends brought to England there were some well-known encyclopedias as well as an abridgement of the elder Pliny. These Bede read; and he found that they contained the answers to many queries about the world that his own mind prompted or that his pupils had asked. Thanks to this stimulus, the scope of his lessons on the almanac and its astronomical prolegomena was gradually extended to include details about the winds, tides and weather, creation and the animals. Isidore and Pliny provided most of the necessary material which was eventually sufficient to form a subject on its own, and was used presumably in the form in which we find it set out in Bede's treatise on the nature of things.*

Alcuin, who succeeded Elbert as master at York, has left us a detailed account of the latter's teaching. Apparently, it covered grammar, rhetoric, law, poetry, astronomy, natural history, arithmetic, geometry, music, and above all the study of the Scriptures. The programme is a wide one; but we can see from the text-books of Bede on the one hand and Alcuin on the other that all these subjects were not regarded as being of equal importance, and that they were not all taught with an equal efficiency. Scripture had of course the pride of place; but on the secular side, grammar and versification received a good deal of attention; rhetoric was little more than the study of the figures of speech found in the Bible; mathematical teaching was centred on the intricacies of the calendar; the music and the law were those of the Church; and natural history was still largely anecdotal. The most fruitful portions of ancient science, the cosmogony and psychology of the Aristotelians were at this period still unknown. It is evident that this range of subjects, limited though it appears in comparison with what men were to study later, represented a considerable advance on the curricula of the earlier Irish schools. Thanks to the activity of a generation of devoted teachers, an essential portion of the classical heritage had been expressed in a simple form which the minds of uninstructed men could quickly absorb. The very first stage in the assimilation of ancient knowledge by new European culture was now over.

III. THE EDUCATIONAL REFORMS OF CHARLEMAGNE
775–814

Meanwhile, on the continent parish priests were as ignorant as their clodhopping parishioners. Boniface heard one baptising a child 'in nomine Patria et Filia et Spiritu Sancta' and wondered ruefully whether the sacrament would be considered valid.* It was obvious that sooner or later some sort of organised teaching would have to replace the haphazard instruction which was all the individual bishops and priests could offer. There were complaints and suggestions from many quarters, but eventually it was a secular ruler who started the ball rolling.

The victories of Charles Martel and his descendants had greatly increased the power of the Frankish monarchy. The kings, being now in a position to organise their territories, were feeling the need for trained subordinates, but the Church, which they hoped would supply support for their power, was plainly unfit to play its part unless its educational system could be overhauled; and the difficulty was to find the right method. Some efforts, whose details are unknown to us, must have been made towards the middle of the century; for about that time the Latin used in the charters sensibly improved.* Much, however, still remained to be done. A letter from Pope Paul I to Pepin, written presumably between 758 and 763,* is commonly quoted in connection with these early attempts at an educational revival. Pepin had asked for books; and the Pope had sent him a volume of antiphons and responds, a grammar by Aristotle (!), a second grammar, a treatise on orthography and another on geometry by Dionysius the Areopagite (!), all of them written in Greek. It is to be presumed that Pepin had for some reason required Greek works; but a less suitable selection for a backward country could hardly be imagined.

Charlemagne, the son of Pepin, brought a number of scholars from Italy, one of whom, Peter of Pisa, was attached to the Palace School. The date of his appointment is uncertain, but occurred almost certainly between 775 and 780. The Palace School had been in existence since the sixth century, and its purpose was to train youths intended for the priesthood.* But now its teaching was reorganised, and laymen were allowed to attend.

This is a good, clear example of the sort of change which we find happening both in England and France during the eighth century. The old domestic system of Church education is improved in a number of small ways which together have the effect of altering it out of all recognition. The part-time teacher, the busy parish priest or bishop, who has to spare a few minutes every day to instruct the novices under his charge, is replaced by the professional who makes the school his life's work; and the casual lessons which must have rested upon the inspiration of the moment give place to a settled, purposive curriculum.

The scheme had great merits; but unfortunately the man whom Charlemagne had chosen to be the first professional master of the Palace School was temperamentally unsuited to initiate a large-scale educational reform. Peter of Pisa came, as his name indicates, from northern Italy, which by this time had suffered considerably from the devastations of war and the upheavals of alien settlement. It is true that these upheavals had not been as violent as the parallel disturbances which had so effectively changed the face of Gaulish society. The cultural traditions of the Empire still lingered on. Their collapse had been admittedly incomplete. But it had gone a long way, and not all the parts of the old order had shown an equal power of survival. The legal relationships which had characterised Roman life, the municipal structure which had been the pride of Roman statesmen, the spoken language itself, all proved remarkably viable. But the mental world of the educated Roman, that intellectual tradition which the schools strove to preserve, had been an anachronism even in the fourth century; it had been already in the time of Ausonius a pattern derived from the past, without firm roots in existing conditions, imposed artificially through the study of the language and literature of an earlier age. The continued maintenance of such a tradition was bound to prove difficult in a period of social chaos, when education is inevitably neglected and men's minds are occupied with the pressing needs of each dangerous moment. At no point therefore had the breakdown been more obvious, at no point had the Roman world found it more difficult to hold its own, than precisely in the realm of the intellect.

After the Lombard invasions we hear of no schools in northern Italy for about a hundred years. Then certain vague figures with claims to learning make their appearance, and history spares them a line or two in its long record of battles and intrigues. There is the Felix mentioned by Paulus Diaconus* to whom King Cuncipert gave a stick ornamented with gold and silver. There is Benedictus Crispus, Archbishop of Milan (681–725) who wrote a poem on medicine for the use of a certain Maurus, and who claims that he taught Maurus the liberal arts.* The Stephanus who wrote a poem on the Synod of Ticino (698) had obviously received at least the rudiments of a literary education for he has a reminiscence of Virgil.* Flavian, the teacher of Paulus Diaconus, seems to have had a school at Pavia during the second and third decades of the eighth century; and we are told of a Lombard law about the same period which ordained that elementary instruction should be given in every parish.

These fragmentary pieces of information appear to hint at a state of affairs where new beginnings co-existed with old survivals. It is evident that on the one hand the Lombards found they could not do without a minimum of learning. Evidently, too, on the other hand, there were small groups in the cities, descendants of the well-to-do Roman population, who tried to keep alive their inherited culture, as an old family might try to keep up a great house which was once the centre of a huge estate, but which now stands merely as a functionless ornament. There were consequently in the Lombard kingdom teachers who struggled to impart the rudiments of reading and writing, while others, fewer in number and attracting fewer pupils, were concerned with the appreciation of the classical heritage.

It was to this latter class that Peter of Pisa belonged. If he was indeed the Magister Petrus whom Alcuin as a young man heard disputing with a Jew at Pavia, and the identification merits a certain measure of doubt, then we must suppose that his interest in theology had waned with the years. For once at the court of Charlemagne he seems to have made no effort to relate his teaching either to the Christian thought or the practical needs of the time. To forward the writing of correct Latin, the composition of elegant verses and above all the appreciation of the classical authors constituted his only concern. He remained at the Palace School for a long period, and within a restricted circle he appears to have exercised a definite influence. It is well known that Charles's closest friends made a veritable cult of the pagan writers. They called each other by classical names; and they went further than any of their immediate predecessors in their imitation of classical models. The breezes of Humanism, which had been still for so long, blow through the poems of Angilbert, of Modoin, of Ermolaus Nigellus with the promise of a new spring;* and it would not be plausible, considering the Christian orientation of the Anglo-Saxon schools and considering Alcuin's own expressed views,* to saddle him with the responsibility for this court fashion, the more so since for a long time, even while he was the general head of the Palace School, the grammar teaching as such seems to have remained in Peter's hands. The balance of probability is rather in favour of the hypothesis that Peter, who had returned to Italy by the time his pupils were old enough to set the tone of the court, was the real originator of this sudden Humanism. It is true that his name is not mentioned to any such purpose, but then his departure may have earned him Charles's displeasure, and courtiers have always been careful not to pay tributes to a fallen star.

But even if we admit Peter's possible claims to have influenced the court writers, his importance for the history of the classical heritage will still lag far behind that of Alcuin. He was at best a man of taste, a champion of the literary art in a world which was not yet ready for such luxuries. Although he was to lend himself later without protest to the fashions and games of his entourage, Charles saw well enough in 780 that he needed more from his educational coadjutor than just skill in cultivating the aesthetic enjoyment of literature. He wanted priests who could read their Bibles, monks who could understand theology, bishops who could deal with the administration of a diocese, and he wanted the Church to provide him with trained civil servants. These aims could only be attained through organisation; and the tasks of that organisation called for a man who would understand the problems involved in educating an élite from among a barbarous and illiterate nation. England was the only country which could furnish a teacher with the necessary experience; and so in 782 Charles persuaded Alcuin, the master at York, to accept the Headship of the Palace School together with the position of his informal adviser on all matters pertaining to the upbringing of the young.*

Alcuin's subsequent services to education were twofold. On the one hand he took a discipline which had been evolved in a single English school, transplanted it to the continent, and then helped to disseminate its use to a number of fresh centres, with the result that the pattern set in York was eventually followed over the whole of Europe. On the other hand, he also improved that discipline while he popularised it, extending its scope to fresh subjects, and developing its techniques to attain a greater efficiency in the field already covered.

The detailed history of the campaign which Charlemagne and Alcuin began in 787 to reform the schools need not concern us here. The capitularies which gave it effect have been frequently described. The secular state helped the Church to impose upon herself a reform beneficial to both; and by virtue of their joint efforts Europe's first large-scale educational system came into being. It was markedly Christian in tone and could hardly be otherwise since it was organised round the monasteries and cathedrals. Charlemagne, however, was sufficiently important to demand attention for his particular needs, and the curriculum which came to be introduced in his empire was in consequence somewhat wider in scope than the one the Church had built entirely to its pattern in England.

The capitularies outline this curriculum only in the most general terms. But we can reconstruct some of its details from Alcuin's own text-books which may be presumed to embody the methods he encouraged in the Palace School and later in his monastery at Tours. It is obvious first of all that great emphasis was put on the teaching of Latin; and that this aim was envisaged from an eminently practical point of view. Alcuin did not follow Capella in requiring the written language to be academic, nor did he follow Cassiodorus in requiring it to be beautiful. He wanted correctness, nothing more. He knew that he had to deal with men some of whom, having taken their vows late in life, were ignorant of any but their mother tongue,* while others, though brought up in a monastery, were still hesitant about reading even the monastic rule in Latin and were certainly unable to write the learned language with any degree of accuracy.

Correct Latin, according to Alcuin, is determined by nature, reason, authority and usage. He borrows these terms from earlier grammarians, and it is not possible to say what precisely he means by them. But it is perhaps significant that he does not repeat the specific injunction of Cassiodorus who had recommended the study of the 'famous poets and orators'.* Alcuin was not primarily interested in the pagan tradition and may indeed have looked upon the pagan authors with a certain distrust. Latin for him was the language of Christianity with its roots in the Vulgate and the Fathers, but still alive in the contemporary speech and writing of educated churchmen.

The grammar commonly attributed to Bede, which we mentioned above, had made use of the question and answer method; so had the commentary on the *Ars Minor* of Donatus by Paul the Deacon. Therefore, the method which Alcuin chose for his text-book on the subject* cannot be said to have been original, but he used it originally. What had been a mechanical dialogue in his predecessors, he made into a drama with characters: a fourteen-year old Frank, a fifteen-year old Saxon who has just enough extra knowledge to answer simple questions, and a master to whom difficulties can be referred. One could not easily make a dry topic more pleasant; and the book had other virtues as well. It was not merely another version of Donatus. It filled out the gaps which a non-Latin speaker was likely to find in the latter by the addition of elementary details and cleared up difficult points by drawing upon Priscian. It combined good scholarship and good pedagogy.

Classes were small, particularly in the monastic schools, but even so the most important single factor which affected every branch of medieval education was the shortage of books. Copying had been neglected during the seventh and eighth centuries; and although reforms were initiated at the time we are discussing, the scribes in the monastic scriptories, writing for the love of God, wrote in too leisurely a fashion to satisfy the needs of men.* Moreover, books even when available were not generally speaking easy to use. The confusion of scripts which had existed before the introduction of the Caroline minuscule and the unavoidable inequalities of calligraphic skill rendered the physical task of reading decidedly onerous. To read was to spell out a text which offered few aids to the eye and none to the memory. So, because the average monastic library possessed only one or two copies of even the more popular works, and because the uninstructed would in any case have found the productions of the average scribe tricky to decipher, the common practice was for the master only to have the text which was being read; and he then used it as a score to refresh his memory.

That is the background against which Alcuin's teaching method must be judged, and where its excellence becomes manifest. The dialogues were read to the class. They learnt the question and answer by heart, and they could then practise saying them, one group asking, another answering, until all were perfectly and almost painlessly fixed in their memories.*

Grammar of this kind taught boys to fit words together; but the words themselves also needed attention. The active vocabulary required by the average cleric comprised hundreds of terms; the passive, thousands. Before Carolingian times very little had been done to organise this mass of material. The British and Irish schools in the sixth century had possessed numerous word lists and if Zimmer's theory is correct* had produced an aid to study in the *Hisperica Famina*, but its language was too exaggerated to be of use later. The Anglo-Saxons on the other hand had done next to nothing. Their only contribution had been a rather crude glossary by Bede.* It was left to Alcuin to make the first important pedagogic advance in this rather neglected field. His method was to approach the central problem of word-learning from several sides at once. He rewrote Bede's little book; he introduced a great deal of conversational material into his grammar so that a boy who had its dialogues by heart was already well on the way to acquiring a competent vocabulary, and finally found time to produce a small work also in dialogue form which provided its readers with a stock of useful synonyms.

Q. What is the head?
A. The peak of the body.
Q. What is the body?
A. The home of the soul.
Q. What is the hair?
A. The head's garment.
Q. What is the beard?
A. The indication of sex, the honour of age.

The questions which are asked by the pupil, Pippin, treat of man and nature, and then finish with definitions of hope, friendship and faith. In the second half, Alcuin asks a few riddles in his turn. They are all simple; 'who is the person you can see only with your eyes shut' being one of the subtlest; and apart from the subsidiary purpose of sharpening the pupil's wits, a favourite activity with all Anglo-Saxon teachers, the aim is just to provide material for word-drills.* As a pioneer effort the work is not without merit, and by its means the difficult passage from the crude glossary to the planned reading book was safely and finally made.

There were the bases on which the medieval study of Latin was to rest; and it is profitable to reflect what effect such an amount of learning by heart must have had upon the minds of those who spent years with their grammar and their phrase book. Every grammatical form, each word with its specialised construction must have lived in their memories very clearly, but at the same time in a curious linguistic vacuum. They must have known the whole language as the present-day student of Kennedy's Grammar knows the masculines in -io.

These linguistic studies, together with a careful reading of the Scriptures, undoubtedly formed the essential kernel of the new education. Alongside them were certain other subjects of less importance. Although Alcuin did not devote a special treatise to versification we can be reasonably sure that it was taught and from an early age. Bede had written of it in some detail, and the technical triumphs of the Carolingian poets, remarkable both for their quality and quantity, would have been scarcely possible had they needed to rely on such uncertain skill as can be derived from self-instruction. Besides we have the striking instance of Walafrid Strabo who is known to have written in a variety of meters before the age of fifteen.*

A more distinctive field was explored in the study of elementary mathematics; and Alcuin's *Propositiones ad acuendos juvenes** give us some idea of how the subject was treated. This little book contains fifty-three questions, some of which definitely require geometrical or algebraic solutions, while others, though they call for a certain crude skill in calculation, are rather exercises in ingenuity. We are told, for example, that three men come to a river with their sisters. It is to be assumed that no girl is safe alone with any male except her brother. There is only one boat, capable of holding two at a time; and the student is asked to show how the party can cross without endangering any girl's virtue. Such simple exercises were introductory to systematic lessons on the *Computus*. The understanding of calendarial calculations was an accomplishment of considerable value at a time when disputes on the fixing of Easter divided the Christian body; and Bede, as we have already seen, had dealt at some length with the problems involved. The existence of a small treatise, *de Computo* by Alcuin's pupil Hraban, provides further evidence of the monks' preoccupation with this study; and the fact that in one manuscript the text is furnished with an interlinear German translation indicates that it was an object of interest to the ignorant as well as to the learned, that it belonged to the primary and not to the secondary level of training.*

The writing of simple verse and prose, practice in simple arithmetic and such insight as the calculations of the *computus* might afford into the mysteries of the stars, extended language learning and interpretative grammar into something which had the marks of a competent, if elementary, education. The curriculum, if such we may call it, was admittedly unequal. The intelligent reading of the Bible, the knowledge of Latin, were accomplishments whose value was well understood and whose mastery was pursued in an elaborate and systematic fashion, by means carefully worked out to achieve the ends desired. Within these limits Carolingian pedagogy was thorough and efficient; but when we get outside them how different the scene becomes, what a falling-off there is in skill and interest alike. We are reminded once again, and with a force which leaves no loophole for doubt, that the world of books was not yet co-extensive with the whole of civilisation, that use of reading and writing was largely confined to a particular class. The monks, it is true, were numerous, forming a substantial portion of every Western community; and their concerns were varied. But when every allowance is made for the part they played in agriculture commerce and administration, the ineluctable fact remains that theirs was an unrepresentative life which had its centre in their specialised religious role. The practical interests of ordinary men found only a feeble echo in their meditative universe and were therefore imperfectly represented in the education they had created and whose fortunes they controlled. We have seen that the teaching of arithmetic and geometry were exceedingly haphazard; and these mathematical disciplines were held in relatively high esteem. The other varieties of worldly knowledge, history, geography, biology, if not totally forgotten, were allowed only a casual mention as far as elementary education was concerned and that generally in connection with the all-important topic of language. From the *Disputatio Pippini* it is possible to gather some crumbs of information concerning man and the physical world, but how dry and how rare these crumbs are compared to the feast we are offered of Latin vocabulary and grammar. A similar picture meets us in some school notes preserved in a manuscript which Manitius ascribes to the years 813–15. They consist of dictated pieces which a pupil was anxious to preserve, just as Hraban preserved his record of Alcuin's lectures at Tours. The subjects treated include the Scriptures, the Liturgy and Canon Law, the *Computus*, Arithmetic and Grammar. There are formulae for letter-writing and prescriptions for medicines; and finally there are some items which may be classed as general: the names of the men who discovered the alphabet, observations on the length of human life, a discussion on the age of Abraham, the names of certain ancient doctors, the number of the Roman provinces, the number of the known languages and the known varieties of snakes.*

The importance of this manuscript is obvious. We catch a glimpse of the normal business of a Carolingian school; and what we see tallies to a nicety with what we can deduce from the text-books. Biblical commentary, grammar, arithmetic and the *computus* were the subjects which received most attention from educational writers, and whose exposition was best attuned to the needs of a still more or less ignorant audience. All our evidence suggests that they should be regarded as the constituents of what we may fairly call the average education of the time, that training which was given in the majority of schools to the majority of the pupils.

The most striking characteristic of the text-books we have discussed so far has been their simplicity, the skill with which they were constructed to meet the needs of a beginner. Now we must pass to certain other works of a manifestly different kind. Alcuin wrote a couple of dialogues on rhetoric and dialectic. But in these the questioner is not a boy. Charlemagne himself assumes the role which in the *de Grammatica* was allotted to a fourteen-year old; and we are left with the clear impression that these are studies for grown men. The classroom walls have fallen away. We are eavesdropping on one of those learned discussions initiated by Charles's omnivorous curiosity. Alcuin, moreover, is content here to summarise the obvious classical sources* and his work does not have the skilful simplifications or show those clear traces of teaching experience which impress us in his more elementary text-books. A similar aura of higher learning hangs over the commentary on Horace's *Ars Poetica*, which has been attributed to Alcuin or his school.

To construct a good and lucid poem, prefer an artificial sequence and spurn the natural. Sequence is either artificial or natural: natural when the narration follows the actual order of events, artificial when the narrator begins not with the beginning but with the middle of his story, as for example when Virgil defers in the *Aeneid* the relation of the events that occurred first and relates instead later happenings. For if he had followed a natural sequence he ought to have spoken first of the fall of Troy and then of Aeneas' coming to the island of Antandros and to other places he visited previous to his arrival at Carthage. Instead he altered this order and described first Aeneas' coming to Carthage, which came naturally second, and kept the destruction of Troy for a more suitable occasion, namely for the moment when Aeneas holds the pleased attention of the guests and then begins: 'All fell silent....'*

Such analyses—and the extract is typical of the work as a whole— are plainly not for the tyro, struggling with difficulties of vocabulary and apparent ambiguities of syntax. They are intended for the advanced student who is interested in the rules of rhetoric; and as we examine them a further point emerges which has its bearing on the more general problem of the Carolingian attitude to the ancient authors. We find simple text-books on grammar, on music, on versification, on arithmetic, on the *Computus*. We find commentaries which explain the difficulties of the Scriptures. But neither Alcuin, nor any of his immediate contemporaries seem to have undertaken the task of similarly commenting the pagan authors from the interpretative point of view, or indeed to have troubled much about the provision of reading matter for their schools. One is inclined to conclude that Alcuin thought that his own dialogues would adequately serve the needs of beginners and that the Scriptures would then be the main pabulum of those who had learnt enough to understand a Latin text. The commentary on Horace quoted above seems to lend some support to this view; for the commentator appears to have had no great linguistic or historical interest in his author. All he is concerned to do is to extract from the *Ars Poetica* a number of rules which he then elucidates and expands. The original meaning of the poem is simplified and distorted and sometimes altogether lost in the process; and the reader who studies the text and commentary simultaneously is likely to find his impression of the first somewhat blurred by the second, his mind permeated by Carolingian rather than Augustan ways of thought.

Hraban Maur, the educator of the generation after Alcuin, was to restate in somewhat more forcible terms the doctrines of St Augustine concerning pagan literature. The useful elements in the secular poets are so much grist to the Christian mill; what is not obviously useful, we wipe from our minds, and that applies above all to any mention of the heathen gods, love or the care of worldly things.*

The Horace commentary affords an admirable example of how these precepts were carried out and the attention of scholars restricted to what was patently useful.

We have looked at Alcuin's teaching in its detail. The evidence of its workings which has survived the obliterating forces of time, is fragmentary. But as we gaze upon the scattered fragments certain traits emerge of what must have been their general pattern. It becomes clear that we ought not to link Alcuin too closely with Petrarch and Erasmus, or see in him the founder of a premature Renaissance. The problems he set out to solve were such as allowed little scope for a cult of antiquity, and his mood was in any case Christian. He was asked to work out the means whereby the Frankish kingdom could be assured of a Latin-speaking priesthood, capable of performing its necessary tasks. So he produced his apparatus of simplified text-books and demonstrated their use in model schools. This part of his achievement, though of vast importance for the future acquisition of classical knowledge (for it made the Latin language a certain possession), did not involve him much in classical studies. He aimed at a level of attainment which fell below the point where the ecclesiastical and the pagan heritage separated. He was also asked to make some contribution to the higher advancement of knowledge. And in that field he followed strictly a somewhat narrow interpretation of Augustine's precepts. He concentrated on the impersonalities of technique: the definitions of logic, the rules and precepts of rhetoric, the facts of mathematics and astronomy. He was prepared to plunder the Egyptians. But how carefully he chose his booty! In the end he rejected more than he took. Though conscious of the value of the great pagan writers, as we can see from his account of the York Library and prepared to countenance the intellectual fashions of the court, he remained distrustful. *Timuit Danaos et dona ferentes*.

IV. THE EDUCATIONAL CROSS-CURRENTS OF THE NINTH-CENTURY

The intellectual life of the Carolingian Age had a dual character. The main stream that watered its fields had its source in Alcuin and brought the calm waters of an ecclesiastically conceived Latin culture. The other stream, thinner but more spectacular, welled from the court and possibly from the teaching of Peter of Pisa. It was specifically classical, and to it we must attribute that flowering of imitative verse and unstinting appreciation of antiquity which we notice first in Charles's court and then a generation later among those who had been in personal touch with members of Charles's circle, in a Lupus of Ferrières, a Walafrid or a Hincmar.

Education does not stop today at the level set by the final degree examinations; and it did not stop in the ninth century at the level attained by the majority of pupils in the average school. That is, it did not come to a dead end. But its character changed. There were several reasons for this, the major one being a sharp fall in the number of students. The monastic schools were at no stage the crowded institutions which the cathedral schools afterwards became; moreover not every pupil in a monastery, who struggled through his grammar, had the ability to advance further, and most of those who did advance chose to concentrate their attention upon theology. Thus, in most schools the groups studying advanced grammar, rhetoric or literature must have been small; and the arrangements for their work must have been informal. Since custom did not demand that those who continued their training should do so without a break, they were likely too to be of different ages. They laboured at their own speed and quite often in their own spare time, having also some other job or study in hand.

Under these circumstances, they must have had advice and help rather than set lessons from their teachers. So we have two educational systems which blend sometimes, but are for the most part distinct: on the one hand the average classroom with its routine, its elementary text-books, and its limited aims; on the other, the individual student guided only by his own taste or the chance enthusiasm of a superior, with no bounds set either to his opportunities or his methods. But we must also remember that on occasion such individual students could look for help to the exceptional school where that rare person, the brilliant teacher who was interested in secular subjects, had managed to gather round him a sufficient number of advanced pupils to form a proper class. It was at this higher level of unorganised study that the second and distinctively secular stream of learning found room to flow. Individual scholars of merit, many of whom were linked by personal ties, kept alive an interest in the pagan writers whom the majority of their contemporaries considered of very minor value. Thus, Servatus Lupus, the book-collector, whom we can fairly describe as the most active humanist of the ninth century, was the correspondent of Einhard and of Hincmar, the master of Heiric of Auxerre, while Rémi in his turn was Heiric's pupil.

The work of Alcuin and the Palace School is all important for the ninth and tenth centuries. The monasteries increased and flourished. At Fulda, at Corbie, at Reichenau, at St Gallen and at dozens of smaller centres, their schools toiled to spread the knowledge of Latin along the lines that Alcuin had indicated. There were no significant changes in method. The Latin-English Glossary compiled by Aelfric of Eynsham round about the end of the tenth century, and the German translations of his contemporary Notker Labeo, suggest that the vernacular was slowly coming to play a greater part in the first stages of Latin teaching. At the same time the subject matter of Aelfric's *Colloquium* which consists of dialogues after the manner of Alcuin but goes far beyond its model in the scope and variety of the vocabulary it offers, and such glimpses as we have of school activities elsewhere, indicate that the average level of attainment was growing ever higher. We hear for example of an episcopal visit to Notker's school at St Gallen where the boys address the visiting bishop in spontaneously composed verse; and a book of model letters dating from about the same period attests the growth of a greater concern with prose style, a preoccupation which is mirrored in the increasing correctness and expressive power of the common run of Latin prose.

But these changes in the degree of educational attainment did not amount to a major change in quality. The essential characteristics of Carolingian culture persisted until the end of the tenth century. The teaching of Latin led up to the study of the Bible which naturally remained the monks' main concern; and the principal achievement of the age was not in its linguistic or secular studies, but in its detailed and painstaking systematisation of what the Fathers had said about the Bible, a systematisation which in its turn was to lead to further difficulties.

The study of the classical heritage for its own sake continued as a subsidiary to this main stream of religious culture. The survival of the classicism which had developed in Charlemagne's court has already been mentioned. It is unlikely, however, that a love of antiquity could have flourished with such vigour in a monastic atmosphere, however much it was supported by the inspirations of personal genius, if it had not from time to time drawn new life from an outside source.

Ninth-century Italy lacked the extensive libraries which the French and German monasteries were rapidly accumulating. She had no schools to compare with Tours, Fulda or Reichenau. Her monks and priests were ignorant by northern standards and there are indications that they found the theology of a Paschasius or a Hincmar somewhat difficult to understand. On the other hand, the Italians still stood closer to the classical past than other nations. Their language had exceptional affinities with Latin, a fact of which one is reminded by the very errors which the Lombard chroniclers make in their grammar and syntax. For it is the forms of a spoken idiom that they introduce into their writing. Moreover, many Roman customs and institutions still survived in the Italian towns; and the prevalence of urban communities, the fact that Italian life had its cultural centre in the city rather than the monastery, made for a more secular outlook which was by that very token less distrustful of the pagan past.

Thus, amid the appearances of general decline, we hear of small groups of educated men like the one in Rome which gathered round the scholar-diplomatist Anastasius and the wealthy John the Deacon. Anastasius certainly possessed an adequate knowledge of Greek and an unusual familiarity with Byzantine sources. His work on church history, the *Chronographia Tripartita* draws heavily on historians like Theophanes and Georgius Syncellus: and his corrections to John the Scot's translation of Dionysius were of undoubted value. John the Deacon had not the same wide learning, but his life of Gregory I and his version of the *Cena Cypriani* show him to have had a lucid and witty mind with some pretensions to literary taste. We find also in the Italian manuscripts of the time a number of poems of such varied types as the *Nobilibus quondam fueras*, the *O Roma nobilis* and the *O admirabile Veneris idolum* which are plainly not works of scholarship, but which nevertheless show traces of classical knowledge. Like the Italian prose of the age they bear the marks of traditional knowledge, unorganised by education and carelessly used. Moreover, it does not seem likely that if ninth-century Italy had sunk into a genuine barbarism, the tenth century could have produced such poems as the *Gesta Berengarii* with its manifold classical allusions, or such writers as Eugenius Vulgaris, Gunzo and Luitprand, the latter the wittiest and the most learned man of his age.

The truth would seem to be that Italy was not so much inferior to the north as different from it in her cultural organisation. England and France possessed an intellectual élite, trained in centres which had been set up to ensure not only the spread of learning, but also the regular multiplication of books. They possessed populations whose way of life, thought and expression had hardly felt as yet the impact of the Roman heritage. The Celtic and Germanic races were still at the threshold of the civilisation which was to be theirs; and as we saw earlier, the completeness of their ignorance and illiteracy had been the reason which made the training of a monastic élite unavoidable. Now when we turn to Italy we find a picture which is different in almost every detail. During the ninth century, the peninsula was poorly supplied with books. Except for a few centres like Novalesa, the monasteries had only small libraries and they were not the homes of organised learning. There was no learned élite, only individual scholars, because the mass of the population had never sunk to that level of ignorance which might have made it necessary for someone in authority to take the educational question seriously in hand. The town-dwellers had retained much of their old Roman pattern of life; Roman institutions, Roman laws and even Latin speech had survived, not indeed in their original form, since much had been lost and much had changed in the course of the years, but in sufficient abundance to make the classical heritage much more accessible in Italy than in France or in England. A citizen of Milan or Padua did not require an elaborate training in order to read the ancient classics. He did not need to spend years over his grammar or laboriously mastering a vocabulary which bore no relation to his daily speech. Once he was literate, once he had familiarised himself with certain differences in usage, the stored-up knowledge of the past lay within his grasp. Even Greek could be learnt with comparative ease by those who like Anastasius had the good fortune to make personal contact with its speakers.

Thus, throughout the Carolingian Age, when travellers crossed the Alps or letters were exchanged with Italian scholars, it was not two countries, but two civilisations that made contact. When the monks from Hraban's monastery came south in search of relics, when the anonymous clerk of Einsiedeln surveyed Pavia and Ravenna, when Gunzo visited St Gallen and Hroswitha corresponded with Luitprand, the northerners, confident in the superiority of their systematic learning, caught glimpses of a world that was less active, less efficient but some-how richer than their own, where the rivers of knowledge that they had trained to speed between restricted banks had spread over a whole country-side in vast and stagnant shallows that yet here and there concealed waters of surprising depth.

Since the Italians were largely unaware of their intellectual advan-tages, their influence would by itself have achieved little. What lent force to the impact of Italian culture upon the monastic communities of the north was the presence in those communities of the Irish emigrants. The Celts of the West, like the Italians, were for the most part free of that Augustinian mistrustfulness which characterised the mainstream of monastic culture. Paganism for an Irishman meant the magical and prophetic practices of the druid bards; the Roman world and all its works, the *de Officiis* nearly as much as the *de Civitate Dei*, figured among the supports of the Christian faith. So the Irish, more indeed than the Saxons and a great deal more than the French, were prepared to make the whole of ancient knowledge welcome. Their curiosity ranged without restriction and was all the bolder because in general it skimmed only the surface.

To describe the learning of Adamnan, Dungal and John the Scot as shallow appears at first sight a gross misstatement. Yet it hides at least a half-truth. These men had delved into problems far in advance of their contemporaries. Their familiarity with abstruse subjects was undoubted and unusual. But behind their displays of academic competence one feels a certain naivety. Everyone who has taught at a university is familiar with the type of brilliant undergraduate who has the latest periodical articles at his finger tips but does not know the major authorities on his subject because he has not had time to do more than skim through them. The work of the Irish scholars has something of the same uneven quality.

The Biblical, grammatical and chronological studies which flourished in Ireland were, if we leave aside the Bible and certain patristic writings, based on Isidore, Macrobius and a few fragmentary texts of ancient grammars and glossaries; and they showed in their often ingenious elaborations the original sparseness of their sources. From the middle of the eighth century onwards as a result of Irish travel in foreign countries the sources available even to those scholars who preferred to stay at home increased in number and improved in quality, while those who were prepared to work abroad had of course ready access to all the growing libraries of Europe. Consequently the standard of Irish scholarship went up by leaps and bounds. But so strong are the bonds of habit that its essential character did not alter. For as the Irish monks widened their mastery of the ancient heritage, so they set their aims correspondingly higher. The known was valued by them only as a stepping stone from which to press further forward into the unknown. In theology, in philosophy, in the sciences of the Quadrivium and even in the modest art of grammar, they hankered by common consent after the unattainable, after a perfect explanation of the Bible, an all-embracing cosmology, a skill which could solve every mathematical puzzle, a baroque rhetoric and a knowledge of Hebrew and Greek.

Their study of this last-named subject typifies both the strength and the weakness of their approach. Greek, as one of the Biblical languages, had always enjoyed a vast reputation among the Irish and had been traditionally considered as one of the components of an ideal education.* The ideal, alas, was manifestly unattainable. But that did not prevent the Irish from doing their best with the insufficient material they had to hand. From their few bilingual texts of the Scriptures, from glossaries, from casual references in Isidore, they collected a strangely assorted vocabulary. The morphological and syntactical framework into which these words had originally fitted was largely unknown to them. A fragment of Dositheus which covered a little more than a part of the conjugations, and Macrobius on the verb were the only Greek grammars available anywhere in Ireland. So, for the most part, they accepted each word in the form in which they had originally found it, mixing together nominatives, accusatives and datives, indicatives and participles, and where they had no authority they often invented. The compiler of that *liber de numeris* which used to be attributed to Isidore, but is now regarded as almost certainly of Irish origin, showed an unusual caution when he wrote: 'The Father, the Son and the Holy Ghost—these three Persons are called by the Hebrews Abba, Ben, Ruha; by the Greeks

Pater, Bar,—but I have not yet discovered how one says Holy Ghost in Greek.'* Many of his contemporaries were less discriminating.

When the focal centre of Irish culture shifted in the Carolingian era to the emigrant groups on the continent, the leading scholars came into occasional contact with Greek-speaking monks and they made use of the opportunity to fill in the gaps in their knowledge. Thus the ninth-century grammar which was produced in the Irish school at Laon deals with all the parts of speech except numerals. But a slight improvement like this was not sufficient to alter the essential character of their Greek studies. The lack of texts and the lack of a sufficiency of teachers were too great obstacles to overcome; and though many of the Irish and their immediate pupils managed to learn a surprising amount of Greek, their attainments remained lexicographical rather than linguistic. Since they were undoubtedly the founders of the early Western tradition in this branch of learning, it is not unreasonable to ascribe to their influence that esoterism which led men to look on Greek rather as a branch of magic than as a language, so that the very letters of the alphabet were individually endowed with mystical meanings.*

The traditional culture of the Italians and the traditional zeal of the Irish worked like a ferment on the somewhat sluggish and restricted intellectual life of the north. Where they combined, as they did spectacularly in the case of John the Scot, they produced remarkable effects. It is true that John's knowledge of Greek, for example, had its limitations. His translation of the Areopagite needed a good deal of correction. Like the majority of his countrymen he did his best to run before he bothered to walk, and his work lacks that sureness of touch in matters of detail which the extent of his undertakings would lead us to expect. Nevertheless, he stands a giant of the pioneering spirit. He explored problems which for three hundred years after him no one was competent to touch, and suggested solutions which even to-day deserve attentive discussion.

John, however, was an exception. Elsewhere the two fructifying traditions did not make so close a contact, or did so in cases where the additional ingredient of genius was lacking; and if we view Carolingian culture in its entirety, we can hardly avoid the conclusion that the influence of the older Celtic and Italian worlds was limited in the main to ornamenting and varying rather than to substantially changing the dominant monastic pattern.

This is a period in whose study the common difficulties of the literary historian are seriously aggravated. The Carolingian writings which have been preserved, and even more the Carolingian writings which are commonly held to deserve attention, are naturally those which possess philosophical or literary merit. But the pursuit of philosophy and literary excellence was (with some exceptions) confined to the representatives of what we have described as the secondary traditions which emanated from Ireland, from Italy or from the brief florescence of the Palace School. Modoin, Angilbert, Servatus Lupus, Dungal and Anastasius are the figures whose eminence catches our eye. The *Historia Langobardum*, the *Vita Karoli*, the *de Divisione Naturae* and the earlier Cambridge Songs are the works we most readily value. Yet these are unrepresentative; and to catch the spirit of the majority we should do better to confine our attention to Alcuin, to Hraban, to Ermenrich, to Notker Balbulus.

The hypothesis that the Carolingian Age provides us with an early example of a Humanist revival of the type which occurred in the fifteenth century cannot be accepted. It is based on a misreading of the evidence. At the same time, however—and this is the fact which makes the interpretation of the period peculiarly difficult—we must avoid the contrary error of denying all importance to the Humanist current. If the Humanist aims did not represent the main interests of Carolingian culture, they nevertheless tended to promote a much more whole-hearted approach to the study of pagan writings than was implied by Hraban's analogy with the treatment meted out to the captive woman in Deuteronomy xxi; and it is to their influence that we must trace that modest increase in classical learning which then followed.

Alcuin as we saw had made less detailed provision for reading than for the other aspects of language study. His various text-books were planned to serve the needs of beginners; and he seems to have envisaged the Scriptures for the general use of more advanced students. If more was needed, there were the Christian writers. Having cherished their works in the York library, he would no doubt have concurred in Hraban's recommending Juvencus, Sedulius, Arator, Alcimus, Paulinus and Fortunatus as poetic models.* It was not that Alcuin discouraged his pupils from wandering outside the Bible and the Fathers, though he did on one recorded occasion express his disapproval of Virgil. It was rather that this branch of pedagogy did not seem to him particularly important and so did not receive his special attention. Consequently, it was here that his successors had most to add.

Some of the additions have already been mentioned. The *Disticha Catonis* whose popularity had grown steadily from the seventh century onwards found its way into the schools, and as the commentary of Rémi of Auxerre shows, came to be common reading for beginners. A somewhat similar fate befell the Fables of Avian* and perhaps, though not until the tenth century, the Eclogue of Theodulus.

Since these texts were read by every schoolboy, the effect of their introduction was to indoctrinate the medieval world with the principles of ancient morality. The dose was admittedly limited and contained nothing obviously unchristian; but its universality gave it a certain importance. If nothing else, then the idea that pagans could be wise and worthy of respect was widely inculcated. More important, however, was the increase in the number of authors read at a more advanced level. A surprising number of classical quotations have been traced in several of the monastic writers. Ermenrich in his letter to Grimald cites or otherwise refers to Lucretius, Virgil, Horace, Ovid and Ausonius. The author of the *Ecloga Theoduli*, who may have been Godescalc, borrows freely from Virgil, Ovid and Capella, as well as from numerous Christian poets. Heiric of Auxerre is familiar with Horace and even a lesser figure like Radbert of Corbie can cite Terence and Seneca. How are we to interpret the significance of these quotations? That they indicate a kindlier attitude to the classics than Alcuin's or Hraban's goes without saying. That they indicate a genuine knowledge of the authors cited is less certain. Their very nature precludes them from being sufficiently exhaustive to prove that any particular book had indeed been read; and the researches of Ullman and others suggest that many at any rate were drawn from anthologies rather than directly from the original sources.*

Several such anthologies are known to have been in circulation from the eighth century onwards. Since the age was ill-supplied with books, their utility requires no proof, and their popularity no explanation. They varied in type. Rémi of Auxerre, whom we find teaching at Rheims round about 893, produced a volume of selections from a single author, the historian Valerius Maximus. In the previous generation, his master Heiric had been responsible for a somewhat similar work drawn from Suetonius as well as from Valerius.* But most of the other anthologists preferred to tap a wider field; and the *Exempla diversorum auctorum* of Mico of St Riquier or the *Collectaneum* of Sedulius Scottus are more truly representative of their work. Mico's collection derives added interest from the fact that it does not stand alone but belongs to a family of related anthologies. Early in the third decade of the ninth century an old Lombard *Florilegium*, containing excerpts from pagan and Christian poets, came into the possession of the monks at Reichenau, who found it sufficiently useful to copy it several times over. One copy went to Laon where it was further multiplied. A second was sent to Mico, who revised it for classroom use, since he wished to specialise in the teaching of prosody, and made a number of additions. How much he added must remain a matter of doubt; for no copyist either of his or of the original manuscript ever felt bound to meticulous exactitude, but omitted and included passages at will. All the versions, however, include passages from pagan and Christian, ancient and medieval writers alike. Ovid, Statius and Virgil, Persius, Martial and Juvenal stand side by side with Prudentius and Fortunatus, Theodulf and Smaragdus of St Mihiel.

The *Collectaneum*, as befits the product of the Irish school, confines itself to prose and betrays a philosophical rather than a literary approach. The extracts from classical authors occupy about a quarter of the collection, rather less than is allotted to contemporary theological texts. Sedulius had evidently fallen under the spell of Cicero; for there are passages of a good length from the speeches, from the *Tusculanae Disputationes* and from the *de Inventione*. Philosophy is represented by Macrobius on the *Somnium Scipionis*, history by the *Scriptores Historiae Augustae*, and technical interests by Frontinus and Vegetius. In addition to these sizeable excerpts, there is also a considerable collection of proverbs and moral sayings, some of which are translated from the Greek. They serve as a further proof of the Carolingian taste for the gnomic. But since they do little but extol the virtues of wisdom as against ignorance, a truism which most of their readers must have taken for granted, one cannot see them as an important influence on human development.

But whatever the merits of individual anthologies, there can be no doubt about the importance of the role they played in disseminating classical knowledge. Nor in view of their existence is it possible to escape the conclusion that what we find in the Carolingian writers must often be the appearance rather than the reality of knowledge, that many of them were after all *homines unius libri*, the book in question having been a patchwork.

The greater the educational importance one attributes to these anthologies (and the present state of our knowledge leaves a very free field for speculation), the more one is inclined to stress the limitations of Carolingian learning. But that is a line of argument which can prove misleading if carried too far, since there is also good evidence that in some places authors were studied in full. Heiric of Auxerre lectured on Persius, Juvenal, Horace and Prudentius, and his commentary on Juvenal was written up and circulated by Rémi, who also performed that service for his other teacher Dunchad's commentary on Capella. Notker, on the other hand, at St Gallen appears to have neglected the pagan writers whom he condemns even more strongly than had Alcuin or Hraban, but to have placed considerable emphasis on the reading of the Fathers and the Christian poets.*

Thus, the picture we form of Carolingian education must inevitably allow room for variety. Some students like Notker's young Salomo at St Gallen left school with little knowledge outside of their grammar; others read anthologies; others again drank deeply of some Christian or even of some pagan author. The one common feature which emerges from this diversity is that between the time of Alcuin and that of Rémi, between the end of the eighth and the beginning of the tenth century, the general standard of educational attainment perceptibly increased, and the study of the classical heritage benefited from this advance. Alcuin having saved classical learning by his exertions, failed to smother its further growth by his example. The lingering survivals of the Roman world in Italy, the curiosity of the Irish, the patronage of enlightened monarchs like Charles the Bald combined to sustain the faltering course of ancient studies. The steady if slow labours of the copyists multiplied the available texts. The researches of individual scholars simplified their interpretation; and the greater knowledge of Latin among the clergy brought them within reach of an ever increasing number of readers. The man who could understand the Bible could also understand Virgil.

With the close of the Carolingian Age, the curtain sinks on the first act of the new Europe's assimilation to its past. We began with a state of ignorance which almost endangered the survival of the Latin-speaking Church. We saw this ignorance combated by the development of an education which necessarily utilised some of the traditional instruments of Roman pedagogy. That education spread from the Celtic to the Anglo-Saxon lands and then to France and Germany, increasing in efficiency at each remove. Its purpose was not the absorption of pagan knowledge, but more strictly the teaching of Latin so that monks could read the Bible and the Fathers, and so that a few men in each generation might be fitted to conduct the administrative business of the Church. But while the educated pursued these general aims, they also learnt to make better use of the classical heritage; and they made their own the greater part of what the ancients had discovered concerning the nature of language. Then with the ninth century the situation altered. It is true that the needs which had been responsible for the rise of monastic education still continued to operate. But they were needs which contemporary learning, having been adequately organised, now found easy to fulfil; and socially there was stagnation. There were no great changes of the sort which might have given rise to fresh educational demands. As a result, for a brief period, a situation existed in which human learning developed in response to its own interests independently of outside pressures.

It is a common belief among scholars that a disinterested curiosity has been the main force behind every advancement of learning. This theory, though it contains a measure of truth, is not altogether innocent of wishful thinking. That human curiosity has always existed and has always exercised its own dynamic admits of no doubt; but history suggests that the force of that dynamic cannot really be compared with the violent impulsions of the political and economic needs which are the main determinants of our destiny. Only at times when the action of those needs was temporarily suspended, when there was a certain favourable disproportion between the capabilities of an educational system and the calls which society made upon it, only that is to say, under quite exceptional circumstances, had curiosity more than a subsidiary role in deciding the direction, though it always contributed substantially to the vigour, of intellectual effort. But in the latter half of the Carolingian Age these exceptional circumstances did obtain, and the Walafrids, the Heirics, the Notkers were not seduced from following their particular bent by any feeling that there were more important problems to be solved. Nor were even the classicists among them seriously hampered by disapproval or active interference, since the nature of their work was as yet too elementary to represent a threat to the social or religious order.

It is true, however, that this halcyon state was not to be of long duration. By the middle of the tenth century the apparent standstill was at an end. The economic and social changes which the slow developments of the ninth century had imperceptibly prepared, were ready to burst upon Europe bringing their harvest of new intellectual and educational requirements. The study of the classical heritage which Walafrid could regard as a harmless pastime, was to impress Anselm of Bisate two hundred years later as a pursuit likely to bring an answer to all his intellectual problems; and Notker's gentle observation that pagan writings were useless was to give place to the diatribes of Peter Damian.

For good or for ill the primary stage in the assimilation of classical culture, which had as its objects the elements common to both the pagan and the Christian traditions, was decisively over. What Europe now needed from the past in the shape of law, philosophy and science was more definitely secular and derived from those sectors of Roman civilisation that patristic Christianity had failed to make properly its own. Bede, Alcuin and Hraban had merely repeated the work of Isidore, as the similarity between the *Etymologiae* and the *de Universo* only too clearly shows. But now the time had come to carry the spoiling of the Egyptians one step—indeed several steps—further, in realms where the practice of the Fathers could offer no guidance. The self-styled pygmies of the Middle Ages were faced with the task of wresting from paganism a contribution to the City of God that the greatest of their authorities had been afraid to contemplate.

CHAPTER IV

THE PRE-SCHOLASTIC AGE

The period from the middle of the tenth to the beginning of the thirteenth century not only witnessed a great number of changes affecting nearly every important field of human experience; but the changes were most subtly connected one to another. Independent in their origins, they became interdependent in their effects; and their interdependence was not of the simple sort which is adequately represented by the familiar analogy of threads uniting to form a pattern. For the threads did not merely cross and recross. It would be more exact to describe them as continually untwisting into their constituent fibres which then reappear in fresh combinations. And they did not just exist side by side; they altered one another's substantial character by their proximity. Moreover—and this perhaps is the circumstance which makes the period most difficult to clarify—the renaissance following from these new departures failed to come to that brilliant fruition which an observer of its first beginnings would have naturally expected. Every change that occurred generated such a vigorous opposition that the innovators had to come to terms everywhere with those who wished to preserve the *status quo*. So there was not a single clear-cut line of growth. There were only a series of false starts. Tendencies which were later to become dominant in the fifteenth and sixteenth centuries showed themselves for the first time. But they met with hostility and were aborted. Nothing developed freely. Every thesis was countered by an immediate and more powerful antithesis.

The new age owed its progressive character to a variety of circumstances. Life was generally more settled. The impetus of the great migrations had worn itself out. The vacuum left by the decline of Roman power, in itself sufficient to attract any number of invaders, had at last been satisfactorily filled. Such marauders as came at this late hour had to fight their way through warlike communities intent on defending their own; for there was again a balance of military force between the West and the East, the South and the forest-covered North. Though the Magyars came on their horses, and the Vikings came in their ships, the civilised area of Europe was probably less disturbed by the activities of tribes from outside its periphery than it had been at any period during the preceding seven hundred years.

At the same time there was a greater measure of internal peace. During this early stage in the development of Europe, more government was tantamount to better government; and the reforms initiated by Charlemagne had done much to promote social stability. Thanks to his far-sighted encouragement of education and thanks also to the example he had set in using educated men as clerks and organisers, there was a notable increase from his time onwards in the administrative effectiveness of central and local authority. By the middle of the tenth century it is possible to find all over Western Europe the beginnings at least of that administrative machinery which is so necessary for the running of civilised life, and which, once established, can absorb a surprising number of shocks and can outlast most natural disasters, civil disturbances and external wars.

One is not surprised therefore, in view of these general improvements, to find Europe in the eleventh century entering upon a period of economic revival. Life having become more settled, the labour which generations of patient cultivators had devoted to clearing and working the land could at last begin to show some results. It was now possible to make a profit out of farming as the system of leasing out lands to individual entrepreneurs adequately shows; and the monasteries at least were often in a position to derive appreciable benefits from their many manors. Thanks to their accumulations of produce, they became in some places centres for local barter, while elsewhere their trading activities contributed to the rising prosperity of some conveniently placed town. For as the countryside grew more wealthy, so urban life also began to flourish. The towns in which a century or two earlier a mere handful of inhabitants had scraped a precarious living inadequately sheltered by half-ruined walls, were now rebuilding their fortifications, could offer security and demand rights for their citizens. They became centres of manufacture and trade; and as time went on more and more organised markets were set up under a charter from the King or from some magnate. These markets and the great fairs connected with them became the focal points of an economic activity that grew every year wider and more intense. The Italian cities had been hard hit in the seventh century by the Arab conquest of the Mediterranean which had cut them off from their traditional customers and suppliers. But now the tide of Islam was at last in retreat. The hundred years that followed Orseolo's fight against the Adriatic pirates saw the Venetian fleet consolidate its control over the sea-lanes, and ships were once again bringing to the peninsula the spices of the Orient and the iron of Spain. The great stream of trade ran from the Baltic to the Mediterranean and by the twelfth century its tributaries were to irrigate the whole of the civilised area of Europe.

Such economic changes had social and political consequences of considerable moment for our enquiry. A new world was coming into existence prepared to make a fuller use of the classical heritage. The epoch was over when the Carolingian grammarians had represented the vanguard of progress; and in their place were men who had other and more impressive interests.

The most significant development from our point of view was the emergence of specialist groups in the legal, medical and philosophical fields. These subjects had been brilliantly studied during the Carolingian period and even earlier; but knowledge of them had been confined to a few remarkable individuals. With the tenth century, however, the number of these individuals had increased, and by the eleventh, they were sufficiently numerous and sufficiently organised to constitute professional groups recognisably similar to their modern counterparts.

The reasons for this sudden development must be sought in the general conditions of the age, and vary slightly for the different specialities.

When it was no longer easy to seize a neighbour's land by force (a possibility always present during the Dark Ages), the rapacious were bound to seek other means. The pen may not be mightier than the sword, but it has often proved an adequate substitute; and those who in the ninth century would have collected an armed band to raid a near-by farmer's crops, in the eleventh harried their victim with ingenious litigation, seeking to dispossess him all the more zealously since a further effect of peace had been to make land more productive and more valuable. Under these circumstances an expert knowledge of the law was necessarily in considerable demand, and the emergence of a class of professional lawyers almost inevitable.

Somewhat similar patterns of cause and effect can be worked out for the other specialist groups. An increase in the number of doctors is a natural concomitant of greater prosperity. When a man has money to spend to relieve himself of pain, spend it he will. Thus, as the ranks of the wealthy grew, there was more employment for doctors, the public demand created more and more lucrative openings which clever men were not backward in filling.

Philosophy benefited in a slightly different way. We must remember that when these developments occurred, philosophy meant in effect the study of logic; and logic was of practical utility in two important fields. It had a general value for the ever-growing body of clerks and officials engaged in administration who could hope to derive a sensible advantage from learning to think clearly; and it had a more definite relevance to the problems which beset the theologians. But while the administrators required at most a superficial knowledge of how to reason, the priests and monks, entangled in the dangerous thickets of conflicting authorities, could not be satisfied with any understanding of the laws of thought which was not most exact and detailed. It is therefore in the popularity of theology that we must seek the major cause of the popularity which logic came to enjoy.

Now in the history of theology we may discern the working of the same influences that were responsible for the revival of medicine and law. The pattern of causes and effects is admittedly not quite the same. It is, however, recognisably similar. Here the function of prosperity was to permit rather than to encourage. The theologians never formed a distinct professional class. But every priest and every monk was potentially a student of the subject. The quiescence of the alarms and disasters which had marked the Dark Ages meant the liberation of this interest. No longer shadowed by the fear of rapine, no longer compelled to devote the best of their energies to ensuring their own survival, the monks in particular were enabled to spend more time on education and more energy on the examination of their faith. The Carolingian period had seen the beginnings of serious theology. But as we shall show later, the method which its theologians followed in their investigations had landed them in a troublesome predicament. They could not reconcile their authorities; and it was their need for a critical technique which led them to logic.

Law, medicine and theology were the three foci of medieval thought; and the medieval exploitation of the classical heritage was determined first and foremost by their needs. The Carolingians had domesticated Latin grammar and had established a place in the school programme for the *Rhetorica ad Herennium* and the *de Inventione*. Now their successors moved on to take cognizance of the *Digest*, the medical corpus and the philosophy of Aristotle. In the mastery of these detailed and difficult works and in the consequent remoulding of the appropriate specialities lay the greatest achievement of these medieval scholars, without which further progress would not have been possible. The Humanists of the

Renaissance were to like describing themselves as pigmies perched on the shoulders of giants; and so indeed they were. Only, from the point of view of cultural history, the precursors whose massive strength supported their showy eminence were not the ancients they so respected, but Irnerius and Bartolo, Constantine the African and Michael Scot, Abélard and St Thomas Aquinas.

The development of the specialities must form therefore the kernel of our chapter. But no more than the kernel. For there were other influences as well which have claims on our notice. The patient accumulation of specialised knowledge was bedevilled and complicated throughout this period by an interest in the classics which derived from a different origin and had a very different end in view. To the stream of solid learning, itself fraught with some danger for the lowlands of a Christian civilisation, there were added the waters of a restless and ever-swelling tributary; and to the men of the time their combined force appeared an imminent menace.

This second current of classical learning did not draw its strength from any specific branch of knowledge. It was fed by interests that ranged over the whole of ancient life and by a variety of aesthetic, literary, ideological and social enthusiasms. It resembled strongly the Humanism of the Renaissance; and we shall not go far wrong if we regard it as a foretaste of that great movement.

Trade was the nerve centre of that economic revival which was transforming Carolingian Europe. But the merchants and craftsmen of the towns who had effective control of this new commercial activity were not in a position either to pursue their aims without hindrance, or to reap the rewards to which they might fairly have aspired. That they had no proper place in the feudal pyramid, the bulk of their wealth not being in land, did not perhaps matter so much. But this legal inconvenience was coupled with other disabilities of a more serious nature. Ecclesiastical law condemned money-lending for profit as usury, and the provision of the credit needed for business had to be left to the Jews who derived obvious benefit from this monopoly, but on the other hand suffered bitterly from their ostracism and from the exactions which periodically stripped them of their wealth. Charters essential for the holding of a regular market were difficult to obtain. The raw materials required for the production of many of the goods most in demand were controlled by the owners of land; and the tasks of collection and transport could be hindered in a thousand ways where the local lords happened to be greedy or turbulent. In the inevitable struggle between country and town, the scales were heavily weighted against the latter.

Such a situation could have only one outcome. Its natural result was that urban communities did their best to escape from feudal tutelage by achieving political independence; and their success in Italy contributed greatly to that country's rapid economic development. When the Milanese rid themselves of their suzerain at the beginning of the eleventh century, they won the first victory for their side in a contest which was to rage at length and with varying fortunes over the whole of Europe, and which furnishes a clear indication that the natural outcome of capitalist prosperity is capitalist rule. Since capitalism during the Middle Ages was still at a primitive stage in its development, compromise could make it possible for the capitalist and feudal elements to co-exist in certain localities to their mutual advantage. Local truces lasted often for quite long periods, but in the last analysis, as the rise of the city states amply demonstrates, the merchants and those who shared their interests, the poorer nobles who tried to augment their resources through trade, the more prosperous villeins who thanks to the practice of commutation were enabled to build up small estates, formed a disruptive element in medieval society.

Alongside the practical disabilities which hampered this class were others of a more ideological character. The values accepted by the majority of men were such that the successful capitalist was automatically deprived of that reward which to many temperaments appears as the most important—namely public esteem. The intellectual epiphenomenon of a world centred on the monastery and the castle, the dominant medieval outlook reserved its admiration for two ways of life and was forced by its presuppositions to exclude all others as inferior. The time had its hero in the contemplative saint rapt from mundane distractions in the solitude of his cell, though this ideal had perhaps an even more powerful appeal when the saintly figure was pictured, like Bernard of Clairvaux, possessed of vast authority, immersed in manifold cares and yet amid the calls and pomps of the world detached and alone with his vision of reality. The force of this conception, its validity as a guide to behaviour, requires no proof. When one remembers how many thinkers and writers during the past hundred years have seen an alternative to the nerve-racking conventions of mass-production culture in the ascetic life, one is not disposed to deny its possible fascination for an earlier and traditionally more religious society. But power even in the Middle Ages was not wholly spiritual, and its most outstanding earthly possessors also received their share of public regard. Aristocratic distinction was honoured. Now in the popular respect accorded to a great noble some part was no doubt played by the actual virtues of the individual or the class, by eminence in war, by superior manners, by the useful habit of command. But generally speaking these qualities were little more than a makeweight. In essence men's homage was paid for another reason. The meaning of the aristocratic ideal depends upon the acceptance of a magic quality in the mere circumstance of birth. Where that ideal is accepted, a person who is born from noble ancestors is thereby exempt without further question from that intimate suspicion of inferiority which clouds the days of his fellows, and the certainty of his confidence draws their admiration like a magnet.

Prevented by their interests from pursuing sanctity and relegated by their humble birth to a permanently inferior station, the merchants, the lawyers, the clerks involved in the minor tasks of administration, the skilled craftsmen who acquired some tincture of education, and above all the socially ostracised Jews, had no hope of winning the whole-hearted esteem of their contemporaries. The particular ends to which they devoted their energies were dismissed as of little worth by the culture they lived in. For some time this had mattered little. The merchants of the Dark Ages had been hucksters who made an uncertain living turning their hand to whatever chance of money-making came their way. Neither they nor their immediate successors were men to expect a great deal from life. But by the eleventh century that situation had changed. In Italy at least commercial activity was on a vastly greater scale; and its material rewards were proportionately larger, so that the want of social recognition was more deeply felt. Nor was this the whole trouble. To be personally admired is not all the successful require. The admiration they naturally seek is one which should extend to their habits and circumstances, which should cover not only their own position, but also all the normal accompaniments and pro-ducts of their way of life. These conditions were satisfied for the feudal lords. The esteem accorded to them did not fall short in any particular. The business of arms in which they spent their days filled their castles with devoted henchmen and with the impressive paraphernalia that surrounds a commanding officer. Their inheritance of lands, their judicial functions, their exacting, if theoretically paternal, sway over a multitude of serfs elicited from those who came in contact with them a reverence which aptly reinforced the claims of their social position.

But how was a merchant to arrange his life in a society which offered him only this aristocratic model for an admired and successful existence? He could not acquire the requisite status and estates; nor was the role of a military leader likely to sit easily on shoulders that had grown bent in the counting house. Feudal tradition offered him no guidance.

The efforts of the burgher class to build up a dignified and pleasant pattern of life attuned to their specific interests and to win popular esteem for that pattern would merit a systematic examination of greater length than can be given here. Stirred by a vague need, rather than consciously aware of a problem to be solved, they tried to imitate the nobility, buying land, building impressive houses, keeping special retainers. But no collection of manors, purchased where opportunity offered, was likely to match in extent or dignity a fief held from the king. No town house, however elaborate, could hope to equal the eminence of a baronial hall. And what prudent merchant, accustomed to watch his money, could endure the cost of such a retinue as wasted the produce of the great feudal estates. The wealth of the merchants, even where equal in quantity, was different in kind from the resources which the nobles had at their command. Commerce brought to those who followed it individual objects of value: rare spices and scents, clothes, furnishing, jewellery. It could bring works of art. The products of luxury and craftsmanship, available in profusion and selected with taste, were the proper materials of capitalist display. But their use took some time to learn.

We have now reached the point where it is possible to indicate the significance of these developments for the classical heritage. The urban populations of the Middle Ages, struggling for independence, searching for a stable form of self-government, could hardly have failed to turn their eyes to the city-states of the past. Rome with its consuls, its senate of notables, its rarely consulted popular assemblies, had an obvious fascination for the nascent oligarchies of Italy. Nor did their interest stop at political matters. In Republican Rome, the leading citizens had been the recipients of the greatest respect, the highest honours which society had to offer, and they had attained this distinction through the practice of civic virtues. Sainthood had not been required of them, nor had they been expected to perform personal feats of arms, so as to keep violent retainers in order by a superior violence. They had been men aware of wealth and its importance, men who had devoted much of their attention to the wise use and the prudent making of money, men in whom the progressive Italian merchants could see their own prototypes. The writings of Cicero with their idealisation of the Roman Republic began to exercise an influence which would have occasioned their author the keenest pleasure. The public spirit, the profound good sense, the urbanity, which Cicero attributes to those he chooses to praise, but above all the picture he paints by almost imperceptible touches—that famous Roman picture— of a life dignified by practical activity and rendered delightful by beauty and learning, opened men's eyes to the possibilities of a culture based on the city-state. Very gradually and hesitantly—for after all Rome had been pagan—there developed first in Italy and then elsewhere a cult of the past radically different from any that had gone before. With immense reservations, and without daring as yet to confess the fact, men were coming to admire antiquity for its own sake.

Two features of this cult deserve particular mention because they had a wider appeal than the rest. We have been speaking so far about the burgher class, and much of what has been said applies with any force only to its Italian representatives. But on two points their admiration for antiquity was shared by other groups and so acquired a greater cultural significance.

The political institutions of the Republic, the privileged status of her leading citizens, their characteristic virtues, the resolution of a Cato, the courtesy of a Laelius, the atmosphere of a society in which debate was at least theoretically mightier than the sword, all had their manifest attractions for men buoyed up by hopes of independence and power. But more potent even than these, in its power to charm minds trained in the hard discipline of the counting house, was the rational temper of the Roman spirit. A merchant has to take facts into account. Heaven knows what disasters would follow if he did not make his plans arguing from past experience that certain causes would have certain effects. The Romans had applied these procedures to the whole field of human life, to politics, to law, to learning and to philosophy as well as to business. Moreover, they had developed the techniques of their rational thinking to a degree far beyond anything that their medieval successors had yet achieved. It is not surprising therefore that Roman rationalism should have ranked as a quality which the Middle Ages were eager to imitate. Nor was this eagerness confined to the Italians or even to the commercial class in general. Other groups, principally the administrators and professional men, were also involved. The former had to organise people and resources to achieve specific ends. The latter had to order and elucidate their respective branches of knowledge. These were aims which required rational thought. The earnest officials and specialists who pursued them may well have been (as far as their conscious intentions went) the faithful servants of the predominant feudal and authoritarian order. But their day-to-day activities had nevertheless the effect of enlarging imperceptibly through a thousand devices and decisions the areas of rationality within that order which was fundamentally irrational if only because its institutions no longer suited the conditions of the time. They were unconsciously engaged on the same task as their merchant contemporaries in the towns; and for them too Rome was an inevitable model. The forces which were moulding the future moved along the usual multiplicity of tortuous paths each of which, winding and obscure, was to reach its destination by taking those who followed it back to the Roman past; and over this question of rationality past and future alike were equally fraught with danger for the unstable present.

A somewhat similar situation arose concerning another aspect of the Roman tradition which was arousing widespread interest. The Carolingian Age had remained largely unaffected by that preoccupation with the sensual world which plays so prominent a part in ancient literature. The Carolingian scholars had been mostly monks whom their ideals and training had protected against the blandishments of pleasure; and we have only to call to mind the conditions under which they and their contemporaries lived, to realise with the utmost vividness why the sentimental and aesthetic refinements of the Roman poets could not have had much meaning for them. Outside the courts of a few great princes, works of art were rare, comfort almost unknown, and the pleasures of the senses existed untutored as a gross gluttony or lust. The age of Alcuin had been well fitted for asceticism. But with the passage of time this situation had radically changed. Wealth had brought greater opportunities for luxury, for aesthetic and social enjoyment; and the spread of education had carried the classics within the reach of the secular clergy and of a great many who were clerics only in name. For these and most particularly for such of them as spent their lives in the elegant courts of the period under the patronage of some great lady, the epicureanism of Horace, the ecstasies and regrets of the elegiac poets acquired a new significance. The Latin poets became in their hands the text-books of an indulgence which the ascetics justly regarded with loathing.

The simple enumeration of the different strands which conjoined made up the medieval interest in antiquity runs the risk of appearing to place too much weight on the political, rationalist, aesthetic and moral elements. The secondary nature of these must once again be emphasised. The real achievements of learning during this period were to be found in the specialities. It was in Salerno, in Bologna, in Paris that the scholars of the time made their great contribution to the understanding of the classical heritage. The general cult of antiquity which calls to mind the Humanism of the Renaissance, and which was in fact historically a beginning of that Humanism, had not as yet the vigour it was to acquire a few centuries later. It did not inspire feats of scholarship, nor did it forward to any impressive extent the assimilation of Graeco-Roman culture. Its importance was of another order. Being the product of disruptive tendencies, its main effect was to render the whole field of classical studies suspect in the eyes of those who wished to preserve the *status quo*. Its existence made evident what might otherwise have remained unrealised, that the Augustinian scheme of spoiling the Egyptians rested on a profound misunderstanding of the essential conditions of cultural growth, and that any large-scale borrowing from classical sources was bound to hasten the fall of that precarious, but to some very desirable, edifice of spiritual and temporal authority which a lucky improvisation had been able to rear on the ruins of the *Pax Romana*.

It will be proper therefore to devote the bulk of this chapter to the new departures in law, logic and medicine, leaving the other aspects of the period to be discussed briefly in a final section. This procedure, which is the opposite of the one generally adopted, may do something to help us to place the different elements, which contributed to the assimilation of classical culture, in their correct order of importance.

I. THE REVIVAL OF ROMAN LAW

The tenth century marked a most fascinating stage in the history of Europe. For the first time since the collapse of the Western Empire, the forces of civil order were sufficiently strong to place a more or less effective check on the more obvious forms of anarchy. It was no longer entirely safe to murder, to rob, to intimidate one's weaker neighbours by a show of local force. But the spirit of anarchy was far from dead. Men were not yet content to serve the public good peacefully in the hope of an eventual reward. Nor would such an attitude have been justified, for authority, while strong enough to restrain violence, was not strong enough to impose any regular pattern of punishment for wrongdoing or recompense for virtue. The ambitious still sought to grab what advantages they could, where they could, irrespective of all considerations of equity or prudence. They still preferred to fight every point to the uncompromising last. The generality of men were still restless, precipitate and intractable. Only now that the use of the sword was restricted, these qualities had to find an outlet in other directions; and the contentiousness of the time expressed itself in countless claims and counter-claims, in ruthless quarrels about rights within a framework of legality.

The career of Ratherius was as typical of the spirit of tenth-century Italy as the career of Petrarch was to be typical of the spirit of the early Renaissance. A German monk with a reputation for learning, he was appointed to his Italian bishopric at a moment when he lay apparently dying of a grave illness. His last days were to be cheered by the possession of an empty honour. But the medicine which had been intended as a palliative worked an unexpected cure. The patient recovered, and to the dismay of all concerned, assumed the responsibilities of his office. From that point on, his existence was a long battle. His superiors cold-shouldered him; his clergy refused him obedience. He was exiled and even imprisoned. But nothing could daunt his combativeness. He had vast stores of knowledge at his command. He possessed an inexhaustible natural energy. Letters and pamphlets investing his case with a halo of eulogy and heaping invective upon his enemies poured from his pen in a steady stream. His flock were rebellious. Very well. Canon law, he averred, was explicit on the point. A bishop had definite rights which could not be violated. He unearthed ordinance upon ordinance and then, convinced of the virtues of attack, took the offensive in his turn. The clerics who had challenged his authority openly kept concubines, a practice sanctioned by Italian custom, but one which was surely immoral. Ratherius ransacked the Fathers for relevant passages. He found that they were unanimous in their condemnation of lust; and he drew up his indictment with an untiring moral zeal. St Augustine, St Jerome, St Gregory, authority followed authority. There could be no doubt on the matter. The clergy of Verona stood convicted of a particularly loathsome sin. He had called them to order; and they had not obeyed. Their persistence in wickedness undoubtedly deserved the direct punishment of Heaven. A mention of the fate meted out to Sodom would not, he thought, come amiss.

Admittedly, there were important issues at stake; but what holds our attention is the intemperance of the struggle. The contestants risked their reputations, their liberty, even at times their lives. They were the manifest descendants of the men who had been willing to hazard everything on the success of a chance foray. Only their weapons were different.

The revival of Roman Law was an indirect result of these conditions. Reading the diatribes of Ratherius and his opponents, one notices that when they wish to drive home their arguments, they make simultaneous use of two distinct techniques. On the one hand, they employ as far as they can the traditional resources of rhetoric. Mistakenly perhaps, but conscientiously, they do their best to clinch their case by an artistic manipulation of words and themes. On the other hand, they invoke the heavy support of authority. They cite from the Fathers or the Canonists to indicate precisely what the law is, and why it gives them support.

The combination is significant. These men who fought such bitter battles over Church authority and Church discipline were all scholars who had been trained to look to the classical heritage for technical aid; and in this instance they did not look in vain. The Greeks and Romans had possessed in the art of rhetoric a most powerful weapon for intellectual warfare; and their writings were filled with its description and its praises. The controversialists of the tenth century, exasperated by their own inexperience, could hardly have failed to take advantage of the lessons which thus lay ready to their hand.

It is not surprising that there was a sudden renewal of interest in rhetorical studies; the reverse indeed would have been remarkable. With the tenth century the third subject of the Trivium, comparatively neglected by the Carolingians, came into its own. The enthusiasm for it was greatest in the Italian schools. But the north did not lag far behind. Gerbert for example, when he was teaching round 980 at Rheims, went so far as to compose a selection of model speeches for his pupils to imitate. The dry rules which had served his predecessors no longer appeared to him adequate.

But these high hopes were followed by disappointment. Rhetoric, as the Romans had taught it, was not at all suited to the specific needs of medieval controversy. Cicero had framed his precepts with the conditions of the forum and the Roman law courts in view. There, an orator had his audience in front of him; and his main concern was to produce an impression at the time of speaking. He could make full use of the fact that men were suggestible—and forgetful. A Ratherius or a Gerbert had a less easy task. They had readers, not hearers, to persuade. Much of what they wrote was addressed primarily to men in official positions whose judgement could not be hurried and was always given with an eye to precept and authority. In these circumstances many of the devices employed in spoken oratory were plainly out of place. No pompous apostrophe, no pretence of emotion, no specious argument, its imperfection veiled by some paradox, was likely to have much effect.

Some time had to pass before this hard lesson was properly learnt. But already in the tenth century Ratherius thought it necessary, as we saw, to support his rhetorical arguments with a heavy apparatus of citations and references drawn from accepted authorities; and as the various issues were fought out in ever greater detail, so this evidential element grew progressively more important.

The Fathers could supply sufficient ammunition for arguments about theology; but disputes on practical matters, even such everyday problems as the eventual disposition of a dowry or the fine to be incurred for breaking a contract could only be settled with reference to the law of the land. So in the secular field controversy took on an increasingly legal tinge, and by the beginning of the eleventh century, the Italian teachers of rhetoric were accustomed to include in their courses a considerable amount of easy legal information. They realised that their contemporaries paid more attention to the matter of an argument than to its form, and adopted this course in a natural wish to serve the interests of their pupils.

Thus, Anselm of Bisate, a typical member of the north Italian ruling caste, who was educated about 1030, tells us that both his own master, Sichelm, and Drogo who had taught Sichelm, had been lawyers as well as rhetoricians. Such a conjunction of attainments was evidently the rule rather than the exception in learned circles. For did not Lanfranc, who was a product of the same tradition, similarly possess an equal mastery over both these disciplines? Anselm indeed is prepared to state dogmatically as a matter of principle that law and rhetoric belong together, being two sides of the same science.*

This development was of the greatest importance. The knowledge of law had previously been handed on through private instruction or apprenticeship and had acquired a rule of thumb character. But now the interest taken in legal problems by the teachers of the liberal arts meant that the subject was studied from an academic viewpoint, by men whose attention was naturally focused on the classical past, and who knew how to interpret ancient texts.

143

European law at the end of the Carolingian epoch was of mixed origin. It contained Roman and Teutonic elements in proportions that varied from place to place. After the decline of the Western Empire and after the first barbarian settlements, there had been for a time considerable confusion; and most of the conquered provinces had possessed two legal systems. The former Roman citizens lived within the framework of their old laws. The conquering Teutons obeyed a primitive tribal code. But little by little the two had blended. Where the general destruction had been great, and the tribesmen numerous, the Teutonic element remained in the ascendant. Where on the other hand the old Roman municipal system had managed to survive, as was the case in Italy and to some extent in southern France, the opposite occurred, and the law also stayed largely Roman.*

But even in these favoured regions the general situation left much to be desired. The Roman laws which had survived in the West through the Dark Ages had done so at the cost of considerable distortion. Moreover, they derived originally from a stage in the development of legal theory anterior to the great recension of Justinian and were for that reason less in accord with the needs of a Christian society. They did not harmonise well with the inevitable later accretions from Teutonic or Christian sources, and the legal system as a whole was marred by vast lacunae. As litigation grew more common, cases were constantly cropping up which the practical lawyers could not settle, for the law they knew gave them insufficient guidance.

Now, as it happened, the grammarians and rhetoricians who had taken up the study of the law were pre-eminently fitted to find the answer to these difficulties. Their professional tendency to find the answer to all problems in the classical heritage led them to investigate the *Institutes*, the *Code*, the *Digest* and the *Novels*, manuscripts of which had fortunately survived. And these monumental works must have appeared to the pioneers who embarked on their study as a limitless storehouse of legal wisdom.

The history of this development is wrapped in obscurity. Only a few scholars are known to us by name; and not one has left a record of his achievements. In this absence of clear evidence, the revival of Roman law has come to be associated with the achievements of a single individual who came rather late on the scene; and we reserve our esteem for Irnerius whose work, though important, was in all probability just the crown of an edifice built by many patient labourers.

Born during the second half of the eleventh century, he was a teacher of the liberal arts who ended up by specialising in law. By his day, it must have become obvious that rhetoric could not make any valid contribution to the settlement of disputes. Legal knowledge was the real essential, and he seems to have realised this and acted upon his discovery.

The tradition which Irnerius represents was responsible for the first essential step in the process by which Justinian law became a part of the European heritage, and we must therefore examine his methods in some detail. Ten treatises of varying importance used to be ascribed to him by nineteenth-century scholars. But these are now known to have been the work of his successors; and it seems that our evidence about his teaching must be drawn from his numerous glosses, many of which are still unpublished, and from two short introductions to the Code and to the Institutes which again may have been compiled by a later copyist out of the typical fragmentary notes of the author.*

These Irnerian glosses are extraordinarily concise, and the assumption is almost certainly right that they were not meant to be read directly by students, but were lecture notes originally composed for Irnerius' own use and perhaps tidied up later so as to make them handy for other lecturers. The living voice was required to give them extension and substance. Having this general characteristic of conciseness in common, they fall in other respects under two heads, for some of them are of a type common in literary commentaries while the rest represent a new departure.

If Irnerius had not been a teacher of the liberal arts, a rhetorician, and like all the rhetoricians of his time, also a grammarian, he could never have carried his task to a successful conclusion. It is interesting therefore to compare his work with let us say the famous Servian commentary to Virgil. There are many features in common. We find in both the type of note whose purpose is to explain the meaning of a difficult word, usually by providing a synonym. We find the brief remarks that clarify an obscure construction, the historical or antiquarian notices that describe in a few words some custom or institution of which the reader is perhaps ignorant. We find also that Servius and Irnerius both employ the same formula to begin a course of lectures on a text,* mentioning in turn the name of the author, the subject-matter of the work, its intention, what part of philosophy it belongs to and its final cause. A barren little programme! But it is instructive to remember, as Kantorowitz points out, that the habit of using this type of preamble was to lead later commentators to devote more attention to examining the theoretical bases of law than they might otherwise have done.

Some of the other types of comment Irnerius favours cannot be traced to grammatical models. There are the *summulae* or notes in which he sums up the whole content of a law, the *continuationes* in which he explains the connection between groups of laws, the *distinctiones* in which he analyses the legally relevant variations of an abstract factual situation, and finally there are those references to other laws by which he supports or contradicts the one he is examining. These commentatorial techniques were either invented by himself or derived from some purely legal source.

The detailed investigation of this apparatus of comment, both literary and non-literary, which has been carried out by several competent legal historians, reveals that Irnerius had two distinct ends in view. He wanted to elucidate the literal meaning of each sentence in his text. He also wanted—and here he went beyond grammatical practice—to give a certain coherence to the subject-matter as a whole. There were matters of vital interest to which the Justinian law accorded a confused or cursory treatment. There were points which it did not settle except by implication, and other points concerning which its explicit or implied rulings were at variance. The *continuationes*, the *distinctiones*, the careful accumulations of parallel laws were intended to bring the light of comparison and clear statement into these dark corners. The techniques we have described as grammatical or literary are concerned for the most part with line by line elucidation. The others (again for the most part) have the larger aim of making the *Digest* coherent. But the dualism is more apparent than real; and to understand the true role of the Irnerian commentary we must bear in mind that these two aspects of it were in a very real sense complemental portions of a single whole. If Irnerius did more than just explain the material before him, if he made additions here and there, what he added was always derived from the existing data of his text. He looked on his role as that of an interpreter pure and simple, concerned to make known but in no way to modify Roman law.

This was also the attitude of the next generation as represented by the Four Doctors. By and large, their approach was the same as that of Irnerius. The innovations they made concerned only the field of technique. It became rapidly evident that the wider tasks of interpretation which Irnerius set himself could not be effectively carried out within the narrow limits imposed by the gloss which in his case were restricted even further by his own extremely laconic style. Thus, first the habit of excessive brevity, and then the practice of confining all comment to brief glosses, were in turn abandoned.

We possess from the pen of Bulgarus an introduction to the Code that treats the general problems involved with a philosophical penetration which the Irnerian preambles had not possessed.* The same eminent jurist also wrote numerous and extensive *summulae, continuationes* and *distinctiones*, which were sufficiently detailed to merit separation from the text so that they were later incorporated into independent collections or *summae*. But most important of all, he composed the earliest known independent treatise on a point which the classical sources had left obscure. His *Ordo Iudiciorum*, a much needed systematic account of legal procedure and principles in the ancient world, established once and for all the undoubted fact that the ancient law books could be usefully supplemented by contemporary writings. Composed some time before 1141, the example it offered was quickly followed, and the second half of the century saw the publication of a steadily increasing number of legal tracts.

Another form of legal literature which developed about this time and contributed indirectly to the better understanding of Roman law was the *quaestio disputata*. Here again, the credit for the invention must go, it seems, to Bulgarus. He encouraged his pupils to discuss imaginary cases, and after they had delivered speeches for the plaintiff and the defendant he would give his judgement. The points debated were reasonably subtle and often amusing. Seia, who has left home after being whipped by her jealous husband, agrees to return when he promises not to repeat the assault on the pain of a substantial fine. However, once back she is whipped again. Is she entitled to claim the money mentioned in the guarantee? Bulgarus thought not. She could not legally demand payment for the fulfilment of her contractual obligation to live with her husband. Such discussions were first introduced no doubt as a lecture-room exercise; but as their usefulness was realised the habit developed of having them recorded by a clerk, so that they could be summarised and circulated for the benefit of future generations of students.* Relating the dry precepts of the Roman jurists to the familiar tangles of everyday life, they helped to effect a closer conjunction between law and behaviour, and the incidental result of that process was to bring the present closer to the past.

It will be convenient to break off at this point our account of the development of law. For with the passing of the Four Doctors, the first stage in that development came to an end. So far the work of legal scholarship had been dominated by a desire to explain and to spread the knowledge and use of the Roman code. It had not to any marked degree been socially critical of that code. Since law and social institutions, law and morality, law and personal conduct are dynamically interdependent, since therefore the imposition of a legal system which had developed under the conditions of a specific society was bound within certain limits to lead to the recrudescence of that society, this purely interpretative and socially uncritical approach to Roman law represented in effect a tendency to revive the past, to assimilate the medieval world more closely to its classical predecessor.

It was not that Irnerius or any of his followers were uncompromising Humanists who cherished the thought of a new paganism. The shortcomings of contemporary law had set them a problem, and they had taken the first step towards its solution. That step had been academic in character. It had necessitated a theoretical exposition; and engrossed in the difficulties of that exposition, they had been not unnaturally blind to the social consequences of their theoretical system. In any case until that system was applied exhaustively in practice, its effects on social relationships and institutions were not evident. Thus, it was quite easy for the twelfth-century glossators to devote their energies to an enterprise likely to revolutionise society without being aware of what they were doing.

The closing years of the century, however, saw the end of this epoch of theory. As the principles enunciated by the Doctors came more and more to be applied in common legal practice, difficulties arose and social implications of the new teaching became increasingly clear. The time was therefore ripe for a change of attitude, for an approach which aimed less at the acquisition of further knowledge about the classical heritage than at the reconciliation of Europe's existing classical endowment with the intellectual and moral system of the day. Such a quest for reconciliation meant in terms of pure classical learning a certain retrogression, a damping down of enthusiasm for the past, the refusal to consider any fresh borrowings from its store, a tendency to attack those who clung to the paths of Humanism. It meant in short the Scholastic spirit.

Here for the first time in this legal connection we meet what is the common pattern of the eleventh and twelfth centuries: a problem, the solution of that problem by recourse to the classical heritage, the realisation that the knowledge which had been thus acquired is likely to endanger the existing intellectual framework and then the beginnings of retreat, the first signs of a coming epoch of cultural consolidation and conservatism which ends in a fear of progress.

II. THE STUDY OF ARISTOTELIAN LOGIC

The study of logic established an unquestioned dominance over philosophy during the lifetime of Abelard. Within the next hundred and fifty years, its empire was extended over nearly all the other branches of knowledge. By the thirteenth century it was affecting the writing of Latin, and by the fourteenth the writing of the vernaculars. The importance of its role as a formative element in late medieval culture cannot be denied; and even if one hesitates to admire a mode of intellectual activity that had constantly to balance the rigidities of the syllogism by the subtlety of endless distinctions, one is never tempted to be blind to its multifarious influence. The particular significance which this cult of logic has for our investigation derives from its connection with Aristotle. For the attempt to master logical techniques resulted in the widespread and efficient understanding of the most comprehensive of ancient philosophers, and made the basic categories of ancient thought an essential part of the European tradition. Logic rather than literary taste forged the strongest link that binds us to Greece and Rome.

By a strange coincidence, this massive irruption of pagan ideas had as its prime cause the specific needs of theology. It was from the citadel of Faith that the call for the natural light of human reason came the most insistently.

During the Dark Ages, men had been content with a very superficial understanding of the sacred text. But when education became more common there followed a vast increase in intellectual sincerity; and as the Carolingian Age drew on, the minds of the monks began to play freely with a variety of problems on which they sought for enlightenment. Since the religious life of the time was centred on the Bible, the questions most to the fore were those which concerned the interpretation of the Scriptural text, and scholars were led to concentrate their best energies on the tasks of commentary.

The different forms taken by these commentaries have only an incidental significance for the development which will claim our attention. It is worth noting perhaps that the text of the Bible was assumed to possess simultaneously a literal and one or more spiritual meanings;

and that the latter were of three kinds: allegorical, anagogical and tropological.* The reason for this variety of methods was the desire for edification. Those who take the sacredness of the Bible to imply that every page, every line must contain something to uplift the soul—and this view was unquestioned in the Middle Ages—have always found themselves face to face with a multitude of minor difficulties, particularly where the Old Testament is concerned. The modern reader with a highly developed historical sense, who is able moreover to benefit from an understanding of Jewish civilisation built up through centuries of research, can train himself to consider incidents that shock his moral susceptibilities within a perspective which robs them of offence or even at times renders them morally edifying. But the contemporaries of St Gregory I or Anselm of Laon were less satisfactorily equipped for this sort of exercise. Though historical explanations of the modern type were used to some extent, they were insufficiently developed to explain more than a minority of the difficult passages. Recourse to allegorical and other such interpretations furnished the only practicable way out of the dilemma.

Even so all was not well. For the Bible could not be regarded solely as an aid to holiness. It was also a fount of doctrine, its meaning had serious implications for Christian belief. The task of interpreting it could not therefore be left to the free play of the individual fancy; and in this field as elsewhere the medieval writers preferred to draw their material from the safe source of the great Fathers. For a time, for the larger part of the Dark Ages that is, the system had worked satisfactorily. Since books were scarce, a commentator could count himself lucky if he found a single authority to guide him on any particular passage. There were no conflicts, no difficulties. But when the monks at the end of the eighth century settled down to the busy multiplication of texts, when quite small monasteries came eventually to possess copies of nearly all the important Fathers, this primitive situation changed. Industrious scholars striving after an ever greater understanding of disputed passages set themselves to assemble texts from a variety of sources, from Gregory, from Jerome, from Augustine; and when they had done so, a new reason for perplexity became manifest. Learning, it appeared, solved some difficulties only to create others. For the Fathers were not always in agreement; and the more excerpts were collected, the more discordant opinions came to light. Already, Hraban Maur had shown himself aware of this danger and had recommended that each citation should be labelled with the name of its author. For then the brethren could choose for themselves and believe a great rather than an inferior authority.* But alas such care was beyond the power of the average scribe, and references tended to be lost in transcription. Moreover, it was sometimes the case that theologians of equal eminence held contrary views. Was St Jerome to be preferred to St Augustine or vice-versa?

This difficulty—like numerous other ninth-century problems—was at a critical juncture made more awkward by the genius of John the Scot. Thanks to the minor miracle of his knowing Greek when everyone else was ignorant of it, he was enabled to introduce into the already dangerous amalgam of conflicting texts the opinions of Eastern Fathers who on many points differed considerably from the Western. The divergencies he discovered were too great to be ignored. Supremely self-confident, he made no bones about acknowledging them and was even prepared to criticise and pass judgement. The Bible was divinely inspired, which made its authority unquestioned. The Fathers, he thought, did not deserve quite the same regard. A commentator might question their conclusions, might even at times with due respect put himself at a level with them. John admittedly was an exception in boldness as in brilliance. But even his more cautious contemporaries, Paschasius and Haimo of Auxerre, took the same line though with greater circumspection. Plainly, none other was open to them. Exegetical science had in the normal course of its development arrived at a point where no further advance was possible if the commentators were not prepared to criticise their authorities. But the age had no well-established canons of criticism; and even the most skilled theologians were guided largely by intuition. Some of John's judgements on his sources had been marvellously subtle; but no one, not even their author, could have described systematically the principles on which they had been made. They remained, as far as future students were concerned, just inspired guesses which another teacher's inspiration could validly contradict. The danger of exposing the authority of the Fathers to the play of such uncertain forces was manifest. In the absence of a generally accepted critical method, any attempt to weigh one patristic text against another was pointless—pointless and appallingly risky; for the conclusions reached could not be permanently established. But where was theology to find the method it so badly needed? The two more advanced subjects of the Trivium, Rhetoric and Dialectic, both dealt with argument and the ordering of ideas. But such knowledge as men had of them, such knowledge for example as was contained in

Alcuin's treatises or Hraban Maur's encyclopaedia, was plainly insufficient. Biblical scholarship lost heart. For a time the school of Auxerre carried on. But the work of Heiric and Rémi made no advance on what had been already achieved; and with the death of the latter, about 908, the line of Carolingian commentators came to a sudden end. For close on a century and a quarter after this date the voice of exegesis is silent; and when we hear it again, it has as its mouthpieces, Lanfranc of Pavia and Berengar of Tours.*

Simultaneously, philosophy, or to be more exact philosophical theology, suffered a parallel eclipse. Thanks largely to the pedagogic efforts of Alcuin and Hraban Maur, it had risen out of the slough into which the Dark Ages had carried it, and had given proofs of a considerable vigour in the Predestinarian controversy that brought disaster upon the unfortunate Godescalc. Unfortunately, the views expressed by both parties to the dispute had verged on heresy. Moreover, the ease with which the contestants demonstrated each other's fallacies, made it clear to their less intellectual brethren that Philosophy was a very poor guide to truth. No ninth century thinker, not even John the Scot, could forge a chain of premisses and deductions that was not immediately assailable; and wisely, after John's death, serious Christians were unwilling to trust the ship of their Faith on such dangerous waters. The creative energies of the tenth-century religious went into beautifying the liturgy and into meditative sermons whose purpose was to rouse the emotions rather than to encourage speculation. Here, as in Biblical exegesis, there had been a breakdown due first and foremost to an insufficient technical understanding of the laws of reasoned thought.

However, other developments were taking place in the meantime outside the strictly theological field, and some hint of these has already reached us. Controversies over simony, over the marriage of priests, over the law of the Church and State, were bringing men to consider the possibilities of ancient rhetoric and dialectic as techniques of persuasion. Since the purpose of the disputants was to achieve momentary triumphs rather than to discover ultimate truths, they had not at first been troubled by the logical imperfection of these techniques. But just as it was to become obvious in another context that legal disputes could not be resolved except on the basis of a comprehensive system of law, so in ecclesiastical controversy also the realisation came that where disputes involved ideas the final arbiter had to be logic. Only the process took the best part of a century. For a long time, rhetoric absorbed the attention of all enquiring minds.

At first, the enquirers were above all the controversialists. Concerned with issues which had not yet been thoroughly investigated, driven by an urgent need to mobilise support for their views, they had turned naturally to the art that claimed to teach the secrets of persuasion; and some time had to elapse before it became clear that the problems under discussion were too fundamental to be settled by verbal jugglery or appeals to emotion. Some time had to elapse, in other words, before the experts took over from the publicists, and serious thought came into its own.

Moreover, it is only fair to the learned of the Middle Ages to note that the change-over from rhetoric to logic might have occurred earlier but for a circumstance which was outside their control. Perplexed as they were by their intellectual difficulties, the theologians might have taken Aristotle for their guide much more readily, had it not been for a certain defect inherent in the Roman tradition on which they relied. The Romans themselves, it must be remembered, had always subordinated logical to rhetorical studies. Quintilian had strongly recommended the former, but only because he thought that practice in argument might benefit the future orator. Being practical men, the Romans could never make up their minds to their own satisfaction about the relative values of the persuasive and the cogent. For the purposes they had in mind, for the debates of the forum and the courts, the appearance of truth served just as well as truth itself. How then was the latter superior? They could not decide; and as far as the Roman tradition was concerned, the problem remained wrapped in a delusive fog. No wonder then that the thinkers of the tenth century found it difficult to solve. The miracle is that they should have solved it at all. They did so in the face of exceptional difficulties. The books from which these tenth- and eleventh-century scholars had to learn their logic were far from satisfactory. They possessed, it is true, the two introductory treatises of Aristotle's *Organon*, namely the *Categoriae* (in an anonymous translation as well as in an epitome falsely attributed to St Augustine) and the *de Interpretatione* (in two translations, by Boethius and Victorinus). They had, it is also true, the commentaries which Boethius had written on the *Categoriae* and the *de Interpretatione* (the double commentary on the latter in two and six books constituting a major logical work), Porphyry's introduction to the *Categoriae* (in two translations by Victorinus and Boethius), two commentaries on this by Boethius and the *de Definitionibus* of Victorinus. But these works, admirable in their detail, covered only a portion, though fortunately the more elementary portion, of the whole subject. They contained most of what Aristotle and his school had said about the possible types of meaning and the possible types of proposition, but very little else.

For all further information, the student had to turn to writings which were much inferior to the above. There was the *de Inventione* of Cicero and the *ad Herennium*, whose incidental comments on logic were vitiated by their overriding rhetorical intention. There were the three general surveys included in the encyclopaedic writings of Capella, Cassiodorus and Isidore, which erring on the side of brevity, were superficial, often obscure and sometimes plainly wrong. There were the abridgements in which Boethius had summarised the more advanced portions of the *Organon* and which were less informative and less known than his fuller commentaries; and finally there were the *Topica* of Cicero. From these incomplete sources, they had to draw their knowledge on such subjects as deduction and induction, the conditions of scientific demonstration and definition, the forms of argument from probable premisses and the commonplace fallacies. It is not surprising, therefore, that they hesitated so long before applying logical analysis to the vital problems of theology.

Nevertheless, by infinitely slow degrees the intellectual revolution on which so much depended was carried to a successful climax. Much work will have to be done on the history of tenth-century thought and in particular on the Italy of Ratherius and Luitprand before the details of what occurred can be made clear. The generation that saw the death of John the Scot still regarded dialectic with good reason as a dangerous helpmate for theology. A hundred and fifty years later the logical analyses of Berengar evoked, it is true, a notable storm, but the usefulness of his method was immediately acknowledged and imitated. Between the lifetimes of Charles the Bald and William the Conqueror there had been a great change. Ecclesiastical controversy had led to an interest in rhetoric, to more reasoned thinking on legal problems and to that partial systematisation of Canon Law which had its monument in Burchard's great collection. Gerbert had been responsible for a revival of mathematics, another science which required ordered thought. The knowledge of dialectic had developed under the aegis of several other branches of learning, and then suddenly it emerged into a brilliant pre-eminence.

The suddenness of that emergence was due to one of those accidents of personality that happily diversify the long, slow developments of history. It was perhaps to be expected that the techniques of rational thought which were gradually becoming known, would at some point win the allegiance of a powerful intellect which found in them the perfect instruments of its activity. But chance and chance alone decreed that the possessor of that intellect was at the same time a man of saintly renown and great personal charm, with a mind at once pliable and tenacious, capable of yielding to opposition, then, after each withdrawal, each capitulation, returning undeterred to its original course; a man moreover of considerable wealth which he knew how to use to the best advantage. Had Berengar of Tours not possessed this peculiar concatenation of gifts, had he been less saintly or an indigent careerist, or proud like Abélard, or endowed with a different temperament, his speedy ruin would have been certain, and his influence would not have survived a brief and tempestuous career. As it was, he lived to a ripe old age, and though condemned by no fewer than five councils, continued to teach to the end the views he was repeatedly forced to abjure. Execrated for his opinions by great numbers of excellent churchmen, he was protected from the worst effects of his contumacy by the devotion of those who knew him well, and could count even Pope Gregory VII among his friends.

Berengar seems to have been convinced that reason was man's best instrument for the discovery of truth, and upheld its claims as the final criterion of belief. He was the first important Christian thinker to do this and the first to work out the implications of such a belief with reference to a specific theological problem. The issue he chose to submit to the arbitrament of dialectic was the old controversy concerning the Real Presence. His studies of the *Organon* convinced him that accidents could not exist without their proper substance, and on the basis of that logical principle he denied the doctrine of transubstantiation. The use he made of dialectic did not, however, stop at that general statement of his position; and his pervasive influence rests rather on the detail of his work. He applied logical criteria to the interpretation of texts and to the deductions he drew from them. Thanks to an ingenious verbal analysis of his sources, he managed to show that patristic opinion supported his view and flayed his opponents for misreading their authorities and for the rashness with which they derived unjustified conclusions from insufficient premises. By the time he finished his attacks, the theological relevance of logical argument was amply demonstrated.

Berengar's striking example gave his contemporaries a better idea of the possibilities which could follow from the use of dialectic and made the question of that use an urgent theological issue. The nature of his

influence becomes patent when we consider the case of Lanfranc.
A famous teacher of civil law at Pavia, a famous teacher of the liberal
arts at Bec, with the reputation of being well-versed in all the latest
intellectual techniques and chosen for that reason by the Curia to con-
trovert Berengar, he did not as a result of this conflict turn his back
upon dialectic. Instead his interest in the new discipline was sharpened;
and his name was to go down to posterity as a dialectician. 'Wherever
the text lent itself to such a procedure', says Sigebert of Gembloux
about Lanfranc's commentary to the Pauline Epistles, 'he based his
expositions, assumptions and conclusions on the laws of dialectic.' *
It is true that Sigebert's words strike the modern student, who is
familiar with twelfth century exegetical techniques, as a rash overstatement. Lanfranc did not, as his successors were to do, reconcile
conflicting authorities by analysing the strict sense and implications of
their meaning. He used his knowledge of logic merely to support
orthodox interpretations which raised no awkward issues. But his
using it at all was under the circumstances significant. For once admitted
as a valid instrument of theological enquiry, logic was certain to be
eventually applied to those problems of authority for whose solution
it was indispensable. The first step was the one which counted; and
Lanfranc makes his support of it quite explicit when he states as a
general principle that prudently employed, dialectic does not threaten
but confirms the mysteries of faith. *

Methods similar to Lanfranc's can be traced in numerous contemporary writings. Many of the men engaged in solving the intellectual
problems of the day, commentators like Drogo, controversialists like
Bernold, tended to favour the new techniques, at least in moderation.
But, at the same time, the unorthodox character of Berengar's opinions
and the scandal of his repeated condemnations, as well as the fact that
dialectic was not yet clearly distinguished from the unreliable argumenta-
tion of rhetoric, made certain circles suspicious of its use. Presumably,
too, the general distrust of pagan values and pagan ideas which we
shall analyse in a later section, contributed something to this unwillingness to see what were after all the instruments of pagan learning
employed in theology. * The reproaches which Rotiland is supposed to
have made to Anselm of Bisate, in which attacks on Anselm's ratio-
cinatory enthusiasm were apparently coupled with accusations of loose
living, were probably typical. * At any rate, they are echoed by Abbot
Williram's grumbles about the shortcomings of those who put their
trust in grammar and dialectic. *

These two opposing tendencies, which the intervention of Berengar had reinforced about equally, were to continue in existence until the final triumph of dialectic after the middle of the twelfth century. The supporters of reason fought an uphill fight, having at the same time to improve their technique, and by defining its scope to remove the valid objections to its use. The correct definition—the one which finally prevailed—was given early on by St Anselm of Canterbury. But another half century had to elapse before it was generally accepted. Lanfranc's description of the relationship between reason and revealed truth had rested on a purely empirical basis. Anselm who was his pupil considered the problems involved from a philosophical standpoint and produced a philosophical definition. He held that the teachings of faith are ultimately rational, in the sense that a perfectly functioning reason could understand them. Human reason, however, is imperfect. There-fore, revealed truth is often beyond our mental grasp. Nevertheless, it can always be understood to some extent even by our limited minds, and our knowledge of it can to some extent be perfected by the proper use of our reason. Under these circumstances it is evident that the man whose reasoning is in harmony with revelation stands a good chance of being right, even in the early stages of his argument, while the man who tries to work independently of the revealed conclusion which he must reach may easily slip into error. According to Anselm, we are in the position of the schoolboy who has seen the answer to his sum printed at the back of the book. He must make his calculations conform to that answer. If he does not, he is certain to be wrong.

Philosophy, though conquering all things by rule and line, was not to clip the Angel's wings but was rather to soar with their help to otherwise inaccessible heights. But Anselm's formula—*credo ut intellegam*—did not achieve a quick popularity for all its power to quieten the fears of poets and mystics, as well as the doubts of his orthodox contemporaries; and while it was gaining a slow acceptance a fresh storm was brewing.

During Anselm's lifetime (*c.* 1033–1109), the canonists had made a quiet but appreciable contribution to the general technique of scientific criticism. Bernold of St Blaise had laid down five rules for the interpretation of conflicting canons, the main purpose of which was to make sure that the circumstances which prevailed when a law was made were taken into account; and Ivo of Chartres, another of Lanfranc's pupils, had used analysis and logic on a large scale to reconcile apparent discrepancies in the multitude of canons and Papal decrees that made up the law of the Church. By the second decade of the twelfth century, the value of the new techniques was evident, and the stage was set for that famous renaissance of dialectic which filled the schools of Paris and which we have learnt to associate with Roscellinus and William of Champeaux, but above all with the supremely intellectual, intransigent and romantic Abélard.

Where Anselm, while believing the universe rational, had doubted men's capacity to understand it without the help of revealed truth, Abélard was sensationally confident. Reason, he thought with enormous certitude, could reach its goal unaided. Leading strings would serve only to hamper its triumphant progress. It was not that he doubted the ultimate verity of the Christian faith. The pious sentences which every so often lend colour to the productions of his astonishing mind were almost certainly sincere. But from the eminence of his speculation he saw the road of dialectic running straight to the City of God. Why then should not all men follow it?

Set against the background of the time, this enthusiasm is easily understandable. Men believed that dialectic could provide a solution to the difficulties which were threatening to wreck theology and law, the two intellectual systems on which their world plainly depended. The disease had been long manifest. The danger of intellectual disintegration had long threatened; and now a cure had been discovered. Dialectic took precedence as a panacea; and we find associated with it that gratitude, that delight, that excessive trust which a panacea properly arouses. Moreover, in the particular case of Abélard we can trace the operation of yet another psychological factor. The temper of his mind was such that the enthusiasm we have described could possess him entirely and rise unhindered to its highest pitch. For he was not troubled, as Anselm had been, by the thought of the fallible human being behind the seemingly passionless argument. The author of the *Scito te Ipsum* was oddly blind to the tortuous influence which desire exerts over our intellectual processes. Attentive only to the precision of his logical instrument, he contemplated with pleasure the careful Aristotelian rules. Their validity was self-evident. If the universe was rational—and surely that could be taken for granted—how could they fail to unravel its innermost secrets step by irrefutable step? This limited, completely objective view of the activity involved in speculation made Abélard the perfect exponent of the new philosophy. He at least found no cause to hesitate or to have any reservations about its excellence.

His *Sic et Non* was a manifesto plainly designed to show the weaknesses of the patristic tradition and to vaunt the saving power of dialectic. He chose a series of problems ranging over the entire field of theology and canon law, and he illustrated each of them with quotations from the Fathers, selecting such opinions as on a superficial first reading, appeared contradictory. The method emphasised the confusion which existed at the very bases of authorised doctrine; and it lent significance to Abélard's claim that logic could smooth out these inconsistencies. If these texts were properly studied, if they were submitted to a rigorous analysis, they could, he asserted, be brought into some sort of harmony.

The criteria which should guide this analysis were stated in his prologue. Some of them were far from new, having been familiar currency among the learned for two or three centuries. Hincmar for instance—to take one of the late Carolingians—had been more or less clearly aware that students ought to avoid all apocryphal and incorrectly copied works, that they ought to interpret all quotations in the light of their original contexts, that they ought to differentiate between true general laws and such as constituted particular exceptions, and that in cases of doubt they ought to be guided by the natural hierarchy of authorities. These were traditional devices, and one suspects that Abélard mentioned them merely in order to tone down the revolutionary character of his remaining proposals. His real interest was for linguistic analysis; and the point he set out to make was that a theologian who wants to interpret the Bible or the Fathers correctly must take into account all the general factors which affect our use of words. Every man, for example, has his own level of subtlety; and it would be wrong to attribute refinements of meaning to a naturally crude and straightforward writer. Every language has its shortcomings; and every writer adds to these in practice his own specific limitations, while those who write with an audience in view reduce their powers of expression still further to the narrow range of the average human intelligence. Language, thought Abélard, was a poor instrument for the expression of mental experience. And from these considerations of its nature he derived his famous final principle that the same word could have a different meaning with different authors: *Facilis autem plerumque controversiarum solutio reperietur, si eadem verba in diversis significationibus a diversis auctoribus posita defendere poterimus.**

In less than fifty years, these devices were to become the common currency of orthodox criticism. But for the moment the impression left by the *Sic et Non* and by the rest of Abélard's work did not depend upon the technical details of what he taught. What counted was his general message, his intention to enthrone dialectic in the place of authority. Students crowded to his lectures because he was the champion of dialectic; and the fury of his enemies fell upon him for the same reason.

Abélard saw himself as the servant of a truth which harmonised with the greater truth of God. But in the eyes of St Bernard he was one who preferred his own fancies to the authority of the saints, and the pagan to the Christian tradition. Nor was St Bernard's percipience at fault. In a sense, the attitude of Abélard and his supporters invites comparison with the uncritical cult of antiquity characteristic of certain fifteenth-century Humanists. It is true that their admiration was reserved for a limited number of books by a single author, but within those bounds it was complete. They were emotionally prepared to follow the lead of the ancient world without serious reservations; and Abélard himself, who may never have realised how justly such an interpretation could be placed upon his teachings, fell a tragic victim to the prejudices it aroused.

His works, when examined in their detail, do not measure up to the boldness of his general programme. Indeed, it is difficult to assess how much he actually contributed to the understanding of logic and the study of Aristotle. The basis of instruction in dialectic was almost certainly the *lectio* or the reading with commentary of an authoritative text—either some portion of the *Organon* or Porphyry or one of the works of Boethius on those two authors. It is plain enough that the value of such a course would depend upon the character of the commentary, and that seems to have been an uncertain factor, decided almost entirely by the inclination of the teacher. If we try to take the logical writings of Abélard for a guide, we shall find that his commentaries fall into two classes. One set is extremely terse, consisting of brief explanations intended to make the text more easy to understand. The other set contains considerable digressions or *quaestiones* in the course of which Abélard develops his own point of view.* Which then are we to take as the more truly representative of his lecturing method? Or did he use first one and then the other? Was it the case that his technique developed? Or did he vary it according to the intelligence of his hearers? And to make the problem even more complicated, there exists yet a third set of notes from Abélard's hand—those published by Cousin in his *Dialectica*—which cover the same ground but summarise rather than comment the authorities they deal with. One is tempted to suggest that Abélard started his career teaching along traditional early medieval lines and gradually worked out a method very similar to the one used in modern universities. But the absence of any definite evidence about the date of his various logical works makes that pleasant hypothesis nothing more than a guess. Nor does it seem likely, in view of the emphasis placed upon authorities even as late as the thirteenth century, that Abélard could really have lectured without his texts. Until we get some further evidence on the subject we shall have to regard the *Dialectica* not as published lectures, but as a book intended for auxiliary private study.

Abélard owes his place in the story of the classical heritage to the fact that the new movement to which he lent the force of his prestige attracted such a large number of students. He was primarily responsible for laying the foundations of that overwhelming popularity which logical studies and therefore the study of Aristotle enjoyed from the first quarter of the twelfth century until the Renaissance. The fact that his contribution to the technical advancement of dialectic is difficult to estimate, and even the greater fact of his personal failure, must remain by comparison matters of small importance. He dragged the once bright hopes of his career from the crowds of Paris to the Paraclete, and from there through the hostilities of St Gildas to the final agonies of Sens and Cluny; but by the time he died, logic, which at the beginning of the century had still to struggle for popular recognition, was firmly established in the main schools of France.

The personal disasters which befell Abélard had indeed surprisingly little effect on the progress of the movement he had helped to start. Aristotle continued to attract students, and between 1125 and 1158 the reputation and the potential influence of the Aristotelian Corpus vastly increased as the remainder of the *Organon* came into common use. The parts arrived in the following order: first, the *Analytica Priora* which deals with the forms common to all types of reasoning and in particular with the syllogism; then the *Sophistici Elenchi* or the list of common fallacies; then the *Topica* which deals with dialectical argument from probable premisses; and last of all, after 1141, the *Analytica Posteriora* which discusses the conditions of scientific reasoning. These works constituted the so-called *logica nova.**

No one has yet compared the writings of the eleventh century with those of the thirteenth from the point of view of the logical processes they employ: and until such a comparison is made, our estimates of the nce exercised by the *logica nova* must remain largely guesswork. ms likely, however, that the great speculative systems of Scholas- could not have been constructed, nor conversely could they have ~~~~ criticised, without an intimate knowledge of the syllogism. It seems also likely that without the new Aristotle the zeal for definitions and deductions which by the end of the twelfth century invaded every branch of knowledge would never have appeared. But these are points which wait for clarification.

Thierry of Chartres' attempt to collect in his *Heptateuchon* the pedagogic material required for a complete arts course gives us an idea of the books used round 1140 in his advanced and efficient school. They included for dialectic the whole of the *Organon* with the exception of the *Analytica Posteriora* (which owing to its difficulty was not added to scholastic programmes until later), Porphyry's introduction to the *Categoriae*, Boethius' *Introductio ad syllogismos categoricos, de Syllogismo Categorico, de Syllogismo Hypothetico, de Differentiis Topicis* and *de Divisione*, Cicero's *Topica* and an anonymous *de Logica Oratio*. Before another twenty years had passed, the content of these books (or as much of it as medieval scholarship could understand) had become part of the current intellectual tradition. Its influence can be seen almost equally in the *Gloss* of Anselm of Laon, in the *Sentences* of Peter Lombard and in the *Decretum* of Gratian, the definitive text-books which crowned several centuries of study in Biblical exegesis, in doctrine and in Canon law. It was discussed and analysed in the *Metalogicon* by John of Salisbury and formed the essential basis of the great controversy about universals. By 1160 the content of the *Organon* and its supporting literature was assimilated so that even the loss of the ancient texts would have made little difference to what was to happen in the future.

III. THE STUDY OF MEDICINE AND NATURAL PHILOSOPHY

The history of medieval logic and the history of medieval law both begin with a formative period when the subject in question was not properly differentiated from other branches of knowledge. By the first quarter of the twelfth century, however, logic had emerged as an independent discipline with its specific problems and its specific techniques; and after the rise of the Bolognese faculty law was established on much the same footing. They became professional interests whose students had little cause to wander outside their own special field. But medical learning which we now have to consider, falls in a different category. It never achieved the independence and academic isolation which characterised its sister disciplines. In a sense, it escaped from the amorphous condition of its first beginnings. It came to rank as a proper field of study, and its practitioners could boast a recognisable professional status. The pre-eminence of the medical school at Salerno was acknowledged throughout Europe. The medical school at Montpellier was founded. But the links which bound medicine to other subjects remained unbroken. Its progress involved the development of a host of other subjects such as chemistry and botany. It depended on the greater understanding of Aristotle, of Avicenna and Averroes whose works raised philosophical and in some cases even theological issues.

We cannot therefore treat the history of medicine in a convenient isolation but must see it as part of a wider field, comprising the whole of what used to be called natural philosophy and impinging consequently on a host of other studies. The contribution which the classical heritage made to progress in this vast area of knowledge was astonishingly complex. Deriving not only from the medical writers, not only from natural historians like Pliny, not only from Aristotle and his commentators, but from Porphyry, from Macrobius, from Dionysius the Areopagite, its myriad threads criss-cross in bewildering patterns. Moreover, the difficulties which always attend the investigation of variety are aggravated in this particular case by a complication of another sort. The material of this scientific and philosophical tradition is not merely complex; it is also, when viewed from the vantage point of the twentieth century, undoubtedly odd.

In the branches of study considered earlier, we have had to examine the utilisation of knowledge for practical ends; and the ends served to determine the means. Scholars like Alcuin, Irnerius and Abélard dealt with what we, whose approach to learning is animated by the same practical purposes, recognise as valid analyses of language and expression, valid relationships in law, valid categories of thought. But now we must move into a field where such valid knowledge is inextricably mixed with speculations and beliefs which strike us as fantastic. We must take into account the curiosities of the early Herbals and at a different level the wilder interpretations of the Neoplatonic cosmology. We must in short come to terms with the essential duality of the Middle Ages.

The manifest structure of medieval culture is well ordered. Its foundations are firmly set in the Christian religion. Its social relationships find their expression in the feudal order. Its art produces the great cathedrals. Its education draws upon the classical heritage. The different departments of ancient knowledge are utilised as the need arises; grammar first, then rhetoric, then dialectic, law, medicine and philosophy. Everything falls into place in a development which is so coherent, which issues ultimately in such imposing achievements, that we can only marvel. The resultant edifice has a magnificence which appropriately recalls the glories of ecclesiastical architecture. Its solidity is undoubted. Its proportions compel admiration. And yet— let our eyes waver, if only for a moment, from the strict contemplation of these structural beauties, and the pillars, the arches, the great roof itself, are likely to fade from our awareness. We behold instead a multitude of incongruous details. The walls, we notice, are masked by eccentric ornament, the nave is piled high with oddly assorted furniture. The light that filters through the great windows produces lurid and distorted reflections. Where order reigned, there is now chaos; and our original vision of a balanced structure turns into a junk-shop nightmare.

Subjective impressions of this type can never be accepted without some reservation. The contrasts they make are too sharply underlined. On the other hand they often contain an element of truth; and the truth adumbrated by this particular impression is of some importance. Medieval culture does give evidence of a certain duality of character. The antithesis of vision and nightmare, cathedral and junk shop, tends perhaps to over-emphasise the difference of its two constituents, by ignoring the effects of their interaction. But the difference undoubtedly existed. In some of the most vital sectors of human activity development was to a great extent orderly and impressive. As we have tried to show, the means available were carefully employed to achieve definite ends. But in certain other sectors, the means were insufficient or the ends too vague; and the spirit of order failed to make its mark. Observation was replaced by guesswork, reason by childish prelogical thought. The result was confusion.

The study of natural philosophy constituted such a sector. The body of knowledge which comprised the facts that now belong to the sciences of medicine, biology, botany and chemistry was linked to magical beliefs on the one hand and to cosmological theories on the other. The reason for these linkages is almost certainly to be found in the great difficulty men had in understanding the relationships of the natural world with which all these subjects dealt. That initial difficulty prevented the development of proper disciplines like those of law and rhetoric; and the absence of a discipline permitted the continued acceptance of magical explanations which may have been psychologically satisfactory, but which had no scientific relevance. It also permitted the free exercise of the human tendency to tackle large rather than small, vague rather than circumscribed problems.

Besides, tradition also played a part. The connections between science and magic, science and cosmology, went back to the ancient world and beyond. Magical interpretations of phenomena had been current ever since the neolithic age; and the Ionians who were the first natural philosophers had never explained anything without at the same time attempting to explain everything. Aristotle himself had studied both cosmology and natural history, while another set of cosmological theories, those of Neoplatonism, had been ably fused by Iamblichus with the traditions of Babylonian magic. In this field the legacy of Greece and Rome was curiously compounded of the logical and the prelogical, the civilised and the primitive. It was not an exclusive product of the outlook which we normally associate with the classical heritage, the outlook characteristic of the city-state. Other forces also contributed to its growth. With the single exception of the Christian religion, natural philosophy was the only field of ancient knowledge which had received the definitive form in which the future was to know it, not from the Hellenic but from the Hellenistic culture, and embodied therefore not only Greek, but manifold Oriental elements.

Nor was this all. For, while ancient rhetoric, ancient law, ancient literature made a direct impact upon the medieval world through the reading of Greek and Latin texts, the natural philosophy of Hellenistic antiquity arrived through the mediation of another and alien culture.

Since we are studying the history of a discipline which flourished in Christian countries, we have not needed so far to pay any attention to what lay outside the boundaries of Christendom. But from many points of view this division of the Mediterranean world into Christian and non-Christian spheres of influence is highly artificial. It can be cogently argued that the area of the Roman Empire continued to form a single unit throughout the Middle Ages, that its different portions were closely interrelated, and that their development was determined by the same general causes.

To the south of Christian Europe lay Islam. The Dark Ages had ended there earlier than they did in the north, and an increased prosperity had stimulated revivals in the different fields of learning, so that by the tenth century, Arab theology, Arab literature and Arab medicine had attained a respectable eminence. At this time the study of scientific subjects met with far less opposition in Islam than under Christian rule. For, although the Arab theologians did not lack the desire to suppress all manifestations of heretical thought, the power they possessed to enforce their wishes was relatively slight. Dependent as they were upon the shifting goodwill of essentially secular rulers and uncertain in their hold over the minds and hearts of their flocks, it was to take them a long time to win their victory over secular culture. Until the middle of the twelfth century, scientific and philosophical speculation remained reasonably free in all the Arab-controlled countries. Admittedly it was confined to small groups of interested men; but for a time these were far ahead of their Christian counterparts in the range of their knowledge. The first Arabic translations from the Greek were made in the ninth century, and during that same period Alkindius (al-Kindi), who lived in Baghdad and then later in Basra, wrote extensively on geometry, astronomy, music, optics, medicine and psychology. He was the earliest of those Arab encyclopedists who made it their business to transmogrify Graeco-Roman knowledge for the use of their fellow-countrymen. Another Baghdad scholar, Rhases, founded a school of medicine which revived the teachings of Hippocrates. In the tenth century there were more translations, more medical writers including Ali al-Abbas and Isaac Israeli, another philosophical encyclopedist Alfarabius (al-Farabi) and the most famous Arab of them all, Ibn Sina, a young contemporary of Gerbert whom the West was to know familiarly by the garbled name of Avicenna.*

These encyclopedists took the whole of human knowledge for their ostensible field. But in practice they concentrated on two main topics: science and cosmology. The world-picture favoured by the Mohammedan theologians of the time was somewhat crude, and generalisations derived from the sciences could not be reconciled with it. So the secular thinkers turned to other cosmologies which offered to provide a more suitable framework. The Neoplatonically inspired system of Avicenna for example postulated a series of intelligences, each generated by the one above it and each conjoined with its appropriate material sphere as a soul with its body. The lowest sphere, that of the moon, was represented as generating the principle responsible for form in this world, while the motion of the spheres, acting as a unit, produced the natural movements of matter. The system may appear fanciful in the light of modern theories, but plainly enough it supplied a comfortable framework in which the puzzling phenomena of growth could be securely viewed. It provided the imagination with a link, defensible at the highest level of generality, between the two somewhat disconnected aspects of the biological process, which men had already observed. The fact that the constituent elements of living creatures came together as a result of the general movement inherent in matter, was brought into a neat relation with the other equally obvious, but almost contradictory, piece of knowledge that these chance accumulations of matter often acquired from some undiscovered source an essentially pre-existent because repeatable form. Avicenna's system did not explain these matters as we understand explanation; but, unlike the theological tradition it did at least acknowledge their existence. It made scientists (and in particular the doctors) feel more at home in the universe.

The reshaping of Hellenistic natural philosophy by the Arab writers probably merits more study than it has so far received. It may be argued that the changes made were for the most part confined to matters of detail, to the addition or omission of facts, to variations of emphasis. But their total effect was far from negligible. There seems some reason to believe that the Hellenistic tradition emerged from the hands of its Arab and Jewish interpreters more materialistic in its general theories and more irrational in its details than it had been earlier. Avicenna's beliefs concerning the permanence of the material world, his restriction of logic exclusively to the field of the data provided by the intellect (thus breaking the connection between thought and ulti-mate reality) and his denial that man could have any positive knowledge about God, all tended to undermine the connection which Christian thinkers had sought to establish between metaphysics and theology, while at a more practical level Jabir, for example, whose writings were to provide European alchemy with its most respected text-books, made liberal additions to such of his Greek sources as have been so far dis-covered, embodying a great deal from the occult science of Syria and the Middle East.

All the more famous Arab scholars seem to have been voluminous writers; and there is no doubt that their encyclopedic compilations contained a wealth of valuable knowledge: some of which was taken from Aristotle, some added from Eastern sources, and some provided by the authors themselves. Avicenna's contributions to clinical theory, to mention only one point, will always assure him a high place in the hierarchy of medical genius. But alongside the gold, there was a great deal of dross; or to put the matter more circumspectly, alongside the treasures of observation, experiment and cogent inference there was a great deal of speculation that bore the imprint of more primitive processes of thought. The reason for this has already been suggested. The problems set by the natural sciences, and the wider problem of explaining the general nature of the universe, were considerably more difficult than the comparable problems of law or logic. Many centuries were to pass before they could be satisfactorily organised, and in the meantime, the temptation to provide pseudo-rational explanations for what could not be otherwise elucidated, was bound to be overwhelming.

The fanciful nature of these currents of thought should not blind us to their significance for the society in which they flourished. If the picture they gave of the world was worthless or almost worthless as a guide to action, it was not by the same token intellectually un-satisfying. Its most obvious characteristic was the ease with which it was accepted; and the reasons for its popularity are not hard to discover. The beliefs, on which it rested, had their roots in everyday experience. The welcome given by the human mind to anthropomorphic cosmo-logies should not be attributed (as it so often has been) to an innate delight in the products of the imagination. It can be accounted for more simply and more rationally. When a writer describes Nature begging Providence to present Matter with the gift of Form, he is explaining the mysteries of creation in anthropomorphic terms that every human being who has ever interceded on another's behalf would readily understand. The two female figures whom Bernard Silvestris makes responsible for bringing man into the world, the wise, beautiful but somewhat aloof Urania and the practical, comforting Physis, are plainly enough the two aspects which a mother wears for any small child. They hark back to an experience which has its place in most people's memories. Other features of the beliefs which nowadays do appear the products of pure fantasy, make sense if we consider them within the specialised circumstances of the age. When few were capable of elaborate calculation, and the majority could merely wonder at results reached by means they could not understand, it was natural to credit numbers with a mystical power; and the alchemists were not behaving unreasonably when they hoped that the addition of some lucky ingredient would eventually turn lead into gold; for does not the com-mon cooking-pot produce transformations which on the face of it are equally remarkable? The popular beliefs of the Middle Ages were not imaginative. They were startlingly prosaic. They reduced the whole complex fabric of the universe to the limits of everyday experience. Hence their wide appeal and the spell they cast particularly over the minds of the half-instructed.

Such was the unusual form of that part of the classical heritage to whose history we must now turn. It reached the West gradually. A considerable body of factual material was available from the very beginning of the Dark Ages in the works of Pliny, Capella, and Isidore. The writings of these Latin encyclopedists were for the most part unaffected by the occultism of the Eastern tradition. They contained only such fanciful stories and theories as ignorance had led their authors to incorporate from the traditions of popular knowledge; and the role they played was in any case of little importance until the ninth century, since neither the Anglo-Saxon nor the early Carolingian educators set much store by science. Bede was sufficiently interested to write his *de natura rerum*, rehashing Isidore and adding substantial quotations from Pliny, but in general facts about the physical world were regarded much as the educational tradition of today regards such subjects as the history of art. They ranked as general information which it was perhaps useful to possess but which were to be taught incidentally if at all. In this respect, however, the increased enlightenment of the later Carolingians brought a certain measure of change. The monastic community, being a small and settled group, tended to pay a fair amount of attention to the health of its members; and there was a growing interest in the various common illnesses and their cures. The popularity of herbal remedies led to the composition of numerous *Hortuli*. Some of these were little more than lists of simples. But the heights, as well as the depths, of the monastic tradition of medical knowledge are to be found in the *Causae et Curae* of Hildegarde of Bingen. She possessed more physiological knowledge than the majority of the medically-minded religious but at the same time she was more inclined to believe in the miraculous and the magical. Did not the Devil sit regularly at the foot of her bed in the shape of a green dog? The same fanciful strain was also prominent in another popular form of literature with a vaguely scientific reference, in those Bestiaries which we now relish for their oddity. Who would be without the tale of the self-immolating phoenix or the pelican that tears its breast to feed its young?

The dissemination of such fancies was encouraged by a similarly irrational element present in the incidentals of the Christian tradition. There were the early saints' lives with their superabundance of miracles whose authenticity was piously accepted even in the absence of serious evidence. There were the shrines with their record of extraordinary cures; and at a more academic level there were the techniques of Biblical exegesis. The discovery of allegorical meanings was essential for the interpretation of the Old Testament and useful for explaining away, as Fulgentius had done, the more obtrusive mythology of the pagan poets. It was to leave its imprint, however, on every realm of thought, and one can see how its emphasis on the possibility of mysterious correspondences could lead to the easier acceptance of a great deal of nonsense. To form the habit of postulating a supernatural significance for ordinary objects or actions is imperceptibly to lose all hold on the sober criteria of judgement that the normal relations of natural phenomena provide. The leap from allegory to magic is only too rapid. A fantastic tale may be the symbol of a truth. We may accept the unicorn that lays its head on the lap of a virgin because its action prefigures the Incarnation. But minds habituated to such beliefs easily passed to others less permissible and lent to words and objects not only a meaning but a power unjustified by experience. So the letters of the Greek alphabet were interpreted as runes. Numbers took on the character of spells; and chemicals became the means of alchemy. While the main currents of Christian teaching formed the pivot round which civilisation developed, certain accidental features of the Christian tradition did much to reinforce irrationalism. By the beginning of the tenth century, the ground was well prepared for the irruption of the more highly organised occult tradition that was linked to the science of the East.

The Arab world marched with the Christian in Spain and southern Italy. Local trade and travel formed the basis of numerous contacts; and as a result there arose a class of deracinated individuals who were equally at home in both cultures. Over a wider field, the Jews acted as mediators. They too had a foot in both camps; and the knowledge that an Isaac Israeli, a Saadja or a Gebirol acquired through his active commerce with the Arab intellectuals was transmitted along a chain of personal contacts, as part of an essential Jewish tradition, to the communities of the north whose members in their turn had close contacts with the learning of Christendom, helped Gundisalvi with his translations, Andrew of St Victor with his Biblical studies.

From 1050 onwards, the slowly developing revival of Western science and medicine, the tradition of the *de Universo*, the *Hortuli* and the *Causae et Curae*, began to draw inspiration from Arabic sources. Medicine was further advanced in Italy than in the north. The Italian doctors treating lay patients in the wealthy towns and therefore financially dependent on the success of their cures, sought more eagerly after fresh knowledge than did their monastic colleagues; and thanks to Italy's contacts with the Moslem south, they were also better placed to obtain the information they needed. Significantly enough it was the southern city of Salerno that became the first centre of medical studies.

At first they explored Latin authorities such as Caelius Aurelianus, whose cautious methodism is reflected in such early Salernitan works as the *Passionarius* of Guariopontus and the *Practica* of Pietro Clerici.* But when this source of information was exhausted they took the opportunity offered by their contacts with the Arab world.

The earliest medieval translator of importance to move to fresh pastures was a certain Constantine who died in 1087. The accounts we have about him suggest that he lived to a ripe old age, so that his most productive period ought perhaps to be placed soon after the middle years of the century. An African by birth, he had travelled widely in the East before settling in Salerno, where he acquired a remarkable reputation. He possessed the principal medical writings of the tenth-century Arab school, and his major service was to produce Latin versions of Rhases, of Ali al-Abbas and of Isaac Israeli. Since these authors were all meticulous Hippocratists, the Salerno faculty learnt a great deal from them about accurate observation and diagnosis. But Constantine also translated a few works by Hippocrates himself—the *Aphorisms* (with Galen's commentary), the *Prognostics*, and the *de Regimine Morborum Acutorum*. So the two sources of medieval learning, the Greek and the Graeco-Arabic, came simultaneously to men's attention.

The work of Constantine caused a revolution in medical practice; but his positive contributions to knowledge, substantial though these were, must on a long view take second place to the importance of the interest he aroused. For doctors everywhere were eager now to have more translations; and the next on the list were obviously the treatises of Avicenna and Aristotle, which were likely to exercise an influence far beyond the medical sphere. Aristotle was not just another Galen or Hippocrates. He was the divine logician. At this very juncture, the beginning of the twelfth century, the enthusiasm for the *Organon* reached its highest peak. The schools of Paris were crammed with the impassioned students of Abélard; and every clerk trained in dialectic, if not every educated man, was anxious to see what treasures lay hid in those writings of the philosopher which were still unknown. This popular cult gave wings to what would have been without it a slow and unspectacular process of professional discovery.

The translation of Aristotelian writings, from the Arabic and the Greek, attracted after 1140 the attention of some very capable scholars and was carried forward at a great rate. Its detailed history is most complicated, and some of the problems it presents may never be solved. To construct a completely satisfactory picture of the spread of Greek and Arabic thought during the twelfth century, we should need to know what works were translated, and the date, authorship and use made of each version. Our information on the first of these points is fairly extensive and will no doubt increase as the literature of the time and the relevant manuscripts are more deeply studied. But the same cannot be said about the other requirements mentioned. There are some versions concerning which we know nothing at all beyond their bare existence. There are a good many which we can ascribe to some particular author. But there are very few which we can both so ascribe and date. Dating has generally to be done in terms of a limit before which the version must have been in existence. In the majority of cases that limit is set by the death of the author, and so may post-date the work by twenty or thirty years! The question of diffusion is equally awkward. Our only means of judging the use made of a translation are the number of times it is cited and the number of surviving manuscripts: types of evidence which lend themselves to error.

At the beginning of the century the traveller Adelard of Bath translated the *Elements* of Euclid and some Arabic works on astronomy and arithmetic. He dedicated these to a Bishop of Syracuse. Before 1155, Hermann of Carinthia translated Ptolemy's *Planisphera* at Toulouse. All these were from the Arabic. Then before 1162 Aristippus, Archdeacon of Catania, translated from the Greek the *Mechanica* of Hero of Alexandria, the *Optica* and *Katoptrica* of Euclid, the *Almagest* of Ptolemy, the fourth book of Aristotle's *Meteorologica*, the *Phaedo* and the *Meno* of Plato. But none of these translations appears to have been widely known.

The decisive effort was made elsewhere. The centre where the largest number of versions were produced, where the truly influential Greek and Arabic books were translated, and from where they were most speedily and liberally supplied to other countries, was the Spanish city of Toledo. Here an Italian, Gerard of Cremona, put into Latin from the Arabic, the *Meteorologica*, books I–III, the *Physica*, the *de Generatione et Corruptione*, and the *de Caelo* of Aristotle, the pseudo-Aristotelian *de Mundo* (Proclus-al Farabi), the *de Causis*, the medical works of Avicenna, certain philosophical writings of Isaac Israeli, and the *Almagest* of Ptolemy. At the same time, a Jew, John Avendeath, working sometimes alone and sometimes in collaboration with

Gundisalvi, Archdeacon of Segovia, contributed to the general stock most of the other writings of Avicenna, including the latter's rehash of Aristotle, the *de Scientiis* of al Farabi and the *Fons Vitae* of Gebirol. A fourth scholar, Hugh of Santalla, was responsible for the translation of sundry minor Arabic writings.

It appears likely that the majority of these versions were produced between 1140 and 1160, and that they soon found their way to Paris. The Toledan translators are known to have received encouragement from Archbishop Raymond who died in 1151. They must have started work prior to that date. A dedication by Hugh of Santalla proves that he produced most of his translations before then; and Gerard of Cremona's *Meteorologica* was known to Aristippus at least a couple of years before the latter's death in 1162. On the other hand Gerard's *Almagest* was published in 1175, and it is to be presumed that he went on working until his death in 1187.

After that we hear only of the Englishman, Alfred of Sarashel who appears, however, to have worked at Toledo. He put into Latin the *de Vegetalibus* and the *de Congelatis* by Avicenna and the *de Plantis* by Nicolas of Dalmas, while at some point previous to 1193 Burgundio of Pisa in Italy translated afresh the *Aphorisms* of Hippocrates and brought out versions of several small essays by Galen.

But this picture we get by adding together all the known works of all the known translators is hopelessly incomplete. A clear indication of its shortcomings is the fact that it contains only about half the translations from Aristotle which we know from the manuscripts to have been in existence. The study made by the late Monsignor Lacombe for the projected edition of the medieval Aristotle versions has revealed that, in addition to the translations already mentioned, there existed before the end of the twelfth century incomplete versions of the *Metaphysica* (I–IV. 4) and the *Ethica Nicomachea* (II and III only), both translated from the Greek and attributed to Boethius, also versions of the *Physica*, the *de Generatione et Corruptione*, the *de Anima*, the *de Sensu et Sensato*, the *de Memoria et Reminiscentia*, the *de Somno et Vigilia*, and the *de Morte et Vita*, all from the Greek, and the *de Differentia Spiritus et Animae* and the *de Plantis* from the Arabic. These last nine together with the *Meteorologica* of Gerard and Aristippus and the former's *de Caelo et Mundo* were bound together in an omnibus volume and plainly formed the hard core of Aristotelian learning up to 1200.

Similar detailed investigations in respect of other Greek and Arabic authors would almost certainly yield analogous results. There may have been far more of Avicenna, Alfarabius and Hippocrates translated than the list we have given suggests.

The labours of scholarship have uncovered a great deal. They will in time uncover more; and the mists which now enshroud the intellectual life of the twelfth century may soon be dissipated. But at the moment all one can safely say is that a large selection of Aristotle's metaphysical, ethical and scientific treatises, together with numerous works by his commentators and expositors, reached Paris in Latin translations between 1160 and 1200, and were most favourably received on arrival.

That welcome was to be expected in view of the scientific enthusiasm which had been aroused and in view also of the general cult accorded to Aristotle. Even the theologians had become convinced of the usefulness of Aristotelian dialectic since Peter Lombard and Anselm of Laon had furnished practical proofs that reason with all its new weapons could still be subordinated to authority, and that authority was strengthened thereby. But the intensity of the welcome was not due to these interests alone. Certain other influences also contributed to the zeal with which the translations were read and to the momentary absence of that suspicion and hesitancy which normally accompanied the medieval reception of a new pagan work.

The mental climate of France in the middle years of the twelfth century owed much of its character to the activities of the school of Chartres. Founded by Fulbert in 990 when the educational initiative had already passed from the monasteries to the cathedral centres, it was yet truly representative of that pious but freely curious and rather dilettante culture which had distinguished the late Carolingian epoch. Set amid conditions of greater prosperity and a more general learning, it retained the spirit of inquiry of its monastic predecessors raised now to a higher power. Medicine, science, mathematics were all studied in addition to exegesis, theology and the usual disciplines of the Trivium. Like the Irish before them, the Chartrains preferred to move on the frontiers of knowledge. In the lifetime of Berengar, they had made their contribution to the rise of dialectic. But then as the triumph of dialectic was assured, their attention had shifted to other and more subtle aspects of philosophy.

While the students of Paris were crowding the lectures of Abélard, a man of remarkable attainments had appeared on the Chartrain scene. The patience, the habit of petty authority, the systematic orderliness which are the necessary attributes of a good schoolmaster, shrivel the spirit. Few teachers, supremely competent in the daily performance of their tasks, are able to pursue simultaneously with such tasks some original and creative line of thought. Fewer still have that unstinted emotional power which characterises the natural leader. In the personality of Bernard of Chartres these incompatible virtues were successfully united. An excellent pedagogue, adept at working out programmes and unflagging in their application (he could apparently teach the whole of Latin grammar within a single year), an original philosopher, expert in the unfamiliar as well as the familiar aspects of his subject, a man of charming piety who valued faith above learning and whose spiritual peace sustained and enriched all around him, he exercised an enormous influence over his many pupils. He wrote little by all accounts, and his few writings have not survived. But contemporary references afford ample proof of his formative role. This man, with his almost magical power over the minds of the young, was unfashionably a Platonist; or would Neoplatonist be a more correct description?

The systems which stem respectively from the teachings of Plato and Plotinus have as their names suggest a great deal in common; and after Rome fell, they were known to the Western world in the first place through the writings of Augustine. Now, Augustine had set the ideas he had borrowed from pagan sources within a Christian framework and had avoided developing their implications, with the result that his teaching belonged as it were to the common field between the two philosophies and could serve with equal ease as the basis of a Platonic or a Neoplatonic elaboration. Since, however, none of Plato's works with the solitary exception of a Neoplatonist translation of the *Timaeus* were available in the West before the twelfth century (and such dialogues as made their appearance after 1100 were few in number and rarely copied) while the doctrines of Plotinus, or extensions of them, could be exhaustively studied in Macrobius or Dionysius, any philosopher who sought to advance from the Augustinian position by drawing more heavily on ancient sources was bound in practice to end up as a Neoplatonist.

Such in the ninth century had been the experience of John the Scot. It is interesting to reflect that this first attempt to give medieval theology a basis in an ancient philosophical doctrine would, if successful, have carried it in a direction far removed from the Aristotelianism that eventually prevailed. But the abstruse character of John's arguments, his failure to find a technical vocabulary competent to express his thought and yet intelligible to his contemporaries, and the fact that Neoplatonic doctrine, however carefully handled, was in the last analysis irreconcilable with Christianity, proved too much for the magnetism of even his intellectual pre-eminence. He failed to win support within the Church; and the suspicions of the council which stigmatised the *de Predestinatione* as 'Scots porridge' in 855, came to a head when in 1225 Pope Honorius ordered all copies of the *de Divisione Naturae* to be officially burnt. So the tradition represented by John existed from the ninth to the twelfth century not in the centre but on the extreme fringe of Christian thought. There, however, it exercised an obvious attraction over those who had a preference for original and subtle speculation. It was admirably fitted by its strangeness, its mystical wealth and the profundity of its metaphysic to appeal to the spirit which reigned at Chartres.

How deeply Bernard himself explored this tradition, we have no means of telling. His avowed aim was to reconcile Plato with Aristotle and the only work he is known to have written was a commentary on the *Isagoge* of Porphyry, which within its strictly logical field was a Neoplatonic interpretation of Aristotle.

But in the writings of Bernard's brother Thierry, and of Bernard's pupil William of Conches, and in the writings of their pupils Bernard Silvestris and Clarembaud of Arras, all the elements of the Chartrain tradition, Christian piety and natural science, the Neoplatonic cosmology and the Aristotelian dialectic, play their appropriate parts. The theme of Thierry's *de Operibus Sex Dierum* is the creation of the world. God the Father, the One and the Eternal, Who contains all things in Himself, figures as the efficient cause of the world. He creates the four elements which are the material cause. God the Son, as Logos, ordering and organising the universe, is the formal cause, while the final cause is the Holy Spirit drawing all things to Him by the love He inspires. William's more compendious *de Philosophia Mundi* starts with a similar conception which he extends and completes by material drawn from the science of his time, from astronomy and medicine in particular, while the more literary *de Mundi Universitate* of Bernard Silvestris is full of references to *Nous* and a personified *Natura*, to *Urania* the queen of the stars and all-knowing *Physis*. We are in an allegorical world where Neoplatonic symbols purport to represent Christian truths. But the symbols have a sharp clarity while their Christian content is left vague for the reader to guess; and at times the narrative seems to speed on, developed for its sake, regardless of the truths it is supposed to signify. The ordering of the stars and planets by *Nous* provides an excuse for the introduction of astronomical details; passages on the plants and on the creation of man have their sources in the text-books of medicine.*

The whole wide field of Chartrain knowledge is in these books. It is true that the combination of the various elements present in the outlook of Chartres is not perfectly achieved. The logic is sometimes slipshod. The Christian identifications are not always exact or satisfying. But the scientific material is subsumed easily enough under the somewhat fanciful cosmology; and it is not surprising that a generation which was eager to apply its new-found logical knowledge to long-standing metaphysical problems, saw in these Chartrain efforts the beginning at least of that synthesis for which the medieval world had so long been hoping, and was fascinated accordingly. But the feature of the Chartrain writings which most strikes the modern reader is their similarity to Arab thought. It has been suggested that some of Avicenna's commentaries reached Paris early enough to be known to Thierry and William of Conches, or that the Chartrains had learnt about the Arab tradition from Jewish sources, much as their contemporary, Andrew of St Victor, familiarised himself with Jewish exegesis by conversing with rabbis. But these hypotheses are unnecessary. The Chartrains had the same interests as Avicenna. They had before them some of the same authorities. The similarity of their conclusions to the teachings of the great Arab is not therefore surprising.

It is not as the expositors but as the heralds of the new movement that the Chartrains have their place in cultural history. A generation totally unfamiliar with Neoplatonic ideas might have found Avicenna difficult to unravel. But the readers of Thierry and William had no such difficulties; and their readers were indeed many. The *de Operibus Sex Dierum* and the *Pragmaticon* dazzled men's imaginations by the magnificence of their syntheses, by their flashes of poetry, and even more by that suggestion which they managed to impart, and which we can still faintly catch, of doors opening upon an unknown horizon. Because they gave a Christian dress to certain Neoplatonic conceptions selected and expressed with caution, Neoplatonism as a system lost some of the discredit which had attached to it in the past. The Chartrains can be compared therefore with equal force to pedagogues who prepare students for a difficult subject by a preliminary course which states its general principles, and to propagandists who break down prejudice against a new point of view by presenting it in a favourable light. In both these ways, they smoothed the path for the readier acceptance of the Neoplatonised Aristotelianism of the Arab commentators.

Simultaneously, however, that same path was being prepared in other ways. Social developments also contributed to forming a climate of opinion favourable—and in this instance too uncritically favourable—to philosophical innovation. The twelfth century saw the emergence of a social group which was never indeed to take on the character and importance of a clearly defined class, but which was to play from that time onwards a vigorous if subsidiary role in the shaping of ideas. As the monastic community ceased to be the dominant social unit of the educational world, the intellectual proletariat made its first appearance.

Earlier, education had been for those who desired it an almost certain passport to a fair measure of worldly success. The number of trained men was small compared to the number of posts where their energies could be usefully employed; and in any case since the majority of the educated were monks, such of them as failed to find an opening merely sank into the peaceful obscurity of a contemplative life. In the twelfth century, however, this comfortable balance was radically disturbed. The main reason for its collapse was probably the crowding of the cathedral schools. The intellectual fascinations of dialectic combined, we may perhaps assume, with one of those periodic bursts of enthusiasm for education which tend to occur at times of increasing prosperity when educational training is seen as an avenue to material advancement. Curiosity coupled with ambition led students in their hundreds to the lectures which only a few had frequented before; and these new recruits to learning did not come exclusively or even largely from the monasteries. The majority of them were seculars; and many had administrative rather than religious ambitions. Consequently, there soon arose a situation similar to the one which in the nineteenth century followed the establishment of the great French professional schools. The supply of educated personnel outran the demand; and we begin to hear of men whose intellects were capable of dealing with abstract problems, who could interest themselves in theology or philosophy, but who were forced to live unsatisfactory lives embittered by failure and uninfluenced by the responsibilities of office.

Having no settled home in a monastery to which custom might have led them to retire, they tended to wander from one patron's court to another hoping always to find some settled position. Such of them as had gift for entertainment became, like Hugo Primas, jesters for a living. The fantastic career of that poet, who is the archetype of all wandering scholars, owed a lot no doubt to his instability of character. With his gifts, he ought to have been able to earn a comfortable canonry. Instead we find him begging for bread and clothes, now fawning on the citizens of Amiens who had given him money, now venting his wrath on Beauvais where he had suffered some disappointment. At one point he is in Rheims where Alberic condescended to make use of his scurrilous pen. Then again he is in Paris. He is kicked downstairs by a patron whom he has irritated by his importunities. He sinks to living on charity in a hostel for the poor and is thrown out even from there into the mud.

> Dives eram et dilectus
> inter pares preelectus:
> modo curvat me senectus
> et etate sum confectus.
> unde vilis et neglectus
> a deiectis sum deiectus
> quibus rauce sonat pectus,
> mensa gravis, pauper lectus,
> quis nec amor nec affectus,
> sed horrendus est aspectus.

Hugo reveals himself as an idle, insolent, greedy and utterly unprincipled individual; but he was more than an individual. He was a type. Others, who lacked his poetic genius, sank as low or even lower. They formed a new category of the unprivileged; but unlike the rest of the poor they were self-conscious and articulate with abilities above their station. They became, as Primas himself had occasion to be, the natural instruments of any unscrupulous patron who wanted assistance in some dishonest scheme; and on a more general level, over all questions of belief, tradition and social interest they were, disappointed and irresponsible, the natural enemies of the established order.

In this hostility and social irresponsibility, they had certain allies. The urban populations were growing; and for the reasons stated earlier, their way of life did not on the whole fit easily into the dominant feudal and religious pattern. Taken by itself, this fact had as yet little importance. For even the richest merchants still lacked the means to grasp at the prizes that the social order would have denied them. Nor were their economic activities at this time of a sort which would have made them resentful of the usury laws. The only effect therefore of the incipient disharmony which divided their outlook from the established standards of their culture, was a certain restlessness, a slightly greater readiness to question accepted beliefs than was apparent in other circles. There were, however, alongside the peaceful average of the merchant class, certain special categories of mankind in whom this tendency to rebel existed in a somewhat accentuated form. The Jews who even where they were well-treated lived the life of social outcasts, who kept their own distinct culture and whose financial dealings left them open to the most shameless victimisation in the name of current morality, had little incentive to feel friendly towards the existing social and moral system. Their communities became to a small extent the centres from which ideas subversive to that system naturally spread. Even if they did not encourage this, for an instinct of self-preservation must have taught them to hide their strangeness, the process was almost inevitable.

A centre of ideas implies an area over which its influence might spread; and in this instance the area in question was provided by the underprivileged among the educated and by certain elements among the skilled craftsmen who were acquiring a modicum of literacy. Jewellers, painters, workers in glass and precious metals formed an aristocracy of the crafts, members of which were often widely travelled and possessed traditional recipes and information about practical processes which made them appreciative of the parallel achievements of Arab science. Such books as Robert Castrensis' translation of the *Liber de Compositione Alchemiae* (1182) and versions of Avicenna's alchemical treatises must have met with a welcome among them* and familiarised them to some extent with the occult and philosophical ideas as well as with the technical skill of the Arabs.

The presence of this underworld of learning meant that the ideas which came in with the Arab and Aristotelian translations could not be kept within the bounds set by the Chartrains. The students had their contacts among the townsfolk and one might expect them to have been drawn into a particularly close relationship with the poorer men who had intellectual interests. So within the schools as well as outside them a mental climate was created, in which bold speculation was likely to flourish. There were, as we have seen, elements in the Arabic tradition which were irreconcilable with Christian belief and many of these elements (though not all) had their basis in a primitive, prelogical way of thinking. As such they were likely to make a particular appeal to the discontented on the one hand and to the half-educated on the other.

The precise course of events which led up to the condemnation of the new Aristotle is not known to us in detail. The immediate reason for it was the scandal caused by the teachings of one Amaury of Bène, a theological lecturer at what had now become the University of Paris.

Amaury died before the storm burst, but his body was ceremonially disinterred for reburial in unconsecrated ground, and a number of his followers, students and tradesmen of Paris, were executed. So far as one can judge from the brief notices which have come down to us, Amaury's doctrines and those of his supposed inspirer, David of Dinant, owed more to John the Scot than to any Arabic source. Amaury was a pantheist who saw the whole world united in God, while David, also a pantheist, postulated not only God but Mind and Matter as well, to be the basis of the universe. The condemnation of Amaury may, moreover, have had a connection with the campaign against the Albigenses which was just beginning in real earnest. But the fact that the Paris Council of 1210 expressly forbade the reading of Aristotle's books on natural philosophy (as well as of any commentaries upon them), and the renewal of this prohibition in the university statutes sanctioned by Robert of Courçon five years later, suggest that Amaury's heresy was regarded merely as the symptom of a more general evil.*

The theory that we have here primarily a condemnation of Amaury provoked by his Albigensian sympathies, in which the Aristotelian doctrines were involved by the mere accident of their having been taught at the same time, is hardly tenable since the prohibition held good only for Paris and lectures on the new Aristotle were permitted to continue in Toulouse, the very storm-centre of the Albigensian movement.* The ban does appear to have been aimed specifically at the use of the translations which had gained currency since 1140; and its authors plainly had in mind the Parisian setting where, as has been suggested, the elements whose views could not be trusted were largely to be found.

Since, within the next fifteen years such eminent Paris masters as William of Auxerre, Archdeacon of Beauvais, Philip of Grève, Chancellor of the University in 1218, and William of Auvergne who was made a bishop in 1228, wrote treatises containing lengthy references to the *de Generatione et Corruptione*, the *de Anima* and the *Metaphysica Vetus*, treatises which moreover discuss the commentaries of Avicenna, Gebirol and Averroes, it is safe to conclude that the prohibition of public lectures did not affect private studies; and indeed the whole situation was clarified in 1231 when Pope Gregory IX restated the condemnation of 1210 to the effect that the ban was to remain in force only so long as the books in question had not been cleared of error, and appointed a commission to perform this task with William of Auxerre as one of its members.

he fact that the Graeco-Roman natural philosophy made its
arance mixed with oriental elements, and the incidental effects of
social conditions which prevailed in Paris, have served to confuse
main issue. But once we set aside these causes of confusion, a familiar
tern emerges. As happened with all more technical portions of the
classical heritage, there was first a period of preparation during which
the need to draw on classical sources was clearly realised, then there
came a period of what we might call discovery when the sources in
question were explored, and this in turn was followed by a final period
of opposition and assimilation. In the case of the Justinian law, the
period of discovery covers the lifetime of Irnerius and the Four
Doctors. The subsequent assimilation is the work of Accursius and the
Bartolists. In the case of logic the dividing line between the periods is
provided by the death of Abélard, in that of natural philosophy by the
events of 1210. For philosophy, however, the task of primary elucidation had been already completed by the Arabs and required merely
translating, so that serious Western commentaries were not produced
until the need to assimilate the new material had become apparent, and
this fact obscures the parallel we have mentioned. Avicenna and his
translators between them did for natural philosophy the same sort of
service as Lanfranc and Abélard had done for logic and Irnerius for law.

No culture can take over material from outside sources uncondi-
tionally, but must remould what it receives to suit its dominant
ideology and its special circumstances. Normally, the processes of
taking over and remoulding are simultaneous. But in the instances we
have been considering, the technical material taken over from the
classical heritage was contained in texts which were rare and hard to
interpret. Before the content of the *Digest*, the *Organon*, or the *Libri
Naturales* could be remoulded for current use, there had to be a sustained
effort of scholarship and explanation. Such an effort though spread
over a number of years, had to be continuous and could only come
about as the natural expression of an enthusiastic desire for knowledge.
It was bound therefore to produce results in the shape of assimilable
information much faster than that information could be organised and
modified for contemporary purposes. Moreover, the mood which
inspired the often herculean labours of the scholars engaged on this
primary task of interpretation, was in itself likely to be hostile to any
idea of remoulding what had been so hardly won. Thus, we find in all
these cases that the appearance of the material to be absorbed and its
eventual assimilation occur not simultaneously, but successively. There

are periods devoted to the discovery of ancient knowledge, followed by periods when further discoveries are discouraged and when the classical material already to hand is transformed and adapted. The former periods all occur between the years 1050 and 1210 and constitute what is often described as the twelfth-century renaissance. This is an epoch when classical studies are on the whole zealously pursued, and antiquity is looked upon with favour. It is a honeymoon which ends in a mood of sobriety when the thirteenth century finds that it has to set its house in order, stop buying and put each new article of furniture in its appropriate place.

IV. THE STUDY OF LITERATURE

The study of literature during this period differed in a number of essential respects from the professional disciplines whose character we have been examining. Where the lawyers, the doctors and the philosophers were breaking new ground, the grammarians and the writers with purely literary aims had the traditions of the Carolingian Age behind them and moved within a pattern largely determined by the past.

It will be remembered that the original motives for the foundation of schools to teach Latin grammar had been the practical ones to ensure that the Bible was intelligently read and that there were a sufficient number of literate priests and monks to deal with the tasks of civil and ecclesiastical administration. These practical motives did not cease to operate with the reign of Charlemagne. But after the ninth century, their effect was rather to guarantee the maintenance of the existing educational system than to influence the new developments which were taking place. For the system satisfied well enough the needs which had called it into being. There were admittedly a few general improvements which it is reasonable perhaps to attribute to the continued dynamic of these needs. The numbers of the educated steadily increased so that there were always more monks capable of undertaking Biblical or theological studies, more potential administrators with each successive generation and the educated men became steadily more proficient in their handling of Latin. The composition of letters, especially of official letters with their conventional formulae, was taught systematically and in meticulous detail. It became, if not properly an art, at least a high grade professional skill; and towards the close of the period, attempts were made by those engaged in diplomatic correspondence to evolve new styles in the hope of combining a greater lucidity with a more obvious charm. But these developments cannot be regarded as of more than secondary importance. Their influence was restricted and gave no proof of vigour even within the narrow field of its exercise. We should not nowadays expect commercial colleges and civil service crammers to maintain the standards of a university English School; and by the same token we must guard against imagining that the medieval desire for literacy could provide the basis for any but the most elementary sort of literary studies. The impulse for further improvement came from another source.

Already the omnivorous reading of a Servatus Lupus, the delighted verse-writing of a Walafrid Strabo had borne little relation to the utilitarian needs of their time. The Carolingian monks had found that literature possessed a charm of its own. It was pleasant to read Virgil or Cicero, pleasant to compose for oneself in imitation of their style. The enjoyment to be derived from such activities pursued within the familiar quiet of one's monastery walls is a common theme of the ninth-century poets.* Walafrid, Florus, Donatus of Fiesole, all emphasise the intimate association which existed in their minds between poetry and monastic peace. They read of the loves of Dido and the wars of Aeneas, but the impressions which came to them from that reading must have fitted in remarkably with the pattern of a pious and gentle life amid a circle of well-known faces; and when they wrote, their pagan rhythms were more often than not used to celebrate the flowers in their gardens or the departures of their friends.* We may safely conclude that the joy which literature gave these *doctos grammaticos presbiterosque pios** was in the main aesthetic.

But as we move towards the twelfth century the emphasis on monastic quiet becomes less marked and another spirit takes its place, a spirit which had made itself felt once already on an earlier occasion in the worldliness of Charlemagne's courts. The invectives which Otloh of St Emmeram and Peter Damian were to hurl against the students of the classics could not reasonably have been aimed at a Walafrid.* But in the new context of a changing culture, they had their proper target.

One result of increased prosperity in Europe had been to encourage habits of luxurious living. Since the exploitation of the continent's economic resources had not been long in progress, only the most powerful, the largest owners of property, possessed an overplus of worldly goods that could be expended in the service of personal enjoyment. The peasants were still living at the level of bare subsistence. The urban populations were only just beginning to put something by from the proceeds of their industry and trade. Wealth in the degree that permitted ostentatious consumption was a perquisite of the great magnates; but they and their hangers-on had not proved backward in making use of the opportunities it afforded. All the more eminent local princes had their little courts where the niceties of life flourished, where they played an important role in forwarding the allied cults of luxury and pleasure. The pattern set by Charlemagne was repeated not only by such kings as Robert II of France (996–1031), but by such lesser folk as the Norman Belesme.* Indeed, the Normans, though exceptionally warlike and brutal, were also exceptionally fond of material show and sensuous delights. The corruption of the toughest proved appropriately the worst; and the life of that society, which in the eleventh century centred round the family of the Conqueror, has much to remind us of that pageant of passion and glitter which romance associates only with the Renaissance.

Men of letters had their place in these aristocratic coteries from their first beginning. Looking back at the parts played by Angilbert and Einhardt in the amusements of Charlemagne or by John the Scot as the table companion of Charles the Bald, one might be led into dismissing the connection as traditional. Traditions, however, have their reasons for survival; and in this case one potent reason was undoubtedly the habit, common in partially educated communities, of using literary men as the instruments of government. Monks and priests who distinguished themselves by their writings were summoned to the side of some powerful magnate to whom they could be useful. They went willingly if they were ambitious, unwillingly if they valued their peace. In either case, once they were established in their new roles, entrusted with some administrative charge or consulted for expert advice, they were drawn into the life of the court. They learnt to defer to the court ladies; and their superior intelligence was likely to make them as important in the organisation of pleasures as they were in the conduct of business.

The tenth and eleventh centuries form one of the great ages of court poetry. The satirist Adalbero of Laon made his fortune in the entourage of Hugh Capet and then attached himself to Robert II. Hildebert of Lavardin who possessed an exceptional number of aristocratic friends stood high in favour with the Countess Adela and with her sister-in-law the wife of Henry I of England. Godfrey of Rheims sings the praises of the same Adela and does not hesitate to assure that her father William the Conqueror owed his victories to Fate's desire to make her a princess.

Forsitan ignores, quod rex de consule surgit,
quid causae fuerit: filia causa fuit.
nam nec honor nec opes nec equi nec scuta nec enses
culmen ad imperii causa fuere duci,
...ut sceptigeri foret Adela filia regis
regem constitui fata dedere patri.*

Harold, it is to be assumed, never knew why his cause was lost.

Much of this poetry has a notable charm and deserves a high place among the artistic productions of the Middle Ages. One may stop to wonder to what degree the knights and ladies were capable of appreciating the compliments of their learned friends. But what concerns us more nearly is the influence of the courts on the poets and through them on the study of classical literature. New themes came into prominence. Alongside the compliments and laudatory epitaphs written to satisfy the great, we find a considerable body of love poetry. This is the age of the *Cambridge Songs*, of Marbod's 'Quae iuvenis scripsi, senior dum plura retracto', of Baudry's sentimental correspondence with the nun, Constance. A few exceptions apart, these so-called love poems are stilted and artificial, uninspired collections of phrases and ideas culled from classical models. They read like school exercises, and it is impossible to discern what relation they bear to any real feeling or experience. What they do serve to show, however, is that for the first time since the collapse of Rome sexual relationships had become a matter of interest which educated men were prepared to discuss at great length.

The material display of the courts furnished another source of inspiration. Buildings, furniture, clothes, all came in for their due share of description and praise. There is a passage in Baudry of Bourgueil about the Countess Adela's bedroom where the poet's technique is strained to the utmost to depict what must have been for the time a scene of fantastic luxury. The ceiling is painted with the constellations and the planets ordered under the signs of the zodiac. The floor sets out the world in mosaic with the marvels of every land and sea. Tapestries crowd the walls in sufficient numbers to depict events from the Old Testament, from classical legend and from Norman history, while the bed itself is adorned with the figures of the Seven Arts. The poet sees this in a vision; and it is not likely that the reality corresponded in any way with the magnificence he describes. But the magnificence is there; vision or reality, it represented Baudry's ideal and reflected to some extent the taste of the patrons for whom he wrote.*

This passage has many parallels in the writings of Baudry's contemporaries. The love of material splendour is deeply imprinted upon the sensibility of the age. It appears in various disguises, marked by obvious differences of temperament and purpose. But it appears in the best as in the worst. Baudry made his fantasies serve as a vehicle for his learning. The frivolous author of the *Versus Eporedienses* described his mistress's couch in the spirit of a salesman, delighting in luxury for its own sake. Alfanus of Salerno was a man of a different stamp. The elevation of his mind carried him beyond the trivial. He was no courtier. He had no interest in the new social world whose tone was set by the wives and daughters of the great. But the ode in which he celebrated the building of the new basilica at Monte Cassino is filled with the detail of a magnificence which only a connoisseur of the beautiful and the expensive could have appreciated so much. He felt the force of the belief which hallowed the material effort; but for him, as for lesser men, the mosaics, the alabaster, the jewelled chalices and the embroidered vestments had a value which was their own.

Moreover, the delights of love and wealth brought with them, as might be expected, their emotional opposites. The silver lining had its attendant cloud; and the keener search for pleasure meant keener disappointments when pleasure was withheld. Even desire satisfied was likely to have its aftermath of remorse. Alongside the idealising love poetry of the time we find a spate of laments about woman's cruelty and faithlessness. We find invectives against prostitutes. We find the poetry of repentance.

> infecunda mea ficus,
> cuius ramus, ramus siccus,
> incidetur, incendetur,
> si promulgas, quae meretur.*

And the griefs of passion have their counterpart in the griefs of property. Earlier poets had mourned in exile the loss of familiar scenes and faces, but Hildebert of Lavardin when driven overseas by the rivalry of the Count of Maine, bewailed in particular his former possessions, his barns bursting with corn, his beehives, his tapestries and his jewels.

> Nuper eram locuples multisque beatus amicis
> et risere diu prospera fata mihi.
> larga Ceres, deus Arcadiae Bacchusque replebant
> horrea, septa, penum, farre, bidente, mero.
> hortus, apes, famulae, pulmento, melle, tapetis
> ditabant large prandia,vasa, domum.
> dextra laborabat gemmis, pomaria fructu;
> prata redundabant gramine, lacte greges.

187

If the forfeiture of these blessings could be a source of lively misery to the Archbishop of Tours, the fact of having no blessings to forfeit tended in general to provoke an even more bitter emotion. A multitude of satires on clerical greed and avarice bear witness to the acute discontent of those who saw the prizes they had learnt to value snatched from their grasp. The note of personal feeling is unmistakable.

The literature of the tenth and eleventh centuries shows us a changing culture. That of the twelfth represents for the first time the lineaments of modern man. Since the creative fancy is unlikely in this instance to have stolen a march on life, we may assume that the representation had its basis in reality. Greedy, vain, lecherous and sentimental, tormented by envy and divided in frustration between anger and tears, that unlovely figure, which for nearly a millennium the common consensus of moralists has held to be typical of our world, *l'homme moyen sensuel*, makes his bow in the songs of the so-called wandering scholars and in the prose satires which are their proper pendant. All shades of sexual emotion, from its first lyrical hesitancies to the last automatic crudities of an exhausted prurience, all the varied attitudes that spring from appetite and ambition, are present in this literary heritage; and it is some time before one realises that they must be considered together as parts of the same pattern. The delicacies imply the horrors. The *Altercatio Phyllidis et Florae* was brought into existence by the same conjunction of forces that produced the beastly Primas. In the insolence that tinges the Archpoet's regretful acceptance of his own depravity the threads for a moment come together. The pattern of the spontaneity that leads to disaster emerges as a unified whole.

> Feror ego veluti sine nauta navis
> Ut per vias aeris vaga fertur avis,
> Non me tenent vincula, non me tenet clavis,
> Quaero mihi similes et adiungor pravis.

And the description of the disease is followed by the diagnosis of one of its major causes.

> Presul discretissime veniam te precor
> Morte bona moriar dulce nece necor.
> Meum pectus sauciat puellarum decor,
> et quas tactu nequeo saltem corde moechor.

This is a far more successful analysis than we shall get in the several hundred pages of the *Education Sentimentale*.

These new trends which appeared in the European character had their influence also on the study of the classics. They were no more than trends, dominant only in individuals and not yet in society as a whole, where they existed alongside the more conventional monastic and aristocratic patterns. But they sufficed to bring those pagan writers who contribute to their development—the love poets and the satirists —into a greater prominence. The library catalogues of the eleventh and twelfth centuries record a striking increase in the copies of Ovid, Horace, Persius and Juvenal which were in circulation. Terence was another notable favourite, while an analysis of the classical quotations of the literature of the time suggests that no works were more widely read and more lovingly remembered than the *Heroides*, the *Ars Amatoria* and the fourth book of the *Aeneid*.*

Men like Hildebert, Marbod and Baudry wrote their elegies and love poems in imitation of Ovid, copying his rhythms and themes with remarkable skill. They gave expression to the new trends which were actually transforming the sensibility of their time; but to place their work correctly we have to see it also as a product of the schools. It betrays in nearly every line the influence of the classroom exercise. The habit of using Ovid as a model was so widespread, so much a part of the accepted poetic routine, that artistic effects could be drawn from comparatively slight deviations. What the reader is primarily intended to enjoy in the correspondence between Baudry and Constance is the contrast between the structure which follows that of the *Heroides* and the sentiments which are unexpectedly chaste. In the next century, the *Comoediae* showed an even greater dependence on their classical originals. Some of these verse tales derived their content unashamedly from Plautus or Terence while the method of treatment was again taken from Ovid; and titles such as the *Ovidius Puellarum* or the *Ovidius Trium Puellarum* underline the fact that the debt was publicly recognised.

At this point one might add also the observation which Zielinski made concerning the influence of Cicero. The greatest of Latin prose writers was fast recovering from that partial eclipse which his fame had suffered during the Dark Ages and the earlier part of the Carolingian epoch. Though he was read primarily as a master of language, and though his ideas were treated as incidental to his style, they must nevertheless have exercised an effect which was all the more pervasive for being unnoticed. His moral doctrines bore such a strong superficial resemblance to the Christian ethic that they calmed the fears of even the most orthodox who were thus led into accepting points of view which in the final analysis rested on profoundly unchristian presuppositions. Virtue is a word which can cover a multitude of ethical aims; and Cicero's praise of it could sound for all the world like Augustine's. Only a philosopher trained in the ways of ancient thought—and there were not many such—was likely to notice that the Will which Augustine applied as a corrective to Nature, was regarded by Cicero as Nature's handmaiden. Only a philosopher was likely to realise that Cicero considered men to be naturally good and not naturally corrupt as was the Christian view. But many who were not philosophers were unconsciously guided through their easy acceptance of Ciceronian forms of thought to look with far greater respect upon humanity and to allow far greater importance to human impulses than they would have otherwise, so that the increasing popularity of Cicero came to lend some subtle but appreciable support to the hedonism we have been describing. The study of Cicero constituted yet another way in which the new Humanism sapped the strength of the supernaturalist beliefs arrayed against it.*

The reading of the schools which had formerly been largely Christian or had moved within the bounds of some accepted anthology, now included material which from the religious point of view could be classed as undesirable. The inevitable consequence of this was that the murmurs of protest against classical studies—Alcuin's 'there is no reason for you to be corrupted by the wanton eloquence of Virgil's language' and Ermenrich's 'let us renounce Maro as a liar'—swelled to a violent chorus. The very high priests of the Ovidian cult were uneasy. They had pangs of conscience and moments of doubt. Baudry felt it necessary to have recourse to the erotic poet's conventional apology and assured his readers that if his verses were frivolous, his heart and mind were pure,* while Marbod, who had always been more inclined to respectability, published in his old age what amounts to a condemnation of Ovid and all his works. Children are beaten at school, he exclaims, and to what purpose? That they might learn about the debaucheries and adulteries of the pagan gods, about lascivious youths and unchaste girls linked in the pursuit of a pleasure we ought to shun. Their simple minds are corrupted and having had a taste of sin, they long to follow the examples they have been given.*

Marbod did not extend his condemnation beyond what was patently immoral. He set a high value on poetry as such and was prepared to maintain that love, provided that it remained chaste, had a place in the lives of the young. But if one of the most popular contemporary poets and the head of the famous classical school at Angers was prepared to go so far in attacking the trends he represented, others with a different background which made them less sympathetic to ancient learning naturally went much further; and in the monasteries all pagan poetry without exception came to be regarded as the possible instrument of sin.

The sermons and letters of the time furnish numerous examples of the deep feeling of guilt which any classical reading was likely to produce. Otloh of St Emmeram relates that at one time he was fascinated by Lucan whom he read outside the monastery gates. In consequence, a whole series of unpleasant manifestations occurred. A hot wind of which nobody else seemed aware seared his skin. He had a vision in which he was harried by a monster; and finally since, ignorant of the meaning of these portents, he persisted in his reading, a huge man came in a dream and beat him black and blue. Such violent hysterical effects seem out of all proportion to their actual cause. Lucan for all his lurid rhetoric is an innocent writer. The situation is only explicable if we take the reading of the *Pharsalia* as the first step towards the indulgence of an unwholesome desire, if Otloh felt it to be the beginning of the road down which the wandering scholars drifted to the Archpoet's hell.

In Italy paganism had even darker associations. If we are to believe certain dark hints in Anselm of Bisate, the pleasure-loving clerks of Lombardy indulged not only in erotic dreams but in magic practices for erotic ends, practices in which the names of the ancient gods commonly figured.* In the story of Vilgardus, a student of Ravenna at the end of the tenth century who, on being accused of heretical beliefs, claimed to have been misled by demons in the guise of Virgil, Horace and Juvenal, the same conjunction of pagan literature, heresy and magic suggestively appears.* It is small wonder that he was condemned, and that the pious looked upon his like with deep suspicion.

During the end of the eleventh and the beginning of the twelfth century, the attack on the immorality of classical studies became outspoken and comprehensive. The dislike of Ovidian immorality became linked with the fears aroused by the excesses of dialectic and led to ancient philosophy, rhetoric and literature being confounded in a single all-embracing denunciation. I reject Plato, cries St Peter Damian. I set no store by Pythagoras. I renounce the works of Aristotle and Euclid. The rhetoricians with their syllogisms and sophistical cavillings are unworthy of this enquiry. The passage occurs in a treatise expounding the advantages of the solitary life. What use would I have, he goes on, for the fantasies of poets who are in any case mad? And the tragic and comic dramatists, the satirists and the orators are named in turn and consigned to the darkness which is properly theirs, besmirched by the dregs of earthly wisdom. Damian prefers to put his trust in the simplicity of Christ. *Christi me simplicitas doceat.** This is an overstatement of the monastic case and bears rather clearly the stamp of the rhetorical training the saint had received in his youth. Nevertheless, it has its importance; for Damian was not alone in holding these sentiments. His younger contemporary Manegold of Lautenbach, writing in 1085, branded the poets as jesters at the marriage feast of idolatry. They worked only for gain and corrupted the minds of sinners with their fantasies.* Herbert of Losinga, the first bishop of Norwich, who died in 1119, relates like Otloh that he was stopped by a dream from the reading and imitation of Virgil and Ovid.* There was a considerable body of anti-Humanist opinion which was bound to give support to the view that monks ought not to learn anything but their psalter.*

It would be wrong, however, to imagine that the cathedral schools were given over to the exclusive cult of erotic poetry or that the monasteries were the homes of an anti-classical obscurantism. These trends had an undoubted importance; but at the same time the old traditions of a classical learning within the bounds of the Christian outlook were maintained and even deepened. For evidence of this we have only to turn to the epic poems and histories of the age. The epic tradition was based in the main on the conscientious study of Virgil, and the extent to which that study was carried as well as the technical triumphs which resulted from it had already been demonstrated in the tenth century *Waltharius*. In Ekkehard's great poem the new wine of German heroic legend sparkles with superb effect in the glass of classical form. Not only the language, but many of the devices through which the story is presented, the carefully planned confusion of the battle scenes, the boasts, the debates, the personal combats, the occasional laments are all Virgilian in their origin. Ekkehard managed to give his borrowed material an unexpected freshness by retaining the Germanic atmosphere of his legend; and his success was of a sort to encourage others to follow his method. They did so with varying skill, but good or bad, they are without exception faithful to their classical sources, to Virgil, Lucan and Statius. No Roman ever knew the tricks of Silver Age rhetoric so thoroughly as the twelfth-century Joseph of Exeter; and the triumph of the medieval epic tradition in the *Alexandreis* of Walter of Châtillon was amply deserved. It furnishes us with solid proof (if proof is needed) that the cathedral schools had interests beyond the composition of light verse, that a vast amount of advanced and capable work must have been done on the structure and style of the more sober forms of classical poetry. These medieval writers knew just as much about the Latin epic as the pundits of the High Renaissance.

The writing of history is another field in which the hard work of the classroom earned notable dividends. Since the time when Einhard imitated Suetonius in his life of Charlemagne, and Rémi of Auxerre edited his master's excerpts from Valerius Maximus, the study of the ancient historians had proceeded with an ever increasing vigour. Justin had been popular since the eighth century; but with the eleventh, Sallust and Livy, and with the twelfth, Caesar, begin to appear frequently in the surviving catalogues. The disputes of the time made the knowledge of earlier arrangements and precedents a vital advantage, and it was this fact even more than a general interest in the past which gave a violent impetus to historical composition. Abbots, Bishops, Princes and even municipalities were ready to encourage students, who on the other hand could not organise their local detail without reference to a wider schema. The local presupposed the general; and history developed in all its branches.

This contemporary effort was bound to lead to a close study of the ancient historians both as models and sources; and we have only to glance at William of Poitiers' panegyric of the Conqueror, with its reminiscences of Sallust, at William of Malmesbury's history of the English kings,* at the early chapters of the *Gesta Treverorum* which repeat nearly everything Caesar said about the tribe, to realise how intimate that study was and how important were its effects. The writers whose field extended beyond the confines of a locality or period owed an even greater debt to the past. The *Chronicon*, in which Otto of Freising made his graphic attempt to write a Christian history of the world, provides most convincing evidence with its many quotations from the *de Officiis* and its many references to Plato, Seneca and Boethius that in some monastic circles the classics were well-known and what is more were highly respected.

All these different attitudes of favour and opposition and compromise had their pendant in an educational system whose character was singularly elastic. The complex motivations of twelfth-century society were reflected in the cathedral schools which formed the focus of that system, and some account of these schools is therefore necessary if we are to have a clear picture of the period. They had risen from small beginnings. The great advances which were made in education between the age of Alcuin and the age of Abélard had been for the most part the work of the monasteries. If the monks and the secular clergy of the eleventh century were, generally speaking, literate and even learned, the credit must go to the movement which produced Fulda, St Gallen and Corbey. But although the initiative had belonged to the religious houses, the bishops had not been altogether idle. Charlemagne's capitulary of 789 had advocated the establishment of schools by the cathedrals as well as by the monasteries. Its injunctions had been repeated in various forms during the succeeding centuries;* and they had had their effect. By the end of the tenth century there were a fair number of cathedral schools alongside their monastic counterparts.

Up to this time many monasteries had followed the practice of accepting outside pupils. A few had even set up special schools for *externi*; but their action had been primarily a response to the emergency created by the lack of educational facilities. When the emergency came to an end with the rise of the cathedral schools, their tendency was to concentrate more and more on the training of their own novices as the rule of St Benedict ordained. The cathedral schools on the other hand, which existed for the training of the secular clergy, could accept all those who had received or intended to receive even minor orders: a class which included many people who had no intention of proceeding to the priesthood. So when the situation arose that large numbers required to learn Latin for non-religious purposes, for use in law or medicine or administration, it was to the cathedral schools that these new recruits automatically flocked, the more so because the latter were physically handy in the cities instead of being tucked away in some remote corner of the countryside.

The great period of expansion for the cathedral schools was between 1050 and 1150. Instead of one master appointed by the Bishop to take charge of a small class of boys, they came to consist of groups of masters, licensed rather than appointed, whose teaching was of a higher standard than had been customary in earlier times, and who attracted much larger numbers of students of all ages. These were the schools from which the Western universities were later to emerge.

The teachers who thus collected round the great cathedrals and the more famous collegiate churches like St Geneviève in Paris gave instruction not so much in the elements of Latin as in advanced grammar which involved the reading of authors; and they also treated rhetoric, the subjects of the Quadrivium which served as a preparation for medicine, elementary law and above all dialectic. Rheims under Gerbert and later the schools of Chartres were famous for their science. Bologna acquired a great reputation first for literary studies and later for Roman law, while Paris became the centre for theology, dialectic and philosophical learning in general. They all served professional rather than strictly religious aims. Even the education they offered to those whose careers were to lie within the Church was primarily technical in character. For theology, especially the philosophical theology of the twelfth century, Canon Law, and the niceties of ecclesiastical administration must in the last analysis be regarded as professional interests. And in addition they seem to have drawn into their classrooms an appreciable number of those who intended to spend their lives in definitely lay pursuits, in legal work, medicine, or municipal and feudal business. Their fundamentally non-religious character was long masked, however, by the fact that their students were all supposed to be clerics. The convenient clerical status conferred by the possession of minor orders enabled them to welcome not only the type of student who even at an earlier date might anyway have attended an ecclesiastical school, but also those categories who formerly would have been educated in a private and unorganised fashion by lay teachers.*

Since these schools were brought into existence by the needs of the professions, it is not surprising that so many of them should have developed a specialist character. It is important to remember in this connection that originally their curriculum had been elementary in character. Their purpose had been to teach Latin; and the new studies were in every case superimposed upon the old. A schoolmaster would happen to be interested in some desirable speciality, in law, science or rhetoric. He would teach this to his older pupils. His reputation would spread; and others who found such studies useful would come to hear him. Sometimes, a famous teacher found himself with so many pupils that he was forced to appoint assistants, and such a one on his death left a tradition behind him. The smaller schools changed their character as they changed their personnel. But some of the larger ones developed along the lines which had first brought them success and became eventually recognised centres for particular subjects. So Chartres never abandoned the scientific orientation given to it originally by Fulbert, though its later masters added literature as a second speciality. Bologna became the great school of law, while Paris at one time had almost a monopoly of philosophical learning.

13-2

Since our purpose is to consider classical studies, we shall do well to divide these schools into two groups: the professional and the literary. For the classical learning of centres like Paris, Bologna and Salerno was necessarily limited by their specialised interests. The lawyers knew their *Digest*, the doctors their Hippocrates and their Galen, the philosophers their Aristotle. They were probably more familiar with these works than any previous scholars had ever yet been with any pagan author. But their knowledge was intensive, not extensive. The only students to gain a broad understanding of the classics were those trained in the few schools where literature was specifically studied as was the case in Chartres or Orléans.

Our best evidence about the teaching of the classics during this period is the famous passage in John of Salisbury's *Metalogicon* where he describes the methods used by Bernard of Chartres.* Every evening Bernard would expound a classical text in the traditional way, that is along the lines followed by Servius. He explained grammatical problems, pointed out the different figures of rhetoric, placing particular emphasis on the use of metaphor and propriety in the choice of adjectives. He analysed the arguments used and supplied any extraneous facts necessary for the understanding of what was said. He arranged his lessons in such a way (presumably by means of a judicious choice of authors) that within a year he would cover the whole of Latin grammar. This lecture was then followed by the setting of prose and verse compositions to be done for the next day. Bernard encouraged imitation. Indeed, most of his remarks on style seem to have been made for the purpose of indicating to his pupils procedures they might follow in their own compositions. And then to wind up with, there was a short colloquy on some religious topic. Next morning, the boys had to repeat what they had learnt the previous day. Their exercises were marked. And they may have practised giving short sermons themselves.*

There are two points about this account which deserve to be noted. The first is that no mention is made of any allegorical or philosophical exposition. As Paré and his collaborators point out the medieval instructor on a religious text was concerned to bring out first the meaning of the words (*littera*), then the surface meaning of the book as a whole (*sensus*) and finally its deeper meaning (*sententia*). Bernard's teaching appears to have stopped short at the second of these stages. The other point we ought to consider concerns the 'imitation' that is mentioned by John of Salisbury. There is no evidence that Bernard's pupils were familiar with the elaborate techniques which we discussed above in connection with Chrysoloras and which the fifteenth-century Humanists used when they 'imitated' an author. All John tells us is that Bernard called the attention of his class to tricks of style which he advised them to work into their own compositions. There is nothing in this passage and nothing in the surviving works of the Chartrains to suggest that they made a conscious effort always to give words their exact classical sense, or that they collected classical expressions until they had enough of them to serve all possible needs. Imitation to them meant the use of correct grammar, the reproduction of definite rhetorical turns like antithesis, metonomy, antimetaboly and so forth. They never contemplated such a revival of classical Latin as would have brought in its train classical ways of thought by the mere process of linguistic assimilation.

Thus, apart from the progress made in the professional disciplines, the general effect of such changes as did occur in the curriculum and methods of the schools was to intensify the absorption of classical material in ways with which our study of the Carolingian period has made us familiar. There was the same somewhat free imitation of the classical genres in prose and poetry. There was the same haphazard borrowing of facts and ideas. Only the field covered by the general reader had been substantially extended.

The elementary course which every schoolboy covered now included in addition to the *Disticha Catonis*, Maximian, Avian, Aesop, the *Ilias Latina* and the *Ecloga Theoduli*. But many, perhaps most, students went beyond these limits. There is a critical excursus in the *Ars Lectoria* of Aimeric (1086) which divides the pagan authors into three classes according to merit. The lowest includes the school texts mentioned above. The highest is reserved for Terence, Virgil, Horace, Ovid, Lucan, Statius, Juvenal, Persius and Sallust. In between, we have Plautus, Cicero, Boethius, Ennius, Varro, the grammarians and the Latin translation of the *Timaeus*. A list of authors recommended for school study which appears in a thirteenth-century manuscript and which has been attributed to the Cirencester abbot, Alexander Neckham, gives a similar picture, adding a few details as to the particular works to be read. In the case of Cicero these are the *de Oratore*, the *Tusculanae Disputationes*, the *de Amicitia*, the *de Senectute*, the *de Fato*, the *Paradoxa*, the *de Officiis* and the *de Natura Deorum*; in the case of Ovid the *Metamorphoses* and the *de Remedio Amoris*. Neither Aimeric nor Neckham claims to be describing the actual curriculum of his day.

Aimeric is trying to make a critical evaluation, Neckham to outline an ideal literature course. The inclusion by the former of Ennius and Varro, by the latter of such works as the *de Natura Deorum* and Seneca's *Declamationes* indicates the somewhat theoretical character of their statements. Nevertheless, it is obvious that the lists they give cannot have been entirely fanciful. The eleventh- and twelfth-century catalogues provide ample evidence for the growing popularity of the eight major school poets, though as far as Ovid is concerned the *Heroides* and the *Ars Amatoria* which Neckham passes over in silence were much better known than the *Fasti* which he recommends. Nor is there any reason to doubt the vogue of Sallust and of such Ciceronian writings as the *de Amicitia*, the *de Senectute*, the *de Officiis* and the *Paradoxa*. The conclusion is inescapable that the contemporaries of Abélard knew far more about the classical literature than did the contemporaries of Alcuin.

Some mention has already been made of the system of imitation which was in common use and which may fairly be described as haphazard by comparison with the Atticism practised in Byzantium. The difference between East and West in this respect was not one of technique but of the degree to which the relevant techniques were employed. Like the Atticists, the scholars of the medieval West analysed their models and picked out words, figures of speech, forms of argument, metaphors, anecdotes and even observable generalities of structure which they stored in their minds or note-books for future use. But while the Byzantine Atticists constructed the whole, or nearly the whole, of their work from these borrowed elements, their Western colleagues were content if they managed to set an occasional gem of classical provenance—an image from Virgil, a phrase from Cicero, a reference to some pagan story—in a mosaic of their own making. The greater freedom of the Western system had its advantages. It enabled the West to produce poetry which is still regarded as worthy of the name, while the Byzantine writers had to be largely content to score their triumphs in prose. It also facilitated the absorption of classical material into the popular culture of the time, by limiting the amount of that material and also by completing at a learned level the first stage in the mixing of classical and contemporary elements.* Even so, as we shall see, more was taken over from ancient sources than could be readily assimilated; and it is evident that if the scholars of the time had followed a more stringent system, if they had copied their authors as the Byzantines copied the Attic orators or as the Renaissance Humanists were to copy Cicero, they would have speedily lost contact with the varied development of their world which was not yet ready for such a thorough-going classicism.

We must not, however, in appreciating the merits of the Western system, neglect the obverse of the medal. The type of imitation generally practised dominated the methods of study outside the professional disciplines and determined therefore the impression made by the reading of the classics. Since the imitation was haphazard, the impression had also something of the same character.

The Western student took as many precious stones as he could from the mosaic of the classical heritage and used these to construct his own patterns. Thus, his learning appears for the most part in the form of illustrations. When John of Salisbury wants to show the value of hardihood, he does so by quoting an anecdote about Scipio Africanus sharing the food of the common soldiers. In another passage he proves the folly of the contemporary passion for hunting by examples which show that neither Caesar nor Alexander took any interest in the chase. The presence of a great number of these references indicates that John knew many of the facts of ancient history. But did his knowledge amount to a real understanding? Liebeschuetz in a recent work examines the references to Scipio and is forced to conclude that they fail to compose a general picture of Scipio's personality. The classical anecdotes torn from their context have a purely rhetorical character. They exist in John's consciousness as a collection of examples to back his moral judgements, which spring ready-made out of his own experience. So, for example, he has a definition of tyranny formulated to cover the rapacious barons who had caused so much suffering in Stephen's reign: a tyrant is one who goes too far in trying to secure for himself a free field of action. By that token Alexander and Caesar were both tyrants. They misused their natural talents through an excessive desire for glory, and John happily condemns in them the sins of Geoffrey of Mandeville.

John's work is typical. He is the medieval classicist as we find him outside the strictly professional fields. His classical knowledge is not narrow, but it is fragmentary and it influences his view of the world from the outside, modifying his opinions here and there, widening his experience but not as yet providing the kernel of his thought. When the Renaissance Humanists eventually decided to write classical Latin and nothing but classical Latin, they forced themselves by so doing to arrange their experience in the categories common to their classical models, with the result that they entered a new world which gradually became their own to such an extent as to transform even their daily thinking in the vernaculars. The absence of this linguistic rigour in the imitation of the Middle Ages meant that the ancient categories of thought were not wholeheartedly adopted. If they had been, then the later Humanist effort would have been rendered unnecessary. Outside of the specialities of law and logic, the twelfth century did not remould its approach to experience in conformity with a classical pattern. It merely traversed the first stage of that process. It gained a general familiarity with classical ideas, mapped out, so to speak, the territory which its successors were to occupy.

V. THE GENERAL CHARACTER OF THE TWELFTH-CENTURY REVIVAL OF LEARNING

We shall find it convenient to draw together at this point the separate threads of the four preceding sections. We have been considering a period when, against a background of material improvement, men discovered that they could benefit from a closer knowledge of the classical heritage and hastened to take advantage of that discovery. Great efforts were made to utilise the information available in the surviving Latin and Greek texts on such specialised subjects as rhetoric, law, logic and medicine. At the same time, the study of the non-specialised and as yet undifferentiated parts of human knowledge subsumed under the heading of grammar, and covering such important topics as history, literary criticism and political thought, was also intensified. As a result, a vast amount of classical material became known to the educated section of the Western world between 1000 and 1150. Since it had been necessary to open schools, to organise the copying of manuscripts and to train scholars who could interpret them, since it had been necessary in short to set going an impressive educational machine, before any of the information contained in the classics could be made available for general use, there arose a certain disharmony between the rate at which that information was eventually produced and the rate at which it could be absorbed. Once the machinery was in motion, it yielded far more material than could be readily or even safely utilised. So the enthusiasm for classical learning was accompanied by a mood of opposition among groups who felt that the professional students were going too fast and too far. The rhetorical zeal of Anselm of Bisate had its critic in Rotiland. The trust which Abélard vowed to dialectic was matched by the distrust voiced by St Bernard; and on the literary side, the cult of erotic poetry in aristocratic circles and among the less-orderly clerks led to those general condemnations of pagan authors which we find in Peter Damian or Manegold of Lautenbach. Then, after 1150 when the interest in logic and medicine combined to promote a widespread study ot Aristotle and his Arabic commentators, the dangers of heresy implicit in these works led to even stronger protests which reached their climax in the official ban in 1210; and during the same period the need to transform Roman law to suit feudal conditions was finally recognised.

It is important to remember that these various anti-classical movements were not co-ordinated, nor were they organised in themselves. They resulted in each field from a spontaneous feeling of distrust aroused by the sometimes excessive enthusiasm of the professional scholars and from an understandable fear lest the framework of Christian civilisation should be undermined by the popularity of pagan ideas. The Church intervened officially only at times when some specific doctrines were threatened, as happened in the case of Abélard and later of Amaury. For a long time this distrust and fear co-existed with the advance of classical studies. The initial opposition against rhetoric faded as the cult of rhetorical argument gave place to a preoccupation with dialectic. The opposition to dialectic faded as the *Organon* was shown to have its uses for Christian learning. But eventually the pendulum swung the other way. The impetus of the classical revival weakened as the needs which had given it birth were one by one fulfilled; its adversaries gathered strength; and by the second half of the twelfth century, caution rather than humanist zeal was coming to dominate the general climate of educated opinion. The age which had produced John of Salisbury and Walter of Châtillon in literature and the Four Doctors in law drew slowly to a close. For the moment indeed the work of classical discovery was done and the work of assimilation was due to begin.

CHAPTER V

THE SCHOLASTIC AGE

The organic character of cultural growth is an observable fact which recent research has done much to underline. Historians and anthropologists have shown from their different standpoints that the various fields of human activity are closely interrelated and dominated in every epoch by certain pervasive tendencies. In the Renaissance there is the spirit of individualism, in the Baroque Age the spirit of centralised order. The life of the Trobriand islanders described by Malinowski centres on the meticulous recognition of reciprocal duties, that of the North American Zuñi on a love of ceremoniousness. By the same token it is possible to note after the middle of the twelfth century the widespread workings of what one might fairly call a spirit of organisation. The object of this organising interest was the whole of human knowledge, but it concentrated more particularly upon that new information which had come to light as a result of the study of classical sources during the preceding two hundred years, and which was still to a great extent an alien element in the existing medieval system.

Various circumstances combined to produce the mental climate of this epoch, which we may perhaps call the Age of Scholasticism after the most eminent of its intellectual products. The essentials of ancient rhetoric, law, medicine, logic and natural philosophy had been laid bare. Further work along the lines followed by an Anselm of Bisate, an Irnerius, an Abélard, a Constantine or a Gundisalvi was not likely to produce memorable fruit. The point had been reached where the specialists were bound to be more attracted by the thought of applying their knowledge to current problems than by a research into the past, whose results might prove of doubtful value; and the impetus which classical studies had derived from the great professional disciplines died slowly away.

Then there was the question of relationship between Christian and pagan thought. Their disharmony has been frequently mentioned in these pages. Presupposing the existence of an ordered universe, the creation of a personal God, the Christian outlook subordinated the self-regarding impulse to a morality based on the Creator's will. Men were expected to find the final purpose of their lives not only outside of themselves, but outside of that immediate environment with which their selfish interests could be most easily identified. The pattern of Christian culture tended to deny the egoist his natural satisfactions and offered socially approved opportunities for development to those whose temperaments inclined them to selfless service. The pagan outlook was less altruistic. It is true that originally the moral systems characteristic of Hellenic culture had their centre outside the individual in the welfare of the city as a whole. But even by the Periclean era the standards of Creon were an anachronism. And it was not to the standards of Antigone that they yielded. If we want to typify the new morality, we must look to Alcibiades. Similarly in Rome by the first century B.C. the typical patriot was no longer a Regulus but a Cato or a Brutus. Self-abnegation had been replaced by committed ambition. Thus, the pattern of culture which the classical literatures reflect differed from the Christian in allowing man's egoistic impulses an ample measure of overt satisfaction. The institutions, customs and values characteristic of the Graeco-Roman Empire were by and large centred on the main-tenance of private interest, modifying its free pursuit only in so far as the safety of the state or the avoidance of disruptive personal conflicts made some sacrifices necessary.

All religious cultures are to be distinguished from their secular counterparts by their pursuit of values which the secular mind considers arbitrary; and the importance of this distinction is manifest. But it must be emphasised that in the particular case of the classical and the Christian ways of life this general distinction was not the only one. The supernaturalism of Christianity had the additional effect of making the culture it dominated not only arbitrary, but also altruistic. Its purposes were located in the sphere to which Spinoza gives the name of Human Freedom as opposed to the sphere of Human Bondage. It tended to encourage those who preferred to live for ends outside of themselves, and conversely to discourage the self-centred. The Christian world was opposed therefore to the pagan not only by its religious emphases but by virtue of its whole configuration.

When we take these facts into account, it becomes obvious that the Christian society of the Middle Ages was bound to have difficulties in using its classical heritage. The adoption of classical ideas, which could not but have an effect on men's actions, was likely to prove disruptive of the Christian pattern; and when these ideas appeared, as they did during the twelfth century, in exceptionally large numbers, the dangers of disruption were multiplied.

It is not intended to suggest that the Christians of the time were aware of the problem in quite these terms. Their objections were particular rather than general. They set their face against single pagan traits or specific groups of traits, against a heretical belief about the nature of matter, against the cult of Ovid, against Abélard's overweening confidence in dialectic. But as the classical heritage came to play a greater and greater part in the intellectual life of the eleventh and twelfth centuries, so the number of points on which exception could be taken to its teachings also increased. While the need was still urgent for information from ancient sources, the men who cried out against the learning of the schools had comparatively little influence. The protests aroused by the irresponsibility of the professional rhetoricians faded out when rhetoric was replaced by law and dialectic as the main objects of humanist interest. The attack on Abélard fell silent when his successors demonstrated the usefulness of his methods. The disapproval aroused by courtly and erotic poetry extended less and less to classical studies as the direct imitation of Ovid was replaced by a tradition of vernacular song. But enough opposition remained to form a weighty background to the new objections aroused during the second half of the twelfth century by the natural philosophy of Aristotle.

We cannot read Peter Damian, Manegold or Bernard of Clairvaux without being convinced that the unchristian character of classical learning was amply realised. At the same time, the history of the great specialities bears clear witness to the need there was for classical knowledge and to the wide enthusiasm which the rhetoric, law, logic and philosophy of the ancients successively kindled. Given such a thesis and antithesis, some men of good will were bound to seek for a compromise, the more so since St Jerome had pointed out the way with reference to a famous text in Deuteronomy (xxi, 11–13).

And seest among the captives a beautiful woman, and hast a desire unto her, that thou wouldest have her to be thy wife; then thou shalt bring her home to thy house; and she shall shave her head and pare her nails; and she shall put the raiment of her captivity from off her, and shall remain in thy house, and bewail her father and her mother a full month; and after that thou shalt go in to her, and be her husband and she shall be thy wife.

The Christian could utilise pagan literature if he was prepared to discard all alien elements that he did not require. It was a method which even so outspoken a critic of the rhetoricians and philosophers as Peter Damian was prepared to countenance.* Nor were practical examples wanting. Had not Prudentius and Sedulius written poetry that was essentially Christian and yet possessed the technical perfection of the best classical verse? Had not Lactantius equalled Cicero? Had not Anselm of Canterbury and Peter Lombard demonstrated the Christian use of logic, making it clear that belief was a necessary preliminary to understanding?

It is not surprising therefore that during the period we shall now study there should have been a conscientious attempt to cut the hair and pare the nails of the captive whom the humanist victories had brought into the medieval house. This time at least the fair prisoner was not to be allowed to master her less civilised conquerors. Something had to be done. The intellectual tradition now contained a vast mass of classical knowledge. It was necessary that this knowledge should be purified of the elements which the Christian conscience was bound to reject. The task, however, was to prove more difficult than Jerome's metaphor led men to believe. Indeed, the metaphor proved totally misleading. Men found that they could not simply sort out the good and the bad, to treasure the former and discard the latter. Much more complicated processes were involved.

The development of logic had given some hint of this. The *Organon* had not been purified in Jerome's sense of the word. If the Aristotelian techniques of argument had appeared dangerous in the hands of Abélard and innocuous in those of Peter Lombard, it was not because Peter had discarded such as appeared to him unchristian. His orthodoxy was not the result of a careful system of rejection. It derived from the Christian nature of his approach, from his determination to maintain intact the teachings of the Church.

The taming of logic had already begun with the work of Anselm of Canterbury even before the enthusiasm for newly discovered parts of the *Organon* had attained its peak. Let us not forget that the danger of the enthusiasm lay in its tendency to go to extremes; the Church could not allow human reason to become the judge of dogma. It could not allow men to reject parts of its teaching because these did not square logically with whatever premises they chose to accept. On the other hand let us not forget that logic, though dangerous, was indispensable for theology, seeing that it provided the only means whereby the contradictions of the Fathers could be reconciled. Anselm of Canterbury had found the famous formula which served simultaneously to justify the utilisation of logic and to indicate the limits within which that utilisation was permissible. The activity of theology was defined as *fides quaerens intellectum*. The theologian was to accept as a matter of faith the teaching of the Church, and was then to have recourse to logic merely in order to construct a rational explanation of what he had learnt by faith. In other words, logic was to be used first to explain contradictions in patristic teaching and secondly to reinforce the edifice of dogma by establishing rational connections between its several parts. It was not, however, at any point to sit in judgement over dogma. It was to be a servant, not a master.

Anselm's suggestions were not immediately accepted. Indeed for a generation or so his work seems to have attracted remarkably little notice: and Abélard, who tended to overvalue reason, had time to explain in the preface to the *Sic et Non* his method of criticism by the confrontation of opposing texts, and was able to enumerate a large number of Scriptural instances to which that method could be applied. Abélard was condemned; but his technique which at first sight appeared too boldly rationalistic proved in the upshot the perfect instrument for carrying the aims of Anselm. It will be remembered that according to Abélard the contradiction between two texts could generally be ironed out by the use of grammatical and dialectical criticism; in other words by quibbles about the meaning of words and distinctions concerning what they implied. Therefore the correctness of established doctrine could always be demonstrated; and that was the line of argument which Abélard's successors, and especially Peter Lombard, chose to follow. Moreover, once the technique was established its use could be generalised. It was no longer applied only in cases where the Fathers differed and where there was real doubt. Misinterpretations were eventually invented for all dogmas and argued away as a matter of scholastic training.

By the middle of the thirteenth century, philosophical ideas were normally presented throughout all the universities of Europe in the form of a *quaestio*, or inquest in which a doctrinally acceptable thesis was defended against objections raised sometimes by the speaker himself but sometimes by a devil's advocate. These objections mostly consisted of an unassailable major followed by a misleading minor premiss whose implications had then to be separated out or distinguished, the incorrect rejected and the correct shown to be in harmony with accepted doctrine. The use of this technique over a period of years made scholastic theology if not logically coherent in all its parts, then at least practically unanswerable by the methods open to Aristotelian logic, for objectors could be led from distinction to distinction until they lost themselves in a maze of argument. By the thirteenth century the new logic was no longer a danger.

In logic the need had been for reorientation. Roman law and Graeco-Arab natural philosophy were to present tougher problems. Like the *Organon*, the teachings of the *Digest* and the Aristotelian *Corpus* formed interconnected systems from which very little could be discarded without injuring the main fabric. On the other hand, they could not be accepted in their totality for they conflicted, the one with feudal usage, the other with Christian belief. Different but equally awkward difficulties existed in the case of literature. The Latin language and the principles of rhetoric could be learnt, as Alcuin had shown, without much reference to the pagan authors. But since Carolingian times, the medieval world had become attracted to the authors themselves, to the excellence of their style which no handbook could replace, to their imagery and their ideas. Here, it would seem at first sight, was a field in which the principle of selection could be effectively applied. Harmless poems or prose writings could be popularised in anthologies. The lascivious or the heathenish could be omitted at least in the school reading of standard works. And to some extent these methods were employed. But they did not suffice to solve the problem. For the unchristian element in many of the most widely read classical works—among which the *Metamorphoses* may be instanced—formed too great a part of the whole to be easily excised. What indeed would remain of Ovid's fantastic poem, if you removed all references to the gods and all passages that deal with sensual love? It is easier to conceive of *Hamlet* without its prince.

To find the answer to these difficulties was the achievement of the Scholastic Age. The three subjects mentioned were tackled independently by different groups of men whose work derived its cohesion not from any overall plan, not from the guidance of a genius, but merely from the vague feelings outlined above. Their success was for that reason all the more remarkable.

I. THE REORGANISATION OF LITERARY STUDIES

The literary culture of the eleventh century had been confined to restricted groups in a small number of centres. It was not until the time of Abélard that the groups had grown larger and the centres more numerous. Guibert of Nogent, a contemporary of Abélard, tells us that in his youth learning was badly neglected. Travellers could pass through town after town without ever finding a schoolmaster. And then he goes on to rejoice at the great change which he himself had fostered and whose result had been to establish a host of schools and to encourage a lively interest in literary studies.*

It will be most convenient to start with the changes which occurred in the teaching of grammar itself, taking the word now in its modern sense to mean merely that systematisation of morphology and syntax which we rely on to facilitate our study of a language. Here the pioneer was a certain Peter Helias (fl. 1140–50) who is reputed to have been the Peter Lombard of his particular field. It will be remembered that great classical grammarians had been descriptive in their methods. Donatus and Priscian, whose works had been the grammatical bible of the centuries previous to the twelfth, trace the general rules of language: that is they establish morphological and syntactical uniformities and note the obvious exceptions with proofs drawn from the best authors. The student of the *Ars Maior* or the *Institutiones* is at every step brought face to face with the fact that the Latin he is learning is the language of Rome's golden age, and that his business is to take these authors for his models. The school of Chartres, as can be seen from the *Heptateuchon* of Theodore, still put its faith in this tradition as late as the middle of the century. But Chartres was the great centre of traditional scholarship; and Peter Helias who taught in Paris worked along other lines. He introduced dialectic into grammar. He was interested not so much in the facts of language as in the causes of those facts. He tried to construct a Latin for which the authority was not usage but reason,* finding logical explanations for the existence of the different parts of speech and for the relationship between them. As a result, he weakened to some extent the traditional authority of the pagan writers as the only proper models of usage, while satisfying the contemporary taste for logic and the contemporary zest for creation. For if language could be derived from logic, the age of Abélard could surely feel itself entitled to embark on the work of linguistic experiment. Since the theories of Helias harmonised with the taste of the moment, they enjoyed a wide popularity, dominated the schools and were displaced only after some fifty years by the more ambitious *Doctrinale* of Alexander of Villedieu which went further along the same lines.

Alexander, a Norman who had studied in Paris and then taught in Brittany, compiled his curious masterpiece round about 1199. The story goes that he based it on the doggerels he had composed to teach grammar rules to his boys and certainly great tracts of it do recall the verses at the end of Kennedy's Primer. Intended for study after the *Ars Minor*, its indisputable handiness must account in part for its great popularity. Otherwise it would hardly have played so great a part in French grammar teaching until the later sixteenth century. Superficially it appears less logic-ridden than the works of Helias, but that impression is dispelled if one considers the book in closer detail. The fact is that Alexander does not feel it necessary, as his predecessors did, to argue about the rational character of language. He takes this for granted. He starts from the assumption that a rational being made the whole of the Latin language at one stroke to fit the created world; and we find him tacitly assuming the correspondence between the rules he expounds and the structure of human experience. He likes to list the categories which figure in his mind as the logical framework of the universe. There must be masculines and feminines. There must be three persons. There must be cases where these are declined. Action must be described in past, present and future and with respect to the various persons. There must be words for all these possibilities. The *Doctrinale* revels in such factual categories, and slurs over or omits the anomalies and the exceptions. Take it as your guide, and you will find yourself reconstructing the Latin language. Appeals to usage are rare. The first part of the book which deals with morphology is empty of citations. The second part which is concerned with syntax, has a few; but generally Alexander prefers to illustrate his rules from examples he has made up himself. For he is concerned not with classical Latin but with the Latin of his time. Anything he considers archaic he is quite happy to dismiss.

> Accentus normas legitur posuisse vetustas,
> Non tamen has credo servandas tempore nostro.*

Medieval culture was becoming conscious of its own value; and Alexander's work reflects this new self-esteem. Influenced by the idea that language could be made into an exact instrument of logical thought and encouraged by his consequent admiration for contemporary writing (which bore the stamp of the contemporary love of logic), he went a long way towards emancipating himself from the traditional belief of the grammarians that the classical authors were the only true guides to correct Latin. This view was not altogether revolutionary. It had been a long-standing convention of medieval scholarship that the style of the Vulgate was to be considered perfect, although in many instances it failed to obey the classical rules;* and this special position occupied by the most honoured of known writings had always made the linguistic pre-eminence of the classics somewhat suspect in medieval eyes. Besides, Alexander did not have sufficient confidence in his novel opinions to make them openly his theme. They appear casually in incidental comments and implied rather than firmly stated, win the reader's adherence by degrees.

The *Doctrinale* was soon followed by a very similar work from the pen of Evrard of Béthune. This book, the *Grecismus*, was also written in verse and also enjoyed a popularity of centuries. Its character will be sufficiently evident from the fact that Priscian is taken to task for not having indicated the reasons for the usages he mentions, in other words for not writing a scholastic grammar.* The *Doctrinale* and the *Grecismus* had a long run.* Rabelais over three hundred years later still needed to attack them. Thanks to their appearance on the scene, one of the avenues by which classical influence had infiltrated into the medieval tradition was effectively blocked. The study of Latin, which a clerical education required, no longer led the young by an automatic and inevitable transition to admire pagan authors. Latin grammar was freed from the bonds that had united it to Latin literature.

Contemporaneously with these changes in the teaching of grammar, there occurred a similar transformation in the teaching of rhetoric. We have already pointed out that the men responsible for these new departures were not in all cases opposed to Humanism, that on the contrary many of them were enthusiastic admirers of the classics. This observation is particularly relevant in the case of the rhetoricians. Matthew of Vendôme, Geoffrey of Vinsauf, Gervase of Melkley, John of Garland, Eberhard the German, quote their Ovid, their Virgil, their Cicero, with great willingness. They are without question widely read in the classical writers; and such of them at least as were connected with the schools of Chartres and Orléans, were often accused by contemporaries of playing with the fire of paganism. But the modern reader cannot help feeling that even if the accusation is justified, their play only served to put the fire out.

With one exception they made their appearance after the middle of the twelfth century.* The exception was Marbod's *de Ornamentis Verborum* which must have been written prior to 1130 and in any case dealt with only part of the subject. Both Marbod and his successors drew heavily on Cicero's *de Inventione* and the *ad Herennium*, the traditional *Rhetorica Vetus* and *Rhetorica Nova* of the Humanist schools. They were reproducing material which had been in pedagogic use for several centuries; and their editor Faral emphasises their links with the past by quoting the famous passage from the *Metalogicon* where Bernard of Chartres is described indicating to his pupils figures of speech, flowers of rhetoric, the use of epithets and the use of imagery.

But even if the study of rhetoric was traditional, scholastic rhetoric was a new departure. First of all, the subject was more intensively studied than had been habitual earlier. The very fact that men like Matthew of Vendôme chose this moment to rewrite the old text-books should tell us something. The grammar books had after all been rewritten and commented time and time again during the Dark Ages and the pre-Scholastic period. Why had works like the *ad Herennium* been, comparatively speaking, neglected? Presumably because the general interest in them had been less. And why were they now republished with such zeal in the second half of the twelfth century? Presumably because there was a revival of interest in systematic rhetoric.

Secondly, the dry formal aspects of rhetoric which admittedly had their place in the classical treatises, were given an extraordinary emphasis. The modern reader finds it wellnigh impossible to form any reasoned judgement about the merits of the various *Poetriae*, Arts of Verse and expositions *de Coloribus*, of which the Scholastic Age was so proud. Sparing in generalisation and avid of detail, they bristle with indigestible technical terms and seem in any case to reflect a type of analysis we have long abandoned as aimless. Admittedly, they are thorough. They have a long tradition behind them. And as we read them, we cannot help wondering whether we should not learn something if we mastered their categories. But the effort always proves too great. Automatically, we bestow upon them the admiration we keep for the bones of the Mastodon.

The reader who wishes for first-hand knowledge of their multitudinous classifications and distinctions can do worse than turn to the *Ars Versificatoria* of Matthew of Vendôme, which is at once a typical example of the genre and more competently written than the rest. Matthew, it will be remembered, taught at Orléans and had received his education from a master trained at Chartres.* His first book is largely devoted to hints on how to invent subject-matter. He deals with generalisations and gives examples of a dozen different types suitable for various occasions. Do you wish to write about the imperfections of human happiness? Then you can model your reflections on Horace's *nihil est ab omni parte beatum*. Or if love is your main interest, you can imitate Ovid's *regnat et in dominos ius habet ille deos*. Next, he lists eleven sources from which you can derive material for describing a person. These are; the person's name (in those cases where it has some appropriate significance), his characteristics (both moral and external), his upbringing, his good and ill fortune, his habits, his typical actions, his interests, his reactions, his power of judgement and his manner of speech. External characteristics are further defined as including such facts as nationality, age, family connections and sex. This theoretical analysis is followed by some typical descriptions composed to illustrate it; and they bear a strong family resemblance to police records. To end with there is a list of nine sources from which a writer may draw material for the characterisation of an event. They include, as we might expect, the time, the place, the manner, and the cause of what has happened and also in the case of minor incidents, their relationship to some major occurrence. That is all we hear about invention; and we may be forgiven if we feel that we have heard too much about some of its aspects and too little in general. Moreover, these somewhat exiguous instructions are not clearly given but are mixed up with extraneous detail about the general problems of arrangement, about turgidity of style and about the use of the zeugma. We have in fact merely the trappings of systematic scholarship. The reality is far away.

The second book has a brief preface. Elegy is evoked to tell us that poetry derives its charm from three sources: from its subject-matter, from the beauty of its words and from the graces of its style. The first has been discussed already, so we pass to the second. The beauty of words for Matthew is to be found exclusively in their sound. He recommends the use of adjectives ending in -alis, -osus, -atus, -ivus, -aris, and verbs like *pilleo, prospero, syncipo, illaquaeo, emancipo, delapido*, because their syllables charm the ear. Here again one is struck by the narrowness of his approach as compared to more modern treatises. There are no generalisations. He is satisfied with giving long lists of examples.

The third book is the most important, and contains the various figures of rhetoric which are grouped under the three headings: *schemata, tropi* and *colores rhetorici*. Under *schemata* he mentions *ʒeugma, hypoʒeuxis, anaphora, epanelepsis, anadiplosis epiʒeuxis, paronomasia, paromoion, schesis onomaton, homoioteleuton, polyptoton, polysyndeton* and *asyndeton*. The first two refer to a syntactical construction where the same word plays a part in several clauses. The next four all concern repetition; when the same word occurs at the beginning of successive lines, when it occurs at the beginning and end of the same line, when it occurs at the end of one line and the beginning of the next. You have a *paromoion* when several words begin, an *homoioteleuton* when several words end, with the same sound. A *polyptoton* is the complement of an *homoioteleuton*. It consists of a series of nouns similar in case but with endings that sound different, while a *paronomasia* is a kind of alliterative parallelism which is best understood through Matthew's own example:

> Fama famem pretii parit amentis nec amantis.

Schesis onomaton on the other hand denotes a parallelism of form rather than sound: noun-adjective, noun-adjective. A *polysyndeton* is a series where all the words are connected by the same conjunction: and an *asyndeton* is a similar series without connections. The *tropi* are more directly concerned with the relations of ideas such as antithesis, the use of the climax, metaphor, periphrasis, allegory, metonomy (which Matthew limits to three types—namely, putting the inventor for the invention, the container for what it contains, the quality for its possessor), the *synecdoche* (putting the part for the whole), and the *energema* or the use of puzzling language.

The colours are thirty-one in number. Some of them repeat the figures previously given. *Antithesis, anaphora, epizeuxis, paronomasia, epanelepsis, schesis onomaton, asyndeton, polysyndeton* and the *climax* all recur in this new list under different names. Others refer to such varied tricks as the repetition of phrases, exclamations, rhetorical questions, internal rhymes, and definitions.

None of the three sections really hangs together. They correspond to traditional divisions and not to any thorough analysis of the technique of expression. Quite apart from the confusion which exists between the *schemata* and the *tropi* on the one hand, and the *colours* on the other, there is no particular reason why *zeugma* should be classed with *anaphora*, or antithesis with metaphor.

Finally, in spite of the confusion of his main text which ought to have allowed for the insertion of any number of stray ideas, Matthew finds it necessary to add an epilogue. This is a hotch-potch of odd hints. It provides advice on how to treat classical subjects, gives warnings against turgidity and looseness of construction and ends with an encouragement to utilise contemporary themes: presumably along the lines of Matthew's own description of a lady:

> Marcia praeradiat virtutum dote, redundat
> Morum deliciis, religione praeit.
> Matronale decus exemplo suscitat, expers
> Fastus, incestus nescia, pura dolis.
> Dotibus innumeris est saturata, modesta
> Verbo, consilio provida, mente virens.
> Lascivos reprimit motus, vestire laborat
> Naturam, sexus immemor esse studet.
> (*Ars Versificatoria*, sec. 55, ll. 1–8)

It is necessary to analyse a book of this type before we can understand the real character of the change which had fallen on classical teaching. Rhetoric had always been taught, but now it dominated the classroom. Bernard of Chartres had pointed out the figures of speech, but his spiritual grandson Matthew plainly had eyes for nothing else. Under this new dispensation, you classified as you read. Here was an *asyndeton*, there an *epanelepsis*. And the meaning tended to vanish.*

The writing of Latin prose had in the meantime come to a great extent under the influence of the specialists in the professional disciplines. Theology had always possessed its own idiom, borrowed from the early Fathers. Now philosophy too vindicated its claim to a special language exempt from the normal rules of classical style. The great advance in logical and metaphysical thought from the time of Abélard to the death of Aquinas gave rise to a multitude of technical terms and to forms of expression which were indispensable to scholastic argument, but which had no parallel in classical usage. The Latin of the Schoolmen which provided the medium for all the philosophical works, as well as for a great many of the sermons, treatises and pamphlets of the later Middle Ages, was a new language, full of innovations. And simultaneously, as the philosophers obtained control over one large sector of prose literature, the lawyers in their turn possessed themselves of another. The art of letter-writing had formed an unimportant sub-division of the ancient rhetorical course. Education in Rome had more complicated aims; and a man who had mastered the technique of composing a speech, was not likely to find his daily correspondence difficult. But now in the twelfth century conditions had changed. Oratory was at a discount. On the other hand, there were a great many lawyers, administrators and men of business who were required to write lengthy and necessarily lucid letters in Latin; and the schools did their best to prepare their pupils for this contingency.

Letter-writing deserves to rank as the most contemporary of all the genres that the Middle Ages attempted. It was dominated by its utilitarian purpose. Letters—especially formal letters, and it was formal correspondence that the medieval schools largely sought to teach—have no existence apart from the occasions that call them forth. They are bound to bear, in content and form alike, the indisputable stamp of actuality. Besides, this was a field in which the classical heritage was short of useful models. The familiar missives of Cicero, which were in any case imperfectly known, offered little guidance to a diplomat addressing an Archbishop, or to a lawyer concerned to elucidate some question of feudal right. Nor had they any information to give on the thorny subject of current social usage; and the official circles of the Middle Ages set great store by proper formulae. There were phrases for beginning and ending a letter, suitable forms of address for different social categories, legal terms, ecclesiastical terms, formulae for felicitation and condolence, for the granting of requests, for their refusal, for their non-committal postponement; and the schools were at special pains to teach these to their pupils. Even at Orléans, which was regarded as the great home of the literary art, the masters devoted infinite time and trouble to the dissemination of this kind of knowledge; and that fact, more perhaps than any other, serves to indicate the change that had come over classical studies. For the letters of the time, elaborate as they were, gemmed with references to the ancient authors, embellished with all the devices of rhetoric, must rank in the last analysis as the products not of art but of artifice; and they did not offer opportunities for imitation on a broad and educationally valuable scale. They may have been constructed in part from classical phrases. They may have embodied occasional classical ideas. But to secure such fragmentary borrowings, your letter-writer did not need to look beyond what was already and commonly known. His craft gave no incentive to extend the bounds of his knowledge, to penetrate anywhere more deeply into the arcana of the past. Moreover, the good writers whose craftsmanship gives us something to admire were relatively few in number. The majority were content to rely on the set formulae which were learnt by heart and reproduced as required, or which they copied from the collections of model letters such as were produced by the school of Orléans; and in Italy there arose a new professional class, the *dictatores*, who made a living by helping others with their correspondence.* They were not teachers, but specialists called in to perform a skilled task; and they naturally made great use of stereotyped and labour-saving forms of expression. The great area of writing which they represented had lost all organic contact with classical literature.

The new departures in grammar teaching were a product of the popular worship of logic. The attention paid to letter-writing had its origins in the administrative needs of a society which was becoming more wealthy and more organised. Of the three developments we have discussed, the increased emphasis on the formal study of rhetoric alone appears to have some direct connection with the distrust which Humanist enthusiasms had aroused and with the scruples of such scholars as Marbod. When a man felt, as Marbod did, that the young were corrupted by pagan stories, it was not unnatural that he should turn instead to those formal elements in classical poetry, which were morally harmless, and should busy himself with writing *de Coloribus Verborum.*

A further proof that this shift of interest was indeed connected with the feelings of disquiet which had long accompanied the cult of pagan verse, is furnished by the fact that other prophylactics were simultaneously applied. Abélard had been told by his critics that a monk ought not to concern himself with ancient literature.* What better answer could there be to such a criticism than to demonstrate that the very stories whose paganism shocked the pious, had their place in the hierarchy of Christian truth?

It had been customary in the Roman grammar schools for the teacher to preface the reading of a fresh work by a few introductory remarks. His aim was to provide that minimum of biographical and bibliographical detail which would be necessary for the proper understanding of the text. This practice had continued during the Middle Ages in Italy and among those Italian masters who came to spread their learning in the north. The information given was morally innocuous enough. But it was not useful from the Christian point of view. It did not help to counteract the pagan ideas in the text. Early in the twelfth century, however, there was a change, and the old style of introduction was abandoned.

Nec te lateat quod in libris explanandis septem antiqui requirebant; auctorem, titulum operis, carminis qualitatem, scribentis intentionem, ordinem, numerum librorum, explanationem; sed moderni quattuor requirenda censuerunt: operis materiam, scribentis intentionem, finalem causam, et cui parti philosophiae subponatur quod scribitur

writes Conrad of Hirschau in a book composed some time before 1150.* As he remarks the seven points demanded by the ancient grammarians had been reduced to four. But the four he names are exceedingly comprehensive. Moreover, there is a radical difference in the type of comment required, the emphasis is no longer on illustrative details. The teacher is expected to make a philosophic judgement on the text he is about to expound and to define its place in the hierarchy of Christian knowledge. The distinction thus established between the intention of the author and the final cause of the work, is significant for the character of this new type of introduction. The *intentio* represents the blind purpose of a human artist; and *finalis causa* stands as that higher aim in the mind of God which allows the book a definite function in His plan for the universe. When the teacher names such a final cause, he fits his text into a scheme which covers the whole of experience and which is dominated in all its particulars by religious beliefs.* Conrad is a valuable witness, just because he was a man of little imagination. We can rely on him to describe the routine instructions which the ordinary teacher was expected to follow. His contemporary, the learned theologian and educationalist, Hugh of St Victor, was a theoretical thinker whose statements are always made with the maximum of generality; and before we can give a meaning to his schematic observations we are often compelled to complete them with material derived from other sources. But on the question of exegesis he has some enlightening comments:

Expositio tria continet: litteram, sensum, sententiam. *Littera* est congrua ordinatio dictionum quae etiam constructionem vocamus; *sensus* est facilis quaedam et aperta significatio, quam littera prima fronte praefert; *sententia* est profundior intelligentia quae nisi expositione vel interpretatione non invenitur.*

To the two stages familiar to us in the teaching of Bernard of Chartres, Hugh has added a third. The master construes the grammar; he elucidates the precise meaning of the passage; he then goes on to expound.... But what does he expound? What interpretation are we to place on this reference to a more profound understanding of the text? Again, the more pedestrian Conrad provides the clue. 'Primum, in hoc opere a docente sensus ponendus est literae, deinde ipsa litera per allegoriam elucidenda inde per moralitatem vita legentis instituenda.'* As has already been mentioned, the habit of allegorical interpretation had arisen first in the case of the Bible. It provided the theologians with an easy means of explaining those stories which appeared to them either pointless or in direct conflict with Christian beliefs. The discovery of allegories is a pleasant mental exercise and one which must have appeared peculiarly acceptable to men who regarded the natural world as the unreal shadow of a higher order. The technique became extremely popular, and by the end of the eleventh century it was being applied to pagan and contemporary authors as well as to the Old and New Testaments.* Its origins are admirably discussed in C. S. Lewis' excellent book.* As soon as men looked for hidden meanings in the Olympian legends that shocked their sensibilities, as soon as Cronus swallowing his children became a figure of all-devouring Time, and the disease-bringing shafts of Apollo were seen as the rays of a pestilential tropical sun, the day of allegory was already at hand.

But we ought perhaps to distinguish at this early point between its two varieties. The interest of C. S. Lewis is largely for the allegory which is a technique of expression. He starts from the fact that during the later centuries of the Empire the Greeks and Romans had become aware of what we might call the combats of the soul. The inner struggles of conscience and impulse are not, he points out, easy to describe. Even Freud writing fifty years ago was driven to use a terminology which, with its Ego, Super-Ego and Id, its thresholds, censors and repressions, strongly suggests the contemporary settings of human crime and drama. So who can blame the ancients for representing the forces of their spiritual life anthropomorphically, to the effect that they talked of bellicose urges as Mars, of love as Amor, of the Super-Ego as Prudentia. The *Psychomachia* of Prudentius, the *de Nuptiis* of Martianus Capella, the *Megacosmos* of Bernard Silvestris, the *Château d'Amour* of Grosseteste all furnish good examples of this type of allegory. But we at the moment are more concerned with an allied but not identical phenomenon. Allegorical expression is one thing. Allegorical interpretation is another. The former can be a convenient method of representing facts which are somewhat troublesome to handle. The latter is the purposeful deformation of literary material whose content for some reason or other does not meet with the author's approval; or alternatively it is an attempt to derive information about some subject close to the allegorizer's heart, from a source which we should consider wholly unsuitable.

In the sixth century a Christian grammarian called Fulgentius took the stories of pagan mythology and extracted from them what he called their useful elements. That is, he treated them as allegorical tales whose point of reference was the life of the soul. He then performed the same service for Virgil. The twelve books of the *Aeneid* were equated with the story of a man's life from babyhood to age in a fantasy that constantly verges on the comical.* This is not allegory in the sense it is used by Prudentius. The *Expositio Vergilianae Continentiae* impresses one rather as the obverse of the *Psychomachia*. What we have is not a spiritual experience represented as a story, but a story interpreted on the spiritual plane, long after it was written. This manner of exegesis became very popular in scriptural studies. The Bible—and especially the Old Testament—contains a multitude of stories which have no obvious religious significance and a few which are even repugnant to the religious mind. To men unversed in the subtleties of historical interpretation, it appeared impossible that any portion of a book which God had inspired, should be valueless or worse. They looked for hidden meanings. Sometimes they traced a parallel between a scriptural narrative and a religious practice, or linked an Old Testament anecdote with an event in the history of the Church. Sometimes they worked out a moral significance. Sometimes they made the historical sense of the text the illustration of a supernatural truth. In all these cases, they made what had been previously valueless into a source of edification.

Given this background, it is hardly surprising that similar techniques came to be applied to the pagan poets. But until the end of the eleventh century the practice seems to have occurred on a small scale only. Then we have Bernard of Utrecht (d. 1099) writing an allegorical commentary to one of the common schoolbooks (the *Ecloga Theoduli*). The homilies which ended Bernard of Chartres' evening lectures may have included a Christian reinterpretation of what had been read, and it may be that we ought to trace back to them this new development in the Chartrain tradition. Allegorical commentaries to the pagan poets became common after the middle of the century, and in the fifties we have Bernard Silvestris, the pupil of Thierry of Chartres, writing a commentary on the first six books of the *Aeneid*, which traces their correspondence with the six stages of human life. Aeneas landing on the Carthaginian shore is the new-born soul at birth. The flames which consume Troy are the devouring passions of youth. The sixth book represents man's passage to the world hereafter. We can see that once such a framework has been constructed, it provides innumerable pegs on which to hang moral homilies and disquisitions calculated to edify a pious student, until the original text disappears beneath a mass of extraneous comment and becomes little more than the excuse for a sermon.*

Thus from Bernard of Chartres to Bernard Silvestris of Tours, from Guibert of Nogent to Matthew of Vendôme, during the vigorous midportion of the twelfth century, the work of the schools underwent a notable change. The curriculum remained much as before, and may indeed have widened. One gets the impression that the number of classical authors who were read steadily increased.* If the best of the medieval Humanists, a John of Salisbury and a Peter of Blois, must be classed as belonging to the pre-scholastic tradition, if a Giraldus Cambrensis whose education in Paris took place round 1160, is still the product of a transitional age,* such scholars as John of Garland and

Eberhard the German have their roots firmly in the new world of the thirteenth century, and the extent of their classical knowledge does not fall far short of the standards set by their illustrious predecessors. Many of the classical acquisitions revealed by the twelfth-century catalogues must have been made in the years preceding 1150 when, for example, we find that a third of the books in the cathedral library at Rouen contained works by ancient authors, and see in the list of the fifty-eight codices which are mentioned the *Ilias Latina*, Horace, the *Metamorphoses* and *Amores*, Cicero, Arator, Juvenal, Virgil, Donatus and Boethius.* But many volumes were acquired later; and it is in the thirteenth century that the classical libraries of the Middle Ages were at their best.

What altered was not the scope but the spirit of classical studies. How bare the *Laborintus* or the writings of John of Garland seem alongside the more colourful productions of what has been called the twelfth-century renaissance! So long as professional studies had attracted men to the classics, Humanism had grown ever more vigorous. Decade by decade it had increased its hold on Western culture. If that process had continued after 1150, its next stage would have been a florescence not unlike the great Renaissance itself. There is nothing inherently absurd in the thought of Petrarch's *Africa* being written a generation after the *Alexandreis* or the *Decameron* a generation after Walter Map. But instead of accelerating, the Humanist advance diminished. The tide which had flowed so strongly for two centuries, hesitated and ebbed away.

The deeper causes of this development will be discussed later. More immediately, it was linked with those formal and utilitarian pre-occupations which had come to play so great a part in the life of the schools. Their impact was considerable; for it came at a moment when it could do the most damage. We can see from Liebeschuetz's careful study of John of Salisbury, whom we fairly regard as a typical twelfth-century humanist, that outside the specialities, the classical learning of the age was focused on the detail rather than on the broad general characteristics of the ancient authors.* The twelfth-century scholars adopted classical instances, classical arguments to illustrate the conclusions of their own experience just as they used classical metres and figures in their essentially medieval poems. Picking and choosing on the basis of an unsystematic knowledge was a necessary first stage in the assimilation of the literary and historical material which the classics had to offer; and already there were signs that the ground was prepared for the next step forward. Walter of Châtillon for example is no pedestrian imitator. He shows a genuine appreciation of the overall form and characteristics of his genre. He reproduces not only the detail, but also the generalities of the classical epic; and his heroes, Alexander and Darius, are truly heroic. They stand above the common run of mankind, not because of birth or success, not even because of warlike skill (for Darius had none), but because of a certain greatness of spirit, a *magnanimitas* which strikes the poet with wonder. Moreover, Walter is not without the pride of the artist. 'Vivemus pariter', he tells his patron, William of Rheims,

> vivet cum vate superstes
> gloria Guilhelmi, nullum moritura per aevum.

The idea of literature as a path to glory was beginning to stir the imaginations of men. It was not confined to Walter. There are traces of its influence in writers so different as Sigebert and Hugo Primas.

The sense of individual greatness, the importance allotted to art, the glorification of the past, the view that literature consists of distinct genres, each of which has its own rules for perfection, the very themes which were eventually to characterise the mental world of the High Renaissance can be found in the twelfth century. But they existed only in embryo; and the shift of interest which occurred at the beginning of the Scholastic period was sufficient to prevent momentarily their further growth.

With the last quarter of the twelfth century, the schools ceased to encourage any advances in the understanding of the classics. We have mentioned in connection with the grammar of Alexander de Villedieu that the thirteenth century was proud of its contemporary culture. This pride left its mark also on their choice of books for school study. The list of classical texts given by Alexander Neckham is impressive. So is the other slightly later list in the *Laborintus*. Claudian, Statius, Ovid, Horace's satires, Virgil all have their place. But they were read alongside Marbod, Vitalis Blesensis, Walter of Lille, Gunther of Paris, Peter of Riga, Geoffrey of Vinsauf, or Matthew of Vendôme; and this in itself was sufficient to prevent that exclusive cult of the past which alone could have provided the impetus for a forward movement of classical studies. The schools helped to preserve the ground that had been gained. They helped also to imprint more deeply on the popular consciousness the rather scattered material that earlier ages had derived from the classical heritage. Some at least of the facts and ideas that had made up the

mental furniture of John of Salisbury found their way into the minds
of the majority of educated men. But this popularisation was not
accompanied by any comparable progress in the discovery of the past.
There the clock stood still; and its immobility was reflected in the new
status of the literary schools. Only at Orléans and Toulouse was
grammar still the main object of study; and as the thirteenth century
drew to its close even these last strongholds of Humanism were to
disappear.

In any case it mattered little whether the classical authors were read or
not. Their subject-matter was hardly likely to make much impression
upon minds already steeped in rhetoric and susceptible to the bewilderments of allegory.* Nor was there in the last analysis much difference
between the rival schools. John of Garland may have satirised the logic-
chopping which prevailed in Paris but all our evidence suggests that
thirteenth-century literature teaching was, for all practical purposes, as
scholastic in Orléans as in the capital.

F. M. Powicke is of the opinion that the university teachers of
the thirteenth and fourteenth centuries must have taken an unofficial
interest in the classics.* He reasons that the classical motifs in the
literature of the time show the ancient authors to have been widely read,
and that such reading must have been encouraged by someone. This is
a view calculated to bring into prominence an aspect of the age which
our argument has somewhat neglected. We have represented Scholasticism as a movement whose purpose was to limit the purely human
interests of medieval man. How can we reconcile this conception with
the rich and varied life which undoubtedly existed during the scholastic
age and with the literature which that life undoubtedly produced?

Along the great roads, in all the towns where markets could be held,
men congregated, exchanged ideas and goods, quarrelled, loved, prayed,
followed their private fantasies to their hearts' content. They told
stories of a Virgil who was the best of poets:

> Tu se' lo mio maestro e il mio autore:
> tu se' solo colui, da cui io tolsi
> lo bello stile che m' ha fatto onore.   (*Inf.* I, 82–5)

—and more even than a poet since he had foretold the coming of
Christ.* They placed Homer, Horace, Ovid and Lucan in the calm of
Limbo. They identified the ancient gods with the Christian devils; and
with slight exaggerations made the incidents of ancient history their
own.*

Quali Alessandro in quelle parti calde
d' india vide sopra lo suo stuolo
fiamme cadere infino a terra salde;
Perch' ei provvide a scalpitar lo suolo
con le sue schiere, acciocche il vapore
me' si stingeva mentre ch'era solo: (*Inf.* XIV, 31–7)

How could they be hostile to the classics when the great arsenal of stories which Ovid and Statius had preserved from the popular traditions of Greece served them still for entertainment?

There seems good evidence that the thirteenth century was more vital, more urgently human and above all more aware of the classical past than any period until the High Renaissance. But that evidence needs to be interpreted with reserve. The classicism of the Scholastic period has a distorted quality. Dante's Virgil is not the painstaking laureate of the Augustan Age. He possesses the attributes of a magician and has something in common with that awesome figure which the medieval imagination successively constructed round the personalities of Gerbert, Michael Scot and Albert the Great. The tales, the anecdotes, the characters that came originally from Statius, or Ovid, or Livy have been medievalised. Similarly, the information which appears in the dictionaries and the encyclopedias is hardly ever faultless. Our word, tragedy, is connected with the Greek *tragos* 'a goat', but the association with goats does not derive, as Ugoccione of Pisa suggests, from a resemblance between one's emotional response to disaster and one's olfactory shrinking from stench.*

Dante and Guillaume de Lorris were able scholars* who had read their ancient authors. So much is undoubted. But it is equally beyond dispute that a great deal of the classical material in their poetry was not derived directly from the original sources but came to them indirectly through the medium of popular tradition. The vigorous Humanism of the eleventh and twelfth centuries had made first the clerks, and then the wider society in which they moved, familiar with the content of the major Latin poets and with some at least of the historians. When Hildebert wanted to imitate Ovid, he had written in elegiacs. Later in the *Carmina Burana* and *Altercatio Phyllidis et Florae** we find Ovidian sentiments presented in non-classical metres; and in the Provençal lyric or the Minnesang they appear in the vernacular.*

Scholasticism affected the schools and the professions. It did not penetrate the life of the people: and vernacular poetry, which lay in the borderland between the popular culture and the academic sphere, largely escaped its restrictive influence. Dante in many respects is the child of a tradition which had died in the schools a hundred years before he wrote.

II. THE REORGANISATION OF PHILOSOPHY

Such was the development of literary studies. The reorganisation of philosophy occurred some time later. The metaphysical and scientific works of Aristotle, the summaries and commentaries of Alfarabi, Avicenna and Averroes did not become widely known until the beginning of the thirteenth century, more than a hundred years after the first revival of Humanism, and so the scholastic effort to bring them into accord with Christianity was similarly delayed. It took the form of a philosophical revaluation which had great technical merits and still serves as the basis of Roman Catholic thought. The excellent histories of B. Geyer and de Wulf describe it in the most minute detail. We, however, shall need to approach it from a different viewpoint, and one slightly wider than theirs. They are concerned with philosophy alone. We shall require to take into account scientific knowledge as well. To the *Summae* of Thomas Aquinas we shall need to add the *Speculum Maius* of Vincent of Beauvais.

The thirteenth century dawned on a philosophical scene of more than customary confusion. The new Aristotle of the *Metaphysics*, the *ethica vetus* and the scientific treatises, from which so much had been hoped fifty years before, had at last arrived. It had come to stay, as all thinking men unhesitatingly realised; but it had come reinforced by the dubious accompaniments of Oriental commentary. New concepts, new interpretations of the universe had made their appearance; and once recognised were not to be lightly dismissed. New questions had been raised which Christianity had to answer if it was to retain its hold over the minds of men. But a great many of these questions and a great many of these concepts seemed to furnish occasions for heresy, implying that human beings could attain to a knowledge of God without Revelation and without guidance from the Church, or alternatively exalting a mundane rationalism at the expense of authority. Pantheism was implicit in some of the Arab writings, materialism in others; and what applied to the Arabs applied at this juncture to Aristotle also. For no one was in a position to distinguish the content of the original texts from the later interpretations and commentaries.

When the condemnation of Amaury in 1204 and the burning of his followers five years later drew public attention to the dangers of heresy, no one knew enough about the issues involved to guarantee that Aristotle, Algazel and Avicenna would not automatically lead their readers into similar religious errors. It is not surprising therefore that the council of 1210, the first official body to enquire into the new learning, should have adopted a restrictive policy and should have forbidden both public discussion and private reading of the *Libri naturales*. But the policy had no hope of success. The clock could not be put back. The flow of translations could not be stopped or their contents forgotten. Already a new commentator seemingly more dangerous than his predecessors was becoming known at least by reputation. Averroes (translated by Michael Scot in 1217) was soon to take his place alongside Avicenna. If disaster was to be avoided (for in a world ruled through ideas a sudden spread of heterodox opinions could spell disaster), then some method of defence other than mere restriction had to be found.

There is some evidence which suggests that the ban as worded by the council of 1210 was raised three years later,* and the statutes which the Papal Legate, Robert of Courçon sanctioned for the Paris University in 1215, mention only that public lectures on Aristotle's metaphysics and natural history were forbidden. After the first flurry of alarm which followed the discovery of heretical beliefs, no one was prepared to embark on a campaign of suppression involving the whole body of Aristotelian learning. But what happened instead is truly remarkable. A large number of scholars, first in Paris and then all over Europe, set themselves to the task of reconciling the metaphysical presuppositions of ancient philosophy with their Christian faith. Their effort received official sanction in 1231 when Gregory IX appointed his commission to purify the *Libri Naturales*, but it was not officially initiated. It was the spontaneous response of men who believing in the value of their civilisation and striving to preserve its coherence, were prepared to meet the challenge of a conflict between their knowledge and their religion by making an energetic attempt to retain both. The first in the field were the Parisian scholars, William of Auxerre, Philip of Grève and William of Auvergne; but their books, written for the most part between 1220 and 1240, took into account only a limited number of the Aristotelian and Arabic works which were in circulation. They were the pioneers. Their successors were to be more systematic.

The achievements of the great Scholastics are too well known in their outline and too complicated in their details for us to describe them here.

It will be sufficient perhaps if we recall that the intellectual effort of the time revolved round two cosmologies: the Neoplatonist and the Aristotelian; and that these rival systems had a good deal in common, with the result that thinkers were constantly slipping from one to the other. The first man to use the whole body of Aristotle's writings to help in the development of his theology was the Franciscan Alexander of Hales whose *Summa Universae Theologiae* belongs to the period between 1230 and 1245. He aspired however to be simultaneously an Aristotelian and a Platonist, so that he attempted to reconcile Aristotle not only to Christianity but also to Plato: and the enterprise was too ambitious to meet with an unqualified success.

His work was carried on by another Franciscan, the more famous Bonaventura who was born half a century after him, and whose cosmology was based on a Neoplatonist conception of Light as the substantial form of all things: a theory which Grosseteste had also held. The weakness of these Franciscan philosophies derived, not so much from any technical failure to reconcile their Neoplatonism with Christianity, but from the ease with which their ideas could be used to justify a mysticism which, relying on an inner light, tended to deny the authority of the Church. So Bonaventura's pupil Petrus Olivi went too far in his speculations and had to be condemned. Men were bound to feel that the Franciscan solutions did not yet represent safety; and the Scholastic synthesis was only achieved when Thomas Aquinas rejected Neoplatonic solutions in favour of a purer Aristotle.

What the Scholastics were attempting to bring into accord with Christianity was not a single classical or Oriental system but a complex of interlocking philosophies of diverse provenance. Taken as a whole, the totality of thirteenth- and fourteenth-century thought can be seen to represent the Christianisation of the material translated from Greek and Arabic sources. But no single philosopher of the period came to grips with that material in all its aspects. With the possible exception of Albertus (who does indeed appear to have included everything, but who failed on the other hand in his efforts at synthesis so that the different currents of non-Christian thought co-exist in his work without commingling*), the Scholastic thinkers were content to select what suited their particular point of view and to embody in their syntheses only what they had selected. The Franciscans concentrated their attention on developing those Neoplatonic elements which had already made their appearance in the works of Augustine. Siger of Brabant made himself the champion of the materialist Aristotelianism of

Averroes. Dietrich of Freiburg and Master Eckhardt specialised in a speculative mysticism that drew heavily on the Neoplatonic ideas in the work of Albertus.

Now within the mental climate and circumstances of the age, Christianity and Neoplatonism were difficult to reconcile even where materialist admixtures, such as existed in the Arab doctrines, did not complicate the issue. The belief (which formed a necessary part of every system derived from Plotinus) that man could attain to an intuitive knowledge of the Godhead, left the door open for an exaltation of private over public religion. Christian philosophies impregnated with Neoplatonism could not, even when they were theoretically orthodox, avoid giving a measure of encouragement to those whose temperaments inclined them to set up a personal vision against the validity of traditional dogmas. Though in particular controversies, men like Ramon Lull could emerge as the champions of orthodoxy against a heretical Averroism, it remains evident that in the last analysis the Neoplatonic world-view was quite as opposed as the Materialist outlook to the essence of medieval Christianity.

The synthesis attempted by Aquinas was in a sense as restricted as the syntheses of his Franciscan or Averroist critics; but his success as the champion of orthodoxy, his present fame as the most remarkable exponent of Scholasticism, derives from the fact that the principle of choice which he adopted led him to exclude the Neoplatonic as well as the strictly materialist elements in the Greco-Arabic tradition. His panegyrists have lauded his powers of argument. It would be more appropriate to emphasise the excellence of his judgement. His genius was to see precisely which parts of pagan philosophy were reconcilable with Christian belief and to bring only these into his system.

The method of Aquinas meant in practice a return to the original works of Aristotle as distinct from their later accretions, and this involved philological as well as philosophical scholarship. It was not sufficient to set aside the Arab commentaries, the translations made from the Arabic had also to be replaced. Already in the twelfth century there had existed a few versions made directly from the Greek, which had in certain cases enjoyed a fairly wide circulation. This original stock had included the *Metaphysica Vetustissima*, covering for the most part the first three books of the *Metaphysics*, and treatises such as the *Physics*, the *de Generatione*, the *Meteorologica* and the *de Anima*. To it the early part of the thirteenth century had added the *Translatio Media* which comprised all but Book XI of the *Metaphysics* and Grosseteste's noble

Nicomachean Ethics. The collection may fairly be regarded as imposing. But many of these early versions were spoilt by inaccuracies; and when Aquinas started his philosophical researches there was still much to be done both by way of correction and in providing translations of works unknown in Latin or known only through the Arabic: tasks which called for a knowledge of Greek and a philological skill of no mean order.

As it happened, circumstances were now propitious for Greek studies. During the greater part of the twelfth century, the Byzantine emperors, fostering the flames of a new-found nationalism, had done their best to discourage contacts with the West; and only a few zealous travellers had managed to surmount the barriers of danger and distance, aided only by their own initiative. Such as did so, had inspired their contemporaries with awe; the monk, Guillaume de Gap who in 1167 had brought back some Hermetic literature to St Denis, Grossolano, the Archbishop of Milan and the Tuscan brothers, Hugo and Leo, who had distinguished themselves in theological discussions at the Byzantine court wore on their return the mantle of an adventurous boldness. But high adventure does not normally attract those whose temperaments fit them for the labours of routine scholarship; and the twelfth-century translators of Aristotle were for the most part men of a different stamp. They had learnt their Greek in South Italy, content to pick up what scraps of linguistic information their own world could offer without venturing further afield to where Byzantium guarded the gates of a more complete knowledge.

But that situation had changed radically with the weakening of Byzantine power after 1190; and the establishment of the Latin Empire a few years later made contacts with the East easy for all who desired them. At first, the world of learning made little use of this accessibility. The men who came in contact with the Greeks and acquired their language were soldiers whose only concern was to control a subject population, monks who hoped to convert their schismatic brethren, and merchants who traded with Byzantine firms. They spoke Greek as Roger Bacon points out, but did not understand the grammar or know how to teach it,* being for the most part semi-educated and inarticulate folk with no thoughts beyond their daily business, remote from the controversies of the schools. It was not until the middle of the thirteenth century, that the Church, conscious of its missionary role, began to encourage the study of Greek among the members of the mendicant orders; and then for the first time in the history of the medieval West, there came into existence a class of men, some of whom at least were professionally equipped to approach the treasures of the Byzantine heritage.

Earlier in the century, Grosseteste had still relied largely on Italian teachers of Greek, although he did arrange to have grammars collected and sent to him from the newly conquered Byzantine territories. But Roger Bacon who lived only a generation or so later (*c.* 1214–94), was able to benefit from his contacts with Greeks or with men who had learnt the language in Greece. For his grammar follows the Byzantine tradition both in pronunciation and in its arrangement of the subject-matter. Indignant passages in the *Opus Maius* as well as in the unfinished *Compendium Studii Philosophiae* make it clear that the enthusiasm for Greek studies, of which Bacon was so zealous an advocate, was limited to a very small number of individuals; but in spite of its limitations it did exist now in a way which had been unknown for hundreds of years.

The work of Aquinas owed much to this new development. His philosophical studies would have been seriously interrupted had he been compelled to acquire a mastery of Greek adequate for his purposes. As it was, he found expert advice close at hand. Among the Dominicans who spent several years in Greece learning the language was a young Fleming, William of Moerbeke. On his return to Italy he met Aquinas at the Papal Court, became his philological adviser and was persuaded by him to undertake the task of preparing a definitive translation of Aristotle. William's version of the *Politics* (*c.* 1260) was followed by his revisions of the scientific works and of the *Metaphysics* as well as by a new rendering of the *Rhetoric*. He also translated a number of Aristotle's Greek commentators, and it was always his texts that Aquinas consulted in preference to any other. Philologists generally perform the humble labour of shaping the stones which other men will use. They are remembered if at all in the shadow of other men's fame; and William has shared the common fate of his kind. But the preparatory nature of his contribution should not blind us to its importance. It is difficult to imagine how the Thomistic synthesis could have come into being without his help.

The *Summae* of Aquinas effectively reconciled the metaphysics implicit in Christianity with the ideas of Aristotle. Neither system is seriously distorted in their meeting, and their accommodation is built up on a logical framework so firm that it cannot be broken at any point but has always had to be undermined from its first foundations by those who have wished to shake it. Aquinas towers above his colleagues and rivals precisely because his synthesis was perfect. No implicit conflicts shattered its stability. For the first time since the Patristic Age, a part of Greek philosophy, imposing in its scope and importance, was firmly welded to the Christian tradition. Aristotle was annexed; and in such a way that the medieval world could continue with its essential character unchanged.

The nineteenth-century revival of Thomism in the Roman Catholic Church has inspired a great mass of painstaking research on the Scholastic philosophers; and the result has been to overemphasise their importance. It is not unusual to find people who talk as if the culture of the later Middle Ages had been little more than a by-product of the thought of Aquinas. Such ideas are manifestly exaggerated, and we need not consider them seriously. But when we dismiss them, we shall do well to remember that wild as they are, the exaggerations of enthusiasm do hide a kernel of truth. There can in fact be no doubt that the philosophical systems of the thirteenth century deserve to rank as the most important achievements of the Scholastic spirit. For we must take into account not only the success of Aquinas, but also the partial successes of his contemporaries. If they did not manage to bring Neoplatonism or Averroist rationalism into as complete an accord with Christianity as he brought Aristotle, they nevertheless elucidated an imposing number of difficulties and reduced the areas of conflict to manageable proportions. Looked at as a whole, the organisation of classical material effected in the schools of philosophy from William of Auxerre to Ramon Lull must strike us as imposing both in its scope and its completeness. Moreover, it derives weight from the nature of the issues discussed. The philosophies of an age are key centres of its thought. Attempting to bring into some sort of logical order the ideas and attitudes that make up the current world-view, they are bound to exercise an influence on every field of knowledge; and the Scholastic adaptation of classical philosophy to a medieval pattern meant that in other spheres too the absorption of the classical heritage would be simultaneously facilitated.

III. THE ORGANISATION OF GENERAL KNOWLEDGE

Logic and the study of Latin literature had received the stamp of Scholasticism back in the twelfth century. But they were not the only sectors apart from metaphysics where the classical revival had made ancient learning available for medieval use. Besides law and medicine (which we shall have to consider in the next section), there existed at the beginning of the thirteenth century a mass of general knowledge which did not yet fall within the range of any speciality; and the part of this knowledge which derived from ancient sources had not so far been properly fitted into a view of life that could give Christianity a dominant place. Here was another sphere of mental activity, diverse and yet undifferentiated which was bound to feel in its turn the impact of the Scholastic effort.

In considering the organisation of what we may perhaps call un-specialised knowledge (the facts of history, political thought, economics, psychology, geography, biology and so forth, which in the medieval period lacked as yet the cohesion offered by properly developed disciplines), we must once again cast our eyes back to the twelfth century and to the work of men like Hugh of St Victor and Thierry of Chartres. These scholars were the successors of those early writers who had epitomised pagan knowledge for Christian use. Learned and systematic, they devoted their energies to doing for the twelfth century what Hraban Maur had done for the ninth. But there was a difference. Their predecessors had been mere collectors, satisfied to amass or at best to classify. They on the other hand were anxious primarily to impose a structure upon knowledge, to subordinate everything to a few general ideas.

The techniques which this purpose required took some time to develop. Thierry's *Heptateuchon* is little more than a massive com-pilation devoid of original value since it merely gives the accepted text-books for each of the seven arts. But the prologue contains some interesting sentiments. Wisdom is the goal of life. Philosophy is the source of wisdom, and to philosophise you require the Quadrivium and the Trivium. The former provides you with material for thought, the latter with the necessary means of expression. Thierry may have been a traditionalist as far as practice was concerned, but in theory he thought already of human knowledge as a single unit, which had a single pur-pose and was related to the final aim of man.

A somewhat similar conception of the unity of knowledge is implicit in John of Salisbury's remark that to count as properly literate a man must be familiar with mathematics and history as well as with the poets and orators.* But the greatest advance as far as the mid-twelfth century is concerned, was made not by a liberal-minded secular clerk, not by a professional philosopher, but by the monk Hugh of St Victor. His

Didascalion is a work of the first importance. It takes a theory which had appeared in Aristotle, which subsequently had been noticed by Boethius and repeated by Gerbert.* It takes this theory which the writers mentioned had played with as it were on the margin of their thought, and binds on it with a firm intention. Hugh, like so many of his contemporaries, was original not because he invented fresh ideas, but because he brought into the limelight ideas that had been known but neglected before. Starting from the Aristotelian hypothesis that all knowledge is one, he elaborated a hierarchical system which invites comparison with the constructions of Auguste Comte. Considering the sciences as groups of techniques aimed at ensuring our mastery in particular fields, he divided *philosophia*, or the totality of man's intelligent response to environment, into four sections. To the first he allotted the theoretical sciences: theology, physics and mathematics. In the second he put the techniques necessary for practical life; in the third, the mechanical crafts, while the fourth was devoted to the arts of expression; that is to grammar, dialectic and rhetoric.* Each of these branches of learning served the general activity of the human spirit; and considered subjectively, they could be seen to constitute its different forms.

The importance of Hugh's scheme lay in its systematic character, in the theoretical subordination of the parts to the whole. He left his readers intensely aware of the natural divisions of human knowledge, and of the relationship that each division bore to the rest. He did not merely develop the existing tradition which made the Trivium preparatory to the Quadrivium on utilitarian grounds or on the excuse that the study of sounds (*voces*) was in its essence ancillary to the study of things (*res*).* He completely transformed men's thinking about the subject by postulating that the aim of the disciplines must be to cover the whole of experience. And in doing so he marked out the lines along which the next generation was to work.

Hugh for all his brilliance was merely a precursor. He talked of organising knowledge but as yet there was none that urgently needed organisation. Miscellaneous facts of a non-scientific character were commonly employed as we have seen to illustrate contemporary opinions. The historical, psychological and political ideas of the ancients were, thanks to the rhetorical techniques of teaching used in the schools, firmly subordinated to a framework of thought that had an essentially medieval character. The scientific facts such as came from Pliny and Varro were disconnected, often fanciful, and without significance for philosophy or theology. But the next fifty years were to see the translation of the scientific and metaphysical Aristotle as well as of Aristotle's Arabian commentators. The age of relative ignorance was at an end. Science with its array of facts had arrived, even though the facts in question left much to be desired. By 1215 the problem of how to subordinate the search for knowledge in the separate sciences to the search for wisdom consonant with the religious ends of man—that awkward problem which had been largely theoretical for Hugh of St Victor—required an immediate practical solution.

When in 1231 Gregory IX repeated de Courçon's prohibition, he did so with the proviso that the Aristotelian books would be examined by a special commission, and lectures on them would be permitted as soon as they had been purged of heresy. As has been said, the labours of this commission need not concern us here. Our interest must be for the private effort which the situation aroused. Many of Aristotle's scientific hypotheses and many of the ideas advanced by his commentators appeared to have anti-Christian, rationalist or materialistic implications. These had to be disproved and the connections between the scientific details of the Aristotelian Corpus and Christian principles at their highest level had to be drawn tighter.

Alexander of Hales, William of Auvergne, John of La Rochelle all took part in this work. But the men effectively responsible for its achievement were Robert Grosseteste and Albertus Magnus.

Grosseteste wrote so many works on scientific topics that even the list of their titles would extend to more than half a page; but his career at Oxford and his eventual preferment as Bishop of Lincoln prove that his orthodoxy was never suspect. He seems to have been one of those men who unite a strong respect for fact with an equally strong inclination to accept the dicta of traditional faith in matters where facts offer no guidance. This dualism of outlook made him the ideal interpreter of Aristotle, and he did in fact manage to rewrite the greatest part of the latter's scientific work without falling into theological error.

While Grosseteste wore out his energies composing treatises on particular topics his younger contemporary, the Dominican Albertus who later received the title of Great, more openly commented Aristotle, using a system of summaries which he adopted from Avicenna and which had the advantage of allowing him to present his author's text alongside his own commentary and alongside references to other commentators. Albertus was a discursive and somewhat dull philosopher whose exact doctrines are not easy to discover. But it is patent that he paved the way for Aquinas. The distinction between *universalia ante rem* present only in the Divine Mind and *universalia in re* immanent after the creative act, which managed simultaneously to avoid the Scylla of Pantheism and the Charybdis of the materialist outlook, was common to them both. And Albertus was largely responsible for organising the scientific work of Aristotle to fit in with that conception.

The measure of Albertus' success is the fact that after him science and philosophy part company.* The metaphysical implications of science are no longer a matter of dispute, so that the presentation of its detailed conclusions can be peacefully left to able popularisers. And such new discoveries as the scientists of the day are competent to make, also fit without trouble into the comprehensive philosophical framework prepared originally for their classical forerunners.* The ideas which at the beginning of the thirteenth century seemed to many to endanger the very existence of the Church, are fifty years later happily described and discussed by a Vincent of Beauvais.*

The *Speculum Maius* composed just after the middle of the thirteenth century is a monument to the triumph of Scholasticism. Vincent in his prologue quotes Jerome with approbation. He sees himself as following Jerome's advice to take the good and to leave the bad and so make secular knowledge suitable for Christians. But in fact his technique is far superior to anything Jerome conceived. He does not merely excerpt. He reinterprets. And he assembles his information in a hierarchical framework.

The first of his three volumes deals with the field of natural knowledge, the second and third discuss the relations between man and the universe.* The subsections are arranged in an order based upon the Bible story of the Creation. Thus the book opens with an account of God as seen by the light of human reason. Next we have summaries of contemporary knowledge in physics and natural history which are concerned with the realm of material creation; and to end the first section, there follows what we might call the natural history of man. It comprises his physiology, his psychology and a description of his means of subsistence. The second volume has for its subject man's relations to his environment and embraces the facts of grammar, dialectic, rhetoric, political science, morals, law and theology. The third volume is supplementary to the second and is devoted to history treated from an ecclesiastical viewpoint. Every field of knowledge is considered primarily with reference to the supernatural. Logic for example is represented as the analysis of relationships which existed first in the mind of God. Morals are a by-product of religion. Their main task is to give institutional form to customs framed in accordance with religious belief. In short, the book is a typical product of the Scholastic approach.

Naturally, it did not stand alone. Vincent had his predecessors, his rivals and his imitators. He is, however, representative. He wrote just at the moment when the Scholastic organisation of knowledge was complete, so that he forms the watershed between discoverers and organisers on the one hand and the popularisers on the other.

IV. THE REORGANISATION IN MEDICINE AND LAW

We have traced the victory of Scholasticism in theology, literature, philosophy and science; there remain medicine and law. They need not delay us long. Grosseteste's and Albertus' rewriting of Aristotle's science had its repercussions on medical learning. The free experimental study of medicine which had characterised the school of Salerno was replaced by an authoritarianism glorifying Galen. It will be remembered that Galen had adapted medical theory to Aristotelian science, and although an experimentalist, had come finally to believe in the dominance of the soul over the body. It is easy to see how this Groddeck-like viewpoint fitted in with the supernaturalist preoccupations of the medieval mind. Galen became the darling of the schools and eminent doctors like Peter of Abano had to have recourse to the most ingenious shifts to fit their observations into the common Galenic mould.

Law had a similar history. During the first half of the thirteenth century, Accursius assembled all existing comment on the *Code*, the *Institutes* and the *Digest* in a single comprehensive survey which was given the name of the *glossa ordinaria* or *magistralis*. Already in the previous two generations the commentary of the Four Doctors had been concerned not only to interpret Roman Law, but also to apply its principles to topics which the Roman jurists had not adequately covered; and Bulgarus in particular had made tentative efforts to show how these principles worked in settling everyday legal problems. By the time Accursius wrote, these extraneous forms of comment, which were not strictly related to the text, had come to form a vitally important element in legal scholarship, so that his *Glossa* was in itself representative of a certain accommodation of the Justinian law to medieval conditions. But Accursius was relatively speaking conservative in his methods. He still looked back to Irnerius; and the trends of the day were more adequately represented by the French school of Jacques de Retigny and by Cino da Pistoia. Their contribution to law consists almost entirely of decisions and opinions on practical problems. Cino was for many years assessor of civil causes in his native city and he brought to his academic studies a vast fund of experience of what actually happened in the courts.

The progress of a discipline which touched upon life at every point was necessarily slow; and the task of adapting and reinterpreting Roman Law was still unfinished when the thirteenth century drew to its close. The Scholastic synthesis in this field lags nearly a hundred years behind the great constructions of Thomistic philosophy. Its main architect is Cino's pupil, that Bartolo on whom Rabelais was to heap such scorn. Like his master, Bartolo spent many years as an assessor or assistant judge, and he was reputed never to make a point in his lectures which he did not relate to some case that had come to his notice. His conclusions always take into account the particular habits prevailing in the Italian cities. So for example he accepts the provisions of canon law with regard to marriage and gives assent to the Tuscan custom which allowed the bastard sons of nobles the same status as their legitimate offspring, a practice contrary to Roman usage. His work is so deeply rooted in actuality that we can derive from it a complete picture of *trecento* social life. No wonder that he appeared barbarous and unclassical to the sixteenth-century Humanists.

V. THE CAUSES OF THE SCHOLASTIC MOVEMENT

The lifetime of Aquinas is the great age of Scholasticism. But to trace the beginnings of the effort which was made to assimilate the classical heritage, we must go back to Peter Lombard and Hugh of St Victor, to a time when the classical revival was still in full swing; and to trace its completion we must move forward to the fourteenth century when the teachings of Petrarch have set the Renaissance in motion. Scholasticism is not so much an epoch as a movement, a stage in the development of European culture which occurs earlier in one field, later in another, but is nowhere omitted. Some of the secondary reasons for this movement have been already mentioned. We have considered the fact that the needs which gave birth to the classical revival had by 1200 all been satisfied, and the further fact that periods of intense cultural borrowing are naturally followed by periods of gradual assimilation. What remains to be explained is why in this particular case the assimilation took the form it did so that the borrowed material was used every time to support rather than to alter existing intellectual patterns. A glance at the fifteenth-century Renaissance will show that given other conditions the opposite is likely to occur. Cultures have been known to alter out of all recognition through the impact of extraneous techniques and ideas.

Scholasticism was in no sense a clerically inspired reaction against dangerous thoughts, along lines with which the eighteenth and nineteenth centuries have made us familiar; but it did have the effect of preserving Christianity from possible attacks, and the impulse which sustained it must be sought in the general belief that the Christian Order was worth preserving. Such an answer, however, runs the danger of appearing too simple. It amounts to little more than the naïve statement that the thirteenth century was an Age of Faith with the result that the classical revival was brought under control, while the Renaissance was an Age of Disbelief with the result that Humanism ran riot; and such a statement does not deserve the status of an explanation. Faith and its opposite are not qualities which come into being inexplicably at the fiat of some universal will. So more must be added.

The spread of religious faith is aided or hindered by observable social conditions. Christianity (which in its first beginnings had played the part of a religion of protest, providing the Roman poor with hope in the midst of desperate circumstances) became during the Dark Ages a guarantee of social stability. The medieval Church stood for order, for the morality which alone made life tolerable, for some measure of public welfare. If medieval men behaved humanely and sensibly, the reason must be sought to a great extent in the authority exercised by the Church. Long years of anarchy had dissipated the natural loyalties on which the tribal communities of the invaders had once depended; and the patterns of moral behaviour imposed by the Roman state had not survived the collapse of its rule. During the confused anarchy of the Dark Ages, there was no civil power sufficiently strong to compel even a temporary obedience, much less enforce permanent rules of conduct. There was only the Church, and the Faith on which the Church's influence ultimately depended.

Thus, during the centuries that follow the fall of Rome, the Christian Faith was treasured not only as the pledge of a personal salvation, but as a social good. It inspired the loyalty which now finds expression in patriotic zeal. Inevitably however (since social values have their roots in social conditions) as the civil state extended its powers, as the kings grew stronger and government more centralised, and men came to look to the secular authorities to guarantee them the peace they desired, so the social loyalty which had lent its support to the Church suffered a gradual decline. Eventually—by the Renaissance—the state was to take the place of the universal Church as the institution which men's desire for safety made them anxious to preserve. But during the period we have been considering in this chapter, that is during the twelfth and thirteenthcenturies, the change from a religiously stabilised community to one organised in secular units was still incomplete. The civil power was stronger than it had been in the Dark Ages, but it was not yet strong enough to stand alone; and in any case men were not accustomed to look elsewhere than to the Church for support. So at this time the loss of religious faith was still looked upon as a social danger. Its widespread abandonment was still envisaged as a major social calamity; and that spiritual devotion which springs from religious experience still received emotional reinforcement from social fears. Consequently, the world of Aquinas had what the world of Erasmus was to lack—an overwhelming desire to retain the Christian pattern of life. It was this desire which determined the character of the Scholastic effort and so has given us the *Summa contra Gentiles*, the *Divina Commedia*, the *Roman de la Rose* and on the reverse of the medal the puerilities of the *viri obscuri*.

CHAPTER VI

COLLAPSE AND NEW BEGINNINGS

When Petrarch was crowned with laurel on the Capitol, the students of Paris were listening to Buridan's lectures on the *pons asinorum*. The event which was to serve future generations as the aptest symbol of the Renaissance coincided in time with the typical pursuits of Scholasticism; and by a similar paradox only three years separate the revolt of the Florentine *popolo* against Walter of Brienne from the battle of Crécy. The proper characterisation of the fourteenth century has therefore been a matter of dispute; and the question has been asked whether the epoch which produced both Ockham's razor and the *Decameron* belongs more typically to the end of the Middle Ages or the beginning of the Renaissance.

The historians who have sought to answer this question have commonly drawn attention to the dividing line of the Alps and presumed the existence of two distinct cultures, one to the south, the other to the north. We can, the argument runs, look upon the Renaissance as evolving in time. We can note how certain books were read, first by a few and then by many, how they were translated and interpreted, imitated and gradually absorbed into contemporary tradition. We can trace the history of techniques from their first introduction to their eventual acceptance as commonplace routines. We can follow the elaboration of particular ideas, which make their début as concepts in some specialised field and were then applied to other spheres of experience. We can note how the culture which we associate with the name of Petrarch became more complex and played a larger role in European life with each passing decade, how each year brought some fresh advance, some new development. But however hard we may put the accent upon the time factor, we must also realise that the spatial unit, in which this movement grew to maturity, comprised a number of separate countries, so that the general history of the period consists of several overlapping local narratives. During the fourteenth and fifteenth centuries, Italy was in the van. France, Germany and England, weakened by long drawn out wars, could not free themselves from a decaying Scholasticism. Then in 1494 came Charles VIII's promenade, which exacerbated the internecine strife of the Italian cities, and during the crises which followed, their Humanism fell into a gradual decline. In the meantime the French soldiers who had paid this mass visit to the peninsula went home with novel ideas, with a love of luxury and a vehement admiration for art; and fired by their discoveries, they began to create a new Italy in France. But the northern Renaissance did not start at the point where its Italian predecessor had stood a hundred and fifty years earlier. When at the end of the fifteenth century Agricola, Linacre and Erasmus returned from their travels impregnated with the Italian outlook and in full command of the current Italian techniques, England, France and Germany crowded into a brief twenty years all the stages of growth which had taken so much longer in the south; and the northern Humanists improved upon what they learnt even before they had properly learnt it. Consequently, the evolution of the Renaissance, over Europe as a whole, went on without a pause.

This account is plausible; but at the same time it is open to one serious objection. It ignores the obvious similarities between Italy and the North. It describes the cult of chivalry for example as the self-conscious affirmation of feudal values forced upon a nobility which felt its power slipping away and so had to bolster up a position of material weakness by the appeal of an ideal. But when we find knights in Froissart who strive to acquit themselves well in order that people may speak of it in future times, or when later Chastellain praises the Duke of Burgundy for his 'haute magnificence de cœur pour estre vu et regardé en singulières choses', are we right to ignore the likeness which seems to link these attitudes to Petrarch's quest for *fama* and *virtus*? Is it not the same spirit that we see working on both sides of the Alps? When Boccaccio was writing learned tomes on famous men and women, the North had its cult of the nine worthies and their female counterparts, glorified Alexander and made a popular hero of du Guesclin. A few such coincidences could be dismissed as insignificant; but in this instance, they crowd upon the mind. Since the love of the ancients has always been considered the distinguishing mark of the Italian *trecento*, let us take a look at the following passage:

Although the novelties of the moderns were never disagreeable to our desires, who have always cherished with grateful affection those who devote themselves to study and who add anything either ingenious or useful to the opinions of our forefathers, yet we have always desired with more undoubting avidity to investigate the well-tested labours of the ancients. For whether they had by nature a greater vigour of mental sagacity, or whether they perhaps indulged in closer application to study, or whether they were assisted in their progress by both these things, the one point we are perfectly clear about is that their successors are barely capable of discussing the discoveries of their forerunners, and of acquiring those things as pupils which the ancients dug out by difficult efforts of discovery.

These words were not written by Petrarch or Salutati, but occur in the *Philobiblon* of the English monk, Richard of Bury (1281–1385), who was the tutor of Edward III.*

We should be ill-advised to accept the argument that these manifestations of the Renaissance spirit in the north may be disregarded since they appeared mixed with scholastic and feudal survivals. For Petrarch was a Christian even more surely than he was a Humanist, as the *Secretum* and the *de Remediis Utriusque Fortunae* reveal. He could write of the superiority of contemplative over the active ideal and pontificate on the inanity of worldly blessings. Salutati, too, shows himself prepared to advance the old medieval hypothesis that Virgil was worth reading because you could find references to the Trinity, to the foundation of the Church and the immortality of the soul hidden in the text; and his arguments on this topic end with a sentence which would not have been out of place in the mouth of Bernard Silvestris: 'Thus, I who am Christian read Virgil, not as one who will remain with him always or for long, but search diligently to find in his word whatever will help me to uprightness of character and right living.'* Even so zealous a Humanist as Bruni, who was the first to envisage the ideal of man's full development, had his medieval moments; and when he is drawing up a course of reading, he recommends Lactantius, Augustine and Jerome as an essential preparation for Cicero and the Latin poets.*

The affinities between thirteenth-century Italy and thirteenth-century France or England are in the last analysis more striking than the contrasts. The Alps did not constitute a cultural boundary at this period any more than they had done earlier. Western Europe was still a cultural unit. The theory we have outlined which would divide that unit into two distinct parts is plainly unacceptable; and yet it provides the only possible answer to the question asked at the beginning of this chapter. If we *are* given the choice of two patterns of life, medieval and Renaissance, into which to fit the thirteenth century, then we must allot Italy to the second and the rest of the West to the first.

The way of escape from this dilemma is to conclude that the question itself is at fault. Its terms of reference are wrong. We ought not to assume that there were two distinct cultures, the Renaissance succeeding the Middle Ages as the day the night. The Renaissance way of life was not the result of a reorientation. It was the result of a long and slow development which can be clearly traced in the preceding centuries. Renaissance man has been described as an individualist, and the historians of the period have noted the spread of capitalist relations in the economic field and the parallel spread of rationality in administration, the general acceptance of materialist values and a greater emphasis on social mobility, conspicuous expenditure and the cult of personal glory. Now all these traits which are accepted as the distinguishing characteristics of the Renaissance, can be found in embryo during the Middle Ages. Not only are they present at that earlier time; but what is perhaps more important, they can be seen to exercise an ever growing influence. The Middle Ages were not capitalistic, in the sense that there was no regular system for the investment of surplus wealth. But the feudal pattern of status and service did not exist in a theoretically perfect form anywhere outside the artificially constructed principalities of the Crusaders; and in its imperfect state it offered individuals ample opportunities to amass property out of all proportion to their status and responsibilities. In Cambridgeshire, for example, the rise of the Dunnings during the eleventh and twelfth centuries was followed by much more spectacular accumulations of the de Quincy family during the thirteenth. Nor were these practices confined to isolated adventurers. While Aquinas was hammering out his condemnations of usury, large numbers of serfs were hastening to commute their works for a money payment so that they might devote their attention to their own plots and produce a saleable surplus. The system of landholding was riddled in all its parts by the activities of private enterprise; and land was the stronghold of feudalism. In commerce, fortunes were even more freely made. The energy and boldness of individuals expected and earned specific rewards whose extent can be readily deduced from the manifest prosperity of the great trading towns.

Such a widespread zeal for money-making could hardly have existed in a society which placed no emphasis on material values; and certain manifestations of the medieval cult of luxury have already been described. They reached their peak at the Sicilian court. There, in a southern setting, the Norman taste for magnificence was allowed unbridled play. Palermo had the reputation of an earthly paradise. Its gorgeous fountains, its seductive pleasure-gardens and decorated buildings delighted the eyes and dazzled the imagination of every traveller. Benjamin of Tudela who visited the city in 1180 tells of an artificial lake in the royal gardens where he saw ships covered with gold and silver which belong to the king who uses them for pleasure trips with his women. In the same park there is also a great palace, the walls of which are covered partly with painted designs, partly with gold and silver; and the paving of the floors is of marble, picked out in gold and silver with all manner of designs. There exists no building like it in all the world.

And these excesses of luxury were the outward sign of the spirit that governed the running of the State as a whole. Its dispositions were guided by the pleasure principle. Everything was rationally organised to secure the maximum of possible well-being; exquisite delights for the king and nobles, but also an unusual material prosperity for the lower orders. It was in Sicily indeed that those rational practices of government which during the Renaissance were to form the necessary corollary of capitalist development emerged for the first time in their full power, though their value had been demonstrated in other places as well, in the England of Henry II for example. The Sicilian kingdom has been called the first modern state. It had no supernatural aims. Four ancient traditions, the Moslem, the Jewish, the Byzantine and the Latin, met to form a new scepticism. The Sicilian intellectuals viewing all beliefs impartially, discarded them all, and worshipped nothing but immediate joys.

Frederick II was the greatest exponent of this spirit. His career affords us startling evidence of that secularism which was trying to displace the monastic outlook, and with that secularism went its inevitable accompaniment of a thirst for personal distinction, that vainglory which the satirists of the time are never tired of attacking.

As we move up the centuries from Charlemagne to Frederick II, we can trace the emergence and then the rapid growth of the social patterns which were to become dominant with the Renaissance. Seen against these broad currents of development, feudal relationships and the supernaturalist social values of the medieval Church appear as forms of merely episodic significance. It is possible to consider them as a stop-gap owing their existence to a temporary need rather than as an expression of the inner character of the society they served.

The development of what we have called Renaissance society had to reach a fairly advanced stage before the secular state, which was its appropriate political expression, could emerge and survive. It was preceded therefore by forms of political organisation which bore no direct relation to it but which rendered possible the immediate maintenance of order. Structurally feudalism appears the antithesis of the Renaissance state; but historically it prepared the way for that institution by creating the necessary preconditions of its growth. In a similar way, even before feudalism had been properly established, the authority of the Church had served to guarantee a measure of peace and had guarded the vulnerable infancy of the secularist world.

Many of the problems which confront us when we try to understand the Middle Ages vanish if we interpret their life in terms of a slowly developing secular culture which has imposed upon it a pattern of relationships extraneous to its secular nature, relationships derived from those social institutions which had grown up to meet the immediate challenge of anarchy. The adoption of this view does not involve denying the cultural value of that feudal and supernaturalist pattern, nor does it call into question the undoubted fact that the certainties of feudal status and monastic other-worldliness provided some temperaments with more satisfactory outlets than they were to find during the Renaissance or can find today. Such considerations of value belong elsewhere. What has been said amounts to no more than a factual analysis. Feudalism and the standards of the *Civitas Dei* may have dominated, but they did not completely permeate medieval society. They were not the expression of its whole life as the culture of Athens was the expression of the life of Athens. They were, even at the moments of their widest acceptance, superimposed upon another and more lasting pattern, upon the Renaissance in embryo.

Scholasticism was an effort at the intellectual level to subsume under a world-view in accord with feudalism and with the medieval form of Christianity the newly discovered classical material that for the most part served the requirements of a growing secular culture. At the intellectual level, the attempt succeeded. For the majority of men still felt their world to depend on the survival of their old institutions. But the ultimate causes of the change which was coming over the world lay beyond the reach of Thomistic thought; and the fourteenth century was to bring the Renaissance.

By 1300, the new order in Italy was on the point of replacing the old. The balance of economic power had shifted to the middle classes. The social attitudes proper to an individualist economy commanded widespread adherence. The peculiar virtues of the entrepreneur—thrift, ingenuity and calculated daring—began to receive the recognition which they had long been denied; and success found its appropriate method of expression in conspicuous display.

The rest of Europe lagged somewhat behind. Since Italy had always been the gateway to the East, the orientation of the trade routes brought her a prosperity which hastened her economic advance. But even apart from that incidental advantage, large units like France and England were bound to find the transition from feudalism more difficult than was the case in the compact Italian city-states. But this difference which affected only their degree of development cannot be held to have made the northern societies different in kind from those of the peninsula. As we have seen, the main traits of Italian life can be traced in the north where they present themselves in a slightly modified but still recognisable form.

The cult of chivalry will serve to illustrate the nature of these identities and modifications. Perhaps the most notable characteristic of the new Renaissance order was the high value given to individual effort and the consequent emphasis placed upon the distinction which was to reward such effort. As far as Italy was concerned, Petrarch's mystique of *virtus* and *fama* (which linked success with an innate merit and gave popular acclaim a magic quality) together with the ample opportunities afforded by the new cult of art for a conspicuous consumption that appeared both 'enviable and uplifting',* was sufficient to provide individualist ambition with the impetus it needed; and since in the peninsula careers were largely open to talent, the relationship between merit and recompense could be presented without complications. In the north matters were not so simple. There the feudal aristocracy was still dominant. It was admittedly open to anyone who could to make a display of his wealth. But greatness fell in a different category. For no middle class adventurer could pretend to himself that he had achieved the reality of distinction in a world where the reins of power were held by those who had inherited their position. Glory manifestly belonged to those of noble birth. Its cult existed—an inevitable product of the prevailing mental climate. But under the circumstances it was almost necessarily limited to a particular class and found expression within the framework of the chivalric ideal which grew corrupted in consequence. By the fourteenth century, the standards of conduct once associated with the name of Godfrey de Bouillon figure as the ideological trappings of an aristocratic self-glorification. We have only to compare the Order of the Garter, founded by Edward III, with some earlier body like the Hospitallers, to recognise immediately the profound change that had come over the whole conception of knighthood. The members of this new Order did not fight the heathen or succour the distressed. Its origins went back apparently to a tourney in which two parties of twelve took part headed respectively by the King and the Black Prince; and it was from its first foundation nothing more than an avenue to social esteem. The picturesque appurtenances of knightly existence, the ceremonies, the insignia, the jousts and processions grew increasingly elaborate. Many of them had been unknown in the eleventh and twelfth centuries; but now they made the nobility the cynosure of every eye, and show clearly enough that the *fama* which Petrarch valued so highly was not absent from the northern scene. Only it was a perquisite of the nobility, and commoners could aspire to it only if, like the Pastons or the Pulteneys, they managed to rise out of their class.*

Thus, Italy was not an isolated unit peremptorily separated from the rest of Europe by the accidents of economic advance. The citizens of the Tuscan and Lombard towns stood at the head of a general movement. The Italian intelligenzia, that found itself so strongly pressed to provide the ideological superstructure of a specifically capitalist culture, can be seen to have put into words the aspirations not only of their compatriots but of the rising middle-class throughout the West. Their writings were in the fullest sense representative of the changing world of their time.

But the formulation of this new world view was necessarily a gradual process. For it could not take place at the level of conscious thought. Contemporary knowledge about the nature of social change was not sufficient to permit a reasoned analysis of current trends or a reasoned statement of current objectives. The intellectuals responded to a vague feeling common to the people around them, which they understood to the precise extent that they shared it. They were in fact expressing and often expressing clumsily their own imperfectly realised aspirations. The new outlook evolved blindly and piecemeal. There were attacks upon the Italian Church and nobles, which still fitted into the old categories of the Guelf and Ghibelline controversy, and which have their counterparts in the anti-clericalism of Southern France as expressed by Jean de Meung, and perhaps in Wyclif's Lollard movement. The traditional order was assailed from many directions and for a variety of motives. But every onslaught, whatever its conscious intention, served in practice the same end. They all helped to bring the Renaissance nearer. Early in the fourteenth century, Convenevole da Prato who was later to have Petrarch for his pupil wrote a poem praising Robert of Anjou.* Ferreto of Vincenza bewailed the lack of a Maecenas to celebrate in his verse,* and between 1306 and 1320,

Giovanni de Matociis, a Veronese scholar, composed a history of the emperors from Augustus to Charlemagne in order to honour famous men.* What is more, writers sought fame for themselves and obtained it. In 1314, twenty-six years before the famous crowning of Petrarch, Albertino Mussato was awarded a poet's crown by the city of Padua. He appears to have done little to deserve it, being more of a grammarian than a poet, but it is the fact of the award rather than the man's merit that we must take as significant.

How long this slow rate of advance might have lasted, and what its eventual outcome would have been, we are not in a position to know. For at this juncture, a remarkable personality came on the scene.

The cult of fame found its high priest in Petrarch. He made his first appearance in the early decades of the fourteenth century as a young Italian poet who had won the admiration of a vast public by those exquisite sonnets which we still associate with his name. It was open to him to spend his life flattered and fêted in all the courts of his day, but occupied only in the exploitation of his unique talent; and if he had lived a hundred years earlier, that would have been the course he would certainly have chosen. But he was profoundly a man of his age. That individualist temper whose first stirrings we have noted among his contemporaries, possessed him in its most fiery and articulate form; and he used the fame won him by his verses to gain public recognition for his personality and his ideas. He was the first man of letters to follow that pattern which a Voltaire, an Hugo and a Shaw have since made so familiar. His vernacular poetry had employed the motifs of the chivalric lyric which, however, he had transformed by infusing a personal reality into the lover's desire and pain; and the ideas he chose to popularise were similarly coloured by his self-dramatisation. He developed the cult of fame and explained its implications. Human talent, he assumed, is certain of recognition if it is properly used; and a genuine public recognition is never accorded to the unworthy. So, glory is at once the proof of a natural excellence or *virtus* and the reward required to bring this excellence to perfection. He also assumed that excellence was a function of the whole personality even where it found expression through some particular talent. It will be evident from what has been said that *virtus* and *fama* in Petrarch's thought bear a strong resemblance to the divine election and the salvation of the Calvinists. Presumably, the two pairs of concepts are based on the same underlying experience. There is a common belief among successful men that their success has derived from some unusual quality in themselves.

Where Mussato had been content merely to claim fame as the reward of his poetry, Petrarch developed the idea that literature not only deserved such recognition but was also able to bestow it. Eloquence was not only the proper expression, but was also the proper guerdon of *virtus*. An eloquent writer could win for himself that acclamation which constitutes fame, and he could also win it for the deeds he described. The quality of excellence originally inherent in the poet passed from him to his work and so came to be associated with his subject. This mystical conception, which had been Pindar's at an earlier epoch, but which Petrarch now formulated independently, left the poet in a unique position. He could really feel himself superior to the rest of mankind and had no reason to blush for his triumphs in the presence of the materially successful. Petrarch made it possible for writers to give whole-hearted support to the new individualism.

His ideas were important in themselves; but what made his influence so vital was the circumstance that his own life provided such startling proof of the validity of his doctrines. He has been called the first modern man; and the description is remarkably just. No writer has ever regarded the foibles of his own character with a more loving eye or took such trouble to explain to others the pattern he had selected for his own behaviour. Free from the burden of domestic ties, he devoted himself to the cult of friendship and the enjoyment of nature. He waxed enthusiastic, somewhat guardedly, about the distant prospect of the Alps, and more genuinely about his own garden. He dramatised his fits of discouragement, his religious scruples, his vigorous good health. But the boldest flights of his histrionic genius were reserved for the part he best loved to play, the role of the famous author sitting at his desk, withdrawn from the world, but conscious of the devoted attention of a million admirers. He was a literary man, and the life he lived and described bore to some extent the stamp of his profession. But many of its traits were such that they could suit any individualist. His independence, his attitude to love and friendship, his delight in solitude and his passion for fame were qualities accessible to all. He provided his generation with a design for living.

In our eyes, however, he figures not only as the typical Renaissance man, the discoverer of a new ethos, but also as the most zealous champion of classical learning; and it now remains for us to discover the link between his individualism and his Humanism. This, however, was more subtle than might at first appear; for neither the general cult of fame, nor the more specific desire for poetic glory, necessitated a revival of interest in the classics. Admittedly, there was the unbroken tradition which made Latin the language of literature; and admittedly many of Petrarch's immediate predecessors who sought for literary fame had chosen to write in Latin. There was Mussato with his poetic crown. There was Giovanni de Matociis with his history of the emperors. Indeed, we can trace the faint stirrings of a new Humanism at the beginning of the fourteenth century some time before Petrarch's influence could have made itself felt. In 1321 when the chair of formal rhetoric was re-established in Bologna, the students petitioned simultaneously for a chair of poetry. The 1328 programme of Toulouse University shows an unusual attention to the teaching of grammar, and in 1343 a salary was bestowed upon a certain Magister Vitale at Bologna for lecturing on Cicero and on the *Metamorphoses* of Ovid.* But if ever any man was in a position to break with that tradition once and for all, the successful author of the *Sonnets* could have done so. He could have lumped the study of Latin with the other medieval practices he abhorred, and he could have established the vernacular as the proper vehicle of the new anti-feudal, anti-scholastic society.* The reason why he did not take this course, the reason why he did precisely the opposite, must be sought partly in the general temper of the individualism he represented and partly in his own experience. For all their energy and confident self-assertion, the protagonists of the new spirit lacked cultural self-confidence. Unable as yet to visualise the new world towards which their aspirations were directed, they clung to what scraps of guidance seemed available; and rejecting Scholasticism were bound to turn to the Latin and Greek authors. Moreover, there were good practical reasons for such a choice. The Humanism of the twelfth century had not yet drawn all that antiquity could teach mankind into the main current of the European tradition. Concerning human behaviour in particular, the new epoch (which stood nearer to Cicero than to Aquinas) had a good deal to learn from the past. So the rebels, and Petrarch with them, for in this respect too he was typical of his age, found it natural to look backwards as well as forwards and to seek in antiquity the seeds of the future.

Moreover, Petrarch himself happened to be attracted to the Latin authors for personal reasons. As an adolescent he had found spiritual comfort in the reading of Cicero and Virgil. They had appeared to him to possess, in a full and harmonious form, the sentiments and attitudes he felt burgeoning obscurely within himself; and he saw the Roman world as the one in which he would have chosen to live. He also accepted whole-heartedly Cicero's estimate of the artistic value of Latin. His naturally fine ear had led him from his boyhood to take great pleasure in the music of words, and finding that his contemporaries neglected the musical aspects of style, while Cicero contrariwise placed great emphasis on them, he became Cicero's worshipper and learnt to regard Latin as the only language in which great art could be produced. He never grew tired of extolling the grace and beauty of the Ciceronian period. Rhetoric was the queen of the Arts for him, and Cicero the king of rhetoricians.

So he raised the cry of 'back to antiquity'. When he received a poetic crown upon the Capitol, he turned that circumstance into an excuse for regarding himself as a Roman citizen. He wrote a letter of praise to Rienzi while the Tribune's affairs were still prospering, and later interceded with the Papal Commission of 1348 as a champion of the Roman people.* The constitution of the ancient republic was in his opinion the model which the new Rome ought to follow; and he advised his adopted countrymen to that effect. He was indeed so fascinated by the republican heroes that eventually he wrote a book in which he out-Livied Livy in his idealisation of the kings and consuls.

We shall not, however, form a correct picture of his Humanism or estimate its vital connection with the rest of his thought so long as we consider only what he liked in the classics. For his rejections were also significant. He always claimed to be an ardent propagandist for the content as well as for the form of classical literature; and when he was overtly stating his creed, he never wavered in his affirmation that all the ancients had written was undoubtedly good. Theoretically, his enthusiasm embraced the whole of the classical heritage. But if we leave his general statements on one side, if we look instead at his judgements on matters of detail, a different picture emerges. He rejected a great deal. He despised for instance the paraphernalia of Aristotelian logic and metaphysics; and aware that this antipathy did not square with his cult of the past, was ready with a subtle excuse for his attitude. Aristotle, he claimed, had been a stylist. He must therefore have written something very different and infinitely more valuable than the corrupt and Averroist texts that we know. This excuse might appear convincing if Petrarch's rejections had stopped with the medieval Aristotle. We find, however, that he went much further. Law was for him as abominable as metaphysics; and here his technical knowledge (he had been trained at Bologna) stopped him from trying to discriminate, as his less informed successors were to do, between the Roman text and the constructions of its commentators.* He embraced the lot in a wholesale condemnation; and he was likewise prepared to throw overboard the totality of existing medical knowledge. 'I do not question', he says, 'that Medicine exists and is of great importance.'* But the medicine he is thus willing to accept is the science of the future. He has nothing but contempt for the authorities of his day including Hippocrates and Galen; and nothing but contempt too for the science of his day which indeed he grossly maligns. The young Averroist whom he attacks in the *de sui ipsius et multorum aliorum ignorantia* is described as knowing how many hairs a lion has on his head, how elephants copulate backwards and how hunters fool tigers with a mirror. What, asks Petrarch, having thus prejudged his case, can be the pertinence of this knowledge? How can it contribute to the good life?*

The passage is important, for the good life is indeed Petrarch's only interest. The above catalogue will have served to show that he throws aside precisely those portions of the classical heritage which interested his medieval predecessors. The technicalities of law, medicine, science and philosophy lie outside his scope. Instead he focuses the attention of his contemporaries on ancient artistic achievement and on the ancient way of life. In his eyes, Cicero is the paragon of eloquence, the *magister vitae*, the writer on friendship and dignified leisure whose *Hortensius* led St Augustine to the study of truth. Virgil is the lover of the countryside, Horace the man who had expressed a wish to flee from the madding crowd. He sees them all as the exponents of his own creed.

Petrarch, like Byron after him, owed his popularity to the fact that he showed his time its future self. His services to contemporary culture included the provision of a *mystique* to justify current aspirations as well as his creating a pattern for individualists to follow. Both were to prove influential beyond his wildest dreams. But his contribution to classical learning, which concerns us more nearly, was of an equal importance. We may legitimately observe that his approach to ancient literature was guided in all its details by his individualist preoccupations, and that he organised classical learning to serve the Renaissance spirit. But we cannot stop at that point. The change of emphasis from the learning of the professional disciplines to the joint study of artistic form and the good life admittedly transformed Humanism into an apt instrument for the furtherance of what we called the new order. But it also had another and most beneficial effect. The twelfth-century scholars had done their work well, and the parts of the classical heritage which had received their attention were by Petrarch's lifetime thoroughly explored. Given the techniques of study available, there was not much more to be learnt from the further investigation of Aristotle, or Galen, or the Justinian law.* So long as Humanism failed to shift its attention to those fields where antiquity still had new treasures to offer, it was after the twelfth century doomed to be sterile. But when we cast our eyes over the huge panorama of medieval learning, we see immediately that the utilitarianism of the specialists and the moral fears of the orthodox had resulted in preventing this necessary readjustment of approach; and the scholars of the later Middle Ages had closed their eyes to all that the Greeks and Romans could have taught them about man the artist and about man as an individual seeking for a pattern of life. The gap, which still remained to be filled in Europe's absorption of its heritage, was in just those sectors to which Petrarch now directed the energies of his disciples; and their Humanism was to complete the process which, begun by the Fathers, had been set into motion again by Bede and Alcuin, and then carried forward to great effect by Constantine the African, Irnerius and the Aristotelians. We must see the Renaissance as adding the last span to the bridge which the Middle Ages had started to construct; and this is the setting in which we must judge the value of Petrarch's services to classical learning.

But let us now turn to the detail of these services. Petrarch's insistence that Greek and Latin were the only suitable languages for literature was admittedly to prove a stumbling-block in the way of that cultural progress to whose support the Humanists were otherwise committed. It was to hinder that natural development of the vernaculars, which was a necessary corollary both of the growth of nationalism and of the spread of education; while the difficulties which it raised for the Humanists, and which increased with the passage of time, will occupy us in a later chapter. One could collect a good deal of evidence to show that in so far as Petrarch made himself the champion of imitation, his influence was not wholly beneficial, but even on this issue his modern critics have been chary of blame.

Son œuvre est calquée sur celle de l'antiquité qu'il a exhumée. Elle manque d'originalité dans la forme et souvent dans le fond; elle prépare une littérature d'imitation, qui entravera presqu'autant qu'elle servira le développement des littératures nationales; mais cette imitation malgré tout est un grand pas en avant....*

For alongside the harshest judgement one can pass on the lifelessness of Neo-Latin literature, there rises always the further question: could

252

the vernaculars have acquired so full a vocabulary in so short a space of time, and could their writers have learnt to use such diverse and fruitful genres, if the age had not served its apprenticeship in reproducing Cicero and composing tragedies after a Senecan model? But in any case Petrarch's influence did not stop with his advocacy of imitation. To assess his work aright, it is essential to remember that he recommended the ancients not only as masters in the art of writing, but above all as masters in the art of living. The stream of books which poured from his pen appear pedantic to the modern reader and were neglected during the High Renaissance. But they impressed his contemporaries; and the circling of their manifold arguments and illustrations converges persistently on this one point, that the ancients can show us the way to live, how to enjoy nature, how to cultivate friendship, how to move *a necessariis artificiis ad elegantiora*. Writers like Cicero treat of virtue; and 'even if our goal is not virtue itself, the path to our right true end lies through human virtues, and not through the comprehension of their nature, but through the love we have for them'.*

Combine these two elements, complete the imitative interest by the ideological, and you have a programme for a new approach to the classics which focuses attention on a hitherto comparatively neglected sector of the ancient heritage. The role of Petrarch in the limited field of classical studies was every whit as revolutionary therefore as the part he played in the whole wide development of European culture. If he was the first modern man, he was also the first modern—or at any rate, the first Renaissance—scholar.

But programmes which involve radical changes are not easy to carry out; and when we turn from the theoretical statements to practical achievements of the fourteenth-century Humanists, it is impossible to avoid a feeling of disappointment. The progress that was made seems derisory alongside the aspirations from which it derived its being. Medieval scholarship had tended to set itself restricted aims; and our survey of the Middle Ages has accustomed us to see advances made in knowledge not through any grandeur of intention, but because the men who actually studied the classical authors were always led by their immediate interest further than they had originally intended. Now for the first time the dynamic came from a theorist and was communicated by him to the workers in the field. For the first time scholars were set a goal well beyond what they could immediately reach. No wonder then, that, by contrast with the twelfth century, the performance of the fourteenth strikes the observer as disappointing.

To judge fourteenth-century Humanism fairly, one must form some idea of the difficulties of its task. Successful imitation cannot be learnt in a day. To reproduce the language or the literary structure of another writer requires an elaborate technique of a sort which in Petrarch's day was known only to the Byzantine Atticists. The desired understanding of the Greek and Roman way of life similarly presupposed a painstaking study of ancient literature and an infinity of attempts to interpret it in contemporary terms. Nor was there any hope of spreading these accomplishments beyond a very small circle of scholars without a vast educational effort involving the introduction of new teaching methods and new curricula. In all these spheres, the fourteenth century made a certain limited advance. But since the goal that Petrarch set was not to be attained until the High Renaissance had done its work, it is not surprising that this early advance did not carry the Humanist banner very far.

Much of the work was done by Petrarch himself. On the strictly linguistic side, his desire to write like Cicero never went beyond a pious aspiration; and if we accept the view that Ciceronianism proved as much of a curse as a blessing, his failure in this respect must be placed to his credit; for he was recommending a procedure whose ultimate implications he did not realise. Where he did make a more solid contribution was in popularising certain classical genres. The interest he took in his own personality led him to appreciate a form of expression which gave prominence to incidental opinions and foibles; and his *Letters* which during his lifetime formed the most important source of his influence revived the familiar manner of Cicero, thus bringing to notice a hitherto neglected element in the classical tradition. He also resuscitated the Epic which had been somewhat forgotten since the great days of the twelfth century. The *Africa* missed the moment when its publication would have had greatest effect. Jealously concealed from the world during the lifetime of its author, it first became known at a time when public taste was already shifting towards a more extreme Humanism, and its reputation never recovered from this initial setback. The nineteenth century echoing Zumbini's judgement classed it with the *Franciade* and the *Henriade* as 'un grande tentativo fallito', the last infirmity of a noble mind, better left unread. Most modern readers of the poem agree that this verdict was unduly harsh. Petrarch had certain merits as a writer of epic. If he does not stir our emotions, he does not on the other hand shock our good taste or our reason. He is not a second Virgil, but he will bear comparison with Walter of

Châtillon or even with Statius. And if we consider the *Africa* not as a work of art, but as a link in a chain that leads to Camoens and Tasso, the impulse it gave to a renewed study of classical forms emerges as a new departure of some importance.

The Petrarch of the *Canzoniere* does not concern us. In his Latin writings he shows himself a competent craftsman, but his main contribution is in the field of ideas. His Latin works, including the *Africa*, are an elaborate footnote to Cicero's ideas on the good life, which they extol, illustrate and bring into accord with Christianity. To read Petrarch is to read a Cicero aware of the implications of his creed and turned apologist. The noblest themes of Latin philosophy, its zeal for an understanding of man's nature, its gratitude for the good things of this world, its emphasis on the role of the will, its firm recognition of the values of art and intellect are all sympathetically treated and exemplified in the *de Ignorantia*, in the *de Remediis Utriusque Fortunae*, in the *Secretum* and above all in the *Letters*. The reconciliation of these views with Christianity is admittedly incomplete; and there were times when Petrarch despaired of satisfying his Augustinian conscience. But on the whole he follows the line that salvation must in any case come through the practice of human virtues, through that living well here and now, which is Cicero's lesson. For Petrarch, like so many of his Humanist successors, tended to emphasise morality rather than theology, to trust in the last analysis a personal relationship with God rather than the authority of the Church.*

When Petrarch besought his countrymen to close their Aristotle and open their Cicero, he was most truly the Father of the Renaissance. His revelation of the Roman outlook had a lasting influence so that we find the ideas and attitudes to which he gave prominence, not only among his immediate disciples, not only in Guarino, Vittorino da Feltre and Machiavelli, but in Erasmus, in Budé, in Ascham and in Montaigne. It is not as the propagandist of imitation, it is not as the champion of antiquity in general, that Petrarch most deserves notice. His greatest service to European culture was to have formulated the Humanist ideology, which we may perhaps define as the noblest elements in Roman morality organised to serve the Renaissance spirit; and for confirmation of this we need look no further than the case of Coluccio Salutati. Latin Secretary to the Florentine Republic for over thirty years, the correspondent of every important Humanist of his day and the most ardent of Petrarch's admirers, Salutati has been described by a modern critic as the man who gave the Middle Ages its *coup de grâce*.*

He has been allotted a place of honour in the forefront of the Humanist battle-line. Yet a few pages back we have had occasion to refer to him as the exponent of an allegorical method of interpreting Virgil; and there is other evidence to show that his valuation of the classics was almost medieval. In the appendix to the modern edition of his letters there is a list of his citations—a list, from which we can gain some idea of the range and direction of his reading. The largest number of references is to the Old Testament, but the New Testament and Cicero come a close second. Virgil is next; and then after a substantial gap, St Augustine, Seneca, Aristotle, Ovid, Horace and Petrarch.* Except for the presence of Aristotle and Petrarch and the prominence given to Seneca, the names correspond to those mentioned by Servatus Lupus four centuries earlier. The authors a man quotes are those who belong to him most intimately; and in so far as the pattern of this intimate knowledge is concerned, Salutati had much in common with his medieval predecessors. Moreover, the very terms in which he praises Petrarch show that he did not, like most later Humanists, accord antiquity an unquestioned pre-eminence. When he states: 'we have in Francesco Petrarca a writer whom we can, I would not say, oppose, but prefer to the ancients and even to the Greeks', he links himself not with Valla and Guarino, but with John of Garland and Eberhard the German.*

It is not necessary, however, to assume the incorrectness of Saitta's verdict. Coluccio Salutati was both a Paladin of Humanism and in some ways a late representative of the medieval tradition. The opposition between these two views of his character can be resolved if we distinguish the precise nature of his Humanist activity and note that he was enthralled, not by the whole, but by one particular aspect of Petrarch's teaching. In a well-known passage written after his idol's death, he praises the latter primarily for providing an example of virtue in his life, manners and reputation. His admiration in short was for Petrarch the moralist, not for Humanist eloquence or classicolatry but for the Humanist ethos.

The *de Viris Illustribus* which Petrarch was writing when he died, was not published until the nineteenth century, but its central conception had been fully expounded in his earlier treatises and formed an important pendant to the moral ideas which Salutati found so impressive. The *Africa* stood as a memorial to Scipio; and the *Letters* furnish a multitude of passages where the same service was performed for other Roman heroes. As Petrarch had not been the first to venture into this field of panegyric, where the Veronese had preceded him, so he was not the last. The time and energy which the Humanists of the fourteenth and fifteenth centuries expended on retracing the lineaments of the Roman great, furnish a striking example of the way in which prevailing cultural attitudes have dominated classical studies.

By 1356 Pastrengo had completed his monumental *de originibus rerum*, more than half of which was devoted to biographical notices on famous authors.* Boccaccio wrote on famous women, and later treated of the sad fate of famous men. He related in an organised fashion the histories of the ancient gods and demi-gods, those heroic figures larger than life, and devoted one book specifically to the defence of poets. Petrarch's ideals—fame, excellence, poetic inspiration and the eternal value of the classics—pervade the whole of his disciple's work. Strangely enough, the author of the *Decameron* was a dry pedant when he came to write in Latin. But if he took upon himself the thankless and uninspiring role of providing the facts to support the Petrarchian thesis, the popularity of his compilations showed that his energies were not misplaced. The *Genealogies* were printed six times between 1473 and 1572; and later both they and the more facile histories of famous men and women, were translated into French. Only one of Petrarch's books, the *de Remediis Utriusque Fortunae* enjoyed an equal renown.*

Salutati and Boccaccio did a great deal to win attention for Petrarch's ideas. But even with the personal influence of the first and the popularity of the second, Humanism remained for a long time a doctrine in vogue among the intelligenzia and made next to no impact on the schools. These had seen little change since the thirteenth century. Grammar, which was taught up to the age of fourteen, and rhetoric were preparatory subjects for the professional disciplines. In the former the course began with the *Psalter* and went on to the *Disticha Catonis*, Aesop, Boethius' *de Consolatione* and Prosper's *Epigrams*. Sometimes the boys were expected to get this material parrot-fashion by heart. And in general the average grammarian impressed his charges by his brutality rather than by his knowledge.* Grammar was followed by a year or more of dialectic, and then at the university level came rhetoric. But at some places of which Florence is an example the course in dialectic was omitted; and in the popular faculty of law, higher education consisted of a strictly professional discipline into which rhetorical studies entered only as a subsidiary. In the *Studio* in Florence, there were professors for civil and canon law, a teacher to impart the elements of grammar, another to train the boys in the formulae needed for legal documents and a rhetorician who instructed them in the arts of persuasion.* It was a closely organised curriculum well defended against innovations. But even in those cities where rhetoric was a university subject, undertaken at the age of sixteen or thereabouts, young men were expected to abandon it within a couple of years for some more profitable branch of study.*

It was not until the end of the century that the influence of Humanism began to spread in the educational world. Then certain individual teachers, working within the established system, sought to give their lessons in grammar or rhetoric a somewhat wider range. Among these innovators, who came under the spell of Petrarch, were Giovanni Malpaghini, who numbered among his pupils Leonardo Bruni, Marsuppini and Poggio—although the latter does not tell us anything to his credit—and Giovanni da Ravenna who, like Petrarch, was determined to devote himself to literature and, like Petrarch, wandered restlessly from place to place. In the intervals of his wanderings he appears, however, to have done some useful work; for during his stay at Padua he trained Guarino and Vittorino da Feltre. As time went on these Humanist teachers developed a theory. Already Giovanni da Ravenna had set forth in his autobiography* ideas on education, which owed a good deal to Petrarch. But it was in 1404 that the new aims were definitely formulated when Vergerio wrote his *de Ingenuis Moribus.** It is true that this treatise was composed after the turn of the century, by which time Vergerio had attended the lectures of Chrysoloras; but he had been teaching for many years previous to his Florentine visit, and we may reasonably assume that he was putting on paper the principles which had guided him throughout his career. Many of Vergerio's contemporaries must have been startled by the originality of his approach. In direct contradistinction to the medieval treatises, the emphasis is placed on the formation of character and not on the acquisition of knowledge. The ideal character envisaged by the author is energetic, highly susceptible to those stimuli of praise and blame which lead to self-improvement, ambitious and eager to learn. Prudence and the ability to mix with one's fellows are singled out for praise; and Vergerio further insists on the importance of that sensitivity to the nuances of behaviour which older men like to see in the young. 'A habit of squandering money thoughtlessly...must be checked.' 'Nothing injures a young man in the eyes of serious people so much as exaggeration and untruthfulness.' 'Solitary temper must be disciplined and on no account encouraged.'* These are ideals and precepts which could find favour in a business college and remind us that the Renaissance Italy was a nation of shopkeepers. Although Vergerio addresses his dedication to Ubertino of Carrara, the pupil he obviously has in mind is the typical merchant's son who will have to make his way in the world by pleasing his father's colleagues, by a strict attention to business and by his eagerness to outdo every competitor. From the examination of character, the book passes to the problems of a curriculum. At first, two reasons are suggested for the study of letters. Literature, Vergerio says, occupies the leisure hours. It saves you from having to while away the time like Domitian by killing flies; and it also teaches a power of expression which is of considerable help to an administrator. Continuing his analysis, he finds, however, another reason which overshadows the two already given. No more mention is made of leisure, and the reader's enthusiasm about the practical value of eloquence is damped by the statement that in the law-courts, the council and the popular assembly oratory is now despised: speed, brevity and homeliness are the only qualities desired. And from this point on, Vergerio puts every argument he can to exalt books as moral guides. History is given particular mention because it provides us with concrete examples of the precepts inculcated by philosophy;* poetry is praised; and the whole Humanist course is represented as a form of basic instruction which everyone, lawyers, doctors, administrators and even soldiers would find beneficial. In short, after numerous shifts and false starts, Petrarch's colours are firmly nailed to the educational mast. The schools are to train men for a new way of life.

On the whole the *de Ingenuis Moribus* is spoilt by its tendency to generalise and its consequent lack of practical, detailed suggestions. Vergerio fails to indicate how long his course will take, what the curriculum will be, and when, if ever, the pupil is to pass to more specialised disciplines. A professor of logic for the greater part of his career, dialectic is the only subject on which he ventures to give concrete advice. Here he recommends a complete reorientation. The student is to have a pragmatic aim. He is to learn to distinguish whether the arguments he comes across in books or in talk are true or the reverse. Although a professional logician, Vergerio seems to have been quite blind to the possibilities of the orthodox Scholastic tradition which still dominated the schools, and which in the north at least had definite creative potentialities.* The work of four hundred years spent in examining the formal relations of the reasoning process is to be summarily abandoned. Nothing could indicate more clearly the unbridgeable cleft between the Humanist and the medieval outlook.

Unimpressive as they are, these theories of Vergerio, and the practice they presumably represent, constitute the high peak of four-teenth-century Humanist achievement in the educational field. Here as elsewhere the age of Petrarch was an age of preparation. The world was told which way to go; but the world was slow in moving.

An incidental feature of Petrarch's career, his attempt to introduce Greek studies into Italy, might serve as a symbol for the whole of his work. He does not seem to have linked his efforts with the Council of Vienne's attempt in 1311 to foster Greek studies or to have learnt much from Barlaam, the pupil of Nicephoros Gregoras who became librarian to Robert of Anjou and encouraged the king to buy manuscripts and translations during the early years of the century.* He started on his own, procured a Homer, and being desirous to read it, persuaded an itinerant Byzantine to give him lessons. His choice of a teacher was unlucky; the man was ignorant and self-seeking, and Petrarch's learning of Greek remained an unfulfilled hope. But so vigorous was his praise of the Greek writers whose works he could not read, and so notable his influence as Helleniser that half a century later the Florentines were prepared to invite a Byzantine scholar to lecture in their city.

The incident is symbolic; for in other fields besides Greek studies the value of Petrarch's contribution lay precisely in the compelling force with which he could formulate a general aim whose implications he only half understood. Just as the economic and social changes that gave rise to the Italian Renaissance affected the rest of Europe to an almost equal extent, with the result that many of the traits of the new Italian outlook can be matched from other countries, so the actual achievements of Italian Humanism were no different in nature and only a little greater in their extent than the slight gains which the classical scholars of the north were able to record. Poggio's remarks suggest that the teaching of rhetoric in Florence under Malpaghini was conducted along tradi-tionally medieval lines; and there is no reason to suppose that judged by strictly Humanist standards the subject was much worse taught at Toulouse. We have had occasion to compare Richard of Bury with his Italian contemporaries. His learning, his enthusiasms for the classics were as vigorous as theirs; and it is possible to see in the *de Vita et Moribus Philosophorum* of his friend, Walter Burley, a not unworthy companion to the *de Viris Illustribus*. Richard had definite views, modelled probably on those of Bacon, concerning the importance of Greek studies, and his knowledge of the language was almost superior to Petrarch's own. This ardent Englishman, as Petrarch described him after their meeting in Avignon, 'not unlearned in literature and with a strong natural curiosity for abstruse and esoteric lore'* matched Vergerio in preferring literature to law and equalled Valla's zeal for the exact study of grammar, while his intimate associate Archbishop Bradwardine was perhaps the foremost mathematician of the century, a distinction to which no contemporary Italian Humanist even aspired.

Up to 1400, the North did not lag noticeably behind Italy in classical learning. The superiority of Italian Humanism derived not from its greater scholarship but from its clarity of aim and from Petrarch's impressive delineation of an idealised Roman way of life, the materials for which came from Cicero, an author whose works were generally available. Had not even the Sorbonne in 1338 no fewer than twenty-four manuscripts of his rhetorical and philosophical writings?

One further point, however, remains to be noted. We have dealt so far with the study of the classics and with the organisation of the schools where the dead hand of habit placed an infinity of obstacles in the Humanists' way. The difficulties they experienced in the working out of their ideas, which required a detailed scholarship, and in the popularisation of their pedagogic aims, which would have transformed education, made them turn all the more eagerly to another field where tangible results were easier to obtain. They collected and copied classical manuscripts with a zeal and assiduity which have added enormously to their fame.

The library catalogues of the twelfth and thirteenth centuries record a substantial increase in the number of classical texts. With the fourteenth, that increase comes to an end. The evidence, as it stands, does not warrant the belief that there was an overall decline in existing stocks; but it does at least preclude the possibility of these stocks having grown to any notable extent after 1300.* The universities were giving all their attention to those specialised studies which were now building their independent constructions on ancient knowledge rather than digging more deeply into classical sources; and the teachers of grammar were drifting more and more deeply into the habit of using contemporary texts alongside their traditional authorities. Already, thirteenth-century educators like Alexander Neckham and Eberhard the German had been accustomed to recommend the *Tobias* or the *Anticlaudianus* for their pupils' reading, and that trend had gone on unchecked; so much so, that in 1366, Priscian was dropped from the Paris arts course to be replaced by the *Doctrinale* and the *Grecismus.** At the same time a new and regrettable spirit of neglect was making itself felt. Books were no longer treasured with the care given them by earlier ages. Since there were more of them, they were more easily allowed to fall into disrepair. Richard of Bury's complaints on the subject are written for effect and were belied by his own practice. Nevertheless, it is difficult to believe that they do not contain a kernel of truth.

> We are expelled from the homes of the clergy [goes the lament of the books]. Our places are seized now by dogs, now by hawks, now by that biped beast whose cohabitation with the clergy was forbidden of old, who [is] always jealous of the love of us.... The coverings anciently given to us have been torn by violent hands...ragged and shivering we are flung away in dark corners or in tears take our place with Job upon his dunghill. We lie as hostages in taverns with no one to redeem us.*

The experiences of the early Humanist book-collectors lend support to this grim picture. Indeed, the mere mention of a manuscript in a catalogue provides no indication as to how and where it was kept or of the extent to which it was available for reading. The relative lack of interest in the classics, and especially in the rarer authors, meant that these suffered to an exceptional degree from any general neglect.

Admittedly Virgil, Lucan, Persius, Juvenal, Statius, Sallust and Valerius Maximus, as well as the better-known works of Terence, Horace, Ovid, Cicero and Seneca could be obtained without much difficulty. The average teacher of grammar could hope for the chance to read them all and to assemble a selection for his private use. Many classical books, however, were available only in large libraries or in jealously guarded private collections, while such authors as Catullus, Lucretius and Tacitus whose survival through the Middle Ages had depended on rare isolated manuscripts still remained, as might be expected, hidden from view.*

The Humanists, whose enthusiasm made them most curious precisely about the authors they did not have to hand, were galled by the restrictions placed on their learning; and while Petrarch was an adolescent with his reputation still to make, certain Veronese scholars were already engaged in collecting and copying the lesser-known works of antiquity. Petrarch converted these desultory efforts into an organised campaign. He hunted up every manuscript that came to his notice, and what was more important, he managed to persuade his friends to do likewise. Among his personal discoveries, if we may give them that name, were several of Cicero's speeches, the letters to Quintus and Atticus and the poems of Propertius. Among the books rare in his own day which he possessed or had at least read, were eight comedies of

Plautus, three decades of Livy, Pliny's *Historia Naturalis*, a mutilated copy of Quintilian, the *Noctes Atticae*, the *Strategemata* of Frontinus, Censorinus, Vegetius' *de Re Militari*, Servius on Virgil and Fulgentius. Guglielmo da Pastrengo and other Veronese friends unearthed for him Varro's *de Re Rustica*, the *Apocolocyntosis*, Vitruvius, Victorinus on the *de Inventione* and the *Historia Augusta*.* Boccaccio sent him the *de Lingua Latina* though that may have been an imperfect copy. The interest that Petrarch had aroused outlived him and indeed gathered force after his death. Years of meticulous collecting enabled Boccaccio to leave to the library at San Spirito a Martial, a complete Ausonius, the *Ibis* of Ovid, a volume of Tacitus, poems from the *Appendix Vergiliana* and possibly the *Verrine Orations* which Petrarch had never seen,* while Salutati was the first of the Humanists to possess the *Epistolae ad Familiares*, the *de Agricultura* of Cato, the elegies of Maximian and the *Aratea*.

So much has been written about this aspect of the Humanist effort that it has come to seem more important than it was in practice. These books which we have just mentioned, had all been known to the scholars of the Middle Ages. We are not concerned with the recovery of literature lost in the sense that the *Medea* of Ovid or missing books of Livy have gone from our ken. Time and again during the medieval period we come across scholars who look for rare manuscripts and then copy them or have them copied. The work of Petrarch and his circle was in this tradition which had been the glory of Tours and Monte Cassino. If the invention of printing had not supervened, their labours would have had to be repeated again and again as had been the case after similar efforts in the past. What they did was to bring certain scarce works within the orbit of the intellectual movement they represented; and given the movement, given an enthusiasm for the classics, that development was nothing unusual.

Moreover, with a few exceptions, the Humanist discoveries concerned works of secondary importance. Even if we move beyond the fourteenth century and take into account the manuscripts which Poggio found at St Gallen and elsewhere, as well as those which Landriani unearthed in Lodi and which Capra found in Milan, their total value remains small in comparison with that great body of Latin literature that was already available in Petrarch's youth. To have recovered the works of Lucretius, Catullus, Propertius and Tacitus, the *Silvae* of Statius and the *Punica* of Silius Italicus, the *Letters*, the *Brutus* and numerous speeches of Cicero, and to have acquired in addition complete texts of the *Institutiones Oratoriae*, the *de Oratore* and the *Orator*, was a matter of great importance for the progress of Latin studies, but it did not alter the character of these studies. Humanism could still have flourished during the fifteenth century, much as it did, even if these writings had not been available.

The hunt after classical manuscripts must count therefore as an incidental rather than as the principal feature of the early Renaissance. It was the impact of Petrarch's ideas and not the energy of Petrarch's researches that decided the course of history.

CHAPTER VII

THE HIGH RENAISSANCE

I. THE POPULARISATION OF A NEW METHOD OF STUDY

When the fourteenth century gives way to the fifteenth, we seem to pass from the gloom of a passage into the brilliant light of a sunlit room. The long process whose stages we have been tracing now reaches its climax. The widened interests of scholarship embrace for the first time the whole of the classical heritage. Not only is the movement started by Petrarch for the recovery of Roman eloquence and the Roman way of life brought to a triumphant conclusion, but the work of earlier ages in law, medicine and philosophy is once again examined, criticised and completed. Moreover, the cultural scene is enriched and complicated at this juncture by the almost simultaneous appearance of two new elements. Greek studies which had so long wilted in obscurity take their place alongside Latin, their long-hidden treasures accessible at last to a multitude of scholars; and the invention of printing radically changes the basic conditions of education and research. The world suddenly wears a different face.

The impressive growth of trade, the collapse of feudal independence, better government and a greater mastery of material resources, new discoveries and new ideals, all played their part in effecting this transformation, which involved the educational field along with the rest. But if our interest goes beyond the mere fact of progress, and we want to understand why the new education took the form it did, we must look beyond the broad social and political factors to a more specific cause. We must look to the work of the teachers. In a sense, the key to the whole complex development of Humanism during the fifteenth century is in a way furnished by the appearance of a certain technique which served to link the two previously disconnected parts of Petrarch's programme. Facilitating the imitation of classical language and style it promoted at the same time the detailed understanding of ancient ways of thought. This was an innovation of the first importance; and so the manner in which this technique was introduced and employed has obviously first claim on our attention.

The tendency to interpret the stylistic aims of the fifteenth century in terms of Bembo's Ciceronianism has done much to confuse our picture of the Renaissance. If we assume Petrarch, Barzizza, Valla and Guarino to have been guided by the same ideal as Bembo, that is by the desire to write a Latin that corresponded exactly to Ciceronian or at least to ancient usage, we are left in the ridiculous position of having to excuse eminent scholars for failing to achieve something that a clever under-graduate can manage without undue trouble; and as a result, the whole movement which centred on the fifteenth-century interest in imitation becomes impossible to explain. We are left to interpret the Renaissance cult of eloquence as a curious by-product of the general enthusiasm for the classics, similar to those irrelevancies that anthropologists point out in primitive culture patterns when some trait is elaborated in an over-weening and asocial fashion.

It will be convenient therefore to abandon the standpoint of nine-teenth-century scholarship, as exemplified in Sabbadini, and to ask afresh what Petrarch meant when he recommended the imitation of ancient authors. Are we to interpret the fourteenth century in the light of the fifteenth and attribute to him a desire for the meticulous repro-duction of Ciceronian usage? Petrarch's main guide was Cicero himself, and Cicero does not make an issue of linguistic accuracy. If he recom-mends imitation, it is as a means of building up an orator's powers of expression. He likes to point out that with a sufficiency of phrases and set ideas at his command a man can talk or write fluently on any subject. His long investigations into the formal characteristics of good writing centre on differences between the Attic and Asiatic manner, on questions of colour and rhythm. Not, it must be emphasised, on correct or in-correct Latin. If Petrarch followed Cicero in these matters, as he almost certainly did, then we must assume that in discussing eloquence he had the same stylistic elements in mind. It is reasonable to believe that when he encouraged his contemporaries to take the classical writers for a model, he meant them to catch the sound of classical Latin; he meant them to make the tone of their writing appropriate to the natural level of the subject as it was in the best classical authors; and he meant them above all to widen their powers of expression, to collect their stocks of phrases on every subject. The advantage of this hypothesis is that the aims we have listed correspond to the actual achievement of writers like Petrarch and Barzizza. The private correspondence of the latter catches for example to perfection the easy style of Cicero in his informal mood. But its language is full of medievalisms. The best passages of Petrarch also possess undoubted power. He is always fluent, and at times he can be moving. Should we not assume that these were the ends he sought rather than a classical exactitude in his grammar and syntax?

If we admit the hypothesis that these early Humanists were merely concerned to find more effective means of expression and had no thought of exactly reproducing the language of Cicero, then we can not only acquit them of the charge of self-sufficiency, but their enthusiasm for eloquence needs no explanation. Petrarch had defined literary distinction as one of the forms in which human genius could find a legitimate outlet; and the honours commonly accorded to the writers of the time furnished the claim with a sound practical basis. Given this background, it was natural that those who chose to write, took Latin as their vehicle of expression. Latin was a language in general use, a learned idiom better suited to their purposes than the vernacular and one which allowed them to imitate their only models, the classical authors, with reasonable ease. None of its rivals had equal claims.

Imitation as preached and practised by Petrarch had made effective writing possible. It had not resulted, however, in men assimilating classical ways of thought. It had been too unsystematic for that specialised purpose which was to play so large a role in the later Renaissance. Petrarch and his friends studied their Virgil and their Cicero as we study books nowadays, relying on the unorganised working of the memory. But a person who studies in this way rarely remembers more than a handful of the facts which a book offers for his attention, and when that book contains unfamiliar ideas or mirrors some unfamiliar forms of sensibility, the likelihood is that he will reach the last page only half aware of the novelties he has encountered. The recovery of a past culture in the course of ordinary reading is therefore a lengthy, if not an impossible, task.

However zealous and however painstaking a fourteenth-century student tried to be, he was not likely to recall much beyond the immediately obvious, surface content of the classics. But the overt statements of the Greek and Latin writers, when they speculate about life or advocate particular values, supply only the vague outline of the knowledge we can get from them about antiquity. The details of the complete picture derive from a more subtle source. To make this point clear it is necessary to call to mind once again that the ancient literatures are constructed out of the fabric of Greek and Roman experience. The impression they give of the universe is organised in terms of the categories, is characterised by the choices and omissions native to Greece and Rome. Certain sensations, feelings and interests receive unusual emphasis. Others, equally important perhaps in our eyes, are peremptorily neglected; and it is only when we have become familiar with the light and shade of these imponderable differences between the Graeco-Roman outlook and our own, that the direct reality of the past takes shape in our consciousness. The pattern of that past emerges only for those who learn to think in its categories and can adopt its sensibility and its standards. But such an identification, involving as it does that abandonment of the student's own world of thought was not to be achieved through the enthusiastic but casual reading of the fourteenth century Humanists.

Petrarch extracted from the works of Cicero an ideology which corresponded to his own outlook. But he took little or nothing that had not already a prior existence in his own mind. He was so little changed by his classical studies that certain modern critics have—with some justice—described him as a medieval thinker. But a few decades after his death we find men who were not indeed slightly altered, but veritably transformed by their Humanism, men whose worlds of thought and expression stood recognisably nearer to Cicero's than to the traditionally educated average of their day; and the cause of this difference between the generation of Petrarch and the generation of Guarino was in the last analysis the appearance and widespread adoption of a pedagogic technique.

Pedagogically, the Renaissance began with Chrysoloras. It will be remembered that this Byzantine schoolmaster came to Italy first of all as a diplomatist to implore Western aid against the Turks, but finding that his private attainments aroused more interest than his public mission, gave lessons in Greek and eventually accepted an invitation to return to Florence in 1396 as a municipally-paid lecturer. The circumstances of his arrival in a non-scholastic capacity and his final scholastic appointment show clearly what importance we must ascribe to the Humanist enthusiasm which had its origins in Petrarch's teaching. It was the demand that created the supply. Without a pre-existent demand for Greek knowledge, Chrysoloras would have come and gone unnoticed, a diplomatic emissary on a diplomatic mission. As it was, however, he proved for once the right man in the right place. Possessed of a magnetic personality, a scholar and a skilled pedagogue, he knew how to exploit to the full the charm that novelty gave to his subject, and the intellectual pre-eminence of Florentine culture brought him in contact with the leading minds of the age. He numbered Guarino, Bruni, d'Angeli and Vergerio among his pupils. He corresponded with

Filelfo and Barzizza; and he became an intimate friend of Niccolò Niccoli. The excellence of his teaching, and its impact on the age are universally attested.* Guarino was to make a cult of his memory to the extent of collecting everything he had written. Poggio who had not been properly speaking his pupil, was to express a wish to write his funeral oration. Vergerio says that he counted every moment his master spent in Italy as a blessing.* And these were not mere words; the influence of Chrysoloras is visible in all their writings.

We have our first glimpse of this influence in a pamphlet on education which Leonardo Bruni dedicated to a daughter of the Count of Urbino.* Being written for a woman this does not discuss rhetorical studies in detail, as rhetoric in all its manifestations—public discussion, forensic argument and logical debate—was considered to belong exclusively to the sphere of masculine activities; but Bruni gives some general recommendations about reading, and these provide him with an opportunity to describe the new method that had come to his notice. Teachers are to look beyond the general structure of the writings they expound. They are to pay more attention to the minutiae on which literary excellence ultimately depends. Students must fix in their minds not only words and syllables, but tropes, figures and all the ornaments of style. It is evident that Bruni wishes to disassociate himself equally from the medieval rhetoricians who followed the *de Inventione* in their analyses of structure, and from the school of Petrarch and Barzizza who concentrated on the widening of the student's vocabulary and on the sound of what was written. The new method which was to replace these traditional techniques is not described with exactitude, but Bruni is plainly aiming at a more comprehensive approach where everything is analysed and everything noticed.

Here, for the first time in the West, we have the love of detail which characterised the Byzantine imitators and a reasoned statement of the belief that eloquence in its various forms depends on the attention paid to linguistic minutiae. Here too we have the first mention of that humble auxiliary without which the most painstaking analysis would have been to no purpose. The material collected in the course of reading is to be written down in a note-book and when the student writes or speaks he must take great care not to use any word which he has not previously recorded.* The age of mnemotechnical aids has begun.

Bruni rushed in where his more able fellow-Humanists still feared to tread. Guarino, the most influential of Chrysoloras' pupils, did not write an account of his methods; and to learn about them we must turn to the memorials of his son Battista and his panegyrist Janus Pannonius.* Guarino, we are told, coupled reading and composition, preparation and practice, from the very start of a boy's education. Beginners read the easy authors using them as models for writing short tales; while more advanced pupils paralleled the study of the more difficult orators and historians by extensive free composition. Reading was always analytical. The matter which needed to be collected was divided into two parts, *Methodice* and *Historice*, the former containing rhetorical forms and idioms, the latter general information.* Each had a note-book allotted to it and as he read, the student jotted down the details that seized his attention. The connection between phrase collecting and composition which Chrysoloras left vague is here made amply obvious. The theory is now complete.

Guarino's pupils put his ideas into practice. They made their meticulous lists of phrases under the headings of form and content, and some of them went so far as to publish what they had compiled. The generation which lived in the middle of the fifteenth century worked at making the Latin legacy available to the public in this convenient note-book form, so that correct composition should be quick and easy, possible not only for the scholar but for the man in the street. Guarino himself is supposed to have composed a book of *florilegia*. His pupil and successor, Sassuelo da Prato, produced his *Commentarii* which according to Prendilacqua classified under suitable headings the finest passages of the Greek and Latin writers on every subject worthy of discussion.*

Sassuelo's interest seems to have been primarily in the non-linguistic aspects of good writing. But about the same time the study of language as such received attention from a man of remarkable genius. Valla, the professor of rhetoric in Rome, produced his *Elegantiae Linguae Latinae*. This book which was to become the Bible of the later Humanists dealt for the most part with the proper construction of individual words, collating sometimes as many as a dozen uses for an ordinary noun. Since it established for the first time strict standards of linguistic accuracy, it laid the foundations of the Ciceronianism which was to flourish at the end of the century. But Valla's aims should not be interpreted in terms of Bembo's programme. We must set him against the background of the Humanist movement as a whole. He made it his task to purify contemporary Latin according to the standards of classical usage. There is no evidence, however, that he considered this accuracy to be the only or even the main requisite of eloquence. His approach was complementary to that of Sassuelo. Working within a highly specialised field, he elaborated one aspect of Guarino's *Methodice* and was in any case rather more concerned with the correct understanding of the ancient authors than with the positive virtue of correct composition. He had made his reputation by showing that the style and contents of the Donation of Constantine were inconsistent with its supposed date. The *Elegantiae* bear many traces of his long battle to establish the primacy of philological over legal studies, a battle which turned on questions of interpretation.

After its first printing in 1471 Valla's work ran into a vast number of editions.* He also had many imitators, among whom Augustinus Datus deserves mention, if only because he was a pupil of Filelfo, and thus united in his person the two main streams of the tradition which flowed from Chrysoloras.* Datus published a volume of *Elegantiolae* which he claims in his introduction to be indispensable because even those who read Cicero often remained poor orators if they were not told what they should look for in the Latin text. He too deals with problems of usage and more particularly of order, but unlike Valla, he gives a list of synonyms as well as advice on construction, and so furnishes evidence to show the close connection which linked philological to rhetorical studies.*

Such was the early development of the new techniques from Chrysoloras to Guarino, from Bruni to Valla, from Chrysococces to Filelfo and Datus. After 1450 the method of Chrysoloras was in general use. Most of the Humanists wrote some form of the *stile a mosaico*, and the theory behind the method was developed in a number of treatises.

Francesco Pico furnishes us with an account which is in part a justification of what the imitators were trying to do. He starts by assuming that the impression made by a piece of writing is the sum total of a number of separate impressions, each of which can be traced to some distinct part or aspect of what has been written. Our earlier discussion on the methods of analysis adopted by Guarino will give us a clue as to the nature of these pebbles into which the mosaic of a poem or prose passage is divided. They include such varied elements as methods of arranging the subject-matter, varieties of argument, ideas, illustrations, metaphors, figures of speech, single words, speech rhythms and even isolated sound effects. Since literary excellence derives ultimately from these elements, good writing depends on their judicious recombination. Admittedly every genre had its appropriate raw materials. The precious stones required to ornament a temple could not properly be used to pave the utilitarian entrance to one's domestic offices. But within the limits set by the demands of suitability, it was possible for an intending writer to choose from his classical models whatever struck his fancy and out of these fragments he could construct a new and pleasing whole.*

This procedure is so alien to modern practice that we cannot easily understand what it implies. One misconception must, however, be avoided. Pico and his like were not plagiarists in the modern sense of the word. They analysed their models too thoroughly and selected their material from too many sources for their works to merit comparison with such blatant appropriations as the early works of Stendhal.

The organisation of the material, which Guarino had included under the rubric *Historice*, also presented certain difficulties and these are discussed by Rodolphus Agricola. Guarino had made no mention of sub-headings; and it is obvious that anyone who applied his methods conscientiously was bound inside a very few years to accumulate an unmanageably large stock of metaphors, anecdotes, epigrams and other illustrative matter. The need was soon felt for a more detailed system of classification, and the cry came loudest and most insistently from the encyclopedic Rhine. Agricola himself remarked that knowledge, alas! was worthless unless you had it at your finger-tips. But he thought he knew how this could be achieved. Let us, he says, arrange our material under certain headings like 'virtue', 'vice', 'life', 'death', 'learning', 'ignorance', 'goodwill', 'hatred', and so forth, which have a general application and are well known to all. Let us class under them everything that we learn and then by repeating these headings we shall call to mind all that they cover.* The idea was not original. It was borrowed from a field of popular scholarship which the Humanists tended to deride, but which had much in common with their own. Since the thirteenth century, preachers had been accustomed to rely on sermon-books for the anecdotes or *exempla* with which they illustrated their arguments, and the material in these utilitarian compilations was normally arranged under headings that represented topics for discussion.* Agricola merely turned to Humanist use a common medieval technique.

The note-book and heading method is also recommended by Vivès, who however applied it rather to the study of language and merely mentioned the rhetorical material which had been his predecessor's chief concern.

Make a book of blank leaves of a proper size. Divide it into certain topics, so to say, into nests. In one, jot down the names of subjects of daily converse: the mind, body, our occupations, games, clothes, divisions of time, dwellings, foods; in another, idioms or *formulae docendi*; in another, *sententiae*; in another, proverbs; in another, difficult passages from authors; in another, matters which seem worthy of note to thy teacher or thyself.*

Vivès is detailed, but the most complete account we possess was composed some twelve years previously by a writer of even greater importance. The whole of the *de Copia* of Erasmus could be quoted in this connection.

The very word *Copia* takes us back to Petrarch and to the fourteenth century's dream of an eloquence which would cover the whole range of the human mind. We are once again reminded that with the possible exception of Bembo all the Humanist imitators had the same, very comprehensive aim. The goal they set before themselves was to write well, writing like the ancients was merely a means to that end. Even Bembo differed from the rest only over a question of fact. He believed that Cicero could serve as a model of eloquence over the whole field that a Renaissance writer might need to cover, while Pico and Erasmus saw that the contemporary consciousness extended beyond the Ciceronian as a larger circle spreads beyond a smaller one with the same centre but a shorter radius.

Erasmus distinguishes the two sides of his subject along the lines which had been traditional since the days of Guarino. In the *Copia Verborum* he deals largely with vocabulary and with the various ways of replacing a word that has already been used, arranging his material in the form indicated by the quotation from Vivès.* But words, he points out, are not the only instruments of eloquence; and in the second half of his treatise, the *Copia Rerum,* he enumerates all the forms in which illustrative material can be presented, naming among others simile, metaphor, fable, apophthegms, gnomes, fictitious narrative and allegory. He discusses in an interesting passage the way in which a single instance can be used to illustrate several morals. You should consider, he tells the reader, the different aspects of your example and ask yourself what topics it can serve. Socrates has been accused by the rascally Anytus and Melitus. This illustrates the stock theme that truth breeds hatred; or it can prove that an outstanding virtue sows the seeds of envy; or again, a third possible theme, that judges respect status rather than merit.* The extreme pliability of the Humanist method is clearly demonstrated. The last part of the *de Copia* is devoted to an account of the method by which these examples are to be collected; and we return once more to Agricola's recommendations. The student is to take a note-book divided into sections under headings, which are then further varied by sub-headings and by stock themes entered under the latter. Reading is then done with a view to extrapolating; and it is suggested that every intending writer should go through the whole of classical literature in this way at least once in his life, presumably before he starts seriously to write.*

Erasmus also has a system for choosing his headings where Agricola had been content to select at random. He explains that some will be provided by the names of the virtues and vices, opposites being classed together for convenience, because instances of the one might be used to illustrate the other by way of contrast. In this class came Piety, Faith, Beneficence and so forth. Each of these can for convenience' sake be further subdivided. Faith for example provides sections entitled 'faith towards God', 'faith towards Man'. And under the latter rubric, Erasmus gives us yet further subdivisions such as: 'loyalty to friends, to masters, to one's enemies.' The rest of the headings come from what he calls 'stock themes'. The examples he gives are 'old age and youth', 'sudden or strange death', 'each to his own taste', 'love and hate', 'monarchy and democracy'.

The *de Copia* has not been accorded the importance it deserves. It provides us in a sense with a clue to the whole of Humanism. Specifying the techniques on which imitation depended, it makes clear what men were attempting not only in Latin, but also in the vernaculars. Without the information it offers, the purport of such works as du Bellay's *Deffense et Illustration* cannot be properly understood. Nor is that information valuable only for the light it sheds on the processes of composition. We have been concerned largely with the way in which classical writings were analysed, for that is the problem which our sources discuss at length. But the analysis with its attendant classifications was only a preliminary. It was meant to be followed by a vast effort at remembering what had been classified.

The whole purpose of the Humanists in transmogrifying Greek and Latin literature into a series of notes was to produce a body of material which could be easily retained and repeated. They made titanic efforts to remember the contents of the note-books they compiled. The Renaissance was the age of memorising. Books were written outlining fantastic schemes for the use of scholars. The mnemotechnician, Leporeus, advised his readers to imagine a wall divided into eight segments in which were noted the facts they wished to remember. They were to picture this wall when they woke up in the morning, and as they passed from one segment to the next, the knowledge noted thereon was supposed to appear. Another of these forerunners of Pelmanism based his system on a game of cards. Their ingenuity was misplaced; but their works survive to show the significance which was attached to the learning by heart of isolated facts—facts which could be arranged in lists.*

When Erasmus suggested that every scholar should at some time or other read through the whole of ancient literature note-book in hand, his advice was based on his own practice, which many others had also followed. The techniques of the *de Copia*, reinforced by detailed memorising, furnish a key therefore, not only to the procedures of imitation and composition, but also to the whole field of classical learning. They determined the manner in which those portions of the classical legacy that the Middle Ages had left on one side were now finally absorbed into the European tradition. We can trace their effects in the seventeenth and eighteenth centuries, throughout the plays of Racine and the pages of Johnson. But before we examine the form which the reflective spirit of Cicero or the fire of Aeschylus assumed on the Procrustean bed of these techniques, it will be convenient to take a look at the material the Humanists were to make their own, and to consider specifically how Greek literature, which contributed so much to that material, had made its appearance in the West.

II. THE ADDITIONS TO THE CLASSICAL HERITAGE

The enthusiasm which sent Poggio climbing up the wretched roads from Constance to St Gallen embraced the whole extent of classical literature. He was prepared to transcribe any author who had written before the seventh century A.D., just as Petrarch had been glad to add Varro and Frontinus to a collection that contained his beloved Cicero. Nevertheless, it is evident that certain of the finds occasioned more pleasure than others. The discovery of the *Institutiones Oratoriae* was a triumph notified in delighted letters to Bruni and Niccoli. The commentary of Asconius on Cicero was deemed sufficiently valuable to be copied three times over. In the same context we may note that the manuscript containing the *de Oratore*, the *Brutus* and the *Orator* became a bone of contention among scholars after its discovery by Landriani in 1421; that the hope of securing a complete Livy inspired Poggio to endless journeys and negotiations; and that Niccoli thought the Ammianus Marcellinus which Poggio had sent him worth copying in his own hand. The poets were given their due; but the orators and the historians seem to have held first place in the Humanist pantheon. This impression is borne out by the *editiones principes*. During the first five years that the classics were printed (1465–9) the presses produced the *de Officiis*, the *Paradoxa*, the *de Officiis* again, the *de Oratore*, Lactantius, the *de Civitate Dei*, the *ad Familiares*, the *de Oratore*, *Brutus* and *Orator*, Apuleius, Gellius, Caesar, Lucan and the elder Pliny—a good selection of prose writers and only a single poet.

But it is in connection with the recovery of Greek literature that the orientation of Humanist interests becomes most obvious. When we come to consider which Greek works were available in Italy before 1450 we find that the prose writers were much better represented than the poets. It is possible to trace over forty manuscripts of Aristotle including copies of all his important books; twenty manuscripts of Plato, three of them complete; twelve of Xenophon including the *Memorabilia, Hellenica, Cyropedia, Oeconomica*; eight of Thucydides, one at least of which was complete; nine of Demosthenes; and six of Theophrastus and five of Herodotus. Among the poets, Homer with nine manuscripts to his credit is the only one to rival the philosophers and historians. The remaining figures are poor by comparison: Euripides, six (none of them complete); Hesiod, seven; Phocylides and Pindar, four (none of them complete); Sophocles, four (only one of which is known to have had all the seven plays) and Aeschylus, four (one with seven, the other with two or three plays). In short, there seem to have been in circulation some hundred manuscripts of the six leading prose writers and only thirty-eight of the six leading poets (see Appendix I, p. 455).

It is true that these calculations must be treated with considerable caution. The evidence on which they rest is of unequal value: for references in letters and catalogues have been added to the rather smaller number of those manuscripts which some positive indication enables us to identify as having been in the possession of one or other of the early Humanists; and the fact that the researches of bibliographers have revealed fewer copies of Aeschylus than Aristotle does not prove beyond question that there had been fewer copies in existence. The evidence of the catalogues must, however, carry a certain weight. The libraries of Guarino and Ciriaco were presumably representative, and although the above evidence is far from reliable as regards any particular author, we should be rash to assume that its errors are such as to have consistently favoured the prose writers against the poets. The main conclusions therefore can probably stand. That the scholars were more interested in prose than in poetry seems fairly certain.

When we consider the translations which were made from the Greek, this impression is confirmed. The translators were popularisers. It lay in the very nature of their activity that they wrote less for the learned specialists than for the common mass of educated men. They addressed themselves perforce to all those who could read Latin; and we may suppose that they selected such authors as they thought would have a wide appeal. When we look at a list of their works, the importance given to Aristotle leaps to the eye just as it does in the case of the manuscripts. He found more translators during the fifteenth century than any other pagan author, in spite of the fact that the medieval versions were still used in the universities. Bruni, Manetti, Theodore of Gaza, George of Trebizond, Argyropoulos, Gregorio Tifernas, Bessarion and Andronicus Callistus, all tried their hand at one or more of his major works.* The Platonic dialogues were neglected by comparison and continued to be so until Ficino began his great rendering in 1463.* Since the majority of the Humanists always expressed a preference for Plato, it appears strange at first sight that for so many decades more attention should have been paid to Aristotle. But we must remember the conditions which governed the activity of the copyists and translators. Many poorer scholars preferred to spend their energies on tasks which had been specially commissioned. Their choice of authors to transcribe or turn into Latin was determined by the tastes of those who paid them; and this was particularly true of the Byzantines whose interest in Greek studies did not presuppose an enthusiastic participation in the ideals of the Renaissance. Humanist scholarship was to a great extent dependent upon patronage, and its character is explained by the nature of its patrons. Before the close of the fifteenth century, few men of advanced Humanist views attained to positions where they had money at their command. High appointments went to those whose outlook conformed more or less to the traditional scholastic norm. The disciples of the old dispensation were still predominant among the dignitaries who controlled or advised upon the disbursement of wealth for the ends of scholarship. This being the state of the world, such of the copyists and translators as needed commissions were bound to seek their patrons among the conventionally-minded. In the absence of stronger support, they were bound to exploit that vague sympathy for

Humanist ideas which marked what we might call the progressive wing of the Scholastic intelligenzia. But when one of these still hesitant sympathisers turned his attention to Greek studies, he naturally favoured the author whose works provided common ground between the Scholastic and Humanist traditions. The prevalence of Aristotelian manuscripts and translations shows the influence of the old order upon new.

Aristotle had pride of place; but the historians also received a good deal of attention; and this line of interest which had for its object the Graeco-Roman way of life seems to reflect to some degree the tastes of the Humanists themselves. Herodotus, Thucydides, Xenophon and Plutarch all figured in the libraries of Guarino and Vittorino. Bessarion possessed every historical writer of note; and here the translators are not Byzantines. The work is done by the Italian scholars. By 1460, not only the four writers mentioned above, but Appian, Arrian, Diodorus Siculus, Polybius and Diogenes Laertius could all be read in Latin. So could the historical orations of Demosthenes and the educational writings of Isocrates. The poets were neglected by comparison. The *Iliad* alone attracted a certain measure of attention.*

After 1460, however, there came a change in emphasis. The Florentine Academy took up Platonic studies. Its labours were crowned by the magnificent translation of the whole of Plato's works, which Ficino completed in 1482; and this interest in philosophy, which we shall discuss later, was matched by a correspondingly greater attention to poetry in both Latin and Greek. While the older generation of Humanists had been largely content to cultivate an impressive prose style, its successors were ready to try their hand at verse and prose alike. Marullus imitated Catullus, Horace and eventually Lucretius, while his contemporary Politian composed with an almost equal facility in Greek, Latin and the vernacular, and declaimed his Latin poems in the middle of his lectures. Men who set much store by their own poetic efforts were not likely to neglect their obvious models. Among the members of the Florentine Academy, Landino annotated Horace and Virgil, Politian lectured on Homer, Hesiod, Virgil, Persius and Statius, Beroaldo edited Propertius.

Simultaneously, more manuscripts with the works of the principal Greek poets appeared in Italy. By 1475 the Vatican Library possessed nine copies of the *Iliad* and four of the *Odyssey*. Hesiod who had been scarcely known during the first part of the century—we hear of five copies in all brought from Constantinople—was represented in the library of Giorgio Valla, catalogued in 1490, by two copies of the *Theogony*, two of the *Works and Days* and one of the *Shield of Heracles*. With regard to the other poets, it will be convenient to refer once again to the Papal Library of 1475 since this is the largest collection of which we have a detailed account. Sixtus IV possessed eight manuscripts of Pindar, three of Aeschylus, ten of Sophocles, seven of Euripides, nine of Aristophanes, three of Theocritus and seven of 'Oppian'. The poets were now as well known as the prose writers (see Appendix I, p. 455).

Moreover, while the first Latin authors printed between 1465 and 1469 had been mostly writers of prose, the Greek *editiones principes* some twenty years later included Homer, Theocritus, the *Works and Days* and the *Anthology*. This is a further sign that tastes had indeed changed.

The differences between the medieval (or twelfth century) and the modern (or fifteenth and sixteenth century) revivals of learning have been variously explained. It has been long established that the texts which Poggio and his friends brought to light had for the most part been known earlier; and there can be little doubt that the twelfth century had nearly as much opportunity to understand and imitate Latin culture as the fifteenth. So the obvious disparity between the two Humanisms has been put down either to the introduction of Greek learning or to the invention of the printing press. For although many years were to pass before the whole of ancient literature became available in print, most of the Latin and a substantial portion of the best Greek authors were in circulation by 1516. Thanks to the efforts of the Aldine Press, learning was no longer tied to the apron-strings of the copyist.

Hundreds of generations have paid tribute to the brilliance of Greece; and one has no difficulty in believing that the sudden discovery of Greek learning and Greek art would have had the power to transform a culture previously ignorant of their treasures. But the facts suggest that what could have happened in theory, did not (as far as the Renaissance is concerned) happen in practice. To begin with, the Western world in the fifteenth century was not ignorant of the Greek tradition. Justinian, Hippocrates, Galen and Aristotle had all been translated. Latin literature, which imitated Greek models, was intimately known; and the Christian philosophy, which owed so much to earlier systems, had already made men familiar with many patterns of Greek thought and feeling. It is true that the writings of Plato and Plotinus, and the works of the Greek poets, orators and historians whom the Humanists expounded, contained elements absent from the medieval outlook; but can we say that these elements were in themselves sufficient to cause an intellectual revolution? Nor must we forget that the dissemination of this new material was comparatively slow. The scholars who could understand their Homer or their Plato in the original were a small and select body; and it would be fair to say that no Greek work found a wide circle of readers until a translation had been prepared. But the majority of the translations date as we have seen from the second half of the century; and if we then allow time for them to be read, time for them to exercise an influence, we are bound to conclude that the new Greek learning could not have made much of an impact before 1480.

Similar considerations suggest themselves with regard to the invention of printing. Most of the Latin *editiones principes* appeared between 1465 and 1475, most of the Greek between 1493 and 1518. Allowing for the period which must necessarily elapse between the publication of a work and its coming into common use, we can fix on the last decade of the fifteenth century as the very earliest point at which the new methods of book production could have exercised an influence upon the increase or the character of learning. But by 1490, the flood-tide of the Italian Renaissance was definitely over. The pattern of the movement had been clearly established; and many of its finest achievements in art and literature had already seen the light of day. The conclusion is inescapable that the Italian Renaissance as such owed little to the newly available Greek learning and even less to the novelties of the printing press. Humanism may indeed have owed the ultimate survival of its ideas to Gutenberg's discovery. If the rapid multiplication of books had not won thousands of fresh disciples for scholars like Valla and Erasmus, their achievements might perhaps have been transmogrified by a new Scholasticism. The invention of printing meant that the development of techniques for spreading ideas had momentarily outrun the development of counter-techniques of conservative control, and in this way it certainly helped to keep alive revolutionary ideas. It certainly fostered, but it did not create the Renaissance.

Thus, we must abandon the conventional hypothesis and seek to explain the special character of fifteenth-century learning by referring to the manner in which the classical legacy was studied. The Humanism of the twelfth century originated in the needs of the specialities. The upper classes and the clerks may have read Ovid or Juvenal and desired to adopt more worldly forms of behaviour. But they were not sufficiently numerous, or sufficiently obsessed by their desires to exercise a commanding influence. It was the urgent zeal of the great professional categories to find solutions for their theological, legal and medical problems that made men put such energy into classical studies; and since their specialities were bound to develop along the lines indicated by Graeco-Roman experience, we get the impression that at this juncture book-learning did shape human destiny. Constantine, Irnerius, Anselm and Abélard were in the fullest sense of the word the leaders of their age. In the High Renaissance, on the contrary, the specialities were not involved. The Humanist effort of the fifteenth century derived its impetus from men's wish to build a world in which individualists could feel at home. The scholars who followed Petrarch concentrated on those sections of ancient literature which offered most support to the ideology that was to form their special contribution to the Renaissance spirit. They sought for heroes, so that in their writings we find Livy valued above Tacitus. They sought to widen their understanding of Petrarch's personal ideal and developed from it the concept of the good life that we see in the *Della Famiglia*, that revealing work where Alberti paints the Florentine merchant class in the fulness of its good sense and sober ostentation. They sought increasingly to master the problems of the city state and to balance the see-saw of liberty and tyranny, so that from Petrarch's letter to Charles IV, the line of succession runs through Bruni's translation of the *Politics* and Guarino's of the *Nicocles*, through the *de Pontificatu* and the *de Liberorum Educatione*, to the *Discorsi sopra la prima deca di Tito Livio*. But most of all, since this was the province where their own individualism found expression, they sought to establish the primacy of art as the finest product of human excellence and the primacy of writers as princes among men. Eloquence was all. Where the twelfth century had seen the Greeks and Romans as paragons of learning, the fifteenth saw them as paragons of human excellence; and this fact is perhaps the key to the general difference between the two periods. It certainly explains one specific disparity. In the twelfth century, the scholars who explored the secrets of the classical past had been the leaders of their generation. The Guarinos and Vallas of the fifteenth were condemned to a humbler role. Since the Renaissance way of life could not in practice conform to any classical precedent, being in the long run always determined by the contemporary situation, the Humanists who tried to bring men back to antiquity found that they were not followed but were in the position of advisers whose counsels are often disregarded. So they turned more and more to this special sphere which was allowed them in the

Renaissance pattern. They glorified the poet and the artist and devoted themselves to the non-utilitarian forms of literature. 'Il faut cultiver notre jardin. . . c'est le seul moyen de rendre la vie supportable.'

III. HUMANISM AND THE SPECIALITIES

Renaissance man approached learning sometimes as a citizen, sometimes as an artist, but always as an individual eager for self-development and self-display. The significant studies of the period were centred on the social, aesthetic and personal interests whose pursuit in the case of the classical heritage was influenced by the technique of literary imitation. The character and use of that technique forms the central topic of the present chapter; but before we continue this main enquiry, it will be convenient to explore certain secondary developments which must be discussed separately if confusion is to be avoided.

The great professional specialities of philosophy, medicine and law presented the Humanists with a difficult problem. Thanks to the enthusiasm which these subjects had aroused during the Middle Ages, they were now allied to elaborate disciplines and possessed their own highly developed methods of study. The understanding of literature in which the Humanists excelled could not do much to solve their highly technical perplexities. Moreover, most of the material that the classical heritage could contribute to their advancement had already been absorbed into their current tradition. Their future progress depended, not on a fresh injection of classical knowledge, but upon men's ability to erect a worthy superstructure upon the foundations that the classics had already supplied.

The specialities constituted a field outside the scope of Humanist studies, but a field which the Humanists nevertheless wanted to make their own. For had they not claimed the whole of life as their province? In view of that claim, they could not neglect such vital portions of human experience as law, philosophy and medical science. Parallel with its main effort which was focused on literary studies, Humanism fought a number of subsidiary campaigns planned to capture the specialities, campaigns to which the Humanist weapons were ill-suited, and which consequently failed in their intention.

Petrarch had started the ball rolling when he wrote the de Ignorantia against the Averroists, and Vergerio had followed him prepared to make a clean sweep of traditional logic in favour of an inspired common sense. But before the Humanists could make a serious attack upon the

Scholastic redoubt, it was natural that they should attempt to resolve the dissensions within their own ranks; and so the battle of the specialities begins with an internecine conflict.

The Byzantine emigrants who came to Italy were divided as to their philosophical loyalties between Plato and Aristotle. The conflict which had rent the Paleologue Church at the end of the fourteenth century rumbled on uneasily among these exiles who in the time-honoured manner of refugees had brought their hatreds with them. When the aged Plethon (sent to champion the Eastern Church at the Council of Florence after nearly fifty years of banishment as a heretic) found that the Florentine scholars listened admiringly to his philosophical expositions, when he saw that he was honoured as a prophet in this far country to which fate had brought him, he could not resist launching a final attack on his enemies. Cosimo dei Medici had flattered him by calling him a second Plato. Very well, Cosimo should be supplied with ammunition to defend Plato's and incidentally Plethon's good name. In a sense, this last ebullition of the old man's combative spirit achieved its purpose. His eulogy of Plato was answered by the Aristotelian Theodore of Gaza and defended cautiously by Bessarion. Gaza composed a second refutation, and again Bessarion provided a defence. This time however he had the unwelcome support of Apostolius, an indigent theologian with ten children and a bitter temper. The latter's contribution was a fine piece of invective whose merits have been underrated. Bessarion disowned it, but it emboldened another poor scholar, George of Trebizond, to reply in kind, accusing Plato of pederasty and Plethon of a carefully dissimulated crypto-Mohammedanism. Greek met Greek to such effect that in the end even the gentle Gaza lost his temper and became scurrilous.

As might have been expected, this descent into scurrility brought nothing but bitterness in its train. The claims of the rival philosophers remained undecided; and as neither party succeeded in convincing the other, the Humanist attack upon Scholasticism was eventually made from two irreconcilable viewpoints. The Aristotelians followed one line, the Platonists another; and their respective fortunes must be separately considered.

Aristotle had been deeply pondered since the days of Aquinas. The weaknesses of his system had given birth to a multitude of distinctions. New problems had shown themselves, and the attempts to solve them had opened new horizons. In logic and in epistemology, modern thought was beginning its advance beyond the classical positions.

Under the cover of traditional disputes, men were already feeling their way towards that philosophical revolution which was to result in the *metodo risolutivo* and the *metodo comparativo*, towards that analysis of experience which would have the control of the material world for its primary aim.

Such were the vast new developments that had grown up round Aristotelian studies; and against this background we must set the fact that the Humanists who first sought to make their mark in this field were for the most part Byzantines. They were not men who had learnt Greek because they were interested in Aristotle, but men who had become interested in Aristotle because they knew Greek, because the most popular of all philosophers seemed to afford good scope for the exploitation of that knowledge which they had gathered without special effort at their mother's knee.

The linguistic criticism of Aristotle might have yielded good fruit, had it been made ancillary to a wider understanding of philosophical issues. But where the Byzantines were concerned, fluency in Greek did not presuppose a general interest in intellectual problems; nor was it necessarily (as it would have been in the case of an Italian scholar) a sign of high intelligence. These Humanists from the East were on the whole reluctant to venture beyond the field of language which seems often to have been their only strong point. They were philologists pure and simple. They encouraged the study of the Greek Aristotle and produced a number of translations. But that was the sum total of their achievement.

A Humanist school which offered so little guidance on the burning philosophical questions of the day was not likely to attract many converts; and it could be argued that the only useful purpose served by the Humanist study of Aristotle was to have shaken men's confidence in the time-honoured Scholastic interpretations and so helped to prepare the way for a general collapse of Scholasticism before the probings of the scientific spirit. But even in this marginal realm of propaganda, the Humanist teachings appear to have been a double-edged weapon. For some philosophers, such as Filelfo's friend, Niccolò Fava and the more famous Leonico Tomeo, used their philological knowledge to discredit rather than to support the forward march of ideas. By diverting attention from the real points at issue, their Humanist criticisms served to keep Scholasticism sheltered from more dangerous attack. So, all in all, the Humanist attempt to transform the Scholastic world from the inside, through the philological study of Aristotle, must be held to have ended in failure.

We must bear in mind however that Lefèvre d'Etaples who was a pupil of Argyropoulus is supposed to have made a serious contribution to the reform of Aristotelian logic. If this is true, and if it could be shown that the reforms he initiated stemmed from his Humanist learning, then the adverse judgement we have passed on the Byzantines would need to be reconsidered. But so far the commentaries of Lefèvre have not been sufficiently studied to enable us to assess either the value of his work or his Humanist debt.

Since the Aristotelians achieved so little, the history of the Platonists shines by comparison. They had more to give; and from the very beginning circumstances favoured their efforts. Cicero is lavish in his praises of the Academy, and Petrarch was led in consequence to set up Plato as his authority against Scholastics though he himself had very little knowledge of Plato's writings. For nearly a whole century the Italian Humanists praised a philosophy which they did not understand and whose tenets they regularly misinterpreted. Petrarch, for example, attached great importance to the belief that men can learn about ultimate reality by studying its intimations within the created universe. *

But the use he made of this originally Platonic theory had little connection with Plato. Impelled by his desire to contradict man's corruption, he cited the understanding of the Absolute as a proof of human superiority; and he never learnt that for Plato the dimness of that understanding had proved human weakness. Nor was this his only misconception. He commonly spoke as if the manifestations of the supernatural in this world were to be recognised by the aesthetic delight they occasioned, while orthodox Platonism presented that recognition as an intellectual process. For all his enthusiasm, Petrarch has no serious claim to rank as a Platonist; nor has Salutati with his belief that right conduct depends on the possession of the right sentiments; nor has Manetti with his ardent championship of human excellence. * They were moralists, not philosophers, and they were throughout their lives largely ignorant of Plato's teachings. Their only connection with him lay in their hope that his writings, when discovered, would provide that metaphysical defence of individualism which they were so zealously seeking.

Two-thirds of the way through the fifteenth century the situation was still the same, as far as Plato was concerned. The enthusiasm of his Italian disciples still subsisted in an atmosphere of dire ignorance. For the Byzantines, like Bessarion, who alone could have dispelled the darkness that surrounded the philosopher were so taken up with his moral character and his relationship to Christianity that their writings gave a most incomplete picture of his thought.* When genuine knowledge of Plato's text was obtained at last during the 'sixties and 'seventies it came from another source.

Cosimo dei Medici's admiration for Plethon bore surprising fruit. Being an organiser of genius he took effective steps to satisfy his interest and encouraged a promising lad, one Marsilio Ficino, the son of his personal physician, to train as a Plato scholar; in 1463 Ficino started on the enormous task of translating the Platonic corpus at which he was to labour for twenty years; and the successful termination of this work meant that Plato was at last available to all who could read Latin. He proved to have much to recommend him. The dialogues were eloquent, striking works of art whose beauty stood in sharp contrast to the crabbed involutions of the Aristotelian treatises. The Socratic method had an undoubted attraction for individualists confident in the accuracy of their own opinions; and as the Byzantine controversy had shown, there were undoubted affinities between Platonism and Christianity: a matter of some concern for a pious generation.

The centre of the new Platonism was Florence where Ficino and Pico della Mirandola, Lorenzo dei Medici, Politian, Landino and L. B. Alberti, formed the circle known as the Platonic Academy.* Both Ficino and Pico, who set the tone for the rest, depended on Dionysius the Areopagite rather than on Plato for the innermost substance of their thought so that the Academicians were if anything Neoplatonist. But the more fundamental trouble was that despite their learning they were not (in any real sense of the word) philosophers at all. Fascinated by the attitudes they wished to justify, they had no interest to spare for making their system coherent or for confuting its opponents. In Pico's *Heptaplus*, a sevenfold commentary on Genesis, we find the Godhead, perfect in its simplicity and unity, and the created worlds which emanate from it in a hierarchical order. The uppermost world of pure mind is devoted to the eternal contemplation of the divine essence. The second or celestial world of the spheres (which, however, derives its movement and light as well as its Being directly from God) observes the intellectual realm above it, transmuting the knowledge it thus acquires into 'forms' and 'qualities' and transmitting their influence to the sublunary realm below. That last realm, our own, is consequently a shadow of truth, a region of darkness and change. To this traditional set of concepts Ficino and Pico added a new one, by insisting upon humanity's special role.* Bound by his physical nature to the lowest of created things, man is nevertheless a microcosm, a fourth world which has the power of containing the other three. He is the mediator of the universe, the interpreter who stands half-way between flux and eternity, and he can reach even to God himself. The final beatitude or possession of the Godhead can be attained by virtue of the divine in man which is in communion with the divine everywhere even at its very source.

The vigorous individualism of the age makes itself felt in this doctrine which gives man such a unique place in the universe; and the more we read Pico and Ficino, the more evident it becomes that their philosophy was merely an apologia for contemporary attitudes. The behaviour patterns they exalt are precisely those which Petrarch had glorified. The typical forms of activity assigned to the divine element in man are love and awareness. Its typical objects are the manifestations of God in the universe. Its typical aim is creation. Poetic fervour which draws inspiration from the sublime to produce literature, and sexual love* which is aroused by beauty for the begetting of children, are both given a divine origin; and so are all forms of enthusiasm whether for glory, for honour or for the love of country since they too are stimulated by lofty aspirations and find issue in creative action.

All this was valueless as philosophy. Aquinas had demolished far cleverer statements of Neoplatonism two centuries before; and no attempt was made to meet his criticisms. Furthermore, the new element in the mixture, that naïve glorification of aesthetic sensibility, energy, love and literary creativeness did not fit in well with the rest. The connections which linked it to the Neoplatonic cosmogony were picturesque rather than logical, and certainly owed very little to Plato.

The teachings of Ficino inspired some fine poetry and some interesting essays, though it is not often that the poems of his disciples attained the philosophical heights of Lorenzo's.

> O Dio, o Sommo Bene, or come fai?
> Chè te sol cerco, e non ritrovo mai.
>
> Lasso, s'io cerco questa cosa o quella
> Te cerco in esse, o dolce Signor mio.
> Ogni cosa per te e buona e bella.
> E muove come buona il mio disio.
> Tu se' per tutto in ogni luogo, O Dio,
> E in alcun luogo non ti truovo mai.*

287

The commoner practice was to identify Absolute Beauty with the poet's lady. *She* was the source whence it spread to the surrounding world:

> Anzi sempre si truova in ogni parte
> Chè ciò che agli occhi è bel da questa viene.
> Varie bellezze in varie cose sparte
> Da al mondo il fonte vivo d'ogni bene;
> E quel che monstran l'altre cose in parte
> In lui tutto e perfetto si contiene:
> E se la simiglianza agli occhi piace
> Quanto è qui più perfetta ogni lor pace.*

Nor is it often that the essays produced by the group have the serious-ness of Landino's *de Summo Bono.* * Florentine philosophy betrayed its fundamental weakness in appealing not so much to the thinker as to the dilettante; and Ficino's writings on love had their offspring in the countless fashionable treatises that formed the reading of the Italian courts. Thanks to the technical deficiencies of his thought, he found his truest disciples, not among the philosophers, but among gentlemen who liked to consider their sexual predilections as strivings towards the Absolute and were anxious to vindicate flirtation as a virtue, even though fornication had to be a vice.*

This preoccupation with mystical fancies and social behaviour weakened the impact of Florentine Platonism as a serious philosophy. But Ficino's translation was to have an influence independently of the school that produced it. For the first time since the decline of Greek studies in the fourth century, Western scholars had the works of Plato before them in an easily accessible form, and the detailed study of the dialogues was bound to have notable results. The development of Humanism during the sixteenth century belongs properly to the next chapter; but certain philosophical trends may be noted here since they follow directly from the events we have been describing and do not bear the distinctive stamp of the Reformation. The work of Lefèvre in France deserves particular mention. Since he was primarily a reformer, the discussion of his Platonism belongs to our next chapter, but he was also a logician and his interpretations of the *Organon* may have owed something to his reading of the dialogues.* In any case, a few years later, Plato's logic was to find an open champion in Pierre la Ramée who peremptorily challenged the Aristotelian dialectic of his day. He deserves credit for having been the first Western thinker to claim a technical understanding of Platonism; but here our generalisations must wait upon a more exact knowledge. The precise significance of

La Ramée's work will not become clear until the Scholasticism he attacked is studied along the lines indicated by Elie, as an important stage in the development of thought.*

Lefèvre, La Ramée and among the Averroists, Zabarella, deserve to rank among the forerunners of Bacon and Galileo. The weaknesses they discovered in the existing structure of thought, the fruitful hints they lighted on but left half-developed, were as essential to Bacon's logic of discovery and to Galileo's method of analysis and construction as manure is to a growing plant. Thus, the new departures of the intellect that Ficino inspired call for our respect. Their influence was slow and indirect; but when their workings will have been fully revealed, they may emerge as an essential tributary in the stream that takes us to Locke and Newton.

The other aspects of sixteenth-century Platonism, which are more directly concerned with religion, literature and social improvement belong to the epoch of the Reformation; and we must pass at this point to the second of the medieval specialities that Humanism tried to penetrate. While blackguarding the precepts of his doctors, Petrarch had placed on record his belief in a true medicine yet to be discovered; and his successors were to occupy themselves with its discovery. But again their task was not easy.

Medicine, like philosophy, had reached the stage where it was developing independently of the classical heritage. A substantial amount of fresh data had been collected since the thirteenth century from dissections and from the observation of patients. Official opinion demanded that these facts (or such of them as had been admitted into the medical books) should be harmonised with the views of Aristotle and Galen; but the reconciliation was made at some cost and meant utilising distinctions and syllogistic arguments similar to those employed in theology. Even so, by the second half of the fifteenth century the Procrustean bed was really too small. The last great doctor who tried to reconcile his conclusions with the scholastic tradition, Peter of Abano, found himself at odds with the ecclesiastical authorities because his arguments were so subtle that they no longer convinced. It was evident to all his critics that his real aim was to preserve the record of his discoveries which were at variance with the accepted canon. But the attack on Peter marked the dawn of a new epoch; the medieval synthesis was breaking down; and Manardi, another fifteenth-century doctor, could take a bolder line. He could openly recommend his fellow-students to abandon the traditional authorities.

The future well-being of millions hinged on this battle between scholastic authoritarianism and the beginnings of scientific method: and if the disciples of Petrarch had remained faithful to the spirit of their master, they would have ranged themselves uncompromisingly on the side of the innovators. But the Humanists of the fifteenth century were less adaptable than their intuitive predecessors. They had become more specifically propagandists for the ancient texts and were men of the Renaissance only in so far as their philological interests allowed. Since all the products of antiquity were sacrosanct in their eyes, they extended their championship to Hippocrates and Galen; and the only support they offered the new movement in medicine was to join its partisans in condemning the Middle Ages, while for their own part they persisted in recommending their usual panacea of a return to the texts.

This approach had its uses, however, for some of the minor writers of the Greek medical corpus were unknown or insufficiently studied; and the Humanists who copied or translated them filled an important gap.* Moreover, the scholastic tradition was based mainly on Galen so that, by widening the field of possible authorities, the Humanist effort aided the innovators. Indeed, Leonicenus, the most able of the fifteenth-century medical translators and the one who placed most value on the Hippocratic Collection, found himself as a result in the same camp as Manardi. Since the partisans of progress had a certain amount in common with the Hippocratic school whose general method they accepted in spite of differences over matters of detail, Manardi had thought it wise to support his revolutionary attitude by advertising his dependence on what was after all an unassailable source.

It is in the work of Rabelais that we can best trace the relationship between the two currents of Humanism and scientific progress. The author of *Pantagruel* went to Montpellier as an enthusiastic young Humanist in 1531; and he tells us that when he lectured on the *Aphorisms* of Hippocrates, he corrected the standard translations after a very old manuscript in his possession. For, he says, they contained many deficiencies and unauthorised additions. Next year he happened to be in Lyons where the printer Gryphius saw his notes and advised their publication. Rabelais agreed; and the corrected version of the *Aphorisms* was then put on the market in 1532.

Rabelais states in his preface that he considers his work a serious contribution to the advance of medicine, since the excellence of his Greek text has enabled him to reveal the true meaning of Hippocrates where others had been misled by incorrect readings. This is the stand-

point of a strict Humanist. An ancient text has been properly elucidated, and now all will be well. But the proof of every pudding is in the
eating. Manifestos have no claim to be taken seriously unless they have
the backing of action; and when one comes to examine Rabelais' little
book, one begins to wonder whether he really set so much store by his
philological labours. For one finds that so far from providing an original
version, Rabelais merely corrected a rendering in general use which
had been made during the fifteenth century by the Humanist Leonicenus. The annotations which Gryphius is supposed to have admired are
mostly single words cited in Greek from the manuscript or are taken
from the Latin of another Humanist translation by Theodore of Gaza.
Nor has the reader any clue as to why Rabelais chooses to give the
Greek for one word rather than another, or why he mentions one point
on which Gaza differs from Leonicenus and neglects three others.*
If the revision of the texts which the medical Humanists officially
advocated had been a serious programme, Rabelais would have been
encouraged to go about the matter in a very different way. The philo-
logically slipshod character of his Hippocrates suggests that the real
interests of the movement lay elsewhere; and we have only to glance
down a bibliography of Rabelais and we shall find a clue to their
orientation. For Rabelais edited also Manardi's plea for a more rational
approach to medicine and was himself an advocate of dissection in the
study of anatomy. Scientific advance rather than the apotheosis of Greek
knowledge was the prime concern of the circles in which he moved.

In law, the situation took longer to clarify. Petrarch's strictures had
been made from the outside. Though he had some knowledge of law,
he had not troubled to weigh the problems or appreciate the very real
achievements of the men he censured. Nor were the Humanists who
followed him any more competent. For over a century they criticised
the lawyers from a purely philological viewpoint because legal studies
fell short of certain philological ideals.*

In law, however, there was more room for this type of criticism
than there could be in philosophy or medicine, as Valla's highly publi-
cised work on the Donation of Constantine amply shows. The dictum
that law consists either in the interpretation of words or in the distinction between what is just and what is unjust* carries a strong
element of truth. Philology has a part to play in legal studies: and in
the fifteenth century its role had a particular importance since the
medieval commentators had made some gross errors owing to their
ignorance of Latin usage.

Thus, many lawyers were prepared to lend a sympathetic ear to the Humanist attacks on their discipline; for although these did not hit the nail altogether on the head, they seemed to have some relevance to difficulties of which men were becoming increasingly conscious. After the middle of the fifteenth century, almost everyone agreed that the study of law was in urgent need of reform. Not only were its traditional techniques of analysis, classification and proof becoming unworkable owing to the increasing complexity of legal material; but society was changing, and the reinterpretation of Roman law to suit feudal conditions, which had been the great achievement of the Bartolists, was rapidly becoming outdated.

To understand what was happening we must cast our eyes back on the legal developments which occurred during the scholastic period. The main purpose of the scholastic lawyers had been to reconcile the principles and decisions of the Roman jurists with the feudal conditions of their own day. It was not enough for them to expound Roman law, they had to put fresh interpretations upon the Roman terms. A practical lawyer of the thirteenth century could not use the *Digest* directly. He needed to have its technical terms linked to some contemporary equivalent. That is why the *Digest* had been replaced in general use by the *Glose* and the *Glose* by the Bartolist commentaries.* Many Italian cities furthermore followed the practice of appointing foreigners to act as judges. The appointment was always for a limited period, and at the end of his tenure, the ex-judge could be hauled before the courts in his turn to justify the decisions he had given. One effect of this practice was to make every magistrate anxious to produce authorities for all his opinions. Nor were ordinary precedents accounted sufficient. Irate city courts questioning a judgement required to be shown more weighty evidence. They had to be referred to the *Digest* (as reinterpreted by Accursius) or to the works of some renowned doctor like Bardo or Bartolo, and the relevance of the authority quoted had to be shown by means of subtle distinctions and arguments. Given this system of referring judgements back to authorities at all costs, legal language was bound to grow increasingly obscure and the mass of material to be examined before an opinion could be formed was bound to become more and more unwieldy.

From the fifteenth century onwards there are numerous complaints about the confusion into which law had fallen owing to the endless multiplication of commentaries,* and some eminent jurists including Jason of Mayne, the professor at Pavia, made efforts to bring some order into the prevailing chaos.* But it is left to one of Jason's pupils, the brilliant Andreas Alciat, to find a solution.

The work of Alciat is of particular interest to us since he passed as a Humanist. We should expect him therefore to place great value on style. But he does quite the opposite. He defends the technicalities of law and argues that excessive attention to style will lead to obscurity.* We should expect him furthermore to lean exclusively on the authority of the *Digest* and to eschew the medieval legists. He does not do so. His aim seems to have been to establish the general principles of jurisprudence, and to do this he was prepared to use medieval as well as classical writings. Throughout his teaching career, he advocated an historical study of law, holding that the manner in which basic principles are applied will vary from age to age, and that both the *Digest* and the Bartolists ought to be studied against the setting of their times.* To his own students he recommended first the reading of the *Institutes*, as an introduction to jurisprudence, and then practice in the application of legal principles to contemporary cases, which, it will be noted, were no longer taken from a feudal setting but from an increasingly capitalistic world.

This Humanism was essentially an attempt to clear the ground for the building of a legal system to suit the economic and social developments of the age. Admittedly, Alciat felt that any scholar attempting the reformulation of contemporary law needed to have a thorough understanding of the Graeco-Roman jurists and of the Graeco-Roman world. The fact that contemporary capitalist society was coming to resemble the ancient Roman more than it did the medieval, made this knowledge doubly useful. Nevertheless, he wanted the *Digest* (and the learning which explained it) to be consulted as an aid and not worshipped as an authority. In this he had the support of Budé whose attitude to the classics was utilitarian; and he did not need to clash with enthusiasts like Deloynes and Brachet who believed that Greek was necessary for any understanding of law.* He could use their results and go beyond them.

The other great jurists of the sixteenth century, Duarein and Cujas, followed Alciat's lead but perhaps the most startling tribute to the influence of his views is a famous passage in Rabelais. Someone has suggested that Pantagruel should be asked to judge the dispute between Baisecul and Humevesne:

Hereunto all the Counsellors and Doctors willingly agreed, and according to that their result, having instantly sent for him, they intreated him to be pleased to canvass the process, and sift it thoroughly, that after a deep search and narrow examination of all the points thereof, he might forthwith make the report unto them, such as he shall think good in true and legal knowledge. To this effect they delivered into his hands the bags wherein were the Writs and Pancarts concerning that suit, which for bulk and weight were almost enough to load four great couillard or stoned Asses; but Pantagruel said unto them, Are the two Lords between whom this debate and process is, yet living? It was answered him, Yes: To what a devil then (said he), serve so many paltry heaps, and bundles of papers and copies which you give me? is it not better to hear their Controversy from their own mouths, whilest they are face to face before us, than to read these vile fopperies, which are nothing but trumperies, deceits, diabolical cosenages of Cepola, pernicious slights and subversions of equity? for I am sure, that you, and all those through whose hands this process hath past, have by your devices added what you could to it *pro et contra* in such sort, that although their difference perhaps was clear and easy enough to determine at first, you have obscured it, and made it more intricate by the frivolous, sottish, unreasonable and foolish reasons and opinions of Accursius, Baldus, Bartolus, de Castro, de Imola, Hippolytus, Panormo, Bertachin, Alexander, Curtius and those other old Mastiffs, who never understood the least law of the Pandects, they being but mere blockheads and great tithe-calves, ignorant of all that which was needful for the understanding of the laws; for (as it is most certain) they had not the knowledge either of the Greek or Latin tongue, but only of the Gothic or Barbarian.

Furthermore, seeing the Laws are excerpted out of the middle of moral and natural Philosophy, how should these fools have understood it, that have, by G—, studied less in Philosophy than my Mule? in respect of human learning, and the knowledge of Antiquities and History, they were truly laden with those faculties as a toad is with feathers. And yet of all this the Laws are so full, that without it they cannot be understood, Therefore if you will that I make any meddling in this process, first, cause all these papers to be burnt; secondly, make the two Gentlemen come personally before me; and afterwards, when I shall have heard them, I will tell you my opinion freely without feignedness or dissimulation whatsoever.*

Pantagruel does not forget to praise the Pandects or to emphasise the necessity for a good knowledge of Roman antiquities; but when he comes to give judgement, he does not refer to the Pandects but consults the general principles of justice and his own native wit to apply them to the case in hand.

Thus we see that the three great specialities, which had been learnt from the classics in the twelfth and thirteenth centuries, were all developing beyond their classical foundations and were all faced with the problem of sloughing off their scholastic forms in order to make that development possible. In all these cases, Humanism working from a wider knowledge of the classics made some contribution to the cause of progress. In philosophy, the Humanists shook off the authority of the scholastic synthesis and promoted the knowledge of Plato's logic. In medicine, they helped to shift the emphasis of authority from Galen to Hippocrates. In law, their philological strictures did good service in sweeping away the formulations of a dying society. It is true that they exaggerated the importance of their role. They were not leaders but merely auxiliaries. The reform of the specialities was initiated from within and largely carried out from within. It would have occurred if Humanism had never existed, if the absorption of classical knowledge had ceased with the thirteenth century. In these fields of learning which the Middle Ages had explored, the Humanist effort was incidental. Its main impetus was directed elsewhere.

IV. HUMANISM OUTSIDE OF THE SPECIALITIES

It was not until the nineteenth century that the specialised disciplines began to proliferate; and the phenomenon of their multiplication was not unconnected with the spell cast by the *Cours de Philosophie Positive*. Locating the principle of progress in the hierarchical interdependence of fields of enquiry, Comte banished the fear that specialisation would result in chaos. He provided an excuse. The accidental fact that a substantial increase in the number of university departments served to open new avenues to academic success, supplied that excuse with the backing of a multitude of satisfied ambitions; and the tendency to subdivide faculties, which Comtism helped to inaugurate, continues unchecked to this day.

This nineteenth-century development separates us decisively from the Renaissance, when knowledge was for the most part undifferentiated. During the fifteenth and sixteenth centuries, a great variety of subjects, which we now place in distinct and water-tight compartments, were all looked upon as the infrangible province of rhetoric and grammar. Only the three specialities which we discussed in the last section had the status of independent disciplines. Everything else belonged together, forming an amorphous mass of material to which literary studies provided the only approach. This lack of differentiation must be kept in mind if we are to understand how Humanism came to exercise such a profound influence. For it explains why the specific Humanist techniques of analysis and synthesis for the purposes of imitation were applied to so vast a sector of human knowledge, and why within that sector their supremacy as instruments of intellectual organisation was virtually unchallenged. If such subjects as history and political thought had possessed their own methods of study, the impact of the Humanist techniques would have been notably less since they would have been counterbalanced by alternative forms of interpretation. But as things were, they had a clear field. In the absence of other disciplines, their power to mould and fashion was for all intents and purposes absolute.

Having surveyed the methods of imitation in an earlier part of this chapter, our task now is to judge of their effects; and for this purpose, we must consider the works of literature which mirror the thought of the period. The poems of Pontano and Sannazaro, Valla's *De Voluptate*, Alberti's *Della Famiglia* and Machiavelli's *Discorsi* sprang from minds that Humanism had deeply impregnated. They are consequently a measure of the Humanists' cultural achievement.

If Humanism did contribute a specific new element to European culture, the extent of its contribution must be sought within the range of the differences which distinguish the literature of the fifteenth century from its medieval predecessor. That fact is indisputable; and viewed in its light the evidence at our disposal must surely tend to banish any doubts we may feel about the validity of the Humanist claims to have reshaped the world. For the differences in question are indeed startling. The writers of the Middle Ages (and for that matter the early Humanists of the fourteenth century) speak to us from an unfamiliar universe. Their voices sound across a gulf, discoursing on problems we do not share, in terms which few men nowadays would consider significant. But let us move only a hundred years nearer into the mid-period of the Renaissance, and this feeling of strangeness vanishes. We recognise ourselves to be once again within the familiar precincts of our own time. Such is the force of these impressions that they quite commonly affect our attitude towards the two groups of writers. We read Petrarch to learn about Petrarch. We read Machiavelli to learn about ourselves. Yet as a recent critic has pointed out* Petrarch and Machiavelli had a great deal in common. Why then do we react to them in such dissimilar ways? The distinction does not seem to derive from the themes treated by the two authors; for no reader of Gide's *L'Immoraliste* can remain long in doubt about the essential modernity of the debate in the *Secretum*. It is without question as topical as any Machiavellian analysis. So we need to look beyond the main themes to the details of their treatment. Petrarch's attitude to life made him a man of the Renaissance; but to illustrate his ideas he drew on the common stock of the Middle Ages, on that presentation of experience which we find in sermon-books, in which fact was inextricably mixed with fancy, with the *magna ex parte falsa* that the *de Ignorantia* deplores. This stock of ideas has passed from our midst. We know it only by an effort of the historical imagination. Machiavelli on the other hand located his thought against that familiar background which meets us also in Montesquieu, in Voltaire, in Dean Stanley and Dr Arnold, where a demagogue can be described by comparing him with Cleon the Tanner, where a tyrant's ambitious favourites are interpreted in terms borrowed from the career of Seianus.

This difference between Petrarch and Machiavelli has an undoubted connection with the methods and aims of fifteenth-century Humanism. The effect of reading the Greek and Roman authors with a view to imitation was precisely to fix in the mind the details of ancient history and ancient life. An eighteenth-century student who grew up in a world whose vernacular literature and daily speech were permeated with classical material could enter into this heritage with no more than he learnt during a brief school education from the composition of themes and the reading of authors; but the Humanists who lived still surrounded by the popular culture of medieval times had to travel further to reach the same goal. It had needed a long and systematic effort to bring them from the state of Petrarch to that of Machiavelli.

If we want to trace how the Humanist practice of imitation affected creative writing, if we want to go behind the scenes and cast an eye on the mechanics of the process whose overt results we have been considering, our best guide is Erasmus; for his works show us the process in all its stages. The *de Copia*, which we have already had some occasion to quote, outlines his method. The *Adages* present us with the fruits of that method as it were in mid-passage, at the moment when the preliminaries of analysis and classification are complete, but before the imitator has sat down to write. And finally, the *Colloquies* and the *Praise of Folly* show us the finished product. They have their shortcomings because Erasmus was an imperfect artist. But there is no doubt that they were meant to be read for pleasure or at least for edification. Despite their occasional crudities, they are works of literature, and they provide us with a clear example of how the material of Humanist analysis was to be used for artistic effect.

Since we have discussed the *de Copia* in an earlier section, it will be convenient at this point to take the theoretical principles of imitation for granted and to turn straightaway to its practical results as we find them embodied in the *Adages*. That enormous work contains so many novelties, so much of the moralist and so much of the scholar, that the elements which link it with the *de Copia* are easily overlooked. But a careful examination shows those elements to be in the majority and their influence on subsequent writers was profound. Erasmus begins by emphasising a fourfold purpose for his work, which is to serve 'ad philosophiam, ad decus orationis, ad persuadendum et ad intelligendos auctores'. He then explains why, instead of collecting all useful metaphors, sentences and anecdotes, in accordance with the principles laid down in the *de Copia*, he has concentrated on adages, which he defines as popular sayings pithily and attractively put. To have included everything would have made the book too long and unwieldy. There had to be some criterion of selection, and adages were in any case peculiarly suited to serve two of the purposes he had at heart: *philosophia* (by which he means education) and the understanding of authors. But he makes it clear that these purposes were secondary; for the rest of the introduction is devoted to the uses of the adage as a form of rhetorical illustration. To be acceptable from this point of view, an adage must be well known: a popular saying, a quotation from poetry or drama, an historical reference or a technical phrase from a common craft or profession. Furthermore, it must be striking, either in its subject-matter or in its structure, a quality generally attained by metaphor.* Such adages possess great persuasive power because they carry with them the authority of the past, and bring to us a wisdom distilled from experience.* At the same time they are worthy ornaments to any piece of writing. And here Erasmus adds a warning. Being ornaments, his adages should be treated as such. They are the salt that renders the dish tasty and should not be introduced by the sackful or dragged in where they are unsuitable. But with a little skill you can make the self-same adage illustrate a variety of points* or alternatively you can construct proverbial figures in imitation of authentic adages. It is the author of the *de Copia* who is talking here.

Writers on Erasmus generally single out for comment those adages which have a moral bearing:* the 'Sileni Alcibiadis', the 'Festina lente', the 'Dulce bellum inexpertis'.* But these are exceptions, and the majority of the articles have a rhetorical purpose. Many of the shorter ones simply enumerate the possible uses of the particular proverb in question;* and in a great many other cases, the moral essay or antiquarian disquisition is prefaced by a note on the rhetorical value of the phrase.* Even the 'Sileni Alcibiadis' derives its form from the rhetorical lesson, for Erasmus proceeds by listing those people who are not what they seem, and to whom the phrase might suitably be applied, until finally he arrives at Christ and the true Christian.

The form in which these quotations were meant to appear in a finished work can be seen in Erasmus' own more literary writings. They are sprinkled with Greek quotations for whose presence there is no excuse, unless we are to regard them as endowed with the authority of the ages and therefore a powerful support to the argument.* In the *Praise of Folly* the Trophonian cave appears as a circumlocution describing the temperamentally mournful. Folly is pictured with the *Mystae*. The numbers of Pythagoras symbolise philosophy. The contrast between Nestor's honeyed voice and the rough tones of Achilles illustrates the superiority of age to youth. Erasmus cites the drunkenness of the gods and turns Stoicism upside down to demonstrate his theme. Plato's misogyny is made to prove the folly of the female sex and his famous golden age when kings would be philosophers is turned to the ridicule of the latter.*

Erasmus began his career as a Greek scholar by translating Euripides and Lucian.* Their appeal for him was admittedly to some extent stylistic, if style be interpreted in the broadest sense of the word. For he was entranced by the colourful world of their bright imagery. 'I am sending you Lucian', he writes to Urswich, 'who will delight you by his novelty, by the variety of his colour, his beauty and his fragrance.' But mostly these Greek writers had the power to move him because of the similarity of their standards to his own. Temperamentally sensitive, attached to understanding, kindness and beauty, and obsessed by a fierce, emotional hatred of their opposites, not the member of a ruling class but an ordinary man of humble or even dubious origins, Erasmus saw the good life as based on the pursuit of happiness among one's equals. He was bound to be attracted to a writer like Euripides or Lucian who derived his ideas and imagery from the common experience of the free citizens of his time, who took his metaphors from the scenes in town or country through which such citizens normally passed, habitually discussed their practical problems and never wearied of speculating on how they ought to behave. Not unnaturally Erasmus found Greek literature to his taste. Not unnaturally he adopted Greek standards and strove to actualise Greek customs. We have seen how he started by translating authors in whom the ideas bearing on this subject appeared in their clearest form; and his next step was to collect the ideas themselves, the traditional wisdom of the Greeks, in his *Adages*. Read carefully, that huge collection presents a more complete picture of the

Greeks than any anthology or ideological study since produced. We see them at war and at their more complicated peace-time occupations, engaged in the extensive ceremonies of their religion, administration and law. We see their amusements, music, gymnastics and drinking, and their simple domestic life which provides the material for so much of their language.* The multiform and disjointed citations bring into prominence facets of the ancient world that its systematic historians too often miss. So, for example, the majority of the metaphors are drawn from agriculture, hunting, the habits of animals or the phenomena of nature;* and we realise that despite their urban preoccupations, the Greeks were more conscious of the country than of the town. The resulting picture of ancient life formed an important background to the principles it accompanied. Its presence helped to prevent the otherwise almost inevitable misinterpretation of the general ideas borrowed from antiquity and provided concrete examples for those who found ideas unpalatable food. Here at last was the hand-book to the past for which five generations had waited, which made the wisdom of the ancients accessible and ready for use.

Without the note-book method and all the work it implied, the Humanist contribution to European culture would have lost much of its importance. The present would have borrowed from the past only such general conceptions, such particular judgements and anecdotes, such individual traits of sensibility as could be casually transmitted in the course of reading and unsystematic imitation. It would not have been possible for men to copy the epics, dramas and histories of the ancients with any degree of exactness or with the hope of producing demonstrably similar effects. For lacking a substantial identity in the details, the accuracy of the general form would not have been sufficient to ensure an acceptable likeness. If the turns of speech, the imagery, the very situations and characters had not been drawn from ancient sources, the mere observance of the unities would not have made the new dramas appear an effective reproduction of their classical prototypes. Deprived of the satisfactions of success, imitators would have been discouraged. They would have looked with inevitably greater favour upon contemporary genres, and the literature of the sixteenth and seventeenth centuries, stripped of its great epics, its classical tragedies, its comedies that derived from Terence, its artistic histories and its formal odes, would have appeared very different to our eyes to-day, freer perhaps and simpler, more charming, but without the strength which comes from the artist's struggle with a difficult form.

Admittedly, the most important developments of the new age, its admiration for enterprise and personal success, the progress of political knowledge and the dawning interest in science, were independent of Humanism and would not have been much affected if Humanist techniques had been less efficient.* But there exist grounds for supposing that in the absence of Humanism the generally accepted conception of man would have laid less emphasis on rational control or on the ultimate power of theory and will to shape the mutinousness of life. For this commonplace rationality, based on an over-simplified view of human nature, had its origins in the ancient world and thus owed its wide acceptance after the Renaissance to the supporting presence of those innumerable fragments of Graeco-Roman thought and sensibility which had come to form an integral part of every man's mental equipment. If there had been fewer of these fragments, Cartesianism in the seventeenth, rationalism in the eighteenth century, might not have gained so speedy or so firm a hold. A deeper understanding of human psychology might have evolved much earlier or might not have evolved at all.

Such speculations are fascinating, but not susceptible of proof. The facts, however, remain. At the end of the fourteenth century, the cultural tradition of the West bore the recognisable imprint of the Middle Ages. By the end of the sixteenth, the medieval elements had been replaced by others drawn from the Graeco-Roman heritage; and in between these two limits of time, we find that the method of study in general use is based on the analysis of the classical texts and the memorisation of linguistic and illustrative detail. That these Humanist studies subserved certain wide aims characteristic of the period as a whole seems almost irrelevant in view of the thoroughness of the methods employed. Admittedly there was some degree of selection, certain aspects of ancient life received more emphasis than others; but once a student had embarked upon the recommended course, once he had started analysing and memorising, the techniques he employed acquired, like some powerful engine, an impetus of their own and took in everything irrespective of its interest, so that the whole or nearly the whole of the classical heritage passed into the common stock of European thought.

CHAPTER VIII

THE END OF THE RENAISSANCE AND THE APPEARANCE OF NEW PATTERNS IN CLASSICAL EDUCATION AND SCHOLARSHIP

I. THE NORTHERN RENAISSANCE

The specific achievement of the Humanists, their bringing within the ambit of contemporary knowledge those sectors of the classical heritage which the Middle Ages had failed to explore, was accomplished in two stages. The earlier representatives of the movement, such as Guarino and Erasmus, had written in Latin and the material they had mastered had been accessible only to the learned. It was left to the sixteenth century to contrive the transference of their gains into a more popular medium so that with the rise of the vernacular literatures the New Learning became familiar to all who could read. When that had happened, the absorption of the classical heritage by European culture may be regarded as virtually complete within the limits set by the techniques of the time. The long process we have been following since the seventh century was at an end. But this crowning of a millennium of patient work had an inevitable corollary. Men's attitude to antiquity changed. As the content of the classical literatures became available in the vernaculars and merged in that common background of ideas which is the starting-point of all new thought, the direct study of these literatures lost much of its old interest. The architects of cultural progress had little incentive to concern themselves with the Greek and Latin authors in particular, since most of what these had to offer was already contained within the contemporary tradition. Nevertheless, the study of the classics was too well established to be peremptorily abandoned. Its place in European life was guaranteed by long-standing custom. So it survived, obeying, however, the general law which governs the survival of institutions that have outlived their original purpose. Bereft of its former function, it took on a new role and became at one level the vehicle of an education intended to preserve existing values, while at another and more difficult level it figured as a self-sufficient speciality, which could be cultivated for its own sake and provided a socially approved field for the demonstration of mental aptitude. These three topics, the emergence of the vernacular literatures, the new education of the *pietas litterata* and the rise of modern scholarship will be discussed in the later sections of this chapter. But before we can come to them, something in the nature of a general introduction is necessary.

Up to this point, it has been possible to treat Western society as a unit. The observable differences between its geographical parts have not been great enough to justify the sacrifice of the advantages incidental to a single chronological exposition. But with the advent of the sixteenth century, that convenience has to be abandoned. Each of the four major countries, Italy, Germany, England and France had its own problems. Each followed a particular pattern of social development; and if Spain is to be included in our survey, Spanish society must fall, thanks to the Moorish wars, in a class wholly apart. Humanism spread unevenly and its growth was in each case modified by purely local factors. The old Europe of the *Pax Romana* was breaking up into the New Europe of the national states.

When we turn our attention to the lands north of the Alps, we find that Humanism made its first appearance in the imperial territories. By 1460, groups of ardent Humanists could be found in a number of centres from Vienna to the Rhineland; and this fact has all the air of a paradox, for the Empire was by Italian standards the most backward area of western Europe. But at this particular juncture, during the middle years of the fifteenth century, England and France, the two countries which stood on the verge of becoming national states, were hindered by the difficulties incidental to their political advance from making progress in any other field. The Wars of the Roses and the Burgundian struggle were eventually to complete the ruin of the feudal magnates. They were preparing the ground for a brilliant future. But their immediate effects were deleterious. For the moment, England and France were bereft of cultural energy; and so it was left to the Empire since it was free from political disturbances of a similar intensity, to take the lead in a temporary but spectacular revival of knowledge. Although the imperial domains were complacently feudal in their general structure, individual towns possessed a great measure of autonomy. Even if they did not enjoy the complete independence of the larger Italian city-states, the life of their citizens approached to some extent the Italian pattern; and they could to that degree share the cultural aims which classical studies were competent to promote. Thus there were posts for Humanists in the German schools and universities, many of which were under municipal control. At the same time, too, the Emperors showed a craving for the externals of that Renaissance absolutism whose essence they plainly lacked. They could not be despots, but they could be and were patrons of learning, and like the d'Este and the Visconti they kept Humanists at their courts.

The Emperor Sigismund gave employment to Vergerio and the more enterprising Frederick III had Aeneas Sylvius for a secretary and poet laureate. The association of the latter pair produced a famous novelette (whose subject was furnished by the adventures of Frederick's Chancellor) and a treatise on education which was written for Frederick's ward. But these achievements were personal to the future Pius II. Court officials, however gifted, are not among the natural propagandists of knowledge; and the imperial patronage of Humanism would in all likelihood have proved unproductive, had it not received support from that humbler quarter which we have mentioned above. Like their English contemporaries, whom we shall have occasion to discuss later, German scholars were in the habit of visiting Italy. But unlike the English, they did not on their return abandon academic life for the tasks of administration or the fat plums of ecclesiastical preferment. Thanks to the independence and the Humanist interests of the cities, their world was so organised that they could profitably continue as scholars.

By 1460 Purbach and Regiomontanus in Vienna, Luder at Heidelberg, and Hegius at Emmerich were all engaged in spreading Humanist ideas. It is possible to dismiss these men as ill-informed and helpless in their comparative isolation. None of them possessed that southern breadth of vision and eloquence which had marked, for example, even the abortive work of Jean de Montreuil. They were dull pedants admittedly; but despite their dullness, we must credit them with one virtue, which more than compensated for their incidental deficiencies. They were sincerely determined to learn from their Italian mentors. That sort of humility which recognises the superiority of another race and makes possible the systematic copying of foreign achievements has often enabled the Germans to move mountains. This was one of the occasions when its usefulness was successfully displayed. The second generation of German Humanists far outstripped the first, and among them there were some whose attainments placed them in the front rank. Even if we accord Wimpheling no more honour than is due to a conscientious grammarian, Agricola must be recognised as a lesser Erasmus, a vivid controversialist who did much to shake scholastic influence; and Reuchlin was without doubt the finest Greek scholar of his day. These men, who rose to prominence in the fourteen-seventies, were Humanists in the full meaning of the word. They spanned the whole range of contemporary knowledge; and it is not surprising that their work ushered in a July of the Renaissance as glorious as its Italian June.

Reuchlin and Agricola paved the way for Sebastian Brant, Celtes, Despauterius and Erasmus. These men, two generations removed from the beginnings of German Humanism, supplemented and completed the work of the Italian fifteenth century while at the same time laying unassailable foundations for the New Learning in the north. Their systematising spirit led them to fill important gaps that the Italians, men of letters rather than teachers, had neglected. Despauterius produced a Latin grammar which resembled the *Doctrinale* sufficiently to be accepted in contemporary schools but which embodied many of the Humanist simplifications, putting its main emphasis on usage rather than logic. Erasmus wrote the first comprehensive account of the techniques necessary for imitation, compiled an excellent reader in the *Colloquies* and a great compendium of illustrative material in the *Adages*. Froben at Basle provided a northern equivalent of the Aldine Press; and their efforts were finally crowned by the opening in 1517 of the *Collegium Trilingue* at Louvain with Busleiden for its Maecenas.

The subsequent history of German Humanism belongs to the sections of this chapter on the schools and scholarship. The most impressive exponents of the *pietas litterata* were to come from Germany, and if Eobanus Hessus was still an old-style Humanist concerned above all with translation from the Greek and imitation, most of his sixteenth-century colleagues, Polmannus, Mycillus, Glareanus, Gelenius, the solemn Camerarius and the encyclopedic Gesner, were editors and antiquarians, the pioneers of that detailed learning which meets us in the monumental commentaries of the Enlightenment. One point, however, deserves notice, for it stems from that political backwardness which has already been mentioned. The Empire fostered a Humanism which remained without its natural accompaniment of a Renaissance; and we are struck by the absence of any serious effort to imitate Latin writers in the vernacular. Some unimportant writings of the satirist Ulrich von Hutten, the uninspired plays of Frischlin, a few traits in the dramatic dialogues of Hans Sachs, a few fables by Alberus and Waldis, are all that Germany has to match the popular literatures of contemporary England and France. It is true that towards the end of the century we find Fischart and his imitation of *Pantagruel*, but the German literary Renaissance does not begin effectively until the Heidelberg school comes into prominence with Zincgref and Opitz after 1600.

If Germany possessed the New Learning without the New Life, France went to the opposite extreme. During the fifteenth century French Humanism had struggled gallantly against overwhelming odds since it received neither civic nor royal patronage. The uncertain spring of that early period, when Pierre Bersuire translated Livy, and Jean de Montreuil pronounced himself a disciple of Petrarch, never ripened into summer. One of Montreuil's friends, Nicolas de Clemanges, lived until 1440, piping the praises of Cicero amid the storms of the Burgundian wars. But eventually that faint voice died away like the rest. An adventurous Byzantine, who ventured to Paris in 1456 hoping to obtain a public lectureship, found that some badly paid private lessons were all that would come his way and departed cursing France for a land of barbarians.* The year 1460, when German Humanism had already taken great strides towards its eventual success, saw the very nadir of Humanist learning in France.

After the coronation of Louis XI, conditions gradually improved. But at first progress moved at a snail's pace. The historian, Robert Gaguin, who had been one of the Byzantine Tifernas' few private pupils, gathered round him a small group of men who took a desultory interest in the new ideas from Italy. Another Byzantine, George Hermonymus, received sufficient support to keep alive, though on one occasion at least he was hauled off to prison for debt and was generally reduced to copying endless psalters and breviaries.* Fichet produced a small grammar. The German Hellenist Johann Wessel is supposed to have taught in Paris round about 1470. But the work of these men represented not so much an advance on what had been achieved earlier, as a painful and not very efficient effort to regain lost ground. They groped their way among uncertainties and judged by the common standards of Humanist learning, they were in every sense inferior to Jean de Montrueil.

Though Lefèvre d'Etaples was inspired to visit Italy in 1486 for the purpose of hearing Argyropoulus on Aristotle, and though the Ferrara-trained Josse Bade lectured at Valence and later at Lyons, it was the expedition of Charles VIII which finally opened French eyes to the glories of the Renaissance. The adventurous gentlemen who crossed the Alps in 1494 to the land of books and statues returned with an enthusiasm which matched the transports of Agricola; and the interpenetration of the two cultures, already marked in centres like Lyons, was suddenly intensified.

If the age of Louis XI had been empty of Humanist learning, it had not been equally empty of those interests and untutored desires which the Renaissance outlook could satisfy; and it is this latter circumstance which probably explains the startling effects of the Italian Promenade. We can glimpse the spirit of Machiavelli in Comines' hard, rational analyses and in Comines' contempt for shibboleths of feudalism. *Où est le profit, là est l'honneur* could never have passed muster as a medieval maxim; and the wish to praise famous men was present in the French biographies of the time no less surely than in the works of Boccaccio. Indeed, France had long been ready for its Renaissance: and once the floodgates of Italian influence were opened the new movement made swift progress.

Enthusiasm for the Italian way of life spread with startling suddenness through the whole of France. The ideas one associates with the Renaissance were eagerly canvassed. They made their appearance in the Latin disquisitions of the Lyons Platonist, Champier, who relied for his information on Ficino and Pico della Mirandola. Champier poured forth encyclopedic tomes in which he reconciled Plato with Aristotle, Dionysius with Christianity and—since he was a doctor—Galen with Hippocrates, seasoning this recondite intellectual fare by occasional discussions of the technicalities of chivalry;* and he seems to have been the centre of an admiring circle. But his influence was at the best secondary for although he was a dilettante whose mind followed the call of every popular interest, he wrote (as his medieval predecessors had done) in that Latin which was a perquisite of the educated few. The real pivot of the new enthusiasm lay elsewhere; and the ideas of the Renaissance were to owe their promulgation primarily to the active pens of the vernacular writers. For the first time in European history the language of the people did not wait for a lead from the language of learning.

The spirit which had transformed Italy found expression in the French writings of Jean Lemaire de Belges and in the French translations of Octovien de Saint-Gelais and Claude de Seyssel. All three were familiar figures in aristocratic circles. They could claim some acquaintance with the ancient writers. They possessed more than a tincture of education; but they were not scholars. At any rate, they would not have willingly devoted their lives to elucidating a manuscript or to perfecting a fine Latin style. Their aim was not to widen the boundaries of Humanist knowledge. What they set out to do was to bring that knowledge (as it existed in the polite courts of Italy) within the grasp of the French high society of their day. Saint-Gelais, the Bishop of Angoulême, was a man of fashion, and his version of the *Heroides* seems to have been planned above all to please the ladies of the court, most of whom would have had some difficulty in reading the Latin original. Seyssel, another bishop, had a purpose which though more serious resembled the aims of Saint-Gelais. His French renderings of Valla's Thucydides and Poggio's Diodorus were intended for the personal instruction of the king. Lemaire was a man of humbler station, a professional writer who served, however, as secretary to a number of distinguished patrons including Anne of Brittany and Margaret of Savoy. He has been described as a colossus with one foot in the Middle Ages and the other in the Renaissance; but the medieval element in his work is little more than a formal shell which cracks and reveals now the Machiavellian ready to analyse the intricacies of a political dispute, now the sensualist fascinated by worldly beauty, now the self-conscious poet who preaches the value of art as the source of personal or national glory. He was more surely than many of his successors a man of the new age. But he was not a Humanist.

He died (or at any rate disappeared from human ken) about 1515; but the movement which he had helped to inaugurate went from strength to strength. The young Clément Marot emerged as an excellent poet after the Renaissance pattern who could reproduce in French the delights of Ovid and Martial. Budé, otherwise a conscientious Latinist, embodied the fruits of his renowned learning in the *Institution du Prince* (1529) written in the vernacular at the request of Francis I; and Rabelais produced his own praise of folly in *Pantagruel*. Long before French Humanism reached its apogee with the great generation of Danès, Toussain, Lambin, La Ramée and Dorat, the French Renaissance was well on its way carried on the wings of a more modern medium. The circumstances and further history of this development will be discussed in the following section. For the moment, however, we must notice the twist which it gave to the New Learning in France.

If we consider the growth of French Humanism and look at it systematically in its entirety we shall come to the conclusion that it followed the same slow course as its Italian and German predecessors. Nor indeed could it have done otherwise; for scholars need to be trained, and the training of a sufficient number to ensure the continuance of a national tradition cannot be the work of a day. In Italy these preliminaries had been hastened by the teaching of Chrysoloras, but in Germany they had occupied the energies of the two generations whose representative figures are respectively Purbach and Agricola. The French effort too was to take the best part of forty years. We can set the beginning of French Humanism in 1491 when Budé is supposed to have embraced a career of learning, in 1492 when Lefèvre produced his first work on Aristotle, or in 1494 when Charles VIII made his promenade; but it was not until 1530, the year when Royal Readerships were established, that we find a generation of scholars who equal in their numbers and attainments the Italian contemporaries of Guarino or the German contemporaries of Erasmus.

But this picture of a slow evolution proceeding by easy stages—dependent at first on the occasional lessons of a visiting Janus Lascaris or on the lectures of the Italian Aleandro and then gathering strength as a native generation of scholars matures—this expected picture into which we can fit the groping Humanism of a Josse Bade or a Bérault, is put altogether out of focus by the prodigious figure of Guillaume Budé. The author of the *Annotationes ad Pandectas* and the *de Asse* was by common consent almost the equal of Erasmus and head and shoulders above any other Humanist of his day. One would expect to find him among the exponents of developed Humanism, not among the groping students of an epoch of experiment.

The paradox can be explained only if we realise that Budé's career stands in sharp contradiction to the forces that were tending to separate the intellectual life of the different nations. He belongs not to French Humanism in particular, but to European Humanism in general. He was indeed one of those rare beings who can instruct themselves primarily from books with only the minimum of outside help. With writings of the Italian and German Humanists at his elbow, he could mount to the level they had attained and move beyond. Such an independent path to knowledge is generally beset by a variety of pitfalls; and it is possible that if Budé had been born twenty years earlier, his autodidact learning would have foundered on the rocks of inexperience. But by 1490 he had just sufficient help from his personal contacts and from his correspondence with men like Lascaris and Erasmus to keep him from straying into unfruitful by-ways. No other French Humanist with the possible exception of Lefèvre came anywhere near equalling his achievement.

French Humanism did not develop evenly. Since it was a comparative late-comer in the field, the various stages of its growth were curiously telescoped. Its early history has a good deal in common with the similar crude beginnings of its Italian and German counterparts. Classical learning spread slowly; and many of the first French Humanists carried the stamp of the Middle Ages, a sign of their kinship with a Salutati or a Purbach. Symphorien Champier is a case in point with his clumsy attempts to produce a universal philosophy, and that Nicolas Bérault who still used the Bartolists to interpret the *Pandects* and was prepared to edit William of Auvergne after Valla's *Elegantiae.* * On the other hand, the influence of Budé, which brought his younger contemporaries in touch with the latest achievements of scholarship, and the general swift spread of Renaissance ideas, thanks to the work of men like Lemaire, meant that even in its embryonic stage French Humanism had some of the characteristics which we regard as typical of the more advanced contemporary developments of classical learning; and the ultimate result of this telescoping was that when the movement came to maturity, which happened after 1530 with the appointment of Royal Readers for Greek and Latin, it shared in every respect the aims and methods which Italian and German Humanism had by then managed to evolve. It showed the same interest in vernacular imitation, the same zeal for textual criticism, the same markedly religious bias. Its further history belongs therefore to the later portions of this chapter; and we must now—moving in space rather than time—turn to England.

England in the fifteenth century suffered from much the same disabilities as her neighbour. She was racked by a civil war which, if more intermittent, was just as destructive as the Burgundian conflict. She too experienced a decline in cultural standards. Petrarch meeting Bury when the latter visited Avignon in 1373 had found him receptive of new ideas. Similarly, despite his medieval education, the author of the *Canterbury Tales* had stood nearly as close as Petrarch himself to the threshold of the Renaissance. But in England even more than in France the promise of the fourteenth century was denied by the fifteenth. Chaucer was succeeded by Lydgate. It is true that there were schools in plenty and that a surprisingly large portion of the population knew how to read and write.* But few progressed from the merely useful to the fields of original learning, and the universities had little to offer by way of inspiring knowledge. It is true also that a substantial number of Englishmen visited Italy and even spent time with Humanists like Guarino. But the best-known of these travellers, the two noblemen whose activities attracted most notice, Humphrey, Duke of Gloucester, and his younger contemporary, the Earl of Worcester, belong to the age of the Grand Tour more than to their own century. They appear to have been learned dilettantes collecting manuscripts, savouring the adulation of scholars, potential Maecenases, but by that very token unlikely to do much good in their homeland where they had so few learned men to patronise.* The other Englishmen who made the Italian journey were drawn into public life on their return home and abandoned the pursuit of learning for the tasks of diplomacy or administration. Grey ended his life as Bishop of Ely, Free as Bishop of Bath. Flemming and Gunthorp both became deans; and the latter moreover was in considerable demand as an ambassador. Even William Selling, the most earnest scholar of the century, who had been taken to Italy by no other motive but his simple enthusiasm for the classics, spent his last thirteen years a prior. The very eminence of these men militated against their being active propagandists for a new method of study. They had too little time to devote to the teaching of complicated literary techniques.

The careers of Gray, Gunthorpe and Free belong to the period before 1480. Selling studied in Italy from 1464 to 1467 and died in 1494. They have never been regarded as anything more than precursors; and it is not until we come to the next generation that we find the men whom all the school-books call the English Humanists. The work of Linacre, Colet, More and Lily has been the subject of much discussion. Their importance has been persistently emphasised; and many people have come to think of their age as the heyday of the New Learning in England. That is the popular impression; but it has much to contradict it. If we pass in review the development of Humanism in the different countries of Europe, we shall see that in each case its period of florescence coincided with the fulfilment of certain conditions. In each case, by the time Humanism can be said to have flourished, the number of its skilled exponents was considerable, and their immersion in classical knowledge had set them free from any trace of medieval influence. But during the early years of Henry VIII neither of these conditions obtained. Interest in Greek and Latin was largely confined to Colet's few friends; and their learning, though considerable, was by no means wholly in accord with Renaissance ideas. Linacre had spent more than ten years in Italy, had graduated in medicine at Padua, studied under Chalcondyles and Politian, had been urged by Ermolaus Barbaro to translate Aristotle and praised by Manutius as a man learned in both Greek and Latin. He devoted his spare time to compiling Latin grammars and composing translations from the Greek which showed an exquisite sense of style, but within the limits of his own profession he was a devotee of the outdated Galenian school which the Humanist doctors of his time had largely abandoned. Lily was a grammarian in the Italian tradition—he had studied under Pomponius in Rome—but his interests did not carry him beyond the technicalities of morphology and syntax. Grocyn and Latimer who had shared Linacre's travels made little use of the knowledge they had acquired. Grocyn lectured on divinity and is supposed to have taught some of his students Greek. Latimer, apart from occasional letters to Erasmus, hid his light of his learning under a bushel.

Indeed, the only members of the group who combined an interest in style with an interest in new ideas and who left written memorials of their work after the approved Humanist fashion were Colet and More. The former deserves to rank as the English Lefèvre, though his linguistic knowledge was more thorough, while his knowledge of logic was more superficial, than the Frenchman's. But he did share Lefèvre's Neoplatonic enthusiasms and Lefèvre's historical approach to exegesis. As for More—his zeal for the New Learning is well attested, and his *Utopia* shows that he must have been at the very least a competent scholar. Moreover, by the time he came on the scene, the best of the Humanists were moving beyond the ideals which could be directly supported from the classics. They were exploring fresh possibilities of a kind that the ancient authorities had not discussed; and in this respect, too, More was among the innovators. His concern for social problems, other than the obvious evils of war, links him with that most original of Renaissance thinkers, the Spaniard Vivès. But despite his originality, he was an ascetic who wore a hair shirt, a persecutor who crushed the Reformers 'like ants beneath his feet'. There is, of course, no logical reason why a man should not uphold simultaneously the excellence of Plato and the authority of the Pope. But most of the Humanists, at this early stage, showed a certain sympathy for the ideas of the Reformation; and More in that sense was exceptional.

Few in number and somewhat unusual in their approach to learning Colet and his friends have all the characteristics by which one learns to distinguish the pioneer. Their personal contacts with Erasmus did not draw them effectively within the orbit of the fully-developed continental Humanism; and the proof of this comes when we consider their successors. In France the efforts of Budé, Aleandro and Scaliger produced by the fifteen-thirties an eminent generation of scholars. In England, the teaching inaugurated by Colet and Linacre produced, even with the help of further voyages to Italy and the Rhine, no one more eminent than Croke, Smith and Cheke.

Erasmus had failed to arouse much interest in Greek during the time he spent at Cambridge (1511–14); but in 1516 Wolsey established a Greek lectureship at Oxford and two years later Fisher, a close ally of More, carried through a similar measure in Cambridge where Croke was made Reader. The opposition which greeted these appointments seems hard to explain. A hostile party who called themselves the Trojans went so far as to heckle and jeer at the champions of Greek in the open street. Why should they have troubled? Or was this just another manifestation of academic conservatism? A passage in Croke's public defence of his subject affords us a clue.* He regarded the university as an institution whose function it was to educate administrators and based his arguments for Greek on its usefulness in the study of the sciences. Such a conception was not likely to have much favour with the partisans of a medieval order. It meant the extension to Oxford and Cambridge of that 'Lawyers' University' which was already flourishing in the Inns of Court; and if Greek was regarded as the thin end of a utilitarian wedge, the advance guard of a 'Queen Elizabeth's Academy', we need not wonder that it met with hostility. At the same time it must be remembered that the year was 1520 and the study of Greek was held to involve a new approach to the Bible, which apart from all questions of heresy constituted an open threat to existing academic methods. If philology was competent to solve questions of faith, logicians were in danger of losing their influence.

In the earlier part of this chapter we traced the fortunes of German Humanism up to 1515 and those of French Humanism up to 1530, taking each to the point where its individual development began to show the trends which are typical of sixteenth-century classical studies. But neither 1515 nor 1530 can serve us as a stopping-place where England is concerned. English Humanism remained unaffected by continental trends until the reign of Elizabeth. It followed a fifteenth- rather than a sixteenth-century pattern. In 1535 Croke was succeeded as Reader in Greek by Thomas Smith who was then twenty-one years of age. Smith was a brilliant scholar, but even so his extreme youth suggests that the post was not held in high esteem. Five years later the Readership was raised to the dignity of a Professorial Chair for John Cheke 'the Exchequer of Eloquence, a man of men, supernaturally traded in all tongues'. Public Orator, Provost of King's College, Cambridge, member of a commission entrusted with visiting the universities, Privy

Councillor and Secretary of State in the nine-day reign of Lady Jane Grey, a zealous supporter of the Protestant cause but driven eventually by fear of the stake into a shameful public recantation and submission to Rome, Cheke was undoubtedly a man able to impress his fellows and an excellent teacher who did much to popularise Greek at Cambridge.

But it is instructive to compare these imposing figures with their contemporaries across the Channel. We look in vain for those works of scholarship, those meticulous editions, those monumental encyclopedias, those ingenious *Adversaria* and *Variae Lectiones*, which record the labours of Lambin, Gesner, Turnèbe and Muret. Cheke, it is true, edited a few of Chrysostom's homilies; but he was more at ease inditing pamphlets against those who dared to disturb the king's peace by protesting against the enclosure of common lands. The account given by Ascham makes it clear that these Cambridge Humanists had not advanced (after the manner of their French and German colleagues) from the study of imitation to the study of texts. In so far as they were scholars they followed the fifteenth-century Italian model. They held to the practices systematised in the *de Copia*, but without the interest which would have led them to add improvements of their own. One cannot help suspecting that their scholarship was largely a means to an end. Croke had made the point that the study of the classics would fit a man for public office, and Cheke had plainly taken him at his word. The accomplishments of that versatile genius had carried him first to university office, and then to those uplands of administration where university politicians meet their professional counterparts; for a moment the highest honours, the realities of power had hovered within his grasp. But it was not to be. Neither his knowledge of the classics, nor his knowledge of the world, had been sufficient to save him from backing the weaker side; and in the bitterness of his exile—his wealth was confiscated and he had to teach Greek in Strassburg for a living—the one consolation which might have proved efficacious was denied him by the vagaries of time. He could not tell himself that in a troubled age those who loved learning for its own sake were just as likely to suffer as the votaries of ambition. For another fifteen years were to pass before Lambin died of shock at the news of St Bartholomew.

The writing of good Latin prose had been the hall-mark and the highest achievement of the second generation of English Humanists. It is not surprising therefore that their successors should have concerned themselves almost entirely with a campaign of translation into

Latin and English and with vernacular imitations of the classics. It was appropriate that Thomas Wilson who praises Cheke's Latin renderings of the *Olynthiacs*, should have been the first to produce an English version of that work. But the story of the translators and the fortunes of the English hexameter belong more properly to the following section. Here our task is to note that thanks to the competing interest of the Reformation and the close connection which existed between the universities and public life, English Humanism did little more than uphold the standards of fifteenth-century Italy in an age which had largely outgrown them and was never the main force behind the English Renaissance which developed more or less independently of classical studies with the help of Italian, French and Spanish models.

Humanism also flourished for a brief moment in the Hungarian kingdom where Cardinal Vitéz, who had studied in Italy before becoming the right-hand man of Matthias Corvinus, tried at one time to establish a university. But the early death of his nephew, Janus Pannonius (1434–72) who had been trained at Ferrara to be that university's cynosure, had delayed the realisation of the project; and soon after Renaissance Hungary collapsed in the general holocaust of Mohács. Spain therefore is the only country which still remains to be considered. The Spanish Renaissance resembles the English and the French rather than the German. The vernacular literature was vigorous and original, while the learned tradition was relatively weak. Consequently the former dominated the latter to an even greater degree than in France. Both the Castilian and the Catalán writers were notably influenced by Italian models from the fourteenth century onwards, when Lopez de Ayala translated Livy. Early in the fifteenth, we find Juan de Mena deliberately imitating Lucan and Virgil as well as Dante and Petrarch; and he does not confine himself to a merely literary imitation, but comes forward as the champion of at least one characteristic Renaissance belief. He stresses the importance of poetry and the poet, for he shares Petrarch's conviction that art is a valid expression of human greatness. From Juan de Mena's time onwards, Spanish poetry and prose derived many of their themes and much of their technique from imitation; and Spanish writers produced several excellent vernacular translations (see Appendix II, pp. 506 ff.). With Encinas who began by translating Virgil's *Eclogues* and then went on to write eclogues of his own, we are on the threshold of the *Siglo de Oro* when Boscán, Garcilaso de la Vega and Luis de Léon express the genuine mood of the Renaissance.

With the solitary exception of the Italian, Spanish was the first great vernacular literature to bear the imprint of Humanism and the imprint went deep. But when we turn from literature to learning, we find that Spanish Humanism never attained to any great distinction. Spain, like her neighbours, was torn by internecine struggles until late in the fifteenth century, and it was only with the reign of Ferdinand and Isabella that conditions became propitious for higher studies. The first Humanists of note were, as elsewhere, men who had studied in Italy. The most famous of them, Antonio of Nebrija, lectured from 1473 at Sevilla and Salamanca, until he was transferred in 1510 to the new university founded by Ximenes at Alcalá de Henares. He prepared the ground for the study of Latin and Greek but the limits of his influence are clearly shown by the fact that Vivès who studied in Spain during the first decade of the sixteenth century left the country a confirmed scholastic and was converted to Humanism later by the influence of Erasmus. The New Learning was hamstrung in Spain, as later in Portugal, by the repressive policy of the Church, which did not allow it to develop until the free-thinking of the fifteenth century had been effectively replaced by the pious and scholarly preoccupations of the sixteenth. It is noteworthy that after 1500 the translators were far less active than in other Western countries, and that Antonio's most eminent pupil, Nunez de Guzman, left his notes on Themistius unpublished while he did not hesitate to trust to print his translation of St Basil's letter on Greek studies.

Spain therefore is again a special case; and the fact confirms the statement made earlier that Northern Humanism was national rather than European. Its parts do not form a unified whole. Even such a brief survey of national developments as we have been able to give shows that the form taken by Humanism differed from country to country; and so did the relations between the Humanist movements and the general spread of Renaissance ideas. The next stage in our enquiry is therefore set against a complicated background which stands in contrast to the relative simplicity of the fifteenth-century Italian scene; and although the imitation of classical writings in the vernacular, the adoption of the Humanist discipline in the schools and the growing interest in technical scholarship are universal traits and characterise the sixteenth century in all the Western countries we shall in considering them have to take into account numerous variations and shifts of emphasis. We shall have to bear local differences in mind.

II. IMITATION IN THE VERNACULARS

The sixteenth century is generally regarded as the first great epoch of cultural nationalism. The growth of centralised authority and the consequent glorification of the State had characterised the Renaissance from its very beginnings. But so long as the new spirit was confined to Italy, these tendencies had little influence on the development of vernacular literature. For Italian and Latin were alike in belonging as truly to Siena as to Florence, to Venice as to Milan. The Italians' love of their language and their national writers remained more or less independent of the patriotisms of the warring cities. 1494, however, brought a great change as a result of the French invasion.

The armies of Charles VIII were dazzled by the spectacle of a culture vastly superior to the one they knew at home. They came to conquer. They remained—in the intervals of conquest—to admire. Humility, however, is not a French virtue; and as soon as the first shock of delight had faded to a more critical awe, the forerunners of Stendhal felt the need to assert their own value. They did this with spirit; and the Italians, their national feelings sharpened by this foreign impact, responded in kind. The result was a long debate, conducted in a hundred places by a thousand acrimonious tongues, whose echoes we hear in Lemaire's *Concorde des Deux Langages*.* The French, having a clear grasp of fact, tended to emphasise the potential rather than the actual excellence of their culture; but neither party was at all content to rest on past laurels. Both were equally determined to advance to a future full of glory.

In Italy there followed the famous three-sided argument as to what form the language of the future ought to take, Florentine usage, the courtly idiom and the Italian of Boccaccio and Dante having their respective partisans in Machiavelli, Castiglione and Bembo. The translators put their hand to the plough. The history of Italian translation goes back to Brunetto Latini; but apart from popular versions of Plautus and Boiardo's Herodotus and Apuleius, there had been little of note during the fifteenth century. The sixteenth was to see the work of Lodovico Dolce and Annibale Caro as well as the productions of a number of minor writers (see Appendix II, pp. 506 ff.). Within the comparatively short space of a hundred years, the greatest part of Greek and Latin literature made its appearance in Italian. Virgil and Ovid, Cicero and Seneca, the Greek historians and the principal writings of the Greek philosophers were all at hand to enrich the minds of ordinary citizens who had not received a classical education. But a foreign work is bound to remain alien to the genius of the language into which it is translated; and the men of the time were well aware of this fact. Consequently, the enthusiasts who laboured to improve the vernacular were constrained to supplement translation by another method. The Humanists who had stocked their minds with classical material for the purpose of writing Latin found it easy to use this material and to employ their techniques of imitation in the new medium of Italian. Indeed, their minds were so profoundly impregnated by classical ways of thought, their sensibility was so finely attuned to its classical model, that they could not help mirroring antiquity whatever the language in which they chose to write. The *Orfeo* of Politian had been the first contemporary drama on a classical theme and with reminiscences of classical authors. But half-opera, half-pastoral it had not conformed to any accepted genre. Ariosto, however, made a more serious attempt to recapture the dramatic concentration of his classical models in the comedies he wrote during the first decade of the new century, and his example proved a valuable source of inspiration. The tragedies of Trissino and Alamanni, who followed Ariosto's lead in a kindred genre, are, it is true, somewhat rhetorical. They are marred by an excessively rigid conception of tragic dignity. Alamanni in particular had such strong views on the need to keep tragic action at a high level that even when he was translating Sophocles, he preferred to omit certain passages which he considered unworthy. He leaves out, for example, the grumblings of the guard in the *Antigone*. But despite these excesses, he and Trissino between them went a long way towards producing a tolerable Italian variant of classical drama.

Furthermore, their efforts were given a specialised and somewhat formal emphasis by the study of Aristotle's *Poetics*. It is true that imitation was never limited to the observance of Aristotle's rules. But the rules came to occupy a central place and writers allowed themselves to be guided by a theoretical conception of what was proper to the genre they were employing. Trissino's cumbersome epic, which describes in twenty-seven books Justinian's conquest of the Goths, was supposed to follow faithfully the critical prescripts of the *Poetics*. Ariosto's *Orlando Furioso*, though chivalric in its subject, also owed the classics a debt; and we find that Tasso in the *Discorsi* which he wrote while composing the *Gerusalemme Liberata* emphasises his wish to reproduce the form and the lofty style of the ancients.* But in practice the borrowings and adaptations went far beyond these generalities. The supernatural element characteristic of Homer and Virgil figures in all the Renaissance epics, now in its original pagan form, now Christianised so that God and His Angels play the part formerly allotted to the Olympian pantheon. Certain effective devices, such as the detailed description of a work of art, and the introduction of crowded battle-scenes and games, recur again and again, while the Homeric simile was so highly valued for the ornamental relief it provided as to be worked almost to death.

To appreciate the importance of these incidental classicisms we have only to turn to pastoral and romantic writing. In a sense, Sannazaro's *Arcadia*, Politian's *Orfeo*, Tasso's *Amyntas* had no classical models. Ancient literature provides no example of a pastoral novel in alternate prose and verse, after the manner of Petronius, or even of a straightforward pastoral drama. But all the same these works had their roots in Theocritus, Virgil and the *Daphnis et Chloë*. Their peculiar blend of the real and the idyllic, where a fantastic world is made plausible by carefully observed details so chosen as not to disturb the fantasy, is without doubt a classical invention. Perfected by Theocritus, it has its origins as far back as Homer. The *Arcadia* with its vivid pictures of country life and landscape, its contests of skill, its half-romantic, half-sensual impression of life is in essence a classical work, for all the originality of its form.

Italian writers in the vernacular had followed ancient models since the days of Boccaccio. But the Promenade of 1494 had the effect of intensifying this trend; for it made this kind of imitation a matter of national honour. Italian, as Speroni indicated in the work which du Bellay was later to copy, had all the potentialities of the classical tongues. A language was not a fixed entity, but the product of human effort, and it was the duty of every writer to add what he could to the glories of the national tradition. The influence of these beliefs, considerable in Italy, were startling in France where the literature of imitation had still to be created.

Translation into French had as long a history as in Italian, going back to the medieval versions of Ovid and to the fourteenth-century work of Oresme and Pierre Bersuire. But now the translators came to their task with a new purpose. They were aware for the first time of a need to be accurate and of a need to catch the artistic spirit of the author they were translating. The best of them was the courtier, Octovien de Saint-Gelais, whose *Aeneid* and *Heroides* in elegant decasyllables were much appreciated by a world of fashion intent on creating an Italian brilliance round the king.

The theory of linguistic development was, as we have seen, first enunciated by Lemaire whose experience went beyond the literary field, for he was not only a poet, but also a courtier, being the personal secretary of Margaret of Savoy. The aim of his *Concorde des deux langages* (1507) was to show that French and Italian could grow in a friendly rather than an unfriendly rivalry. The attempts he makes to reconcile their claims to distinction are less significant, however, than the fact that the possibility of linguistic and cultural development is already taken for granted. There was in any case a notable difference between the Italian and French line of approach. While the former were debating the relative merits of three alternative idioms all of which had good claims to be considered as a possible literary language, the French were more concerned with the question of giving flexibility and range to what was still a rather bare medium. The desire to create a national literature modelled on the classics had come to Italy when a great part of that literature was already in existence; but it had come to France at the very beginning of her Humanist effort. French imitation is therefore self-conscious and systematic; and we can learn a good deal from it about the nature of the processes involved.

A more detailed and purposeful manifesto than Lemaire's poetic vision appeared in 1529 when Tory's *Champ Fleury*, a treatise on orthography which contrived at the same time to be a panegyric of the French language, sketched out a definite programme of improvement. Its publication gave a great impetus to the study of French grammar; but its most important service was perhaps to make clear the methods and limits of vernacular imitation.* Here we are back once again in the world of the *de Copia*, for according to the *Champ Fleury* borrowing is to take two forms, the one concerned with words, the other with illustrative material: and the theories of Tory have their pendant in the practice of Rabelais.

That François Rabelais was the greatest comic writer of the sixteenth century—and perhaps of all time—must remain outside the scope of our enquiry. The genius which shaped his ends was his own contribution. We are concerned with what he took from others. Borrowings from other authors constitute a major portion of his work—or more accurately—provide the raw material which he moulded into an artistic whole, shaping it to maintain interest through variety in accordance with principles of construction which have now been largely abandoned to the radio and music hall. He took Latin or Greek words and turned them into French. He took Latin or Greek ideas, which had captured his attention in the course of his reading, and turned them with strange embellishments to stranger uses. He illustrated his fanciful arguments by classical anecdotes and supported his wildest opinions by classical references. He was a humorist; but if we disregard the incongruities inseparable from humorous writing, it is easy to see that he employed a type of material which a student who followed the precepts of the *de Copia* would naturally have to hand, and that his handling of this material corresponded in every detail to the recommendations of Erasmus.

The reappearance of the *de Copia* is not surprising in this context. The generation to which Rabelais belonged grew to maturity in the shadow of that magisterial treatise. The influence of school-books is often underrated because we tend to think primarily of their effects on behaviour. Books, we say, do not determine how we act towards our fellow-men: and that is true. They do not, or if they do, it is to an infinitesimal extent. But social behaviour is only one aspect of life. Other aspects also deserve notice; and there the dusty primers of our schooldays, the solid compilations of our later training play a more decisive part. They shape the character of our attention. They fix our minds in the habit of noticing certain facts and neglecting others. They furnish us with categories of reasoned interpretation which are necessarily exclusive. In short, they mould our experience.

Rabelais, it is plain, knew the *de Copia* well; and the Humanist rubrics of *verba et res* offer the most convenient framework for analysing his debt to the classics. On the linguistic side, he limited his borrowings—for the most part—to vocabulary. One is tempted to assume that he had too keen an appreciation of spoken French to wish to meddle with its syntax. Sainéan, the most painstaking student of his language, has listed hundreds of his coinages and adaptations.* Some of these have established themselves; others, like *pastophores* and *hypophetes* never had any hope of survival. In a vast number of cases, usage refused to accept his lead.

It was easy to state in theory how the vernacular should be enriched. Henri Estienne was to put the matter in a nutshell: 'Comment donc ne sera-t-il loisible d'emprunter d'un autre langage les mots dont le nôtre se trouvera avoir faute?' But in practice, the pitfalls were many. Rabelais, as we have seen, went further than his contemporaries would follow. No one could judge, however, what public taste would accept;

and under the circumstances, the method of offering a large number of possible coinages for inspection, in full awareness that the majority would be rejected, had perhaps some merits. Moreover, if Rabelais set his ceiling too high, he did nevertheless recognise that there was a ceiling. For we find him condemning those pedants who spoke a jargon that was more Latin than French. He realised well enough that borrowing must not be allowed to destroy the unique essence of the language which was being improved.*

But the main effort of Rabelais' imitation was in any case directed elsewhere. His style was his own; a highly personal tissue of changing moods, exaggerations and parodies, balanced and contrasted by his superb sense of rhythm. Admittedly it contained classical elements, but then it contained everything, even the homely terms of his native Touraine. It was in the field covered by the *Copia Rerum*, in his use of illustrative material, that he shows himself most vigorously an imitator.

Quotations and references spatter the pages of his story. It may be regarded as natural that having been trained as a doctor, he likes to make an elaborate display of medical authorities, and brings up two, three, four of them at a time, Aristotle, Hippocrates, Xenophon, Galen, all in a bunch, to support some quite unimportant theory.* But he piles up his illustrations just as freely outside of this special field, in instances where his citations are merely ornamental. The classical writers serve him as a source for innumerable colourful anecdotes. Phaethon driving up to the sun, Midas finding his gold a curse, Diogenes arguing with Alexander, Socrates drinking his hemlock, are used to illustrate his remarks and enliven his narrative.* Some of these stories were taken from his own reading. Many, however, came from compendia like the *Adages*.* But whatever their source, they all bear the marks of having been at some point excerpted into note-books under the usual rhetorical headings. Rabelais even more than Erasmus handed on what he had learnt in much the same form as he had learnt it. The contents of his note-books (and other people's note-books) appeared to him too valuable not to be passed on verbatim to his readers.

At the same time, however, it would be wrong to assume that none of his classical learning had become incorporated into the deeper levels of his thought. Like Erasmus he was a devotee of the Greek view of life, a champion of moderation and natural happiness. Like Erasmus, he glorified the character of the reasonable man and in the words and actions of his heroes set before his readers ideals of gentleness and shrewd common sense. Gargantua spares the vanquished. Pantagruel counsels the just payment of debts; and the enthusiastic pilgrims are told to stay at home and do their proper work. 'Allez vous en, pauvres gens, au nom de Dieu le Créateur, lequel vous soit en guide perpetuelle, et dorénavant ne soyez faciles à ces otieux et inutilles voyages. Entretenez vos familles, travaillez chascun en sa vocation, instruez vos enfants. . . .' No greater abandonment of medieval standards could be imagined. In the Abbey of Thélème each member of the society was to follow his own nature, to do what he wished. It was the keystone of Rabelais' creed that in a well-born and well-brought-up man obedience to instinct would inevitably result in correct behaviour; and in that he stood near to Aristotle but monstrously far from Augustine.

The close connection between the work of Rabelais and the programme of the Pléiade is not often realised. Rabelais did not make a show of being an imitator of the ancients. He laid so little emphasis on his work as a transmitter of classical culture and was at the same time so successful in his original story-telling and satire, that his services to Humanism have been generally underrated. The Pléiade on the other hand did everything they could to emphasise the importance and novelty of their borrowed material. They represented themselves as the first champions of classical standards in French literature, and consistently made light of the real originality which marked most of their writings. As a result, Rabelais has the reputation of an independent genius, while we regard Dorat, Ronsard and du Bellay as the great exponents of imitation. In fact, they added only one item to the programme which Rabelais had already carried out before them. He had not tried to reproduce the general form of any ancient genre, since the novel which was his particular interest had no settled pattern in ancient times. They on the other hand made the revival of classical genres the focal point of their enterprise. But that was the only innovation for which they were responsible.

Ronsard and his friends were little more than schoolboys when they first formulated their famous programme; and the responsibility for their ideas goes back, as they themselves freely admit, to the man who had charge of their education, that is to a Humanist, a scholar of the first rank and an expert practitioner of all the usual techniques. Dorat was the guiding spirit behind the *Deffense et Illustration*, the *Cléopatre Captive* and the *Odes*.

Now Dorat's own Pindaric odes were an elaborate patchwork. In the one he dedicates to Ronsard, the rhythm of the strophe recalls the twelfth Pythian; and Ronsard's name is brought in by a device which

Pindar often employs. The poet is made to exclaim that he has sung enough about the gods, he will now pass to his hero. Another Pindaric touch introduces the myth by way of a simile. Besides these borrowings which concern the general structure, there are a multitude of others in the imagery and the ideas. Song is associated, as in Pindar, with honey and with sleep. It is the reward of glory and a balm that soothes. The hero is the flower of his race. His fame derives from the feasts where he is praised, from the stars and from the gods. The poet receives his powers from nature. He cannot learn his craft and is envied by those not so gifted. But for a certain distressingly pedestrian quality in the words, which kills both the rhythm and the ideas, we might be reading one of the Epiniceans.*

But these elements which Dorat has picked out are precisely those that Ronsard also imitates. The classical borrowings in the *Odes*, as analysed by Laumonier, fall into five classes: rhythm, style, imagery, myth and history, ideas. Those in the first class are admittedly inconsiderable. French is not a language which depends for its effects on the alternance of long and short syllables, so Ronsard could not follow Dorat and model his lines more or less exactly on the Greek. His debt to the classics in this particular field is therefore of a more subtle kind. What he learnt from Pindar and Horace was the value of rhythmic patterns. He became aware that unity could be combined with variety. How that combination was to be achieved in French, was a matter he had to work out for himself. But the general conception came from his reading.

When we come to consider style and structure we find that the main features of the original Epiniceans are faithfully reproduced. Thus the *Ode au Seigneur de Carnavalet* begins with the usual Pindaric invocation to a deity. Then in true Pindaric fashion, Carnavalet himself, the hero, is abruptly introduced.

> Dirai-je l'expérience
> Que tu as en la science,
> Ou ta main qui sçait l'adresse
> De façonner la jeunesse....

Next comes the myth which makes the centrepiece of the poem, and this is followed by a further reference to the hero and by an epode to the Muses which balance as in Pindar the two introductory items. Admittedly, Ronsard does not always follow the Pindaric structure in such meticulous detail. He often omits the invocation or alternatively the myth; for he is on the whole disinclined to permit himself the sharp transitions from one topic to another, which are a necessary accompaniment of Pindar's technique. But even where he does not follow his model entirely he goes some of the way; and he certainly does his best to maintain that elevation of style which is the most notable characteristic of the Greek poet.

Elevation of style depends to a great extent on imagery and the choice of subject-matter; and it is here perhaps that the French stands closest to the Greek. Pindar derived his imagery for the most part from such phenomena of light and movement as entered into his daily experience, from architecture, from the games themselves and from the common life of his day on the land, in the cities and as travellers saw it by road and sea. Laumonier's analysis shows that all these spheres of sensitivity yielded Ronsard a substantial number of images.* He succeeded therefore in entering into Pindar's world. And images were not the only key with which he unlocked the doors of the past. Ronsard, like most of his contemporaries, regarded myths as allegories: 'La poésie n'estoit au premier âge qu'un théologie allégorique.' It was an opinion he shared with Dorat. Valuing the classical stories for their content as well as for their plastic beauty, he used them freely, sometimes retaining his model complete as in the tale of Bellerophon which adorns the *Ode au Carnavalet*, sometimes adapting the Greek original to suit his subject, sometimes contenting himself with a mere reference,* but always instructing his reader in the intricacies of Greek legend or presupposing a prior knowledge. These odes are meaningless to a man who is not a Humanist.

Images and myths belong to the preconscious levels of the human mind. To them we must add, even in poetry, the formulated concepts of the conscious intellect. In this realm too Ronsard's borrowings were considerable.

The *Odes* are full of sentences which reproduce the gnomic sayings in the Epiniceans. Man is ephemeral, and God alone remains stable; man's fortune is uncertain, now ill, now good; it is a fine thing to reward noble deeds with lasting praise; great deeds are not to be accomplished easily; and so on. All Pindar's common themes are fully represented.

Ronsard wrote many more odes than Dorat, so his borrowings can be analysed at greater length. But the resemblance between their methods is obvious. The elements they imitate are similar in kind; and behind their work we can see the *de Copia* and the whole tradition of the Humanist imitators. Ronsard is a Pindarian, as Bembo was a Ciceronian.

Later the members of the Pléiade were to revise their methods, moved no doubt by the *Odes'* poetic failure. Du Bellay had in any case never liked mechanistic imitation and already in his early *Deffense et Illustration de la Langue Française* had laid great stress on Quintilian's contention that an imitator should know his models well enough to reproduce the elements he required without help from note-books and without even remembering exactly where each gem came from.* He preferred to compose without adventitious aids, without even any conscious efforts of memory, and to introduce only such classical material as came spontaneously to his pen. Gradually his friends followed suit; the later writings of the Pléiade belong not to the second but to the third stage of the assimilatory process. They add very little to the classical material already contained in the French tradition, but they repeat, develop and familiarise what is already there. In the *Hymns* of Ronsard, in the *Mimes* of Baif and especially in Desportes we see the beginning of the neo-classical age when antiquity will put on a seventeenth-century costume.

We have examined the work of Rabelais and the Pléiade because it is representative of imitation in its extreme form, but countless other writers followed the same paths. Classical anecdotes, allusions and citations appear in the pages of Henri Estienne and Montaigne almost as frequently as in *Gargantua*. They abound likewise in Bacon's *Essays* and in the *Anatomy of Melancholy*.* All the writers who received a Humanist education set themselves at some time or other to imitate the ancients, and when they did so they consciously or unconsciously transferred to their vernacular efforts some of the methods they had been taught for imitating in Latin. By this means they made generally available a mass of classical material which others who were not trained Humanists could borrow in their turn

Shakespeare is of particular interest because he stands at the furthest possible remove from such conscious imitators as Dorat or Ronsard and yet is manifestly influenced by the classical tradition. Here is a man who has travelled far from the Middle Ages, further indeed than Ariosto or Rabelais. We cannot take him for anything but the product of the Humanist ferment. But if a Humanist is one who has studied the classics extensively, he is no Humanist. The problem of Shakespeare's learning has been discussed at very great length ever since the eighteenth century; and many attempts have been made to provide 'small Latine and lesse Greeke' with a precise denotation.* It appears indisputable that Shakespeare knew some Latin. He had certainly ground his way through a few classical works at school and may have retained enough to read the language fluently in later life. Indisputably too he had little understanding of Greek. He had read the *Metamorphoses* in Golding's translation, though with occasional references at least to the original. He had read the plays of Seneca: and here again it is open to question whether he used the English *Ten Tragedies* or the original text. He had read North's *Plutarch* and certain of Plautus' plays including the *Amphitruo* which was not, so far as one knows, available in English. He was familiar with bits and pieces of other authors, especially Virgil. But when we turn from direct reference to the larger field of general comprehension, we find that while Shakespeare's Romans are indeed Roman and carry their Stoicism with an authentic solemnity, his Greeks are hardly Greek; which seems to suggest that it is not to North alone that we owe the verisimilitude of the Roman plays. For if North had been responsible for that verisimilitude then it is difficult to see why the Greece of the plays should lag so far behind the Rome in reality since he supplied material for both. Nor of course could the *Metamorphoses* or even the ten Senecan tragedies account for the difference. There must have been some other factor involved.

The question of how much classics Shakespeare knew is difficult to solve because it is unimportant. Living at the end of the sixteenth century, he did not need to take his classical material from Latin sources. By then Humanism, and more especially the work of the translators and the vernacular imitators, had transformed the fabric of men's outlook.

There had been Readers in Greek at Cambridge since 1518 and Regius Professors since 1540. The first generation of English Humanists had been succeeded by a second; and during the first years of Elizabeth, this second generation, the brilliant Cambridge circle of Cheke, Ascham, Thomas Smith, Mulcaster and Wilson, gave place in its turn to a third of almost equal distinction. It is true that by this time Oxford and Cambridge, which had flourished during the first part of the century, were once more in the doldrums. The economic disorders of the period were hitting the colleges hard, and the number of teachers and students declined. The consequent retrenchment had particularly bad effects on classical studies which were not properly integrated into any standard course. By 1555 it was possible for Sir Thomas Pope to express the view that no good purpose would be served by founding a Greek lectureship in Trinity College, Oxford—'as the times will not bear it now', and thirty years later Greek was hardly known to anyone at

St John's College, Cambridge, which had been one of its principal homes.* But many Elizabethan translators worked outside the universities and pursued what had become a private interest. Gascoigne, Kinwelmersh and Phaer were lawyers, Marlowe and Thomas Watson were men of letters, Hall a politician. There were also some writers like Adlington, Thomas Nichols and Sir Thomas North who were not classical scholars but produced English versions based on existing Italian or French translations.

By 1600, the main works of Virgil, the *Satires*, *Epistles* and *Ars Poetica* of Horace, the *Metamorphoses*, *Tristia* and *Heroides*, Valerius Flaccus, the *Andria*, the *Tragedies* of Seneca, most of the historians and military writers, most of the philosophical writings of Cicero, Pomponius Mela, Seneca's *de Beneficiis* and *de Remediis Fortuitorum*, much of Pliny's *Natural History*, the *Golden Ass*, the *de Consolatione Philosophiae*; and (turning to the Greek) the *Batrachomyomachia*, a substantial portion of the *Iliad*, six idylls of Theocritus, the *Antigone*, the *Phoenissae*, a great many historians, Isocrates' *Nicocles*, *ad Demonicum* and *ad Nicoclem*, the *Olynthiacs* of Demosthenes, the *Ethics*, the *Politics* and the *Problems* of Aristotle, Plutarch's *Lives* and some of the essays from the *Moralia*, a few of Lucian's minor pieces, Heliodorus and the *Daphnis et Chloe* were all available in English. Moreover, anyone who was familiar with French could read in that language in addition the whole of Livy, Herodotus and Xenophon, a good deal of Plato, the rest of the *Moralia* and one or two of the plays such as the *Electra* of Sophocles, the *Iphigenia in Aulis* or the *Hecuba* (see Appendix II, pp. 506 ff.), and readers of Italian could command an even wider choice. Considered in their entirety, the vernacular translations cover an enormous field. With the exception of Greek lyric poetry and drama, the whole of the classical heritage was within the grasp of a travelled man though he possessed small Latin and less Greek.

At the same time also a great deal of classical material had become available in the writings of the imitators. By Shakespeare's day More's *Utopia* had been translated into English, and Sidney had written the *Arcadia*, full of reminiscences of Sannazaro and the *Diana* of Montemayor. Spenser, deeply steeped in Baptista Mantuanus, Politian and the Pléiade as well as in the classics, produced the *Shepheard's Calendar* in 1579 and the *Faerie Queen* by 1596, while Elyot's *Governour*, Ascham's *Scholemaster*, Thomas Wilson's *Arte of Rhetorique*, Lyly's *Euphues* and even the writings of Greene and Nashe must also have done much to spread Humanist ideas. Humanism was no longer the esoteric possession of a few. It leavened the whole of England's intellectual life.

Shakespeare therefore is a product of a world that had learnt through imitation. The fragments which others excerpted from the classics had come to him along a thousand devious paths to form the essential fabric of his outlook. He, Montaigne and Sir Thomas Browne may stand as our exemplars of the sort of mind that the Renaissance eventually produced. Just as the classical learning of the Middle Ages had crystallised in Dante, so the wider and more profound Humanism of the fifteenth and sixteenth centuries precipitated this new brilliance that stands at the threshold of our own epoch.

III. 'PIETAS LITTERATA'

At the beginning of the Renaissance, there were privately run elementary schools in most Italian towns. They catered for the middle-class boy whom his parents destined for a legal or administrative career and who therefore had to learn Latin. The masters in these schools seem to have been at the best pedants, at the worst sadistic brutes, and the Latin they taught was not the language of Cicero, but that utilitarian idiom which we find in the business letters of the period. At the same time, there were numerous *studia* or centres of higher education which, however, varied enormously both in their character and their importance. Some like Bologna were old-established universities with a broadly based curriculum. Others, like the *Studio* in Florence, seem to have been little better than specialist schools.* The Humanists made themselves felt in both the elementary and the more advanced field. But the extent of their influence has probably been overrated.

We find Voigt stating that, in spite of the criticisms which Petrarch and his followers levelled against the jurists and the doctors, these faculties were always prepared to welcome the partisans of the new learning and even to provide them with jobs. The success of Marsuppini's teaching in Florence, the enthusiastic reception accorded to Filelfo in Bologna, and the founding of Ferrara University round the school established by Guarino, certainly support that view. Nevertheless, we should be rash to accept it without further qualification. There were certain contributory circumstances which Voigt did not take into account and which would make the welcome he describes less significant than he believed it to have been. As we saw at the end of our last chapter, the cult of rhetoric preceded and was largely independent of

Humanism. It was a by-product of that increased complexity which characterised all political and social relationships from the thirteenth century onwards. States had ever more complicated dealings with other states, business houses embarked on more elaborate transactions, private individuals pursued more extensive aims, and above all the Church saw its wide interests enmeshed in ever subtler intrigues. The normal activities of every-day living could not be pursued without the aid of reports, letters and statements of policy, which had to be clearly and persuasively phrased. So the art of writing came once again into high esteem. Diplomatists like Peter of Vinea cultivated an impressive epistolary style. But they were not Humanists. Far from turning to antiquity for their models, they tried to write elegantly in the Latin of their own day. In view of this revival of rhetorical studies, before the time of Petrarch it would be unreasonable to assume that all the chairs of rhetoric we hear about in the fourteenth century were founded in response to Humanist demands, or that their appearance is proof of a popular desire to study the past. Many of them were probably set up because men had come to feel that the ability to express one's ideas was an important accomplishment in its own right, whether one imitated Cicero or not. Many of the fourteenth- and early fifteenth-century teachers of rhetoric were not Humanists; and such disciples of Petrarch as were appointed to these posts seem to have lectured along conventional rather than strictly Humanist lines. Gasparino da Barzizza, for example, who taught at Pavia, Venice, Padua, Ferrara and Milan, made a great parade of his enthusiasm for Cicero, but when he came to write in Latin, he worked on the lines laid down by the thirteenth-century *dictatores* and regularly employed medieval turns of phrase. These appointments cannot therefore be regarded as so many tributes to the new movement. Men like Malphagini, Barzizza and Vergerio held their posts in the *studia* not because of their Humanism, but rather in spite of it. They were there because they could do another job which the academic world of the time considered worth doing.

Later, we find a Filelfo, a Guarino, a Chalcondyles called in to lecture at a university on the ancient authors in order to give the student a taste of the new Humanist ideas. But these appointments are of a temporary nature. The Humanists have often been accused of restlessness because they moved time and time again from one city to another. It would be fairer to regard their journeyings as actuated by the need to earn a living. For the *studia* seem to have employed them on a short-term basis, as visiting lecturers, and not as permanent members of the staff. Their ideas were considered interesting. It was fashionable to go and hear them; and the more famous among them had large audiences. But one may wonder whether they ever had pupils long enough or under such conditions that they could embark on serious teaching. Their opportunities were for publicity rather than for instruction.

Moreover, teachers of rhetoric and Humanist lecturers alike were all badly paid. Pietro da Muglio, Petrarch's friend who held a chair at Bologna, received only one-eighth of the salary allotted to his more important colleagues in the faculties of civil and canon law,* while the celebrated fee offered to Filelfo to tempt him to give an extraordinary course of lectures, also at Bologna, in 1439, the fee which was renowned as the largest ever earned by a Humanist, and which in any case he was to have for only six months, appears in fact to have been very little more than the normal half-yearly stipend of a law professor. Plainly, the Humanists were not the monarchs but just the hangers-on of their academic world.

A handful only held permanent appointments. The chair of Greek at Florence was occupied almost without a break from 1429 to 1493;* and at the newly-founded *Studium* of Ferrara, Guarino could teach rhetoric for an untroubled twenty-four years (1436–60). But it needed the enlightened patronage of the Medici and the d'Este to make even these minor triumphs possible. In most places, the old dispensation held firm.

The situation in elementary teaching was very similar. There must have been hundreds of small private schools in Italy; and very few of them were in Humanist hands. Here again Humanist practice provided rather a model for the future than the dominant educational pattern. Guarino's school at Ferrara (1429–36) and Vittorino's at Mantua (1423–46) were famous in their own day and have remained so in ours, but they were only two among many.* Both were originally founded to provide a suitable setting for the education of the local princelings whom their enlightened parents preferred to bring up in a Humanist rather than a traditional atmosphere. Humanism with its glorification of the individual was calculated to appeal to these self-made rulers who had risen through skill and kept their position by intrigue and display. Thanks to this patronage, the work of Guarino and Vittorino attracted a great deal of notice. Their methods received the blessing of fashion, were admired and to some extent copied. If we wish to study the educational practices of fifteenth-century Humanism, it is to these two schools that we must turn. For there are no others. But it would be foolish to regard them as the typical educational institutions of their period.

Guarino was first and last a teacher of classics. His purpose was to form scholars capable of construing a difficult passage or writing a handsome oration. It was Vittorino who introduced that all-round education which we regard as typically Humanist, who laid a great emphasis on the training of character, who refused to take more pupils than he could personally supervise and had a nineteenth-century respect for the virtues of cold air and games. Yet such is the vanity of educational aspirations that while Guarino's intellectuals proved themselves in later life men of probity and honour, the favourite pupils of Vittorino included Valla, the future prophet of Hedonism, Beccadelli, the future author of the *Hermaphroditus* and the dubious Platina, two of whom at least never quite cleared themselves of the suspicion of homosexuality.

But in the literary field there was little to choose between the methods of the two teachers. Vittorino had been Guarino's pupil for more than a year and had learnt a great many of his techniques. A knowledge of grammar was acquired first of all partly through the study of a systematic treatise and partly as a result of analysing chosen passages which were dictated and learnt by heart.* There is some evidence that Vittorino used translation exercises from the Italian to drive home the rules of accidence and syntax while Guarino preferred to train his pupils in making up extempore the sentences to illustrate their grammar.* Both placed great emphasis on accent and enunciation; for they considered reading aloud healthful and an aid to the memory. In both schools, the pupils kept note-books into which they entered the words they learnt, together with notes about usage, according to the method which Guarino had been taught by Chrysoloras. Besides reading with an eye to the grammar, they also read for content, and collected passages suitable for illustration, especially moral instances and striking anecdotes.* In short, they followed implicitly the analytical technique which we have described above.

Latin was studied for daily use; but Greek was learnt more as we learn it today. Passive knowledge was valued above active; and though prose composition was practised, it was regarded as a memory aid rather than an end in itself.* The Greek authors were pillaged for material which the learner hoped one day to use in Latin. Style in Greek remained a secondary consideration; and that had the fortunate effect of allowing a wider range of works to be read: Lucian, Plutarch and Isocrates. In both languages the emphasis was on the moralists and historians. The former helped the conquest of vice while the latter provided the best possible training for public life not only through precept but through example. Vittorino at any rate never forgot that the classics he taught were only a means to an end, and that his final aim had to be to produce men capable of living successfully. The utilitarian bent of both his and Guarino's teaching is obvious.

These schools are the only ones we know which genuinely reflected the spirit of the High Renaissance, which made the re-living of antiquity and the development of the individual their primary aims. The next Humanist foundations which come to our notice belong to a different age and have a different character.

Throughout the fifteenth century, Christianity and Humanism had been in conflict. The three long dialogues of the *Secretum* in which the author of the *Africa* discusses his problems with an unsympathetic St Augustine, constitute one of the oddest as well as one of the most depressing of imaginary conversations. We feel from the beginning that Petrarch's position is hopeless, that he must submit, and that his submission must in the nature of things prove hypocritical: which was indeed the case. And where Petrarch failed how could others succeed? Traversari and Vittorino were pious men. Bessarion and Bembo rose to be cardinals. But they never achieved more than a personal compromise, holding the divergent aims to which their lives were devoted side by side in a sort of tension, condemning on the one hand the attacks against Humanism, censuring on the other the moral excesses of the Pomponios and the Beccadellis. Vittorino's failure to implant Christian principles into many of his prominent pupils clearly indicates the difficulties of this attempt to keep a middle way and to serve two incompatible masters.

For at the time they were incompatible. The Christian Church had its eyes fixed on the feudal past. Individualism was abhorrent to the zealous upholders of its traditions, whether the individual's self-assertion took the form of private enterprise beyond the limits set by the usury laws, or made a deeper claim to exercise private judgement in the specifically religious sphere. The Humanists for their part were influenced by the aspirations and outlook of the newly emergent capitalist class. Alberti's insistence that riches must be employed *in cose magnifiche e onestissime* shows to a nicety how the Humanist ideas served the worldly of their generation. *Il Magnifico*, Palmieri tells us, must expend his money for honourable and glorious purposes, not private but public, such as buildings and the adornment of churches, theatres, galleries and public ceremonies. The superiority of these conceptions to the ostentatious display which characterised the Burgundian court stands to the credit of Petrarch's followers. It is their finest achievement; but at the same time it shows with an unmistakable clarity the closeness of the links which bound them to the nascent capitalism of their day. One is driven to ask could they have done so much for a category of men with whom they were not in sympathy? And was not their own cult of eloquence a type of the universal quest for fame and success? Cast for the role of propagandists, some of them tended to exaggerate both in their writings and their lives the traits which it was their function to recommend. *Voluptas est bonum undecunque quaesitum* urged Valla, a statement which was remembered when the qualifications that had accompanied it were forgotten. While these attitudes lasted the chasm between the two ideologies, Christian and Humanist, remained unbridgeable.

Such had been the situation in the fifteenth century; but by the beginning of the sixteenth, both parties had shifted their ground, so that a synthesis between their views had for the first time become possible. The causes of this change were complex. The very success of that social revolution to which the Humanists had given their support operated to transform their outlook. The back of the old order was broken. The world of the individualist was at last a possibility. But this meant that the character of the Renaissance had to alter. Values which have served as ideological battering-rams against the past are rarely of much use when men come to build the positive foundations of a new society. Destructive elements have to be modified to suit the needs of co-operative living.

A striking example of the sort of change which was taking place is furnished by that key concept of early Renaissance propaganda, Petrarch's ideal of the hero. The work of the Florentine Neoplatonists, philosophically negligible, had, through its impact on this ideal, an immense cultural significance. If Pico della Mirandola and Ficino failed to establish the identity of earthly and heavenly beauty in arguments which would satisfy a conscientious philosopher, they did lead men to focus their attention on the higher rather than the lower varieties of aesthetic enjoyment, on happiness rather than on pleasure; and their very frivolities, their tendency to concern themselves with etiquette rather than metaphysics, added to the extent of their influence. One of their circle was the Pulci whose *Morgante Maggiore* has long been reckoned among the most remarkable products of the fifteenth century. The satire of this mock epic, whose heroes are a Rabelaisian giant and a monstrous Panurge, is ostensibly directed against the exaggerations of medieval chivalry. But as Walser has indicated, if we read with attention, we discover traces of a new view of man which shows up the falsity of Petrarch's success stories just as plainly as it castigates the more patent follies of the chivalric ideal. This is the conception which Ariosto was later to develop. Ariosto's Orlando has his share of resounding triumphs; but he is at his greatest at the moment of apparent failure. Our feelings for him are most keenly roused when his love for the worthless Angelica has sent him mad; and that was the poet's undoubted intention. By the end of the fifteenth century men had learnt to envisage success in subjective rather than objective terms. They remained individualists. But Humanists and all, they located the goals of their strivings outside the sphere of simple material advantages and pleasures. Even the business men of the time were affected by these trends; and we shall find them turning away from Mammon simple to pursue the Mammon of Righteousness instead.

In a generation which placed such value upon high ideals, the cynicism of the early Humanists would have been out of place. The typical scholar of the later fifteenth century was never tempted to cock a snook at convention or to show that he respected nothing but his own advantage. The revolutionary stage of the Renaissance had passed. Also the rising middle classes were now in a position to visualise the sort of world they wanted, and they could see that the measures required for its attainment were of a practical nature. They no longer needed guides or propagandists. So the bonds which had linked classical learning with the forces promoting social change correspondingly slackened.

Once Humanist aims had taken on these new forms, the obstacles which still hindered the creation of an ideological synthesis with Christianity were all on the side of the Church, and there the problem was solved by the Reform movement. Luther in Germany, Lefèvre in France, Erasmus in the Low Countries, concurred in making the personal relation of the soul to God the centre of religious life. In the political disputes between Church and State, in the attacks on institutional abuses, in the ever more complicated theological controversies which characterised the age, we can trace, both among the schismatics and among their Catholic sympathisers, a general tendency to value the spirit rather than the letter, so that the private judgement of the conscience has a larger voice in determining man's duty and the choice between right and wrong. Protestantism was religious individualism. *Homo sum*, Luther might have said, *et nil divinum a me alienum puto*. The Roman Church also, shaken by the attacks against it, was moved to put its house in order. Abuses were swept away, and by subtle changes of emphasis, the pattern of Catholic life was widened to make room for the strivings of the individualist. At the same time both Churches, Catholic and Protestant, embarked on a campaign to assert their control over all fields of intellectual activity: and where Humanism was already in possession, compromise could not be avoided.

Let us now recapitulate the changes that had taken place. On the one hand, the aspirations of the emergent middle class had altered and had become less narrowly egotistical with success, and their influence pressed less vigorously upon the Humanists who tended more and more to devote themselves to a type of scholarship without ideological significance. On the other hand, the character of Christianity itself had assumed a more individualistic tinge. The Neoplatonist who was guided in his conduct by his vision of an ideal not of this world, and the Protestant who was guided by his conception of the Divine Purpose, were no longer ideologically irreconcilable. The synthesis which Petrarch had found impossible of attainment, and which Vittorino could achieve only for his own self without being able to communicate it to his pupils, had become a reality.

We have now arrived at the point where we can study that synthesis in the work of Erasmus, who was perhaps its greatest theoretical exponent. When we referred to him earlier, it was as the man who did a good deal to perfect and popularise the techniques of literary imitation, so that he must be given much of the credit for the successful absorption of ancient ideas by the emergent European cultures. But his activities and interests were many-sided; and he stands at the beginning of the new age as well as at the end of the old.

Erasmus dominated his age. He is the greatest man we come across in the history of education. Those particular qualities of sympathy, mental grasp and imagination which an educator requires if he is to be completely successful, are in practice rarely found together. He possessed them all in a perfect combination and on a gigantic scale.*

Moreover, he belonged to an age and to a society which, if strongly individualistic, was also strongly moral. In the daily conduct of the merchant classes of northern Europe, public charity and respect for law existed harmoniously alongside business ruthlessness. The educator who sought to develop these conflicting tendencies in the young pursued a clearly marked course. He had before him any number of living examples to illustrate his ideal and to impress both on his own mind and on the minds of his pupils precisely what limits had to be set to the imitation of the ancients and the imitation of Christ.

The theory of the *pietas litterata* rested upon two arguments, one of which was contributed by history while the other came from philology. Erasmus was careful to point out that the Christian culture had developed out of the Greek, that the best of the Fathers had derived much of their learning from pagan philosophy and that the very structure of Christian dogma was not exempt from the influence of pagan thought. The argument was not new. It had been put forward several times during the previous century; but Erasmus made a great deal of it, and he was supported by Budé who summarised much of the evidence in an exceptionally learned, if somewhat indigestible, three-volume treatise.* To this was added a second argument from philology, which was more specifically the work of Erasmus himself. The Italian Humanists had taken examples from the ancient writers to bolster the daring self-assertion or the even more daring self-indulgence which were fashionable in their day; and men like Cardinal Dominici had therefore regarded classical studies as a manifest cause of scandal and offence. But now Erasmus looked deeper. His *Adages* constituted a more or less complete survey of moral ideas in antiquity and provided firm grounds for the belief that the ancients, or at least the best of them, taught an ethic as near as makes no matter to the Christian. A thorough study of their writings could, Erasmus concluded, only strengthen a scholar's virtue. All one needed was a little care to make sure that none of the less philosophic writers like Martial should ever fall into the hands of anyone too young or too ignorant to appreciate their flippancy at its true worth. Christianity was crowning the achievement of Greece and Rome. The best of their culture led up to it and was therefore in harmony with its dictates.

Such was the theory; but the strength of the new programme lay not so much in any theory as in its method, and here again Erasmus took the lead. He set forth his plans in a series of treatises which make good reading even after the lapse of over four hundred years: the *de Ratione Studii* (1511); the *de Pueris Instituendis* (1529); the *de Civilitate Morum Puerilium* (1530); and incidentally the *Colloquies* (1516) and the *Encheiridion Militis Christiani* (1515). These books which deal specifically with education and moral training must be read in conjunction with his numerous others on rhetoric, especially the *de Duplici Copia Verborum ac Rerum*.* Erasmus wanted to introduce into the schools the traditional Humanist method, which Chrysoloras had brought to Italy and Guarino had improved, the analysis of texts and the excerption, memorising and reproduction of their constituent elements. But since this method was likely to train out-and-out admirers of the ancients rather than sincere Christians (it had after all produced Valla, Beccadelli and Janus Pannonius), he went on to suggest certain safeguards.

The first guarantee of piety was to come from the early training of the child; and in making this recommendation, Erasmus resembled his predecessor Quintilian and his successors, the Jesuits. He believed in the formative influence of the first six years of life. His practical suggestions for early education were commonplace. They could have been put forward by any intelligent Humanist and add up to little more than warnings against the chatter of maidservants, over-indulgence and bad example, with the proviso that the child should be entrusted to a wise and well-paid tutor at the earliest possible opportunity.* But they derive a certain importance from the ideals that are placed before the parents. Erasmus was quite clear in his mind that it was a father's duty to bring up his child as a good citizen and a good Christian, that truthfulness, hardihood, temperance and modesty were the qualities for which everyone should strive, and this conception was to have an influence far outside the specialised realm of early childhood.

Although Erasmus devoted a good deal of thought to the upbringing of infants, he remained, like all educators until the nineteenth century, an amateur in that enigmatic field. But on the subject of secondary education and particularly on the subject of classical studies, his knowledge was comprehensive and profound. What he had to say on this point formed the kernel of his system.

Long before the sixteenth century, the Scholastic Age has sought to organise pagan learning to suit the needs of a Christian society; and the most instructive approach to the proposals of Erasmus is to compare them to the methods adopted by the contemporaries of Bernard Silvestris and Vincent of Beauvais. It will be remembered that the Scholastic Age had guarded its young against the infection of pagan ideas by insisting upon the formal study of texts and on the use of allegory. Faced with the same problem of bringing up Christians on pagan material, Erasmus abandoned the first but retained the second of these safeguards.

He refused explicitly to restrict classical learning to stylistic analysis. When the attention is fixed on 'unusual words, archaisms, innovations, ingenuity in handling material, distinction of style, historical and moral instances and proverbial expressions, the note-book being at hand to record them',* very little else will be noticed; and Erasmus was aware of this. 'It is true that in reading an author for vocabulary and style the student cannot fail to gather something besides',* he tells us in the *de Ratione Studii*. But he makes it clear that in his opinion the something will not amount to much; and unlike the Scholastics he is not satisfied with such meagre fare at the classic board. He insists on a second reading 'for content', when the student is to have note-books to hand with headings drawn from the *de Copia Rerum*: agriculture, architecture, the art of war, cookery, precious stones, mountains, rivers, cities, trees, plants, animals, dress, appliances and so forth,* ready to excerpt the sort of information that is found in the *Adages* and so to build up an understanding of the classical world.

On the other hand, while he was unwilling to go as far as the Scholastic Age had done over the question of allegorical interpretations, he did decide to recommend their use. Since so many of the pagan myths were admittedly offensive, he felt it necessary to suggest some way of making them edifying. To calm the consciences of his more earnestly Christian supporters, he was prepared to state that all ancient poetry and a good deal of ancient philosophy was 'allegorical'. Fortunately, the realist spirit of the sixteenth century prevented this from being a major surrender of Humanist principles. Allegory had lost its appeal; and the Reformers who were first to put the plans of Erasmus into practice had even less inclination than most of their contemporaries to think along such antiquated lines. But the fact that Erasmus was willing to make the concession shows the paramount influence of traditional Christian ideas in the movement he represented.

A reliance on allegorical interpretations and an excessive attention to form had been the principal scholastic weapons against the pagan influences of antiquity. But thirteenth-century teachers had also made a very definite effort to replace the ancient texts by more contemporary ones. On this point again Erasmus refused to follow their lead. He had, however, an alternative to offer. He recommended selection. That method had been barred to the Scholastics, who had not possessed enough texts, and were bound to utilise whatever came to hand. In this respect, the invention of printing had worked a great change. There were large numbers of Greek and Latin books available; and schoolmasters could now pick and choose. They could now take what was edifying and avoid the rest.

Erasmus advised that the ordinary course of school reading should be limited to Lucian, Demosthenes, Herodotus, Aristophanes, Homer, Euripides in Greek, and to Terence, some carefully selected Plautus, Virgil, Horace, Cicero, Caesar and Sallust in Latin.* In another work, he recommended letting the very young start with chosen passages from Seneca and from the *Apophthegmata* and *Moralia* of Plutarch.* But he never suggested that these authors should be studied at length. Was it because, for all their attraction, they were moralists whom many pious people regarded as dangerous? He expressly barred philosophy from his school course; and one notes that Catullus, the elegiac poets and the satirists were also left unread, presumably for moral reasons. Another interesting omission is Livy, the favourite of the Italian Humanists. His heroes had too close associations with the Italian ideal of *virtù* which had come to be considered dangerous; and his usefulness for the scientific investigation of Roman history in terms of political conditions and movements was not yet appreciated, certainly not by Erasmus. Machiavelli wrote his *Discorsi* on Livy only four years after *de Ratione Studii* and considerably before several of Erasmus' major educational works. But the rift between Humanism and advanced contemporary thought was already so wide that the significance of these new developments completely escaped the great Dutch Humanist. History for him remained a storehouse of anecdotes which could point a moral or illustrate an opinion; and if the anecdotes were unsuitable, if their moral effect was doubtful, then the historian in question was better unread.

Erasmus takes a much wider view than the Scholastics of the value of the classical heritage. They had looked upon the classical authors as a convenient source of certain types of technical information, and had been largely concerned to ensure the passage of that information into the minds of the young, unaccompanied by dangerous ideas. He, on the contrary, found an element of positive good precisely in the ideas and general outlook of the pagan world. It is important to notice, however, that he did not, like most of the fifteenth-century Humanists, accept that world in its entirety. He selected; and the rejection of certain authors was to be in consequence the keynote of the *pietas litterata*.

The first school which tried to put these ideals into practice was Colet's foundation of St Paul's. This was apparently established by 1512 though the statutes were not drawn up until six years later. Judging by the regulations he approved, Colet was prepared to go even further than Erasmus in his concessions to piety. The life of the school was organised round learning to write and speak a correct near-Ciceronian Latin, and the Humanist methods of note-taking and repetition were in general use. But Colet favoured the reading of Christian authors such as Lactantius, Prudentius, Sedulius, Juvencus, St Augustine and St Jerome, while the pious Baptista Mantuanus was given a prominent place in the recommended list of authors.*

One gets the impression that Humanist though he was Colet still regarded the classics as a somewhat risky instrument of education. Or perhaps he felt it best to pander to a backward public opinion. He certainly failed to realise how morally innocuous the study of the ancient writers could be made if the texts were carefully selected and the emphasis was placed on language rather than on content. The credit for that discovery was to belong more to the heirs than to the friends of Erasmus, and so to the actively Protestant rather than to the still hopefully Catholic generation among the Reformers.

The history of Protestant education during the sixteenth century has been told in terms of personalities and institutions. Its chroniclers have made great men like Luther and Melanchthon, or great schools like the Strassburg Gymnasium their units of study; and this practice has had the effect of obscuring the strict sequence of educational development. Reading Paulsen, Schmidt, Bonet-Maury, Kueckelhahn, Sandys, Woodward, Le Coultre and their successors, one can easily slip into the error of believing that the eighty years after Rudolf Agricola's return from Italy in 1479 formed a unified period whose end was distinguished from its beginning only by the greater popularity of the Humanist discipline and not by any changes in technique. So, for example, Bonet-Maury, the historian of the Brethren of the Common Life would have us regard them as pioneers of Humanism because they used the grammar of Despauterius and because Sturm praised the curriculum of a school with which they were connected. But Sturm's stay at the Brethren's school in Liège came at a comparatively late date, that is between 1521 and 1524, well after the founding of St Paul's; and the use of Despauterius' grammar in place of the *Doctrinale* could not under any circumstances have occurred before 1512. There is no satisfactory evidence that the Brethren were anything but medieval in their methods during the fifteenth century; and indeed the lurid account which Erasmus gave of conditions of Deventer proves the backwardness of their pedagogy. Moreover, the careful reader may permit himself certain doubts even about the 1521 curriculum. It is true that the boys began Greek in the fourth of the eight classes, and that the imitation of ancient authors figured specifically on the programme. But the study of Greek seems to have been so speedy that one suspects its thoroughness. The boys were supposed to master the grammar in two years; and their work on imitation was done in a class primarily devoted to the traditional subjects of dialectic and rhetoric, while the two top classes spent all their time on logic and theology. There is nothing to suggest that Humanist text-books were used, or that the pagan authors were thoroughly studied; and the very considerable attention which was given to logic suggests that the religious teaching of the Brethren had not lost its scholastic stamp. In short, the course seems to have been predominantly medieval in form and subject-matter with only a few concessions to the theories of the Humanists; and the Brethren appear to have made precisely the sort of compromise which one expects from an established educational organisation faced with a new movement that is winning popular support. They jumped early on the Humanist band-waggon, but they were not among its first drivers.

The temptation to attribute the achievements of the sixteenth century to the later decades of the fifteenth ought to be resisted whether we are considering educators like the Brethren or individual prodigies of learning like Hegius, Reuchlin and Agricola. The schools and universities of the North knew only the first tentative flickers of Humanism before 1500. There were the few enthusiasts who had visited Italy, the few teachers of Greek, the few experimentalists who desired reform, but their influence for good or ill was very slight. Then during the next twenty years came the theoretical work of Erasmus and the foundation in England of St Paul's which demonstrated that the *pietas litterata* could work in practice. But it was not until after 1520 that the methods and aims of the new movement effectively began to transform the German schools. And this eventual triumph was due as much to the support of Luther as to any pronounced success on the part of the general Humanist propaganda.

Luther's educational writings are refreshingly clear-headed. He stated the views of an intelligent outsider, as later Rousseau was to do, on matters which generally find only professional teachers to discuss them. He had no professional axe to grind. There was no branch of study which he desired consciously or unconsciously to popularise or preserve. God and Germany occupied all his thoughts; and it was only because the worship of the former and the prosperity of the latter seemed to require the presence of educated men, that incidentally he came to take an interest in education. Piety was his first concern; and he advocated making the Bible the staple reading of every school. But the Bible in German or even Latin was not good enough. God must have had some specific purpose, Luther thought, when He arranged for His Word to be written first in Greek and Hebrew. It was reasonable to assume that those languages possessed a special virtue, some power of expression denied to lesser tongues; and it was therefore men's duty to learn them. This belief made him look with favour upon the Humanists who on their side also advocated the study of the Biblical languages and the reading of the Scriptures in the original. He did not imagine that every student would be mentally fitted to perform these difficult tasks, but he felt that he could demand their accomplishment from a substantial portion of the clergy: and the more so, since another essential prerequisite for the progress of religion was that this clergy should be able to preach.

Like all religious revivals, Protestantism depended for its success on the ability of its champions to communicate their own enthusiasm by means of the spoken word; and this was not an easy aim to achieve. The techniques which the Scholastic Church and in particular the Mendicant Orders had worked out to train their preachers, were unsuitable for Luther's purposes. A work like the *Summa Predicantium* contained a great deal that Protestants considered doctrinally unsound as well as lacking in contemporary appeal. Luther had to cast round for alternatives; and again it was Humanism with its elaborate apparatus for the teaching of rhetoric that seemed best able to provide the higher education he wanted. It was evident, for instance, that the *exempla* of the *Adages* which emphasised the Christian elements in ancient civilisation could be easily turned to the service of an individualist Protestant piety. What objection could there be then to bringing in Erasmus to replace John of Bromyarde?

Besides, Luther had yet another good reason to make him champion the Humanist approach. Those rational techniques which had proved so successful in Italy were just being introduced into German business and administration; and Latin being still the language of affairs, the need for men who possessed a lucid and persuasive Latin style was keenly felt. But how were such men to be found? Once again, the education recommended by the Humanists seemed to provide the answer. It appeared that their programme could serve not only the good of

Protestantism but the good of Germany also. After his Faith, his country was the interest nearest to Luther's heart; and the possibility of benefiting both at the same time had an attraction which proved irresistible. He set himself unhesitatingly to advocate a Humanist programme for the schools, demanding only that it should retain a strong tinge of piety; and his enormous prestige decided the matter.

We find Luther in a moment of honesty and insight comparing himself to the rough labourer who clears a way through a wood, hewing down the undergrowth and digging out the tree-stumps by main force. 'And then', he goes on to say, 'Philip Melanchthon comes along in his neat and quiet way to till and sow, plant and water, doing with great joy the tasks for which God has so richly endowed him.' The career of Melanchthon is interesting because it reflects so clearly the different stages in the growth of German Humanism. Born in 1497 he went at the age of ten to the grammar school at Pforzheim where he was given lessons in Greek by Simler outside of the normal course. Simler was one of the early enthusiasts for Humanism in Germany and the author of a creditable Greek grammar. But the very fact that he had to teach his pet subject privately shows how little headway the new movement had made, even in centres of educational advance.* The young Melanchthon's interest in the classical languages was then further aroused by his great-uncle Reuchlin. That eminent Hebraist was living at Stuttgart during this period, and there is no suggestion that he actually taught his young relative. But he encouraged the boy with good advice, the present of a lexicon and the magic of his learned example.

In 1509 Melanchthon went to Heidelberg and from there to Tuebingen, following in both places the traditional university course in logic and scholastic philosophy. His Humanist education, or rather self-education, began in earnest after he had taken a master's degree in arts and settled down to lecture first on grammar and later also on rhetoric. Conditions were such that it was possible for him to work and teach as a Humanist within the framework of the existing curriculum for those subjects. The circumstance that even during the heyday of Scholasticism the best known classical writers had been retained as possible texts for school reading alongside the patristic and contemporary authors who were more in favour, now made deviations from the scholastic pattern considerably easier. Melanchthon could choose to give his courses on Virgil and Terence, Livy and Cicero, without arousing undue opposition; and while he taught, he also improved his own knowledge. Since his hearers were young and ignorant, he had to spend most of his time on vocabulary, morphology and syntax; but he no doubt emphasised the importance of following ancient usage and avoided the common practice of treating grammar as if it were a branch of logic. By 1518 he had a fair reputation as a Humanist.

The next step was all important. Luther had commenced his career of reform during the previous year and was now intent on building up support for his ideas. Realising how greatly Humanism could contribute to the ends he had in view he allied himself with Spalatinus, a Humanist of good standing who had a certain sympathy for the reformers. Their joint pressure persuaded Frederick of Saxony to found lectureships in Hebrew and Greek at Wittenberg; and Reuchlin whose advice was inevitably sought recommended his nephew for the latter post.

Melanchthon's inaugural lecture at Wittenberg has been erroneously described as a manifesto containing all his later ideas in an embryonic form. Nothing could be further from the truth. At that time, his intellectual development was far from complete, and he was not in a position to produce a blueprint of his future work. The lecture is in fact a somewhat tame and cautious composition in which he is content to tell his audience of that great benefit which can accrue from reading Aristotle and the Scriptures in the original. It helps us, however, to envisage what Melanchthon thought before he met Luther, and hence the nature of Luther's influence upon him.

Luther soon realised that Reuchlin's great-nephew was a genius and set to work to arouse his interest for theological reform. The two men became fast friends. Their attraction was mutual; their gifts almost equal. But as always the more forceful character took the lead. Within a year, Melanchthon presented himself to be examined for his first degree in theology, and having obtained this, he gave, as was the custom, a course of divinity lectures. His views were calculated to please the most extreme section of the reforming party, and his exposition of them was so convincing that Luther immediately persuaded Frederick to appoint him professor of theology as well as lecturer in Greek. Thenceforth he was a member of two faculties, and this circumstance led to a profound revolution in his thought. He had been accustomed to talk in vague and hopeful generalities about the usefulness of classical studies for theology. Now he came to know in the course of his daily work the thousand practical connections which existed between the two. Men had been idealising Christian Humanism for over a hundred years; but he was the first to be in sober fact a Christian Humanist.

Three influences are apparent in the formation of Melanchthon's educational philosophy; and each of them reflects an aspect of his own experience. From his scholastic university course within the framework of the Trivium and Quadrivium, he retained the idea that the essential function of learning was to give a complete and well co-ordinated picture of the world. From his Humanist studies he derived a clear conception of the part which language plays in understanding, and finally from his friendship with Luther and his reformist activities, there sprang an overmastering love of religion and an attendant desire to subordinate all knowledge to religious ends. His mind was the meeting-place of three traditions, the Medieval, the Humanist and the Protestant. All the basic concepts of his thought can therefore be found elsewhere, in any number of earlier writers. But his special contribution was to reconcile what had previously proved irreconcilable within the bounds of a single workable discipline.

The easiest way to understand the achievement of Melanchthon is to compare him with Erasmus. Humanist education always centred round the cult of eloquence. Just as the whole of medieval philosophy was presupposed in a single sentence of Boethius, so the whole of Humanism with its manifold variations was to some extent implicit in Quintilian's conception of the perfect orator. The *Institutio Oratoria* had described a discipline whose aim was to produce virtuous men skilled in all branches of knowledge and capable of presenting their ideas in brilliantly persuasive words. Petrarch's imagination had been fired by the romantic aspects of this ideal and particularly by the thought of a highly developed personality impressing itself upon its inferiors. He had contemplated with delight the power and the glory that would come to a speaker who could sway thousands, while the technical aspects of rhetoric had not interested him. His successors on the other hand, the Humanists of the fifteenth and early sixteenth centuries, were as much concerned with the technical aspects of eloquence as with the prizes it could win. But still eloquence remained to them an end in itself. For all his piety, Erasmus never succeeded in subordinating his Humanism to any external purpose; and he too considered the personal development which resulted from a study of the classics to be sufficient justification for the labour involved. Not so Melanchthon. Protestant and northerner as he was, the cult of personal development beyond a certain stage, that is beyond the stage normal in his generation, struck him as dangerous. He preferred therefore to emphasise that other aspect of Quintilian's definition which up to his time had been comparatively neglected. He dismissed as unworthy the desire to impress, stripped his orator of all those qualities which make for success on the rostrum and left him a scientist writing in his study. Knowledge and lucidity were the qualities he valued. His pupils were not to be great men; he was content that they should be well-instructed.

The educational writings of the fifteenth-century Humanists contained much that is brilliant and a good deal that is sensible; but their general effect was marred for the reader by a want of logic in the argument. They all suffered from precisely the same defect. On the one hand, they eulogised Graeco-Roman civilisation and recommended it as a fit object of imitation and study. On the other hand, they sang the praises of the ancient languages and sought to persuade everyone to write Latin like Cicero. But the connection between these two essentially distinct aims, between cultural imitation on the one hand and linguistic imitation on the other, was never defined. No attempt was made to explain why the ancient literatures provided the best key to the ancient civilisations, or why for example a student who wished to understand the Romans would attain his aim more surely by learning to use the language of Cicero than he would by amassing facts about Roman law or Roman economic organisation.

Melanchthon found an answer to this particular problem. We have only to read his comments on Homer, Hesiod or Pindar to realise that he found a place and indeed a very important place for purely literary works in the hierarchy of factual knowledge. He saw that such writings whether in prose or verse were our best record of men's behaviour and outlook. The *Iliad* and *Odyssey* embodied much of the wisdom that primitive humanity had accumulated over centuries. Pindar mirrored the habits of early Greek society. Aristophanes was our authority for the life of Athens.*

Melanchthon came very near to putting forward that argument which must always stand as the most valid defence of non-specialised literary studies. For he implied (even if he did not state in so many words) that life is too complex to be described in terms of specialities, and that if we wish to discover how a society lived, we must supplement the data we glean from the economists, the sociologists and the historians by the reading of its literature. For there alone, in those casual productions of the fancy, shall we be able to find a record of how people felt and behaved in the face of the manifold trivial incidents that make up the totality of human experience. An anthropologist who claimed to know a present-day native culture without having done field-work on the spot would be instantly discredited. Personal contact is admitted to be essential for the understanding of a society. But when we turn to the great civilisations of the past, it is their literature that provides this personal key. Nothing else can show us the ancient patterns of culture with an equal wealth of detail. And Melanchthon sensing this framed his theories accordingly.

He was able to put forward an apologia for classical studies which formed a unified whole, and he had no need either to adopt the fanciful ideals of Ciceronian imitation or to jettison literary studies altogether in favour of some dim scholastic curriculum based on the specialities. The balanced view to which he had attained presented, however, one difficulty. The earlier Humanist interest in language and style had to some extent withdrawn the student's attention from the pagan subject-matter. Melanchthon's method was bound to have precisely the opposite effect. Once people began to take a lively interest in the content of the classics, the problem of the divergencies between paganism and Christianity was certain to arise. Taking a leaf out of Erasmus' book, Melanchthon met this difficulty by selecting his authors. His own preference was for intensive rather than extensive study, for a few books well-known rather than for a nodding acquaintance with many, and he was quite content that the average schoolboy should limit his reading to Donatus, the *Disticha Catonis*, the *Paedologia* of Mosellanus, a selection from the *Colloquies* of Erasmus, Terence, the respectable plays of Plautus, Virgil, the *Metamorphoses*, the *de Officiis* and the *Epistolae ad Familiares*.* To these were added, in the Humanist schools he tried to found in Nuremberg and Eisleben, the *de Copia* of Erasmus, Livy, Sallust, selected dialogues of Lucian, and readings from Hesiod and Homer.* For university courses he had of course a wider field in view. The 1546 regulations for Wittenberg prescribe the most important poets and the main works of Cicero as essential for the Latin course, while the professor of Greek is to lecture on Homer, Hesiod, Sophocles, Euripides, Theocritus, some of Demosthenes' speeches and one historian.* Melanchthon's own lectures during the forty-eight years of his teaching life ranged as one expects over a wide field. It would have been surprising indeed if over so long a period his vivid personal interests had not drawn his attention to a number of different writers. But even so nine-tenths of his Latin courses were devoted to Cicero, while in Greek, Aristotle's *Ethics*, Demosthenes' speeches and the *Iliad* claimed a disproportionate amount of his time. He never lectured on Aeschylus, gave only one course on Aristophanes, one on Theocritus and two briefly on Sophocles, and he neglected the historians altogether except for occasional lectures on Thucydides.*

By this strict limitation of the field in which he drew his pupils' attention to ancient ideas, he solved for his time what we might term the problem of paganism. A practical Christian was not likely to find anything objectionable in Cicero or Demosthenes. Those ideals of public life which occupy so great a space in their works could be fed without harm to the young of any civilisation. The discrepancies between Aristotle's *Ethics* and Christianity had been explained away centuries before; and the *Iliad* was too fanciful in its setting, too remote from civilised normality, for its bolder presuppositions to make a sharp impact upon the untrained mind of an ordinary student. The points on which it conflicted with Christianity could be dismissed as the inevitable defects of a primitive outlook.

One is bound to regret the contrast between the breadth of Melanchthon's theory and the evident limitations of his practice. He started from the assumption that the task of Humanist teaching was to make the ancient world live anew through the study of its literature; and it is reasonable to suppose that he shared the views of Budé and Erasmus concerning the natural conformity between Greek and Christian thought. As far as his theory went, there was nothing to prevent him from bringing into the classroom the methods which had produced the *Adages*. There was nothing to prevent him from encouraging every student to explore the entire field of Greek and Roman life. But when he did enter the classroom, when he faced the lads who were to be the spiritual leaders of a Protestant Germany, he abandoned his theory and preferred the counsels of an excessive caution. He lost all confidence in the value of the classical heritage, and instead of trusting that an adequate knowledge would be a bar to misinterpretation, he selected his material by rule of thumb methods, ready to reject whatever seemed to conflict with Christian belief.

In short then, while Melanchthon's thought is the crown and ultimate clarification of fifteenth-century Humanist theory, his teaching belongs to the tradition of the *pietas litterata*, and we can observe that he narrows the field of classical knowledge prescribed by Erasmus. He jettisoned a great deal of the Graeco-Roman heritage; and his successors were to jettison even more.

The most distinguished of the Protestant teachers who followed in Melanchthon's footsteps was Johann Sturm. Born in 1506 in Luxemburg, educated by the Brothers of the Common Life and later at the new Humanist College at Louvain, he earned a laborious living as a private teacher in Paris until that conversion to Protestantism which led to his being invited in 1535 to take charge of the municipal school at Strassburg. The city had ranged itself early on the side of the Reformation, and, since 1524, its pastors had been demanding that adequate arrangements should be made to ensure a high level of general literacy (without which a Bible-reading religion could not survive) as well as proper instruction for their own successors. The magistrature had responded to these demands with fair energy. It had given its approval to one senior and three sizeable junior schools besides sundry smaller ones scattered round the town. It had engaged lecturers on a large variety of subjects including Hebrew, Greek, geography and mathematics. But the system had remained unorganised. Its parts did not work smoothly together; and it was as an organiser that Sturm was called in to help.

He followed Melanchthon in holding that the purpose of education was to train the young in a wise and eloquent piety.* But he did not share that eminent teacher's revolutionary interest in factual knowledge; and his conception of the Humanist discipline suffered in consequence. In his eyes, as in the eyes of all the great Protestant educators of the period, a teacher's first duty was to inculcate sound religious and moral principles. Once this Christian outlook had been firmly established, it was then to be bolstered by carefully selected material drawn from the classics, and the arts of expression were to be very fully taught. Since Latin was the learned language of the time, that meant the detailed teaching of Latin.

Soon after his arrival in Strassburg, Sturm persuaded the magistrates to combine the existing schools into one large Gymnasium of about five hundred pupils. The junior section of this was to consist of nine classes in which pupils could be graded according to their proficiency. Six was the normal age for commencing the course, and most boys were expected to complete it by fifteen, which meant a yearly promotion. During this time, they learnt a fluent and correct Latin, enough Greek to read Demosthenes, a sufficiency of rhetoric, the rudiments of dialectic and a little geography. Sturm placed great weight on the ability to speak Latin. So much so that he forbade the use of the vernacular except for necessary explanations in the very lowest classes, and drove the boys to begin their studies by learning long vocabularies and phrase lists, such as we find in his own *Onomasticon Puerile*.* He did not, however, share the aesthetic ideals of the Italian Humanists. The very fact that he was primarily interested in speech shows that he thought of Latin as a means of communication and not as a magical medium for the creation of deathless works of art. Similarly when the boys came to study rhetoric and dialectic, Sturm and his assistants emphasised the application of the rules rather than the rules themselves. Endless spoken and written exercises constituted the main activity of the school.

Reading was restricted. During the first three years of the course which were devoted entirely to Latin, the boys studied certain selected letters, the *de Amicitia* and the *de Senectute* of Cicero, selected poems from Horace, Catullus and Tibullus, and the *Eclogues* of Virgil. They also started the *Aeneid*. Greek made its appearance in the fourth class at the end of which the second *Olynthiac* was read. The later half of the course then included: in Latin, the rest of the *Aeneid*, more Cicero, Caesar, Terence, Sallust and certain plays of Plautus; in Greek, Demosthenes, Aeschines, the *Organon* and the *Rhetoric* of Aristotle and a few of Plato's dialogues. Furthermore, if we are to judge by Sturm's published commentaries, the teachers laid far more emphasis on meaning as such than on the ideas under discussion.*

The senior section of the school consisted of six successive classes, and here the lectures were public so that anyone could attend. The entire course would have provided some training in all the specialities including law and medicine. But the majority of the students probably heard one or two professors at the most. Unfortunately, we know very little about the teaching offered in Latin and Greek. It was supposed to cover the major authors. But again it appears to have been largely formal.*

The high respect in which his contemporaries held Sturm, the notable success of his school, strike us as strange in view of the uninspired dryasdust character of his teaching. Yet it may have been his very dullness that made him popular. A Humanist who was also a thinker, like Melanchthon, was bound to tax the intelligence of his hearers. Sturm made no such demands. He paraphrased simple texts in even simpler language, explaining each word and each usage. Nor was it his intention to train brilliant stylists. The Latin he taught was an idiom suitable for everyday use which was well within his pupils' power to learn.

The significance of the discipline he created will become clearer perhaps when we consider the work of some of his contemporaries who were moving along the same lines. One stands out in particular. Mathurin Cordier was older than either Sturm or Melanchthon, but his development had been slow. He was fifty years of age before he contributed seriously to the progress of education. Born in 1480, he published his first important work, the *de Corrupti Sermonis Emendatione* in 1530.

This book helps us to see in its true perspective the effort of the Protestant Humanists to popularise the use of correct Latin. It consists of fifty-eight sections, each dealing either with some aspect of human experience such as 'religion', 'work', 'pleasure', 'bodily functions' or with some division of language such as 'adverbs', 'irregular verbs', 'verbs which take special cases'. In each section Cordier gives a number of faulty expressions as used in the Paris Schools of the period, followed by alternative ways of rendering the same ideas in a more classical idiom.

Many of the usages he condemns can only be understood if one translates them word for word into French. 'Do not say', he implores, '*ego bene transibo me de te* or *est totum* or indeed *chiffravit reparationes ad latrinas.*' Here plainly is the obverse of Rabelais' *écolier limousin*. It was the fashion in the non-Humanist schools to bespatter the language of learning with vernacular idioms and coinages. The simplified 'modern' Latin that the scholastics introduced four centuries earlier had degenerated into a bastard jargon that had no excuse for its existence. Cordier could count on a good deal of support when, under the influence of Humanist ideals, he proposed replacing this linguistic monstrosity by an equally simple but correct Latin taught, as Sturm planned to teach it, through the medium of a few carefully selected, morally innocuous classical works.

Humanists in the past had done their share in transforming the economic and the political system. They had introduced new ideals of behaviour, new feelings and new tastes. They had made writers conscious of form, and great men interested in their own eminence. They had found Europe a continent of learned universities and left it a continent of learned courts. They had revolutionised painting, literature and science. They had changed the character of men's sensibility; and their zeal for correct Latin had been a means to these more impressive ends. But their successors, like the Sturms and the Cordiers, concentrated on that means to the exclusion of all else. The only feature of the original Humanist tradition which they included in their educational programme was to inculcate the use of correct classical Latin. Two hundred years earlier, the attainment of that aim would admittedly have involved the reading of innumerable classical authors. But by the fourth decade of the sixteenth century there were grammars, dictionaries and phrase-books in plenty; and there were so many copies of every well-known author that teachers were no longer compelled to read what came to hand, thereby exposing their pupils to all sorts of influences, but could pick and choose, taking for class use only what suited their own ideas of propriety.

The new Humanism was far less revolutionary than the old; and proof of this can be found in Cordier's career. From 1514 onwards he taught grammar in a number of Paris Colleges including the notorious Sainte-Barbe. He counted as a Humanist but he earned his living peacefully enough in the very stronghold of Scholasticism; and it was there that he evolved the methods of instruction which his book illustrates. If these methods had diverged noticeably from the medieval tradition, he could not have employed them without scandal. But the *de Corrupti Sermonis Emendatione* is not a collection of Latin phrases bearing on various topics which might be expected to give some picture of the Roman mind. It is basically a collection of French phrases, either in the original, or in a corrupt Latin translation, for which Cordier has painfully unearthed a classical equivalent. Moreover, the book is full of pious exhortations scattered haphazard among the grammar. In the chapter on 'Going and Returning' we find for example:

Swearing is not permitted to Christians even in jest, for the Apostle, inspired by the Holy Ghost, has given them this precept: 'Let all bitterness, and wrath, and anger, and clamour, and railing, be put away from you, with all malice; and be you kind one to another, tender hearted, forgiving each other even as God also in Christ forgave you.'

And a little further on—

'But fornication and all uncleanness and covetousness, let it not be named among you, as becometh saints; nor filthiness, nor foolish talking, or jesting which are not befitting; but rather giving of thanks.'

And sometimes Cordier goes beyond the inculcation of a general piety to the preaching of his own opinions. At the end of the section on religion, he attacks the dances which the Church allowed in the streets on St Stephen's Day. He warns the young against believing that such dances are religious because they are held officially for a religious reason. They are the snares which the devil spreads to catch miserable souls whom he might torture. And he expresses the hope that Francis I will soon forbid such practices.

Cordier's next undertaking was a commentary on the *Disticha Catonis*. That little collection of moral platitudes had been used as a first Latin reading book since the days of Alcuin and had been regarded with favour even during the Scholastic Age. Erasmus had produced an edition in 1513 of which he was very proud, and he told Budé that in his opinion 'Cato' said far wiser things than Scotus. Cordier was more intransigent in his piety. He disapproved of 'Cato' as too pagan, regretted that custom forced him to use the *Distichs* and wrote his commentary to contradict rather than to illustrate them. So he appended a French translation to those aphorisms with which he agreed; but where he disagreed, he left the translation out, and he did his best to discredit 'Cato' as unchristian. The *Distichs* were published in 1533 while Cordier was at Nevers where he had gone three years before. Soon after he passed on from there, having spent some time in Paris, to the Collège de Guyenne at Bordeaux, then to Geneva, to Neuchâtel and finally to Lausanne. In these last three places the curriculum followed the Strassburg model. Only there was more emphasis on religion, and the standards of classical learning were appreciably lower. At Geneva, Greek was taught exclusively from the New Testament; at Neuchâtel it was not taught at all. At Lausanne where Cordier stayed longest (1545–57) the senior school with its public lectures was devoted entirely to theology. Greek was confined to the last two years of the junior course, the students reading Aesop, Cebes, Lucian's *Dialogues of the Dead* and selections from Herodian, Xenophon or Plutarch. In Latin the first three classes did not progress beyond 'Cato' and the *Letters* of Cicero, probably in Cordier's own selection which omitted everything but the familiar chit-chat. The fourth class read the *de Amicitia* and some Terence; the fifth, parts of Ovid's *Tristia* and *Epistolae ex Ponto*, parts of the *Aeneid*, the *de Officiis* and Caesar's *Commentaries*; the sixth made a beginning with Horace and the *ad Herennium*; while the seventh and highest crowned its work with some of the easier speeches from Cicero and Livy. The authorities were plainly content if the boys knew Latin and could follow the Greek text of the New Testament with a commentary. No more was required for a theological career.

During his stay at Lausanne, Cordier published two books which tell us a good deal about his methods. His *Selections from Cicero'*

Letters for the use of beginners are taken from the *Epistolae ad Familiares*, the fourteenth and sixteenth books being the ones most fully represented. But except for some of the short notes to Terentia and Tiro, hardly any letters are given in full. Not only the passages which contain difficult Latin (which are usually the most interesting), but all those dealing with politics are summarily omitted. Cordier's intention seems to have been to provide his boys with suitable phrases for their everyday correspondence, and he was not concerned to keep much beyond the routine salutations, the assurances of goodwill and the offers of service with which Cicero greased the wheels of his personal relationships. The Commentary is plainly a product of the same principles that had guided the choice of material. It consists sometimes of a paraphrase in simpler Latin, but mostly it gives just the French translation.* There are no historical or geographical explanations, no attempt is made to describe when or where the letters were written, and the structure of Roman society is arbitrarily equated with that of Cordier's own world. The praetors become '*prevosts*', the senate '*le parlement*', the *tribuni militares* '*les caporaux*'. The Roman past is of no interest to Cordier. All he wants from it is the language for contemporary use.

The Cicero selection which appeared in 1556 was followed seven years later by the most important of Cordier's school text-books, the *Colloquiorum Scholasticorum libri iiij ad pueros in sermone Latino paulatim exercendos* which, published first by Henri Estienne, was translated into French, English and German and reprinted again and again until the middle of the nineteenth century so that nearly a hundred separate editions have been traced. These colloquies are little conversations arranged in an ascending order of difficulty and intended (as in all Cordier's exercises) to teach the grammar and vocabulary of Latin for daily use. The first book contains the declensions, the conjugations and a few word-lists followed by short dialogues to ensure repetition. The second is more advanced. The pieces deal with special topics, such as the parts of the body and the terms to be learnt are introduced in the text. The third book, more advanced still, contains conversations between the *praeceptor*, obviously Cordier himself, and his pupils on subjects to do with the running of the school, while the fourth has for its purpose the teaching of Christian morality. The form is one which several writers had attempted since the first introduction of Humanism into the schools. Similar easy dialogues for the teaching of Latin had been written by Petrus Mosellanus (1517), Erasmus (1524), Adrian Barland (1525), Ravisius Textor (1529), and Vivès (1539). They must all take their place alongside Alcuin's text-books and the scholastic *Grecimus* and *Doctrinale* as attempts to teach Latin independently of the classics.

If popularity can provide a trustworthy criterion of judgement, then Cordier was more successful in this enterprise than any of his predecessors. His success must be ascribed to his real ability as a teacher, to the pedagogic skill with which he graded his material, but partly also to his unashamed sermonising; for during the next several centuries European parents were to consider that a priggish morality was the ideal mental food for their young. 'Lend me a pen', says Poitevin to Joshua. 'I don't want to'—'Remember that some day you will ask me for something and I shan't give it to you'—'But don't you know that Jesus Christ has told us to repay evil with good?'—'I have not learnt that yet'—'You must learn it if you wish to be His disciple'—'That is what I desire above all things'—'Then learn to imitate the Master'—'I shall learn by and by'—'You had better begin now while you have time'—'You are too hard on me. My mother says that I am not eight yet'—'One is never too young to do good'.* It is plain enough that Cordier knew children; but one might argue that he encouraged their worst instead of their best inclinations.

We have now passed in review the four leading exponents of the *pietas litterata*: Erasmus, Melanchthon, Sturm and Cordier. This order in which their names have been placed is significant for two reasons. Erasmus was a more zealous Humanist than Melanchthon, Melanchthon than Sturm, Sturm than Cordier. On the other hand, their success and influence as practical educators was in inverse proportion to their Humanist zeal. Erasmus was a theorist whose ideas were never applied as he formulated them. Melanchthon was both theorist and organiser, but he was forced to make endless compromises in his organising, and what he achieved in practice was only a pale shadow of what he had outlined in theory. Sturm, a less competent thinker than either, did found one very successful school which apparently served as a model for many others. But his imitators never really tried to equal the high standards which he had set. So it was Cordier, the practical teacher with narrow interests who exercised the greatest ultimate influence, leaving his mark on the many schools in which he had worked and writing text-books which were used for generations. It is Cordier whom we must see as the real representative of the Humanism that eventually won itself a place in the educational system of Europe.

For the extreme Protestant schools were not the only ones to set strict limits upon their classical studies. The same spirit reigned on the other side of the fence. In this matter the Catholic reformers were at one mind with their opponents. Both looked back to St Augustine. In 1546 the Jesuit college at Gandia, which had been founded for the education of members of the society, opened certain of its philosophy and arts lectures to secular students. The experiment proved successful, and Ignatius Loyola realised that educational work could be a powerful instrument for the furtherance of the aims he had at heart. Two years later, the Society opened another centre at Messina for the education of the youth of the city. There was a grammar class in three sections, and classes in rhetoric, logic, Greek and Hebrew. The fathers insisted on regular attendance. The course was arranged progressively. Grammar had to be studied, then rhetoric, and then only could the student pass to other subjects; all in direct contravention to the existing Italian practice which allowed everyone to attend what lectures he chose, so that many listened to disquisitions on philosophy before they even knew how to write.*

By 1551 there were Jesuit colleges in Rome, Bologna, Ferrara, Florence and Venice, and a programme was drawn up for their guidance based largely on the experience of the teachers at Messina. According to this programme, there were to be seven classes in grammar. The first five were to spend all their time on morphology and syntax in Donatus and Despauterius. The sixth, while continuing with syntax, was to read selections from Cicero's *Letters*, and Terence or Virgil's *Eclogues*. The seventh was to add the *de Amicitia* or the *de Senectute*, Ovid's *Tristia* and *Epistolae ex Ponto*, and Sallust, if Terence was not read. Repetition and written exercises were both to be used so as to make sure that the pupils remembered what they had been taught.* Promotion from one class to the next could take place within the year except after the last year of grammar when the student went on to a new section of the course, which was called the Humanities class. Here the *de Copia* and the *de Conscribendis Epistolis* of Erasmus were read alongside Horace's *Ars Poetica* and Cicero's *Tusculanae Disputationes*. Greek was started with readings from Aesop and surprisingly enough from the *Plutus* of Aristophanes. The Humanities class was followed by one in rhetoric, where the work was largely practical. The students wrote a speech a week, and read precepts excerpted from Quintilian, the *ad Herennium*, some of Cicero's *Orations* and an historical author.* When they could do this, they were considered fit to leave or to attempt more difficult studies.

It is in its choice of authors that this whole programme bears such a strong resemblance to its Protestant predecessors. Technical treatises on rhetoric occupy a disproportionately large place, while the historians and poets are neglected. Terence, whose plays were recommended for study in 1551, was banned at a later date. Both St Ignatius and Father Nadal, the head of the Messina College, were worried at the thought of young boys under their care reading about licentious love, and they independently tried to sketch out plans as to how classical authors could best be expurgated for use in schools. Finally in 1551 Ignatius commissioned Father Frusius to produce suitable editions of Terence, Horace and Martial. Frusius surveyed the field and said that he could do the last two authors without great difficulty, and he did indeed produce an expurgated Martial which appeared in 1558 and ran to eighteen editions. But Terence presented a more serious problem. The best suggestion he could make was that the illicit passions which formed the theme of the plays should be transmogrified into pure conjugal love. But this proposal was insufficiently drastic to meet the requirements of Ignatius, and the matter ended with the imposition of an absolute ban.*

The Jesuit schools proved unprecedentedly popular. By 1551 there were over a hundred and fifty of them in the different Catholic countries, and the General had on his table requests for sixty more.* Efficiency and method had scored a signal triumph in a field where those qualities had been notably lacking. Education came to count among the Society's chief concerns, and considerable energy was devoted to its organisation. The *Constitutions* of 1551, the *Ratio Studiorum* of 1586, and the revised versions of 1591 and 1599, all introduced changes into the first scheme of studies which Nadal worked out at Messina. But the changes were not fundamental. The general approach stayed the same.

The length of the course remained unsettled, varying from five years for the most intelligent to a possible eight for the stupid. But the usual age for finishing one's classical studies was about sixteen. After that serious students went on to philosophy and scholastic theology. The Jesuits did not offer any higher instruction in the Humanities.

The list of authors prescribed by the *Ratio Studiorum* of 1599 is a good deal longer than the one we extracted from Nadal's programme; it is to be noticed, however, that many of the works it mentions are to be read in selections or 'provided that any expurgated edition is used'. Selected pieces from Catullus, Tibullus and Propertius and some of the easier books of Virgil ('provided that *Aeneid* IV and certain Eclogues are not read') and the *Odes* of Horace, suitably expurgated, figure in the reading of the Humanities class. But it would be an error to assume that the historians for example were studied in any detail. The time allowed for their perusal was half an hour a day on alternate days during the first part of the year, which gives a hundred hours in all, allowing for vacations, holidays and the like. Most modern schools would assign that much time to the reading of two short set books!

The greatest divergence between the practice of Messina and the later *Rationes* concerns, however, the organisation of Greek studies. In the revised curriculum, Greek is begun simultaneously with Latin, and the Greek authors listed for the two top classes include Isocrates, Plato, Plutarch, Demosthenes, Homer, Hesiod and Pindar as well as many of the early Fathers. This is an impressive programme so long as we do not consider the actual time-table. That tells another story. Out of the possible 4500–5000 teaching hours of the normal course, 800–900 only were spent on Greek.* Plato, Synesius, Plutarch and Homer were supposedly read after the first three hundred hours; and yet after three hundred hours of Latin the boys were still spelling out the easiest letters of Cicero and were considered incapable of translating Ovid! Why should they have made so much more progress in one language than another? It is obvious that the Greek programme given in the 1599 *Ratio* is too ambitious in its implications. The authors must have been read in very easy selections and with a good deal of help from the teacher.

In practice, the Jesuits set much the same limits on their Humanism as Cordier had done. Their reading of authors was selective; their explanations rhetorical. Literature was studied for the sake of composition and for no other reason.* The appendix to the 1591 *Ratio* warns the teacher against digressions into history or antiquities. His task is to teach the use of words. Moreover, there are clear indications that the performance of that task was not highly honoured, the Humanities being regarded as a relatively unimportant subject. The professors of Latin and Greek being made to feel inferior to their colleagues while their students were habitually impatient to move on to the more esteemed courses in philosophy.*

When Rabelais compared the medieval and Humanist forms of education, he set a reality whose defects he exaggerated against an unrealised ideal. When that ideal was realised, when Humanist schools made their appearance all over Europe under the aegis of the rival Churches, they patently lacked in practice the attractions which had belonged to them in theory. It is true that they taught a Latin which conformed to classical usage and also taught a certain amount of Greek. But we cannot assign any great educational importance to these changes unless we are prepared to argue that there is some extraordinary virtue in the mere elements of Greek, or that classical Latin far surpasses its medieval counterpart as a pedagogic instrument, even when it is inculcated more or less independently of its authors. For the new schools were nearly as careful as the old to avoid giving a recognisable picture of the pagan way of life. The traits which had most clearly characterised the Humanism of the Renaissance were the ones most vigorously excluded from the ambit of the *pietas litterata*. The Cordiers and the Nadals had no wish to see a revival of the Roman past. They did not aspire to the delights of universal genius. They did not, and being religious men they honestly could not, regard literature as the most significant of human activities. In Jesuit and Protestant schools alike, religious beliefs, the promptings of conscience and the problems presented by the Bible or theology took first place in everyone's mind. Literature came a poor second and was often despised. It could hardly have been otherwise; for a great number of the pupils at these schools were destined either for the Roman Catholic priesthood or for the Protestant ministry. They were bound to be absorbed in their vocation and to regard as distracting studies that had not a specifically religious content.

There was in the last analysis no great difference between the Scholastics and the Reformers (or Counter-Reformers) as far as their attitude to the classics was concerned. Cordier was another Bernard Silvestris, Nadal another Neckham. But there existed a certain number of other schools in which religious feeling was not so strong so that classical learning was allowed a more important place.

The Protestant and Jesuit schools were markedly successful in adapting Humanist education to serve religious needs; and it has been convenient therefore to consider their work as a whole independently of the national developments which had gone far by this time to divide Europe into a number of separate compartments. But now we must turn back to the complexities of the historical picture. For not only did certain countries, like France and England, escape to some extent the full force of the religious movement which produced the *pietas litterata*, but the movement itself developed unequally. Protestant Humanism was some thirty years ahead of its Catholic counterpart. The Reformation preceded the Counter-Reformation.

The educational life of Germany and Switzerland was completely dominated from 1520 onwards by the Protestant tradition which we have described above. The schools of Spain retained their medieval character until the arrival of the Jesuits and so require no special mention. But the remaining four countries of western Europe, Italy, France, the Netherlands and England all show individual variations on the main pattern of Christian Humanism which in some cases were of great importance for classical studies.

Italy is the least interesting. By the end of the fifteenth century, Italian education had lost that medieval character which it had still possessed in the days of Guarino. Most of the teachers were Humanists; but by an unlucky chance, the manner in which education was organised rendered their Humanism largely ineffective. The advanced training provided by the distinguished scholars of the period was given in the form of open lectures where neither the initial attainments of the audience nor their progress was adequately checked. The only systematic teaching was that offered by the men who taught young boys the rudiments of Latin and who sometimes included a few lessons on Greek; and at that elementary level, Italian Humanism lacked the effectiveness of the northern tradition. The years between 1480 and 1550 were wasted. The Humanist education which Petrarch had envisaged was never established; and when eventually the Jesuits opened their college in Messina, they entered upon a heritage of muddle.

The *pietas litterata* did not make its appearance in Italy until half-way through the sixteenth century. It came as we have seen with the Jesuits. French education on the other hand was influenced by the pioneers of Protestant teaching even before 1530. Sturm worked out his system in Paris. Cordier taught at Sainte-Barbe. But their methods, which Germany was to welcome, received a curious twist in the country of their origin. France was a battleground where the struggle of the rival faiths was still undecided. Circumstances were such that few cared to commit themselves too deeply on one side or the other; and the French authorities, although Catholic, did not attack the Reformers with the systematic zeal that was to distinguish the Inquisition in Spain and Italy. Extreme measures were not employed as a matter of course. Persecution had an intermittent character; and for long periods of time Protestants could hold important posts if they avoided making a public parade of opposition. Consequently, we come across many Humanists with known Protestant sympathies who nevertheless taught in the French universities and schools. Such men were bound to have a lively interest in the methods used by their German co-religionists. But we find that they were hampered by certain restrictions. Their safety depended on their caution. They could not permit themselves to propagate the views they had at heart.

The educational consequences of this situation were curious. Like all illogical compromises, it produced unexpected and illogical results. One of the centres where the Protestant Humanists came together was the Collège de Guyenne at Bordeaux. This school where Montaigne was to spend some years as a pupil rose out of obscurity under the guidance of Andreas de Gouvea. In 1535, five out of the twelve teachers working there secretly preferred Geneva to Rome; and it is not surprising therefore that the curriculum followed to a great extent the pattern of Strassburg. It is true that in the place of Sturm's eight junior and six senior grades, Gouvea had twelve and two respectively; and the senior section seems to have studied philosophy only. But the juniors spent most of their time on Latin and, as in Strassburg, far more attention was paid to the active use of the language than to the reading of authors (which explains Montaigne's complaint that he was allowed to leave school unaware of the delights of literature). The *Disticha Catonis* and selected works of Cicero and Terence comprised the whole Latin reading of the first seven classes. Ovid was introduced in the eighth, and Horace in the final year. The teaching of Greek followed a more or less parallel course. By the time they reached the senior school the students were able to understand Aristotle in the original. Progress was probably slower, and the general standard of attainment for any particular age less than Sturm had considered proper. For until they were seventeen or eighteen, the boys learnt nothing but the ancient languages, except that the two top classes had one hour of history a day from Justin and Livy. But these were unimportant differences. As far as the mechanics of the curriculum went the Collège de Guyenne was a Protestant school. Its unique character sprang from another source.

Since the Collège de Guyenne was in Catholic France, its professors though sympathetic to the Reformation could not give rein to their religious feelings; and there seems to have been little of the energetic piety which characterised the new education in Protestant lands. Gouvea followed Sturm in limiting his classical curriculum to formal studies, but he did not complement this limited course by the intensive religious instruction which the Strassburg plan took for granted. His pupils were left empty of ideas; and the result of this one-sided regimen was to give their interests a markedly aesthetic orientation. Thanks to the efforts of the Protestant educationists, the classical discipline had been stripped of its ideological components. It had been reduced to the study of language and style and made ancillary to a religious upbringing. Now, in Bordeaux, the religious element was also removed. The new truncated, style-centred Humanism was left to develop in a vacuum. According to the practice of the time, the acting of plays was a regular feature of the school year, and in the absence of more serious concerns, this artistic activity took on a great importance. The Scottish Humanist Buchanan, who joined Gouvea's staff in 1539, wrote two Latin tragedies modelled on the Greek and Latinised two plays by Euripides which went to swell the school repertoire. Buchanan, however, was a more headstrong Protestant than most of his colleagues. In spite of Gouvea's restraining influence, he poured the wine of evangelism into his formally impeccable plays so that after five years, the authorities began to look askance at him, and he was compelled to leave. Jovial, energetic and immensely learned, he occupies a place of honour among the successors of John the Scot, as one of the many northerners who revivified the intellectual life of France; and though his further adventures do not concern us here, it is pleasant to note that he eventually returned home to witness the triumph of the Scottish Church for which he had laboured and suffered. At Bordeaux, his enforced departure necessarily deepened the impression that style was the only safe study; and his successor Muret was a man likely to benefit by the warning of his example. Muret was only twenty-one when he came to teach at the Collège de Guyenne in 1546. Many years later his lectures on Plato were to call down on him the wrath of the Roman Inquisition because of their unorthodoxy, but at this point in his life he was still a brilliant youth concerned only to make a name for himself by utilising his remarkable knowledge of Latin. He was a stylist first and last, and his play on Julius Caesar carried on the tradition which Buchanan had inaugurated.

From Bordeaux Muret moved to Paris where he had a post at the College de Boncourt. His career links the experiment of Gouvea with the parallel developments which were making themselves felt in the capital, and his literary genius made a notable contribution to both. Humanism was flourishing in Paris where the Royal Readers provided a higher education which was based exclusively on the classics. But although these Readers were without exception distinguished scholars, they too experienced the inevitable pressure of contemporary fears and suspicions. Avoiding the discussion of ideas, they concentrated on linguistic and literary criticism; and the lesser lights who surrounded them followed suit.

Dorat at the Collège de Coqueret, Muret at the Collège de Boncourt, encouraged the pupils to study the classics as literary models. Their teaching was based on the established techniques of imitation, which they applied, however, in a narrower field than Erasmus had originally recommended. The poets were their gods. They immersed themselves in Homer, in Pindar and in Horace. They imitated Euripides and Seneca, and caught up on the tide of the national Renaissance, the ultimate result of their work was to give us the Pléiade, that revival of classical poetry without its prose, a Humanism wrapped in the swaddling-clothes of the sublime.

In England, developments followed an analogous, if not quite parallel course. Thanks to the reforms of Henry VIII and Edward VI which destroyed some and reorganised others of the four hundred odd cathedral, grammar and chantry schools in the kingdom, the old system of education received a shaking which made the acceptance of new ideas comparatively easy. By the second half of the century most of the larger foundations had adopted a more or less Humanist curriculum.

We possess a certain amount of evidence concerning Eton and Westminster; and although it would be rash to assume that they were altogether typical, we may regard them as representative of an important trend in sixteenth-century English education. Both schools placed great emphasis on the speaking and writing of correct Latin. Both included rhetorical treatises such as the *Epitome* of Susenbrotus among their text-books, and at Westminster, the boys were specifically required to follow the advice of Erasmus. They were told to collect in their note-books figures of speech, antitheses, epithets, synonyms, proverbs, similes, comparisons, anecdotes, descriptions of times, places and persons, fables, witty sayings and apophthegms; in short, all the usual illustrative matter of rhetoric. But while the lower forms like their compeers in Strassburg studied Erasmus, Cordier and Vivès in preference to the classics, the older boys read more widely than Sturm or the Jesuits would have approved and in particular they read more poetry.* The literary tradition was strong in England. England had compromised on the religious issue. She had embraced neither extreme. Her schools were not pressed to inculcate religious zeal and so the classical discipline avoided those stringent limitations which were imposed upon it elsewhere. As we noted earlier, English Humanism had been dominated by the ideals of the fifteenth century during its heyday at the end of Henry VIII's reign. Cheke and his fellows were the real heirs of Italy. When the French Humanists turned to the details of philological scholarship in a world grown unfriendly to ideas, these Englishmen continued to proclaim the value of Greek as a training for diplomacy. The careers of Cheke and to some extent Ascham lent colour to this belief, and the memory of their triumphs continued to exercise an influence far into the reign of Elizabeth. The Roman Catholics and the Puritans whose absorption in religious controversy was likely to lead them to neglect other more mundane interests, sent their children out of the country to get their education on the Continent, and so the English schools were organised to satisfy those more moderate members of the middle class who did not hanker to be saints or theologians, but who did want to see their sons succeed in the world of affairs. So the English schools retained not only a measure of literary enthusiasm, but an interest in the political and social life of the ancient world: and the Inns of Court were full of men who retained a lively love of the classics.

But it was the habit to make small Latin and less Greek suffice. So in effect the same diminution of the Humanist programme took place in England as elsewhere. The reasons for it may have been different, but the ultimate result was the same. A few hundred pages of Cicero and Demosthenes, a few hundred lines of Virgil and Homer, with extracts from the historians and the elegiac poets, and perhaps a tragedy by Euripides or a comedy by Terence, came to represent the sum total of the Graeco-Roman legacy for all but a chosen few classical scholars. In the long run, the divorce of classical learning from the latest advances in knowledge, a divorce which was made inevitable by the general orientation of European scholarship, came to exercise its influence. The later years of Elizabeth failed to produce a second Croke or a second Sir Thomas More whose learning would have shown how the classics could help men to solve contemporary problems; and as a result men's interest in Greece and Rome lost its earlier vigour. The classical discipline came to be regarded as a mere pedagogic instrument, while scholarship, divorced from education and from life, found itself transformed into a specialised interest, the most highly skilled of all intellectual crafts, whose devotees were delighted to escape from the present in order to add their mite to the service of posterity.

So, by 1600, the Humanist revival was over; and one glance at European education in the post-Reformation period is sufficient to show that the Humanists won a pyrrhic victory. They had brought classical studies into the schools, but only at the price of compromising on all their original aims. Rabelais had dreamt of a Humanist discipline which would use time-saving methods and yet develop the whole man, body and soul, giving him a grasp of ancient and modern knowledge, but training him above all in judgement and the power to act. Seventy years later, there was a Humanist curriculum in every grammar school, but the dream was as far from fulfilment as ever. These new apparently Humanist schools were devoted to an outworn rhetoric and were, at the best, breeding-grounds for textual scholars. They had not the purpose or the power to train supermen perfect in all they undertook and capable of setting the world to rights.

Yet we should do wrong to conclude that the new education was therefore a failure. It seems to have suited the needs of the age. Supermen after all make poor citizens. A Caesare Borgia would be a disruptive force in any society; and a world of Caesares is inconceivable. By the seventeenth century men had learnt how to compromise about individualism, how to allow so much of it and no more. And it is not altogether fanciful to suppose that an early and carefully limited acquaintance with the Humanist interpretation of the ancient world, when set against the explicit claims of religious obedience and the unspoken pressures of society, gave something like the right amount of encouragement to individualist attitudes and aspirations. Certainly, it did not interfere in any way with the prevailing pattern of behaviour. It possessed the negative but essential virtue of not disturbing the *status quo*. For when a new culture is evolving, as happened during the early Renaissance, the social group which aims to establish fresh norms generally tries to make some positive use of education. But when the process of evolution is complete, when the new pattern has gained widespread acceptance, that positive purpose can be abandoned; and all a society with a stable culture requires from its educational system is this passive quality of not running counter to the spirit of the age; and that the *pietas litterata* certainly avoided doing.

Moreover, it is to this limited study of the ancient writers that we owe in part at least the classicism of the French *grand siècle* and the English Augustan writers. Obviously, there were other forces at work as well. The temper of the age, the elements drawn into the European tradition during the Renaissance, and in particular the current reinterpretations of ancient literary theory, played a not inconsiderable part in shaping the achievement of a Racine or an Addison. But it would be

366

foolish to neglect altogether the contribution of the schools. An early education which accustomed the mind to regard good writing as the meticulous application of rules, which insisted on polish and propriety and represented its antique heroes as rational and urbane, was bound to sow the seeds of the attitude we label classicism. In an unfavourable atmosphere these seeds would have come to nothing. But in the propitious mental climate of the late seventeenth and early eighteenth centuries they flourished magnificently. The Humanism of the schools, being an integral part of contemporary culture, made a serious contribution to the literature in which that culture found expression.

With the Classical Age, the long struggle of the Church and Humanism in the educational field came to an unspectacular end. During the first half of the eighteenth century, classical studies declined to such an extent that a competent knowledge of Greek became a scholarly rarity. When they revived again, it was in an altered form. The positive element in scholarship after 1750 was that historical, anthropological and archaeological interest which eventually produced such valuable results in the development of those specialities. But that vivifying interest which once again linked ancient studies with the progress of knowledge did not spread to the educational field. During the later part of the eighteenth and most of the nineteenth century, the classics that were taught in the schools and universities, so far from being a danger to any accepted system of thought, were the harmless instrument of contemporary educational fashions and were used to inculcate a taste for rhetoric in France, patriotism in Germany and a public school morality in Dr Arnold's England.

This final, inglorious finish should not, however, blind us to the significance of the struggle. Being concerned primarily with the use that was made of the classical legacy, we have described the forms of humanist education sponsored by the representatives of the Christian tradition always in terms of limitations imposed upon a possible whole-hearted Humanism. The aim of this book has been to show the impact of the dominant ideologies of each period upon general education; and no other method of description would have served for that purpose. The only way to make obvious the influence of social pressures upon the classical curriculum was to set the content of each new classical discipline against a theoretical totality. But this method of presentation should not be considered to imply value judgements of a type which would in any case lie outside the competence of a work whose only purpose has been to trace the mechanics of educational development. The statement that the schools in the scholastic period made a very restricted use of the classical legacy should not, for example, be taken to mean that scholastic education was consequently bad.

If we look at the struggle between Christianity and Humanism in its broadest aspects, we are bound to conclude that the efforts made by the Christian Churches to restrict the unfettered use of pagan material were no less important for the cultural and social progress of Europe, than the contrary efforts of the Humanists to make that material a part of the European heritage. The spread of Humanist ideas was closely connected in practice with the growth of economic individualism. Now, it is evident that a wholly individualist society is exposed to grave inner tensions which will split and ruin it unless they are counterbalanced by a cohesive force which can engage the loyalty of individuals against their own immediate interests. Patriotism fulfilled that function in ancient Greece and Rome. But the medieval world knew no patriots since there were no national states; and it was the Church which stood in their place, as the cohesive force of medieval society. The higher morality of religion was the only guarantee of social behaviour. The well-being of medieval Europe required that the growing individualist tendencies of its society should be effectively subordinated to Christian principles; and Humanism which was the educational expression of those tendencies had therefore to be christianised.

The school programmes of the Scholastic Age and again of the Reformation can be regarded as the by-products of the two great attempts which were made to impose a Christian pattern upon an increasingly individualist world. Though both attempts eventually failed, they both enjoyed their moments of success, and during those moments they gave European society a stability which it would not have possessed without them, and which, since the nineteenth century, the solitary force of national loyalties has not been able to replace. Patriotism in fact functioned adequately as a cohesive element only so long as it was still reinforced to some extent by the influence of religion: that is, until the present era.

If we had wished to make value judgements, we should have had to place the Christian effort in a different perspective from the one which appears in these pages. The purpose of this enquiry has not been to judge, but merely to analyse. We have been tracing the use which was made of the classical heritage and the forces which determined the fortunes of that heritage. The Christian tradition has figured therefore as a limiting factor which checked men's curiosity and set bounds to their zeal to learn from the pagan past. The further circumstance that such a check may have been beneficial lies outside the scope of our analysis.

IV. THE NEW SCHOLARSHIP

The third trend which characterised the sixteenth century was the new orientation given to the work of the professional scholars. Earlier scholarship had been concerned partly with imitation, partly with its attempt to contribute something of value in the specialised fields which the Middle Ages had already explored. By 1520 these specific aims were largely fulfilled. Imitation was reduced to a science, firmly founded in a series of excellent grammars and hand-books. Medicine was shaking off the hampering chains of Galen and about to embark on a lively period of independent growth. Law was similarly on the threshold of a new age when it would be guided by 'common sense and the *Institutes*'. Apart from a few good texts and translations of Greek medical writers, and apart from a certain amount of yet undiscovered information concerning those aspects of Roman life that had a relevance for law, Humanism had no more to contribute in these fields where its work had been so important. Of the realms that had called for its scholarship for a hundred years one alone now remained. Philosophy, and in particular Platonic philosophy, still required attention.

The history of sixteenth-century Platonism has already been mentioned in connection with La Ramée's contributions to the study of logic. He was a Frenchman; and in general the focus of Platonic learning shifts during this period from Italy to France and England. The scholars of Bembo's generation (1470–1547) continued in the traditions of the Florentine Academy and contributed little original work that was of much note. The sack of Rome in 1527 proved a grievous disaster which had a profoundly discouraging effect on the intellectual life of the peninsula; and after 1550 the Inquisition and the Index were distinctly unfavourable to those forms of classical scholarship that had a close connection with contemporary thought. Thus Italian Platonism stagnated.*

France took up the cause that Italy let drop. Slowly but surely the texts on which speculation depended were made available to northern scholars. It is true that Ficino's mystical works were published long before his great translation; and when the latter did appear, the editions (1519 and 1522) were small owing to the cost and did not reach many hands. But the third edition of 1533, the fourth of 1536, the appearance of individual Platonic works, some in Greek, some in Latin, and finally a number of excellent French versions to some extent remedied this state of affairs.*

French Platonism was certainly ahead of its German and English rivals. In the early part of the century, German Humanism had looked to Reuchlin for guidance where Greek studies were concerned; but when Reuchlin visited Italy in 1490, he had been more interested by the Cabbalistic than by the Platonic aspect of Pico's studies; and this fact may account for the distrust with which his pious colleagues regarded the Florentine school. The name of Plato is missing from the list of authors recommended for study at Wittenberg in 1546; and as late as 1550 no work of his had been translated into German.

In England, the situation was nearly as bad. It is true that prejudice was absent, but indifference reigned in its stead. Plato remained the possession of a select few. If Colet had been impressed by the ideas of Ficino, and if More had imitated the *Republic* in his *Utopia*, their example had not been followed. Ascham's account of the revival of Greek studies in Cambridge when Cheke was appointed Professor of Greek (1540), is probably exaggerated. He was writing about his friends whom he would naturally wish to flatter; and in any case he gives Plato only a casual mention. The dialogues may have been read at Cambridge round about 1540; but it does not seem likely that they were read by many; and the lack of English translations suggests that the number may have been very small indeed.

Italian Platonism was in decline, though it retained some traces of its formerly vigorous life. In France the movement was on the upgrade; and it was growing in England also but to a much lesser extent. These geographical variations are, however, of little importance. Wherever the study of Plato was pursued, it had much the same character. The want of technical accuracy which had marked the fifteenth-century Florentine school spread to all its intellectual heirs; and that is the fact which demands our attention.

The reading of Ficino produced a turmoil in men's ideas which found expression in original thought on current issues. It contributed little to the technical advance of philosophy, but offered useful solutions for problems which were troubling the conscience of the age. Lefèvre and Colet, who rank as Ficino's leading disciples in the north, were theologians whose aim was to revive religious feeling and who made their Platonism an instrument of that revival.* In Ficino's *Theologia Platonica* the philosophical concepts of Christianity are somewhat arbitrarily identified with the philosophical concepts of Plato and Plotinus. Philosophy is pursuit of truth. God is truth. Therefore philosophy is religion. But Christian practice was left out of the picture. Lefèvre's approach (and to some extent Colet's) was altogether different. Their Platonism was a background, first to a mystical piety which encouraged a direct appeal to God, and secondly to an historical study of the Scriptures; in other words to a Christianity that had already much in common with the individualist religion of the Reformers.

This religious orientation was ultimately to prove dominant; but for a time its primacy was disputed by another current of Platonic thought which took its rise this time specifically from the *Republic*. More's *Utopia* borrowed Plato's poetic concept of an ideal society and used its framework to propound rational solutions to social problems. Echoes of his inspiration are to be found in Rabelais (though the inhabitants of Thélème do not form a proper society, for they are kept by the labours of others) and also in the educational writings of Ascham and Mulcaster. But in spite of its brilliant beginnings, this line of interpretation remained secondary.

The greatest number of the French Platonists (and they had no compeers in England) followed the lead of Lefèvre. The centre of the movement was the court of Marguerite de Navarre. Lefèvre in his old age, Despériers and Dolet, the translators, Heroët, the poet of Platonic affinities, all benefited from her protection. Marguerite had two great interests, religion and love. Like so many women, she derived abiding happiness from what she conceived as a personal relationship to God; and she had been attracted therefore to the doctrines of Lefèvre, who not only followed the general practice of emphasising the individual's direct responsibility to God (which betrays the common origin of the Humanist Renaissance and its apparent opposite, the pious Reformation), but also incorporated in his teachings a considerable element of mysticism. Marguerite had been influenced by Lefèvre's disciples, Roussel and Briçonnet in her early formative years and her contacts with them continued throughout her maturity. The so-called Platonic element in her religion was an echo of their mystical teachings, whose sources went back in part to Ficino, but in part through Lefèvre to the older tradition of the Rhineland mystics. 'Be kind, be kind and you will be saints' Ruysbroek had said, and Marguerite would have echoed him.

To this religious amalgam she added another which was to some extent of her own making. As Lefèvre had reshaped the theology of the Florentines, so she took their social tenets and gave them a novel content. The spiritualisation of love as we find it described in the fourth book of *Il Cortegiano* is an abstract concept. The Italians were concerned with the nature of beauty and with the relative worth of the satisfactions it offered. If Bembo condemns sensual love, it is because:

> Doing, a filthy pleasure is, and short;
> And done, we straight repent us of the sport.

Et taedet Veneris statim peractae—the attitude is subjective and takes only the man into account. Marguerite was a woman who lived in a rough society. What great lord of any later age, having a princess for his guest, would put her in a room with a secret door so as to rape her in the middle of the night and be turned from his design only by the most determined physical resistance of the lady and her maid? What modern husband hearing his wife retail this anecdote of her youth would remark that the lord should have killed the maidservant and used force to accomplish his purpose? Marguerite's interest was not for the dichotomy of spiritual and sensual love, but for the contrasts of selfishness and consideration. In her way she was an early champion of women's rights, wanting to see established a relationship between the sexes in which the dignity and happiness of the weaker were fairly respected.

She subtly blends these ideas with the usual concept of Platonic love. Her poems and the *Heptaméron* contain therefore an Italian Platonism which has been doubly changed, its cosmological speculations leavened with piety, its metaphysics of love applied to a social problem. No one followed Marguerite in her feminist preoccupations. Her client Heroët was a conventional Neoplatonist, and the *Parfaicte Amye* is no more than an echo of the Florentine poets. But her particular brand of mysticism was shared by all her circle. It is instructive to consider that many of the translators and students of Plato were suspected of Protestant sympathies, that the precise location of Lefèvre's theology between the orthodox and the heretical has remained a puzzle for scholars, that Dolet was burnt in the Place Maubert, La Ramée murdered in the St Bartholomew massacre and Despériers was saved from the charge of Protestantism only because he was thought an atheist. Platonic thought in France was largely subordinated to the interests of religion.

Thus, the one field in which learning still pursued its fifteenth-century course became within a very short time a religious battle-ground. Just because Platonism could affect men's beliefs and conduct, just because it popularised ideas that had a contemporary relevance, it was involved, like the Humanist education of the schools, in the struggle of the rival creeds. Its fate serves therefore as a suitable introduction to the general history of Humanist scholarship during the period. It was the exception which emphatically proved the rule.

The main purposes of sixteenth-century scholarship were to establish correct texts of the ancient authors and to elucidate their exact meaning. The famous Humanists of the period pored over manuscripts, bringing a vast linguistic and historical knowledge to bear on problems of reading and interpretation. They made their famous inspired guesses whose inspiration, however, had to rest on the tedious preparatory labours of years. In this work they followed a long-standing tradition. As Sir John Sandys has shown, they used and added to stores of knowledge which had been collected by Alexandrian, Byzantine and Italian scholars, by Aristarchus and Aristophanes, by 'Suidas' and Arethas, by Filelfo and Guarino. But they differed from their predecessors and more especially from their immediate predecessors, in one important respect. Scholarship played a secondary role in the work of a Guarino or an Erasmus. It was subordinated to wider interests, to the cult of fame through eloquence, to social and religious preoccupations. But in the life of a Turnèbe or a Casaubon, the settling of *Hoti's* business took precedence of all else.

We noted earlier, when considering Shakespeare, that by the last quarter of the sixteenth century the long task of appropriating the classical heritage was virtually over; and it had for nearly fifty years before then been the chosen task of popular writers rather than of technical scholars. From about 1520 onwards, the scholars as such were free to follow their own interest. They were no longer pressed to satisfy urgent demands from outside sources as they had been ever since the days of Desiderius of Vienne. They were not called upon to provide the material for the training of Biblical exegetes or logicians or lawyers. They were not drawn in to support a middle-class revolution. The heritage which was their speciality had now given to the world all that it could for the moment conveniently give, and from this point on, their studies were without an immediate practical relevance.

Moreover, just as classical learning in general was becoming dissociated from the mainstream of contemporary thought, so Humanism in particular, the specific product of fourteenth- and fifteenth-century needs, found its usefulness suddenly at an end as those needs were satisfied. The ambitious who wanted to learn how to write now had all the guidance they required in the works of Erasmus or could take their models from the vernaculars. The seekers after a design for living could read their Castiglione or their Elyot. They no longer needed to turn for help to the Humanists of the moment. The movement initiated by Petrarch was killed by its own success.

If the growth of human societies was governed by strictly utilitarian considerations, classical studies would at this juncture have dwindled into insignificance. But since social patterns once established tend to survive and even develop by the mere weight of habit, that likely result did not occur. Besides the adoption of the classical discipline as the standard vehicle of education also made, as we shall see, for the survival of Greek and Latin scholarship which took on the new, if not very important, role of providing school studies with their indispensable specialist background. Thus, from the economic point of view, the scholars were safe, while in general they were left to their own devices as to what they would study.

This theoretical freedom had, however, certain limitations. After the middle of the sixteenth century, a man who knew his ancient authors, his ancient history, and nothing else, could not contribute much to the advancement of other fields of knowledge. Grosseteste, the Aristotelian, had without further trouble been able to stand forth as the finest scientist of his day. But Victorius, who knew his Aristotle far better than Grosseteste, could not three hundred years later hope to vie with Galileo.

In these circumstances, the classical cobblers were more or less compelled to stick to their specialised last. They devoted themselves to the preparation and interpretation of texts and to completing their knowledge of antiquity beyond the degree that had been sufficient to serve the needs of the Renaissance. For this purpose they built on foundations that the fifteenth century had incidentally constructed, on the careful study of language initiated by Valla, on the archaeological researches of Ciriaco, Schedel and Flavio Biondo, and above all on the work of the men who prepared the first printed editions.

If the external events had been responsible for the growing isolation of classical learning as a self-sufficient speciality, the invention of printing had a good deal to do with the particular form that isolation eventually took. In earlier ages, the scholar who corrected a manuscript or explained a confused passage must have been conscious that he worked largely for himself. The slow rate at which books were produced, the danger of fresh errors creeping in with every copy, left very little ground for the hope that any particular emendation or commentary would become definitive. The best the critic could expect from his labours was to make one family of manuscripts out of many carry a more accurate version. So textual criticism was regarded as a necessary but rather thankless occupation, undertaken to benefit one's own studies and one's own immediate pupils. Printing changed all that. A reading once established, a difficulty once elucidated, became patently a permanent possession. The advances of philological learning were plainly visible; and scholars were naturally attracted to what was an obviously fruitful field.

The imposing edifice of learning reared by sixteenth-century scholarship shows what human curiosity and the human love of perfection can achieve when once the attendant circumstances are wholly favourable. Both textual criticism and the study of ancient institutions in which the century excelled owed their first beginnings to a wish to satisfy popular demand. The educated public which Aldus and Froben sought to serve called for accurate printed texts, and the lawyers faced with the problems of a society which was freeing itself from feudalism were anxious for more exact knowledge about the political and social arrangements of ancient Rome. But once the scholars were set properly to work collating manuscripts and smoothing out the tangled skeins of incorrect syntax, they persisted in their tasks long after the *editiones principes* had satisfied the avidity of the reading public. The high standards of accuracy which had been established in the first place by the editors of the Greek texts who had risen to the challenge of an exceptionally difficult task, were rapidly adopted by their colleagues working on the easier Latin authors. The triumphs of Chalcondyles, Lascaris and Musurus were equalled by Politian, Merula and Beroaldo. By 1520, the great work of printing the classics was for the most part complete. But the tradition continued to develop. Perfection was pursued for its own sake; and the giants of French scholarship, from Longolius to Casaubon, poured the immense resources of their knowledge in an endless series of editions and commentaries. For classical studies had won themselves an unassailable position thanks to their past services to the progress of the Renaissance; and the classical student could now labour free from all uneasiness in the assurance of that esteem which is normally given only to those who serve ends dear to the public heart. For a brief period he was to receive that esteem and social recognition even though his interests no longer had a direct social relevance. These were the favourable circumstances to which we referred earlier. Complete freedom was conjoined with a complete social acceptance; and the results were remarkable.

Similarly, the men who explored the intricacies of Roman economics and imperial administration did not stop when they had settled the legal difficulties which had originally prompted their enquiries. By the end of the fifteenth century this line of research had come to engage the energies of many able minds, most notable of whom was perhaps Guillaume Budé. Standing half-way between Petrarch and the pure scholars of the late sixteenth century, he belongs patently to an age which resembles our own, when a new kind of society is being built. If he laid considerable stress on the formation of character, it was the education of princes that primarily held his interest because he felt that the prosperity of states depended upon their rulers. If he championed the claims of eloquence against the crudities of the Sorbonne, it was as an instrument of knowledge because he felt that facts had no value when they were not clearly expressed. And if he sought tirelessly for information about Greek and Latin, or about the Greek and Roman past, it was always for some practical purpose. His researches were intended to serve the lawyers, administrators and theologians.

Budé's first important book was the *Annotationes ad Pandectas* published in 1508. Jettisoning once and for all the medieval reinterpretation of Roman law in feudal terms, he elucidated the original significance of his text with reference to the social and economic conditions that had actually prevailed in ancient times, and to which the conditions of his own day bore a marked similarity. By doing this he not only established the contemporary relevance of Roman law, which Italian jurists like Jason de Mayne had for some time suspected without being able to prove; but he also placed the study of it on a systematic basis, so that within the next half century Alciat and Cujas could lay the foundations of modern jurisprudence. Budé had been trained as a lawyer, so the character of the *Annotationes* is not surprising. His next book was also intended to help his professional colleagues; for by that time it had been established that the interpretation of Roman legal usage required a knowledge of the society it served. The question of the real value of Roman measures of weight and money had long troubled scholars, and confusion on this vital point had prevented any proper understanding of the Roman economic system. Budé undertook to collate and sift the evidence and after six years of patient labour, summarised his conclusions in the *de Asse et partibus eius* (1514). The book proved extremely popular, passing through ten editions in twenty years and establishing Budé's reputation as one of the most learned men of his day. After that his fame placed obstacles in the way of his scholarship. For he was employed on diplomatic work. His correspondence grew in volume; and from 1520 onwards he had to spend a great deal of time supervising the royal library. Nevertheless, he struggled though more slowly with another enormous task: the compilation of a dictionary of Greek legal terms, which finally appeared in 1529 as the *Commentarii Linguae Graecae*. Like all Budé's writings, it is a hotch-potch of notes interspersed with short essays, some of which run to over a thousand words. The stylists and the wits condemned it, and the treasures of shrewd observation that lighten its pages have not been sufficient to save it from oblivion. But it was welcomed by the lawyers of the time, by the students of Greek and by every man who had the progress of knowledge at heart. It fascinated Alciat, Rabelais and Turnèbe; and many of its conclusions, as well as the incidental brilliant ideas scattered at random through its notes, can be found repeated in their writings.

Budé's researches were continued after his death, but with a diminished vigour that reflected their lessening practical importance. Gradually, but inevitably, classical scholarship drew away from other subjects and used its established techniques to put its own house in ever finer order. The information provided by the ancient authors was summarised in a number of spheres that had received scant attention earlier. Glareanus wrote on geography; Charles Estienne on botanical names; J. C. Scaliger on literary criticism. The discovery of the *Fasti Capitolini* in 1547 brought chronology, on which Glareanus had already done some useful work, back into the limelight and the next decade was filled with loud arguments of Robortelli and Sigonio. The archaeological descriptions of Biondo's *Italia Illustrata* were amplified by such successors as Marliano, Agustin and Ligorio.* The glory that had been Greece, the grandeur that had been Rome, were neatly embodied in vast handbooks where seekers after knowledge could find their facts without trouble. The *Bibliotheca Universalis* of Conrad Gesner (1545–1549) was an immense biographical dictionary of all Greek, Latin and Hebrew writers, coupled with an encyclopaedia of the Arts and Sciences. Gesner intended it for the use of scholars in all branches of knowledge; but already much of its information was of a sort which would interest only those who studied antiquity for its own sake. The links between classical studies and the more advanced forms of contemporary knowledge were fast disappearing.

The Italian sixteenth century has been justly described as the *saeculum Victorianum*. The Florentine Vettori, or Victorius to give him his more usual name, was not only the most eminent scholar of his generation, the editor of numerous Greek and Latin texts, the definitive commentator of Aristotle, and the author of thirty-eight books of *Variae Lectiones*; he was also the perfect type of the men who in Italy and elsewhere had come to dominate classical learning. Robertelli, the author of the first treatise on textual criticism,* Nizzoli and Majoragio, the two giants of Ciceronian commentary, the restless and versatile Muret, the copious Lambin, the careful Joseph Scaliger and the nervous Casaubon, all conformed to the pattern of Victorius. With vast knowledge and painstaking accuracy, they brought text after text to a state of near perfection. When they tried to move outside of their special field, they met with disapproval and often persecution. The fate of Dolet and La Ramée has already been mentioned. Buchanan was driven from place to place, perhaps deservedly for he lived as a reformer in a Catholic country. Muret was forbidden in Rome to lecture on Plato, and Paleario fell a victim to the Inquisition. Eventually most of them made a virtue of necessity and retired so far within their ivory tower that contacts with life became painful. J. J. Scaliger was unable to face an audience; and when Casaubon came to stay with the Warden of Merton, who was a worldly scholar after the manner of Cheke, he looked upon his host with wonder and a considerable measure of dismay.

So the study of the classical heritage entered on a new phase which was to be ennobled by the names of Bentley and Porson, Jowett, Housman and Wilamowitz. It was to provide opportunities still for the exercise of integrity, patience and wit, for rare erudition and exquisite taste, for all the noblest of the human virtues; but the period of its greatest services to mankind was definitely over. From this time on, classical learning belonged to those branches of knowledge whose contribution may be relevant to progress in the future, but which are luxuries in the present; and it had been far otherwise. During that dark millennium whose story we have examined, the scholars had been the indispensable agents of cultural advance. Not only the triumphs of literature, but law, craftsmanship, science and administration itself had a necessary basis in their work. The flowering of the Renaissance had owed to them the broad perspectives of its rationality and the taste that excused its luxuries. The greatness of an Alcuin, an Irnerius, a Petrarch, measured in personal terms, may fall below the standard achieved by a Scaliger or a Casaubon; but seen in the perspectives of history, they are unique. Never have mere students of books been in a position to give so much.

The movements we have described in the latter half of this chapter, the ordering of education under the aegis of the *pietas litterata* and the new orientation of scholarship, constitute the two halves of a single process, whereby classical learning was adapted to its new role. From 1600 onwards, the classical discipline served to maintain the civilisation it had built up, by giving each generation that understanding of anti-quity which the Humanist origins of culture demanded, while for the next two hundred years scholarship existed partly as a survival, and partly as a necessary adjunct to the education of the time. With the nine-teenth century this situation was to change again. New specialities were to arise making necessary a fresh approach to the classical heritage for new types of information, while a certain decline in the educational popularity of the classical discipline was eventually to make the pursuit of its traditional enquiries less attractive so that our own time is once again an epoch of change.

The persistence with which the classical heritage was explored until it had yielded the best that it could give is little short of amazing. But perhaps the most arresting feature of its whole long history is the way in which that exploration was conditioned at every turn by the pressure of immediate requirements. It was always some urgent practical need that set the scholars to their task and gave their curiosity, which other wise lost itself in aimless roamings, a definite and fruitful purpose. It was always some practical need, to preserve some desired *status quo*, that acted as a bar to the pursuit of researches which went beyond what was immediately useful. The history of learning is not a free field. It is the history of society.

CHAPTER IX

EDUCATION AND THE CLASSICAL HERITAGE

We have seen how the educational possibilities of the classical heritage came to light one by one in a succession determined by the challenge of events, and how they developed in a manner directly dependent upon social needs.

For some time after the break-up of the old order, the memorials of the Graeco-Roman past lay scattered in a thousand manuscripts, inscriptions, monuments and works of art which could not be interpreted without expert study. Roman civilisation survived in every town, in every village almost, but it was as useless to their inhabitants as an outcrop of coal to a shivering savage. Western man had little understanding of the extent or value of his intellectual inheritance.

The first discoveries of what Latin literature had to offer were made in the eighth century, by which time the virtual disappearance of the imperial schools had led to such a decline in education that the clergy were no longer competent to read their Bibles. Further retreat down the road of ignorance would have endangered the entire fabric of the Church's authority; and at that point, under the pressure of dire need, some of the ancient grammar curriculum was brought back into use. It is true that the Christian writers of the patristic age held first place as text-books and as models for literary imitation. But the pagans were not forgotten. Donatus and Priscian were read for the rules of syntax and prosody. Virgil was popular. Suetonius inspired one famous work —Einhard's *Life of Charlemagne*; and even mathematics, history and natural science came in for a certain measure of attention. By the beginning of the ninth century, the classical heritage was universally accepted as an excellent instrument for teaching first the Latin language which was the official medium of the Church, secondly the art of writing in that language, and thirdly that modicum of general knowledge which Carolingian man felt he required.

The next step forward was taken two hundred years later when growing prosperity had brought in its train a demand for legal and medical information, and when the theologians discovered that dialectic was needed to solve their difficulties. After a fresh crisis of learning, the Justinian Code, the Medical Corpus and the philosophy of Aristotle became the objects of keen professional interest, and about the same time the aristocratic courts of the period began to cultivate those aesthetic delights which are conventionally regarded as the appropriate accompaniments of luxury and leisure. The clerks who fluttered round the aristocratic flame, as indigent parasites or as cultured friends, made these delights their chief preoccupation. The successful among them revived the seductions of Ovid. The unsuccessful found relief in elegiac lamentation or in imitating the rages of Juvenal. There was a rebirth of erotic, elegiac and satirical poetry. The life of the cities and courts took on a new fullness; and the classical literatures were further established in public esteem, on the one hand as a mine of useful knowledge, on the other as a guide to pleasure and beauty.

The Humanism of the twelfth century was followed by the organising fervour of the Scholastics, by a hundred years of consolidation and a hundred years of slow decline. The gifts which the classical heritage still held in store were temporarily neglected. The haste of intellectual advance halted and took breath.

Meanwhile, the fortunes of Greek studies in the East had followed a line analogous to the Western history just described. The ancient literature, which the Dark Ages had tended to forget, was restored to a place of honour in the schools at the end of the ninth century since the victorious Iconodules saw in Hellenism a support against the Eastern beliefs that had threatened to undermine their Church. This revival, like its twelfth-century analogue in the West, was concerned primarily with practical information. It produced encyclopedias, and when their stored-up knowledge was conveniently to hand, dwindled into nothingness. The further development of Byzantine learning, its exploration of the poetic and personal universe of the past, came a hundred years later, as the by-product of an emergent nationalism. Worshipping the literature of Athens because it was Greek, the generation of Psellus accepted every ancient author, the literary as well as the informative, with equal zeal. It accepted them, however, for a culture which was concerned only to preserve and not to create, for a culture which was hamstrung by the Byzantine folly of clinging to a language too difficult to learn.

The final stage therefore in the development of classical studies was reached only after the union of Byzantine and Western knowledge in the fifteenth century. The life of the Italian cities was dominated during that period by the needs of the rising middle class. The new capitalists wanted to consolidate their mastery of the material environment, and so set great store by accurate means of expression and calculation. They lived in cities and so were concerned to discover the best forms of civic life. They possessed immense wealth and so became interested in the arts which create the only unique possessions. To serve these ends, their intellectuals uncovered the last secrets of the classical heritage. The Renaissance revealed to an amazed world those elements in classical poetry, history and speculation that bore on the personal life. Humanism became equated with the free and full development of the individual.

When the classical student of today considers this long record, considers how much his speciality gave Europe in the past, he is bound to ask himself what relevance, if any, that past has to the future. Which of the intellectual treasures that delighted our ancestors would be welcome to students now?

To answer this question, in so far as it can be answered, we must retrace the narrative of the preceding pages with the requirements of the twentieth century at the forefront of our minds.

The first of the educational potentialities of the classical heritage to come to light was its usefulness for teaching a correct and forceful Latin. The Carolingians, who were dependent on Latin as a medium of communication, derived considerable benefits from their grammar course. But here, it is immediately obvious that we could not expect similar advantages. We no longer compose our learned books in Latin. Our diplomacy takes its language from Washington; and any attempt to put the clock back would end in ignominious failure.

The centuries which followed the Carolingian Age valued the ancient writings primarily as source books of practical knowledge. The works which were their chief authorities are still on our shelves; but once again it is clear that we cannot expect to find them as useful as they were in the past. The medical, mathematical and scientific achievements of Greece and Rome have been so firmly incorporated into the groundwork of our present disciplines and have been so far surpassed by present-day research that their specific study is no longer relevant for the subject they once glorified. The modern doctor, mathematician or scientist who wants to extend the boundaries of his speciality will not find much to help him in the classics. We cannot expect a new Salerno or a new rush of enthusiasm for the physiological treatises of Aristotle.

The medieval period had, it is true, jurists and dialecticians as well as scientific experts; and it is also true that ancient law and philosophy have not been superseded as completely as ancient medicine. The specialist still finds the Greek philosophers illuminating and the *Digest* worthy of serious study. Moreover, both the Greek philosophers and the Roman law books can serve the beginner as a useful introduction to the fields of enquiry which they represent. But the triumphs of classical learning in the age of Irnerius and Abélard could not be revived on this slight basis. The specialists whose researches would demand linguistic knowledge of the sort provided by the classical discipline are too few in number to justify the presence of Latin and Greek as subjects in a competitive curriculum, while instruction in elementary law and philosophy can be just as easily given by means of translations as by recourse to the original texts.

The benefits that the men of the Middle Ages derived from their classical studies have little relevance for us; and it is plain that we must either find in antiquity something more than our ancestors discovered, or our classical learning must derive its main justification from the realm which was so brilliantly exploited during the Renaissance. We have seen that we cannot model ourselves on Alcuin or Grosseteste; but there is still Petrarch to consider.

The Renaissance approach was complex. It had at least two main facets: the aesthetic and the personal, a preoccupation with form and the development of the personality. The two must be considered separately; and it will be convenient to take the former first.

The general run of medieval writing before the Renaissance is marked by certain recurrent faults. It tends to be shapeless and repetitive. There are too many distinctions in the plainest argument, too many digressions in the simplest narrative. Descriptive passages contain too many words which 'neither strike, pierce, nor possess the sight of soul'. Impetus is sacrificed to a passion for detail unless—as happens of course in the greater masterpieces—the unaccountable felicities of genius intervene to correct a defective technique. The literature of the seventeenth century on the other hand, written after the Renaissance, is notably free from these particular faults. Even the lesser writers are aware that a literary work ought to aim at making a unified impression and that at all stages the combination of details counts for more than the details themselves. They are in consequence lucid where their medieval predecessors, who have a superior knowledge of logic, often leave the reader in a mental fog.

This difference reflects the achievement of the Humanists. Their signal merit was to have switched the attention of their contemporaries from the theory of logic and rhetoric to the more fruitful practice of imitation. The notebook system of Guarino involved an anatomising of classical literature which had much in common with the analyses of the medieval scholars; but it was not theoretical. The extracts which sought to cover the whole field of language and human experience were carefully memorised. Since some of them dealt with the use of particular words, while others provided illustrations and developments of common themes, the effect of this memorising was to transform the student's manner of thought, and this had manifest repercussions on literary composition.

The eagerness of the Humanists to revive a correct classical Latin led them to watch the meanings of words and to trace with particular attention how the same word often takes on a subtly different sense in different contexts. They learnt to think in phrases and hammered out a linguistic instrument—the Latin of the Renaissance—which was lucidly adequate for all the ordinary needs of communication. It is true that their emphasis on a past usage which did not yield precise definitions would not have earned the approval of an exact logician. But where the devotee of Aristotle could write with exactitude only about theology or metaphysics (since the defining of his terms was too laborious a process for him to extend it beyond the fields which interested him most), the Humanists with their less impeccable methods could cover the whole range of contemporary experience and communicate their ideas reasonably well on a large number of subjects.

Similarly, the conscious intention to produce works of art rivalling those of the ancients led to that greater awareness of the general characteristics typical of each literary genre, which we notice in the seventeenth century. When the medieval poet Alfanus of Salerno imitated Horace, his imitations were Horatian only in their metres. When the Humanist poet Ronsard imitated Pindar, he paid little attention to the details of metre but was at great pains to keep the pattern of strophe, antistrophe and epode. He also followed the Pindaric arrangement of themes, thus emphasising the general rather than the particular features of his model. It was a change in method without which the development of the classical French drama, for example, would have proved impossible.

No good purpose would be served, however, by retailing in detail all that the Humanist writers gained from their study of the classics. What Humanism made its own has since become a part of the European heritage; and from the viewpoint of present needs, the gains of

Humanism are of less interest than the method which made them possible. The lessons which great literatures can teach us about the mystery of creative writing are admittedly inexhaustible. The interplay of experience and artistic expression in a literary work of genius will never be fully understood. Too many details are involved; and that is why a method such as imitation, which demands a great knowledge of detail, merits serious notice. We have no reason to suppose that the Humanists managed to learn all that imitation could reveal. They were primarily concerned to remedy certain defects in their technique of writing and looked no further than their immediate problems. If we were to study the classical masterpieces with the same attention to detail as they did and with the impulse to create works as good as the ones we read, it is not impossible that we too would discover solutions to the new problems that vex us.

The aesthetic interest of the classics cannot be lightly dismissed, nor can the cultural, which was the second string to the Humanist bow. We have had occasion to mention above the part played by experience in the construction of a work of literary art. Whatever else it may be, literature is also an interpretation of experience, an interpretation that tells us a great deal also about the interpreter. As we know, this was a point which the Humanists amply realised. Many of them read the classics primarily for the purpose of getting an insight into the Greek and Roman outlook on life; and the moral attitudes with which our immediate history makes us familiar—the abounding confidence of Petrarch, the calculating opportunism of Machiavelli, the scepticism of Montaigne and the defensive self-affirmation of the Neo-Stoics—which have their modern parallels in the ideas of Gide, Sorel, France and Sartre—all drew sustenance from classical sources. We have antiquity to thank that our culture includes these many variations on the Humanist outlook which takes the individual as its final court of appeal and envisages him as a responsible being face to face with an independent and often recalcitrant environment.

So there exist at least two good reasons why this cultural approach to the classics, which interested the Renaissance, should still be of interest today. Not only are we bound to experience a certain curiosity about a culture which contributed so much to our own, but we cannot reasonably blind ourselves to the fact that a line of enquiry which proved eminently successful in the past is unlikely to have lost all its original value; and to these two reasons a third might be added. Our generation has fallen under the spell of the social sciences.

The study of society, which fifty years ago was still the preserve of philosophical amateurs, has become a professional interest which—to judge by the number of books produced—commands a vast audience; and the Graeco-Roman world, which we know better than any other culture possessed of a high degree of material civilisation, could obviously provide the sociologist with information unobtainable elsewhere. Sociology is a still indeterminate field of learning to which philosophers and moralists, economists, demographers, political theorists, students of religion, students of administration and students of crime have all added their mite. But perhaps the greatest contribution to its advance has come from the allied and more clearly defined field cultivated by the anthropologist, who does his research living rigorously among the primitive peoples he wants to survey. It has been proved true once again that nothing illuminates so vividly as comparison; and the organisation of primitive societies has given us the best insight we have into the complexities of our own world. But if the Manus, the Trobriand and the Pueblo cultures have been able to furnish us with precious categories of interpretation and richly suggestive parallels, could we not expect a more advanced society, such as the Graeco-Roman, to perform this same service with an even greater efficiency? Ancient culture had its spiritual centre in the small independent city; and the life of Roman or Athenian citizens satisfied many of the impulses which we must obviously neglect in the mass states of today. If the field-worker could visit Greece or Rome as he visits the tribes of New Guinea, the value of his researches would be beyond question.

It follows therefore that the interest of classical studies for the sociologist (and for that modern public which looks to him for enlightenment) depends upon the extent to which the classical heritage can illuminate its parent culture; and it is here that the experience of the Renaissance appears relevant. The Humanists of the fifteenth century impressed the categories, the values, the very sensibility of the ancients upon the minds of their pupils and disciples. They remoulded the outlook of educated Europe so well that the products of the seventeenth-century schools stood nearer to Cicero than to the medieval monks who had been their immediate predecessors. *L'espace cornélien c'est la Cité* remarks a recent critic of Corneille, M. Octave Nadal. This achievement of the Humanists argues an extraordinary understanding of their models, an understanding which far surpasses the normal knowledge of the historian.

In many ways the past is outside our grasp. We cannot cross-question the dead, measure their intelligence or count the incidence of their daily activities. We can analyse the working of institutions. We can reconstruct the development of ideologies. We can trace the ebb and flow of custom and taste. But there is always a danger that these analyses and reconstructions may prove incorrect because they are too theoretical. Based upon a twofold selection (since the historian picks out a particular class of facts after vicissitudes of survival have already limited the field of what is available) they remain hypotheses which other hypotheses based on a slightly different set of data can easily replace. The conclusions of the economic, the political and even the religious historian must remain uncertain if they cannot be checked against a more direct and personal knowledge of the past. The student of the social sciences who deals with the present is often saved from advancing an incorrect theory about the nature of an institution or a belief because of his direct acquaintance with the people in whose lives that institution or belief plays a functional part. The historian lacks that safeguard—over a great portion of his field of study.

In certain cases however—and the golden ages of Athens and Rome constitute one of these exceptions—an extensive literature, broad in its choice of topics and competent in its execution, can to some degree replace the personal contact which is denied to the historian in its ordinary form.

> Non omnis moriar; multaque pars mei
> Vitabit Libitinam.

The poet's claims of immortality have some foundation in fact. The two ancient literatures preserve the two languages of antiquity in the complex vigour of their heyday. The evocative compressions of the poets, the fireworks of the orators, the logical arguments and the long sober passages of narrative which we find in verse and prose alike, enshrine the living speech which was their source; and as the spoken word reflects the mind of the speaker, they can be said to enshrine, along with the speech, the intellectual universe of antiquity. Their linguistic fabric holds in suspension the essence of Greece and Rome, so that they could inform us about the life of the ancient cities and tell us all we need to know, even without the innumerable facts about ancient ideas, values and forms of sensibility which they overtly transmit. The data furnished by the classical philosophers and the historians are incontrovertibly precious. The classical legends which present the prelogical experience of a people who had just risen out of the Neolithic mist are perhaps more precious still. But in the last analysis these overtly expressed conceptions are of less importance than the information we derive incidentally from the manner in which they are presented. The obvious content of literature is less significant than the mechanism of thought and language employed by its authors. Attic Greek is our surest guide to Athens, classical Latin our surest guide to Rome. Nothing mirrors the nature of a civilisation so clearly as its habitual medium of expression.

The relevance of literary studies for historical understanding has been exhaustively discussed since Taine first brought the topic to popular notice; and it is agreed nowadays in general terms that the historian cannot safely neglect the evidence provided by philology. This general view requires, however, a measure of qualification. Not every form of literary study is equally useful. History demands cultural insight; and that insight can come only through the recognition of thousands of tiny details from which the common categories of thought and feeling are built up in their living reality. The systematic encouragement of this recognition was the main virtue of the Humanist techniques described in the preceding chapters.

We have some reason to suppose therefore that classical studies could be made to serve that sociological interest which appears a typical feature of the modern outlook. Whether that interest will continue, and how far its influence will be felt in the educational field, are matters of conjecture which only the future can decide. But since such a development is at least possible, it is worth noting that there would be room for the classical discipline in a curriculum centred on social enquiry.

The more closely one examines the question, the more good reasons one finds to recommend the classical discipline. The conclusion which necessarily emerges from all theoretical enquiries is that the ancient literatures still have much to teach us. But when we put theory aside and look at the practice of our grammar schools we find that Greek studies have declined since the beginning of the century while the position of Latin as a major subject is persistently attacked. Many people believe that in another fifty years the two ancient languages will have vanished from the secondary curriculum. Now, it has been argued that this modern failure to recognise the educational potentialities of Greek and Latin is due to certain obvious defects in our modern methods of classics teaching; and the charge is not without foundation. We seem to have retained the dull preliminaries of the old Humanist course only to stop short at the very point where the Humanists began to acquire their vivid and satisfying knowledge of the past; and even if we did not stop short there, it is unlikely that we should ever equal the Humanist achievements, since we lack that final purpose which breathed life into their work. We do not read the classics in order to learn to write or in order to solve our daily problems of conduct. We have been half-hearted in our following of tradition, and at the same time we have made next to no effort to develop that type of approach which would canalise the contemporary interest in sociology. The present classical curriculum is unsatisfactory, and the necessary but highly specialised study of textual criticism does perhaps exercise too great influence over what should be an educational discipline. But these shortcomings which would justify a call for reform cannot, when we set them against the well-known and admitted benefits of classical learning, wholly explain the all too common tendency to reject that learning.

The student of the classics who is concerned about the future of his subject would be well advised therefore to turn his attention to what is often called, for want of a better name, the intellectual climate of the age. The past fortunes of the classical heritage are there to show us how social aspirations and interests can affect the course of education; and the present comparative neglect of the classical discipline originates in causes of the same broad order. It derives from an outlook deeply rooted in our whole present way of life.

The opponents of Greek and Latin take as their basic principle the view that the first task of a modern educator is to fit his charges for the complex activities of industry, commerce and administration. Taking this for granted, they go on to argue that schools should therefore place greatest emphasis on those subjects whose theory provides a background to scientific, technological and professional training. They do not altogether disdain the old Arts curriculum (for they admit that educated men necessarily have some interests beyond the vocational) but they would prefer to restrict the number of hours allotted to its pursuit. It is impossible to avoid the conclusion that Arts subjects rank in their opinion with those recreational activities which enlightened firms arrange for their staffs on the principle that all work and no play makes Jack a dull boy. But no firm would consider the play more important than the work; and so for those who think along these lines, the Arts subjects, relegated almost to the rank of hobbies whose function it is to make leisure more interesting, appear as mere ancillaries to the real business of education. As far as they are concerned, the classical discipline which requires a vast expenditure of time and energy is a luxury beyond our educational means.

From the strictly practical point of view, this popular modern outlook is an anachronism. Its origins go back to the days of 'whiskey
money' and the early polytechnics when our grandfathers faced the
problem of setting up for the first time some form of scientific and
technical education. Then the point at issue was how to train a minority
of future specialists, men whose work would lie wholly in the laboratory
or the machine shop; and all the propaganda which was produced in
favour of a preponderantly scientific curriculum must be interpreted in
the light of that all-important limitation. Today, however, the curriculum of the nineteenth-century science student is recommended for
the majority of our more intelligent children at the secondary level.
What had been planned as the training of a specialised class is now
advocated for the education of an extensive élite. As has happened
often before, in the logic schools of the Middle Ages for example, there
is a move to universalise a speciality which the public imagination has
clothed in a halo of romance; and this is happening without reference
to the fact that a great number of tasks in industry and commerce and
certainly in the civil and municipal services require for their performance only a small amount of scientific, technical or economic information, but demand primarily an understanding and judgement which the
currently admired forms of scientific, technological and commercial
training are ill-equipped to develop.

The belief that science, technology and vocational knowledge belong
together and their elements constitute the best possible school discipline
for our times cannot be justified on practical grounds; and if we want
to discover the reason why it is cherished by so many of our contemporaries, we must look not in the practical realm, but in the realm
of values and ideas. During the five centuries which followed the
advent of the Renaissance, social progress depended on the success of
the efforts made by individuals, and the liberal Humanism of the period
had for its aim to justify and encourage the enterprising, the genius and
the hero. Since then, the past sixty years have seen the rise of enormous
administrative and industrial organisations, each of which is concerned
to satisfy some specialised social or economic need, and whose impact
upon our lives is so marked and so persistent as to dwarf for us all but
the most outstanding individual contributions to human progress. The
nature of man's daily experience has altered, and the inferences which
we have unconsciously or half-consciously drawn from our circumstances are leading us to set aside the once admired possibilities of
individual development and to prize instead the massive organisations

which require our homage. So far this process has hardly reached the level of conscious reason, and when we formulate our emergent values we still employ categories acceptable to the individualism which originally formed our minds. Sometimes an organisation is identified with the whole of society, and its service is represented as socially useful; or doing one's job is identified with keeping one's self-respect and is thus given an absolute value. But such formulations merely mask a feeling whose bald reality man's intellect is not yet ready to accept; and what their advocates demand is in practice nothing less than that each of us should be fully at the disposal of the organisation he happens to serve.

The significance of this shift in human values will become apparent if we consider the character of the firms, corporations, Government Boards and Authorities that proliferate around us. They exist, as we have said, to carry out specialised tasks, and the policies of those who direct them are determined not by any overall conception of humanity but by the pressures of a particular need, which may be to sell more goods, to dig more coal, to collect a larger audience, to win higher rates of pay, or to provide some statutory service at minimum cost. Everything is planned with reference to consumers, listeners, readers, wage-earners and other such abstractions. The energies of millions are mobilised for fragmentary ends which take no account of that harmony of purposes and interests which each individual must of necessity try and establish within his own experience. Moreover, the labours which these great organisations demand are if anything even more specialised than the ends they pursue. The techniques of the assembly line have had an influence far beyond industrial practice. The majority of able men who have mastered some skill or professional competence are expected to spend their working hours performing with the exactitude that comes from repetition a small succession of tasks, to which they are bound for the rest of their lives since experience is regarded as a man's main qualification for employment, and a specialist knows only his speciality. They are also expected more and more to centre not only their working hours but the whole of their lives round their specialised task. The successes of industrial psychology have encouraged the view that eating and sleeping, exercise and amusement the satisfaction of intellectual curiosity and the relief of emotional tension are processes analogous to the oiling and maintenance required by the machines which are the workers' inanimate counterparts. They are necessary for efficiency; but they are to be provided for efficiency's sake.

Society always wears a double face as far as the individual is concerned. It furnishes certain services and demands others in return. But the services furnished by modern society provide only for certain selected needs while the services demanded similarly involve only a small number of each person's capabilities. The citizen of a modern state, absorbed in his specialised tasks, has been justly compared to the ant or the bee; but if we consider his leisure rather than his work, we may prefer to liken him to a customer at a fair surrounded by a ring of barkers, each of whom is competing for his full attention, so that he goes from one to another, deafened by their clamour, and never has a chance to think of what he is or what he wants. The ant-heap and the fair seem to belong to different worlds. Fundamentally, however, the man who has come to resemble an ant and the befuddled fair-goer suffer the same kind of frustration. Both find that a part of their being has been elevated above the whole. The importance of some limited trait, impulse or interest has been over-emphasised at the expense of an inner harmony and the integrating power of the will.

If we take this characteristic of modern life into account, and if we come to see that the ethics of fragmentation are threatening to replace the ethics of Humanism, the educational trends of our time will become easier to understand. The traditional Arts curriculum still—in spite of the defects foisted upon it by the current love of specialisation—inculcates a view of life which respects individual responsibility and the individual integration of human experience. It is therefore in conflict with the forces described above, and we need not be surprised to find it pushed aside in favour of a scientific and technical training which can be more easily reconciled with the desire and pursuit of the partial. Technology has no concern with ethical presuppositions, while the scientific tradition which stresses the importance of a disinterested search for truth, says nothing about the personal needs of the seekers and so remains neutral in the struggle which the older disciplines cannot avoid.

It seems therefore that the dislike of Arts studies, which is implicit in so many contemporary pronouncements, derives in the last analysis from causes beyond the control of any teacher or student. There is reason to suppose that if the trends which distinguish our century from its predecessors continue unchecked, the classical discipline may disappear from our schools, as the most intractably Humanist of all the Humanities. Nevertheless the classical scholar has a choice beyond mere acquiescence in a regretted but inevitable collapse. The time for dignified despair has not yet come.

If we examine what men have said and written during the past hundred years, we shall find that these social and economic developments which threaten Humanism have already called forth a multitude of protests. Nineteenth-century capitalism was bitterly castigated for treating its workers as if they were economic pawns, and the totalitarian states of our own time have been similarly attacked for judging their citizens on political grounds alone and killing, imprisoning or exiling thousands because they happened to be 'bad security risks'. We do not conceal our indignation at the suffering which is caused when a civil or a military bureaucracy overrides personal needs for the sake of administrative convenience, or when the sensational press corrupts the young on the excuse that its sole function is to provide entertainment which will sell. We deplore the nagging taste for luxury which its advertisers stimulate on the ground that their task is to arouse public demand; and we are appalled at the emptiness of our churches since religion does not attract a generation brought up to avoid hard thinking about the moral problems that occupied the minds of their forefathers.

Echoes of these discontents can be found in all the major writers of the past hundred years from Baudelaire to Orwell, and taken together they represent an impressive total. The conflict we can trace in our schools is not just another example of a hopeless struggle waged by an outworn tradition against a triumphant new order. Those social developments, which are the ultimate cause of the present attacks on Humanism, have aroused an opposition which is firmly rooted in an awareness of present injuries; and in view of this opposition, the triumph of the order they herald appears neither assured, nor altogether desirable. Humanism can be convicted of the atrocious crime of having a long history; but at the same time it stands in the closest alliance with needs and impulses generated by the very trends which would destroy it; and the classical student should bear this in mind before he despairs of his subject.

NOTES

4]

writes Professor Highet. G. Highet, *The Classical Tradition* (Oxford, 1949); J. E. Sandys, *A History of Classical Scholarship* (Cambridge, 1903–8).

we find comprehensive surveys. O. Gruppe, *Geschichte der klassischen Mythologie und Religions-geschichte waehrend des Mittelalters im Abendland und waehrend der Neuzeit* (Leipzig, 1921); J. Borinski, *Die Antike in Poetik und Kunsttheorie vom Ausgang des Klassischen Altertums bis auf Goethe und Wilhelm von Humboldt* (Leipzig, 1914 and 1924).

29]

the notes to classical authors. W. G. Rutherford, *A Chapter in the History of Annotation* (*Scholia Aristophanica,* vol. III) (London, 1905), pp. 97–179.

32]

attract capable men. The following are the key dates: Between A.D. 70 and 80. Vespasian fixes the salaries which municipalities must pay to the teachers they employ, and establishes in Rome a chair of Greek and a chair of Latin rhetoric paid by the State (Suetonius, *Vespasiani Vita,* c. 18). Antoninus Pius (138–61) orders every Italian city to employ teachers and extends to the provinces the salary scales fixed for Italy (J. Capitolinus, *Vita Pii,* II, 3). There does not seem to have been a general law applicable to all the provinces; but we have in the Theodosian Code the law of Gaul that 'the most populous, powerful and famous cities' were to employ grammarians and rhetoricians (*Cod. Theod.* XIII, 3, 11 in *Corpus Iuris Romani Anteiustiniani* II, ed. Haenel).

362. Julian orders that in the case of public teaching appointments all nominations must be submitted to the emperor (*Cod. Theod.* XIII, 3, 5).

425. Theodosius and Valentinian order that teachers in the public service must not hold classes outside the institutions to which they are attached (*Cod. Theod.* XIV, 9, 3).

33]

the proportion was twenty to eight. Ausonius, *Commemoratio Professorum Burgidalensium* and *Cod. Theod.* XIV, 9, 3. As far as the West is concerned we hear a good deal more about grammatical than rhetorical studies (cf. Ausonius, *Liber Protrepticus;* Paulinus of Pella, *Eucharisticus;* Augustine, *Confess.* I, 14, 23). Against the work of Servius, Donatus and Macrobius, rhetoric can only set the second-rate compilations of a Sulpicius Victor and a Fortunatianus. The great text-books of Isodore and Martianus Capella do of course deal with rhetoric but only as one department among many. Their intention is encyclopedic, and they are obviously designed to serve the grammarian rather than the rhetor.

the Bordeaux master, Ausonius. Cf. in particular Ausonius, *Liber Protrepticus* and the *Commemoratio* mentioned in the note above.

a less qualified assistant. The following texts refer separately to the 'litterator' or 'primus magister' and the 'grammaticus': J. Capitolinus, *Vita Antonini, Scriptt. Hist. Aug.* IV, 2; Augustine, *Confess.* I, 13. On the other hand, Ausonius describes his first master Macrinus as a grammarian, *Prof.* X, and mentions a certain Crispus who taught the elements to children but figured at the same time as an expert on poetry and history, *Prof.* XXI. In another place he says that he himself took children from a very early age, and he was a most distinguished rhetorician: 'Multos lactantibus annis / ipse alui' (*Liber Protrepticus*, ll. 67, 68).

34]

the educated provincial. The Gauls in particular seem to have had difficulties with their Latin. Cf. Sulpicius Severus, *Dialogi*, I, 26 (*P.L.* XX, 200): 'Sed dum cogito me hominem Gallum inter Aquitanos verba facturum, vereor ne offendat vestras nimium aures sermo rusticior'. Also Julian, *Misopogon*, ed. Hertlein (Leipzig, 1875), p. 440, where he speaks about ἡ Κελτῶν ἀγροικία. Later in the same chapter he classes together Gauls, Syrians, Arabs, Thracians and Mysians as all lacking in culture (*ibid.* p. 449).

35]

such studies bring worldly wisdom. Cum studia saecularium litterarum magno desiderio fervere cognoscerem, ita ut multa pars hominum per ipsa se mundi prudentiam crederet adipisci... (Cassiodorus Senator, *Institutiones* I, 1, ed. R. A. B. Mynors, Oxford, 1937).

36]

replace philosophy by astronomy. St Augustine mentions his plans for a work after the manner of Varro's *Disciplinae* and lists the topics he intended to treat in *Retract* I, 6. He never completed this, and of the parts he wrote, only about half—the dialogue on music, the abridgement of the section on grammar, and the introductions to the rhetoric and logic—have survived. For Capella's list see the titles of *de Nuptiis Mercurii et Philologiae*, Books III–IX written between 410 and 427; Cassiodorus gives his in *Institutiones* II, praef. 5 (written *c.* 543).

figure in several roles. For example, Claudius Marmertus is described as 'Orator, dialecticus, poeta, tractator, geometer, musicusque' (Sidonius, *Epist.* IV, 11) and he was a philosopher as well (*ibid.* V, 2). Polemius was an orator, a poet, a philosopher, and an astronomer (*Carmen* XIV), while an unnamed headmaster was not only a skilled musician, but a geometer, mathematician and astrologer (*Carmen* XXII, Introd.).

Proclus a philosopher and a poet. We possess in addition to the Orations of Themistius a part of his early work, the *Paraphrases of Aristotle*. On Hypatia see the monograph of W. A. Meyer (1886), p. 34. Seven of the Hymns of Proclus have been preserved in addition to his philosophical commentaries.

37]

contemporary works they inspired. The following table has been compiled from the medieval catalogues studied by Manitius. The figures indicate the number of copies mentioned in each century.

	800–900	900–1000	1000–1100	1100–1200	1200–1300	1300–1400
Cicero,						
ad Herennium	1	—	6	13	4	5
de Rhetorica	6	2	9	32	35	35
de Oratore	3	—	1	3	3	2

The title *de Rhetorica* refers generally to the *de Inventione*, but may on occasion have been used for the *ad Herennium*. The point of the comparison, however, is to indicate how greatly the two schematic works taken together outnumbered the more subtle and artistic *de Oratore*. Cf. M. Manitius, *Handschriften Antiker Autoren in Mittelalterlichen Bibliothekskatalogen* (Leipzig, 1935).

39]

allusions and epigrams. Quotations, allusions, anecdotes, epigrams are all classed under the two headings *gnome* and *chreia*. These terms are so different from the ones we use as to be somewhat confusing. *Gnome* is the all-inclusive word. It can denote every reference that is made to events or sayings external to the topic under discussion provided that such a reference is made for a moral purpose and with reasonable brevity. *Chreia* refers more specifically to witty sayings.

a grammatical fault. Sidonius, *Ep.* II, 10, 1 Tantum increbruit multitudo desidiosorum ut, nisi vel paucissimi quique meram linguae Latiaris proprietatem de trivialium barbarismorum robigine vindicaveritis, eam brevi abolitam defleamus interemptamque.

41]

acting in character. An analysis of the commentary on the second book gave the following results:

		(%)
Comments on points of language	Morphology	6
	Derivations	1
	Syntax	9
	Meaning of words	27
	Meaning of phrases	13
Comments on non-linguistic points	Historical, literary and antiquarian allusions	16
	'Psychological' explanations	12
	Metre, readings, etc.	3

49]

Jewish sources. J. Sandys, *A History of Classical Scholarship*, vol. 1 (Cambridge, 1903), p. 325.

power to dispel prejudice. Clement of Alexandria, *Stromata* VI. Chapters 8 and 18 are particularly relevant.

50]

that lesser figure Bishop Synesius. His interests, however, were more pagan than Christian and it was much against his will that the Bishopric of Ptolemais was pressed upon him.

the minds of its readers. Basil of Caesarea, πρὸς τοὺς νέους ὅπως ἂν ἐξ Ἑλληνίκων ὠφελοίντο λόγων, in *Epistolae*, ed. Deferrari (Loeb Series, London, 1934), vol. IV, p. 378. See also Gregory Nazianzen, *Funebris Oratio in laudem Basilii Magni*, cc. 17–23 (Migne, *P.G.* XXXVI, 519–28).

not to be countenanced. Tertullian, *de Idololatria* 10 (Migne, *P.L.* I, 675) Huic necessitas ad excusationem deputatur quia aliter discere non potest. Cf. also his *de Spectaculis* 18 (*P.L.* I, 650).

51]

the writings of the two Latin Fathers. For the impression made upon Jerome by contemporary events see *Epistolae*, ed. Hilberg, III, 161 (CXXVIII, 5) (Vienna, 1918).

no Christian but a Ciceronian. Jerome, *Epistolae*, ed. Hilberg, I, 190 (XXII, 30).

a class of boys. For his justification of such teaching see *Ep.* I, p. 700 (LXX). For the fact: *Rufini Apologia in D. Hieronym.* II, 10 (*P.L.* XXI, 592).

53]

of potential value. Augustine, *Retractationes*, I, 3 (*P.L.* XXXII, 588).

adequately equipped. Augustine, *de Doctrina Christiana*, IV, 2 and 20 (*P.L.* XXXIV, 89 and 107).

54]

no foothold in their memory. Augustine, *de Doctrina Christiana*, books II and III. Although in the fourth book of this work he is to argue that a Christian writer does not require pagan models for his style, in these books he emphasises that we must know a good many rhetorical turns which can be learnt only from authors if we are to understand the subject-matter of the Scriptures. See in particular *P.L.* XXXIV, 80 (book III, 29).

the reading of Virgil and Ovid. Ennodius, *Ep.* IX, 9 Erubesco ecclesiastica profitentem ornamentis saecularibus (*P.L.* LXIII, 152). Claudius Victor, *de perversis suae aetatis mortibus* (*P.L.* LXI, 970):

Paulo et Salmone relicto
Quod Maro cantatur Phoenissae et Naso Corinnae
Quod plausum accipiunt lyra Flacci aut scena Terenti,
Nos, horum nos Causa sumus; nos turpiter istis
Nutrimenta damus flammis.

55]

a skilled rhetorician for all that. Zschimmer, *Salvianus und seine Schriften*, p. 43 (Halle, 1875).

56]

avoid solecisms and barbarisms. Gregory the Great, *Moral. libri sive Expos. in Lib. Job, Epist.* V (*P.L.* LXXV, 516) ipsam loquendi artem quam magisteria disciplinae exterioris insinuant servare despexi. Nam sicut huius quoque epistolae tenor enunciat, non metacismi collisionem fugio, non barbarismi confusionem devito, situs motusque et praepositionum casus servare contemno, quia indignum vehementer existimo, ut verba caelestis oraculi restringam sub regulis Donati.

62]

a variety of secular subjects. The only authority for the curriculum is a life of the Patriarch Germanus which describes the twelve teachers as possessing ἅπασαν γνῶσιν τῆς τε θύραθεν καὶ τῆς καθ' ἡμᾶς φιλοσοφίας (ed. Papadopoulos-Kerameus, *Anecdota Hellenica*, Constantinople, 1884, pp. 1–17).

63]

another and yet wider field. The later persecution of the Paulicians by the Iconoclasts should not be regarded as evidence that their views were dissimilar. It is a common phenomenon for the moderates of a revolutionary party to attack the extremists.

65]

support his policy. Patria Constantinopoleos, ed. Preger, in *Scriptores Originum Constantinopolitanum,* p. 226.

withdrawn from higher education. The story of the fire is given by Georgius Monachus (ed. de Boor, II, p. 742) and by *Patria Constantinopoleos* (ed. Preger, p. 226), but is omitted by the earlier authority for the incident, the Life of the Patriarch Germanus. For a list of the other authorities who mention the episode and a discussion of the evidence see F. Fuchs, *Die Hoeheren Schulen von Konstantinopel im Mittelalter Byz. Archiv,* Heft 8 (1926), pp. 8–18.

a poor substitute for wide reading. The Ἐπαρχικὸν βίβλιον compiled by order of Leo the Wise and containing the rules under which the various professional corporations functioned makes it clear that the object of grammar school training for lawyers was only to give them sufficient mastery of the written idiom to avoid bad errors in drafting: παιδευθῆναι δὲ καὶ τὴν ἐγκύκλιον παίδευσιν ὡς ἂν μὴ διαμαρτάνῃ μὲν ἐν ταῖς ἐκδόσεσιν, ὀλισθαίνῃ δὲ καὶ περὶ τὴν λέξιν.

    J. Nicole, *Le Livre du Préfet* (Geneva, 1893), p. 14. The continued use of the *Progymnasmata* is attested by the appearance of fresh commentaries during the tenth and eleventh centuries which suggests that they could not have been wholly neglected during the previous 200 years.

the accent on every Greek word. πάλαι γάρ μοι διαπονουμένῳ τὰ γραμματικὰ καὶ ἑκαστῆς λέξεως τὴν ἁρμόδιον κανόνα ἀπὸ τῶν φοιτητῶν ἀπαραιτήτως ἐπιπραττομένῳ (Theognostus, *Orthographia*, ed. J. A. Cramer, *Anecdota Oxon.* II (1885), pp. 1–165).

68]

the sample was representative. Arethas who is supposed to have been a pupil of Photius, though at a somewhat later period, had obviously the same interests as those suggested by the *Myriobiblon*. The only writers he is known to have annotated or had copied apart from the Fathers are Plato, Dio Chrysostom and Lucian. Again there is no mention of the poets.

70]

paved the way for a future Atticism. To his correspondent Amphilochus who has asked for advice about the best models to follow in letter writing, Photius recommends Plato as unsurpassable, 'Phalaris', 'Brutus' and Libanius. It is plain that he did not distinguish between the usage of different epochs, but was willing to accept any idiom that had the authority of a respectable writer. He goes on to suggest to Amphilochus that he should read St Basil and St Gregory Nazianzen because their writings are not only models of style but a possible source of edification. εἰ δὲ βούλει σὺν τῷ χαρακτῆρι καὶ πολλῶν ἄλλων καὶ μεγάλων συλλέξαι ὠφέλειαν ἀρκήσει σοι βασίλειος ὁ γλύκυς καὶ ὁ κάλλους εἴ τις ἄλλος ἐργάτης Γρηγόριος καὶ ἡ ποικίλη καὶ τῆς ἡμετέρας αὐλῆς μοῦσα 'Ισίδωρος ὃς ὥσπερ λόγων οὕτω δὲ καὶ ἱερατικῆς καὶ ἀσκητικῆς πολιτείας κανών ἐστι χρηματίζειν ἀξιόχρεως (*Epp.* II, 44 in *P.G.* CII, 862).

Personally, he never read for literary ends alone, and his letters do not contain many hints of his linguistic interests. Now and then, writing to the Metropolitan Paul of Laodicea, to Amphilochus, or to the Abbot Theodore who was reputed to have a great love of Homer, he touches on the topic of style or corrects a solecism. But for the most part he is a monk addressing his fellow monks in the manner to which they are accustomed (cf. *Epp.* II, 38, 48, in *P.G.* CII, 854 and 866).

71]

neglect of the authorities. Cedrenus, ed. Bekker, II, p. 326 (Bonn, 1889) [ὁ Κωνσταντῖνος]...τὰς γὰρ ἐπιστήμας, ἀριθμητικήν, μουσικήν, ἀστρονομίαν, γεωμετρίαν, στερεομετρίαν, καὶ τὴν ἐν πάσαις ἔτοχον φιλοσοφίαν, ἐκ μακροῦ χρόνου ἀμελείᾳ καὶ ἀμαθίᾳ τῶν κρατούντων ἀπολωλυίας οἰκείᾳ σπουδῇ ἀνεκτήσατο.

revel in their solecisms. The historians in question are Georgius Monachus, Genesius, Kameniates, and Leo the Deacon.

72]

a polemical work directed against the Atticists. Paris Bibl. Nat. Coislinianus 345. The anonymous treatises have been given the name of *Lexica Segueriana* after a possessor of the manuscript (ed. L. Bachmann, *Anecdota Graeca*, vol. I, Leipzig, 1828).

a large number of later writers. K. Krumbacher, *Geschichte der byzantischen Literatur* (Munich, 1897), pp. 566–70.

a satire in the manner of Lucian. The *Philopatris* can be found in the appendix to the works of Lucian, ed. C. Jakobitz (Bibl. Teub. 1876), vol. III, pp. 411–25.

74]

the troops in the field. The growing importance of the landed aristocracy is clearly illustrated in the circumstances attending the election of Isaac Comnenus. The votes of the generals assembled in secret conclave fell on the veteran Cataclon whose reputation was based exclusively on his military career. Declining the honour, he suggested to his colleagues that it was not politic to neglect the claims of birth and fortune in favour of the narrow interests of a military caucus; and his intervention secured the election of Comnenus, then the most distinguished of the aristocratic leaders.

treatises on the characters in Homer. Krumbacher, *op. cit.* p. 525.

the personal enterprise of individuals. Ἐσπούδαζον ὡς αὐτοτελεῖς are the words Psellus uses to describe the activity of these private teachers (*Chronographia*, ed. K. Sathas in *Bibl. Gr. Med. Aevi*, vol. IV, p. 36 (Paris, 1872–90)); cf. also Anna Comnena, *Alexias* V, 8, ed. A. Reifferscheid, vol. I, pp. 177–8 (Leipzig, 1884).

the threshold of the Humanist age. For a full account of Mauropus summarising all the evidence see J. M. Hussey, *Church and Learning in the Byzantine Empire (867–1185)* (Oxford, 1937), ch. 2.

75]

Nicetas and Mauropus as his assistants. For an admirable survey of the career and character of Psellus see J. M. Hussey, *op. cit.* pp. 37–102; the details concerning the foundation of the university can be found in F. Fuchs, *op. cit.* pp. 23–35. Cf. also A. Rambaud, 'Michael Psellos', *Revue Historique*, vol. III (1887), pt. 2, pp. 241–82. Most of our information concerning Psellus comes from his own writings, of which there is no complete edition. The theological works can be found in *P.G.* cxxII. The *Chronographia*, the *Funeral Orations*, the *Panegyrics* and the letters are in the edition by K. N. Sathas, vols. IV and V. The best bibliography is given by E. Renauld, *Etude de la langue et du style de Psellos* (Paris, 1920).

76]

composed his examples himself. Psellus, *de Operatione Daemonum*, ed. F. Boissonade (Nuremberg, 1838), pp. 73, 78, 85, 124, 135, 140, 144, 147.

78]

the subjects in which Psellus and his colleagues had given instruction. The evidence for the curriculum of the Patriarchal School during the eleventh century is vague. It rests on the following evidence:

(*a*) A statement by Psellus in a letter written to a Metropolitan of Thessalonica who is described as τῷ γεγονότι μαΐστωρ τῶν ῥητόρων— οὐδὲν ὁ ῥήτωρ ὅτι μὴ γλῶσσα λαμπρὰ κἂν λέγῃ, κἂν γραφῇ καὶ παιδεύσῃ ῥητορικήν, κἂν φιλοσοφίᾳ τὸν νοῦν ἀσχολῇ (*P.G.* cxxII, 1161).

(*b*) The fact that the οἰκουμενικὸς διδάσκαλος (the title given to the principal of the Patriarchal School) round about 1080 was the grammarian Nicetas of Heracleia.

(c) A sentence in Anna Comnena's *Alexias* where she appears to be talking of the past and includes among the noted grammarians τοὺς γεγονότας τοῦ ἱεροῦ καταλόγου τῆς μεγάλης παρ' ἡμῖν ἐκκλησίας (ed. Reifferscheid II, 294).

But there seems little doubt that during the next century the Patriarchal School did equal the secular foundation of Monomachos in the number of subjects taught. We have fairly conclusive evidence:

(a) Anselm of Havelberg who visited Constantinople in the reign of John Comnenus (1118–43) says: Fuit autem idem archiepiscopus Nechites praecipuus inter duodecim didascalos qui iuxta morem sapientum Graecorum et liberalium artium et divinarum scripturarum studia regunt (*P.L.* CLXXXVIII, 1141).

(b) Michael Italicus who was Head of the School also in the reign of John Comnenus describes himself as teaching arithmetic, geometry, astronomy, music, philosophy (including the doctrines of Pythagoras, Plato, Aristotle and the Stoa) and literature (including epic, tragedy, comedy, satire, the historians and the orators) (Cramer, *Anecdota Graeca*, Oxon. III, 167).

(c) Michael's statement is further supported by Theodore Prodromus who describes him using Plato and Aristides as models in his rhetoric classes, and also teaching grammar, Platonic and Aristotelian philosophy, arithmetic and geometry (Theodorus Prodromos, *Epistolae*, in *P.G.* CXXXIII, 1297).

(d) Eustathius was master of rhetoric some time after 1182 (J. Draeseke, 'Eustathios und Michael Akominatos', *Neue kirch. Zeitschr.* XXIV (1913), p. 497). He gave instruction in grammar, metric and poetry, cf. also *P.G.* CXXXV, 517 n.b, and 425.

its historian, Nicholas Mesarites. Nicolas Mesarites, 'Beschreibung der Apostelkirche' in A. Heisenberg, *Grabeskirche und Apostelkirche* (Leipzig, 1908), vol. II, pp. 90–5, which gives a detailed account of the school's curriculum.

79]

his sixteenth or seventeenth year. Georgius Acropolites left the grammar school and commenced his rhetorical studies at sixteen (*Opera*, ed. Heisenberg (Leipzig, 1893), vol. I, p. 49). Nicephorus Blemmydas did so at seventeen (Blemmydas, *Curriculum vitae*, ed. Heisenberg, p. 2).

harmful to serious studies. For detailed accounts of schedographia see Krumbacher, *op. cit.* p. 590; F. Fuchs, *op. cit.* p. 46; S. D. Papademetriu, *Theodorus Prodromos* (Odessa, 1905), pp. 413f. A slighting reference to the practice will be found in Anna Comnena (ed. Reifferscheid, p. 294). She was the writer who considered it an injurious innovation. There exists a twelfth-century example of schedography in a Vatican manuscript entitled Λογγιβάρδου τοῦ σόφου παρεκβολαῖον τῆς σχεδογραφίας.

hidden meanings to light. Psellus, *Allegoriae*, ed. Boissonade (Lyons, 1851), pp. 343–4, 365–6.

80]

the tomb of Zeus has still to be located. *Ibid.* p. 348. The story is of course well known. It appears in Cicero, *de Nat. Deorum* III, 21.

the stone over Tantalus' head. *Ibid.* p. 349.

the approach of winter. Tzetzes, *Allegoriae Iliados* XV, ed. Boissonade (Lyons, 1851).

his work was appreciated. *Ibid. Prolegomena,* 32–5. One proof of its popularity is its imitation during the following century by Constantine Hermoniacus.

81]

not taught in the schools. The grammarian John Doxoprates wrote an introduction to the *Progymnasmata* which illustrates their popularity in the period (Krumbacher, *op. cit.* p. 462).

a sophistical rather than a systematic treatment. Heisenberg, *op. cit.* p. 90.

the Escurial Manuscript Krumbacher, *op. cit.* p. 470.

82]

short trochaic lines with eight accentual feet. E. Legrand, *La guerre de Troie par Constantine Hermoniacos* (Bibl. gr. vulgaire V, Paris, 1890).

83]

invading the field of literature. M. Triantaphullides, Νεοελλινικη Γραμματικη-ιστορικη εισαγογη (Athens, 1939), pp. 29–46. For the best known examples of this new demotic literature see Hesseling-Pernot, *Poèmes prodromiques* (12th cent.); J. Schmitt, *Die Chronik von Morea* (13th cent.); W. Wagner, *Carmina Graeca medii aevi*; πουλόλογος (14th cent.).

all cultured and intelligent people. Theodorus Metochites in C. Sathas, Μεσαιωνικὴ βιβλιοθήκη, τόμος Α σελ.πϛ΄.

84]

Artificiality declined. We still possess an example of the style in vogue at the end of the thirteenth century in the *Melete* and the *Progymnasmata* of Georgios Pachymeres (*Progymnasmata,* ed. Rhetores Graeci, C. Walz, vol. 1549–96; *Melete* in *Anec. Gr.* ed. Boissonade, vol. V, pp. 350ff.). He used the ecclesiastical idiom but enlivened it by phrases from Homer.

the elucidation of the more obscure texts. Tzetzes, περὶ Ῥημάτων αὐθυποτάκτων, ed. (in part) Bekker, *An. Gr.* III, 1088–90; Gregory of Corinth, περὶ τῶν Ἰδιωμάτων τῶν διαλέκτων, ed. H. Schaefer (Leipzig, 1811).

learning Greek as a dead language. Maximus Planudes, περὶ Γραμματικῆς and περὶ Συντάξεως, ed. Bachmann, *An. Gr.* vol. II (1828); Joannes Glykys, περὶ Ὀρθοτήτος συντάξεως, ed. A. Jahn (Bern, 1849); Manuel Moschopoulus, Ἐρωτήματα γραμματικά (Milan, 1493).

meaning and use of the words. L. Voltz, 'Die Schriftstellerei des Georgios Lekapenos', *Byz. Zeitschr.* II (1893), 221–34.

86]

the only efficient scholar in Constantinople. For the criticisms of Gennadius see Hardouin, *Concil. Coll.* IX, 449 and Sp. Lampros, Παλαιολόγια καὶ Πελοποννησιακά II, 3 (Athens and Leipzig, 1912). For those of Filelfo, *Epistolae* V, 30.

such eminent men? The following table is not without interest:

Master	Pupils
Gemistus Plethon	Marcus Eugenianus (who organised the opposition against the union of the Churches), Gennadius, Bessarion.
Manuel Chrysoloras	Guarino, Giacopo di Scarparia, (and in Italy) Roberto Rossi, Niccolo Niccoli, Leonardo Bruni, Carlo Marsuppini, Ambrogio Traversari (?), Vergerio, Uberto Decembrio, Poggio.
Joannes Chrysoloras	Guarino, Filelfo, Francesco Ferrato, Louis de Fréjus.
Georgius Chrysococces	Filelfo, Bessarion.
Joannes Argyropoulus	Gianmario Filelfo, (and in Italy) Palla Strozzi, Politian, Reuchlin.

87]

in communion with theirs. On the school of Plethon, see F. Fuchs, *op. cit.* pp. 70–1; a description of his teaching is given by Gennadius, *op. cit.* II, 20, 15.

ideas and tastes of the past. In medicine, Joannes Actuarius, writing between 1328 and 1341, had revived the system of Galen (Krumbacher, *op. cit.* p. 615); in astronomy, both Metochitas and Melitoniotes had made extensive use of ancient sources (*ibid.* pp. 623–4).

88]

memory failed to do its work. R. Sabbadini, *Epistolario di Guarino Veronese,* II, 269 f. (Venice, 1916). The letter is too long to be cited in full, but the following is perhaps the most important passage: 'Quodsi inter legendum quicquam aut ornate dictum aut prudenter et officiose factum aut acute responsum ad instituendam ornandamque vitam pertinens offenderis, ut id memoriter ediscas suadebo; idque ut recordationi firmius inhaereat tenaciusque servetur, non satis erit dixisse semel, verum de more Pythagoreum quod interdiu didiceris reminiscendum erit vesperi; et aliquo desumpto mensis die erit praeceptorum omnium renovanda memoria. Firmandae quoque lectorum memoriae vehementer proderit si quem delegeris quocum lecta conferas et in lucubrationum tuarum partem communicationemque vocaveris; haec namque recordationis vis atque natura est, ut iners esse nolit et in fatigatione levetur in dies. Has ad res salubre probatumque praestatur consilium ut quotiens lectitandum est paratum teneas codicillum tamquam fidelem tibi depositarium in quo quicquid selectum adnotaveris, describas et sicuti collectorum catalogum facias; nam quotiens visa placita delecta repetere constitueris ne semper tot de integro revolvendae sint chartae, praesto condicillus erit qui sicuti minister strenuus et assiduus petita subjiciat.'

89]

the words of the immortals. Sir Frederick Harrison, Rede Lecture for 1900, quoted by Sandys, *op. cit.* I, p. 427.

93]

the confusions of Babel. Certain scholars have held that Irish Latin can be found in its most extreme form in the *Hisperica Famina*. The origin, purpose and even the meaning of that strange work remain as yet a mystery. If the hypotheses of its sixth-century date and Irish authorship are to be accepted, then its coinages like *cantamen, congelamen, doctoreus, gaudifluus, frangorico,* its misuse of existing words like *forceps* for *os, vernia* for *laetitia,* its borrowings from Greek like *Trices,* and *idor,* from the Hebrew like *iduma,* and *gibra* (which gave *gibrosus*), and from no known language at all like *domesca, sennosus, gigna,* or *charassus,* do indeed provide a most striking instance of tendencies one can trace in the generality of Irish compositions; but if on the other hand we are to believe that the *Hisperica Famina,* the *Lorica* attributed to Gildas and certain other similar writings have a connection with the mystifications of the grammarian Virgil and are the products of a movement active over the whole of Europe, then the problems involved become a hundred times more baffling. It is possible that the last agonies of Graeco-Roman culture produced an orgy of intentional unreason. Such phenomena are not unknown; but on the whole it may be more accordant with observable fact to ascribe the appearance of irrationality to the over-ambitious efforts of genuine ignorance. For a detailed account F. J. H. Jenkinson, *The Hisperica Famina* (Cambridge, 1908), should be consulted. H. Zimmer 'Neue Fragmente von Hisperica Famina aus Handschriften in Luxemburg und Paris' in *Nachrichten der Kais. Gesell. der Wissen zu Göttingen* (Phil.-hist. Klasse) 1895, p. 158 puts forward the theory that we may possess the remains of a rather elaborate school text-book. If that is the case, then the *Hisperica Famina* provides an interesting sidelight on the methods used in the Celtic schools. Chapters 6–13 of the version in the Vatican MS. sketch the occupations of a normal day, chapters 14–17 treat of the sky, the sea, fire and the winds, chapter 18 of clothes, chapter 19 seems to describe a hut, chapter 20 a writing tablet, chapter 21 an oratory and chapter 24 a hunt. If the book is indeed an aid to learning, intended to provide students with appropriate vocabularies, then we have here a foretaste of that pragmatical method of linking the literary language with daily life which Alcuin and particularly Aelfric were later to exploit.

after he had left his homeland. For these classical citations and reminiscences see in particular *Mon. Germ. Hist. Epist.* vol. III (*Epp. Merov. et Karol Aevi*), ed. W. Gundlach, pp. 156–7, 159, 164, 166–7, 182 ff.

95]

in a manuscript of the Georgics. M. Manitius, *Geschichte der lateinischen Literatur des Mittelalters*, vol. I, p. 293.

96]

the follies of secular literature. Gregory the Great, *Registrum Epistolarum*, ed. P. Ewald and M. Hartmann, in *Mon. Germ. Hist. Epist.* I–II (Berlin, 1891–9), XI, 34, p. 303.

97]

such schools still abounded. There is good evidence that the Roman schools were still in existence in fairly large numbers on the eve of the Lombard invasions in 568. Venantius Fortunatus went to a school in Ravenna where he learnt both grammar and rhetoric (biographical introduction to his *Vita Martini*, I, 29–33, also Paulus Diaconus, *Hist. Lang.* II, 13). He was born between 530 and 540, so his schooling must have come between 535 and 555. Gregory the Great was supposed to have shone in grammar, rhetoric and dialectic during his schooldays round about 550 in Rome (Paulus Diaconus, *Vita Gregorii*, c. 1 Disciplinis vero liberalibus hoc est grammatica, rhetorica, dialectica, ita a pueritia est institutus ut quamvis hic eo tempore potissimum florerent studia litterarum nulli in urbe hac putaretur esse secundus). And finally there are the *Institutiones* of Cassiodorus. Written probably between 546 and 555 (Traube, *Textgeschichte der Regula Benedicti*, p. 95) they mention the popularity of literary studies—'mundani auctores celeberrima procul dubio traditione pollerent' (Cassiodorus, *Institutiones* I, 1, ed. R. A. B. Mynors (Oxford, 1937), p. 3). Furthermore, since the book shows obvious signs of a later revision (cf. part I, c. 17 and c. 30) and this passage is left unrevised, we may conclude that Cassiodorus remained of this opinion even during the latter part of his long life.

the madness of princes.... Gregory of Tours, *Opera*, ed. W. Arndt and B. Krusch in *Mon. Germ. Hist. Script. rer. Merov. I* (Hamburg, 1884–5), *Hist. Franc. Praef.*

99]

a controlling position in the hierarchy. Pupils of Aidan, the first British Bishop of York (635–51) occupied at some time or other the following sees: London, Lichfield, Lindisfarne, Hexham, York (Bede, *Hist. Eccl.* III, 26, 28; IV, 12, 23).

100]

their own mother tongue.... Bede, *Hist. Eccl.* IV, 2.

as he did his mother tongue. Ibid. V, 8, 20 and 23.

103]

rules for determining quantity and stress. See the last part of the *de Septenario* of Aldhelm (*P.L.* LXXXIX, 201 ff.); also the first part of Bede, *de Arte Metrica* (Keil, *Gramm. Lat.* VII, p. 227). For the importance attached to a correct pronunciation when singing or speaking see Aldhelm, *Epist. Heddae P.L.* LXXXIX, 95).

dedicated to the service of God. Bede calls Latin, Greek and Hebrew the three sacred languages.

104]

one by Boniface. W. Levison, *England and the Continent in the Eighth Century* (Oxford, 1946), p. 70.

all simple. Cunabula grammaticae artis Donati a Beda restituta (*P.L.* XC, 613). This may not be by Bede since he does not mention it in the list he gives in *Hist. Eccl.* 24. It is interesting both for the simplicity of its arrangement and its use of a question and answer method. The other grammatical work by Bede, the *de Orthographia* (Keil, *op. cit.* VII, 261) is largely a word list which deals with the spelling and gives grammatical facts about individual words. Tatwine, *de Octo Partibus Orationis*, not published. M. Roger, *L'Enseignement des lettres classiques d'Ausone à Alcuin* (Paris, 1905), p. 332.

the intervals of episcopal business. John of Beverley, Bishop of York, 686–721. For the story of his teaching see Bede, *Hist. Eccl.* V, 6.

105]

Bede's treatise on the nature of things. Bede, *de Temporibus Liber* (*P.L.* XC, 284). The date of this work which deals with the concept of the world, the elements, the firmament, the zones, the planets, the sun and moon, comets, winds, tides, weather and animals is doubtful. Cf. chs. 14 and 25.

106]

would be considered valid. M. Tangl, *Die Briefe des hl. Bonifatius*, vol. I, p. 140 (Berlin, 1916).

the Latin used in the charters sensibly improved. M. Bonnet, *Le Latin de Grégoire de Tours*, p. 83 n. 4.

written presumably between 758 and 763. Mon. Germ. Hist. Epist. vol. III (*Epist. Merovingici et Karolini Aevi*, ed. Gundlach, p. 529) Direximus itaque excellentissime praecellentiae vestrae et libros, quantos reperire potuimus: id est antiphonale et responsale, insimul atrem grammaticam Aristolis, Dionisii Ariopagitis geometricam, orthografiam, grammaticam, omnes Graeco eloquio scriptas. Bouquet, *Recueil des Historiens des Gaules*, V, 513, inserts *libros* after *Areopagitae* and *scriptores* for *scriptas*: which would suggest that perhaps the books were not all in Greek. The attribution of these unusual works to the Areopagite is a not uncommon medieval trick. All writers of the name of Dionysius tend to be lumped together under the name of the most famous.

107]

youths intended for the priesthood. J. B. Pitra, *Histoire de St. Léger* (Paris, 1846), pp. 24–34.

108]

the Felix mentioned by Paulus Diaconus. Paulus Diaconus, *Historia Langobardum* VI, 7.

taught Maurus the liberal arts. G. Hoerle, *Fruehmittelalterliche Moench- und Klerikerbildung in Italien*, p. 38 (Leipzig, 1914).

a reminiscence of Virgil. Manitius, *Geschichte der lateinischen Literatur des Mittelalters* (Munich, 1911), vol. I, p. 199.

109]

the promise of a new spring. Angilbert's elegiacs to Pippin of Italy are full of Ovidian reminiscences (*Mon. Hist. Ger. Poetae Lat. Aevi Kar.* I, 358 ff.; cf. also Raby, *Secular Latin Poetry*, Oxford, 1934); Modoin of Autun and Ermolaus Nigellus both imitated the *Tristia* of Ovid (Raby, pp. 203–22; Manitius, *op. cit.* vol. I, pp. 549 and 552). C. H. Beeson, *A Primer of Medieval Latin*, pp. 155–9, gives an interesting analysis of Einhard's portrait of Charlemagne showing how its phrases are drawn from a number of separate descriptions by Suetonius. Peter of Pisa had probably left the Palace School by the time Einhard arrived, for that was not until 794 or even later; but over exactitude in imitation, the principle counts for a good deal, and the advice of a man like Angilbert as well as his example could have easily been responsible for the decision of Einhard to model his style on the ancient historians. Even his technique of phrase borrowing could have been taken over from the methods which Angilbert and Peter's other pupils used in their poetry.

Alcuin's own expressed views. *Alcuini Vita*, c. 10 sufficiunt divini poetae vobis, nec egetis luxuriosa sermonis Virgilii vos pollui facundia.

the upbringing of the young. Alcuin's career at the court of Charlemagne is curiously paralleled by the experiences of Sir Robert Morant in Siam some years before the end of the last century. Morant was engaged originally as a tutor for the crown prince, but after four years, we find him not only reorganizing the whole of Siamese education, but installed as a confidential adviser to the king with a voice in matters far outside the educational sphere (B. Allen, *Sir Robert Morant*, London, 1934). Such are the golden opportunities which a primitive state affords its teachers.

110]

ignorant of any but their mother tongue. Bede, *Epistola ad Egbertum* (*P.L.* XCIV, 659).

famous poets and orators. Cassiodorus Senator, *Institutiones* II, I, ed. R. A. B. Mynors (Oxford, 1937), p. 94.

his textbook on the subject. Alcuin, *Grammatica* (*P.L.* CI, 858).

111]

to satisfy the needs of men. J. W. Thompson, *The Medieval Library*, (Chicago, 1939), p. 31.

almost painlessly fixed in their memories. We must remember, however, that these lessons were the boys' first introduction to a new language; and in England and Germany at any rate their daily speech bore no resemblance to Latin. It is difficult to see how under the circumstances the use of the vernacular in the early stages could ever have been avoided. Alcuin's dialogues have many pedagogic virtues, but they are not arranged according to the principles demanded by the direct method. They do not start from the demonstrable, or build up to abstractions when the names of visible objects have become familiar. Their Latin would be quite incomprehensible to a beginner; and we have in fact sure indications that English and German were used in teaching. Many of Hraban Maur's educational works have an inter-linear German translation in some early manuscripts (Manitius, *op. cit.* p. 301). The well-known *Colloquium* of Aelfric of Eynsham (*c.* 955–*c.* 1035) is similarly accompanied by an Anglo-Saxon text. Both Hraban and Aelfric produced vernacular-latin glossaries. We can assume that in the early stages the first reading of a new text was always followed by an immediate translation; and in the case of Alcuin's dialogues the probable procedure was for each question and answer to be read out separately. The master would then make the meaning clear either in the vernacular or, when the boys had come to know enough, in Latin. The class would then repeat question and answer until they were remembered. If the Roman tradition was followed the boys probably replied first of all in chorus; and then one was chosen to interrogate and another to give the explanations, one took the part of the Frank and another took the part of the Saxon while the master supervised. So step by step over a very long period the necessary amount of grammar was learnt. H. M. Dubois, *Aelfric* (Paris, 1943). W. J. Chase, *The Ars Minor of Donatus* (Madison, 1926).

if Zimmer's theory is correct. See above, p. 404.

112]

crude glossary by Bede. Bede, *de Orthographia* (Keil, *Gramm. Lat.* VII, p. 261).

material for word-drills. Alcuin, *de Orthographia* (Keil, *op. cit.* VII, p. 295): on the *Disputatio Pippini cum Albino scholastico*, cf. Wilmanns, *Zeitschrift für deutsches Altertum*, XIV, p. 544.

113]

before the age of fifteen. In the ninth-century MS. Sangall 869, the scribe is careful to distinguish Strabo's adult poetry from the productions of his early teens.

Alcuin's Propositiones ad acuendos juvenes. *P.L.* CI, 1145–60.

the secondary level of training. P.L. CVII, 269.

114]

the known varieties of snakes. Manitius, *Geschichte der lateinischen Literatur des Mittelalters*, vol. I, p. 254.

115]

the obvious classical sources. The *de Rhetorica* summarises Cicero's *de Inventione*, while the *de Dialectica* combines material from Isidore, Boethius and pseudo-Augustinian *Categoriae*. Cf. Manitius, *op. cit.* vol. I, pp. 282–4.

All fell silent.... Scholia Vidobonensia ad Horatii Artem Poeticam, ed. Zechmeister (Vienna, 1887).

116]
the care of worldly things. Hraban Maur, *de Clericorum Institutione*, III, 18
(*P.L.* CVII, 394).

122]
an ideal education. G. Calder, *Auraicept na n-Eces: The Scholar's Primer*
(Edinburgh, 1917).

123]
Holy Ghost in Greek. Laudensis 444 (A. Eckstein, *Analekten zur Geschichte
der Paedagogik*, Prog. der lat. Hauptschule in Halle, 1861).

endowed with mystical meanings. The best account of Greek studies outside
Italy during the early Middle Ages is given by B. Bischoff, 'Das Griechische Element in der abendlaendischen Bildung des Mittelalters',
Byzantische Zeitschrift, Band 44 (Munich, 1951). He cites the following
lists of interpretations for the Greek alphabet:

alfa	agricola	agricola
beta	vetus	beatitudo
gamma	virga	virga correctionis
delta	correctionis	bonitas
epsilon	hec	latitudo
zeta	scientia	preciositas
eta	filiorum	edificatio
theta	possessio	ignis obscurus
iota	in	auris sive aurum
kappa	populis	prudentia
lambda	mee	ignis
mu	legis	templum
nu	exclamatio	retributio
xi	doctrinae	multiplicitas
o	omnis	corona
pi	exultans	gratia
ro	figura	lucerna
sigma	signorum	vis orationis
tau	amicorum	edificium
u	amor	potestas
phi	totus	scintilla
chi	circulus	oculos
psi	laus	species
omega	mirabilis	finis

124]
poetic models. Hraban Maur, *de Clericorum Institutione* III, 18 (*P.L.* CVII,
396).

125]
the Fables of Avian. E. K. Rand, *Johannes Scotus* (Munich, 1906), p. 97, is
of the opinion that Rémi also provided Avian with a commentary.

original sources. E. K. Ullman, 'Classical Authors in medieval Florilegia', *Classical Philology,* XXIII (1928)–XXVII (1932).

from Suetonius as well as from Valerius. For the classical citations and references mentioned in this paragraph see Manitius, *op. cit.* vol. I, pp. 410, 499, 500–1, 503, 515, 573.

127]

the Christian poets. E. Duemmler, *Das Formelbuch des Bischofs Salamo III v. Konstanz* (Leipzig, 1857) pp. 65–6.

143]

two sides of the same science. Anselm of Bisate, *Rhetorimachia,* ed. E. Duemmler, p. 17. Cf. Milo Crispinus *Vita Lanfranci* (*P.L.* CL, 39) Eruditus est in scholis liberalium artium et legum secularium ad suae morem patriae.

144]

the law also stayed largely Roman. H. Rashdall, *The Universities of Europe in the Middle Ages,* ed. F. M. Powicke and A. B. Emden (Oxford, 1936), vol. I, p. 95; M. Thurot, *L'organisation de l'enseignement dans l'Université de Paris,* makes the suggestion (p. 3) that Southern France should be included along with Italy as one of the areas where law remained largely Roman.

145]

fragmentary notes of the author. H. Kantorowicz, *Studies in the Glossators of the Roman Law* (Cambridge, 1938), pp. 33–7.

lectures on a text. This is assuming that the two introductions which have come down to us under the name of Irnerius are indeed to a substantial extent his own work.

147]

the Irnerian preambles had not possessed. H. Kantorowicz, *op. cit.* pp. 46–50.

future generations of students. Ibid. p. 81.

150]

allegorical, anagogical and tropological. All these three forms of explanation involved establishing an analogy one term of which was a person, thing or event mentioned in the Biblical text. The analogy was called allegorical when its other term had its origin in this world, as for example when the city of Jerusalem was taken as a type of the Church militant. It was called anagogical when its other term derived from the supernatural sphere, as in a comparison between Jerusalem and the Church triumphant. A tropological explanation had a moral significance; as Jerusalem had to suffer for its sins, so the soul of sinful man must expect suffering.

151]

a great rather than an inferior authority. Hraban Maur, *Enarrationes in epist. B. Pauli,* Praefatio altera (*P.L.* III, 1276) Sunt enim eorum sensus in aliquibus concordantes, in aliquibus discrepantes. Unde necessarium reor ut intentus auditor per lectorem primum recitata singulorum auctorum nomina ante scripta sua audiat, quatenus sciat quid in lectione apostolica unusquisque senserit, sicque in mentem suam plurima coacervans, potest de singulis iudicare quid sibi utile sit inde sumere.

152]

Lanfranc of Pavia and Berengar of Tours. B. Smalley, *The Study of the Bible in the Middle Ages* (Oxford, 1941), pp. 29–31.

156]

the laws of dialectic. Sigebert of Gembloux, *de Scriptoribus Ecclesiasticis* (*P.L.* CLX, 582) Lanfrancus dialecticus et Cantuariensis archiepiscopus Paulum apostolum exposuit et ubicumque opportunitas locorum occurrit, secundum leges dialecticas exponit, assumit, concludit.

the mysteries of faith. Lanfranc of Canterbury, *Glossa in Epist. B. Pauli* (*P.L.* CL, 1578) Perspicaciter...intuentibus dialectica sacramenta Dei non impugnat sed cum res exigit si rectissime teneatur, astruit et confirmat. Cf. also his *Liber de Corpore et Sanguine Domini* c. 7 (*P.L.* CL, 417).

the instruments of pagan learning employed in theology. This theory may be held to derive a certain support from the fact that St Peter Damian confounds philosophers, rhetoricians and poets, Aristotle, Cicero and Terence, in his sweeping condemnations of pagan literature. Obviously at this early stage the different elements of the classical heritage were not easy to distinguish.

probably typical. Anselm of Bisate, *Rhetorimachia*, ed. E. Duemmler (Halle, 1872), pp. 17–19.

grammar and dialectic. William of St Ebersberg, *Expositio super Cantica canticorum, Quellen und Forsch. zur Sprach- und Kulturgeschichte*, XXVIII, p. 12.

159]

a diversis auctoribus posita defendere poterimus. A lucid analysis of these rules as well as an example of their practical application, drawn from Abélard's commentary on the Epistle to the Romans, will be found in J. G. Sikes, *Peter Abélard* (Cambridge, 1932), pp. 98–9. Sikes, however, had not the whole of Geyer's work at his disposal and tends to underestimate the importance which Abélard placed on dialectic. In any case, much of what he says on pp. 86–8 contradicts his earlier assertions.

160]

Abélard develops his own point of view. The commentary mentioned is the *Logica 'Ingredientibus'*, the second the *Logica 'Nostrorum petitioni'*, so called after the words with which the manuscripts begin. Cf. B. Geyer, *Beitraege zur Geschichte der Philosophie des Mittelalters*, XXI, 1–305, whose introduction discusses the problems arising out of Abélard's teaching of logic

411

161]

the so-called logica nova. J. Ghellinck *Le Mouvement Théologique du XII*^e *siècle* (Bruges, 1948).

166]

the garbled name of Avicenna. For a convenient short account of Arabic and Jewish thought see B. Geyer, *Ueberwegs Grundriss der Geschichte der Philosophie*, Teil 2 (*Die Patristische und Scholastische Philosophie*), (Berlin, 1928), pp. 287–342.

171]

the Practica *of Pietro Clerici.* A. Castiglioni, *A History of Medicine* (New York, 1947), pp. 299–305.

177]

the text-books of medicine. No account of the Chartres school is entirely satisfactory. The detailed narrative of A. Clerval, *Les Ecoles de Chartres* (Paris, 1895), misses the wood for the trees. Ueberweg-Geyer, *op. cit.* pp. 226–48 should be consulted wherever possible. Geyer does not however indicate the position of the school in the cultural development of the age. A good description of the poetical work of Bernard Silvestris can be found in F. J. E. Raby, *Secular Latin Poetry* (Oxford, 1934), vol. II, pp. 5–13. Cf. also E. Gilson, 'La Cosmogonie de B. Silvestris', *Speculum*, III, 5–24 and on the *Heptateuchon*, B. Haureau, *Notices et extraits*, I, 52–68.

180]

a welcome among them. The practical detail which distinguishes the Latin Geber of the thirteenth century from the Arabic Jabir, suggests that the chemical traditions of the East were reshaped round about 1200 in circles well acquainted with the use of the materials involved, which could have been only those of the skilled craftsmen.

181]

the symptom of a more general evil. According to the Paris Council of 1210: nec libri Aristotelis de naturali philosophia nec commenta legantur Parisiis publice vel secreto (cf. H. Denifle, *Chartularium Univ. Paris.* (Paris, 1889), vol. I, p. 70). According to the statutes of 1215: non legantur libri Aristotelis *de methafisica* et *de naturali philosophia* nec summe de eisdem, aut de doctrina magistri David de Dinant aut Amalrici heretici aut Mauricii hyspani. The Mauricius in question was almost certainly Averroes (Denifle, vol. I, pp. 78–9).

the Albigensian movement. A letter issued by the masters of Toulouse in 1229 expressly states: libros naturales, qui fuerant Parisiis prohibiti, poterunt illic audire qui volunt naturae sinum medullitus perscrutari (Denifle, vol. I, p. 131).

184]

a common theme of the ninth-century poets. A good example of this connection is found in the lines where Walafrid condoles with his master Grimald for the happiness the latter is missing by having to leave his monastery to serve at the court:

> quamvis subter agas regum tabularia vitam,
> non te praetereo: specubusne latebis, Homere?
> novi namque Sicana tibi spelea placere,
> solus ubi Musis Musarum et amore fruaris.
>
> *de Imagine Tetrici*, ll. 227–30,

in *Mon. Germ. Hist. Poet. Lat. Aevi Carolini* (Berlin, 1884), vol. II, p. 377.

the departures of their friends. Among the well-known poems which deal with these subjects, one might cite the *Hortulus* of Walafrid Strabo, the *ad Colmanum* of Donatus, the *o cur iubes, pusiole* of Godescalc.

doctos grammaticos presbiterosque pios. Sedulius Scottus, *Mon. Germ. Hist. Poet. Lat. Aevi Car.* vol. III, p. 168.

aimed at a Walafrid. Ermenrich's indirect attack, denigrating the lovers of Virgil by running down Virgil himself, may, I think, be so dismissed as the product of an over-literal mind (Ermenrich of Ellwangen, *Epistola ad Grimaldum*, in *Mon. Germ. Hist. Epist.* vol. V, pp. 536 ff.).

185]
the Norman Belesme. In this monstrously cruel and rapacious family, the women were as powerful as the men, and vanity or pleasure dictated most of their crimes.

186]
fata dedere patri. Quoted by F. J. E. Raby, *op. cit.* vol. I, p. 315.

the patrons for whom he wrote. P. Abrahams, *Les Œuvres poétiques de Baudri de Bourgueil* (Paris, 1926), pp. 197–231.

187]
si promulgas, quae meretur. *Analecta Hymn. Medii Aevi*, I, 409.

189]
the fourth book of the Aeneid. Admittedly there was a general increase which affected all books; but the authors mentioned seem to have benefited from it to a disproportionate extent. Virgil is mentioned 27 times in the catalogues of the ninth century, 33 times in those of the eleventh, 72 times in those of the twelfth. The analogous figures for Terence are 1, 10, 25; for Ovid 3, 24, 77; for Horace 4, 34, 27; for Persius 3, 19, 32; for Juvenal 4, 16, 29. These calculations refer only to the catalogues mentioned by Manitius; but they may perhaps be regarded as representative even though not complete. See M. Manitius, *Handschriften antiker Autoren in mittelalterlichen Bibliotheks-katalogen* (Leipzig, 1935).

190]
the supernaturalist beliefs arrayed against it. T. Zielinski, *Cicero im Wandel der Jahrhunderte* (3rd ed. Leipzig, 1912).

his heart and mind were pure. P. Abrahams, *Les Œuvres poétiques de Baudri de Bourgueil*, p. 341:

> sed quicquid dicam, teneant mea facta pudorem,
> cor mundum vigeat, mensque pudica mihi.

the examples they have been given. Marbod of Rennes, *Liber Decem Capitulorum* (*P.L.* CLXXI, 1695):

> ad pueri propero lacrimas, quem verbere saevo
> iratus cogit dictata referre magister,
> dediscenda docens quae confixere poetae,
> stupra nefanda Iovis, seu Martis adultera facta,
> lascivos recitans iuvenes, turpesque puellas,
> mutua quos iunxit sed detestanda voluptas,
> imbuit ad culpam similem rude fabula pectus,
> praeventusque puer vitii ferventis odore
> iam cupit exemplo committere foeda deorum.

191]

the names of the ancient gods commonly figured. Anselm of Bisate, *Rhetorimachia* (ed. Duemmler), II, pp. 38–9.

heresy and magic suggestively appears. Rudolfus Glaber, *Historia*, II, 12 (*P.L.* CXLII, 614). Vilgardus is described as exceptionally assiduous in his grammatical studies; and he was accused of having made the rash statement that the poets were unimpeachable guides to conduct. If that was indeed the totality of his misdoing, we should be justified in regarding him as a martyr who suffered for the cause of classical studies. But Glaber goes on to report that opinions similar to those of Vilgardus were widespread in Italy, that the 'heresy' led to numerous executions and having spread from Sardinia to Spain needed there again to be stamped out by force. A singular career for a literary cult! And one is led to wonder what other interests were involved.

192]

Christi me simplicitas doceat. Petrus Damianus, *Dominus Vobiscum* (*P.L.* CXLV, 231): Platonem latentis naturae secreta rimantem respuo, planetarum circulis metas, astrorumque meatibus calculos affigentem: cuncta etiam sphaerici orbis climata radio distinguentem Pythagoram parvipendo: Nichomachum quoque tritum ephemeridibus digitos abdico: Euclidem perplexis geometricalium figurarum studiis incurvum aeque declino: cunctos sane rhetores cum suis syllogismis et sophisticis cavillationibus indignos hac quaestione decerno. Tremant gymnici suam iugiter amore sapientiae nuditatem: quaerant peripatetici latentem in profundo puteo veritatem.... Quid enim insanientium poetarum fabulosa commenta? Quid mihi tumentium tragicorum cothurnata discrimina? desinat iam comicorum turba venena libidinum crepitantibus buccis effluere, cesset satyricorum vulgus suos clarnos captoriae detractionis amaris dapibus onerare: non mihi Tulliani oratores accurata lepidae urbanitatis trutinent verba: non Demosthenici rhetores captiosae suadelae argumenta versuta componant: cedant in suas tenebras omnes terrenae sapientiae faecibus delibuti: nil mihi conferant sulphureo caliginosae doctrinae splendore caecati. Christi me simplicitas doceat, vera sapientium rusticitas ambiguitatis meae vinculum solvat.

corrupted the minds of sinners with their fantasies. Manegold of Lautenbach, *Contra Wolfelmum*, c. 9 (*P.L.* CLV, 158B): Proficiente et invalescente diaboli seminario, subsecuta est poetarum turba qui tanquam ioculatores ad nuptias idolatriae concurrentes, figmentis et immodestis laudibus animas vana sectantium oblectati sunt. Causa enim quaestus ad adulandum et maledicendum parati sceleratos principes et violentos praedones deificando, et inflatorum verborum tinnitu et sententiarum ornatu, nulla veri puritate munito, inutili memoriae et inani gloriae serviendo obscaena et turpia quibusdam involucris adornarunt et prout natura singulorum viguit alii comedi, alii lyrici, satyrici, tragoedi effecti multis phantasmatibus animas peccantium seduxerunt.

But the whole treatise with its extensive attacks on ancient philosophy deserves to be read.

the reading and imitation of Virgil and Ovid. Herbert of Losinga, *Epistolae*, ed. R. Anstruther (London, 1846), pp. 53–7 verum inter manus tuas unde Ovidianae falsitates et Virgilianae adinventiones. indecenter enim eodem ore Christus praedicatur et Ovidius recitatur.

not to learn anything but their psalter. William of Hirschau, *Prefatio in sua Astronomica* (*P.L.* CL, 64). Cum nobis monachis nihil liberalis scientiae praeter psalterium licere asserant.

193]
William of Malmesbury's history of the English kings. He makes use of Caesar, Livy, Pliny and Suetonius as well as quoting some of the classical poets. Cf. M. Manitius, *Geschichte der lateinischen Literatur des Mittelalters* (Munich, 1931), vol. III, p. 467.

194]
during the succeeding centuries. We may note in particular the Capitulary of Lothair in 825 establishing schools in eight of the principal Lombard cities (*Mon. Germ. Hist. Legum Sectio* II (Hanover, 1883), Tomus I, p. 327) and the decree of Pope Eugenius II in 826: in universis episcopis subiectisque plebibus et aliis locis in quibus necessitas occurrerit, omnis cura et diligentia adhibeatur ut magistri et doctores constituantur, qui studia literarum liberaliumque artium ac sancta habentes, dogmata assidua doceant (*Mon. Germ. Hist. Legum Sectio* III (Hanover and Leipzig, 1908), Tomus II2, p. 581). For further texts see Manacorda, *Storia della scuola in Italia* (I, *Il medio evo*), vol. II, pp. 41–69. Also A. Dresdner, *Kultur- und Sittengeschichte der italienischen Geistlichkeit* (Breslau, 1890); G. Salvioli, *L'instruzione publica in Italia* (Florence, 1912); Rashdall, *op. cit.* vol. I, pp. 90–1; P. Mandonnet, 'La crise scolaire au début du xiiie siècle et la fondation de l'ordre des Frères Précheurs', *Rev. d'Hist. Ecc.* I, XV (1914), pp. 34–49.

194]

rule of St Benedict ordained. On the monastic schools in general see U. Berlière, *L'ordre monastique des origines au xiie siècle*, ch. 3; also 'Ecoles claustrales du moyen âge', *Bulletin des Lettres de l'Académie Royale de Belgique* (1921), pp. 550–72; G. G. Coulton, 'Monastic Schools in the Middle Ages', reprinted in *Medieval Studies*, no. 10 (London, 1913); A. F. Leach, *The Schools of Medieval England* (London, 1915) with the criticism by A. G. Little in the *English Historical Review*, XXX, pp. 525–9. We hear that at Bec in Lanfranc's time *oblati* in the monastic schools received their education free while external students paid (Manacorda, *op. cit.* vol. II, pp. 44–6); D. Knowles, *The Monastic Order in England* (Cambridge, 1949), pp. 487–8.

195]

educated in a private and unorganised fashion by lay teachers. It is not easy to decide what importance we ought to ascribe to private teaching during the tenth and eleventh centuries. The question has been frequently debated; and basing their opinion on the undoubted fact that we possess no definite evidence about the existence of lay schools even in Italy before the thirteenth century certain historians among whom we must number Manacorda (*op. cit.* vol. I, p. 129), have held that earlier lay instruction was negligible in its extent. On the other hand, we know that as early as the tenth century there was an educated professional class of lawyers and doctors, some of whom at least do not appear to have taken even minor orders. Dresdner, who does his best to prove the ignorance of the Italian nobility, quoting such sources as Witholm, *Vita Bened. Clus.* 10 (*Mon. Germ. Hist. Scriptores* XII, 206), the *Vita S. Nili*, 35 (*Acta SS. Scpt.* VII, 304), and Peter Damian, *Opera* (ed. Caetanus) II, 432, is nevertheless perfectly prepared to admit the existence of educated laymen who were jurists and doctors, and indeed considers that Damian's remark (*Opusc.* LVIII, 3): quia tu in seculo non imum obtines locum, nec potes prorsus effugere, ut aliquando ...de litteratoriae disciplinae studiis non attingas—must have been addressed to one of them (A. Dresdner, *op. cit.* Excursus, 'Ueber die italienischen Laienbildung in 10 und 11 Jahrhundert'). If we agree that they received their training privately, it would seem to follow that a large number of people, parents, tutors and professional men must have devoted an appreciable amount of time to their upbringing. Admittedly, it is possible to argue that the range of this private teaching need not have been so great since the ecclesiastical system left numerous loopholes. At the schoolboy stage the distinction between a layman and a cleric or monk must have been not one of actual legal status, but of intention; and in many cases the intention must have been vague, especially where the sons of noble families were concerned. In the tenth century, for example, the future St Dunstan went from the Glastonbury cloister, where he was educated, to the court of Aethelstan, and it was only after his expulsion from the royal household that he became a monk. But even with this proviso, the amount of private teaching given must have been considerable. Indeed, Manacorda's view seems to rest on what is in the last analysis a verbal quibble. His argument is based on considerations of name and legal status rather than on realities. We know that in the smaller monastic schools, the master could count himself lucky if he had half a dozen novices of all ages to instruct, so that he must in effect have been giving individual tuition. Was such a master in a very different position from the tutor in a noble family who had perhaps half a dozen youngsters under his care, or from the professional man who undertook the training of half a dozen apprentices? Yet there must have been many such; for we have no reason to suppose that conditions in Italy at this date were very different from those prevailing in Byzantium. To give the name of school consistently to the monastic establishments and to deny it to the classes run by private individuals and so to underestimate the importance of the latter in comparison to the former, seems therefore to involve a certain blindness about what must have actually happened. There was a private system of education, especially in Italy, which was not enormous in its extent, which was not comparable to the system run by the Church, but which was nevertheless far from negligible.

196]

the methods used by Bernard of Chartres. John of Salisbury, *Metalogicon,* I, c. 24 (*P.L.* CXCIX, 854) (in C. C. Webb's edition the passage appears on pp. 55–6): Sequebatur hunc morem Bernardus Carnotensis, exundantissimus modernis temporibus fons literarum in Gallia, et in auctorum lectione quid simplex esset, et ad imaginem regule positum ostendebat; figuras grammaticae, colores rethoricos, cavillationes sophismatum, et qua parte sui propositae lectionis articulus respiciebat ad alias disciplinas, proponebat in medio; ita tamen ut non in singulis universa doceret, sed pro capacitate audientium dispensaret eis in tempore doctrinae mensuram. Et, quia splendor orationis aut *a proprietate* est, id est, cum adiectivum aut verbum substantivo eleganter adiungitur, aut *a translatione,* id est, ubi sermo ex causa probabili ad alienam traducitur significationem, haec, sumpta occasione, inculcabat mentibus auditorum. Et quoniam memoria exercitio firmatur, ingeniumque acuitur ad imitandum ea quae audiebant, alios admonitionibus, alios flagellis et poenis urgebat. Cogebantur excoluere singuli die sequenti aliquid eorum que precedenti audierant; alii plus, alii minus; erat enim apud eos precedentis discipulus sequens dies. Vespertinum exercitium, quid declinatio dicebatur, tanta copiositate grammaticae refertum erat, ut si quis in eo per annum integrum versaretur, rationem loquendi et scribendi, si non esset hebetior, haberet ad manum, et significationem sermonum, qui in communi usu versantur, ignorare non posset. Sed quia nec scolam nec diem aliquem decet esse religionis expertem, ea proponebatur materia quae fidem edificaret et mores, et unde qui conuenerant, quasi collatione quadam, animarentur ad bonum. Novissimus autem huius declinationis, immo philosophice collationis, articulus pietatis vestigia preferebat; et animas defunctorum commendabat devota oblatione psalmi qui in poenitentialibus sextus est et in oratione Dominica Redemptori suo. Quibus autem indicebantur preexercitamina

puerorum in prosis, aut poematibus imitandis poetas aut oratores proponebat, et eorum iubebat vestigia imitari, ostendens iuncturas dictionum
et elegantes sermonum clausulas. Si quis autem ad splendorem sui operis
alienum pannum assuerat, deprehensum redarguebat furtum; sed poenam
sepissime non infligebat. Sic vero redargutum, si hoc tamen meruerat
inepta positio ad exprimendam auctorum imaginem, modesta indulgentia
conscendere iubebat, faciebatque, ut qui majores imitabatur, fieret posteris
imitandus. Id quoque inter prima rudimenta docebat et infigebat animis,
quae in economia virtus; quae in decore rerum, que in verbis laudanda
sint; ubi tenuitas et quasi macies sermonis, ubi copia probabilis, ubi
excedens, ubi omnium modus. Historias, poemata persurrenda monebat
diligenter quidem et qui velut nullis calcaribus urgebantur ad fugam; et
ex singulis aliquid reconditum in memoria, diurum debitum diligenti
instantia exigebat. Superflua tamen fugienda dicebat; et ea sufficere que
a claris auctoribus scripta sunt.

practised giving short sermons themselves. John uses the word *collatio* twice
in this passage, first with reference to the short sermon which ended
Bernard's evening lectures, and then with reference to one of the activities
he prescribed for his pupils during the morning lesson: prosas et poemata
cotidie scriptitabant, et se mutuis exercebant *collationibus*, quo quidem
exercitio nichil utilius ad eloquentiam, nichil expeditius ad scientiam et
plurimum confert ad vitam, si tamen hanc sedulitatem regit caritas, si in
profectu litterario servetur humilitas (*Metalogicon* (*P.L.* cxcix, 856)).
Both Paré and Webb are of the opinion that the word should be given a
different meaning in these two passages, that the *collationes* composed by
Bernard's pupils were not sermons but general exercises by means of
which they showed off their knowledge to each other in friendly rivalry.
But would a writer of John's calibre who is usually careful in his use of
technical terms give a word such different connotations in the same short
passage without explaining his intention? And it does not appear alien to
the generally religious character of Bernard's teaching that he should have
expected his pupils to demonstrate their rhetorical skill in the form of
a model sermon. Such a *collatio* would be a test of learning, would
provide opportunities for emulation and would yet serve the purposes of
piety. There are some grounds for interpreting the passage to mean that
at the end of the morning lesson the students took it in turns to give a
short sermon which each tried perhaps to make as rhetorically perfect as
possible so as to outdo those who had spoken on earlier occasions.

198]
the mixing of classical and contemporary elements. During the Renaissance
the Humanists kept their works free from contemporary turns of speech,
and this admixture occurred for the most part when material drawn from
the classics found its way into vernacular literature. Thus, the task of
welding the present to the past fell rather to the dilettantes who used the
fruits of scholarship and was not, as it had been in the Middle Ages, a
monopoly of the serious scholars.

204]

was prepared to countenance. Petrus Damianus, *Sermo VI de S. Eleuchadio*
(*P.L.* CXLIV, 541) Mulieri quippe caesariem radimus, cum rationabilis
disciplinae sensus superfluos amputamus... Quae etiam vestem deponere
in qua est capta praecipitur, ut superdictam fabularum et quorumlibet
figmentorum exuat superficiem ac solidam verae rationis exhibeat veritatem.

208]

a lively interest in literary studies. Guibert of Nogent, *de Vita Sua* I, 4 (*P.L.*
CLVI, 844A) Erat paulo ante id temporis et adhuc partim sub meo tempore
tanta grammaticorum raritas, ut in oppidis pene nullus, in urbibus vix
aliquis reperiri potuisset, et quos inveniri contigerat, eorum scientia
tenuis erat, nec etiam moderni temporis clericulis vagantibus comparari
poterat. This refers to a period about 1060. Writing half a century later
he says (*Gesta Dei per Francos* (*P.L.* CLVI, 681)) Cum enim passim videa-
mus fervere grammaticam et quibusque vilissimis prae numerositate
scolarum hanc patere noverimus disciplinam, horrori fuit... hanc nostri
gloriam temporis non scribere.

not usage but reason. Cf. the passage in the commentary on the *Doctrinale*
which is known as the Glosa notabilis: 'Primus inventor grammaticae
positivae fuit metaphysicus et naturalis philosophus, quod ille considerans
diversas proprietates, naturam et modos essendi rerum, rebus imposuit
diversa nomina' (quoted Reichling, *Das Doctrinale des Alexander de
Villa Dei* (Berlin, 1893)).

209]

has credo servandas tempore nostro. D. Reichling, *Das Doctrinale des Alexander
de Villa Dei* (Berlin, 1893), ll. 2330–1. Cf. also Johannes Januensis,
Catholicon Scias quod, licet quaedam nomina inveniantur auctoritate
veterum quandoque in masc. genere, quandoque in neutro, ut hic punctus,
hoc punctum et hic catinus, hoc catinum, non tamen debent dici incerti
generis, quia masculinum talium nominum iam cessavit, quia non utimur
nisi neutro genere istorum nominum (quoted by Reichling in the above
edition of the *Doctrinale*, p. 139).

failed to obey the classical rules; So we find John of Garland, a contemporary
of Alexander, writing:

> Pagina divina non vult se subdere legi
> Grammatices, nec vult illius arte regi.

Cf. Thurot, *Notices et extraits de divers manuscrits latins pour servir à
l'histoire des doctrines grammaticales au moyen âge.* (*Notices et extraits des
manuscrits de la Bibl. Impér. et autres bibl.* XXII, 2) (Paris, 1868), p. 526.

210]

a scholastic grammar. Evrard of Béthune, *Grecismus*, ed. Wroebel, p. ix
Cum Priscianus non docuerit grammaticam per omnem modum sciendi
possibilem, in eo sua doctrina est valde diminuta. Unde constructiones
multas dicit, quarum tamen causas non assignat, sed solum eas declarat per

auctoritatem antiquorum grammaticorum. Propter quod non docet, quia illi tantum docent, qui causas suorum dictorum assignant.

Equally popular, and similar in their approach to the subject, were the commentaries on Priscian by Robert Kilwardby, a Paris Master of Arts who became Archbishop of Canterbury in 1271; and the lexicographers with their traditional enthusiasm for 'explaining' words, also contributed to the growing impression that language was essentially a logical construction. There was a great vogue for etymological dictionaries. The Dominican Balbi of Genoa, whose *Catholicon* was placed as a book of reference in French Churches, derives 'laicus' as follows: popularis, et dicitur a laos quod est populus, vel potius a laos quod est lapis: inde laicus est lapideus quia durus et extraneus est a scientia litterarum. He and others who followed the same line attempted to relate the etymology of each word to the function of the person or thing denoted by it. And their influence is clearly seen in the strange metaphors which crept into the literature of the day: Pontifex interpretatur 'Pontem faciens', et presbyter, 'Prebens iter'. Faciunt enim pontes et itinera ultra tempestuosa flumina huius mundi (quoted by G. R. Owst, *Preaching in Medieval England*, p. 38).

the Grecismus *had a long run.* Reichling, *op. cit.*, mentions 228 manuscripts which contain either the whole, or a part, or commentaries on, the *Doctrinale*. He considered 28 to date from the thirteenth century, 53 from the fourteenth, 144 from the fifteenth and 3 from the sixteenth. There were in addition 279 printed versions, 163 of which belong to the period before 1500. The *Grecismus* was printed eight times in France, 1487–1500.

after the middle of the twelfth century. These treatises on rhetoric have been collected by Faral in a single volume of great interest, and it is there the reader must go for details (E. Faral, *Les Arts Poétiques du xiie et du xiiie siècle*, Bibliothèque de l'Ecole des Hautes Etudes, Fasc. 238, Paris, 1924).

211]

a master trained at Chartres. He was a pupil of Bernard of Tours, who was a pupil of Thierry of Chartres.

214]

the meaning tended to vanish. Most of these distinctions derive of course from the *de Inventione* and the *ad Herennium*, so the statement about the novelty of the scholastic rhetoric may appear to require some further support. In effect, the categories of the *de Inventione* constituted only a small part of the training given in the Roman schools as we can see from Cicero's other treatises and from Quintilian. During the early Middle Ages, the *de Inventione* and the *ad Herennium* were in general use, but their influence was tempered by two circumstances. First, there were not many students sufficiently advanced to read them. Secondly, the free and easy teaching methods of the time did not lend themselves to the imposition of a technique which involved elaborate analyses while reading. It was only the increase in the size of the schools after 1100 that made the study of systematic rhetoric possible. A master would not trouble to dissect a text for one or two advanced pupils. But the method would be labour-saving for anyone faced with a large class.

215]

helping others with their correspondence. C. H. Haskins, *Medieval Culture* (Oxford, 1929), p. 170. The two great centres for the production of model letters and treatises on letter-writing were Bologna which catered particularly for the requirements of the jurists, and Orléans. The leading practitioner of the art in Bologna was the grammarian Buoncompagno, who in 1215 produced an *Ars Dictaminis* in seven volumes. For a bibliography see J. de Ghellinck, *L'Essor de la littérature latine au xiie siècle* (Paris, 1946). Bernard Silvestris, the teacher of Matthew of Vendôme, who figures as an educational innovator in a number of fields, composed a *Summa Dictaminum* in verse which was later abridged in prose (C. V. Langlois, *Bibl. de l'école de Chartres* (1893), pp. 225–37).

216]

ancient literature. Abélard, *Hist. Calam.* c. 8 (*P.L.* CLXXVIII, 140) Mihi semper objiciebant quod proposito monachi valde sit contrarium saecularium librorum studio detineri.

a book composed some time before 1150. Conrad of Hirschau, *Dialogus super auctores sive Didascalion* (ed. Schepps, Würzburg, 1889).

217]

dominated in all its particulars by religious beliefs. Cf. F. Ghisalberti, 'Arnolfo d'Orléans, un cultore d'Ovidio nel secolo XII' in *Memorie del R. Istituto Lombardo di Scienze e Lettere*, XXIV (1932), pp. 157–234. Arnulf wrote in his commentary on the *Fasti*: Ut evidencius appareant quae in serie huius libri disposita sunt, antequam ad litteram accedamus, compendiose quaedam sunt praelibanda, hec scilicet: quis sit titulus operis, que causa suscepti laboris, que intentio scribentis, que utilitas legentis, cui parti philosophie supponatur. (Quoted by L. Delisle, 'Summa Dictaminis', *Annuaire-bulletin de la Société de l'histoire de France*, 1869, p. 148.)

nisi expositione vel interpretatione non invenitur. Hugo of St Victor, *Didascalion*, III, 9 (*P.L.* CLXXVI, 771 D).

per moralitatem vita legentis instituenda. Conrad of Hirschau, *op. cit.* p. 46.

the Old and New Testaments. Notably of Plato; see Abélard, *Dialectica* (ed. Cousin, *Œuvres inédits d'Abélard*, Paris, 1836), p. 475. But Bernard of Utrecht (d. 1099) used allegory in his commentary on the *Eclogue* of Theodulus, a ninth-century poem which was widely read in schools (J. Frey, *Ueber das mittelalterliche Gedicht Theoduli Ecloga und den Kommentar des Bernhardus Ultraiect*, Münster, 1904.

C. S. Lewis's excellent book. C. S. Lewis, *The Allegory of Love* (Oxford, 1938).

218]

constantly verges on the comical. Fulgentius, *Mythologiarum lib. III; Expositio Vergilianae Continentiae* (ed. R. Helm, Teubner Series, 1898). On the influence of Fulgentius see H. Liebeschuetz, *Fulgentius metaforalis* (Leipzig, 1926).

219]

little more than the excuse for a sermon. Commenti Bernardi Silvestris super sex libros Eneidos Virgilii (ed. G. Riedel, Greifswald, 1924). The history of this medieval practice of allegorical thinking has yet to be written. We may regard it as a curious divagation of the human mind. But it has the interest of being perhaps the only intellectual technique which men have used extensively and have now completely abandoned. If we grant certain presuppositions and in particular the existence of a Creator who desires to instruct us in theology and morality through the medium of the natural world, we shall not find anything unreasonable or extravagant in methods employed by the allegorizers. They furnish us with telling examples of a failing common in the history of thought, the tendency to transfer explanations valid in one sphere of discourse to other spheres where they do not apply. The sociologies of Barcelo and H. C. Carey have their place alongside the commentaries of Bernard Silvestris and John Myrc's *Festiall.* The classical world made its contribution to allegorical thinking largely through the medium of Macrobius' *Commentary on the Somnium Scipionis* and the *Mitologiae* of Fulgentius; and there can be no doubt that the Neoplatonic conception of the universe provided a philosophic justification for many an extravagance. In this dangerous borderland it is hard to distinguish the influence of Plato from that of his successors.

Omnis mundi creatura nostrum statum pingit rosa,
quasi liber et pictura nostri status decens glosa,
nobis est in speculum; nostrae vitae lectio;
nostrae vitae, nostrae mortis quae dum primo mane floret,
nostri status, nostrae sortis defloratus flos effloret
fidele signaculum. vespertino senio.

ergo spirans flos expirat
in pallorem dum delirat,
oriendo moriens;
simul vetus et novella,
simul senex et puella,
rosa marcet oriens.

(Alan of Lille, quoted Raby, *op. cit.* vol. II, p. 15.)

The original statement of the Platonic theme is impressive, but even in this short and lovely poem, the elaboration of the allegory borders on the extravagant. The later developments of this type of writing, the dreams and visions which represent the progress of the soul, the personified virtues and vices of the morality plays, the habit of stretching the original parallel to cover every tiny detail, are familiar features of medieval literature. The sermon writers had been the first to discover the uses of allegory and they remained its most hardened exponents. 'Lust consumes the body. It destroys the tongue of confession... the eyes of the intelligence, the ears of obedience, the nose of discretion, the hairs of good thoughts, the beard of fortitude, the eyebrows of holy religion...': MS. Add. 21253, fol. 27*b*, quoted by G. R. Owst, *Preaching in Medieval England* (Cambridge, 1926), p. 26. For the classical sources of allegory see in particular: M. Schedler, *Die Philosophie des Macrobius und ihr Einfluss auf die Wissenschaft des christlichen Mittelalters* (Münster, 1916); and L. K. Born, 'Ovid and allegory' in *Speculum*, IX (1934), pp. 362–79.

the number of classical authors who were read steadily increased. Conrad of Hirschau, *Dialogus super auctores sive Didascalion* (ed. Schepps, Würzburg, 1889), writing at the beginning of the twelfth century, gives the following list: Donatus, Cato, Aesop, Avianus, Sedulius, Juvencus, Prosper, Theodulus, Arator, Prudentius, Tullius (Cicero), Sallust, Boethius, Lucan, Horace, Ovid, Juvenal, Homer (the *Ilias Latina*), Persius, Statius and Virgil. He claims that these writers were regularly read. Eberhard the German, *Laborintus*, ll. 599–686 (ed. E. Faral, *Les Arts Poétiques du xviie et du xviiie siècle* (Paris, 1924), pp. 358–61) recommends all the above authors except Cicero, Sallust, Juvencus and Prosper, but adds Claudian, Martianus Capella, Maximianus, Sidonius Apollinaris and Dares as well as a host of contemporaries. The Englishman, Alexander Neckham (*Gonville and Caius MS.* 385, part I, quoted C. H. Haskins, *Medieval Science*, p. 372), omits from the authors who figure in Conrad's list Aesop, Avianus, Persius, Lucan, the *Ilias Latina*, the Christian poets and Boethius. On the other hand, he adds Martial, Petronius, Livy, Quintus Curtius, Suetonius, Seneca, Quintilian, Pompeius Trogus (Justin's Epitome), Solinus, Sidonius and Symmachus.

the product of a transitional age. John of Salisbury (1110–80) quotes Cicero extensively, but also Seneca, Terence, Virgil, Ovid, Horace, Persius, Juvenal, Martial, Petronius, Suetonius, the elder and younger Pliny, Quintilian, Frontinus, Gellius, Apuleius, Florus, Justin, Publilius Syrus, Sidonius Apollinaris, the *Scriptores Historiae Augustae*, Ausonius and Claudian (Manitius, *Geschichte der lateinischen Literatur des Mittelalters*, vol. III, p. 225).

Peter of Blois, his friend and pupil (1135–1204) quotes in addition to the poets: Cicero (except for the speeches), Valerius Maximus, Seneca (the *Letters*), and Macrobius. He also claims to have read Curtius, Livy, Tacitus (the *Histories*) and Suetonius (Manitius, *op. cit.* vol. III, pp. 293, 299).

Giraldus Cambrensis (1147–1222) refers to an imposing number of pagan authors. The *de Principis Instructione* alone contains reminiscences of Suetonius, Seneca, Publilius Syrus, Martial and Servius, in addition to the more usual poets and prose writers.

220]

Virgil, Donatus and Boethius. Mémoire sur les bibliothèques des archévêques et du chapitre de Rouen (Précis analytique des travaux de l'académie de Rouen 1851–2), pp. 477–8.

the broad general characteristics of the ancient authors. H. Liebeschuetz, *Medieval Humanism in the Life and Writings of John of Salisbury* (London, 1950).

222]

the bewilderments of allegory. E. K. Rand, 'The Classics in the 13th century', *Speculum* IV (1926), pp. 249–69. L. J. Paetow, *The Arts Course at Medieval Universities with special reference to Grammar and Rhetoric* (Illinois, 1910); *Two medieval Satires of the University of Paris: La Bataille des vii arts of Henri d'Andeli and the Morale Scholasticum of John of Garland* (Berkeley, California, 1927). B. L. Ullman, 'A project for a new edition of Vincent of Beauvais', *Speculum* VIII (1933), pp. 312–26.

an unofficial interest in the classics. Powicke and Emden, Rashdall's *Medieval Universities*, vol. I, p. 73 n.

foretold the coming of Christ. On the Virgil legend see Comparetti, *Vergilio nel medio evo* (1872).

made the incidents of ancient history their own. The Alexander story was popular from the ninth century onwards.

223]

one's olfactory shrinking from stench. Oda (quod est cantus vel laus) componitur cum *tragos* (quod est hircus et dicitur hic *tragedia*—e); id est hircina laus, vel hircinus cantus, id est fetidus; est enim de crudelissimis rebus, sicut qui patrem vel matrem interficit, et comedit filium, vel e contrario et hujusmodi. Unde et tragedo dabatur hircus, id est animal fetidum non quod non haberet aliud dignum praemium sed ad fetorem materie designandum (from the thirteenth-century *Magnae Derivationes* of Ugoccione of Pisa). For a description of this work see Paget Toynbee, *Dante Studies and Researches*, p. 97.

were able scholars. Cf. A. Renaudet, *Dante Humaniste* (Paris, 1952); J. H. Whitfield, *Dante and Virgil*, Oxford, 1949.

'Altercatio Phyllidis et Florae.' Notably perhaps such poems as the 'O comes amoris, dolor' (J. A. Schmeller, *Carmina Burana* (Stuttgart, 1847), p. 225), the 'Dum Diana vitrea' (*ibid.* p. 124) and the 'Abmittamus studia' (*ibid.* p. 137). One may mention also

> artes amatorie iam non instruuntur,
> a Nasone tradite, passim pervertuntur;
> nam si quis istis utitur, more modernorum
> turpiter abutitur hac assuetudine morum.
>
> Naso meis artibus feliciter instructus
> mundique voluptatibus et regulis subductus
> ab errore studuit mundum revocare,
> qui sibi notus erit, docuit sapienter amare.

appear in the vernacular. H. Brinkmann, *Geschichte der lateinischen Liebesdichtung in Mittelalter* (Halle, 1925). A. Jeanroy, *Les Origines de la poésie en France au moyen âge* (Paris, 1925).

225]

raised three years later. B. Geyer, *Friedrich Ueberwegs Grundriss der Geschichte der Philosophie*, Zweiter Teil, p. 350.

226]

co-exist in his work without commingling. Cf. B. Geyer, *Ueberwegs Grundriss der Geschichte der Philosophie*, Zweiter Teil (Berlin, 1928), p. 416: 'laufen in der Gedankenwelt Alberts die Verschiedenen Stroemungen des Aristotelismus, des arabischen Neuplatonismus und der augustinischen Tradition unverbunden nebeneinander her. Es ist nicht ohne Interesse zu sehen, wie die gennanten Richtungen in dem albertischen Schulkreise auch unverbunden weiterwirkten.'

228]

know how to teach it. R. Bacon, *Opera Hactenus Inedita* I; *Opus Tertium* (ed. J. S. Brewer), p. 33 (London, 1859).

231]

the poets and orators. John of Salisbury, *Polycraticus* VII, 9 (ed. Webb, p. 126).

232]

repeated by Gerbert. Boethius, *In Porph.* (*P.L.* LXIII, 1112). On Gerbert, see Richer, *Historiae* III, 55–61 (*P.L.* CXXXVIII, 105–7).

to grammar, dialectic and rhetoric. G. Paré *et al.*, *La Renaissance du xiie siècle* (Paris, 1933), p. 100, state Hugh's system in tabular form:

$$
\text{Partitio artium (} Philosophia \text{)}
\begin{cases}
scientia\ theorica = \begin{cases} theologia \\ mathematica = \begin{cases} arithmetica \\ musica \\ geometria \\ astronomia \end{cases} \\ physica \end{cases} \\
scientia\ practica = \text{solitaria, privata, publica} \\
scientia\ mechanica = \text{lanificium, armatura etc.} \\
scientia\ logica = \begin{cases} grammatica \\ dissertiva \begin{cases} demonstratio \\ probabilis \begin{cases} dialectica \\ rhetorica \end{cases} \\ sophistica \end{cases} \end{cases}
\end{cases}
$$

On the unity of philosophy, see Hugh of St Victor, *Didascalion* II, 31 (*P.L.* CLXXVI, 764C); and on the active character of learning, *ibid.* II, 1 (*P.L.* CLXXVI, 572C).

ancillary to the study of things (res). William of Conches, *de Philosophia Mundi* IV, 41 (*P.L.* CLXXII, 100).

234]

science and philosophy part company. Also of course the fact that after 1255 the University of Paris was recommending the forbidden books of Aristotle for its arts course.

prepared originally for their classical forerunners. The fact that Roger Bacon was responsible for certain advances in scientific thought and was condemned in 1277 appears at first sight to militate against this conclusion. But the reasons for Bacon's condemnation are not certain, and it may well have been due to the intemperate manner in which he criticised his contemporaries. He had accused Aquinas, for example, of 'a childish vanity and a voluminous superfluity'.

discussed by a Vincent of Beauvais. J. Bourgeat, *Etudes sur Vincent de Beauvais* (Paris, 1856). Bonterre, 'Vincent de Beauvais et la connaissance de l'antiquité classique au xiie siècle', *Rev. des Quest. Hist.* XVII, 1875.

man and the universe. The fourth, the *Speculum Morale*, was not written by Vincent but dates from early in the fourteenth century.

241]

the tutor of Edward III. Richard of Bury, *Philobiblon*, trans. E. C. Thomas (London, 1902), p. 65.

uprightness of character and right living. Coluccio Salutati, *Epistolario*, ed. F. Novati (4 vols. 1892–1911), vol. I, p. 304.

the Latin poets. W. H. Woodward, *Vittorino da Feltre and other Humanist Educators* (Cambridge, 1897), p. 125.

245]

enviable and uplifting. I have borrowed this phrase from a recent analysis of the spirit that prompted American art collectors like Mellon and Kress, a class of men who had much in common with the Italian patrons of the fourteenth and fifteenth centuries. See S. N. Behrman, *Duveen* (London, 1952).

246]

managed to rise out of their class. It is not unusual for an attitude which derives from some condition common to two societies to find a different expression in each of them. Thus, the isolation of intellectuals in an industrial society has been noted by both English and modern Russian writers. The cure favoured by the Russians is for the intellectual to immerse himself in the dusty interests of some small community, and one may perhaps assume that this line of action which has been so widely advertised (cf. the novel *Happiness* by P. Pavlenko, that is supposed to have sold by the million in the U.S.S.R.), is in some cases at least actually followed. In Victorian England, on the other hand, Leslie Stephen, according to his latest biographer (N. Annan, *Leslie Stephen*, London, 1951), combated his sense of isolation by cultivating a universally admired physical prowess in the Trinity Hall Boats and the comradeship of the Alpine Club.

a poem praising Robert of Anjou. G. Voigt, *Die Wiederbelebung des classischen Altertums*, vol. I, p. 24.

to celebrate in his verse. In the preface to his *Historia rerum in Italia gestarum*, ed. Muratori (Scriptt. IX, 1051).

247]

in order to honour famous men. R. Sabbadini, *Le Scoperte dei codici Latini e Greci* (Florence, 1905), pp. 2–3.

249]

the Metamorphoses *of Ovid.* L. J. Paetow, *The Arts Course at the Medieval Universities*, Univ. of Illinois Studies (1910).

anti-scholastic society. It is interesting to speculate what would have happened, if he had made the opposite choice, if he had espoused the vernacular and put his trust in the spontaneous creativity of his day. The history of literature would almost certainly have been very different. We should not in all probability have had tragedies and comedies on the classical model. We should not have had Ronsard's *Pindaric Odes* or Milton's *Paradise Lost.* The languages of Europe—especially French and English—would have had fewer words of Latin origin, and a less latinised syntax. And presumably our categories of thought would also have been affected. One day someone will undertake the tedious but important piece of research of tracing and classifying the expressions that came into the languages of Europe from Latin and Greek between 1400 and 1600: and then we shall discover how precisely our way of thinking has been influenced by concepts which have their origins not in our experience but in conditions peculiar to Greek and Roman life.

250]

champion of the Roman people. F. Petrarch, *Epp. rer. fam.* XI, 16 and 17. J. H. Whitfield, *Petrarch and the Renaissance* (Oxford, 1943), p. 36, notes that Petrarch's appeal to Charles IV describes the emperor's power to save Rome as different only in degree from Rienzi's. 'If a Tribune could achieve so much, what shall the name of Caesar do' (*Epp. rer. fam.* XVIII, 1). This is a very different attitude from Dante's, who considered that no one but an emperor could help Italy. Petrarch's attitude is an earnest of his thoroughly individualist outlook.

251]

the constructions of its commentators. One ought to note perhaps that in Petrarch's day, and certainly at the time when he received his training at Bologna, the tradition of contemporary law stood closer to the *Digest* than was the case later. The Bartolists had not yet done their work.

Medicine exists and is of great importance. Petrarch, *Epp. rer. Sen.* XII, 2, 1002 Ego vero et esse Medicinam et magnum aliquid esse non dubito. But cf. *ibid.* V, 4, 844 and XII, 2, 1004 for his opinions on current medical knowledge.

contribute to the good life? Petrarch, *De ignorantia*, 24.

252]

the Justinian law. The career of Roger Bacon seems to afford a certain amount of evidence for this statement. Although he was deeply learned in all his sources, his main contributions to science consist not in his interpretations of Aristotle and Alkindi, but in original discoveries. Science had by the thirteenth century reached the stage where to advance was to go beyond the classical level of achievement, and the same was largely true of logic, Aristotelian metaphysics, medicine and law. With only the contemporary techniques of interpretation at its disposal, Humanism had no more to achieve in these fields.

un grand pas en avant.... Nolhac, P. de, *Pétrarque et l'Humanisme*, p. 16.

253]

through the love we have for them. Petrarch, *De sui ipsius et multorum aliorum ignorantia,* ed. Capella (1906), p. 68.

255]

the authority of the Church. It is worth noting (if only as another factor in the collapse of the thirteenth-century synthesis) that during the early part of Petrarch's career, William of Ockham, pursuing his speculations within the framework of scholastic thought, so sharply reduced the number of theological truths demonstrable by reasoning, that in the end he left no rational basis for belief. Religion for his nominalist successors was a matter of mystical faith, an attitude which had much in common with the Humanist approach as the doctrines of Lefèvre d'Etaples and the *Apologie de Raimond Sebond* were later to demonstrate.

gave the Middle Ages its coup de grâce. G. Saitta, *L'Educazione dell' Umanesimo* (1928), p. 17.

256]

Horace and Petrarch.

Classical authors		Patristic, medieval and contemporary	
Cicero	64	Old Testament	75
Virgil	57	New Testament	64
Seneca	24	St Augustine	31
Aristotle	22	Petrarch	20
Ovid	22	St Jerome	14
Horace	20	Dante	10
Valerius Maximus	16	Boethius	9
Terence	11	St Gregory	8
Suetonius	10		
Juvenal	9		
Macrobius	9		
Pliny	8		
Livy, Plato, Plutarch	7 (each)		
Persius	6		
Lucan	5		

No other author occupies over five lines.

Eberhard the German. It is interesting to note, as a sidelight on the so-called backwardness of the northern Renaissance, that while Salutati, the Italian, preferred a contemporary writer to the ancients, the Englishman Richard of Bury, half a century earlier, adopted a much more cautious attitude. 'Although the novelties of the moderns were never disagreeable to our desires...yet we have wished with more undoubted avidity to investigate the well-tested labours of the ancients' (*Philobiblon,* trans. E. C. Thomas, p. 65).

257]

biographical notices on famous authors. Sabbadini, *Le Scoperte dei codici latini e greci nel secoli xiv e xv* (Florence, 1905), p. 7.

enjoyed an equal renown. F. Buisson, *Répertoire des Ouvrages pédagogiques du xvi⁰ siècle* (Paris, 1886), p. 71; also *British Museum, Catalogue of books printed in France 1470–1600* (London, 1924), pp. 71–2, 348.

his brutality rather than by his knowledge. Giovanni da Ravenna, *Rationarium Vitae*, ch. 7 (in R. Sabbadini, *Giovanni da Ravenna*, Florence) 'quippe cum essem ordinis secundi, cunctorum latina carmina antecedentium Catonis, praeterea Prosperi, Boetii quidquid legeretur complecti mente et reddere compellebat'. The same authors are mentioned in Giovanni Dominici's *Regola del governo di cura familiare* (Florence, 1860). The order, however, is different. First came the *Psalter*, and then the latinati read Cato, Aesop, Boethius' *de Consolatione*, Prosper. The same biography of Giovanni of Ravenna tells in lurid detail of the punishments inflicted upon the boys: imprisonment on frosty nights naked in an unheated cellar, daily floggings also naked until the blood flowed, and one atrocious case where a lad was suspended for hours trussed hand and foot in a well. All this was between the ages of six and ten.

258]

the arts of persuasion. E. Walser, *Poggius Florentinus: Leben und Werke* (Leipzig, 1914), pp. 8–9. The decree authorising the reappointment of Giovanni Malpighini to the post of rhetoric teacher is of particular interest: considerantes quod ars rhetorica non solum omnium scientiarum persuasorium instrumentum est sed rerum publicarum maximum ornamentum. The date is 1397 (Gherardi, *Statuti della Universita e Studio fior*, Vieusseuz Firenza, 1881, p. 369).

more profitable branch of study. Compare the famous story of Petrarch's father burning his son's library of Latin authors and compelling the lad to spend seven years studying law (Petrarch, *Epp. rer. sen.* XVI, i). Giovanni da Ravenna was much criticised by his friends for his unwillingness to sacrifice rhetoric for law (*Rationarium Vitae* c. 17). Poggio also picked up his literary training in his spare time (Poggius Florentinus, *Epistolae*, XIII (III, 185 ff.), ed. Ton).

in his autobiography. *Rationarium Vitae*, see note on p. 257 above.

when Vergerio wrote his de Ingenuis Moribus. This date is in dispute. It depends upon a reference to fighting at Brescia. W. H. Woodward takes this to refer to the siege in 1404 (*Vittorino da Feltre and other Humanist Educators* (Cambridge, 1905), p. 113). C. A. Combi, *Epistole di P. P. Vergerio Seniore* (Misc. Publ. della R. Deputazione Veneta di Storia Patria, ser. 4, vol. V, p. xix), refers it to the Battle of Brescia in 1392. The latter dating would put the writing of the book before Vergerio's contacts with Chrysoloras and render the above apology unnecessary.

on no account encouraged. P. P. Vergerio, *de Ingenuis Moribus* (English trans. in W. H. Woodward, *op. cit.* pp. 99–100).

259]

inculcated by philosophy. Vergerio, *loc. cit.* p. 106.

definite creative potentialities. Scholasticism was to retain some of its dynamic in logical studies as late as the sixteenth century. Cf. H. Elie, *Le Traité 'de l'Infini' de Jean Mayor* (Paris, 1936).

260]

during the early years of the century. One notable order was for a translation of Aristotle from Bishop Rouberto of Reggio. Cf. Jules Gay, 'Notes sur l'Hellénisme sicilien', *Byzantion* I, p. 215.

261]

abstruse and esoteric lore. Petrarch, *Epp. rer. fam.* III, I.

any notable extent after 1300. The catalogues edited by Manitius may be assumed to constitute a representative sample of what the libraries of the period contained. The following table summarises some of the trends they indicate.

Author or Work		Number of times mentioned		
		Twelfth century	Thirteenth century	Fourteenth century
Terence	(complete?)	25	6	9
	(part)	7	9	I
Virgil	(complete?)	36	7	13
	(*Aeneid*)	9	11	7
	(*Georgics*)	9	4	—
	(*Eclogues*)	15	12	8
Horace	(complete?)	18	17	10
	(*Epistles*)	3	9	9
	(*Ars Poet.*)	3	7	16
	(*Satires*)	—	7	5
Ovid	(complete?)	5	2	8
	(*Heroides*)	16	17	6
	(*Epp. ex Ponto*)	11	9	4
	(*Tristia*)	2	5	5
	(*Ars Amat.*)	6	7	3
	(*Rem. Amor.*)	7	12	11
	(*Metamorph.*)	10	16	7
	(*Fasti*)	4	6	10
Lucan	(complete?)	28	29	13
Persius	(complete?)	32	17	11
Juvenal	(complete?)	29	13	12
Sallust	(complete?)	31	25	13
Caesar	(complete?)	8	5	4
Cicero	(*Rhetoric*)	35	35	35
	(*de Offic.*)	7	8	15
	(*de Senec.*)	16	13	11
	(*de Amic.*)	25	20	11
Seneca	(*Epistolae*)	12	13	15

See M. Manitius, *Handschriften antiker Autoren in mittelalterlichen Bibliothekskatalogen* (Leipzig, 1935).

replaced by the Doctrinale *and the* Grecismus. Denifle and Chatelain, *Chartularium Universitatis Parisiensis* I (Paris, 1889–97). The *Morale Scolarium* of John of Garland was also studied in Paris as early as 1241.

262]

no one to redeem us. Richard of Bury, *Philobiblion*, trans. E. C. Thomas (London, 1888), c. 4, p. 171.

hidden from view. R. Sabbadini, *Le Scoperte*, pp. 11–12, 23–7.

263]

the Historia Augusta. *Ibid.* pp. 4, 5, 26.

which Petrarch had never seen. Ibid. p. 33.

269]

universally attested. C. di Rosmini, *La Vita e Disciplina di Guarino Veronese* (Brescia, 1805) vol. I, pp. 3–7; vol. II, pp. 29 ff; R. Sabbadini, *La Scuola e gli Studi di Guarino Veronese* (Catania, 1892), pp. 14–16, 213–20.

spent in Italy as a blessing. P. P. Vergerio, *Epistole* (a Crisolora), p. 201.

a daughter of the Count of Urbino. Leonardus Aretinus, *de Studiis et Literis*, ed. H. Baron, in *Leonardo Aretinos Humanistische und Philosophische Schriften* (Quellen zur Geistesgeschichte der Mitt. und der Ren.) (Leipzig, 1928) vol. I, pp. 7–10.

has not previously recorded. Leonardus Aretinus, *op. cit.* p. 8 . . . diligenter curabitque ut quotiens ei loquendum sit aliquid vel scribendum, nullum ponat verbum quod non antea in aliquo istorum reppererit.

270]

his panegyrist Janus Pannonius. B. Guarinus, *de Modo et Ordine Docendi et Discendi*, trans. by W. H. Woodward in *Vittorino da Feltre and other Humanist Educators* (Cambridge, 1905), expressly says that he is describing his father's methods, as does Janus Pannonius in his *Panegyricum Guarini* which can be read in the *Delitiae Poetarum Hungaricorum*. These pamphlets are excellently paraphrased in Rosmini's and Sabbadini's books on Guarino. A translation of the Panegyric with long but somewhat unoriginal introductory matter will be found in I. Hegedüs, *Guarinus és Janus Pannonius*.

the latter general information. B. Guarinus, *op. cit.* p. 163. Grammaticae autem duae partes sunt quarum alteram Methodicem quae omnium orationis partium formulas, id est methodus declarat; alteram Hystoricem quae historias et res gestas pertractat, appellant, eas formulas multis ex libris quae extant capescere licebit, sed magna ex parte compendium illud optimi parentis mei ad id iuvabit, ubi sicut nihil superfluum ita omnia facile reperientur quae ad orationem recte studendam conducere videantur.

every subject worthy of discussion. Quoted by Rosmini, *op. cit.* vol. I, p. 114. I have not been able to find this volume anywhere.

431

271]

a vast number of editions. F. Buisson, *Répertoire des Ouvrages pédagogiques du xvie siècle* (Paris, 1886), lists over sixty exclusive of selections, which appeared before 1550. Besides the *Epitome* by Erasmus there was also a selection by Bonus Accursius and a verse version by Raverini.

the tradition which flowed from Chrysoloras. Guarino and Filelfo were the two Italian scholars who came most closely in contact with Byzantine learning. They had both studied in Byzantium; and if Guarino was the beloved disciple of Chrysoloras, Filelfo had married the daughter of J. Chrysoloras, the master's nephew and successor. Datus who had studied under Filelfo and had then imitated Guarino's pupil, Valla, united the two traditions.

linked philological to rhetorical studies. Augustini Dathi Senesis, *Libellus de Elegantia cum Commentariis et Additionibus solitis.* Et alter *de Antiphrasi et Floribus Ciceronis* (Paris, 1518). As an example of his synonyms: Tu mihi carus es: ego te amo. Tu mihi iucundus es: ego te delector. Sed oblecto et delecto non similiter construuntur. Nam dicimus 'delectat me hae res'. Sed 'oblecto me hac re' ut 'delectat Socratem vitae integritas', 'Pyttacus sese virtute et doctrinae oblectat' et 'ego me oblecto ruri'.

272]

a new and pleasing whole. Cf. the controversy on imitation between Bembo and Francesco Pico printed in Bembo, *Opera*, vol. III (Basel, 1556), p. 5 (the quotation is from Pico's letter): Carpebant ex unoquoque quantum satis esse videbatur ad phrasim vel constituendam vel ornandam quae tamen essent vel propriae cognata naturae vel commoda materiae quae tractaretur.

all that they cover. R. Agricola, *de Formando Studio Epistola* (Cologne, 1532), p. 12 certa quaedam rerum capita habeamus, cuiusmodi sunt 'virtus', 'vitium', 'vita', 'mors', 'doctrina', 'ineruditio', 'bene volentia', 'odium', et reliqua id genus quorum usus fere communis ad omnia et tanquam publicus sit.... Certe quaecumque discimus ad ea redigamus et repetendis capitibus illis ea quoque quae ad ea redigimus repetantur.

topics for discussion. See G. R. Owst, *Preaching in Medieval England*, ch. 7. In addition to the well-known *Gesta Romanorum*, we find the *Exemplorum Liber* (ed. A. G. Little, 1908) and the *Speculum Laicorum* (ed. J. T. Welter, 1914). But the most competent of all these handbooks is an English production, the *Summa Predicantium* by John of Bromyarde. This volume contains thousands of exempla and might fairly be called the medieval equivalent of the *Adages* of Erasmus which it strongly resembles. Its material is grouped under *loci communes*, or topics, those general Christian themes which are every preacher's stock-in-trade. Bromyarde arranges them alphabetically: Abiecti et depressi; abiicere; ab infantia; abstinentia; abusio; absolutio, accidia; accedere; accipietis virtutem supervenientis Spiritus Sancti; accusatio; acquisitio;... and so forth. Under each heading, he gives a short summary of the points a preacher might wish to mention and the *exempla* by which they can be illustrated.

Under '*absolutio*' for instance he lists the offences which demand papal or episcopal absolution, as well as doubtful cases and cases of invalid absolution. Nearly every point is illustrated by quotations and *exempla*, the latter usually of homely sort. The priest, who has given an invalid absolution, is compared to the doctor who effected a superficial cure and who on the patient's relapse and subsequent death was severely punished for his negligence. The book contains very few references to the classics. Its interest for us derives from the method of arrangement that is used.

273]

worthy of note to thy teacher or thyself. J. L. Vivès, *Introductio ad Sapientiam*, quoted by Foster Watson in *Vivès on Education* (Cambridge, 1913), which attributes the invention of note-books and headings to Vivès.

the quotation from Vivès. D. Erasmus, *de Copia Verborum et Rerum*, ch. VII in *Opera Omnia* (ed. 1703), I, 6 Porro duplicem esse copiam non arbitror obscurum esse... Quarum altera consistit in Synonymis, in Heterosi... altera in congerendis, dilatandis, amplificandis argumentis, exemplis, collationibus, similibus dissimilibus, contrariis, atque aliis hoc genus modis quos suo loco reddemus accuratius, sita est.

status rather than merit. *Ibid.* p. 102 Iamsi partes exempli circumspicias, quot locos licebit elicere? Accusatus per invidiam ab Anyto et Melito perditissimis civibus. Locus communis est; veritas odium parit. Item alter: insignis virtus conciliat invidiam. Rursum alius: apud iudicis plerumque plus valet nobilitatis ratio quam respectus honesti....

274]

before he starts seriously to write. *Ibid.* pp. 100, 101 Ergo qui destinavit per omne genus auctorum grassari (nam id omnino semel in vita faciendum, ei qui velit inter eruditos haberi) prius sibi quam plurimos comparabit locos.... Ergo posteaquam tibi titulos compararis, quot erunt satis, eosque in ordinem quam voles digesseris, deinde singulis suas partes subjiceris, rursum partibus addideris locos communes sive sententias, iam quicquid usquam obvium erit, in ullis auctoribus praecipue si sit insignius, mox suo loco annotabis.

275]

facts which could be arranged in lists. Buisson, *Répertoire des Ouvrages pédagogiques du xvie siècle*, names five mnemotechnicians writing before 1520: Mattiolus di Mattiolis, *de Memoria Perficienda* (written 1475 and printed in Venice, 1526); Adamus Naulius, *Artis Memorandi Thesaurus* (Paris, 1518); Wenceslas Neander, *Artifitiosa Memoria* (Leipzig, 1518); Guillelmus Leporeus, *Ars Memorativa* (Bonn, 1520 and Paris, 1523 and 1527); J. Rombersch, *Congestorium Artificiosae Memoriae* (Venice, 1520), but there were others also. Each propounds a different system but all start from the same presupposition: namely that the body of human knowledge consists of separate disconnected facts the significance of which is fully understood in isolation. Consequently they never try to assemble facts according to their natural affinities into connected systems explicatory of some aspect of the universe; instead they force their material into artificial groups which fit in with their particular system of mnemonics. The peak of absurdity is reached by an Italian, Giulio Camillo. Although he was concerned with words and not facts, his methods illustrated to a nicety the trends we have been describing. Wishing to produce a word-list, he chose as his principle of classification the human body; all words concerned with solid bodies were classed under the title 'bone'; 'blood' covered everything to do with heat; 'the lungs' the words appertaining to the air. This system proved insufficiently elastic, so he replaced it by a theatre divided into seven sections, each named after one of the planets, and containing all words akin to the properties attributed to that planet. Thus he covered the whole universe (Sturm to Bucer, Nov. 1533, quoted in C. Schmidt, *La Vie et Travaux de J. Sturm*, p. 252).

277]

one or more of his major works. The main translators of Aristotle were:

Leonardo Bruni: *Oeconomica* (1419/20); *Ethica* (before 1416); *Politica* (1438).

F. Filelfo: *Rhetorica* (1430).

G. Manetti: *Ethica* and *Magna Moralia* (before 1459).

Theodore of Gaza: *Problemata* and *de Animalibus* (probably between 1447 and 1455); *de Caelo* (before 1472).

George of Trebizond: *de Animalibus* and *Rhetorica* (probably between 1447 and 1455); *Problemata* (before 1484).

J. Argyropoulos: *Ethica, Politica, Oeconomica, Logica Physica, de Anima* and *de Caelo* (all between 1440 and 1480).

Gregorio Tifernas: *Ethica* (c. 1450).

Bessarion: *Metaphysica* (1455).

A. Callistos: *de Generatione et Corruptione* (c. 1472).

M. Palmieri: *Meteora* (before 1475).

Ermolao Barbaro: *Rhetorica* (after 1480).

his great rendering in 1463. The main translators of Plato were:

Leonardo Bruni: *Apology* (1424/8), *Crito* (1423/7), *Gorgias* (1409), *Phaedo* (1404/5) and *Phaedrus* (part, 1424), *Epistolae* (1427), *Symposium* (part, 1435).

Rinucci da Castiglione: *Axiochus, Crito, Euthyphro.*

P. C. Decembrio: *Respublica* (1439—this translation was begun by his father, Uberto Decembrio).

George of Trebizond: *Parmenides* (date unknown) and *Leges* (between 1450 and 1455).

Antonio Cassarino: *Respublica* (date uncertain—see P. de Nolhac, *La Bibliothèque de Fulvio Orsini*, p. 221).

Marsilio Ficino: *Opera Omnia* (1463–82).

278]

attracted a certain measure of attention. Among the historical writers translated were:

Appian: *Romaica* by Pier Candido Decembrio, c. 1457.

Arrian: *Anabasis* by P. P. Vergerio, *c.* 1440, corrected by Bartolomeo Fazio, *c.* 1456.

Dio Cassius: *Historia* by N. Leonicenus, 1526.

Diodorus Siculus: *Bibliotheca Historica* by Poggio Bracciolini, before 1455.

Diogenes Laertius: *Vitae Philosophorum* by A. Traversari, *c.* 1435.

Herodotus: *Historia* by L. Valla 1452–5 (incomplete).

Plutarch: *Vitae*, eight by L. Bruni; one by Aurispa; two by J. d'Angeli; five by Filelfo, fifteen by Guarino, three by L. Giustiniani, two by F. Barbaro, thirteen by L. da Castiglionchio, all before 1450. A complete version was made by Campano, *c.* 1470.

Polybius: *Historiae* paraphrased by L. Bruni in *de Primo Bello Punico* 1421; translated by Perotti 1455 (Books I–v).

Thucydides: *Historia* by L. Valla, 1450–2.

Xenophon: *Hiero* (1403),*Hellenica* and the *Apologia Socratis* paraphrased by L. Bruni before 1440; *Cyropedia* paraphrased by Poggio, 1437, translated by F. Filelfo, 1471; *Agesilaus* and *Lacedaemoniorum Respublica* translated by F. Filelfo before 1460; *Oeconomica* by L. da Castiglionchio before 1447.

To these we might add the following works of historical interest:

Aeschines: *Pro Diopithe* (1406); *in Ctesiphontem* (1412); *de Falsa Leg.* (before 1421) by L. Bruni.

Demosthenes: *de Corona* by L. Bruni, 1407 and by L. Valla, 1460. *Olynthiacs* I–III, *de Pace, de Falsa Legatione* (before 1421), two Philippics (before 1444) by L. Bruni. *Olynthiacs*, a *Philippic* and *de Corona* (part) by Rinucci.

Isocrates: *Euagoras* and *Nicocles* by Guarino, *c.* 1435.

Lysias: two speeches by F. Filelfo, 1429.

Plutarch: *de Liberorum Educatione* by Guarino, 1411; *Quod principem deceat* by Rinucci after 1423.

Strabo: *Geographia* by Guarino, *c.* 1440 and the later books also by Gregorio Tifernas, *c.* 1455.

Translations of poetical works and of authors of purely literary interest are by comparison few. Rinucci translated three, Aurispa two and Guarino three essays by Lucian. Portions of the *Iliad* had been put into Latin prose by L. Bruni and P. C. Decembrio, and a more substantial prose rendering of Books I–XVI was made by L. Valla, 1442–4. The task of producing a verse translation was entrusted by Nicholas V to Carlo Marsuppini who finished the first book only. He did, however, translate the *Batrachomyomachia*.

Apart from a number of scientific works (among which the *de Plantis* of Theophrastus and the *Tactica* of Aelian by Theodore of Gaza, *c.* 1455; the *Almagest* of Ptolemy and the *Conic Sections* of Apollonius of Perga by Regiomontanus, 1461–7; the *Almagest* by George of Trebizond and the *Geographia* of Ptolemy by J. d'Angeli; the Onesander by N. Sugundino (1456) and the Latin Galen (Venice, 1490) deserve special notice) the versions listed above constitute together with the philosophical books mentioned in the note (see p. 434), the great bulk of the translations produced prior to 1490. We have little reason to doubt that the interest of translators was primarily in the circumstances of Greek history and Greek life.

285]

within the created universe. On the general ignorance about Plato as late as 1465, see the introductory chapters of Bessarion's *In Calumniatorem Platonis,* ed. L. Mohler (Paderborn, 1937).

ardent championship of human excellence. Coluccio Salutati, *Epistolae,* ed. Novati, 5 vols (Rome, 1891–6), vol. I, pp. 212, 246; Gianozzo Manetti, *De Excellentia et Dignitate Hominis* (Basel, 1532).

286]

a most incomplete picture of his thought. The best account of these Byzantine Platonists is given by N. A. Robb, *The Neoplatonism of the Italian Renaissance* (London, 1935), pp. 48–54. The moderation and scholarly characters of Bessarion's work has, however, led Miss Robb into giving it more praise than it deserves as an exposition of Plato.

the circle known as the Platonic Academy. The history of the Florentine Academy can be found in A. della Torre, *Storia dell' Accademia Platonica di Firenze* (Florence, 1902). For an analysis of its philosophical doctrines consult N. A. Robb, *op. cit.* pp. 83–175; also G. Saitta, *Filosofia Italiana del Umanesimo* (Venice, 1928); A. Humbert, *Les Origines de la Théologie moderne* (Paris, 1911).

287]

humanity's special role. Cf. in particular Pico's treatise *de Hominis Dignitate* (1436) in *Opera,* vol. I, p. 320; and Ficino's *Theologia Platonica* (1468–74), I, 6; III, 2; XIII, 1 (in *Opera,* vol. I, Basel, 1576).

sexual love. M. Ficino, *In Convivium Platonis de Amore Commentarius,* Or. II, 7 (*Opera,* vol. II, p. 1327) Utrobique igitur amor est. Ibi contemplandae hic generandae pulchritudinis desiderium. Amor uterque honestus improbandus? Uterque enim divinam imaginem sequitur. Elsewhere, however, Ficino often condemned physical love, and Pico certainly denied it all value.

E in alcun luogo non ti truove mai. Lorenzo de' Medici, *Opere,* vol. III (Florence, 1823), p. 79 (*Laude* I).

288]

Quanto è qui più perfetta ogni lor pace. Ibid. vol. I, *Selve d'Amore* I, stanza 27, p. 16.

Landino's de Summo Bono. Cristoforo Landino, *Questiones Camaldulenses* (Schuerer, 1508). These dialogues, written about 1470, are probably idealised accounts of discussions which actually took place between members of the academy. Lorenzo, Alberti and Ficino are the principal speakers. The second *quaestio,* treating of the relations between happiness and pleasure, is probably the best of the four.

fornication had to be a vice. Lorenzo Savino, *Di alcuni trattati e trattatisti d'amore italiani* (Naples, 1909–14). The *trattati* range from such respectable productions as the *Asolani* of Pietro Bembo (printed by Aldus, 1505) to Equicola's dubious *Libro di natura d'Amore* (printed at Venice, 1525). Like the *Heptaméron* of Marguerite de Navarre which they helped to inspire, their interest was social rather than philosophical.

his reading of the diologues. See below, note to p. 289. Lefèvre has attracted a good deal of attention as a reformer, and most of the books about him deal with the theological aspects of his thought: e.g. C. H. Graf, *Essai sur la vie et les écrits de Jacques Lefèvre d'Etaples* (Strassburg, 1842); J. Barnaud, *J. Lefèvre d'Etaples et son influence sur les origines de la Réformation française*; and M. M. Phillips, *Erasme et les débuts de la Réformation française* (Paris, 1934). Lefèvre started his Aristotelian studies by writing a paraphrase of the *Physics* in 1492. This was followed by an introduction to the *Metaphysica* (1493), an edition containing three translations of the *Magna Moralia* (1497) and by his first major work, an introduction to the *Organon* (1498). The introduction to Aristotle's ethical works was written in 1502 and that to the *Politics* in 1512. He also produced an introduction to the mathematical works of Boethius, an astronomy and a music which indicate the scientific trend of his interests and lend plausibility to the hypothesis that he may have helped to prepare the way for Galileo.

Certain passages in Lefèvre's works where he expresses a desire to reconcile Plato and Aristotle (cf. the Introduction to the *Ethics* (1502), p. 1), and his editing Ficino's translation of the *Liber de potestate et sapientia Dei* of Hermes Trismegistus (1503), have led to his being regarded as a Platonist. Imbart de la Tour put forward this theory that Lefèvre was converted to Platonism during his visit to Italy in 1500, but this has been denied by Renaudet (*Revue d'hist. moderne* (1909)) who pointed out that the most important of Lefèvre's Aristotelian works are after that date. A. Lefranc ('Le Platonisme en France', *Revue d'hist. littéraire*, 1896) also takes the view that Lefèvre's Platonism was very half-hearted. In any case, one ought to distinguish between the possibility that Lefèvre was influenced by Plato's logic, and the possibility (or probability) of his having been attracted by Neoplatonism. At the moment neither question can be answered with any degree of certainty.

289]

the development of thought. The best full-length work on Pierre la Ramée is still Ch. Waddington-Castus, *Ramus: sa vie, ses écrits et ses opinions* (Paris, 1855). A fresh assessment of his importance is most urgently required. F. P. Graves, *Petrus Ramus and the Educational Reformation of the sixteenth century* (New York, 1912) provides some useful data showing how closely La Ramée copied the ideas of Vittorino and other Italian Humanists, but it does not add to our understanding of his logic. On the Scholasticism of the sixteenth-century Sorbonne, whose importance is just coming to be realised, see H. Elie, *Le Traité de l'Infini de Jean Mayor* (Paris, 1938).

290]

filled an important gap. One curious fact about the medical translations is that separate sets were made in Italy during the fifteenth century and in England and France during the sixteenth. Peter of Abano, Leonicenus and Theodore of Gaza were prominent among the Italian translators. Guillaume Cop, the pupil of Celtis and later physician to the German nation, translated the *Praecepta salubria* of Paul of Aegina (1511), the *Praesagia* and the *de Ratione Victus* of Hippocrates, (1511) and several works of Galen (1513).

Linacre translated Galen's *de Sanitate Tuenda* (1517), *Methodus Medendi* (1519), *de Temperamentis* (1512) and three other treatises (1528).

Jean de Rueil translated Dioscorides *de Medicinali Materia* and *de Virulentibus Animalibus* (1526); according to Ste Marthe he was responsible for the publication in France of the works of Hippocrates, Galen, Euclid, Celsus and Pliny. Gonthier of Andernach was the great systematic translator for Germany. Between 1520 and 1540 he produced versions of nearly all the major medical works.

291]

neglects three others. For a detailed account of Rabelais' annotations see my 'Rabelais' edition of the Aphorisms of Hippocrates' in the *Modern Language Review*, January 1940.

certain philological ideals. Valla, letter to Candido Decembrio (*Opera Omnia*, Basle, 1543, p. 633) Horum quos dico iurisperitorum nemo fere est, qui non contemnendus plane ac ridiculus videatur: ea est ineruditio in illis omnium doctrinarum quae sunt libero homine digna, et praesertim eloquentiae...ea hebetudo ingenii, ea mentis laevitas ac stultitia, ut ipsius iuris civilis doleam vicem, quod pene interpretibus caret, aut quod his quos nunc habet, potius non caret. *Traversari* (v, 18, p. 254, ed. Mehus, Florence, 1759) potius iurisconsultos veteres quam commentatores ignavos tibi hauriendos atque imitandos moneam. Habent illi in se plurimum dignitatis, veterumque elegantiam praeferunt quam novi isti interpretes in tantum abest, ut consequi potuerunt ut per imperitiam linguae saepenumero non intelligant quidem. Alioquin hisce studiis nequaquam absque cultiorum detrimento studiorum vacare posses. Si enim antiqua illa, et limatoria ingenia professionem iuris licet claram, et oratori quoque, teste Cicerone, pernecessariam, non usquequaque praedicabant, multumque illi deesse ad gratiam orationis testabantur; quum tamen illi ipse iuris consulti essent peritissimi; quid ipsi statuere possumus, quum vix reliquiae nudae ac tenues supersint, illaeque ipsae tanta barbaria interpretum violentur?

what is just and what is unjust. Valla, *Elegantiae* III, Praefatio 80, in *Opera* (Basel, 1465) Ut enim Quintilianus inquit: Omne ius aut in verborum interpretatione positum est; aut aequi pravique discrimine.

292]

the Bartolist commentaries. Cf. J. Flach, 'Cujas, les Glossateurs et les Bartolistes', *Nouvelle Revue hist. de droit*, vol. VII (1883), pp. 205–27.

the endless multiplication of commentaries. G. Chiappelli, 'La Polemica contro i legisti', *Archivo Giuridico* (1881), v, 26, p. 1.

293]

some order into the prevailing chaos. A. Alciat, *Parerga* v, 26 (quoted E. Viard, *André Alciat*, Paris, 1926).

lead to obscurity. A. Alciat, *de Verborum Significatione*, Dedicatio (Lyons, 1565), 910–11: Erunt forte qui maiorem elegantiam requirent, et ob latinae maiestatis condignam a me rationem non habitam, diem mihi dicent, quod nimis plana humilisque nostra oratio non schematis ornetur non dictionibus ex antiquitate repetitis abundet, non Ciceronianorum verborum maiestate refulgeat. Sed hi velim sciant haec ab eo minime expetenda esse, qui manibus quotidie Bartolos, Baldos, Alexandros, hujusque farinae auctores verset quique humanitatis studia non ex professo, sed obiter quandoque, et aliud agens, intervisat. Ad haec scenae me servire necesse fuit; quotus enim quisque ex legalibus mystis nostra legeret, si praeter anxiam legum scrutationem, cornu quoque copiae in manibus habendum illi esset, unde et antiqua vocabula addiscere et figuratos loquendi modos percipere necesse haberet? Vix eorum convicia ferre possum, quotidieque cum eis iurgandum est, qui qualemcumque hanc meam dictionem tanquam obscuram calumniantur illudque a vulgo exclamant, indoctius loquare sed apertius. Quid hi quaeso facerent si paulo elegantiore stylo nostratia haec constarent? Abiicerent manibus tanquam aenigmata, et inter Heracliti et Lycophronis tenebras connumerarent. Nec immerito quidem id mihi accideret qui cum Ulpiani et Pauli planissimos et absque illo sermonis scrupulo compositos commentarios declaraturum me profiterer obscuriora ipsis auctoribus tradidissem interpreteque ipse vel potius natatore aliquo Delio, indigerem. . . . Sed cum quaelibet ars sua habeat vocabula, nobis necessario nostris utendum. . . .

the setting of their times. Alciat did some research himself on Roman institutions. In 1523 he published two monographs: *de Constitutione Romani Imperii* and another *de Magistratibus Civilibusque et Militaribus Officiis* (see E. Viard, *op. cit.* pp. 181–2).

any understanding of law. Cf. J. Paquier, *Jérome Aléandre de sa naissance à la fin de son sejour à Brindes* (Paris, 1896). Charles Brachet's father was unwilling to allow him to study Greek under Aleander when the latter was in Paris in 1513, but was convinced by a letter from Budé's friend Deloynes, who persuaded him that Greek was necessary for an understanding of law. There is also extant a letter from Charles Brachet to Deloynes in which he talks about 'les lettres grecques sans lesquelles toutes les autres études sont incomplètes'.

294]

without feignedness or dissimulation whatsoever. Rabelais, *Pantagruel* x (Bohn Library, London, 1849).

296]

a recent critic has pointed out. J. H. Whitfield, *Petrarch and the Renaissance* (Oxford, 1943), p. 33.

298]

generally attained by metaphor. Erasmus, *Opera*, vol. II, pp. 2B–3E.

a wisdom distilled from experience. *Ibid.* vol. II, p. 6A.

a variety of points. He enumerates the application of the adage 'pertusum dolium' as follows: vel ad obliviosum, vel ad profusum, vel ad avarum, vel ad futilem, vel ad ingratum traduci potest. . . Breviter ad omnia in quae quocunque modo haec similitudo competit, accomodes licebit. Illa ratio ferme communis omnibus, quoties a persona ad rem, aut contra, sit deflexio. Ad personam hoc pacto. Proverbium est Μὲδε Ἡρακλῆς πρὸς δύο (Ne Heracles quidem adversus duos). Ego vero Thersites magis quam Heracles, qui possim utrique respondere. Ad rem torquebitur hoc modo. Proverbio dictum est μήδ' Ἡρακλῆς πρὸς δύο, ego qui possim pariter et morbo et inopiae tolerandae par esse? (Erasmus, *Opera* vol. II, p. 10A.)

a moral bearing. So far as I know the *Adagia* have not been studied in detail. The best account is given by J. B. Pineau, *Erasme, sa pensée religieuse* (Paris, 1924), but his examination is limited to the ethical and religious ideas.

the 'Dulce bellum inexpertis'. *Opera*, vol. II, pp. 770C, 397C, 951B.

the particular proverb in question. *Mortuum flagellas*: in eos qui obiurgant illos, qui nihil prorsus obiurgatione commoveantur: sunt qui vita defunctos insectantur ac lacerant (*Opera*, vol. II, p. 172D). Or again: Δικτύῳ ἄνεμον θηρᾷς Reti ventos captas: de frustra laborantibus: aut qui stulte sequuntur ea, quae nulla sit assequendi spes; aut qui rem inanem inaniter captant. Nam utre contineri ventus potest, reti nunquam.

Further examples may be found on every page of the *Adagia*, but see in particular *utre territus*, p. 239E; *Bacchae more*, p. 241D, *bis septem plagis Polypus contusus*, p. 583C, *filius degenerans*, p. 922A.

the rhetorical value of the phrase. *Ibid.* pp. 277E, 901F.

299]

a powerful support to the argument. As an example of the method we might quote this from the *de Civilitate*: Sed nec id (quod vult) ex toto eligat disco, quod solent liguritores, sed quod forte ante ipsum iacet, sumat: quod vel ex Homero discere licet apud quem creber est hic versiculus: οἴδ' ἐπ' ὀνείαθ' ἑτοῖμα προκείμενα χεῖρας ἴαλλον (*Opera*, vol. I, p. 1039C).

the ridicule of the latter. *Opera*, vol. IV, pp. 405C, 409C, 412D, 414B, 417A–C; similar references to Greek will be found in the Colloquies. A disease is described as returning with the frequency of the Euripus (*ibid.* vol. I, p. 633A). There are references to lines of Homer, *ibid.* p. 635C, to the Pythagorean custom of meditation, *ibid.* p. 649B, to the opinions of Homer on hunger, *ibid.* p. 665B, to the gardens of Alcinous, *ibid.* p. 676B, to the Lapithae, *ibid.* p. 688D, to the old age of Tithonus, *ibid.* p. 733C, as well as countless Greek words and allusions.

Erasmus also made a collection of parables and metaphors from classical writers. In the introduction he refers at length to the practical value of his book: Caeterorum ornamentorum singula suam quamdam ac peculiarem adferunt gratiam et commoditatem dictioni, metaphora sola cumulatius praestat universa, quam exornationes reliquae singula (*ibid.* pp. 559–60); but here he makes no reference to the educative value of his examples. Their purpose does not go beyond the limits of rhetoric.

translating Euripides and Lucian. Erasmus did not commence his Greek studies until 1499, and the translations from Euripides were his first serious work (*Epp.* I, ed. Allen, p. 365). Before they were completed he commenced another and easier task, a version of three speeches one by Libanius and two *incerto auctore* in November 1503 (*Epp.* I, 390). His *Hecuba* and *Iphigenia* did not appear till 1506 (*Epp.* I, 417). Then came the translations from Lucian which were spread over a long period.

1506   *Toxaris,* dedicated to Foxe.
         Timon, dedicated to Ruthall.
         Gallus, dedicated to Urswich (sometimes dated 1503).
May   *Pro Tyrannicida,* dedicated to Whitfield.
July   *de Mercede Conductis.* Trans. in Paris.
         Alexander. Brought almost complete to Paris.
Nov.   *Cnemon et Damippus* (trans. in Italy).

Zenophantes et Callidemides.	*Venus et Amor.*
Menippus et Tantalus.	*Mars et Mercurius.*
Menippus et Mercurius.	*Mercurius et Maia.*
Menippus, Amphilochus et	*Doris et Galatea.*
Trophonius.	*Diogenes et Alexander.*
Crates et Diogenes.	*Menippus et Chiron.*
Nireus et Tersites.	*Menippus et Cerberus.*
Charon et Menippus.	*Hercules Gallicus.*
Diogenes et Mausolus.	*Eunuchus.*
Simylus et Polystratus.	*de Sacrificiis.*
Lapithae.	

All the above were published at this point by Bade in Paris, January 1506.

1511 Nov.   *Icaromenippus,* dedicated to Ammonius.
         Saturnalia and
         Epistolae Saturnales ⎱ Warham.
         Cronosolon
1512 Nov.   *Astrologia*
         de Luctu ⎱ dedicated originally to Boerio.
         Abdicatus
1514 May   Bade's second edition includes all the above.

Cf. C. R. Thompson, *The Translations of Lucian by Erasmus and St. Thomas More,* New York, 1940

300]
the material for so much of their language. War metaphors are to be found in the following: *Non bene imperat* (*Opera,* vol. II, p. 25 E); *infixo aculeo*

fugere (p. 27 B); *Bonus dux bonum reddit comitem; neque caecum ducem neque amentem consultorem* (p. 799 A), etc.

Legal metaphors: *lex in manibus* (p. 1108 E); *sycophanta* (p. 515 F); *adactum iusiurandum* (p. 766 A), etc.

Metaphors from religion are countless: *Cicernus Bacchus* (p. 599 B) is a good example of the type, but there is one on nearly every page.

Metaphors from state activities: *a fabis abstineto* (p. 18 B); *capere civitatem* (p. 1061 F); *magistratus virum indicat* (p. 389 F).

Domestic metaphors: *Sileni Alcibiadis* (p. 770 C); *quis aberret a ianua* (p. 236 D); *cumini sector* (p. 408 B); etc.

These are examples selected at random. They do not constitute an exhaustive list.

the phenomena of nature. Country life:

Agriculture: *haud impune vindemiam facies* (p. 453 C); *annus producit, non ager* (p. 46 A); *terra amat imbrem* (p. 510 B); *in aqua sementem facis* and *arenae mandas semina* (p. 170 C).

Animals: *echino asperior* (p. 547 D); *ab equis ad asinos* (p. 273 B); *leonem stimulas* (p. 51); *una hirundo non facit ver* (p. 299 C).

Hunting: *sine canibus et retibus* (p. 1140 C).

Natural phenomena: *minutula pluvia imbrem parit* (p. 112 A); *nox humida* (p. 855 E).

301]

if Humanist techniques had been less efficient. It is not intended to deny, however, that the progress of science did benefit from the work of the Humanists, as the history of astronomy clearly shows. Purbach in Germany was badly hampered by not having the full works of Ptolemy at his disposal, while the ideas of both Regiomontanus and Copernicus were radically transformed as a result of years in Italy where they may have come in contact with the teachings of Byzantine astronomy.

306]

cursing France for a land of barbarians. L. Delaruelle, 'Grégoire le Tifernate', *Mélanges de l'Ecole Française de Rome* XIX.

endless psalters and breviaries. H. Omont, 'Georges Hermonyme de Sparte', *Mémoires de la Société de l'Histoire de la France* XII (1885).

307]

the technicalities of chivalry. Symphorien Champier (1472–1539), a Lyons doctor, was a dilettante who wrote as easily about history, medicine or the technicalities of chivalry as about philosophical topics. His *de Triplici Disciplina* (1508) is a treatise on Orphic theology. It was followed eight years later by the *Symphonia Platonis cum Aristotele et Galenicum Hippo-crate*, an elaborate account of the philosophies concerned, and in 1532 by the *Periarchon de principibus utriusque philosophiae*. These expositions of classical ideas were interspersed, however, by numerous volumes on history, genealogy and *la malice des femmes*. In the width and temper of his mind, Champier was a forerunner of Rabelais (P. Allut, *Etude bio-graphique et bibliographique sur Symphorien Champier*, Lyons, 1859).

310]

after Valla's Elegantiae. L. Delaruelle, 'Nicolas Bérault', *Le Musée Belge*
XIII (Louvain, 1909).

knew how to read and write. Sir Thomas More estimated in the sixteenth
century that every second man was literate. But then he lived in the south
of England (see A. R. Myers, *England in the Late Middle Ages* (London,
1952), p. 227).

311]

so few learned men to patronise. Certainly, most of Humphrey of Gloucester's
patronage was given to Italians. He helped one Clement who had taught
in Rome to obtain a post at Oxford, encouraged Bruni to translate the
Politics of Aristotle, and received the dedication of Decembrio's version
of the *Republic* and Lapo di Castiglionchio's version of some of Plutarch's
Lives (Sandys, *History of Classical Scholarship*, vol. II (Cambridge, 1908),
p. 221).

313]

his subject affords us a clue. He delivered two public lectures in 1520:
*Orationes duae, altera a cura qua utilitatem laudemque graecae linguae
tractat, altera a tempore qua hortatus est Cantabrigenses ne desertores essent
eiusdem* (Paris, 1520).

317]

Lemaire's Concorde des Deux Langages. Jean Lemaire de Belges, *La
Concorde des Deux Langages*, ed. J. Frappier (Paris, 1947). See in
particular Lemaire's preface.

318]

lofty style of the ancients. Borrowings of a formal character were notable in
the imitations of Pindar which were first attempted by Trissino (*Rime*
composed *c.* 1515, but not printed until 1529) and then more effectively
by B. Tasso (*Ode*, 1531 and 1534) and by L. Alamanni (*Opere Toscane*,
1532–6). The last named also tries, however, to copy Pindar's subjects.
See H. Hauvette, *Luigi Alamanni: sa vie et son œuvre* (Paris, 1903).

320]

limits of vernacular imitation. Geofroy Tory, *Le Champ Fleury* (1529,
modern edition, Paris, 1931). It was followed by Jehan Palsgrave's
L'Eclaircissement de la langue françoise (London, 1530), Jacques Dubois'
In Linguam Gallicam Isagoge (1532), Daniel Martin's *Grammatica
Linguae Gallicae* (1533) and Charles de Saulles' *de Differentia Vulgarium
Linguarum et Gallici Sermonis Varietate.*

321]

coinages and adaptations. L. Sainéan, *La Langue de Rabelais* (Paris, 1922–3).

322]

the unique essence of the language which was being improved. This condemnation of the jargon in which the vernacular was heavily mixed with Latin

was not, however, entirely due to the Humanists' recognising that imitation must have its limits. They were influenced by the fact that the practice did not form part of their programme of linguistic reform, though it may occasionally have served the reformers' ends. The motive for it was pedantic display rather than a desire to enrich the pedant's own language; and in Italy its origins go back to before the sixteenth century. We can trace it in such works as the *Hypnerotomachia Polyphili* of Francesco Colonna. In France, too, it must have existed before 1529 otherwise there would have been no point to Tory's attack, mocking in the words which Rabelais was to borrow the gentlemen who 'despumaient la verbocination latiale' (Tory, *op. cit.* (Avant-propos de G. Cohen), p. xviii).

some quite unimportant theory. Rabelais, *Gargantua*, c. 10; cf. also c. 3 (on the possibility of eleven months' children); c. 8 (on the effect of emeralds on virility and on the original nature of man); c. 10 (on the virtues of sunlight).

enliven his narrative. Rabelais, *Pantagruel*, c. 2; *Tiers Livre*, Prologue, c. 10; cf. also for this kind of illustration, *Gargantua*, c. 10 (a stratagem of Pericles); c. 14 (Alexander and Bucephalus); *Pantagruel*, Prologue (the Amaurots); c. 17 (the customs of the Babylonians); c. 18 (the ideas of Plato); c. 30 (the tale of Er). *Tiers Livre*, c. 14 (Artemidorus on dreams); c. 15 (an epilogue by Aesop).

came from compendia like the Adages. The problem of the Rabelais' sources has been discussed at some length. It was suggested by L. Delaruelle (L. Delaruelle, 'Ce que Rabelais doit à Erasmus et à Budé', *Revue d'histoire littéraire de France*, 1904) that the greater part of them was taken from contemporary collections, such as the *Adagia* and *Apophthegmata* of Erasmus, Budé's *Adnotationes ad Pandectas*, the *Officina* of Ravisius Textor, the *Magnum Collectorium Historicum* of Guy de Fontenay: and he traced a certain number. The late W. F. Smith followed this up by making a systematic list of the instances from Erasmus (W. F. Smith, 'Rabelais et Erasme', *Revue des Etudes Rabelaisiennes* VI (1908); cf. also H. Schoenfeld, 'Rabelais and Erasmus', *Publications of the Modern Languages Association of America*, n.s. 1 (1893)). Their thesis has been vigorously opposed by Sainéan (*La Langue de Rabelais*, Introduction) who claims that Rabelais could have taken the citations straight from his sources and blames L. Delaruelle in particular for not having examined his evidence sufficiently. He does not, however, embark on the desired analysis himself. The problem is incapable of an accurate solution, for while there are a limited number of quotations which cannot be traced to any compendium, and a number whose origin in Budé or Erasmus is obvious from the phrasing, there are also many border-line cases which could come either from the originals or from compendia. Less than half of the longer references have been thus traced to compendia, and we must therefore in the present state of our information accept the rest as drawn from the original sources.

324]

we might be reading one of the Epiniceans. The first of Dorat's *Carmina Pindarica* appeared at the end of the 1550 edition of Ronsard's *Odes et Bocage* (*ad P. Ronsardum Io. Aurati Ode*). It is printed by P. Laumonier in the second volume of his new edition of Ronsard, p. 216. The second was published in 1558, in a collection called *Triumphales Odae* dedicated to the Cardinal of Lorraine, and can also be read in Dorat's collected works, Io. Aurati, *Poematia* (Paris, 1586), *Odarum Liber* II, p. 209. (P. de Nolhac, *Ronsard et l'Humanisme* (Paris, 1921), p. 50, is wrong when he says that it appeared in the collection entitled *Le Tombeau de Marguerite de Valois*, Paris, 1551. The ode by Dorat in that volume is not Pindaric but Horatian.)

325]

substantial number of images. P. Laumonier, *Ronsard, Poète Lyrique*, pp. 316–27. So we have imagery drawn from light in the deeds 'qui flamboient comme l'aurore'. Poetry is described as 'flèches sorties de son carquois decochées de son arc' which 'darde la gloire'. Or again as 'un bateau qu'il fait passer à force de rames parmi les mers d'un renom'; metaphors which combine, as do many of Pindar's own, sensitivity to movement with pictures taken from a soldier's or from a sailor's life. We have also the architectural metaphor: 'et nul mieux que moi par ses vers me batist dedans l'univers les collonnes d'une mémoire'; country life is not neglected: 'comme on ne conte les fleurs du Printemps, ni les couleurs qui peignent la verte place'.... The Muse comes from 'un heureux tige' and men 'fleurissent et se fanent'. It is also to be noted that in most cases he uses these images in the same way as Pindar. For example, the latter often joins metaphors descriptive of movement with the philosophical concept of flux. This recurs in Ronsard in the famous Epode beginning 'autour de la vie humaine' (Ronsard, *Œuvres*, ed. Laumonier (Paris, 1924), vol. I, p. 89). The association of song with glory on the one hand and on the other with rest after struggle also occurs many times and actually forms the theme of the myth in the *Ode à Michel de l'Hospital.*

contenting himself with a mere reference. Ronsard, *Œuvres*, ed. Laumonier: for the Bellerophon myth see vol. I, p. 93; another myth given in full is the story of the struggle of the Titans against Zeus from Hesiod (*ibid.* III, p. 129). For adaptations of a Greek original to suit his subject, see the tale of Apollo and Cythera from *Pyth.* IX, 9–70, changed to that of Apollo and Florence (*ibid.* vol. I, p. 66); the tale of Apollo and Pytho from Callimachus adapted to describe Mme Marguerite's victory over Ignorance (*ibid.* p. 75); apart from these direct imitations, the myth or rather mythic reference remained one of the Pléiade's favourite methods of illustration. It was excessively used by Ronsard in his sonnets, and one or two of the *Amours* are pastiches of references. Ronsard introduced the procedure but it soon became popular with his friends. Baif for example can collect four references into as many lines:

> Encore nous ayons les furies d'Ajax,
> Et les cris depiteux de l'accort Promethée
> Et le jaloux courroux de l'ardente Medée
> Et du chast Hippolyt l'execrable trepas.
>
> (*Poésies Choisies*, ed. Becq de Fouquières, p. 276)

and even the moderate du Bellay refers in one poem to Achilles, Agamemnon, Orpheus, Nestor and Prometheus.

326]

remembering exactly where each gem came from. du Bellay, *Défense et Illustration de la Langue Française* I, c. 8:

'Mais entends celuy qui voudra imiter, que ce n'est chose facile que de bien suivre les vertus d'un bon auteur, et quasi comme se transformer en luy.... Je dy cecy pource qu'il y en a beaucoup en toutes langues qui, sans penetrer aux plus cachées et interieures parties de l'auteur qu'ils se sont proposé, s'adaptant seulement au premier regard et s'amusant à la beauté des mots, perdent la force des choses.'

Cf. also *ibid.* cc. 3, 7. We find similar ideas in the correspondence between Pico and Bembo (P. Bembo, *de Imitatione* (*Opera*, vol. III, Basel, 1550)).

in the Anatomy of Melancholy. Henri Estienne (1531–98) in his *Apologie pour Hérodote* combined scholarship with vehement satire much along the lines of the *Praise of Folly*. On Michel de Montaigne (1533–92) see P. Villey, *Les Sources et l'Evolution des Essais de Montaigne* (Paris, 1908).

with a precise denotation. For a short bibliography see G. Highet, *The Classical Tradition* (Oxford, 1949), pp. 617–18. The most detailed work on the subject is T. W. Baldwin, *William Shakespeare's Small Latin and Lesse Greeke* (Urbana, Ill., 1944).

328]

one of its principal homes. J. E. B. Mayor and T. Baker. *The History of the College of St John the Evangelist, Cambridge*, vol. I, p. 180. The one exception seems to have been Andrew Downs who became Professor of Greek in 1586 and moved to Trinity.

329]

specialist schools. E. Walser, *Poggius Florentinus: Leben und Werke* (Berlin, 1914), pp. 8–10.

331]

the faculties of civil and canon law. G. Voigt, *Die Wiederbelebung des Klassischen Altertums*, vol. II (Berlin, 1893), p. 47. His surviving commentary on Seneca gives us an idea of the medieval character of his teaching.

almost without a break from 1429 to 1493. We hear of the following professors of Greek at Florence: 1429–34 Filelfo; 1431–44 Marsuppini (who continued lecturing, however, after his appointment in 1444 to the office of Chancellor); 1456–71 Argyropoulos; *c.* 1471 Andronicus Callistus; 1471–91 Chalcondyles; 1484–94 Politian; 1492–5 J. Lascaris.

only two among many. The information about these two schools has been collected by W. H. Woodward in *Vittorino da Feltre and other Humanist Educators* (Cambridge, 1905) and in *Studies in Education during the age of the Renaissance* (Cambridge, 1906). The first of these books contains a valuable translation of Battista Guarino's *de Ordine Docendi et Studendi*, in which Battista describes the methods his father used. Woodward lays rather too much emphasis on the Christian elements in Vittorino's teaching whose efficacy is somewhat belied by the later career of the Humanist's pupils. The student will therefore do well to consult for himself B. Platina, *Commentariolus de Vita Victorini Feltrensis* (ed. T. A. Vairani, in *Cremonensium Monumenta Romae extantia* (Rome, 1778)) and F. Prendilacqua, *Intorno alla vita di Vittorino da Feltre*, translated and edited by G. Brambilla (Como, 1871).

332]

dictated and learnt by heart. Woodward, *Vittorino*, pp. 45, 164, 169.

sentences to illustrate their grammar. Ibid. pp. 54–5.

moral instances and striking anecdotes. Vittorino's pupil Sassuelo da Prato appears to have compiled a book of examples from history useful in illustration. On Guarino's approach to the subject-matter see Battista Guarino's account in Woodward, *Vittorino*, pp. 169 ff.

rather than an end in itself. Battista Guarino in Woodward, *Vittorino*, pp. 167–8. Battista actually recommends the translation of Latin into Greek as a method for appreciating the virtues of the *Latin* author.

336]

on a gigantic scale. He wasted time and energy on a dispute which added little to the totality of his achievement. We have seen how the position of Latin as the only language of learning led Petrarch and his followers to make it the vehicle of artistic effort and to introduce Graeco-Roman elements into their contemporary Latin rather than into Italian. Their successors then argued bitterly whether the Latin they used was to be Ciceronian or not. The debate was pointless. Ciceronian and unciceronian Latin were equally out of date. The future lay with the vernaculars. Erasmus was drawn into writing pamphlets against the Ciceronians; and some of the historians of his educational work, Sandys and Woodward in particular, have laid undue emphasis on these productions whose interest was at the best transient. By doing so they have blurred the perspective of their accounts and have cast a veil of fatuousness over the more important aspects of their hero's work. The greatness of Erasmus did not lie in his preferring a broader to a narrower variety of Latin. He had far more significant lessons to teach.

337]

somewhat indigestible, three-volume treatise. G. Budé, *de Transitu Hellenismi ad Christianismum* (Paris, 1535).

447

338]

especially the de Duplici Copia Verborum ac Rerum. F. Buisson, *Répertoire des Ouvrages Pédagogiques du xvie siècle* (Paris, 1886), pp. 232–4, gives over 30 editions of this treatise in less than 50 years. To the editions listed there may be added one by Dolet (Lyons, 1540) and another by Gryphius (Lyons, 1555), which are in the British Museum.

the earliest possible opportunity. Erasmus, *de Pueris Statim ac Liberaliter Instituendis* in *Opera*, vol. I, pp. 490–9.

339]

at hand to record them. Erasmus, *Opera*, vol. I, p. 522 B.

to gather something besides. *Ibid.* p. 522 A.

dress, appliances and so forth. *Ibid.* p. 522 D and E.

340]

Caesar and Sallust in Latin. *Ibid.* p. 522 D.

Moralia *of Plutarch.* *Ibid.* vol. IV, p. 587.

341]

the recommended list of authors. The Statutes of St Paul's School and Colet's *Catechyzon* printed in J. H. Lupton, *A Life of John Colet*, pp. 271 ff.

344]

centres of educational advance. Camerarius, *de Vita Melanchthonis*, ed. Strobel (Halle, 1777), p. 9. On Simler see A. Horawitz, *Griechische Studien* I (Berlin, 1884), pp. 14 ff.

347]

our authority for the life of Athens. Corpus Reformatorum V, 569, XI, 400–13, XIX, 187. Cf. also D. Hartfelder, *Philip Melanchthon als Praeceptor Germaniae*, Monumenta Germaniae Pedagogica VIII (Berlin, 1889), pp. 355–67.

348]

the Epistolae ad Familiares. Hartfelder, *op. cit.* pp. 421–2.

readings from Hesiod and Homer. *Ibid.* pp. 431–6.

one historian. P. Melanchthon, *Academiae Wittenbergensis Leges, 1546,* Corpus Reformatorum X, 1010.

349]

occasional lectures on Thucydides. Hartfelder, *op. cit.* pp. 555–66, gives a useful chronological list of Melanchthon's public lectures.

350]

a wise and eloquent piety. 'Propositum a nobis est sapientem atque eloquentem pietatem finem esse studiorum' (J. Sturm, *de Literarum Ludis Recte Aperiendis* (Strassburg, 1538), p. 104).

351]

in his own Onomasticon Puerile. J. Sturm, *Onomasticon Puerile Argentinense* (Strassburg, 1571). Cf. also his *Neanisci* (Strassburg, 1570).

the ideas under discussion. Sturm's own commentaries were purely verbal. See C. Schmidt, *La vie et les travaux de Jean Sturm* (Strassburg, 1855), pp. 285–99.

largely formal. J. Sturm, *Epistolae Classicae* (Strassburg, 1565), pp. 220, 275.

355]
the French translation. The full title of Cordier's selections from Cicero is the *Principia latine loquendi scribendique, sive selecta quaedam ex Ciceronis Epistolis, ad pueros in lingua latina exercendos, adiecta interpretatione Gallica et (ubi opus visum est) Latina declaratione* (Crispinus, Geneva, 1556). There was an edition in 1575 in which the French was replaced by an English translation. A good account of the book can be found in J. Le Coultre, *Maturin Cordier* (Neuchâtel, 1926), pp. 293–302.

356]
never too young to do good. Cordier, *Colloquiorum Scholasticorum Libri* IV (Stephanus, Geneva, 1564). The quotation is taken from Book I, 30 Habesne duas aut tres....

357]
before they even knew how to write. A. de Polanco, *Chronicon Societatis Jesu,* vol. IV, p. 101 (in *Monumenta Historica Societatis Jesu* (Madrid, 1894)).

remembered what they had been taught. The famous *concertationes* were in effect just another form of repetition, the boys being divided into teams and answering each other's questions.

an historical author. This account of the organisation at Messina is given in a long letter from Father Hannibal Coudret writing on behalf of Nadal to Polanco, the secretary of Ignatius. In *Litterae Quadrimestres ex universis praeter Indiam et Brasiliam locis in quibus aliqui de Societatis Jesu versabantur Romae missae,* vol. I (Madrid, 1849), pp. 349–58.

358]
the imposition of an absolute ban. A. P. Farrell, *The Jesuit Code of Liberal Education* (Milwaukee, 1938), pp. 56, 63.

requests for sixty more. 'Provinciae cunctae habent...collegia centum sexaginta duo' (*Litterae Annuae Societatis Jesu 1586–7,* Introduction (Rome)).

359]
800–900 only were spent on Greek. This calculation has been based on the analysis of the 1599 *Ratio Studiorum* by A. P. Farrell, *op. cit.* ch. 14.

for no other reason. 'Imitatio est anima praelectionis', says the 1591 *Ratio.* An excellent analysis of the rhetorical character of Jesuit teaching will be found in Farrell, *op. cit.* pp. 262–79, 296–301.

the more esteemed courses in philosophy. The first few pages of the section 'de studiis humanitatis' in the *Ratio Studiorum* of 1586, c 10, shed a flood of light on the inferior position which grammar studies actually occupied in the Jesuit schools. 'Dolent vero plerique omnes haec studia magna ex parte apud nostros concidisse, ut bono aliquo Grammatico aut Rhetore, aut literarum Humaniorum perito nihil plane sit rarius, aut difficilius inventu: Fiet autem difficile magis in dies, nisi huic malo Superiorum sedulitas vigilanter medeatur. Ex iis autem quae ad id conferre videntur, pauca nunc attingemus. Et primo quidem non impune ferendum esset ab iis, qui studiis altioribus vacant, contemni et plane irrideri Grammaticos et Rhetores: idem enim literas humaniores reddit odiosas.' The other complaints listed are that the grammar and rhetoric teachers were not allowed to sit with the professors of theology and philosophy at school festivals, that all the hackwork of running the domestic side of the school was put on to their shoulders, that in any case they were overworked and received too few holidays, that their living conditions were inferior to those of the other teachers, that they did not get the books they required, that the public lectures given by them were not attended by their superiors, and that they were habitually passed over for promotion. All these conditions, says the *Ratio*, must be remedied—'ut aboleatur opinio quorundum, qui de studiis humanioribus parum honorifice loquuntur, aut sentiunt'. On the unpopularity of grammar studies among the students see A. Astrain, *Historia de la Compañía de Jesús en la Asistencia de España*, vol. IV (Madrid, 1902–20), pp. 9, 10.

364]

they read more poetry. This information appears in the Eton *Consuetudiarium* of the headmaster, William Malim (1560) which is described in Lyte, *The History of Eton College*, ch. VII, and in the Statutes of Westminster School for 1560 (in Leach, *Educational Charters*, pp. 496 ff.).

369]

Italian Platonism stagnated. It must, however, be noted that Italy was the only country to match France in the field of Platonic translations. Nine dialogues and a part of the *Republic* were translated and published in France between 1542 and 1558, and against this achievement we must set the eight dialogues which were translated and published in Italy during the same period. The translators, however, have not the distinction of the French.

370]

remedied this state of affairs. For French editions of Plato see Appendix II, p. 506; also Abel Lefranc, *Grands Ecrivains de la Renaissance*, ch. 2, 'Le Platonisme et la littérature en France' (Paris, 1914). The French editions of Ficino's mystical works predate the appearance of his translation of Plato in France by ten to twenty years. The *de Triplici Vita* appeared in 1496, the translation of Hermes Trismegistus in 1494 with a fresh edition in 1502, the *Apologia* of the second-century Christian Platonist, Athenagoras in 1498, the *de Religione Christiana* in 1510. To these one must add Landino's *Quaestiones Camaludenses* (Petit, 1511); Ficino's translation of Plato was not published until 1519 (Jean Petit), and the second edition was in 1522 (Bade). It was followed during the next two decades by several translations of individual works into Latin (1520, *Timaeus* (Chalcidius); *c.* 1520, *Axiochus*; 1535, *Charmides* (Politian); 1538, *Laws*) and by numerous editions in Greek (1527, *Cratylus* and *Apologia* (both edited by Cheradame); 1530, *Axiochus*; 1532, *Timaeus*; 1539, *Apologia*; 1542, *Timaeus*; 1544, *Symposium*), and by the two new editions of Ficino's complete translation in 1533 and 1536.

an instrument of that revival. Colet (1467–1519) is supposed to have nourished a great affection for the writings of Ficino (Sandys, *A History of Classical Scholarship* vol. II, p. 229), while More's *Picus, Erle of Myrandule* is evidence of a similar interest on his part. For a discussion of the Platonic elements in the *Utopia* see Lupton's edition (Introduction, pp. xlviii ff.). For Ascham's praise of Greek studies at Cambridge see *Epistolae*, p. 74 (quoted Sandys, *loc. cit.* p. 232).

377]

Marliano, Agostino and Ligorio. Alciat's contribution to the study of law has been discussed above. See also E. Viard, *André Alciat* (Paris, 1926). On Glareanus see H. Schreiber, *Glareanus* (Freiburg, 1837); also C. Bursian, *Geschichte der klassischen philologie in Deutschland* (Munich, 1883), pp. 154 ff. He wrote a *de Geographia et Cosmographia Principiis* in which he explained many of the obscurities which had puzzled his predecessors. On the Estiennes in general see A. Renouard, *Annales de l'Imprimerie des Estienne* (Paris, 1843). The botanical dictionaries which Charles produced (notably the *de Hortensi Libellus*, and the *Seminarium* (both 1536) deserve to be better known than they are. J. C. Scaliger's *Poetice* (Lyons, 1561) was the first systematic attempt to summarise classical theories on the art of poetry. (Cf. E. Lintilhac, *De J. C. Scaligeri poetice* (Paris, 1887); J. E. Spingarn, *Literary Criticism in the Renaissance*.)

378]

the first treatise on textual criticism. F. Robertelli, *de Arte sive Ratione Corrigendi Antiquos Libros Disputatio*, reprinted in Scioppius, *de Arte Critica* (Amsterdam, 1572).

APPENDICES

GREEK MANUSCRIPTS IN ITALY DURING
THE FIFTEENTH CENTURY

The evidence used in this appendix comes from three sources of unequal value.

(*a*) Some existing manuscripts are marked in such a way that we know them to have been in fifteenth-century Italy. They are signed by the men who copied or owned them, or they carry other indications of their early wanderings. These marked manuscripts have been objects of interest to scholars for the past two hundred years. Francesco Barbaro's have been noted by Mittarelli, Filelfo's by Omont, Constantine Lascaris's by Iriarte, Leoni's by Dorez, Manetti's by Stevenson, Lorenzo dei Medici's (rather uncertainly) by Mueller, Niccoli's and Vespucci's by Rostagno, and Rudolf Blum has recently traced in the Laurentian Library over fifty codices which had once belonged to Antonio Corbinelli. Where such identifications can be made, we are on firm ground. We have the name of an owner and an exact knowledge of what he possessed. Unfortunately however the manuscripts in question are relatively few in number.

(*b*) To complete our picture we have to turn therefore to information of a less satisfactory kind. We have to consult the book-lists and catalogues of the period, which tend to provide only vague indications of what each manuscript contained. More often than not, they give only the author's name or some indefinite title like 'dialogues', 'speeches' or 'plays'. Moreover, only one of these lists refers indisputably to the first half of the century. This is an account of the manuscripts possessed by Aurispa in Rome during July 1421, which was found by Omont in Cod. Leid. gr. 48. Published in the *Centralblatt für Bibliothekswesen* IV (1887), it has been reprinted in Sabbadini's edition of Aurispa's letters. Another similar list of the manuscripts owned by Ciriaco found in Cod. Paris gr. 421 and also published by Omont may refer to a period before 1450, but here the date is less certain. The rest of the lists and catalogues are undoubtedly later. We have the catalogue of the Vatican Library at the death of Nicholas V in 1455 (published by Muentz and Fabre); the list of the manuscripts left by Guarino, who died in 1460 (published by Omont); the catalogue of the library bequeathed by Zomino to the city of Pistoia, compiled in 1460 (published by Zaccaria);

the catalogue of the library left by Palla Strozzi to the Monastery of St Justina in Padua, 1462 (published by Ferrai); the catalogue of the library bequeathed by Domenico Malatesta to the Convent of St Francis at Cesena in 1464 (published by Muccioli); the catalogue of the library bequeathed by Bessarion to the Convent of St Mark in 1468 (published by Omont); the catalogue of the Vatican library in 1475 during the pontificate of Sixtus IV (published by Muentz and Fabre); two complementary catalogues of the library of Federigo d'Urbino who died in 1482 (published respectively by Stornajolo and Guasti) the catalogues of the Medici library (published by Piccolomini) and in particular the inventory of Lorenzo's Greek books by Janus Lascaris (published by Mueller); and finally two complementary catalogues of the library of Pico della Mirandola, who died in 1494 (published by Calori-Cesis and Kibre).

(c) The evidence of the catalogues is supplemented by the fragmentary information which we obtain from the letters of the Humanists, which is of particular interest for the first part of the century where the catalogues fail us. We shall have occasion to quote the correspondence of Ambrogio Traversari, which contains the lists of acquisitions sent by Aurispa and Filelfo to Florence when they returned from the East in 1424 and 1427, the correspondence of Francesco Barbaro, edited by Quirini, the correspondence of Filelfo, and for the end of the century the correspondence of Politian. The letters, however, have all the defects of the catalogues. The information they give about the content of the manuscripts they mention is far from precise; and the history of Rinucci's Archimedes is a sufficient warning that claims which they make cannot be accepted without question.

Furthermore, since it is obvious that a translator must have had a text to follow, the dates of the translations have been added wherever the number of texts in circulation has not been so large as to render that information without interest.

The attempt which has been made to arrange the information from these varied sources calls for some apology. Only a few of the marked manuscripts are dated, and when we come to the catalogues we find that not all of them can be assigned to a particular year. The method adopted in the case of the undated manuscripts has been to assign them to the year in which their first known owner died unless there is external evidence to suggest an earlier date; and the undated catalogues have been similarly placed under the date when the owner of the library died. This method has the defect of presenting a large number of manuscripts at dates considerably later than the ones at which they probably made their first appearance, but it has the merit of certainty.

Where the further history of a particular manuscript is known, its adventures are given under the date of its first mention. The further history of the libraries has, however, been left unrecorded to avoid excessive repetition and may be noticed here. Antonio Corbinelli's books were preserved after 1425 in the library of the Badia in Florence. Ciriaco's were almost certainly sold on his death c. 1450. Some of Niccoli's were preserved in Florence, while Manetti's passed indirectly into the Palatine Library. The collections of Guarino (which passed in part at least to his son Battista), of Zomino (which was left to the Monastery of St James in Pistoia), and of Bessarion (which went to St Mark's in Venice) did not receive the care given to Corbinelli's bequest and many of the manuscripts passed into other hands even during the fifteenth century. An even worse fate attended the library of Palla Strozzi which, left to the Monastery of St Justina in Padua, was scattered without trace during the next hundred years. The library of Domenico Malatesta on the other hand was faithfully preserved in Cesena. When we consider the larger collections of the second half of the century, we find that the Papal and Medicean Libraries continued to grow, and although they lost some books, the majority of their acquisitions were retained. The Urbino Library remained intact until it was plundered in 1502 by the soldiers of Caesare Borgia; even then, a considerable portion was saved and remained partly in the city and partly at Castel Durante until annexed by Pope Alexander VII between 1658 and 1667. Giorgio Valla's books were bought by the collector Alberto Pio of Carpi, while Pico's went to Venice where they were destroyed by fire in the seventeenth century.

Turning from the construction of the appendix to the information it contains, we see that Italy was rich in Greek manuscripts. The impression given by a list confined to the works of the classical Greek authors may, however, prove misleading, if our purpose is to form some idea of the popularity of Greek studies. The Greek works mentioned here contributed only a small portion of the entire stock of fifteenth-century manuscripts. Even within the strictly classical field, the Latin authors far outnumbered the Greek. Bessarion was the only man to possess more Greek than Latin authors and some important collectors neglected the older language altogether. There were no Greek manuscripts in the Gonzaga Library in 1407, and none in the d'Este Library of 1436. Ercole I d'Este, whose private collection numbered about 700 volumes in 1495, possessed only two in Greek and one of them was a copy of the Psalms. Moreover, in nearly every library and certainly in the great Papal collections the non-classical writers outnumbered the classical. Even an avowed Humanist like Pico della Mirandola had more medieval and patristic than strictly classical texts and read his Greek historians in translation rather than in the original. The evidence of the manuscripts amply confirms the hypothesis which has gained ground since the days of Burckhardt and Sandys, that Greek studies, however influential and however zealously pursued, were in their pure form never more than the interest of a small minority.

Another point on which the history of the manuscripts throws a certain amount of light is the division of that interest between the different portions of the Hellenic legacy. Apart from a few well-known exceptions, as for example the works of Anacreon, the *Oresteia*, the *Oedipus Coloneus* and *Trachiniae*, the *Electra* of Euripides, the *Lysistrata* and *Thesmophoriazusae*, Bion, the *Meditations* of Marcus Aurelius, the treatise *On the Sublime* and the *Daphnis and Chloe*, the principal Greek writings of the ancient world were available in a substantial number of manuscripts by the end of the century. But fifty years earlier the situation had been very different. At that point the manuscripts of the poets were still very thin on the ground. The items in this appendix do not record with any certainty when a particular manuscript first appeared in Italy; but they may serve for a rough guide. We hear of four manuscripts of Aeschylus before 1450 and nine after. For Aratus the corresponding figures are one and five; for Aristophanes five and thirty-four; for Callimachus two and five; for Euripides six and twenty-six; for Hesiod seven and nineteen; for Homer nine and forty-nine; for Lycophron none and five; for Moschus one and three; for Musaeus none and five; for Nicander two and eight; for Nonnus one and none; for Oppian three and eleven; for Orpheus three and six; for Phocylides four and three; for Pindar three and twenty-five; for Quintus Smyrnaeus none and five; for Sophocles four and thirty; for Theocritus three and fifteen; for Theognis none and two. But when we come to the prose writers the proportions are somewhat different. The figures for Demosthenes, for example, are nine and twenty-nine, for Plato twenty and twenty-five for Xenophon twelve and twenty-six. As for Aristotle, we hear of over forty manuscripts in circulation before 1450. The interest in the prose writers came earlier; and if, reckoned over the whole century, the popularity of works of poetry and prose is roughly the same (e.g. we find as many manuscripts of the *Works and Days* as of the *Cyropedia*), it is nevertheless true to say—taking into account the greater volume of prose writing—that the emphasis in Greek studies must have been noticeably different from what it is today. For now we leave much of the prose unread while every student makes his way through the more important poets. Among the poets Homer occupied an unquestioned first place. He alone enjoyed during both parts of the century a popularity equal to the principal prose writers. Among the latter, the first place goes to Aristotle. Not only were his works zealously copied by the Byzantine scribes, not only were they sought after by minor collectors like Piccinino, Pietro Vitali and Francesco da Castiglione, but they also crowded the libraries of the keenest Humanists. Palla Strozzi owned three copies of the *Physica*, Manetti six separate manuscripts containing twenty-nine of the works, while Bessarion possessed eighteen works, four of them twice over. Humanism took a long time to move away from the medieval pattern of interests.

It must be emphasized, however, that these figures are derived only from the manuscripts of which there is some mention. Our libraries today contain a great number of Greek manuscripts of the fifteenth century and earlier which have not yet been connected with any particular collector or library. Some of them may be identical with the manuscripts mentioned in the catalogues which it has not been possible to identify. Others may have reposed in collections outside of Italy. The notes left by Janus Lascaris of the libraries he had seen on his travels (cf. Mueller, *op. cit.*) do suggest that even as late as the end of the fifteenth century the number of Greek manuscripts in the East may still have been greater than the stocks possessed by the libraries in the West.

The short references in the list of manuscripts are to the following works:

ADDA, G. D'. *Indagini storiche, artistiche e bibliographiche sulla libreria visconteo-sforzesca del castello di Pavia* (Milan, 1875).

AURISPA, G. *Carteggio*, ed. R. Sabbadini (Rome, 1931).

BANDINI, A. M. *Catalogus codicum graecorum Bibliothecae Mediceae Laurentianae* (Florence, 1768–70).

BARON, H. *L. Bruni Aretino: Humanistisch-Philosophische Schriften* (Leipzig, 1928).

BERTONI, G. *La Bibliotheca Estense di tempi de duca Ercole I* (Tenno, 1903).

BLUM, R. *La Bibliotheca della Badia Fiorentina*, Studi e Testi no. 155 (Vatican, 1951). For the list of A. Corbinelli's library see pp. 102–4.

CAROLI-CESIS, F. *Giovanni Pico della Mirandola* (Mirandola, 1897). For the list of Pico's library see pp. 32–76.

DELISLE, L. *Le Cabinet de manuscrits de la Bibliothèque Nationale* (Paris, 1868)—for the manuscripts of A. Petrucci, vol. I, p. 229.

DOREZ, L. 'La Bibliothèque de Pier Leoni', *Revue des Bibliothèques* (1894), pp. 73–90.

FERON, E. and BATTAGLINI, F. *Codices Manuscripti Graeci Ottoboniani Bibliothecae Vaticanae* (Rome, 1843).

FERRAI, L. For the list of Palla Strozzi's library see Mazzatinti, G. *Inventario*, vol. II below.

GUASTI, C. 'Inventario della Libreria Urbinate compilato nel secolo XV da Federigo Veterano', *Giornale storico degli archivi toscani*, VI (1862) and VII (1863). The Greek manuscripts are given in VII, pp. 130–54.

HEIBERG, J. L. 'Beitraege zur Geschichte Georg Vallas und seiner Bibliothek', *Beihefte zum Centralblatt fuer Bibliothekswesen*, XVI (1896).

HEINEMANN, O. VON. *Die MSS. der herz. Bibliothek zu Wolfenbuettel*, I, ii, no. 902—manuscript belonging to Aurispa.

IRIARTE, J. *Regiae Bibliothecae Matritensis Graeci MSS.* (Madrid, 1769).

KIBRE, P. *The Library of Pico della Mirandola* (New York, 1936).

LOCKWOOD, D. P. 'De Rinuccio Aretino graecarum litterarum interprete', *Harvard Studies in Classical Philology*, XXIV (1913), pp. 51–109.

MARTIN, A. 'Les MSS. grecs de la bibliothèque malatestiana à Cesena', *Mélanges d'archéologie et d'histoire*, II (1892), pp. 227–8.

MARTINI, E. *Catalogo dei manoscritti greci esistenti nelle biblioteche Italiane* (Milan, 1893–1902).

MAZZATINTI, G. *Inventario dei manoscritti italiani delle bibliotheche di Francia* (Rome, 1896). For the library of Palla Strozzi see vol. II (ed. L. Ferrai) pp. 549–661.

MERCATI, J., etc. *Codices Vaticani Graeci* (Rome, 1923–50).

MITTARELLI, J. B. *Bibliotheca Codicum Manuscriptorum Monasterii S. Michaelis* (Venice, 1779). For the surviving codices of F. Barbaro see p. xvii.

MUCCIOLI, G. M. *Catalogus Codicum Manuscriptorum Malatestinae Caesenitae Bibliothecae* (Cesena, 1780–4).

MUELLER, K. K. 'Neue Mittheilungen ueber Janus Lascaris und die Mediceiische Bibliothek', *Centralblatt fuer Bibliothekswesen* (1884), vol. I, pp. 333–412.

MUENTZ, E. and FABRE, P. *La Bibliothèque du Vatican au xve siècle* (Paris, 1887).

NOLHAC, P. DE. *La Bibliothèque de Fulvio Orsini* (Paris, 1887).

OMONT, H. 'Catalogue des mss. grecs des bibliothèques des Pays-Bas', *Centralblatt fuer Bibliothekswesen*, vol. IV, p. 187. For the lists of manuscripts owned by Aurispa in 1421 and Ciriaco.

—— 'Inventaire des mss. grecs et latins donnés à S. Marc par le Cardinal Bessarion en 1468', *Revue des Bibliothèques*, vol. IV (1894), pp. 129–87.

—— *Inventaire sommaire des manuscrits du fonds grec de la Bibliothèque nationale*, vols. I–IV (Paris, 1888).

—— 'La bibliothèque grecque de Francesco Filelfo', *La Bibliofilia*, vol. II (1900), pp. 136–40.

—— 'Les mss. grecs datés des XVe et XVIe siècles de la Bibliothèque nationale', *Revue des Bibliothèques*, vol. II (1892), pp. 1–32.

—— 'Les mss. grecs de Guarino et la Bibliothèque de Ferrara', *Revue des Bibliothèques*, vol. II (1892), pp. 79 ff.

PICCOLOMINI, E. 'Delle condizioni e delle vicende della libreria Medicea privata', *Archivio stor. ital.*, ser. 3, vol. XXI, pp. 106–12.

QUIRINI, A. M. *Diatriba Praeliminaris ad F. Barbari et Aliorum ad Ipsum Epistolas* (Brescia, 1741–63).

ROSTAGNO, E. and FESTA, N. 'Indici dei codici greci Laurenziani non compreso nel catalogo dei Bandini', *Studi Itali della filologia classica*, I, 129–96. For the manuscripts of Francesco da Castiglione see nos. 149, 167, 197, 200–2; for Niccoli's, pp. 176–96.

—— 'Indici codicum graecorum Bibliothecae Laurentianae supplementum', *ibid.* VI. For the manuscripts of G. A. Vespucci see pp. 147–8.

SABBADINI, R. *Biografia Documentata di Giovanni Aurispa* (Noto, 1891).

—— *Le Scoperte dei Codici Latini e Greci ne' secolo XIV e XV* (Florence, 1905).

— 'L'ultimo Ventennio della Vita di M. Crisolora', *Giornale Ligustico* (1890).

STEVENSON, H. *Codices MSS. Palatini Greci Bibliothecae Vaticanae* (Rome, 1885). For the manuscripts of G. Manetti see pp. xxvi and xxxi and nos. 159–69, 172–5, 177–80, 182–4, 186–7, 190–4, 197, 323.

STORNAJOLO, G. *Codices Urbinates Graeci Bibliothecae Vaticanae* (Rome, 1895). For the Index Vetus of Federigo's library see pp. cix–cxxv.

TRAVERSARI, AMBROGIO (Ambrosii Camaludensis). *Epistolae et Orationes*, ed. L. Mehus (Florence, 1759).

VECCHI, B. DE. 'I Libri di un Medico Umanista fiorentino del secolo xv', *Bibliofilia*, XXXIV (1933), 293–301. For the manuscripts of Bartolo di Tura di Bandino.

ZACCARIA, F. A. *Bibliotheca Pistoriensis* (Turin, 1752). For the manuscripts of Zomino see pp. 193–4.

PROSE WRITERS

ACHILLES TATIUS

1425 Cod. Laur. C.S. 627 of the *Clitiphon et Leucippe* in the library left by A. Corbinelli (Blum, *op. cit.*).

AELIAN OF PRAENESTE AND AELIAN TACTICUS

c. **1420** Cod. Vat. Pal. gr. 260, containing the *de Proprietatibus Animalium* marked as belonging to Lionardo Giustinian. (For approximate date see Traversari, *Epp.* VI, 4, 7.)

1427 MS. mentioned in the list of those brought back by Filelfo (Traversari, *Epp.* XXIV, 32).

1444 MS. of the *Tactica* used by Aurispa. In 1451 this was in the hands of F. Barbaro (Aurispa, *op. cit.* p. 168).

1455 MS. of the *de Proprietatibus Animalium*, mentioned in the catalogue of the library of Nicolas V (Muentz, *op. cit.*).

1457 Cod. Paris gr. 2524, containing the *Tactica* dated and marked as copied for G. de Vollaterrana by Ioannes Rosos. (Omont, *Les MSS. grecs datés*).

1468 MS. containing the *de Proprietatibus Animalium*, mentioned in the catalogue of the library left by Bessarion to St Mark's (Omont, *Inventaire*).

1475 MSS. of the *Variae Historiae*, the *de Proprietatibus Animalium*, and the *Tactica* mentioned in the catalogue of the library of Sixtus IV.

Before **1480** Cod. Pal. gr. 360, containing excerpts from the *Variae Historiae* marked as copied by M. Apostolios (Stevenson, *op. cit.*).

1490 MS. containing *the Variae Historiae*, mentioned in the library of Giorgio Valla (Heiberg, *op. cit.*).

Before **1492** MS. of the *de Proprietatibus Animalium* in the catalogue of Lorenzo dei Medici's library (Mueller, *op. cit.*).

AESCHINES

1425 Cod. Wolfenbuettel Helmst. 920, containing the letters and three speeches owned by Aurispa (Heinemann, *op. cit.*).

1425 Cod. Laur. C.S. 84, containing the *in Timarchum* in the library left by A. Corbinelli (Blum, *op. cit.*).

1427 MS. containing speeches and letters, mentioned in the list of those brought by Filelfo from Byzantium (Traversari, *Epp.* XXIV, 32).

1450 Cod. Laur. Acq. 50, containing the *in Timarchum*, *in Ctesiphontem* and *de Falsa Legatione*, marked as owned by Francesco da Castiglione (Rostagno, *Indici-Suppl.*).

Before **1459** Cod. Vat. Urb. gr. containing the *in Timarchum*, *in Ctesiphontem*, *de Falsa Legatione* and letters possibly owned by Manetti (Stornajolo, *op. cit.*).

1462 MS. of Aeschines among the books left by Palla Strozzi (Mazzatinti, V, p. 570).

1468 MS. mentioned in the catalogue of the library presented by Bessarion to St Mark's (Omont, *Inventaire*).

1475 MS. containing speeches and letters, mentioned in the catalogue of the library of Sixtus IV (Muentz, *op. cit.*).

1481 MS. of speeches in the catalogue of the library of Lorenzo dei Medici (Piccolomini, *op. cit.* p. 285).

Before **1482** MS. containing speeches and letters in the library of Federigo d'Urbino (Guasti, *op. cit.*).

Before **1492** MS. of Aeschines and one of his speeches (Codd. Laur. LX, 4 and 9?) in the catalogue of the library of Lorenzo dei Medici (Mueller, *op. cit.*).

Before **1494** MS. of Aeschines owned by Ermolao Barbaro (Mittarelli, *op. cit.*).

APHTHONIUS

1425 Cod. Laur. C.S. 51 of the *Progymnasmata* in the library left by A. Corbinelli (Blum, *op. cit.*).

Before **1481** Cod. Paris gr. 2978 of the *Progymnasmata* marked as owned by Filelfo (Omont, *Bibliothèque de Filelfo*).

1492 MS. of the *Progymnasmata* in the catalogue of the library of Lorenzo dei Medici (Mueller, *op. cit.*).

APOLLONIUS DYSCOLUS

1424 MS. of Apollonius Dyscolus in the list sent by Aurispa to Florence (Traversari, *Epp.* XXIV, 53).

Before **1462** MS. acquired in Italy by Filelfo through Palla Strozzi (Sabbadini, *Scoperte*, p. 48).

c. **1480** Cod. Laur. Aedil. 223, copied by Scutariotes and marked as owned by G. A. Vespucci (Rostagno, *Indici-Suppl.*).

1482 MS. of Apollonius Dyscolus (Cod. Laur. LXIX, 37?) in the catalogue of the library of Lorenzo dei Medici (Mueller, *op. cit.* For the date Piccolomini, *op. cit.* p. 285).

1495 Cod. Paris gr. 2547, copied by C. Lascaris (Omont, *Les ms. grecs datés*, p. 30).

APOLLONIUS OF PERGA

1427 MS. of Apollonius of Perga in the list sent by Filelfo to Florence (Traversari, *Epp.* XXIV, 32).

1455 MS. of Apollonius of Perga and one of the *Geometria* in the catalogue of the library of Nicolas V (Muentz, *op. cit.*).

1468 MS. of the *Conica* in the catalogue of the library left by Bessarion (Omont, *Inventaire*).

1475 MS. of the *Conica* in the catalogue of the library of Sixtus IV (Muentz, *op. cit.*).

APPIAN

Before **1455** MS. of Appian used by P. C. Decembrio for his translation.

1468 MS. mentioned in the catalogue of the library left by Bessarion to St Mark's (Omont, *Inventaire*).

1469 MS. in the possession of Paul II, probably the same as above. Filelfo asked for the loan of it (Filelfo, *Epp.* fo. 210).

1475 Two MSS. in the catalogue of the library of Sixtus IV (Muentz, *op. cit.*).

Before **1482** MS. in the catalogue of the library of Federigo d'Urbino (Guasti, *op. cit.*).

ARCHIMEDES

1423 MS. entitled *de instrumentis bellicis et aquaticis* supposedly by Archimedes which has never come to light, mentioned as owned by Rinucci da Castiglione (Aurispa, *op. cit.* p. 161).

1468 MS. entitled *Diversa Opera Geometrica* of Archimedes in the catalogue of the library left by Bessarion (Omont, *Inventaire*).
1490 MS. of Archimedes seen by Janus Lascaris in the library of Giorgio Valla (Mueller, *op. cit.* p. 383).

ARISTARCHUS

1421 Cod. Ven. A. Marcianus 4534 of the commentary on the *Iliad* in the list of those owned by Aurispa in Rome (Aurispa, *op. cit.* p. 160).

ARISTIDES

1421 Cod. Vat. gr. 1298, containing almost the complete works of Aristides, dated 1421 and marked as having later belonged to Niccolo Tomeo.
1425 Codd. Laur. C.S. 9, 83 and 185 together containing 44 speeches in the library left by A. Corbinelli (Blum, *op. cit.*).
1427 MS. mentioned in list of those brought back by Filelfo (Traversari, *Epp.* XXIV, 32).
1455 Seven MSS. of speeches and one MS. of *Rhetorica* in the catalogue of the library of Nicolas V (Muentz, *op. cit.*).
1460 MS. mentioned among those left by Aurispa (R. Sabbadini, *Biografia di G. Aurispa*, pp. 170–3). Contains speeches.
1460 MS. mentioned in the list of those left by Guarino to his son Battista (Omont, *MSS. grecs de Guarino*).
1461 Cod. Vat. Urb. gr. 122, dated and marked as owned by Benedictus de Auctariis of Vicenza containing 28 minor works (Stornajolo, *op. cit.*).
Before **1465** Cod. Malatest. XXVII, 3 of 57 speeches in the library of D. Malatesta Novello (Martin, *op. cit.*).
1468 Seven MSS. of speeches, two of unspecified contents and one containing the *Panathenaicus* mentioned in the catalogue of the library left by Bessarion to St Mark's (Omont, *Inventaire*).
c. **1470** Cod. Vat. gr. 1394 of minor works owned by B. Lorenzo (Nolhac, *op. cit.* p. 228).
1475 Thirteen MSS. of works, two containing part of the works, and one with twenty-five speeches, contained in the catalogue of the library of Sixtus IV (Muentz, *op. cit.*).
Before **1482** MS. of the speeches in the catalogue of the library of Federigo d'Urbino (Guasti, *op. cit.*).
1490 MS. mentioned in the catalogue of the library of Giorgio Valla (Heiberg, *op. cit.*).
Before **1492** Two MSS. of Aristides and one of his speeches (perhaps Cod. Laur. LX, 9) in the catalogue of the library of Lorenzo dei Medici (Mueller, *op. cit.*).
Before **1494** Three MSS. of speeches in the catalogue of the library of Pico della Mirandola (Kibre, *op. cit.*).

ARISTOTLE (INCLUDING SUPPOSITIOUS WORKS)

1402 Cod. Paris gr. 1851, containing Aristotle *de Anima* and the *de lineis insecabilibus* dated and marked as copied at Milan (Omont, *Les MSS. grecs datés*).

1407 MS. containing the *Physica*, mentioned as lent by Bruni to Niccoli (Sabbadini, *Scoperte*).

1415 Cod. Vat. Pal. gr. 260, containing the *de Partibus Animalium, de Proprietatibus Animalium* and *de Animalium Historia*, marked as having belonged to Giustinian. It is probably the MS. mentioned in the list he sent to Traversari in 1415 (Traversari, *Epp.* VI, 7).

1415 MS. of the *de Mundo* probably brought by Rinucci da Castiglione from Constantinople (Lockwood, *op. cit.*).

1416 MS. of the *Ethica Nicomachea* used by Bruni for his translation (Baron, *op. cit.*).

1419 MS. of the *Oeconomica* used by Bruni for his translation (*ibid.*).

1421 MS. of 'some works' in the list of those owned by Aurispa in Rome (Aurispa, *op. cit.* p. 160).

1421 MSS. containing the *Eudemian Ethics, de Vaticinatione per Somnium, de Miris Auditis, Rhetorica ad Alexandrum*, mentioned in the list sent by Aurispa to Florence (Traversari, *Epp.* XXIV, 53). Also the *Rhetorica* (*ibid.* 38). A second copy was made in this year of the *Rhetorica* and the *Eudemian Ethics* (Aurispa, *op. cit.* p. 75).

1425 Cod. Laur. C.S. 47 of the *Rhetorica* and *Rhet. ad Alex.*, also three other MSS. (one of the *Logica*) in the library left by Corbinelli (Blum, *op. cit.*).

1427 MSS. *Ethica Eudem. et Nicomach., Magna Moralia, Oeconomica Politica, Physica, Metaphysica, de Anima, de Historia Animalium, de Partibus Animalium, Rhetorica*, mentioned in the list of MSS. brought back by Filelfo from Constantinople (Traversari, *Epp.* XXIV, 32).

1428 Cod. Paris Supp. gr. 1285, containing the *Rhetorica* (probably the one mentioned above), marked as having belonged to Vittorino. For a mention of its sale see Filelfo, *Epp.* fo. 5 v. (quoted Sabbadini, *Scoperte*, p. 61). Eventually it went to F. Barbaro (Omont, *Bibliothèque de Filelfo*).

1432 MS. containing the *Meteora* and the *Metaphysica*, mentioned as belonging to Pietro Vitali (Traversari, *Epp.* VIII, 42).

1432 MS., contents unspecified, mentioned as bought by Palla Strozzi (Vespasiano, *Vite*, p. 272).

1432 MSS. containing several works of Aristotle (one no doubt the *Rhetorica* mentioned above), mentioned as seen in Vittorino's library by Traversari (Traversari, *Epp.* VIII, 50).

1437 Two MSS. of *Ethica*, mentioned as in the possession of Niccoli (Traversari, *Epp.* VIII, 22). The date of this letter is uncertain but it must have been written before Niccoli's death in 1437.

1438 MS. of the *Politica* used by Bruni for his translation (Baron, *op. cit.*).

Before **1440** MS. containing the *Ethica* and the *de Anima*, mentioned in a list of MSS. belonging to Ciriaco of Ancona (Omont, *Centralblatt* IV, p. 187).

1441 MS. of the *de Anima* copied by Palla Strozzi (Mazzatinti, *op. cit.* II, 570).

1442 MS. of the *Physica* copied by Palla Strozzi (*ibid.*).

1442 Cod. Vat. Pal. gr. 159 of the *Logica* dated and marked as copied by Scutariotes for Manetti (Stephenson, *op. cit.*).

Before **1444** Cod. Vat. gr. 1339, marked as owned by G. Piccinino.

1445 Cod. Leid. Scalig. 26, containing the *Politica*, dated and marked as copied for Filelfo by Sgouropoulo (Omont, *Centralblatt* IV, 193).

1446 Cod. Vindobona philos. gr. 75, dated and marked as belonging to Guarino.

c. **1450** Cod. Laur. (Acquisiti) 4 (*Politica, Rhet. ad Alexandrum*), 43 (*de Interpretatione*), 65 (*Mechanica*), 67 (*de Memoria*), 68 (*de Generatione*), 66 (*de Sensu*) owned by Francesco da Castiglione (Rostagno, *Indici*).

1452 MS. of the *Problemata* sent to the Papal Library by Niccolò Perotti (Muentz, *op. cit.* p. 113).

Before **1454** MS. of the *Rhetorica* marked as owned by Francesco Barbaro (Mittarelli, *op. cit.*).

1455 MSS. of the *Logica* (three copies), *de Caelo et Mundo* and *de Generatione et Corruptione* (two copies each), *de Anima, Ethica Nichomachea, Magna Moralia, Meteora, Physica* and *Rhetorica* in the catalogue of the library of Nicholas V (Muentz, *op. cit.*).

1457 MS. of the *Naturales Auditus* sent by Aurispa to Alfonso of Aragon (Aurispa, *op. cit.* p. 148).

1457 MS. of the *Problemata* obtained by Poggio for Guarino (*Spicilegium Romanum*, X, 357).

Before **1459** Codd. Vat. Pal. gr. 160 (*Politica, Rhetorica, Rhetorica ad Alexandrum, Epp. ad Alexandrum et Olympiadem*), 161 (*de Physico Auditu, de Caelo, Meteora, de Generatione et Corruptione, de Anima*), 162 (*de Dogmatibus, de Miris Auditis, de Cosmographia, Mechanica*), 163 (*de Sensu et Sensato, de Memoria et Reminiscentia, de Somno et Vigilia, de Vaticinatione per Somnium, de Longitudine et Brevitate Vitae, de Motu Animalium, de Generatione Animalium, de Partibus Animalium, de Incessu Animalium*), 164 (*Metaphysica, Problemata Physica*), 165 (*Ethica Nicomachea, Ethica Eudemia, I–III, V–VII, Oeconomica*), 323 (*Ethica Eudemia* (a second copy)), copied by Scutariotes and marked as owned by Manetti (Stephenson, *op. cit.*).

1460 MSS. of *Ethica* and *Logica* owned by Zomino (Zaccaria, *op. cit.* pp. 43–4).

1462 Two MSS. of the *Physica* left by P. Strozzi (Mazzatinti, *op. cit.* IV, 570).

1462 MS. containing the *Rhetorica* and also the *Rhetorica* of Trophonius, dated and marked as copied by Constantine Lascaris in Milan (Iriarte, *op. cit.* no. 111, p. 442).

Before **1464** MS. X 88, At 512, in the Library of Columbia University, New York, marked as belonging to Cosimo dei Medici (Ricci and Wilson, *Census of Medieval and Renaissance MSS. in the U.S. and Canada*, p. 1266 (New York, 1935). Contains the *Logica*.

1464 MS. containing the *de Mundo, de Fortuna, de Fato* and also Alexander of Aphrodisias, *de Iis qui Sunt in Potestate Nostra*, dated and marked as copied by Constantine Lascaris in Milan (Iriarte, *op. cit.* no. 119, p. 428).

1468 MS. containing all Aristotle's works except for the *Organon*, also separately the *de Mundo*, *Physica* (2 copies), *de Anima*, *de Motu Animalium*, *Logica* (3 copies), *de Caelo et Mundo*, *de Generatione et Corruptione* (2 copies), *Meteora* (2 copies), *Rhetorica* (6 books), *Politica*, *de Historia Animalium*, *Magna Moralia*, *Ethica Eudem.*, *Metaphysica*, *de physico auditu*, *Ethica Nichom.*, *Problemata*, mentioned in the catalogue of the library which Bessarion left to St Mark's.

1470 MS. containing the *Opera Varia Pleraque Physica* dated and marked as copied by Constantine Lascaris in Messina (Iriarte, *op. cit.* no. 119, p. 428).

Before **1475** Cod. Vat. gr. 1334, containing the *de Insomniis* of Aristotle, marked as copied for Filelfo by Gaza, therefore belonging to the period before the latter's death (Nolhac, *Bibliothèque*).

1475 Cod. Laur. LXXXI, 7 (Bandini, *op. cit.* III, 224), containing the *Nicomachean Ethics*, dated and marked as copied by Ioannes Rosos.

c. **1475** Cod. Laur. LXXXI, 12, containing the *Ethica Eudem.* and the *Magna Moralia*, marked as copied by Ioannes Rhosos, undated but likely to belong to the same period as the *Nicomachean Ethics* above.

1475 MSS. containing *Logica* (complete, 12 copies), *Logica* (part only), *Physica* (8 copies), *Rhetorica* (2 copies), *Magna Moralia*, *Ethica*, *Parva Moralia*, *Parva Naturalia*, *de Generatione et Corruptione*, *de Caelo et Mundo*, *de Partibus Animalium*, *Meteora*, *de Anima* (2 copies), *Metaphysica* (2 copies), *Physiognomia de Rebus Inauditis*, *de Historia Animalium*, *Analectica*, *Varia*, mentioned in the catalogue of the library of Sixtus IV (Muentz, *op. cit.*).

Before **1480** Cod. Vat. Pal. gr. 83, marked as copied by Scutariotes (Stephenson, *op. cit.*).

Before **1480** Cod. Vat. Pal. gr. 74, containing the *Logica* and Cod. Vat. Urb. gr. of the *Meteora*, undated but marked as copied by Michael Apostolios who died in 1480.

c. **1480** Cod. Vat. gr. 1343, containing the *Nicomachea Ethica*, *Oeconomica de virtute* (Nolhac, *op. cit.* p. 197), and marked as copied by Rhalles in Rome.

Before **1481** Cod. Laur. LXXI, 13 and 20, containing the *Ethica Eudem.* and the *Magna Moralia* and also Cod. Vat. Urb. gr. 108 (*de Miris auditis*) owned by Filelfo (Bandini, *op. cit.* II, 538).

Before **1482** Codd. Vat. Urb. gr. 37 (*de Caelo*, II, *de Generatione et Corruptione*, *Meteora*, *de Sensu et Sensato*, *de Memoria et Reminiscentia*, *de Somno et Vigilia*, *de Vaticinatione per Somnium*, *de Longitudine et Brevitate Vitae*, *de Iuventute et Senectute*, *de Vita et Morte*, *de Coloribus*, *Ethica Nicomachea*), 42 (*Ethica Nicomachea*, I–VII), 43, fo. 1 (*Ethica Nicomache*) 44 (*Ethica Nicomachea*, *de Lineis Insecabilibus*, *Mechanica*), 47 (*Rhetorica ad Alexandrum*, *Rhetorica* and *Poetica*), 50 (*Problemata Physica*) and also MSS. of the *de Caelo*, *de Iuventute et Senectute*, *de Longitudine Vitae Animalium*, *de Partibus Animalium*, *de Vita et Morte Animalium*, *Ethica Eudemia*, *Logica* (with separate copies of the *de Interpretatione* and *Analytica*) *Meteora*, *Oeconomica* and *Politica* marked as owned by and/or in the catalogue of the library of Federigo d'Urbino (*Stornajolo*, *op. cit.* and Guasti, *op. cit.*).

1490 MSS. containing the *Magna Moralia*, *Ethica*, *Physica*, *Parva Naturalia* and the *Organon*, mentioned in the catalogue of the library of Giorgio Valla (Heiberg, *op. cit.*).

Before **1492** MS. of the complete works and MSS. of the *Analytica Priora* (Cod. Laur. LXXII, 10?), *Analytica, de Caelo et Mundo, de Partibus Animalium, de Physico Auditu, Ethica Eudemia* (Codd. Laur. LXXXI, 15 and 20?), *Historia Animalium* (Cod. Laur. LXXXVII, 27?), *Logica, Physica, Poetica, Problemata, Rhetorica* (two copies—Codd. Laur. LX, 10 and 18?) in the catalogue of the library of Lorenzo dei Medici (Mueller, *op. cit.*).

1492 Cod. Paris gr. 1857, containing the *Poetica* and the *Rhetorica*, dated and marked as copied by Ioannes Rosos in Rome (Omont, *Les MSS. grecs datés*).

Before **1494** Cod. Laur. LX, 15, containing the *Poetica* and another Cod. Laur. LXXXI, 6, containing the *Politica* undated but marked as having belonged to Angelo Politian who died in 1494 (Bandini, *op. cit.* II, 604 and III, 223).

Before **1494** MSS. of the *Analytica Priora et Posteriora, de Anima, Ethica Nicomachea, Logica* (incomplete), *Meteora, Politica* and *Rhet. ad Alex.* in the catalogue of the library of Pico della Mirandola (Kibre, *op. cit.*).

Before **1495** Cod. Vat. gr. 1305 (*de Plantis*) copied by, and 1391 (*Topica*) annotated by, Ermolao Barbaro and two copies of the *Historia Animalium* in his possession (Mueller, *op. cit.* 387).

ARRIAN

1421 MS. of the *de Alexandro*, mentioned in the list of those owned by Aurispa in Rome (Aurispa, *op. cit.* p. 159).

1427 Cod. Lau. LXX, 34, containing the works of Arrian and Diodorus Siculus, dated and marked as copied by Chrysococces for Garathon (Bandini, *op. cit.* II, 691).

1432 MS. mentioned as seen by Traversari in Vittorino's library (Traversari, *Epp.* VIII, 50).

c. **1440** MS. of the *de Alexandro* used by Vergerio for his translation.

1468 MS. containing the *de Alexandro* and the *in Epictetum*, mentioned in the catalogue of the library left by Bessarion to St Mark's.

1475 MSS. of the *de Alexandro* and *in Epictetum* in the catalogue of the library of Sixtus IV (Muentz, *op. cit.*).

Before **1482** MS. of the *de Alexandro* in the catalogue of the library of Federigo d'Urbino (Guasti, *op. cit.*).

1485 Cod. Laur. LX, 5 of the *in Epictetum* dated and marked as copied by Scutariotes and owned by Politian (Bandini, *op. cit.*).

1490 MS. containing the *in Epictetum*, mentioned in the catalogue of the library of Giorgio Valla (Heiberg, *op. cit.*).

Before **1492** MS. of Arrian (Cod. Laur. LXX, 90), in the library of Lorenzo dei Medici (Mueller, *op. cit.*).

Before **1494** MSS. of the *de Alexandro* and *in Epictetum* in the catalogue of the library of Pico della Mirandola (Kibre, *op. cit.*).

ATHENAEUS

1424 MS. of an extract (*de Coenis*) from the *Deipnosophistae* in the list sent by Aurispa to Florence: later this was in the library of Bessarion (Aurispa, *op. cit.*).

1475 MS. in the catalogue of the library of Sixtus IV (Muentz, *op. cit.*).

1482 Cod. Paris gr. 3056 of the *Deipnosophistae*, dated and marked as copied by E. Barbaro (Omont, *MS. grecs datés*).

CEBES

1482 MS. of the *Tabulae* in the library of P. Leoni (Dorez, *op. cit.*).

DEMOSTHENES

c. **1400** Two MSS. mentioned as given by Chrysoloras to L. Bruni and Roberto Rossi respectively (Sabbadini, *Scoperte*). Contents not specified. One may have included the *de Chersoneso* which Bruni translated in 1405.

Before **1414** Cod. Vat. gr. 1368, dated and marked as copied at Milan, containing *de Corona, Philippics* I and II, *de Pace* (Nolhac, *op. cit.* p. 145).

1415 MS. of the *Olynthiacs*, one *Philippic* and the *de Corona* (incomplete), probably owned by Rinucci da Castiglione (Lockwood, *op. cit.*).

1424 An almost complete MS. of the works in the list sent by Aurispa to Florence (Aurispa, *op. cit.*; Traversari, *Epp.* XXIV, 32).

1425 Codd. Laur. C.S. 136 (16 speeches) and 168 (speeches nos. I–XXXIV, LVIII, LX and LXI), also one other MS. of Demosthenes in the library left by A. Corbinelli (Blum, *op. cit.*).

1427 MS. mentioned in the list of those brought by Filelfo from Constantinople (Traversari, *Epp.* XXIV, 32).

c. **1450** Cod. Lau. (Acquisiti) 70, containing speeches 14–18, 21–25, 60, marked as having belonged to Francesco da Castiglione (Rostagno, *Indici-Suppl.*, p. 202).

1451 Cod. Malatest. XXVII, 2 of 57 speeches, bought by J. Galeotti in Constantinople. This soon passed on to the library of D. Malatesta (Martin, *op. cit.*).

1452 MS. of the Private Orations, mentioned as bought by Perotti for Nicolas V (Muentz, *op. cit.* pp. 113–14).

1455 Five MSS. of speeches, mentioned in the catalogue of the library of Nicolas V. One of these was presumably the MS. of the Private Orations bought in 1452 (Muentz, *op. cit.*).

1458 MS. of Demosthenes taken by Angelo Decembrio to Spain (Capelli, *op. cit.*).

Before **1459** Cod. Vat. Pal. gr. 172, containing 30 speeches marked as owned by Manetti (Stephenson, *op. cit.*).

1460 MS. of speeches, mentioned in the list of those left by Guarino (H. Omont, *Revue de Bibliothèques* II (1892)). Contents unspecified.

1460 MS. of speeches, mentioned in the list of those left by Aurispa (R. Sabbadini, *Biografia di G. Aurispa*, pp. 170–3).

1462   Cod. Paris Coislin 324, containing the complete works of Demosthenes, dated and marked as copied by Ioannes Rhosos (Omont, *MSS. grecs datés*).

Before **1465**   Cod. Malatest. XXIX, 3 of the *Olynthiacs* and *Philippics* in the library of D. Malatesta Novello (Muccioli, *op. cit.* p. 107).

1468   Two MSS. of 'works', two of 'speeches', one of fifty speeches and one of thirty-two speeches mentioned in the catalogue of the library left by Bessarion (Omont, *Inventaire*.)

1475   Six MSS. of speeches. Contents unspecified and one of 'orationes procuratoriae', mentioned in the catalogue of the library of Sixtus IV.

Before **1482**   MS. containing 24 speeches in the catalogue of the library of Federigo d'Urbino (Guasti, *op. cit.*).

1484   Cod. Paris gr. 2939, containing the *Philippics* and the *de Corona*, dated and marked as copied by Nicolas Vlastos (Omont, *MSS. grecs de la Bibliothèque Nationale*).

1485   Cod. Laur. LIX, 46, containing the *de Falsa Legatione*, dated and marked as copied by Ioannes Rosos.

Before **1487**   Cod. Paris gr. 2999 of *Olynthiacs* I–III, *Philippics* I, II and IV, *de Corona*, *de Pace*, *de Chersoneso*, *de Falsa Leg.*, *in Leptinem*, marked as owned by A. Petrucci (Delisle, *op. cit.*).

1487   MS. containing the complete works of Demosthenes except for some private speeches, dated and marked as copied by Constantine Lascaris (Iriarte, *op. cit.* no. 31, p. 131).

1490   MSS. of the *de Falsa Legatione*, *de Corona*, *in Androtium*, *in Aristocratem*, *in Leptinem*, *in Mediam* and *in Timocratem*, seen by Janus Lascaris in the library of Battista Guarino (Mueller, *op. cit.* p. 382).

Before **1492**   Two MSS. of Demosthenes (one perhaps Cod. Laur. LXIX, 8) and a MS. of the *Philippics* (perhaps Cod. Laur. LXIX, 39) in the catalogue of the library of Lorenzo dei Medici (Mueller, *op. cit.*).

Before **1494**   Cod. Laur. (San Marco) 314 of *Oratio* no. 4, marked as owned by Angelo Politian (Rostagno, *Indici*, p. 182).

Before **1494**   MS. containing some speeches in the catalogue of the library of Pico della Mirandola (Caroli-Cesis, *op. cit.*).

DIO CASSIUS

1421   MS. of the *Historia* in the list of those owned by Aurispa in Rome (Aurispa, *op. cit.* p. 160, also Traversari, *Epp.* XXIV, 53).

1438   MS. owned by Guarino (Sabbadini, *Scoperte*, p. 45).

1468   MS. of the *Historia*, books XXX–LVIII and another of books XLIV–LIX in the catalogue of the library left by Bessarion (Omont, *Inventaire*).

1469   MS. in the library of Paul II, mentioned by Filelfo (Filelfo, *Epp.* fo. 210).

1475   Two MSS. (one incomplete) of the *Historia* in the catalogue of the library of Sixtus IV (Muentz, *op. cit.*).

Before **1481**   MS. in the possession of Filelfo (Sabbadini, *Scoperte*, p. 48).

Dio Chrysostom

1424 Cod. Laur. C.S. 114 of all the speeches in the library left by A. Corbinelli (Blum, *op. cit.*), marked as having belonged to Aurispa (Rostagno, *Indici*).

1427 MS. mentioned in the list of those brought back by Filelfo (Traversari, *Epp.* XXIV, 32). Contents not specified.

1431 MS. of Dio Chrysostom owned by Filelfo which Aurispa tries to borrow in 1431 and 1438. Probably Cod. Laur. LXIX, 22 of the *Rhetoricae Meditationes* which is marked as owned by Filelfo (Aurispa, *op. cit.* pp. 73 and 97; Bandini, *op. cit.* II, p. 538).

1460 MS. of the *de Ilio Capto*, mentioned in the list of books left by Guarino to his son Battista (Omont, *Revue des Bibliothèques* II, 1892).

1468 MS. containing eighty speeches and others described as speeches, mentioned in the catalogue of the library left by Bessarion to St Mark's.

1475 MS. mentioned in the catalogue of the library of Sixtus IV (Muentz, *op. cit.*). Contents not specified.

Before **1482** MS. of Dio Chrysostom in the catalogue of the library of Federigo d'Urbino (Guasti, *op. cit.*).

1490 MS. containing five speeches, mentioned in the catalogue of the library of Giorgio Valla (Heiberg, *op. cit.*).

1491 Cod. Paris gr. 2960, dated and marked as copied by F. Vernardo at Verona (Omont, *Les MSS. grecs datés*).

Before **1492** MS. of Dio Chrysostom (perhaps Cod. Laur. LIX, 22 or LXXXI, 2) in the catalogue of the library of Lorenzo dei Medici (Mueller, *op. cit.*).

1493 Cod. Vat. gr. 1336 of *Moralia* marked as copied by M. Musurus (Nolhac, *Bibliothèque*, p. 150).

Before **1494** MS. of Dio Chrysostom in the catalogue of the library of Pico della Mirandola (Kibre, *op. cit.*).

Diodorus Siculus

1424 MS. of many books of the *Historia* in the list sent by Aurispa to Florence (Traversari, *Epp.* XXIV, 53).

1427 Cod. Laur. LXX, 34, containing the works of Diodorus and Arrian, dated and marked as copied by Chrysococces for Garathon (Bandini, *op. cit.* II, 691).

Before **1455** MS. of Diodorus used by Poggio for his translation.

1455 MS. of Book III mentioned in the catalogue of the library of Nicolas V (Muentz, *op. cit.* p. 341).

1468 MS. containing books 1–5 and 11–20, mentioned in the catalogue of the library left by Bessarion to St Mark's.

1469 MS. in the library of Paul II mentioned by Filelfo (Filelfo, *Epp.* fo. 210).

1475 Three MSS. containing the works and one part of the works of Diodorus, mentioned in the catalogue of the library of Sixtus IV (Muentz, *op. cit.*).

Before **1481**   Cod. Laur. LXX, 18, marked as owned by Filelfo (Omont, *Bibliothèque de Filelfo*).

1488   MS. of Diodorus in the library of Lorenzo dei Medici (Piccolomini, *op. cit.* p. 287).

Before **1492**   Two MSS. (one perhaps Cod. Laur. LXX, 16) in the catalogue of the library of Lorenzo dei Medici. One of these was almost certainly the MS. mentioned in 1488 (Mueller, *op. cit.*).

1495   MS. mentioned as being in the library of Ercole I d'Este (Bertoni, *op. cit.* pp. 235–82).

DIOGENES LAERTIUS

1415   MS. of Diogenes Laertius, mentioned as owned by F. Barbaro (Traversari, *Epp.* VI, 14).

1416   MS. of the *de Vita Philosophorum*, copied by Giustinian (Traversari, *Epp.* VI, 25). A copy of this work is mentioned as being in Giustinian's possession in 1425 (*ibid.* VI, 27).

1421   MS. of the *de Vita Philosophorum* in the list of those owned by Aurispa in Rome (Aurispa, *op. cit.* p. 160). It does not appear on the list he sent to Florence in 1424; but there was a copy in his possession in 1431 (*ibid.* pp. 12 and 73).

1423   MS. of the *de Vita Philosophorum*, mentioned as brought by Antonio Massa from Constantinople (Traversari, *Epp.* VI, 23).

1425   Two MSS. of the *de Vita Philosophorum*, mentioned as used by Traversari in his translation. One belonged to Guarino and the other was a copy made from this in Florence (*ibid.* VI, 23).

Before **1439**   MS. mentioned by Traversari as owned by Filelfo (*ibid.* XXIV, 38). This may have been Cod. Vat. Urb. gr. 108 which is marked as owned by Filelfo (Stornajolo, *op. cit.*).

Before **1459**   Cod. Vat. Pal. gr. 182 of the *de Vita Philosophorum*, marked as owned by Manetti (Stephenson, *op. cit.*).

Before **1465**   Cod. Malatest. XXVIII, 4 of the *Vita Platonis* in the library of D. Malatesta Novello (Muccioli, *op. cit.* p. 102).

1468   MS. of the *de Vita Philosophorum* in the catalogue of the library left by Bessarion (Omont, *Inventaire*).

1475   MS. of the *de Vita Philosophorum* in the catalogue of the library of Sixtus IV (Muentz, *op. cit.*).

Before **1482**   MS. of the *de Vita Philosophorum* in the catalogue of the library of Federigo d'Urbino (Guasti, *op. cit.*).

1490   MS. of the *de Vita Philosophorum* seen by Janus Lascaris in the library of G. Valla (Mueller, *op. cit.*).

DIONYSIUS OF HALICARNASSUS

1424   MS. of Dionysius's *Super Significationibus Dictionum* in the list sent by Aurispa to Florence (Traversari, *Epp.* XXIV, 53). Sabbadini thinks that this may have been the now lost Attic Lexicon of Dionysius of Halicarnassus (Aurispa, *op. cit.* XVIII).

1425 Cod. Laur. C.S. 100 of the *de Compositione Nominum* in the library left by A. Corbinelli (Blum, *op. cit.*).

1427 MS. containing the *de Numeris et Characteribus* and another of unspecified contents included in the list of those brought back by Filelfo (Traversari, *Epp.* XXIV, 32).

1455 MS. of the *de Antiquitate Romae*, mentioned in the catalogue of the library of Nicolas V (Muentz, *op. cit.*).

1460 MS. containing the *de Lysia* and another of unspecified contents, mentioned in the list of those left by Guarino to his son (Omont, *Revue des Bibliothèques*).

1468 Two MSS. of the *de Comp. Nom.*, one of the *de Rhetorica*, and one of unspecified contents, mentioned in the catalogue of the books left by Bessarion (Omont, *Inventaire*).

1469 MS. of Dionysius of Halicarnassus copied by A. della Toffe for Pope Paul II who also owned a second copy (*Le Vite di Paolo II*, ed. G. Zippel, IX, 1).

1475 Two MSS. containing the *de Antiquitate Romae* (see under 1455 and 1469 above) and another of unspecified contents, mentioned in the catalogue of the library of Sixtus IV (Muentz, *op. cit.*).

Before **1482** Cod. Vat. Urb. gr. 47 of the *de Compositione Nominum* and two other MSS. of Dionysius of Halicarnassus in the library of Federigo d'Urbino (Stornajolo, *op. cit.* and Guasti, *op. cit.*).

1490 MS. of *de Viris Illustribus*, seen by Janus Lascaris in the library of Giorgio Valla (Mueller, *op. cit.* p. 382).

Before **1492** MS. of Dionysius of Halicarnassus (Cod. Laur. LIX, 15?) in the catalogue of the library of Lorenzo dei Medici (Mueller, *op. cit.*).

DIOPHANTUS

1455 MS. of the *Arithmetica* in the catalogue of the library of Nicolas V (Muentz, *op. cit.*).

1468 MS. of Diophantus in the catalogue of the library left by Bessarion (Omont, *Inventaire*).

DIOSCORIDES

1435 MS. of Dioscorides brought by Tortelli from Constantinople (Tortelli, *Orthographia*, under 'Hippocrates').

1455 MS. of the *de Materia Medica* in the library of Nicholas V (Muentz, *op. cit.*).

1468 Three MSS. mentioned in the catalogue of Bessarion's library (Omont, *Inventaire*, etc.).

1470 MS. containing the *de Qualitatum Temperamentis*, the *de Herbarum Virtute*, *de Medicamentis Succedaneis* and the *de Lapidibus*, dated and marked as copied by Constantine Lascaris at Messina (Iriarte, *op. cit.* no. 110, p. 431).

1475 MS. containing some of the works of Dioscorides, mentioned in the catalogue of the library of Sixtus IV (Muentz, *op. cit.*).

Before **1481** MS. acquired by Filelfo in Italy (Sabbadini, *Scoperte*, no. 34, p. 48).

473

Before **1482**   Cod. Vat. Urb. gr. 66, fo. 1 of the *de Materia Medica* in the catalogue of the library of Federigo d'Urbino (Guasti, *op. cit.*).

Before **1489**   MS. of Dioscorides mentioned by Politian as in the library of Lorenzo dei Medici (Politian, *Epp.* I, 11, cf. Mueller, *op. cit.* p. 353).

Before **1494**   MS. of Dioscorides in the catalogue of the library of Pico della Mirandola (Kibre, *op. cit.*).

EPICTETUS

Before **1489**   Cod. Laur. Redi. 15 of the *Encheiridion* marked as copied by A. Damilas and L. Lauretano (Rostagno, *Indici Suppl.*).

EUCLID

1455   Three MSS. of *Geometria* (probably the *Elementa*) in the catalogue of the library of Nicolas V (Muentz, *op. cit.*).

1468   Three MSS. of the *Elementa*, one each of the *Data*, *Optica* (*Catoptrica*) and *Phaenomena* and one entitled *Alia Geometrica* in the catalogue of the library left by Bessarion (Omont, *Inventaire*).

1475   Four MSS. of *Geometria* (probably the *Elementa*), two of the *Optica* and one entitled *Ledomena* in the catalogue of the library of Sixtus IV (Muentz, *op. cit.*).

1482   MS. of *Geometria* in the catalogue of the library of Lorenzo dei Medici (Mueller, *op. cit.*; for the date see Piccolomini, *op. cit.* p. 256).

Before **1492**   One MS. of Euclid, one of his *Arithmetica* and one of his *Geometria* in the catalogue of the library of Pico della Mirandola (Kibre, *op. cit.*).

GALEN

1433   MS mentioned as in the possession of Pietro Tommasi (Traversari, *Epp.* VIII, 46).

1454   MS. of the *Methodus Medendi* marked as owned by F. Barbaro (Mittarelli, *op. cit.* p. 154).

1455   MSS. of the *Methodus Medendi* and *Opera*, mentioned in the catalogue of the library of Nicolas V (Muentz, *op. cit.*).

1468   MSS. containing the *de Nutrimentis*, *Commentarium Aphorismi Hippocratis* (2 copies), *Microtechnic.*, *de Reg. San.*, *de Medicam.*, mentioned in the catalogue of Bessarion's library (Omont, *Inventaire*, etc.).

1473   Cod. Paris gr. 2160 of the *Methodus Medendi* dated and marked as copied by I. Rosos (Omont, *MSS. grecs datés*).

1475   Two MSS. containing works by Galen, mentioned in the catalogue of the library of Sixtus IV (Muentz, *op. cit.*). Also one MS. containing the commentary on the *Prognostica* of Hippocrates.

Before **1482**   MS. containing the *de usu partium*, *de inventione medicinae* and the *de virtute ciborum* in the catalogue of the library of Federigo d'Urbino (Guasti, *op. cit.*).

1487   Cod. Laur. LXXV, 8, dated and marked as owned by Politian (Bandini, *op. cit.*).

Before **1492**   MS. containing a large number of works (perhaps Cod. Laur. LXXIV, 5) in the catalogue of the library of Lorenzo dei Medici (Mueller, *op. cit.*).

Before **1494**   MSS. of the *Ars Parva*, the commentary on the *Aphorisms* of Hippocrates, the *de usu partium* and the *Introductorium* in the catalogue of the library of Pico della Mirandola (Kibre, *op. cit.*).

HARPOCRATION

1455   MS. in the catalogue of the library of Nicolas V (Muentz, *op. cit.*).

HELIODORUS

1455   Two MSS. of the *Ethiopica* in the catalogue of the library of Nicolas V (Muentz, *op. cit.*).

1468   Three MSS. of the *Ethiopica* in the catalogue of the library left by Bessarion (Omont, *Inventaire*).

1475   MS. of the *Ethiopica* in the catalogue of the library of Sixtus IV (Muentz, *op. cit.*).

HEPHAESTION

1424   MS. of the *de Maetris* in the list sent by Aurispa to Florence (Traversari, *Epp.* XXIV, 53).

1468   Two MSS. of the *de Metris* in the catalogue of the library left by Bessarion (Omont, *Inventaire*).

1475   MS. of the *de Metris* in the catalogue of the library of Sixtus IV (Muentz, *op. cit.*).

1490   MS. of Hephaestion seen by Janus Lascaris in the library of Ermolao Barbaro (Mueller, *op. cit.*).

HERMOGENES

1425   Cod. Laur. C.S. 51 of the *Rhetorica* in the library left by A. Corbinelli (Blum, *op. cit.*).

1427   MS. of Hermogenes in the list sent by Filelfo to Florence (Traversari, *Epp.* XXIV, 32).

1455   Seven MSS. of *Rhetorica* and one of *Theorica* in the catalogue of the library of Nicolas V (Muentz, *op. cit.*).

1458   Cod. Vat. Ottobon. gr. 22 of the *Rhetorica* owned by Palla Strozzi (Feron, *op. cit.*).

1475   Nine MSS. of *Rhetorica* in the catalogue of the library of Sixtus IV (Muentz, *op. cit.*).

1481   Cod. Paris gr. 2978 of the *Ars Rhetorica, de inventione oratoria* and the *de formis oratoriis*, marked as owned by Filelfo (Omont, *Bibliothèque de Filelfo* and *Inventaire sommaire*).

1491   Cod. Paris gr. 2960 of the *Ars Rhetorica*, dated and marked as copied by F. Vernardo at Verona (Omont, *MSS. grecs datés* and *Inventaire sommaire*).

1492   MS. of *Rhetorica* in the catalogue of the library of Lorenzo dei Medici (Mueller, *op. cit.*).

HERO

1421 MS. of the *de Iaculis* (? the *Belopoieica*) in the list of those owned by Aurispa in Rome (Aurispa, *op. cit.* p. 160).

1468 MSS. of the *Pneumatica*, *Mechanica* and *Belopoieica* in the catalogue of the library left by Bessarion (Omont, *Inventaire*).

1490 MSS. of the *Pneumatica*, *Geometria* and *Metrica* seen by J. Lascaris in the library of Giorgio Valla. These are probably the MSS. seen the following year by Politian (Mueller, *op. cit.* pp. 356 and 383).

HERODIAN AND HERODIAN TECHNICUS

1421 MS. of the *de Differentia ling.* in the list of those owned by Aurispa in Rome (Aurispa, *op. cit.* p. 154. Traversari, *Epp.* XXIV, 53).

1425 Cod. Leid. Gronov. 88 of the *de Octo Caesaribus* in the library left by A. Corbinelli (Blum, *op. cit.*).

1468 MS. of unspecified contents and another of the *de Octo Caesaribus*, mentioned in the catalogue of the library of Bessarion (H. Omont, *Inventaire*, etc.).

Before **1481**   Cod. Laur. LVIII, 19 of the *de Nominibus et verbis* marked as owned by Filelfo. He also had a MS. of the *de Differentia Linguarum* (Piccolomini, p. 287).

HERODOTUS

1421 MS. of Herodotus in the list of those owned by Aurispa in Rome (Aurispa, *op. cit.* p. 160).

1423 MS. mentioned by Rinucci da Castiglione in the preface to his translation of the Axiochus (in Cod. Amb. M4 sup. fl. 100 and 104v.), therefore presumably brought by him from Constantinople on his return in 1423. Contents not specified.

1425 Cod. Laur. C.S. 207 (complete) in the library left by A. Corbinelli (Blum, *op. cit.*).

1427 MS. included in the list of those brought back by Filelfo from Constantinople in 1427 (Traversari, *Epp.* XXIV, 32). Contents not specified.

1432 MS. seen by Traversari in Vittorino's library in 1432. May of course be one of the above (Traversari, *Epp.* VIII, 50). Contents not specified.

c. **1440** MS. included in the list of those belonging to Ciriaco of Ancona round about 1440 (Omont, *Centralblatt* IV, 187).

c. **1452** MS. of Herodotus used by L. Valla for his translation.

1455 MS. mentioned in the catalogue of the library belonging to Nicolas V (d. 1455) (Muentz, *op. cit.*).

1457 Cod. Vat. Pal. gr. 176, containing books I–IX and marked as bartered by Aurispa to Billiotti in Rome in 1457.

1460 MS. included in the list of those left by Guarino to his son Battista in 1460 (Omont, *MSS. grecs de Guarino*).

1468 MS. included in the list of those left by Bessarion to St Mark's in Venice in 1468.

1475 Two MSS. included in the catalogue of the library of Sixtus IV (Muentz, *op. cit.*).
1480 Cod. Vat. gr. 1359, containing the complete works of Herodotus copied by Demetrius Rhalles in 1480.
Before **1482** MS. of Herodotus in the catalogue of the library of Federigo d'Urbino (Guasti, *op. cit.*).
1487 MS. containing Herodotus I–IX, marked as copied by Constantine Lascaris at Messina in 1487 (Iriarte, *op. cit.*).
1490 Three MSS. included in the catalogue of the library of Giorgio Valla (Heiberg, *op. cit.*).
Before **1492** MS. of Herodotus (Cod. Laur. LXX, 32?) in the catalogue of the library of Lorenzo dei Medici (Mueller, *op. cit.*).

HIPPOCRATES

1427 MS. of the *Letters* in the list of those brought back by Filelfo from Constantinople (Traversari, *Epp.* XXIV, 32).
1448 MS. mentioned as purchased by L. Valla and as having once belonged to Robert of Sicily (Sabbadini, *Rivista di filologia* XX, p. 332).
1455 MS. of the works of Hippocrates and another of part of his works mentioned in the catalogue of the library of Nicolas V (Muentz, *op. cit.*).
1457 Cod. Vat. Pal. 170, 192, containing twenty-two works of Hippocrates, given by F. Biliotti to Aurispa in exchange for books unnamed.
Before **1459** Cod. Vat. Pal. gr. 192 of *Opuscula*, marked as owned by Manetti (Stephenson, *op. cit.*).
1468 Two MSS. of the *Aphorisms*, mentioned in the catalogue of Bessarion's library (Omont, *Inventaire*, etc.).
1475 MSS. containing (i) the works of Hippocrates (3 copies), (ii) part of the works, (iii) *Aphorisms*, (iv) *de Alimentis*, in the catalogue of the library of Sixtus IV (Muentz, *op. cit.*).
Before **1492** MS. of Hippocrates (Cod. Laur. LXIV, 1?) in the catalogue of the library of Lorenzo dei Medici (Mueller, *op. cit.*).
Before **1494** MSS. of the *Letters* in the catalogue of the library of Pico della Mirandola (Kibre, *op. cit.*). The 1498 catalogue also mentions a MS. entitled *Opera* (Caroli-Cesis, *op. cit.*).

IAMBLICHUS

1424 MS. containing 'many works' in the list sent by Aurispa to Florence (Traversari, *Epp.* XXIV, 53).
1468 MSS. of the *de Secta Pythagorae* and *in Epistolam Porphyrii* in the catalogue of the library left by Bessarion (Omont, *Inventaire*).
1475 MS. of the *de Secta Pythagorae* in the catalogue of the library of Sixtus IV (Muentz, *op. cit.*).
Before **1482** Cod. Vat. Urb. gr. 44 in the library of Lorenzo dei Medici (Stornajolo, *op. cit.*).
Before **1492** MS. of the *de Secta Pythagorae* in the catalogue of the library of Pico della Mirandola (Kibre, *op. cit.*).

ISOCRATES

c. **1400**   MS. Ambros. D 422, copied by Manuel Chrysoloras (Nolhac, *op. cit.* p. 144).

1424   Cod. Wolfenbuettel Helmst. 920, containing three letters in the list sent by Aurispa to Florence (Traversari, *Epp.* XXIV, 53 and Aurispa, *op. cit.* p. 29).

1425   Cod. Laur. C.S. 23–4 together containing all the works except the *Panathenaicus* in the library left by A. Corbinelli (Blum, *op. cit.*).

1455   Two MSS. mentioned in the catalogue of the library of Nicolas V (Muentz, *op. cit.*).

Before **1459**   Cod. Vat. Pal. gr. 187 of 18 speeches marked as owned by Manetti (Stephenson, *op. cit.*).

1460   Two MSS. of speeches and one described as containing some speeches mentioned in the list of the library left by Guarino (Omont, *Centralblatt* IV, 187).

1460   MS. of Isocrates in the library of Zomino (Zaccaria, *op. cit.* p. 43).

Before **1465**   Cod. Laur. (San Marco) 314 owned by T. Gaza (Rosbagno, *Indici*).

1468   MS. of speeches in the catalogue of the library left by Bessarion to St Mark's (Omont, *Inventaire*).

1475   MS. of speeches and two MSS. described as containing 'some works', in the catalogue of the library of Sixtus IV (Muentz, *op. cit.*).

Before **1482**   Two MSS. of Isocrates in the catalogue of the library of Federigo d'Urbino (Guasti, *op. cit.*).

1482   MS. of speeches in the library of Lorenzo dei Medici (Piccolomini, *op. cit.* p. 285).

1490   MS. described as containing some speeches, mentioned in the catalogue of the library of Giorgio Valla (Heiberg, *op. cit.*). Contents not specified. Also mentioned is one MS. of the *ad Demonicum*.

Before **1492**   Three MSS. of speeches (one perhaps Cod. Laur. LVIII, 12 and 14) in the library of Lorenzo dei Medici (Mueller, *op. cit.*). Cf. under 1482 above.

Before **1494**   Two MSS. of Isocrates in the catalogue of the library of Pico della Mirandola (Kibre, *op. cit.*).

JOSEPHUS

1468   Three MSS. of the *Bellum Iudaicum* and one of the *de Antiquitate Iudaica* in the catalogue of the library left by Bessarion (Omont, *Inventaire*).

1475   MS. of the *Bellum Iudaicum* and two of the *de Antiquitate Iudaica* in the catalogue of the library of Sixtus IV (Muentz, *op. cit.*).

Before **1482**   Two MSS. of the *Bellum Iudaicum* in the library of Federigo d'Urbino (Guasti, *op. cit.*).

Before **1492**   MSS. of the *Bellum Iudaicum* and the *de Antiquitate Iudaica* (Codd. Laur. LXIX, 2 and 17?) in the library of Lorenzo dei Medici (Mueller, *op. cit.*).

1493   Cod. Vat. gr. 1304, annotated by Ermolao Barbaro (Nolhac, *op. cit.* p. 166).

JULIAN THE APOSTATE

1432 MS. containing the *Panegyrics* on Constantine and Eusebia and the *Symposium* seen by Traversari in the library of Vittorino (Traversari, *Epp.* VIII, 50).

1468 MS. of some speeches in the catalogue of the library left by Bessarion (Omont, *Inventaire*).

1475 MS. of Julian in the catalogue of the library of Sixtus IV (Muentz, *op. cit.*).

Before **1482** MS. of the *Misopogon* in the catalogue of the library of Federigo d'Urbino (Guasti, *op. cit.*).

1490 MSS. of the *Panegyrics* on Constantine and Eusebia in the library of the Giustina monastery and an incomplete MS. of the *Symposium* in the library of Giorgio Valla seen by J. Lascaris (Mueller, *op. cit.* pp. 386 and 388).

Before **1494** MS. of the *de Sole* in the catalogue of the library of Pico della Mirandola (Kibre, *op. cit.*).

LIBANIUS

1416 Cod. Pal. gr. 282, containing 63 works owned first by L. Giustinian and later by Filelfo (Sabbadini, *Scoperte*, p. 64 and Stephenson, *op. cit.*).

1425 Codd. Laur. C.S. 7 and 172, containing the *Orationes ad Theodosium* and six letters in the library left by A. Corbinelli (Blum, *op. cit.*).

1427 MS. of Libanius in the list sent by Filelfo to Florence (Traversari, *Epp.* XXIV, 32).

Before **1449** Cod. Vat. Urb. gr. 84 of letters and speeches marked as owned by Garathon (Stornajolo, *op. cit.*).

1455 One MS. of the works, six MSS. of the letters and three of the speeches in the catalogue of the library of Nicolas V (Muentz, *op. cit.*).

Before **1460** Cod. Paris gr. 2772, containing three letters marked as owned by Guarino (Omont, *Inventaire sommaire*).

1462 MS. containing many letters in the catalogue of the library left by Palla Strozzi (Mazzatinti, *op. cit.* II, 570).

1468 Three MSS. of the speeches, three of the letters and two entitled *Declamationes* in the catalogue of the library left by Bessarion (Omont, *Inventaire*).

1475 Eight MSS. of Libanius (one marked incomplete), seven of his letters and one entitled *Declamationes* LX in the catalogue of the library of Sixtus IV (Muentz, *op. cit.*).

Before **1480** Cod. Vat. Pal. gr. 248 (*Declamationes* II and letters) and 360 (*Declamationes* III) marked as copied by M. Apostolios (Stephenson, *op. cit.*).

Before **1482** MS. containing *Monodiae* III and two MSS. of letters in the catalogue of the library of Federigo d'Urbino (Guasti, *op. cit.*).

c. **1485** Cod. Laur. San Marco 316 of four speeches and seven letters marked as owned by G. A. Vespucci (Rostagno, *Indici*, p. 183).

c. **1485** Cod. Vat. gr. 1394 owned by Giovanni Lorenzi (Nolhac, *op. cit.* p. 228).

Before **1492**   Three MSS. (one perhaps Cod. Laur. LVII, 44) in the catalogue of the library of Lorenzo dei Medici (Mueller, *op. cit.*).
Before **1494**   MS. of *Declamationes* in the catalogue of the library of Pico della Mirandola (Kibre, *op. cit.*).

'Longinus'

1468   MS. of *On the Sublime*, mentioned in the catalogue of the books left by Bessarion to St Mark's.
1490   MS. of *On the Sublime*, mentioned in the catalogue of the library of Giorgio Valla (Heiberg, *op. cit.*).
1491   Cod. Paris gr. 2960, containing *On the Sublime* dated and marked as copied by F. Vernardo at Verona (Omont, *Les MSS. grecs datés*).

Longus

1425   Cod. Laur. C.S. 627 of the *Daphnis et Chloë* in the library left by A. Corbinelli (Blum, *op. cit.*).

Lucian

1415   MS. containing three dialogues brought by Rinucci da Castiglione from Constantinople (Lockwood, *op. cit.*).
1423   MS. described as containing *Risus et Seria Omnia*, mentioned in the list sent by Aurispa to Florence (Traversari, *Epp.* XXIV, 53).
1425   Codd. Laur. C.S. 77 and 88 with 65 of the works (28 duplicated) in the library left by A. Corbinelli (Blum, *op. cit.*).
1427   MS. mentioned in the list of those brought back by Filelfo (Traversari, *Epp.* XXIV, 32). Incomplete.
c. **1454**   Cod. Vat. Pal. gr. 73, fo. 2, marked as owned by F. Barbaro. Containing 34 minor works (Stephenson, *op. cit.*).
1455   MSS. containing: (i) part of the works of Lucian, (ii) minor works, and (iii) letters mentioned in the catalogue of the library of Nicolas V (Muentz, *op. cit.*). There is also one MS. of Lucian mentioned whose content is unspecified.
Before **1459**   Cod. Vat. Pal. gr. 174, containing 83 works marked as owned by Manetti (Stephenson, *op. cit.*).
1460   MS. mentioned in the list of those left by Guarino to his son Battista (Omont, *MSS. grecs de Guarino*).
1468   MSS. containing: (i) some of Lucian's works (3 copies), (ii) 164 speeches, (iii) speeches, (iv) another selection of speeches, mentioned in the catalogue of the library left by Bessarion (Omont, *Inventaire*).
1475   Seven MSS. containing Lucian's 'works' and one containing a selection, mentioned in the catalogue of the library of Sixtus IV (Muentz, *op. cit.*).
Before **1481**   MS. Cod. Laur. LVII, 6, supposedly in Filelfo's hand, therefore written before his death in 1481. Contains *Opera varia*. Also Cod. Paris gr. 2110 of the *Jupiter Tragoedus* (Omont, *Bibliothèque de Filelfo*).

c. **1482**   MS. Cod. Vat. 1322, almost complete and marked as belonging to Raffaelo Regio who became professor at Padua in 1482.

1490   MSS. containing *opera plura* and the *Solecistes*, mentioned in the catalogue of the library of Giorgio Valla (Heiberg, *op. cit.*).

Before **1492**   Two complete MSS. (one perhaps Codd. Laur. LVII, 28 and 46) and two other MSS. one containing two dialogues in the catalogue of the library of Lorenzo dei Medici (Mueller, *op. cit.*).

Before **1494**   MS. of the *Amores* in the catalogue of the library of Pico della Mirandola (Kibre, *op. cit.*).

LYSIAS

1427   MS. of one speech, mentioned in the list of those brought by Filelfo from Constantinople (Traversari, *Epp.* XXIV, 32).

1464   MS. of many speeches in the catalogue of the library left by Palla Strozzi (Mazzatinti, *op. cit.* II, 2).

1468   Two MSS., one of the *Epitaphios*, in the catalogue of the library presented by Bessarion to St Mark's (Omont, *Inventaire*).

Before **1492**   MS. of the *Apologia* (Cod. Laur. LVII, 4) in the library of Lorenzo dei Medici (Mueller, *op. cit.*).

MAXIMUS OF TYRE

1425   Cod. Laur. C.S. 4, containing all the speeches in the library left by A. Corbinelli (Blum, *op. cit.*).

Before **1446**   Cod. Laur. LXXXV, 15, marked as owned by L. Giustinian (Bandini, *op. cit.* III, 276).

1455   MS. of *Opuscula* in the catalogue of the library of Nicholas V (Muentz, *op. cit.*).

1468   MSS. of the speeches, the *quid est deus secundum Platonem* and other works in the catalogue of the library of Bessarion (Omont, *Inventaire*).

1492   MS. of Maximus of Tyre in the catalogue of the library of Lorenzo dei Medici (Mueller, *op. cit.*).

NICOMACHUS OF GERASA

1425   Cod. Laur. C.S. 30 of the *Arithmetica* in the library left by A. Corbinelli (Blum, *op. cit.*).

1455   MS. of the *Arithmetica* in the catalogue of the library of Nicolas V (Muentz, *op. cit.*).

1468   Five MSS. of the *Arithmetica* in the catalogue of the library left by Bessarion (Omont, *Inventaire*).

1475   Two MSS. of the *Arithmetica* in the catalogue of the library of Sixtus IV (Muentz, *op. cit.*).

Before **1494**   MS. of the *Arithmetica* in the catalogue of the library of Pico della Mirandola (Kibre, *op. cit.*).

PAUSANIAS

1454 MS. mentioned among those possessed by F. Barbaro (Traversari, *Epp.* VI, 10).

1468 MS. of the *Descriptio Graeciae*, mentioned in the catalogue of the library left by Bessarion (Omont, *Inventaire*, etc.).

1497 MS. Paris gr. 1399 of the *Descriptio Graecae* I–X, dated and marked as copied by Hypselas in Milan (Omont, *Les MSS. grecs datés*).

PHILO

1425 Codd. Laur. 59 and 107, containing 12 works in the library left by A.Corbinelli (Blum, *op. cit.*).

1427 MS. mentioned in the list of those brought back by Filelfo (Traversari, *Epp.* XXIV, 32), includes the *Vita Moyesi*.

1455 Two MSS. mentioned in the catalogue of the library of Nicolas V (Muentz, *op. cit.*).

Before **1459** Cod. Vat. Pal. gr. 183, containing 38 works marked as owned by Manetti (Stephenson, *op. cit.*).

1462 MS. of Philo among the books left by P. Strozzi (Mazzatinti, II, 570).

1468 Two MSS., one containing works and the other speeches, mentioned in the catalogue of the library left by Bessarion to St Mark's.

1475 Two MSS. mentioned in the catalogue of the library of Sixtus IV. (Muentz, *op. cit.*).

Before **1492** MS. of the *de Alexandro* in the catalogue of the library of Lorenzo dei Medici (Mueller, *op. cit.*).

PHILO OF BYZANTIUM

1444 MS. of *ad Aristonem* owned by Aurispa. By 1451 this was in the hands of F. Barbaro (Aurispa, *op. cit.* p. 168).

PHILOSTRATUS THE ATHENIAN AND PHILOSTRATUS OF LEMNOS

c. **1417** MS. of the *Vita Apollonii* mentioned as owned by F. Barbaro (Traversari, *Epp.* VI, 10).

1425 Cod. Laur. C.S. 155 of the *Vita Apollonii* in the library left by A. Corbinelli (Blum, *op. cit.*).

1427 MS. of the *Vita Apollonii* in the list sent by Filelfo to Florence (Traversari, *Epp.* XXIV, 32).

1455 MS. of the *Heroica* in the catalogue of the library of Nicholas V (Muentz, *op. cit.*).

1468 MSS. of the *Vita Apollonii*, *Vitae Sophistarum*, *Imagines* and *Heroica* in the catalogue of the library of Bessarion (Omont, *Inventaire*).

1475 Two MSS. of Philostratus, two of the *Heroica* and one of the *Imagines* in the catalogue of the library of Sixtus IV (Muentz, *op. cit.*).

Before **1482** Cod. Laur. Redi. 15 of the *Imagines*, 1–17, copied by Damilas and Lauretano (Rostagno, *Indici-Suppl.*).

Before **1489**   Cod. Laur. Redi. 15 of *Imagines* marked as copied by Danislas and Lauretano (Rostagno, *Indici*, p. 219).
Before **1494**   MS. of the *Vita Apollonii* in the catalogue of the library of Pico della Mirandola (Kibre, *op. cit.*).

PHRYNICHUS

1425   Cod. Laur. C.S. 8, containing selections in the library left by A. Corbinelli (Blum, *op. cit.*).

PLATO

c. **1400**   MSS. containing some unspecified dialogues, mentioned as presented by Manuel Chrysoloras to P. P. Vergerio (R. Sabbadini, *L' ultimo ventennio della vita di Manuel Crisolora*, pp. 5–6 (Florence)) and to Roberto Rossi (Filelfo, *Orationum in Cosmum Medicem*, Lib. I, quoted Sabbadini, *Scoperte*, p. 51).
1405   MS. containing the *Gorgias* and the *Cratylus*, mentioned as deposited by Bruni with Niccoli (Sabbadini, *Scoperte*, p. 52). Another containing the *Phaedo* was used for his translation.
1415   MS. containing the *Axiochus*, *Crito* and *Euthyphro* probably brought by Rinucci da Castiglione from Constantinople (Lockwood, *op. cit.*).
1418   MS. of *Opuscula* (including the *Protagoras*), mentioned as copied by Bartolommeo da Montepulciano (Traversari, *Epp.* XXIV, 9).
Before **1424**   MSS. of the *Apologia*, *Crito* and *Phaedrus* used by Bruni for his translations (Baron, *op. cit.*).
1424   MS. containing the *Definitiones*, mentioned as belonging to Rinucci da Castiglione (Traversari, *Epp.* VIII, 28). Copied by Traversari.
1424   Two MSS. containing Plato's complete works in the list sent by Aurispa to Florence (Traversari, *Epp.* XXIV, 53).
Before **1425**   MS. of the *Respublica* used by Uberto Decembrio for his translation.
1425   Codd. Laur. C.S. 42, 54, 78, 103, 180, containing between them all the works except the *Clitipho*, *Hippias Maior et Minor* and *Menexenus* with the *Crito*, *Apologia* and *Euthyphro* in triplicate and the *Parmenides* in duplicate in the library left by A. Corbinelli (Blum, *op. cit.*).
1426   MS. containing the *Clitipho*, *Respublica*, *Timaeus*, *Critias*, *Phaedrus* and *Leges*, mentioned in the catalogue of the Visconti Library (D'Adda, *Indagini*). It belonged to Petrarch.
1427   MS. containing the *Letters*, mentioned in the list of those Filelfo brought back from Constantinople (Traversari, *Epp.* XXIV, 32).
1432   MS., content unspecified, mentioned as seen by Traversari in Vittorino's library (Traversari, *Epp.* VIII, 50).
1435   MS. containing all Plato's works, mentioned as given by John Eugenicus to Cassarino in Constantinople (E. Legrand, *Les cent-dix lettres grecques de F. Filelfe*, p. 140).
1444   Cod. Vat. Urb. gr. 32 of the *Axiochus*, *Clitipho*, *Euthydemus*, *Hippias Maior et Minor*, *Laches*, *Lysis* and *Theages* dated and marked as copied by L. Bruni, later in the library of Federigo d'Urbino (Stornajolo, *op. cit.*).

Before **1454**   MS. of the dialogues marked as owned by F. Barbaro (Mittarelli, *op. cit.*).

c. **1454**   MS. containing the *Phaedrus, Symposium, Philebus, Parmenides, Euthyphro, Apologia, Crito, Phaedo, Cratylus* and the *Letters,* marked as in the library of F. Barbaro (Quirinus, *op. cit.*).

1455   Four MSS. containing Plato's works and others containing the *Leges,* the *Letters* and 'dialogues', mentioned in the catalogue of the library of Nicolas V (Muentz, *op. cit.*).

Before **1459**   Cod. Vat. Pal. gr. 173 (*Apologia, Phaedo, Alcibiades* I, *Gorgias, Meno* and excerpts), 175 (*Timaeus, Alcibiades* I and II, *Hipparchus, Amatores, Theages, Charmides, Laches, Lysis, Euthyphro, Protagoras, Critias*) and 177 (*Minos* and *Leges*) marked as owned by Manetti (Stephenson, *op. cit.*).

1460   MS. containing the *Dialogues,* another containing 'some dialogues', a third containing 'many dialogues' and a fourth containing the *Leges,* mentioned in the list of books left by Guarino to his son Battista (Omont, *MSS. grecs de Guarino*).

1460   MS. containing the *Timaeus,* mentioned in the list of those left by Aurispa (R. Sabbadini, *Biografia,* pp. 170–3).

1462   MS. of Plato taken by Palla Strozzi to Padua (Vespasiano, *Vite,* 910).

1463–80   Complete MS. of Plato used by Ficino in Florence for his translation.

Before **1465**   Cod. Malatest. XXVIII, 4 of the *Respublica* in the library of D. Malatesta Novello (Muccioli, *op. cit.* p. 102).

1468   Two MSS. containing the complete works of Plato, one containing thirty-eight dialogues and MSS. of the *Leges* and the *Respublica,* mentioned in the catalogue of the library Bessarion left to St Mark's (Omont, *Inventaire*).

1475   MS. containing all Plato's works, three MSS. each containing a part of his works, three MSS. of Dialogues, two MSS. containing eighteen dialogues and one containing twenty-five dialogues, mentioned in the catalogue of the library of Sixtus IV (Muentz, *op. cit.*).

1480   MS. dated 1480, containing the *Respublica* and *Letters* as well as some excerpts from other dialogues, dated and marked as copied by Constantine Lascaris at Messina (Iriarte, *op. cit.* no. 36, p. 138).

Before **1481**   MS. of the *Respublica* (Piccolomini, *op. cit.* p. 287) and Codd. Paris gr. 2110 (*Axiochus and Gorgias*) and Laur. LXXXI, 20 (*Definitiones*) owned by Filelfo (Omont, *Bibliothèque de Filelfo*).

Before **1482**   Codd. Vat. Urb. gr. 33 (*Cratylus* and *Philebus*) and another MS. of the *Cratylus* in the library of Federigo d'Urbino (Stornajolo and Guasti, *opp. cit.*).

1486   MS. of Plato in the catalogue of the library of Lorenzo dei Medici (Piccolomini, *op. cit.* p. 287).

1488   MS. of the *Leges* in the library of Lorenzo dei Medici (*ibid.* p. 287).

1490   MS. of the *Parmenides,* mentioned in the catalogue of the library of Giorgio Valla (Heiberg, *op. cit.*).

1492 A complete MS. of Plato (perhaps Codd. Laur. LIX, 1 and LXXXV, 9), also MSS. of the *Leges* (perhaps Cod. Laur. LXXX, 17, and cf. under 1488 above) and the *Respublica* (perhaps Cod. Laur. LXXX, 7) in the catalogue of the library of Lorenzo dei Medici (Mueller, *op. cit.*).

PLOTINUS

1424 MS. of the complete works in the list sent by Aurispa to Florence (Traversari, *Epp.* XXIV, 53).

1427 MS. of Plotinus in the list sent by Filelfo to Florence (Traversari, *Epp.* XXIV, 32).

Before **1433** MS. of Plotinus in the library of Pietro Miani (Sabbadini, *Scoperte*, p. 63).

Before **1446** Cod. Laur. LXXXV, 15, containing *Enneades* I–VI marked as owned by L. Giustinian (Bandini, *op. cit.* III, 276).

Before **1454** MS. of Plotinus marked as owned by F. Barbaro (Mittarelli, *op. cit.*).

1462 MS. of Plotinus in the catalogue of the library left by Palla Strozzi (Mazzatinti, *op. cit.* III, 570).

1468 Two MSS. of Plotinus in the catalogue of the library left by Bessarion (Omont, *Inventaire*).

1490 MS. of Plotinus seen by Janus Lascaris in the library of Giorgio Valla (Mueller, *op. cit.* p. 383).

1492 MS. of Plotinus in the catalogue of the library of Lorenzo dei Medici (Mueller, *op. cit.*).

PLUTARCH

c. **1400** MS. given by M. Chrysoloras to P. P. Vergerio (Sabbadini, *L' ultimo ventennio*, pp. 5–6.

1405 MS. containing some of the *Lives* deposited by Bruni with Niccoli (Luiso, *op. cit.*).

1408 MS. seen by Traversari in the library of P. Miani (Traversari, *Epp.* VIII, 47). Contents not specified.

1415 MS. of the *Quid principem deceat* probably brought by Rinucci da Castiglione from Constantinople (Lockwood, *op. cit.*).

1419 MS. Cod. Laur. LXIX, 34, containing ten of the *Lives*, dated and marked as belonging to Buondelmonti.

c. **1420** MS. of Plutarch, mentioned as brought from the East by Bartolommeo di Montepulciano (Traversari, *Epp.* XXIV, 9).

1423 MS. of the *Lives* and one of rare works in the list of MSS. sent by Aurispa to Florence (Traversari, *Epp.* XXIV, 53).

1425 Codd. Laur. C.S. 169 and 206 (together containing all the lives except the *Agesilaus, Pompey, Galba* and *Otho*), also 26 and 47 (together containing 23 *Moralia*) in the library left by A. Corbinelli (Blum, *op. cit.*).

1427 MS. of the *Moralia*, mentioned in the list of those brought back by Filelfo (Traversari, *Epp.* XXIV, 32).

1429 Cod. Laur. LXIX, 1, of the *Lives*, dated and marked as copied for Vittorino by Gerardo at Mantua (Bandini, II, 622).

1432 MS. of the *Lives*, seen by Traversari in Vittorino's library (Traversari, *Epp.* VIII, 50).

1433 MS. now Cod. Pal. gr. 168, 169 and Cod. Amb. R. 68, containing fifteen *Lives* dated and marked as belonging to Pier Candido Decembrio.

1433 MS. of the *Moralia*, seen by Traversari in the library of P. Tommasi. (Traversari, *Epp.* VIII, 46).

1434 MS. mentioned as taken by Palla Strozzi from Florence to Padua (Traversari, *Epp.* VII, 9).

1436 Cod. Laur. v. 7, containing *Apophthegmata, de Oraculorum Defectu, de Homero*, etc., dated and marked as copied for Filelfo (Bandini, *op. cit.* II, 306).

1437 Codd. Vat. Pal. gr. 167 (*de fortuna et virtute Alexandri* and nine *Lives*) and 169 (6 *Lives*) dated and marked as owned by Manetti (Stephenson, *op. cit.*).

Before **1444** Cod. Vat. Urb. gr. 97 of the *Lives* and *Moralia* marked as owned by L. Bruni (Stornajolo, *op. cit.*).

1444 Cod. Vat. gr. 1309, containing thirteen pieces from the *Moralia*, the letters of Phalaris, etc., dated. Owned by Ciriaco (Nolhac, *op. cit.* p. 164).

1455 Four MSS. of Plutarch's complete works, and other MSS. separately of the *Moralia*, part of the *Moralia*, the *Lives*, thirteen *Lives*, six *Lives*, mentioned in the catalogue of the library of Nicolas V̂ (Muentz, *op. cit.*).

1457 Cod. Vat. Pal. gr. 170, 192, containing the *Moralia*, dated and marked as given to Aurispa by F. Biliotti. (Stephenson, *op. cit.*).

1460 MS. containing some of the *Lives*, mentioned in the list of books left by Guarino to his son Battista (Omont, *MSS. grecs de Guarino*).

1460 MS. containing *Apophthegmata Rom. et Gr., Apophthegmata laconica, Antiqua Laced. institutio, Vita Homeri*, dated and marked as copied by Constantine Lascaris in Milan (Iriarte, *op. cit.* no. 62, p. 233).

1464 MS. containing the *de Fato*, dated and marked as copied by Constantine Lascaris at Milan (Iriarte, *op. cit.* no. 119, p. 428).

c. **1465** MS. Cod. Vat. Gr. 1308, containing five minor works, marked as belonging to Leonore di Leonori (Nolhac, *op. cit.*).

1468 MSS. of the *Moralia*, forty-eight *Lives*, *Opuscula*, mentioned in the catalogue of the library left by Bessarion to St Mark's (H. Omont, *Inventaire*, etc.).

1475 MSS. of the *Moralia* (6 copies), part of the *Moralia* (2 copies), three *Lives* (3 copies), two *Lives*, selections, mentioned in the catalogue of the library of Sixtus IV (Muentz, *op. cit.*).

1480 Cod. Laur. LVI, 4, dated and marked as copied by A. Damilas (Bandini, *op. cit.* II, 301), containing part of the *Moralia*.

Before **1481** Codd. Laur. LVI, 7 (the *Apophthegmata*) and LXXX, 22 (31 *Moralia* and the *Lives of Galba and Otho*), marked as owned by Filelfo (Bandini, *op. cit.* III, 211).

Before **1482** Two MSS. of the *Lives* and two MSS. of the *Moralia* in the catalogue of the library of Federigo d'Urbino (Guasti, *op. cit.*).

1482 MS. of Plutarch in the library of Lorenzo dei Medici (Piccolomini, *op. cit.*).

Before **1489**   Cod. Laur. Redi. 15 of the *Consolatio ad Apollon*, copied by Damilas and Lauretano (Rostagno, *Indici*, p. 219).
1490   Two MSS. of the *Moralia*, mentioned in the catalogue of the library of Giorgio Valla (Heiberg, *op. cit.*).
Before **1492**   MS. of the *Lives* and a MS. of the *Moralia* in the catalogue of the library of Lorenzo dei Medici (Mueller, *op. cit.*).
Before **1494**   Cod. Laur. LVII, 4, containing 26 *Moralia* and 6 *Lives* marked as owned by A. Politian (Bandini, *op. cit.*).

POLLUX

1421   MS. of the *Onomasticon* in the list of those owned by Aurispa in Rome (Aurispa, *op. cit.* p. 160).
1428   MS. of the *Onomasticon* borrowed by Aurispa from Filelfo (*ibid.* p. 64).
1468   Three MSS. of the *Onomasticon* in the catalogue of the library left by Bessarion (Omont, *Inventaire*).
Before **1480**   Cod. Laur. Aedil. 224, marked as owned by G. A. Vespucci (Rostagno, *Indici-Suppl.*).
Before **1481**   Cod. Laur. XXVIII, 32 of the *Onomasticon* marked as owned by Filelfo (Bandini, *op. cit.* II, 55).
Before **1482**   MS. of Pollux in the catalogue of the library of Federigo d'Urbino (Guasti, *op. cit.*).
Before **1499**   Cod. Laur. Ashburn. 1439, containing excerpts from the *Onomasticon*, marked as copied by M. Ficino (Rostagno *Indici-Suppl.*)

POLYBIUS

1421   MS. of Polybius used by Bruni for his paraphrase (Baron, *op. cit.*).
1425   Cod. Brit. Mus. 11.728 of the *Historia* in the library left by A. Corbinelli (Blum, *op. cit.*).
1427   MS. mentioned in the list of those brought back by Filelfo from Constantinople (Traversari, *Epp.* XXIV, 32).   Contents unspecified.
1455   MS. mentioned in the catalogue of the library of Nicolas V (Muentz, *op. cit.*).   May have been the one used by Perotti in his translation.
1460   MS. mentioned in the list of books left by Guarino to his son Battista (Omont, *Les MSS. grecs de Guarino*).   Contained six books only.
1468   MS. mentioned in the catalogue of the library left by Bessarion to St Mark's (Omont *Inventaire*).
1475   MS. mentioned in the catalogue of the library of Sixtus IV (Muentz, *op. cit.*).
Before **1482**   Two MSS. of Polybius in the catalogue of the library of Federigo d'Urbino (Guasti, *op. cit.*).
1488   MS. of the *Historia* (perhaps Cod. Laur. LXIX, 9) in the library of Lorenzo dei Medici (Piccolomini and Mueller, *op. cit.*).
1490   MS. of Polybius seen by Janus Lascaris in the library of Ermolao Barbaro (Mueller, *op. cit.*).

PORPHYRY

1433   MS. of the commentary on Ptolemy's *Musica* seen by Traversari in the library of Pietro Tommasi (Traversari, *Epp.* VIII, 46).

Before **1454**   MSS. of the *Isagoge* and the commentary to Ptolemy's *Musica*, marked as owned by F. Barbaro (Mittarelli, *op. cit.*).

1468   MSS. of the commentaries on Aristotle's *Categoriae* and Ptolemy's *Musica* in the catalogue of the library left by Bessarion (Omont, *Inventaire*).

Before **1480**   Codd. Pal. gr. 72 and 360 of the *Isagoge* copied by M. Apostolios (Stephenson, *op. cit.*).

Before **1482**   Two MSS. of the *Isagoge* and one of the *Vita Plotini* in the library of Federigo d'Urbino (Guasti, *op. cit.*).

1490   MS. of the commentary on Ptolemy's *Musica* seen by J. Lascaris in the library of Giorgio Valla (Mueller, *op. cit.*).

Before **1492**   One MS. of Porphyry and one of the *Commentary* on the *Categoriae* in the catalogue of the library of Lorenzo dei Medici (Codd. Laur. LXXII, 3 and LXXI, 30?) (Mueller, *op. cit.*).

PROCLUS

1424   MS. of the complete works in the list Aurispa sent to Florence (Traversari, *Epp.* XXIV, 53).

1425   Codd. Laur. C.S. 78 (the commentary on the *Parmenides*) and 103 (*de Theologia Platonis*) in the library left by A. Corbinelli (Blum, *op. cit.*).

1427   MS. entitled *in Platonem* in the list Filelfo sent to Florence (Traversari, *Epp.* XXIV, 32).

Before **1459**   Cod. Vet. Pal. gr. 178, containing the *Hymns* and marked as owned by Manetti (Stephenson, *op. cit.*).

1468   One MS. of the complete works and others of the *Astronomia* (contents unspecified), *Geometria*, *de Theologia Platonis*, 'Christomachia' (perhaps the *Institutio theologica* is intended), the commentaries on the *Timaeus* (2 copies), on the *Parmenides* and on the *Alcibiades* I and one MS. entitled vaguely commentary on Plato in the catalogue of the library left by Bessarion (Omont, *Inventaire*).

1475   MS. of the commentary on Ptolemy's *Tetrabiblon* in the catalogue of the library of Sixtus IV (Muentz, *op. cit.*).

1487   Cod. Paris gr. 2452 dated and marked as copied by I. Rosos (Omont, *Les MSS. grecs datés*).

1489   MS. of the commentary on the *Timaeus* lent to Demetrius Chalcondyles by Lorenzo dei Medici (Mueller, *op. cit.*).

Before **1492**   Two MSS. of the commentary on the *Timaeus* (one Cod. Laur. XXVII, 20?) in the catalogue of the library of Lorenzo dei Medici. Cf. under 1489 above (Mueller, *op. cit.*).

Before **1494**   MSS. of the commentary on Euclid's *Elementa* and the *Hymns* in the catalogue of the library of Pico della Mirandola (Kibre, *op. cit.*).

Ptolemy

1405   MS. of the *Geographica*, mentioned as deposited by Bruni with Niccoli (Sabbadini, *Scoperte*, p. 52).

1431   MS. owned by Giordano Orsini in Rome (Nolhac, *op. cit.*).

1433   MS. of the *Musica* seen in the library of Vittorino (Traversari, *Epp.* VIII, 50) and another in the library of P. Tommasi (D'Adda, *Indagini*, p. 149).

1434   MS. mentioned as taken by Palla Strozzi to Padua (Traversari, *Epp.* VII, 9). Contents not specified.

c. **1440**   MS. of the *de Astrologia*, included in the list of MSS. possessed by Ciriaco of Ancona (Omont, *Catalogue*).

1454   MS. of the *Musica* owned by F. Barbaro (Mittarelli, *op. cit.*).

1455   Three MSS. of the *Almagest* and one of the *Geographia* in the catalogue of the library of Nicolas V (Muentz, *op. cit.*).

Before **1460**   An incomplete MS. of Ptolemy in the library of Zomino (Zaccaria, *op. cit.*).

1465   MS. of the *Tabulae*, mentioned as in the possession of Dominico di Dominicis (Nolhac, *op. cit.* pp. 168–9).

1469   MSS. of (i) *Geographia* (2 copies), (ii) *Musica* (3 copies), (iii) *Tabulae*, (iv) *Quadripartitiones* (2 copies), (v) *Magna constructio*, mentioned as included in Bessarion's library (Omont, *Inventaire*).

1475   Five MSS. of the *Almagest* (one incomplete), three of the *Musica*, one of the *Geographia* and one(?) of the *Tetrabiblum* in the catalogue of the library of Sixtus IV (Muentz, *op. cit.*).

Before **1480**   Cod. Vat. Pal. gr. 314 of the *Geographia* marked as copied by M. Apostolios (Stephenson, *op. cit.*).

Before **1482**   MS. of the *Geographia* in the catalogue of the library of Federigo d'Urbino (Guasti, *op. cit.*).

1490   MS. of the *de Astrolabe*, mentioned in the catalogue of the library of Giorgio Valla (Heiberg, *op. cit.*).

Before **1492**   MS. of the *Musica* and one of the *Tetrabiblum* in the catalogue of the library of Lorenzo dei Medici (Mueller, *op. cit.*).

Sextus Empiricus

1427   MS. mentioned in the list of those brought back by Filelfo (Traversari, *Epp.* XXIV, 32).

1468   MS. of Sextus Empiricus in the catalogue of the library left by Bessarion (Omont, *Inventaire*).

1475   MS. of Sextus Empiricus in the catalogue of the library of Sixtus IV (Muentz, *op. cit.*).

Before **1492**   Three MSS. of Sextus Empiricus (one perhaps Cod. Laur. LXXXV, 11) in the catalogue of the library of Lorenzo dei Medici (Mueller, *op. cit.*).

Strabo

1423   MSS. of the *de Situ Orbis* and the *de Condit. Civitatum*, mentioned in the list of books sent by Aurispa to Florence (Traversari, *Epp.* XXIV, 53).

1427 MS. mentioned in the list of those brought back by Filelfo (Traversari, *Epp.* XXIV, 32). Not in his possession by 1441 (*Epp.* fo. 32).

1444 Cod. Eton 141, containing *Geograph.* books I–IX and MS. Cod. Vat. Laur. LXX, 15, containing books XI–XVII, acquired by Ciriaco and used later by Guarino (1451).

1456 MS. mentioned in a catalogue of the library of Ludovico III of Ferrara (E. Motta in *Bibliofilia* VII, 129 (1886)). Contents unspecified.

1468 MS. of the *Geographia*, presumably complete, another of books 10–12, another of books 11–17, and another of excerpts, mentioned in the catalogue of the library left by Bessarion to St Mark's.

1475 MS. mentioned in the catalogue of the library of Sixtus IV (Muentz, *op. cit.*).

Before **1481** Cod. Escurial, T. II, 7, marked as owned by Filelfo (Omont, *Bibliothèque de Filelfo*).

Before **1482** MS. in the catalogue of the library of Federigo d'Urbino (Guasti, *op. cit.*).

Before **1492** Two MSS. of Strabo in the catalogue of the library of Lorenzo dei Medici (Mueller, *op. cit.*).

Before **1494** Cod. Laur. XXVIII, 19 of the *Geographia* marked as owned by Politian (Bandini, *op. cit.*).

Synesius

1455 MS. containing the *Letters* (2 copies), mentioned in the catalogue of the library of Nicolas V (Muentz, *op. cit.*).

1468 MSS. containing the *Speeches* and the *Letters*, mentioned in the catalogue of Bessarion's library (Omont, *Inventaire*).

1475 MSS. containing the *Letters* (2 copies—almost certainly the ones mentioned above in the Papal Library in 1455) and *Opera Varia*, mentioned in the catalogue of the library of Sixtus IV (Muentz, *op. cit.*).

1475 Cod. Vat. gr. 1334, containing three works of Synesius, copied by Gaza for Filelfo and therefore belonging to the period preceding the former's death (Omont, *Bibliothèque de Filelfo*).

Before **1481** Cod. Laur. LVII, 6, supposedly in Filelfo's hand.

Before **1482** MS. of the *Letters* in the catalogue of the library of Federigo d'Urbino (Guasti, *op. cit.*).

Before **1487** Cod. Paris gr. 2465 of the *Laus Calvitii*, marked as owned by A. Petrucci (Delisle, *op. cit.* I, 266).

1490 MS. containing the *Letters*, mentioned in the catalogue of the library of Giorgio Valla (Heiberg, *op. cit.*).

Before **1494** Cod. Laur. LIX, 35 of 79 letters, marked as owned by A. Politian (Bandini, *op. cit.*).

Themistius

1402 Cod. Paris gr. 1851 of the commentary on Aristotle's *de Anima*, dated and marked as copied in Milan (Omont, *MSS. grecs datés*).

1462 MS. of the *Orationes* and a MS. of the commentary on Aristotle's

Physica in the catalogue of the library left by Palla Strozzi (Mazzatinti, *op. cit.* II, 570).

1468 An incomplete MS. of *Orationes*, two MSS. of 'commentaries on Aristotle', and one MS. each of the commentaries on the *Analytica Posteriora*, *de Anima* and *Physica* in the catalogue of the library left by Bessarion (Omont, *Inventaire*).

Before **1482** MS. of six speeches in the catalogue of the library of Federigo d'Urbino (Guasti, *op. cit.*).

1490 MS. of the commentary on the *de Anima*, seen by J. Lascaris in the library of G. della Torre (Mueller, *op. cit.* p. 384).

1491 Cod. Paris gr. 2960 of *Orationes* VII, X, IX, V and IV, dated and marked as copied by F. Bernardo at Verona (Omont, *MSS. grecs datés* and *Inventaire Sommaire*).

Before **1494** MS. of *Orationes* in the catalogue of the library of Pico della Mirandola (Kibre, *op. cit.*).

THEOPHRASTUS

1421 MS. of some works in the list of those owned by Aurispa in Rome (Aurispa, *op. cit.* p. 160).

1423 MS. containing *Opuscula*, mentioned in the list sent by Aurispa to Florence (Traversari, *Epp.* XXIV, 53).

1425 Cod. Laur. C.S. 110 of the *Characters* in the library left by A. Corbinelli (Blum, *op. cit.*).

1427 MS. containing *Opuscula*, mentioned in the list sent by Filelfo to Florence of the MSS. he had brought back from Constantinople (Traversari, *Epp.* XXIV, 32). Probably Cod. Vat. Urb. gr. 108.

1430 MS. containing the *de Plantis*, seen by Traversari in Niccoli's possession (Traversari, *Epp.* VIII, 35).

Before **1455** MSS. of the *de Animalibus*, *Ethica*, *Metaphysica* and *Rhetorica* used by Bessarion, Tifernas and Gaza in their translations.

Before **1459** Cod. Vat. Pal. gr. 162 of the *de Plantis*, *Metaphysica* and five minor works marked as owned by Manetti (Stephenson, *op. cit.*).

1460 MS. mentioned in the list of those left by Guarino to his son Battista (Omont, *MSS. grecs de Guarino*).

1462 MS. of the *de Plantis* in the catalogue of the library left by Palla Strozzi (Mazzatinti, *op. cit.* II, 570).

1468 MS. of the *de Plantis*, mentioned in the catalogue of the library left by Bessarion to St Mark's (Omont, *Inventaire*).

1475 MS. Paris gr. 1639, containing the *Characteres*, dated and marked as copied by Demetrius Leontaris in Italy (Omont, *MSS. grecs datés*).

Before **1481** Cod. Vat. Urb. gr. 108 of the *Metaphysica* and minor works marked as owned by Filelfo (Omont, *Bibliothèque de Filelfo* and *Inventaire Sommaire*).

Before **1482** MS. of the *de Plantis* in the catalogue of the library of Federigo d'Urbino (Guasti, *op. cit.*).

Before **1492** MS. of Theophrastus and one of the *de Plantis* in the catalogue of the library of Lorenzo dei Medici (Mueller, *op. cit.*).

THUCYDIDES

c. **1400**   MS. mentioned as given by Manuel Chrysoloras to P. P. Vergerio (R. Sabbadini, *L' ultimo ventennio*, pp. 5–6).

1407   MS. mentioned as lent by L. Bruni to P. Miani (Sabbadini, *Scoperte*, p. 52).

1415   Cod. Vat. Urb. gr. 92, dated 1415, with a note that it was left to Francesco Barbaro by his father. Complete.

1417   MS. mentioned as sold to Niccoli by Aurispa in 1417 (Traversari, *Epp.* VI, 8).

1425   Codd. Brit. Mus. 11.727 and Laur. C.S. 179 of the *Historia* in the library left by A. Corbinelli (Blum, *op. cit.*).

1427   MS. included in the list of those brought back by Filelfo from Constantinople (Traversari, *Epp.* XXIV, 32).

1432   MS. seen by Traversari in Vittorino's library (Traversari, *Epp.* VIII, 50).

c. **1435**   MS. mentioned as given by John Eugenicus in Constantinople to Cassarino (E. Legrand, *Les cent-dix lettres grecques de F. Filelfo*, p. 140).

1450   MS. of the *Historia* used by L. Valla for his translation.

1455   Three MSS. mentioned in the catalogue of the library of Nicolas V (Muentz, *op. cit.*).

1468   MS. mentioned as included in the library of Bessarion, left to St Mark's in Venice (Omont, *Inventaire*).

1475   Four MSS. mentioned in the catalogue of the library of Sixtus IV (Muentz, *op. cit.*).

1479   Cod. Vat. gr. 1293, containing a complete Thucydides and the *Hellenica* of Xenophon, copied by D. Rhalles in 1479 (Nolhac, *op. cit.* p. 147).

Before **1482**   Two MSS. of Thucydides and two of the speeches from the *Historia* in the catalogue of the library of Federigo d'Urbino (Guasti, *op. cit.*).

1490   MS. of Thucydides seen by Janus Lascaris in the library of Ermolao Barbaro, probably Cod. Paris gr. 1305 which is marked as copied by the latter (Mueller, *op. cit.*).

1492   Three MSS. of Thucydides (two perhaps Codd. Laur. LXIX, 16 and 2) in the catalogue of the library of Lorenzo dei Medici (Mueller, *op. cit.*).

XENOPHON

1405   MS. mentioned as deposited by L. Bruni with Niccoli (Luiso, *op. cit.*).

1407   MS. mentioned as lent by Bruni to P. Miani (Luiso, *op. cit.* p. 44).

1417   MS. of the *Agesilaus* copied at Florence for F. Barbaro (Traversari, *Epp.* VI, 6).

1417   MS. mentioned by Traversari as containing some of the rarer works in the possession of Guarino (Traversari, *Epp.* V, 33, dated 1417).

1424 Two MSS. containing 'nearly all Xenophon's works', mentioned in a list sent by Aurispa to Florence (Traversari, *Epp.* XXIV, 53). That list also mentions separately a MS. of the *Hippica*.

1425 Codd. Laur. C.S. 110 and 112 containing all the works except the *Agesilaus* and the *Hellenica* in the library left by A. Corbinelli (Blum, *op. cit.*).

1427 Cod. Laur. LV, 19, dated 1427, as copied in Constantinople for Filelfo (Bandini, *Catalogus cod. gr. Bibl. Laur.* II, 306). It contains the *Oeconomica*, the *Symposium* and the *Cyropedia*. This may be reasonably identified with the 'works of Xenophon' mentioned in the list that Filelfo sent to Florence during that year (Traversari, *Epp.* XXIV, 32).

1428 Cod. Paris Suppl. gr. 1285, marked as having belonged to Vittorino. For a mention of its sale see Filelfo, *Epp.* fo. 5 v. (quoted Sabbadini, *Scoperte*, p. 61).

Before **1437** Cod. Laur. (S. Marco) 330, containing the *Hellenica* and marked as having belonged to Niccoli (Rostagno, *Indici*, p. 186).

c. **1450** Cod. Laur. Acq. 58 of the *Cyropedia* and the *Anabasis* marked as owned by Francesco da Castiglione (Rostagno, *Indici*).

1455 MS. mentioned in the catalogue of the library of Nicolas V (Muentz, *op. cit.*). Contents not specified.

Before **1459** Cod. Vat. Pal. gr. 184 of the *Cyropedia*, *Oeconomica* and *Hiero* marked as owned by Manetti (Stephenson, *op. cit.*).

1460 MS. of the *Cyropedia* in the library of Zomino (Zaccaria, *op. cit.* p. 44).

1460 Two MSS. containing Xenophon's complete works, mentioned in the list of books left by Guarino to his son (Omont, *MSS. grecs de Guarino*).

1464 MS. of Xenophon in the library left by Palla Strozzi (Mazzatinti, II, 570).

Before **1465** Cod. Malatest. XXVIII, 1 of the *Anabasis*, *Cyropedia*, *Hiero* and *Oeconomica*, in the library of D. Malatesta Novello (Martin, *op. cit.*).

1468 MS. containing the complete works of Xenophon; others containing the *Oeconomica*, the *Symposium*, the *Hellenica*, *Memorabilia* and *Cyropedia* in the library left by Bessarion to St Mark's (Omont, *Inventaire*).

c. **1470** Cod. Laur. LXXXI, 12, marked as belonging to G. A. Vespucci (Bandini, *op. cit.* III, 226).

1474 Cod. Paris gr. 1639, of the *Cyropedia* and the *Anabasis*, dated and marked as copied by Demetrios Leontaris (Omont, *Les MSS. grecs datés*).

Before **1475** Cod. Vat. gr. 1134, containing *Hipparchicus*, *Hiero*, *Lac. Resp.*, *de Equitatione*, marked as copied by Gaza for Filelfo and therefore belonging to the period before the former's death (Omont, *Bibliothèque de Filelfo*).

1475 Three MSS. of the *Cyropedia*, mentioned in the catalogue of the library of Sixtus IV (Muentz, *op. cit.*).

1479 Cod. Vat. gr. 1239, containing the *Hellenica*, dated and marked as copied by Demetrios Rhalles (Nolhac, *op. cit.* p. 147).

Before **1481** Cod. Vat. gr. 1337 of the *de Resp. Lacedaem* and the *Cyropedia*, marked as copied by Filelfo (Omont, *Bibliothèque de Filelfo*).

Before **1482** MS. of Xenophon, one of the *Hellenica* and two of the *Cyropedia* in the library of Federigo d'Urbino (Guasti, *op. cit.*).

1490 MS. containing the *Memorabilia, de Vectigalibus, Symposium*, in the catalogue of the library of Giorgio Valla (Heiberg, *op. cit.*).

Before **1492** Two MSS. of Xenophon in the catalogue of the library of Lorenzo dei Medici (Mueller, *op. cit.*).

1493 Cod. Vat. gr. 1336, containing the *Memorabilia*, dated and marked as copied by M. Musurus (Nolhac, *op. cit.* p. 150).

Before **1494** Two MSS. of the *Cyropedia*, one of the *de Rep. Lacedaem*, one of five dialogues and one of letters in the catalogue of the library of Pico della Mirandola (Kibre, *op. cit.*).

POETS

AESCHYLUS

1424 Cod. Laur. XXXII, 9 of seven plays by Aeschylus, mentioned as sent by Aurispa to Niccoli (Aurispa, *op. cit.* p. 163).

1425 Codd. Laur. C.S. 71, 98 and 172 each containing the *Prometheus*, *Persae* and *Septem* in the library left by A. Corbinelli (Blum, *op. cit.*).

1431 Laur. CXI, 5 (Bandini III, 421), containing *Prometheus* and *Septem*, marked as belonging to Niccolo Martinozzi.

1455 MS. of Aeschylus, mentioned in the catalogue of the library of Nicolas V (Muentz, *op. cit.*).

1462 MS. containing *Prometheus*, *Septem* and *Persae*, copied by C. Lascaris (Martini, *Catalogo* I, 336).

c. **1465** MS. of Aeschylus marked as owned by Leonori (Martini, *op. cit.* I, 335).

1468 MS. Ven. Mar. 468, containing *Prometheus*, *Septem* and *Persae*, known to have formed part of the library given by Bessarion to St Mark's.

1475 Three MSS. of Aeschylus, mentioned in the catalogue of the library of Sixtus IV (Muentz, *op. cit.*).

Before **1481** Cod. Laur. XXXI, 1 of Aeschylus, marked as owned by Filelfo (Bandini, II, 72).

Before **1492** MS. of Aeschylus in the catalogue of the library of Lorenzo dei Medici (Mueller, *op. cit.*).

APOLLONIUS RHODIUS

1418 MS. of Apollonius owned by F. Barbaro (Traversari, *Epp.* VI, 10).

1423 MS. Laur. XXXII, 16 of *Argonautica* I–IV, bought by Filelfo from the wife of Chrysoloras.

1424 Cod. Laur. XXXII, 9 of the *Argonautica*, sent by Aurispa to Florence (Aurispa, *op. cit.* p. 163).

1427 MS. of *Argonautica*, mentioned among those brought back by Filelfo— probably the one acquired in 1423 (Traversari, *Epp.* XXIV, 32).

Before **1459** Cod. Vat. Pal. gr. 186 of the *Argonautica*, marked as owned by Manetti (Stephenson, *op. cit.*).

1460 MS. of *Argonautica*, mentioned in list of books left by Guarino (Omont, *MSS. grecs de Guarino*).

1464 MS. of *Argonautica*, copied by C. Lascaris in Milan.

1468 MS. of *Argonautica*, mentioned in the catalogue of the library of Bessarion (Omont, *Inventaire*).

1470 MS. of *Argonautica*, mentioned as belonging to G. A. Vespucci (Rostagno, *Indici*, Suppl., no. 35).

Before **1482** MS. of Apollonius Rhodius in the catalogue of the library of Federigo d'Urbino (Guasti, *op. cit.*).

c. **1485** MS. Ricca. 53 k ii 13, containing the *Argonautica*, copied by I. Rosos. Date uncertain.

1490 Two MSS. of *Argonautica* in the library of G. Valla (Heiberg, *op. cit.*).

1498 Cod. Paris gr. 2844 of the *Argonautica*, dated and marked as copied by L. Cyathus in Florence (Omont, *Les MSS. grecs datés*).

ARATUS

1427 MS. of Aratus in the list sent by Filelfo to Florence (Traversari, *Epp.* XXIV, 32).

1454 MS. of the *Phaenomena* dated and marked as copied by Scutariotes. Later owned by Politian (Bandini, *op. cit.*).

1468 MS. of Aratus in the catalogue of the library left by Bessarion (Omont, *Inventaire*).

1488 Cod. Paris gr. 3066 of the *Phaenomena*, dated and marked as copied by I. Rosos (Omont, *Les MSS. grecs datés*).

Before **1492** Two MSS. of Aratus in the catalogue of the library of Lorenzo dei Medici (Mueller, *op. cit.*).

ARISTOPHANES

1408 Cod. Vat. Pal. gr. 116, containing the *Plutus*, *Clouds* and *Frogs*, marked as bought in that year by Guarino in Constantinople (Stephenson, *op. cit.*).

1415 MS. of the *Plutus*, probably brought by Rinucci from Constantinople (Lockwood, *op. cit.*).

1423 MS. of Aristophanes, mentioned in the list sent by Aurispa to Florence (Traversari, *Epp.* XXIV, 53).

1425 Cod. Laur. C.S. 140 of the *Clouds*, *Frogs*, *Knights* and *Plutus* in the library left by A. Corbinelli (Blum, *op. cit.*).

Before **1450** MS. of Aristophanes, mentioned in the list of those belonging to Ciriaco (Omont, *Catalogue*).

Before **1454** MS. of Aristophanes in the library of F. Barbaro (*Studi Ital. di filogia class.* IV, 467).

1455 Seven presumably complete and one incomplete MS. of Aristophanes, mentioned in the catalogue of the library of Nicolas V (Muentz, *op. cit.*).

c. **1460** MS. of eight plays of Aristophanes, mentioned among those left by Guarino (Omont, *MSS. grecs de Guarino*).

c. **1465** MS. containing the *Plutus*, *Clouds* and *Frogs* and another containing the *Plutus* alone, marked as having belonged to Leonoro di Leonori (Martini, *Catalogo* I, 314, 355).

1468 MSS. containing seven and three plays respectively, mentioned in the catalogue of Bessarion's library (Omont, *Inventaire*).

1475 Nine presumably complete MSS. and one incomplete MS. of the works of Aristophanes, mentioned in the catalogue of the library of Sixtus IV (Muentz, *op. cit.*).

Before **1482** Two MSS. of Aristophanes in the catalogue of the library of Federigo d'Urbino (Guasti, *op. cit.*).

1485 Cod. Laur. XCI, 7, containing the *Plutus*, *Clouds* and *Frogs*, marked as copied by Ioannes Rosos.

c. **1490** Two MSS. containing the *Comedies* of Aristophanes and two containing the *Plutus* and the *Clouds*, mentioned in the catalogue of the library of G. Valla (Heiberg, *op. cit.*). One is probably Cod. Vat. Ambr. gr. 480.

1490 MS. of the *Knights*, seen by J. Lascaris in the library of Ermolao Barbaro (Mueller, *op. cit.*).

Before **1492** MS. of Aristophanes in the catalogue of the library of Lorenzo dei Medici (Mueller, *op. cit.*).

Before **1494** MS. of three comedies in the catalogue of the library of Pico della Mirandola (Kibre, *op. cit.*).

CALLIMACHUS

1423 MS. of Callimachus, mentioned in the list sent by Aurispa to Florence (Traversari, *Epp.* XXIV, 53).

1427 MS. of Callimachus, mentioned among those brought back by Filelfo (Traversari, *Epp.* XXIV, 32).

1464 MS. of the *Hymns*, copied by C. Lascaris in Milan.

1468 MS. of *Hymns* in list of Bessarion's library (Omont, *Inventaire*).

1490 MS. of Callimachus, mentioned in the catalogue of the library of G. Valla (Heiberg, *op. cit.*).

Before **1494** MS. of the *Hymns* in the library of Pico della Mirandola (Kibre, *op. cit.*).

1496 Cod. Vat. gr. 1374, copied by G. Moschus at Corcyra.

DIONYSIUS PERIEGETES

1425 Cod. Laur. C.S. 7 of the *Orbis Descriptio* in the library left by A. Corbinelli (Blum, *op. cit.*).

After **1453** MS. of the *Orbis Descriptio* copied by M. Apostolios (Martini, *op. cit.* I, p. 155).

Before **1460** Cod. Paris gr. 2772, containing the *Orbis Descriptio* owned by Guarino (Sabbadini, *Scoperte*, p. 45).

1468 MS. of Dionysius Periegetes in the catalogue of the library left by Bessarion (Omont, *Inventaire*).

1475 MSS. entitled *de Urbe Roma* and *Orbis Descriptio* in the catalogue of the library of Sixtus IV (Muentz, *op. cit.*).

1490 MS. of the *Orbis Descriptio* in the library of Giorgio Valla (Heiberg, *op. cit.*).

1492 MS. of Dionysius Perigetes (perhaps Cod. Laur. XXVIII, 25) in the catalogue of the library of Lorenzo dei Medici (Mueller, *op. cit.*).

Euripides

1413   Cod. Laur. C.S. 71 of *Hecuba, Orestes, Phoenissae* (part), bought by Aurispa in Chios (Aurispa, *op. cit.* p. 3) and sold in 1417 to Niccoli (Sabbadini, *Biografia Documentata*, p. 11).

1417   MS. of Euripides, mentioned as bought by Niccoli from Aurispa (Traversari, *Epp.* vi, 8).

1425   Cod. Laur. C.S. 11 and 98 (containing *Hecuba, Orestes* and *Phoenissae*, no. 98 adding *Andromache* lines 1–40); also Cod. Laur. C.S. 172 (containing *Electra, Hecuba, Helena, Heraclidae*, last 50 verses, *Hercules Furens, Orestes* and *Phoenissae*) in the library left by A. Corbinelli (Blum, *op. cit.*).

1427   MS. containing seven tragedies by Euripides, mentioned among those brought back by Filelfo (Traversari, *Epp.* xxiv, 32).

Before **1437**   Cod. Laur. (San Marco) 226, containing the *Hecuba*, and in part *Orestes, Medea, Phoenissae, Alcestis, Andromache* and *Rhesus*, marked as belonging to Niccoli (Rostagno, *Indici*).

c. **1450**   MS. of Euripides, mentioned among those owned by Ciriaco (Omont, *Catalogue*).

Before **1454**   Cod. Vat. gr. 1421 owned by F. Barbaro (Mercati, *op. cit.*).

1455   Four complete and one incomplete MS. of Euripides, mentioned in the catalogue of the library of Nicolas V (Muentz, *op. cit.*).

1460   MS. of Euripides, mentioned in the list of those left by Guarino (Omont, *MSS. grecs de Guarino*).

1468   Two MSS. of the works of Euripides also separately MSS. of five tragedies and three tragedies, mentioned in the catalogue of the library of Bessarion (Omont, *Inventaire*).

1475   Seven MSS. of Euripides, mentioned in the catalogue of the library of Sixtus IV (Muentz, *op. cit.*).

Before **1481**   Cod. Laur. xxxi, 1, containing the *Rhesus, Iphigenia in Tauris, Iphigenia in Aulis, Bacchae, Supplices, Cyclops, Heraclidae, Hercules Furens, Helena, Ion* and *Electra*, marked as owned by Filelfo (Bandini, ii, 72).

Before **1482**   MS. of Euripides in the catalogue of the library of Federigo d'Urbino (Guasti, *op. cit.*).

1482   MS. of Euripides in the library of Lorenzo dei Medici (Piccolomini, *op. cit.* p. 285).

Before **1487**   Cod. Paris gr. 2795 of *Hecuba, Orestes* and *Phoenissae*, also 2809 of *Alcestes, Andromache, Hecuba, Hippolytus, Medea* and *Orestes*, marked as owned by A. Petrucci (Delisle, *op. cit.*).

1490   MS. containing the *Hecuba, Orestes* and *Phoenissae*, mentioned in the catalogue of the library of G. Valla (Heiberg, *op. cit.*).

Before **1492**   Three MSS. of Euripides (cf. under 1482 above) in the catalogue of the library of Lorenzo dei Medici (Mueller, *op. cit.*).

Hesiod

1423   Cod. Laur. xxxii, 16 (Bandini, v, 140), containing the *Theogony* and the *Works and Days*, marked as bought by Filelfo from the wife of Chrysoloras.

1425 Cod. Laur. C.S. 15 of the complete works and Laur. C.S. 8 of the *Works and Days* in the library left by A. Corbinelli (Blum, *op. cit.*).

1427 MS. of Hesiod, possibly the one mentioned above, listed among those brought by Filelfo from Constantinople (Traversari, *Epp.* XXIV, 32).

Before **1449** MS. of Hesiod (probably Cod. Vat. gr. 39) in the possession of Garathon.

1450 Cod. Laur. (Acq.) 60 of the *Works and Days* marked as having belonged to F. da Castiglione (Rostagno, *Indici*).

c. **1450** MS. of Hesiod, mentioned in the list of those belonging to Ciriaco (Omont, *Centralblatt für Bibliothekswesen* IV, 187).

c. **1454** Cod. Vat. gr. 1421, containing the works of Hesiod, marked as having belonged to F. Barbaro (cf. Quirini, *op. cit.* p. xxxii).

1455 Three complete MSS. and one incomplete MS. of Hesiod, mentioned in the catalogue of the library of Nicolas V (Muentz, *op. cit.*).

Before **1459** Cod. Vat. Pal. gr. 190 of the *Works and Days*, marked as owned by Manetti (Stephenson, *op. cit.*).

Before **1460** Cod. Paris gr. 2772, containing *Works and Days* and the *Shield of Heracles* by Hesiod, marked as having belonged to Guarino who died in that year.

Before **1460** MS. of Hesiod, mentioned as left by Aurispa who died in that year (Archivo di Stato, Modena, *Registro di Investiture* X, fo. 278; R. Sabbadini, *Biografia Documentata*, pp. 157–67).

1460 MS. of Hesiod, left by Zomino (Zacaria, *op. cit.*).

c. **1465** MS. of Hesiod owned by Leonori (Martini, *op. cit.* p. 325).

1466 Cod. Vat. gr. 1384, containing the *Works and Days* (Nolhac, *op. cit.* p. 150).

1468 Works of Hesiod, mentioned among the MSS. given by Bessarion to St Mark's (Omont, *Inventaire*).

1475 Two MSS. of Hesiod in the library of Sixtus IV (Muentz, *op. cit.*).

1490 Two MSS. of the *Works and Days*, two of the *Theogony* and one of the *Shield of Heracles*, mentioned in the catalogue of the library of G. Valla (Heiberg, *op. cit.*).

Before **1492** MS. of the *Works and Days* and the *Shield of Heracles* in the catalogue of the library of Lorenzo dei Medici (Mueller, *op. cit.*).

Before **1494** MS. of Hesiod and another of the *Hymns* in the catalogue of the library of Pico della Mirandola (Kibre, *op. cit.*).

HOMER

1400 MS. of *Odyssey*, mentioned as being in the possession of P. P. Vergerio (R. Sabbadini, *L'ultimo ventennio*, pp. 5–6).

MS. of Homer, mentioned as being in the possession of Palla Strozzi (Traversari, *Epp.* VII, 9).

1405 MS. of Homer, mentioned as deposited by Bruni with Niccoli (Sabbadini, *Scoperte*, 52).

1421 MS. of Homer, mentioned as shown by Aurispa to a friend (R. Sabbadini, *Giornale Storico*, Suppl. 6, p. 77). Sabbadini thinks that this MS. was probably the Cod. Ven. A. Marcianus 454.

1424 MS. of the *Hymns*, mentioned in the list sent by Aurispa to Florence (Traversari, *Epp.* XXIV, 50, 53, 61).

1425 Cod. Laur. C.S. 48 and 193 of the *Iliad* and Laur. C.S. 52 of the *Odyssey* in the library left by A. Corbinelli (Blum, *op. cit.*).

1426 MS. of Homer, mentioned in the catalogue of the Visconti Library at Ferrara. It had belonged to Petrarch (D'Adda, *Indagini*).

1427 MS. of Homer, mentioned in the list of those brought by Filelfo from Constantinople (Traversari, *Epp.* XXIV, 32).

1452 Cod. Ricciardanus 3020, containing the *Batrachomyomachia* and the *Hymns* III–XXIII, marked as copied in that year by Scutariotes.

1452 Cod. Laur. XXXII, 18, containing the *Iliad* marked as copied by Scutariotes.

1455 Two MSS. containing the complete works of Homer, two MSS. containing part of the works and two MSS. of the *Iliad*, mentioned in the catalogue of the library of Nicolas V (Muentz, *op. cit.*).

Before **1459** Cod. Vat. Pal. gr. 179 of the *Iliad*, marked as owned by Manetti (Stephenson, *op. cit.*).

1459 Cod. Laur. XXXII, 22*a*, containing the *Iliad* and the *Batrachomyomachia*, marked as copied by Georgios Presbyter (Bandini II, 173).

1460 Two complete MSS. of the *Odyssey*, one MS. containing eight books of the *Odyssey*, and one complete MS. of the *Iliad*, mentioned in the list of books left by Guarino (Omont, *MSS. grecs de Guarino*).

MS. of Homer, mentioned in the catalogue of the library of Zomino (Zaccaria, *op. cit.*).

1464 MS. containing the *Hymns*, marked as copied in that year by C. Lascaris at Milan.

Before **1465** Cod. Malatest. XXVII, 2 of the *Odyssey* in the library of D. Malatesta Novello (Martin, *op. cit.*).

c. **1465** Cod. Laur. XXXII, 18, containing the *Iliad* and the *Odyssey*, marked as copied by Ioannes Rosos.

Cod. Laur. XXXII, 6 (Bandini II, 130), containing the *Iliad*, *Odyssey* and *Hymns* III–XXIII, marked as copied by Ioannes Rosos.

Cod. Ricc. 53 kii. 13, containing the *Hymns* III–XXIII, marked as copied by Ioannes Rosos.

c. **1465** MS. of *Batrachomyomachia*, belonging to Leonoro di Leonori (Martini, *Catalogo* I, 314).

1468 Cod. Vat. Urb. gr. 137, containing the *Iliad*, also one other MS. of the *Iliad*, two of the *Odyssey*, one of the *Hymns*, one of the *Batrachomyomachia*, one containing two unidentified books of Homer, and two containing some of Homer's works, mentioned in the list of books left by Bessarion (Omont, *Inventaire*, etc.).

1470 MS. of the *Hymns*, mentioned in the possession of G. A. Vespucci (E. Rostagno, *Indici-Suppl.*, no. 35).

Before **1475** Cod. Laur. XXXII, 1, marked as copied by Gaza for Filelfo and containing the *Iliad* and the *Batrachomyomachia* (Bandini, II, 121).

1475 Nine MSS. of the *Iliad* and four of the *Odyssey*, mentioned in the catalogue of the library of Sixtus IV (Muentz, *La Bibliothèque du Vatican*).

Before **1480** Cod. Laur. XXXII, 23 (Bandini, II, 174), containing the *Odyssey*, marked as having belonged to Filelfo.

Before **1480** Cod. Laur. Aedil. 220, marked as copied by Scutariotes (Rostagno, *Indici Suppl.*).

1480 MS. of the *Iliad* and *Odyssey* acquired by Lorenzo dei Medici from Giuliano (Piccolomini, *op. cit.* p. 285).

Before **1482** Three MSS. of the *Iliad* and one of the *Odyssey* in the catalogue of the library of Federigo d'Urbino (Guasti, *op. cit.*).

1482 Incomplete MS. of Homer in the library of Lorenzo dei Medici (Piccolomini, *op. cit.* p. 285).

1484 MS. of the *Odyssey* (incomplete) deposited in the Papal Library by Benedictus Crispus (Muentz, *op. cit.* p. 294).

1488 MS. containing the *Iliad*, marked as copied by C. Lascaris (Iriarte, *op. cit.* no. 96, p. 382).

1489 Cod. Laur. Redi 15 of the *Batrachomyomachia*, dated and marked as copied by Damilas and Lauretano (Rostagno, *Indici-Suppl.*).

1490 MSS. of the *Iliad*, *Odyssey* and *Hymns*, mentioned in the catalogue of the library of Giorgio Valla (Heiberg, *op. cit.*).

Before **1492** Three MSS. of the *Iliad* and two of the *Odyssey* (one set perhaps Laur. XXXII, 4 and 6) in the catalogue of the library of Lorenzo dei Medici (Mueller, *op. cit.*).

Before **1494** MSS. of the *Iliad* and the *Hymns* in the catalogue of the library of Pico della Mirandola (Kibre, *op. cit.*).

Before **1500** Cod. Vat. Pal. gr. 246, marked as copied by Lampudes (Stephenson, *op. cit.*).

LYCOPHRON

c. **1454** Cod. Vat. gr. 1421 of Lycophron, belonging to F. Barbaro.

1460 MS. of Lycophron, mentioned in list of books left by Guarino (Omont, *MSS. grecs de Guarino*).

1468 Two MSS. of Lycophron, in list of Bessarion's library (Omont, *Inventaire*).

1490 MS. of Lycophron, in list of library of G. Valla (Heiberg, *op. cit.*).

Before **1492** Two MSS. of Lycophron in the catalogue of the library of Lorenzo dei Medici (Mueller, *op. cit.*).

MOSCHUS

1423 Cod. Laur. XXXII, 16, containing the works of Moschus, marked as bought by Filelfo from the wife of Chrysoloras.

1468 MS. of Moschus, included in the catalogue of Bessarion's library (Omont, *Inventaire*).

c. **1480** Cod. Laur. *Aedil,* 220 of the *Amor*, marked as having belonged to G. A. Vespucci (Rostagno, *Indici Supplementum*, no. 35).

c. **1485** Cod. Ricc. 53 k ii 13, containing the *Amor*, marked as copied by I. Rosos. Date uncertain.

MUSAEUS

1464 MS. of *Hero and Leander*, copied by C. Lascaris in Milan.

1468 MS. of *Hero and Leander*, mentioned in the catalogue of Bessarion's library (Omont, *Inventaire*).

c. **1485** Cod. Ricc. 53 k ii 13, containing *Hero and Leander*, copied by I. Rosos. Date uncertain.

1490 MS. of Musaeus seen by J. Lascaris in the library of G. della Torre (Mueller, *op. cit.* p. 385).

1491 MS. of Musaeus seen by Politian in the library of Pietro Leoni (Dorez, *op. cit.* p. 91).

NICANDER

1410 MS. of Nicander, mentioned as given by Barbaro to Traversari (Traversari, *Epp.* VI, 4–7, 10–17).

1423 Cod. Laur. XXXII, 16, containing the *Theriaca* and *Alexipharmaca*, bought by Filelfo from the wife of Chrysoloras (Bandidi, II, 140).

c. **1454** MS. of Nicander, mentioned as belonging to F. Barbaro (Quirini, *op. cit.*).

1455 Two MSS. of Nicander, mentioned in the catalogue of the library of Nicolas V (Muentz, *op. cit.*).

1468 MS. of *Theriaca*, mentioned in the catalogue of the library of Bessarion (Omont, *Inventaire*).

1475 MS. of Nicander, mentioned in the catalogue of the library of Sixtus IV (Muentz, *op. cit.*).

1490 Two MSS. of the *Theriaca* and one of the *Alexipharmaca*, mentioned in the catalogue of the library of G. Valla (Heiberg, *op. cit.*).

1490 MSS. of the *Theriaca* and *Alexipharmaca* seen by J. Lascaris in the library of E. Barbaro (Mueller, *op. cit.*).

NONNUS

1423 Cod. Laur. XXXII, 16, containing the *Dionysiaca*, bought by Filelfo from the wife of Chrysoloras (Bandini, II, 140).

1427 MS. of *Dionysiaca*, probably the above-mentioned among those brought back by Filelfo from Constantinople (Traversari, *Epp.* XXIV, 32).

OPPIAN APAMENSIS AND OPPIAN OF CORYCUS

1423 Cod. Laur. XXXII, 16, containing the *Cynegetica* and the *Halieutica*, bought by Filelfo from the wife of Chrysoloras (Bandini, II, 140).

1423 MS. of *Cynegetica* and *Halieutica*, mentioned on list sent by Aurispa to Florence (Traversari, *Epp.* XXIV, 53).

1425 Cod. Bodl. West 28476 of the *Halieutica* in the library left by A. Corbinelli (Blum, *op. cit.*).

1455 MS. of Oppian, mentioned in the catalogue of the library of Nicolas V (Muentz, *op. cit.*).

c. **1460**   MS. of Oppian (probably the one containing the *Cynegetica* and *Halieutica* which Aurispa had in 1423), mentioned in the list of the books he left to his heirs (Sabbadini, *Biografia documentata*, pp. 157–67).

1468   Two MSS. of Oppian whose content in unspecified and one MS. of the *Cynegetica* and *Halieutica*, mentioned in the catalogue of Bessarion's library (Omont, *Inventaire*).

1475   Seven MSS. of Oppian, mentioned in the catalogue of the library of Sixtus IV (Muentz, *op. cit.*).

Before **1482**   MS. of the *Halieutica* in the catalogue of the library of Federigo d'Urbino (Guasti, *op. cit.*).

1488   MS. containing the *Cynegetica* and *Halieutica*, copied by C. Lascaris (Iriarte, *op. cit.* no. 57, p. 192).

1490   MS. of the *Cynegetica* and *Halieutica*, mentioned in the catalogue of the library of G. Valla (Heiberg, *op. cit.*).

1490   MS. of the *Cynegetica* seen by J. Lascaris in the possession of Ermolao Barbaro (Mueller, *op. cit.*).

Before **1492**   Two MSS. of the *Halieutica* in the catalogue of the library of Lorenzo dei Medici (Mueller, *op. cit.*).

'ORPHEUS'

1424   MS. of the *Argonautica*, *Hymns* and possibly the *Lithica* in the list sent by Aurispa to Florence (Aurispa, *op. cit.* p. 11).

1425   Cod. Laur. C.S. 4 of the *Argonautica* and the *Hymns* in the library left by A. Corbinelli (Blum, *op. cit.*).

1427   MS. of Orpheus in the list sent by Filelfo to Florence (Traversari, *Epp.* XXIV, 32).

Before **1459**   Cod. Vat. Pal. gr. 178 of the *Argonautica* and *Hymns* marked as owned by Manetti (Stephenson, *op. cit.*).

1468   MS. of the *Argonautica* in the catalogue of the library left by Bessarion (Omont, *Inventaire*).

c. **1480**   MS. of the *Argonautica* and *Hymns* in the library of G. A. Vespucci (Rostagno, *Indici-Suppl.*).

Before **1492**   Two MSS. of the *Argonautica* in the catalogue of the library of Lorenzo dei Medici (Mueller, *op. cit.*).

Before **1494**   MSS. of the *Argonautica* and the *Hymns* in the catalogue of the library of Pico della Mirandola (Kibre, *op. cit.*).

PHOCYLIDES

1421   MS. of Phocylides, mentioned in the list of MSS. owned by Aurispa (Aurispa, *op. cit.*).

1423   Cod. Laur. XXXII, 16 mentioned as bought by Filelfo from the wife of Chrysoloras (Bandini, II, 140).

1423   MS. of Phocylides, mentioned in the list sent by Aurispa to Florence. This is probably the same as the one we hear of in 1421 (Traversari, *Epp.* XXIV, 53).

1426 MS. of Phocylides, mentioned in the catalogue of the Visconti Library (Nolhac, *op. cit.* p. 150).
1468 MS. of Phocylides, mentioned in the library left by Bessarion (Omont, *Inventaire*).
1490 MS. of Phocylides, mentioned in the catalogue of the library of G. Valla (Heiberg, *op. cit.*).
1491 Cod. Vat. gr. 1336, probably owned at this time by P. C. Decembrio (Nolhac, *Bibliothèque*, p. 150).

PINDAR

1423 MS. of Pindar, mentioned in the list sent by Aurispa to Florence (Traversari, *Epp.* XXIV, 53).
1425 Cod. Laur. C.S. 8 and 94 together containing the complete works in the library left by A. Corbinelli (Blum, *op. cit.*).
1427 MS. of Pindar, mentioned among those brought back by Filelfo (Traversari, *Epp.* XXIV, 32).
Before **1454** Cod. Vat. gr. 1421, marked as owned by F. Barbaro (Mercati, etc., *op. cit.*).
1455 Two MSS. of Pindar, mentioned in the catalogue of the library of Nicolas V (Muentz, *op. cit.*).
Before **1459** Cod. Vat. Pal. gr. 390 of the *Olympians*, marked as owned by Manetti (Stephenson, *op. cit.*).
1460 MS. of Pindar, mentioned in the list of books left by Guarino (Omont, *MSS. grecs de Guarino*).
1462 MS. of *Olympians*, copied by C. Lascaris (Martini, *Catalogo*).
c. **1465** MS. of Pindar, owned by Leonoro di Leonori (Martini, *op. cit.*).
1468 MSS. of *Olympians* and *Isthmians* as well as two other MSS. of Pindar, in the catalogue of Bessarion's library (Omont, *Inventaire*).
1475 Eight MSS. of Pindar, in the catalogue of the library of Sixtus IV (Muentz, *op. cit.*).
1480 Cod. Vat. gr. 1313, marked as belonging to Giglio de Tiferno, a nephew of Gregorio Tifernas.
Before **1482** MS. of the *Olympians* and *Pythians* in the catalogue of the library of Federigo d'Urbino (Guasti, *op. cit.*).
1490 MSS. of *Pythians* and *Nemeans*, mentioned in the catalogue of the library of G. Valla (Heiberg, *op. cit.*).
1490 MS. of Pindar seen by Janus Lascaris in the library of Alessandro Benedetti (Mueller, *op. cit.*).
Before **1492** Three MSS. of Pindar (one marked incomplete) in the catalogue of the library of Lorenzo dei Medici (Mueller, *op. cit.*).

(For PROCLUS see page 488 above.)

QUINTUS SMYRNAEUS

Before **1468** MS. of Quintus Smyrnaeus, originally taken by Bessarion from the monastery of S. Niccolo at Casoli (C. Diehl, *Melanges d'Arch. et Hist.* VI, pp. 173–88 (1886)), mentioned in the catalogue of his library (Omont, *Inventaire*).

Before **1484** Cod. Laur. LVI, 29 (Bandini II, 330), containing the works of Quintus Smyrnaeus, copied by George of Trebizond.

1496 MS. containing the works of Quintus Smyrnaeus, copied that year by C. Lascaris at Messina (Iriarte, *op. cit.* no. 57, p. 192).

1496 Cod. Vat. Ottobon. gr. 103 of book I copied by C. Lascaris (Feron, *op. cit.*).

1497 MS. Vat. gr. 1420, marked as copied in that year by Giovanelli from C. Lascaris' copy at Messina.

SOLON

1490 MS. of Solon, mentioned in the catalogue of the library of G. Valla (Heiberg, *op. cit.*).

SOPHOCLES

1413 Cod. Laur. C.S. 71 of the *Ajax*, *Electra* and *Oedipus Rex*, bought by Aurispa in Chios (Aurispa, *op. cit.* p. 3) and sold 1417 to Niccoli (Sabbadini, *Biografia Documentata*, p. 11).

1424 Cod. Laur. XXXII, 9 containing seven plays sent by Aurispa to Niccoli (Aurispa, *op. cit.* p. 163).

1425 Codd. Laur. C.S. 7, 11 and 98, each containing *Ajax*, *Electra* and *Oedipus Rex* in the library left by A. Corbinelli (Blum, *op. cit.*).

1450 MS. of Sophocles, mentioned in the list of MSS. belonging to Ciriaco (Omont, *Catalogue*).

1455 Four complete and one incomplete MSS. of Sophocles, mentioned in the catalogue of the library of Nicolas V (Muentz, *op. cit.*).

1460 MS. of Sophocles, mentioned in the list of books left by Guarino (Omont, *MSS. grecs de Guarino*).

1460 MS. of Sophocles, mentioned among the books left by Aurispa (Sabbadini, *Biografia*, pp. 157–67).

1468 MSS. of Sophocles, containing seven, six, four and one of the plays respectively in the catalogue of Bessarion's library (Omont, *Inventaire*).

1475 Ten complete and three incomplete MSS. of Sophocles, mentioned in the catalogue of the library of Sixtus IV (Muentz, *op. cit.*).

Before **1481** Cod. Laur. XXXI, 1, containing all the plays except the *Oedipus Coloneus*, marked as owned by Filelfo (Bandini, II, 72).

Before **1482** Two MSS. of Sophocles in the catalogue of the library of Federigo d'Urbino (Guasti, *op. cit.*).

Before **1487** Cod. Paris gr. 2795 of *Ajax*, *Electra* and *Oedipus Tyrannus*, marked as owned by A. Petrucci (Delisle, *op. cit.*).

1490 One MS. with some plays and one with the *Antigone*, mentioned in the catalogue of the library of G. Valla (Heiberg, *op. cit.*).

Before **1492** MS. of Sophocles in the catalogue of the library of Lorenzo dei Medici (Mueller, *op. cit.*).

THEOCRITUS

1423 Cod. Laur. XXXII, 16, containing nineteen idylls of Theocritus, bought by Filelfo from the wife of Chrysoloras (Bandini, II, 140).

1425 Cod. Laur. C.S. 15 of *Idylls* I–XIV in the library left by A. Corbinelli (Blum, *op. cit.*).

1427 MS. of Theocritus, probably the above-mentioned, among those brought by Filelfo from Constantinople (Traversari, *Epp.* XXIV, 32).

1455 Two MSS. of Theocritus, mentioned in the catalogue of the Vatican Library (Muentz, *op. cit.*).

Before **1459** Cod. Vat. Pal. gr. 190 of *Idylls* I–X, marked as owned by Manetti (Stephenson, *op. cit.*).

1460 MS. of Theocritus in the catalogue of the library of Zomino (Zaccaria, *op. cit.*).

c. **1465** MS. of eight idylls of Theocritus, marked as having belonged to Leonoro di Leonori (Martini, *op. cit.* I, 355).

1475 Three MSS. of Theocritus, mentioned in the catalogue of the library of Sixtus IV (Muentz, *op. cit.*).

Before **1481** Cod. Laur. LVIII, 19, marked as owned by Filelfo (Mueller, *op. cit.* p. 382).

1490 MS. of Theocritus, mentioned in the catalogue of the library of G. Valla (Heiberg, *op. cit.*).

Before **1492** MS. of Theocritus in the catalogue of the library of Lorenzo dei Medici (Mueller, *op. cit.*).

Before **1494** MS. of Theocritus in the catalogue of the library of Pico della Mirandola (Kibre, *op. cit.*).

Before **1494** Cod. Laur. XXXII, 46, containing eighteen idylls and marked as having belonged to Angelo Politian who died in that year.

1496 MS. containing the works of Theocritus, marked as copied in that year by George Moschus in Corcyra.

1498 MS. of Theocritus in the library of Renato Trivulzi (Motta, *Libri di Casa Trivulzio*, pp. 8 ff.).

THEOGNIS

1490 MS. of Theognis, mentioned in the catalogue of the library of G. Valla (Heiberg, *op. cit.*).

Before **1494** MS. of Theognis in the catalogue of the library of Pico della Mirandola (Kibre, *op. cit.*).

THE TRANSLATIONS OF THE GREEK AND ROMAN CLASSICAL AUTHORS BEFORE 1600

The following list of translations does not claim to be exhaustive. It has been compiled from easily accessible sources; and its main purpose is to present the information there available in a compact form so that students may see at a glance how much work had been done on each author, and how the rate of translation varied from one country to the next.

The capital letters which appear after the name of certain translations indicate where the work is mentioned:

[B.M.] = British Museum Library Catalogue.
[B.N.] = Bibliothèque Nationale Catalogue.
[A.] = Argellati's *Biblioteca degli Volgarizzatori* (Milan, 1767).
[P.] = J. A. Pellicer, *Bibliotheca de Traductores Españoles* (Madrid, 1768).
[L.] = G. Lanson, *Manuel Bibliographique de la Littérature française moderne* (Paris, 1921).
[R.] = D. Rubio, *Classical Scholarship in Spain* (Washington, D.C., 1934).
[H.] = C. L. Penney, *List of Books printed before 1601 in the Library of the Hispanic Society of America* (New York, 1929).

The majority of the unmarked items are mentioned in:

English translations

H. B. Lathrop, *Translations from the Classics into English from Caxton to Chapman* (Madison, Wisconsin, 1933).
H. R. Palmer, *List of English Editions and Translations of Greek and Latin Classics printed before 1641* (London, 1911).

German translations prior to 1550

L. S. Thompson, 'German Translations of the Classics between 1460 and 1550', *Journal of English and Germanic Philology*, XLII (1947), pp. 343–63.

French translations, 1540–50

R. Bunker, *A Bibliographical study of the Greek Works and Translations published in France during the Renaissance: The Decade 1540–1550* (New York, 1939).

French translations of Virgil

A. Hulubei, 'Virgile en France au XVIᵉ siècle', *Revue du Seizième Siècle* XVIII (1931), pp. 1–77.

Translations and imitations of Plautus and Terence

K. Reinhardstoettner, *Plautus. Spaetere Bearbeitungen plautischer Lustspiele* (Leipzig, 1886).
H. W. Lawton, *Térence en France au XVIᵉ siècle* (Paris, 1926).

Spanish Translations

M. Bataillon, *Erasme et L'Espagne* (Paris, 1937).

The following should also be consulted:

G. Highet, *The Classical Tradition* (Oxford, 1948).
J. Sandys, *The History of Classical Scholarship*, vols. I and II (Cambridge, 1903).

The columns give under the name of each author: first, the translations of his complete works (if such existed); and then, the translations of individual works in order of their first appearance in the vernacular. The purpose of this arrangement is to make it possible for the reader to see which works were available by any particular date. The titles of suppositious works have been placed in brackets. The words 'not printed' should be taken to mean 'not printed before 1600'. Many of the translations which the Renaissance left in manuscript have been published since by scholars like Argellati and Hartfelder. Details of such publications will be found in the authorities cited above.

TRANSLATIONS OF GREEK AUTHORS

AUTHOR	ENGLISH	FRENCH
ACHILLES TATIUS	*de Clitiphonis et Leucippes Amoribus* by W. Burton, 1597	*de Clitiphonis et Leucippes Amoribus* (Extracts) by C. Colet, 1545 [B.N.] V–VIII by J. de Rochemare, 1573 [B.N.] (Complete) by F. de Belleforest, 1575 [B.N.]
AELIANUS TACTICUS	—	*de Militaribus Ordinibus* by N. Wolkyr, 1536 [B.N.]
AELIANUS OF PRAENESTE	*Varia Historia* by A. Fleming, 1576	—
AESCHINES	—	—
ALEXANDER TRALLIANUS	—	*Liber* XI etc. by S. Colin, 1556 [B.M.]
ANACREON	*Carmina* (No. 31) by R. Greene (in Alcida), 1588	*Carmina* by R. Belleau, 1556 [B.N.]
ANTHOLOGIA GRAECA	*Epigrammata* (61) in T. Kendall (*Flowers of Epigrams*), 1577	—
APHTHONIUS	—	—
APPIANUS	*Historia Romana* by W.B., 1578	*Historia Romana* (most) by C. de Seyssel, *a.* 1520 (printed 1544) [B.N.]; (rest) by des Avenneles, 1560 [B.N.]
ARISTOPHANES	—	*Plutus* by J. A. de Baif (not printed and now lost), *c.* 1560*
ARISTOTELES	(*de Astronomia*) printed by R. Wyer, 1535 *Ethica* by J. Wylkinson, 1547 (*Problemata*) anon., 1595 *Politica* by I.D., 1598 *Organon* by T. Blundeville, 1599 (paraphase)	*Oeconomica* by N. Oresme, *c.* 1375 (printed 1489) [B.M.]; by S. Loewenborsch, 1532 [B.N.]; by G. Bonnin (sometimes attributed to E. de La Boétie), 1554 [B.N.] *de Caelo* by N. Oresme, *c.* 1375 (printed 1488) [B.N.] *Ethica* by N. Oresme, *c.* 1375 (printed 1488) [B.N.]; by Le Plessis, 1563 [B.N.] (*Secreta Secretorum*) anon., 1497 [B.N.]

* Becq de Fouquières, *Poésies Choisies de Baif* (Paris, 1874), p. xxxix.

INTO THE VERNACULARS BEFORE 1600

GERMAN	ITALIAN	SPANISH
—	*de Clitiphonis et Leucippes Amoribus* (Extracts) by L. Dolce, 1546 [B.N.] (Complete) by F. A. Coccio, 1563 [B.N.]	—
—	*de Militaribus Ordinibus* by F. Ferrosi, 1551 [B.N.]; by L. Carani, 1552 [B.N.]	—
—	*Varia Historia* by G. Laureo, 1550 [B.N.]	—
—	*In Ctesiphontem* anon., 1520 [A.]; by a Florentine gentleman, 1554 [B.N.]	*In Ctesiphontem* by P. Simón Abril (not printed), *a.* 1595 [R.]
—	—	—
—	—	—
—	—	—
—	—	*Progymnasmata* by P. Simón Abril, 1584 [R.]
—	*Historia Romana* (complete) by L. Dolce, 1559 [A.] (Incomplete editions): *Bellum Civile etc.* by A. Braccio, 1519 [A.] *Bellum Illyricum* by G. Ruscelli, 1563 [A.]	*Historia Romana* (complete) by D. de Salazar, 1536 [B.M.]; by J. Bartolomé, 1592 [P.] (Part) by J. de Molina, 1522 [B.M.]
—	*Comediae* by B. and P. Rosetini, 1545 [A.]	*Plutus* by P. Simón Abril, 1577
Oeconomica anon., 15th cent. (not printed) *Ethica Eudemia* anon., 15th cent. (not printed) *Problemata* anon., 1483 [B.N.]	*Ethica* by Brunetto Latini (?), *a.* 1290 (printed 1568) [B.N.]; anon., 1464 [A.]; by G. Manente, 1538 [A.]; by B. Segni, 1550 [B.N.] *Rhetorica* anon., 15th cent. [A.]; by A. Bruccioli, 1545 [A.]; anon., 1548 [B.N.], 1549 [A.]; by B. Segni, 1549 [A.]; ptd. B. L' Imperiale, 1551 [A.]; by A. Caro, 1570 [A.] *Ethica* (Bruni's Latin), 1418 (Baron, *Bruni*, p. 103)	*Ethica* by Don Carlos de Viana, *a.* 1462 (printed 1509) [B.M.]; by B. de la Torre, 1493 [R.]; by J. de Sepulveda [R.]; by P. Simón Abril (not printed), *a.* 1595 [R.] *Politica* by Don Carlos de Viana, *a.* 1462 (printed 1509) [B.M.]; by P. Simón Abril 1584 [R.] *Oeconomica* by Don Carlos de Viana, *a.* 1462 (printed 1509) [B.M.]

AUTHOR	ENGLISH	FRENCH
Aristoteles (*cont.*)		(*de Mundo*) by L. Meigret, 1541 [B.N.]; by P. Saliat, 1541 [B.N.]; anon. 1542 [B.M.] *Problemata* (section thirty) by M. Riflant, 1542 (Complete) anon., 1554 [B.N.] *Politica* by L. Le Roy, 1568 [B.M.]
Arrianus		*Historia Alexandri* by C. Vuitart, 1581 [B.M.]
Artemidorus	*Oneirocritica* by T. Hill, 1563 (epitome translated from the French)	*Oneirocritica* (complete) by G. Tory, 1529 [B.N.]; (epitome I to IV) by C. Fontaine, 1546
Cebes	*Tabula* by F. Poyntz, *c.* 1535	*Tabula* by G. Tory, 1529 [B.N.]; by G. Corrozet, 1543 [B.M.]

GERMAN	ITALIAN	SPANISH
	de Coloribus anon., 1535 [A.] *(Secreta)* by G. Manente, 1538 [A.]	*Rhetorica* (part) by F. de Escobar [R.] *Mechanica* by Hurtado de Mend-oza, *a.* 1575 [R.]
	Physiognomia by G. Manente, 1538 [A.]	
	Politica anon., 15th cent., [A.]; by A. Bruccioli, 1547 [A.]; by B. Segni, 1551 [B.N.]	
	Poetica by Bernardo Segni, 1549 [A]; printed B. L'Imperiale, 1551 [A.]; by A. Castelvetro, 1570 [B.N.]; by A. Picco-lomini, 1572 [A.], (corrected) 1576 [A.]	
	Meteorologica by B. Fausto, 1542 [A.]; by L. Dolce, *a.* 1568 [A.]; ptd. G. Marescotti, 1573 [A.]	
	de Anima anon., 1549 [A.]; by Sansovino, 1551 [A.]; by A. Bruccioli, 1557 [B.N.]; by L. Dolce, *a.* 1568 [A.]	
	Physica by A. Bruccioli, 1551 [B.M.]; by L. Dolce, *a.* 1568 [A.]; by P. del Rosso, 1578 [A.]—a paraphase	
	de Caelo (et Mundo) by A. Bruccioli, 1552 [A.]	
	de Virtute et Vitio by M. G. Ballino, 1564 [B.N.]	
	de Generatione et Corruptione by L. Dolce, *a.* 1568 [A.]; by A. Bruccioli, 1552 [A.]	
	Problemata I–III by A. Piccolo-mini, 1571 [B.N.]	
	Mechanica anon., 1573 [A.]	
	Metaphysica by B. Varchi (not printed, no date) [A.]; by A. Bruccioli (no date) [A.]	
	Organon by B. Varchi (not printed, no date) [A.]	
	Parva Naturalia by B. Segni (not printed, no date) [A.]	
—	*Historia Alexandri* by P. Lauro, 1544 [A.]	—
—	*Oneirocritica* by P. Lauro, 1540 [A.]	—
—	*Tabula* by F. Coccio, 1530 [A.]	*Tabula* by F. de Tamara, 1549 [R.]; by A. de Morales, 1588 [R.]; by P. Simón Abril, *a.* 1595 [P.]

AUTHOR	ENGLISH	FRENCH
DEMOSTHENES	*Olynthiacae, Philippicae*, by T. Wilson, 1570	*Philippicae* by J. Lallemant, 1549; by L. Le Roy, 1555 *Olynthiacae* by L. Le Roy, 1551
DIOCLES	*ad Antigonum* by H. Lloyd, 1550	*ad Antigonum* by A. Juliani, 1546
DIODORUS SICULUS	*Historia* by T. Stocker, 1569 (from the French, XVIII–XX)	*Historia* by C. de Seyssel XVIII–XX, 1530; I–III by A. Macault, 1536; XI–XVII by J. Amyot, 1554 [all B.N.]
DIOGENES LAERTIUS	*Vitae Philosophorum* by G. H. Burley (?), *a.* 1490, cited L. S. Thompson, etc.—an error for W. Burley's Latin *de Vitae Philosophorum*?	—
DIONYSIUS OF HALICARNASSUS	—	—
DIONYSIUS PERIEGETES	*de Situ Orbis* by T. Twine, 1572	*de Situ Orbis* by B. Saumaize, 1597 [B.N.]
DIOSCORIDES	—	*Materia Medica* by M. Mathée, 1553
EPICTETUS	*Encheiridion* by J. Sandford, 1567	*Encheiridion* by A. du Moulin, 1544 [B.N.]; by A. Rivaudeau 1567 [B.N.]; by J. A. de Baif (not printed), *a.* 1571;* by G. du Vair, 1591 [B.N.] *Altercatio* by J. de Coras, 1558 [B.N.]
EUCLID	*Elementa* by R. Candish, fl. 1556; by H. Billingsley, 1570	*Elementa* I–VI by P. Forcadel, 1564 [B.M.]; VII–IX by P. Forcadel, 1565 [B.N.]
EURIPIDES	*Phoenissae* by F. Kinwelmersh and G. Gascoigne, acted 1566 (printed 1572)	*Troades* by J. Amyot (?), 1542 (?) (not printed) *Hecuba* by Bochetel (sometimes attributed to L. de Baif), 1544 *Iphigenia in Aulide* by J. Amyot (?), 1545–7 (?) (not printed); by T. Sebilet, 1549 *Medea* by J. A. de Baif, *a.* 1570 (not printed)*

* Becq de Fouquières, *Poésies Choisies de Baif* (Paris, 1874), p. xxxv.

GERMAN	ITALIAN	SPANISH
Olynthiaca I by J. Reuchlin (not printed), 1495 *Philippicae* I–IV by H. Boner, 1551	*de Corona* anon., 1520 [A.]; by a Florentine gentleman, 1554 [B.N.] *Philippicae*; *Olynthiacae*; *de Chersoneso* etc. by F. Figliucci, 1550 [A.]—a paraphrase *In Leptinem* by a Florentine gentleman 1555 [A.] *de Fals. Leg.*; *in Meid.*; *in Androt.* by the same, 1557 [A.]	*de Corona* by P. Simón Abril (not printed), *a.* 1595 [P.]
—	—	—
Historia by Herold, 1554	*Historia* from L. Bruni's Latin version, 1526 [A.]; by F. Baldelli, 1575 [A.]	—
Vitae Philosophorum anon., 1490 (from Burley, *v.* English column)	*Vitae Philosophorum* anon. 1480 [B.N.]; by the brothers Rosetini, 1545 [B.N.]; by F. A. Vinitiano, 1598 [B.N.]	—
—	*de Urbe Roma* by F. Venturi, 1545 [A.]	—
—	—	—
Materia Medica by C. Jacobus, 1546	*Alexipharmaca* anon., 1539 [A.] *Materia Medica* by F. da Longiano, 1542 [B.N.]; by M. Montigiano, 1547 [A.]; by A. Matthioli, 1548 [B.N.]	*Materia Medica* by A. de Laguna, 1555 [B.M.] *Alexipharmaca* by J. Jarava, 1557 [B.M.]
Encheiridion by J. Schenk, 1534	*Encheiridion* by M. G. Ballino, 1564 [B.N.]	*Encheiridion* by Gomez de Castro [R.]; by Sanchez de las Brozas [R.]
—	*Elementa* by N. Tartalea, 1543 [A.] *Perspectiva* by E. Danti, 1573 [A.]	*Elementa* by R. Zamorano, 1576 [B.M.] *Perspectiva* by P. A. Onderiz, 1585 [B.M.]
Iphigenia in Aulide by H. Bebst, 1584 [B.N.]	*Electra* by A. Parma, n.d. [A.]; *Alcestis* by H. Giustiniano, 1599 [B.N.] *Hecuba* by L. Dolce, 1543 [B.N.]; by G. Trissino, *a.* 1550 (printed 1560) [A.]; by G. Gelli, *a.* 1563 [A.]; by G. Balcianelli, 1592 [A.] *Iphigenia in Aulide* by L. Dolce, 1551 [A.]	*Hecuba* by Pérez de Oliva, *a.* 1533 [R.] *Medea* by P. Simón Abril, *a.* 1595 (printed 1599) [P.]

AUTHOR	ENGLISH	FRENCH
EURIPIDES (*cont.*)		
GALENUS	*Methodus Medendi* (complete) by T. Gale, 1586 (Partial editions): book IV by Copland, 1541; book III by G. Baker, 1579 *de Mixturis* by W. Turner, 1568 *Elementa* by J. Jones, 1574 *de Compositione Medicamentorum*, book III by G. Baker, 1574	*Methodus Medendi*, books III, IV and VI anon., 1537–9 [B.N.]; books I–VII by G. Chrestien, 1540; (six books) by J. Canappe, 1554 [B.N.] *de Curandi Ratione* by P. Tolet, 1540 *de Motu Musculorum; de Ossibus* by J. Canappe, 1541 [B.N.] *de Tumoribus* by P. Tolet, 1542 *de Simplicium Facultatibus* (complete) by E. Fayard, 1548 [B.N.]; books V and IX by J. Canappe, 1542 *de Compositione Medicamentorum*, books I–III by J. Brèche, 1545; by M. Grégoire, 1545; book IV by M. Grégoire, 1549 *de Ratione Medendi*, book II by G. Chrestien, 1549 [B.N.] *Commentaria in Aphorismos* by J. Brèche, 1550 [B.N.] *de Alimentorum Facultatibus* by J. Massé, 1552 [B.N.] *Commentaria in Hippocratis 'de fracturis'* anon., 1555 [B.N.] *de Foetuum Formatione* by G. Chrestien, 1556 [B.N.] *quod Animi Mores*, etc. by I. Le Bon, 1557 [B.N.] *de Usu Partium* by C. Dalechamps, 1566 [B.N.] *de Anatomicis Administrationibus* by C. Dalechamps, 1572 *de Parvae Pilae Exercitio* by Fourbet L'Aisné, 1599 [B.N.]
HELIODORUS	*Aethiopica* (Complete) by T. Underdowne, 1587 (Partial editions): book IV by J. Sandford, 1567; book I (part) by A. Fraunce, 1591	*Aethiopica* by J. Amyot, 1547
HERMES TRISMEGISTUS	—	*de Potestate Dei* by G. du Préau, 1549 [B.M.]; by F. de Foix, 1579 [B.M.]
HERMOGENES	—	—
HERO		

GERMAN	ITALIAN	SPANISH
Liber Introductorius anon., 1509	*Phoenissae* by Guido Guidi, n.d. [A.]; by L. Dolce, 1560 [A.] *Medea* by L. Dolce, 1557 [A.] *de Simplicium Facultatibus* by Z. Saracino, 1537 [A.] *de Cognitione Artium* by L. Dolce, 1548 [A.] *Methodus Medendi* by G. Tarchagnota, 1549 [A.]; *de Animi Affectuum Agnitione* by A. Firmiano, 1558 [A.]; by F. Betti, 1587 [A.] *de Alimentorum Facultatibus* by F. L' Imperiale, 1560 [A.]; by J. Saccheto, 1582 [A.] *de parvae pilae exercitio* anon., 1562 [A.]	—
—	*Aethiopica* by L. Ghini, 1556 [A.]	*Aethiopica* by F. and J. de Vergara (not printed) 1548; anon., 1554; by F. de Mena, 1587 [B.M.]
—	*de Potestate Dei* by T. Benci, 1545 [A.]	—
—	*de Figuris Orationis* by G. Camillo, 1594 [A.]	—
—	*Pneumatica* by G. Aleotti, 1589 [A.]; by A. Giorgi da Urbino, 1592 [A.] *Automatopoietice* by B. Baldi, 1589 [A.]	—

AUTHOR	ENGLISH	FRENCH
HERODIANUS	*Historia* by N. Smith, 1550	*Historia* by J. Colin, 1541 [B.N.]; by J. de Vintimille, 1554 [B.M.]
HERODOTUS	*Historia* I, II by B.R., 1584	*Historia* I–III by P. Saliat, 1552; IV–IX by P. Saliat, 1556
HESIODUS	—	*Opera et Dies* by R. Le Blanc, 1547 [B.M.]; by L. Daneau, 1571 [B.M.]; by J. A. de Baif (in *Etrennes de Poésies*), 1574; by Le Gras, 1586 [B.M.]
HIPPOCRATES	*Aphorismi* by H. Lloyd, 1550 *Prognostica* by P. Lowe, 1597 *de Natura Hominis* anon., 1599 (from the French of J. de Bourges)	*Praesagia* by P. Verney, 1539 [B.N.]; by J. Canappe, 1552 [B.N.] *de Natura Hominis* by J. de Bourges, 1548; *de Structura* by La Fargue, 1580 *Aphorismi* by J. Brèche, 1550 [B.N.]; by J. Bomier, 1596 [B.N.] *de Articulis*; *de Fracturis* anon., 1555 [B.N.] *de Ulceribus* by F. Lefèvre, 1555 [B.N.] *de Genitura* ed. J. Dubois, 1559 [B.N.] *de Officina Medici* by F. Lefèvre, 1560 [B.N.] *Iusiurandum* by G. de Chauliac, 1595 [B.N.]
HOMERUS	*Ilias* I–IX by A. Hall, 1581; I–VII and the 'Shield of Achilles' by G. Chapman, 1598 (*Batrachomyomachia* by C. Johnson, 1580, into Latin)	*Ilias* (paraphrase) by J. Samson, 1530; I–X by H. Salel, 1545. *Scutum Achilleis* by J. Colin, 1547; XI–XII by H. Salel, 1554; XII–XVI by A. Jamyn, 1574; XVII–XXIV by A. Jamyn, 1580 *Batrachomyomachia* by A. Macault, 1540 [B.N.]; by G. Royhier, 1554 *Odysseia* I, II by J. Peletier, 1547; VIII (extracts) by J. du Bellay, 1556; I–III by A. Jamyn, 1584
ISOCRATES	*Ad Nicoclem* by Thomas Eliot, 1534; by T. Forrest, 1580 *Ad Demonicum* by Bury, 1557; by T. Forrest, 1580; by J. Nuttall, 1585 *Epistolae* (selected) by A. Fleming, 1576 *Nicocles* by T. Forrest, 1580	*Ad Demonicum* (extracts) by C. de la Fontaine, 1543; by L. Le Roy, 1551 [B.N.] *Ad Nicoclem* (extracts) by J. Brèche, 1541 [B.N.]; by L. Macault, 1544; by L. Le Roy, 1551 [B.N.]

GERMAN	ITALIAN	SPANISH
Historia by H. Boner, 1531	*Historia* anon., 1522 [B.N.]; by L. Carani, 1551	*Historia* by F. Flores, 1532 [B.M.]
Historia by H. Boner, 1535	*Historia* by M. M. Boiardo, 1533 [B.N.]	—
—	—	—
—	*Iusiurandum*; *Aphorismi* by L. Filalteo, 1552 [A.]	—
Ilias (the fight between Paris and Menelaus) by J. Reuchlin, 1495 (not printed); (extracts) by C. Bruno, 1544 *Odysseia* by S. Schaidenreisser, 1537	*Batrachomyomachia* by C. Marsuppini, *a.* 1472 (printed 1492) [A.] *Odysseia* (complete) by G. Bacelli, 1581 [A.] (Paraphrases) by L. Dolce, 1572 [B.N.]; ix, x by Ferrante Caraffa, 1578 [A.] *Ilias* i–vii by G. Bacelli, 1581 [A.] (Printed editions): i by F. Gussano, 1544 [A.]; i–v by P. La Badessa, 1564 [A.]; i–v by F. Nevizano, 1572 [A.]; (paraphrase) by L. Dolce, 1572 [B.N.]; i–xii by B. Leo de Piperno, 1573 [A.]	*Ilias* (paraphrase) anon., *c.* 1440; by J. de Mena, *c.* 1440 *Odysseia* i–xiii by G. Pérez, 1550; xiv–xxiv by G. Pérez, 1556 [B.M.]
Ad Demonicum anon., 15th cent. (not printed); by W. Pirckheimer, 1519 *Ad Nicoclem* by J. Altensteig, 1517	*Ad Nicoclem* by G. Brevio, 1542 [B.N.]; by L. P. Rosello, 1552 [A.]; by F. Sansovino, 1561 [A.] *Ad Demonicum* by B. Crisolso, 1548 [A.] *Nicocles* by L. P. Rosello, 1552 [A.]	*Panegyricus* by P. Mejia, 1542 [R.] *Ad Nicoclem* by D. Gracian, 1570 [R.]

AUTHOR	ENGLISH	FRENCH
ISOCRATES (*cont.*)		*Nicocles* by L. Meigret, 1544; by L. Le Roy, 1551 *Epistolae* by L. de Matha, 1547 *Panegyricus* by P. A. de Vuasigny, 1548 *De Pace Servanda* by M. Philippes-Robert, 1579 [B.N.]
JOSEPHUS	—	*Opera* by F. Bourgoing, 1562 [B.N.]; by J. le Frère, 1569 [B.N.]; by G. Genebrard, 1578 [B.N.]; by A. de La Faye, 1597 [B.N.] *Bellum Judaicum* by C. de Seyssel, 1492 [B.N.]; by de Herberay, 1553 *Antiquitates Judaicae* by G. Michel, 1539 [B.N.]
JULIANUS APOSTATA	—	*de Caesaribus* by B. Grangier, 1580
LONGUS	*Daphnis et Chloë* by A. Day, 1587	*Daphnis et Chloe* by J. Amyot, 1559
LUCIANUS	*Menippus* by J. Rastell, *c.* 1520 *Cynicus* by T. Elyot, *a.* 1535 *Toxaris* by A.O., 1565 *Galatea et Polyphemus* by G. Fletcher, 1593	*Opera* by F. Bretin, 1583 [B.N.] *Muscae Encomium* by G. Tory (no date) [B.N.] *Dialogi* (30) by G. Tory, 1529 [B.N.] *Opuscula* by S. Bourgoyng, 1529 *de non credendo calumniae* by S. Bourgoyng, 1529 *Philopseudes* by L. Meigret, 1548 [B.M.] *Toxaris* by B. de Vigenère, 1579 [B.N.]
LYCURGUS	—	—
LYSIAS	—	*In Eratosthenem* by Philibert Bugnyon, 1576 [B.N.] *Contra Mercatores Frumentarios* by P. Bugnyon, 1579 [B.N.]
MOSCHUS	*Idyllae* (one) by B. Barnes, 1593 (from the French)	*Idyllae* (one) anon., *a.* 1593
MUSAEUS	*Hero et Leander* (adapted) by C. Marlowe, 1593	*Hero et Leander* by C. Marot, 1541
ONOSANDER	*Strategicus* by P. Whitehorn, 1533	*Strategicus* by J. Charrier, 1546 [B.N.]

GERMAN	ITALIAN	SPANISH
	Orationes (complete) by M. P. Carrario, 1555 [B.N.]	
Opera by K. Hedio, 1531; by E. Lautenbach, 1571 [B.N.] *Bellum Judaicum* by M. Adam, 1546 [B.N.]	*Bellum Judaicum* anon., 1493 [B.N.] *Antiquitates Judaicae* by P. Lauro, 1544 [A.]; by F. Baldelli, 1581 [B.N.]	*Antiquitates Iudaicae* anon., 1554 [B.M.] *Bellum Judaicum* by Fernandez de Palencia, *a.* 1492 (printed 1536) [P.]; by J. M. Cordero, 1557 [B.M.] *In Apionem* by Fernandez de Palencia, 1492 [H.]
—	—	—
—	*Daphnis et Chloe* by A. Caro, *a.* 1556 (not printed till 1784)	—
Dialogi Mortuorum (No. 12) by J. Reuchlin, 1495 (not printed); by J. zu Schwarzenberg, 1536 [*Lucius*] by N. von Wyle, 1499 *Charon* anon. (not printed), 15th cent. *Scipio* by R. Philesius, 1507 *Opera* (a selection) by J. Galenarius, 1512 *Somnium sive Gallus* by D. von Plieningen, 1515 (*Facetiae*) by D. von Plieningen, 1516 *Timon* by J. Schenk, 1530 *Philopsendes* by H. Ziegler, 1545	*Timon* by M. M. Boiardo, *a.* 1494 (printed 1500) [A.]; by N. da Lonigo, 1525 [A.] (*Lucius*) by M. M. Boiardo, *a.* 1494 (printed 1523) [A.] *Scipio, Alexander, et Hannibal* anon., n.d. [A.] *Dialogi* (28) by N. da Lonigo, 1525 [A.] *Vera Historia* by N. da Lonigo, 1525 [A.] *de mercede conductis* by G. Roselli 1542 [B.N.] *Tragopodagra* by G. M. Scotto, 1552 [B.N.] *Macrobii* by F. Anguilla, 1572 [A.]	*Icaromenippus* by J. de Jarava, 1544 *Vera Historia* anon., 1551 [B.N.] *Dialogi* (some) by P. Simón Abril (not printed), *a.* 1595 [P.] *Tragopodagra* by J. C. de Sepulveda [R.]
(One speech) E. Lautenbeck, 1550	—	—
—	—	—
—	*Idyllae* (one, *Amor Fugitivus*) by G. Benevieni, 1515 [A.]; by L. Alamanni, *a.* 1556; (same) by T. Tasso, *a.* 1595 [A.]	—
—	*Hero et Leander* by B. Baldi, 1590	—
Strategicus anon., 1532 [B.N.]	*Strategicus* by Fabio Cotta, 1546 [B.N.]	*Strategicus* by D. Gracián, 1567

AUTHOR	ENGLISH	FRENCH
OPPIANUS APAMENSIS	—	*Cynegetica* by F. Chrestien, 1575 [B.N.]
PAULUS AEGINITA	—	*de Chirurgica* by P. Tolet, 1541 [B.N.]
(PHALARIS)	—	*Epistolae* by C. Gruget, 1556 [B.N.]
PHILO	(One essay) by L. Humfrey, 1563	*Opera* by P. Bellier, 1575 [B.M.] *de Mundo* anon., 1542 [B.N.]; by P. Saliat, 1542 [B.N.]
PHILOSTRATUS (THE ELDER)	—	*Imagines* by B. de Vigenère, 1578 [B.M.] *Vita Apollonii* by B. de Vigenère, 1599 [B.M.]
PLATO	(*Axiochus*) by Edw. Spenser, 1592 (Palmer gives this as from a French trans. ed. P. de Mornay)	*Lysis* by B. Desperiers, 1540/1 (printed 1544); by B. de Vigenère, 1579 [B.N.] *Crito* by Simon Vallambert, 1542 [L.]; by P. du Val, 1547 [B.M.]; by J. Le Masle, 1582 [B.N.] (*Hipparchus*) by E. Dolet, 1544 [B.N.] (*Axiochus*) by E. Dolet, 1544 [B.N.] *Io* by R. Le Blanc, 1546 [B.M.] *Apologia* by F. Hotman, 1549 *Timaeus* by L. Le Roy, 1551 [B.M.] *Phaedo* by L. Le Roy, 1553 [B.M.] *Respublica* I, II, X by L. Le Roy, 1555 [B.M.]; (complete) by L. Le Roy (printed 1600) [B.M.] *Symposium* (extract, the Androgyne) by H. Héroet, 1542 (Complete) by M. Héret, 1556 [B.M.]; by L. Le Roy, 1558 [B.N.] *Leges* III (extracts) by L. Le Roy, 1562 (1566) [B.N.] (*Theages*) by P. Trédéhan, 1564 [B.N.]
PLUTARCH	*Moralia* (individual essays): *de Tranquillitate Animi* by T. Wyatt, 1528; by T. Blundeville, 1561; by J. Clapham, 1589 *de Educatione Puerorum* by T. Elyot, 1530; by T. Blundeville, 1561; by E. Grant, 1571	*Moralia* (complete) by J. Amyot, 1572 [B.M.] (Individual essays): *Praecepta gerendae reipublicae* by G. Tory, 1532 [B.M.] *Coniugalia Praecepta* by J. Lodé, 1536 [B.M.]

GERMAN	ITALIAN	SPANISH
—	—	—
—	—	—
—	*Epistolae* (from the Latin version of L. Bruni by B. Fonzio, 1471) [A.]; anon., 1525 [A.]	—
—	*Vita Mosis* by S. Fausto, 1548 [B.N.]; by G. Ballino, 1560 [A.] *de Mundo* by A. Ferentilli, 1570 [A.]	—
—	*Vita Apollonii* by L. Dolce, 1549 [B.N.]; by F. Baldelli, 1549 [B.N.]; by B. Galandi, 1549 [A.]	—
—	*Symposium* by E. Barbarasa, 1544 [B.N.]; by C. Bartolo, 1544 [A.]; by G. Sorboli, 1590 [A.] *Lysis* by F. Colombi, 1548 [B.N.] *Io* by N. Trivisani, 1548 [A.] (*Axiochus*) by Vincentio Belprato, 1550 [B.N.] *Respublica* by P. Fiorimbene, 1554 [B.N.]; anon. (not printed), 1558 [A.] *Phaedrus* anon. (not printed), 1558 [A.]; by F. Figliucci, 1564 [A.] *Timaeus* by S. Erizzo, 1558 [A.]; anon. (not printed), 1558 [A.] (*Hipparchus*) by O. Maggi, 1558 [A.] *Parmenides*; *Leges* anon. (not printed), 1558 *Phaedo* anon. (not printed), 1558; by S. Erizzo, 1574 [A.] *Euthyphro*; *Apologia*; *Crito* by S. Erizzo, 1574 [A.]	*Phaedo* by P. Díaz de Toledo, 15th cent. [R.] *Gorgias*; *Cratylus* by P. Simón Abril *a.* 1595 [R.]
Moralia (complete) by M. Herr, 1535; by Xylander, 1550 (Selections) by G. Burckhardt, 1521 *Vitae* (1) by Philesius, 1508 [B.N.]; (8) by H. Boner, 1530; (? others) by H. Boner, 1541	*Moralia* (individual essays): *de Educatione Liberorum* by N. Segondino, 1501 [A.]; ptd. J. Stuppio, 1599 [A.] *Consolatio ad Apollonium*; *de Amicitia*; *de Curiositate*; *de Discrimine Odi*; *et Invidiae*;	*Moralia* (complete) by D. Gracián, 1542 [R.] (Individual essays) *Apophthegmata* by D. Gracián, 1533 [B.M.] *Vitae* (part) by Fernandez de Palencia, 1491 [B.M.]; (two

AUTHOR	ENGLISH	FRENCH
PLUTARCH (cont.)	de Sanitate Tuenda ptd. R. Wyer, 1530; by J. Hales, 1543 de Capienda ex Inimicis Utilitatem by T. Elyot (?), 1535 (?); by T. Blundeville, 1561 Vitae (complete) by Sir T. North, 1579	de Fortuna Romanorum by A. Chandon, 1536 (?) Memorabilia Mulierum anon., 1538 [B.N.]; de Educatione by J. Colin, 1537 de Tranquillitate Animi by J. Colin, 1538 [B.N.] de Immodica Verecundia by F. Legrand, 1544 [B.N.] de Discrimine Amici et Adulatoris by A. du Saix, 1537 [B.N.] de Cohibenda Ira; de Curiositate by P. de St Julien, 1546 [B.N.] Utrum Graviores sint Animi Morbi by P. de St Julien, 1546 [B.N.] de Sanitate Tuenda; de Virtute et Vitio; de Animalium Ratione; de Capienda ex Inimicis Utilitatem; Dialogus Ulixis et Grylli by E. Pasquier, 1546 [B.N.] de Vitanda Usura by A. du Moulin, 1546 [L.] de Anima by L. Le Roy, 1552 [B.N.] Moralia (a selection) by F. Le Tort, 1578 [B.M.] Vitae (complete) by des Avenelles (an epitome), 1558 [B.M.]; by J. Amyot, 1559 [B.M.] (Individual lives): (4) by L. de Baif, 1530 [L.]; (8) by G. de Selve, 1543 [B.M.]; (4) by A. Chandon, c. 1545
POLYBIUS	Historia book 1 by T. Watson, 1568	Historia I–v by L. Meigret, 1542 [L.]; vI by L. Meigret, 1545 [L.] (Complete) by L. Meigret, 1558 [B.M.]
PROCLUS	de Sphaera by W. Salysburie, 1550	de Sphaera by Elie Vinet, 1544 [B.N.] de Motu by P. Forcadel, 1565 [B.M.]
PTOLEMAEUS	(Compost) anon., 1550 (from the French)	(Compost) anon., a. 1550

GERMAN	ITALIAN	SPANISH
	de Principi Requiri Doctrinam; *de Virtuti et Vitio*; *Quaestiones Romanae*; *Si Oportet in Convitio Philosophare* by P. Lauro, etc., 1543 [A.]	lives) anon., 1547 [B.M.]; (complete) by F. de Encinas, 1551 [R.]; (eight lives) by J. Castro Salinas, 1562 [R.] (Individual lives) by D. Gracián and F. de Encinas, 1551
	Memorabilia Mulierum anon., 1543 [A.]; anon., 1570 [A.]	
	Coniugalia Praecepta anon., 1543 [A.]; by M. A. Gandino, 1586 [A.]	
	de Celeritate Animalium by B. L' Imperiale, 1545 [A.]	
	Apophthegmata F. da Longiano, 1546 [A.]; by B. Gualandi, 1565 [A.]	
	de Amore Patris in Filium by G. Ballino, 1564	
	(Complete): by L. Domenichi, 1560 [B.N.]; by Marcello Andrini (not printed), 1561 [A.]; by M. A. Gandino, G. M. Gratii, A. Massa, G. Taracagnotta, 1598	
	Vitae (complete): by B. Jaconello de Riete, 1482 [B.N.]; by L. Domenichi, 1555 [B.N.]; by S. Sansovino, 1564 [A.]	
	(Selections): by L. Giustiniani, 1505 [A.]	
	(A compendium): by D. Tiberto, 1543 [A.]	
—	*Historia* by L. Domenichi, 1546 [B.N.]; (selection) by P. Strozzi, 1552	—
—	*de Sphaera* by G. Scandianese, 1556 [B.N.]; by E. Danti, 1573 [B.N.]	—
—	*Geographia* by P. Mattioli, 1548 [B.N.]; by G. Ruscelli, 1569 [A.]; by L. Cernoti, 1597 [B.N.]	—
	Planispherium by H. Bottigaro, 1572 [B.N.]	

AUTHOR	ENGLISH	FRENCH
SOPHOCLES	(*Antigone* by T. Watson, 1581, into Latin)	*Electra* by L. de Baif, 1537 *Antigone* by Calvy de la Fontaine, 1542 (?); by J. de Baif, 1572 (L.) *Trachiniae* by J. de Baif (not printed and now lost), *c.* 1565*
STRABO	—	—
SYNESIUS	*Laus Calvitii* by A. Fleming, 1579	—
THEMISTIUS	—	—
THEOCRITUS	*Bucolica* (6) anon., 1588	*Bucolica* XXI by C. Marot, 1549
THEOPHRASTUS	—	—
THUCYDIDES	*Historia* (complete) by T. Nichols, 1550	*Historia* (complete) by C. de Seyssel, 1527
XENOPHON	*Oeconomica* by G. Hervet, 1532 *Cyropedia* I–VI by W. Barker, 1560 (?)	*Anabasis* by C. de Seyssel, 1529 *Cyropedia* by J. de Vintimille, 1547 [B.M.] *Oeconomica* by G. Tory, 1531; by de Ferris, 1562; by E. de La Boétie, *a.* 1563 (printed 1571)

* Becq de Fouquières, *Poésies choisies de Baif* (Paris, 1874), p. xxxix.

GERMAN	ITALIAN	SPANISH
—	*Opera* by A. Dell' Anguillara, 1566 [A.] *Antigone* by L. Alamanni, 1532 [A.]; by Guido Guidi, n.d. [A.] *Oedipus Rex* by Guido Guidi, n.d. [A.]; by A. Dell' Anguillara, 1565 [A.]; by O. Giustiniano, 1585 [A.]; by M. P. Angeli, 1589 [A.] *Electra* by Guido Guidi, n.d. [A.]; by Erasmo de Valvasone, 1588 [A.]	*Electra* by F. Pérez de Oliva, 1528 [R.]
—	*Geographia* part i by A. Bonacciuoli, 1562; part ii by A. Bonacciuoli, 1565	—
—	—	—
—	*Orationes* xiv anon., 1542 [A.]	—
—	—	—
de Characteres by Pirckheimer (no date)	*de Plantis* by M. A. Biondo, 1548	—
Historia (complete) by H. Boner, 1533	*Historia* (complete) by F. de Soldo Strozzi, 1545 [A.]	*Historia* (complete) by D. Gracián, 1564 [B.M.]; by Castro de Salinas (not printed) [R.]
Hiero by A. Wernher, 1502 *Cyropedia* by H. Boner, 1540	*Opera* by A. Gandini, 1588 [A.] *Cyropedia* by J. Poggio, 1521 [A.] *Oeconomica* by A. Giustiniani, 1536 [A.]; by L. Domenichi, 1547 [A.] *Anabasis* by L. Domenichi, 1547 [B.M.] *Agesilaus; Hiero; Memorabilia; Apologia Socratis; Lacedaemoniorum Respublica* by L. Domenichi, 1547 [A.] *Hellenica* by F. di Soldo Strozzi, 1550 [A.] *Hippike* ptd. F. Ziletti, 1580 [A.]	*Opera* by D. Gracián, 1552 [B.M.] *Oeconomica* by F. Tamara, 1546 [B.M.]; by J. Jarava, 1549 [B.N.] *Cyropedia* by A. Agustin, a. 1586 [R.]

TRANSLATIONS OF LATIN AUTHORS

AUTHOR	ENGLISH	FRENCH
APULEIUS	*Metamorphoses* by W. Adlington, 1566	*Metamorphoses* by J. Michel, 1522 [B.N.]; by L. Louveau, 1586 [B.N.]
AUSONIUS	*Epigrammata* in T. Kendall, *Flowers of Epigrams*, 1577	—
BOETHIUS	*De Consolatione Philosophiae* by Alfred the Great, *c.* 900; by G. Chaucer, *a.* 1380 (printed 1479); by J. Walton, 1410; by G. Colville, 1556	*De Consolatione Philosophiae* by J. de Meung, *c.* 1300 (printed 15th cent.); anon., 15th cent. attributed to Charles d'Orléans [B.N.]; by R. de St Trudon, 1477 [B.N.]; by M. de Mente, 1578 [B.N.]
CAESAR	*Bellum Gallicum* anon., 1530 (part); by A. Golding, 1565; I–IV by C. Edmundes, 1600	*Bellum Civile* by de l'Aigue (printed 1531) [B.N.]; by B. de Vigenère, 1589 *Bellum Gallicum* by R. Gaguin, *c.* 1488; by B. de Vigenère, 1576 [B.M.]
CASSIODORUS	—	*Historia Ecclesiastica* by L. Cinaeus, 1568 [B.N.]
CATULLUS	—	—
CELSUS	—	—
CICERO	*De Amicitia* by J. Tiptoft, ptd. 1481; by J. Harington, 1550; by T. Newton, 1577 *De Senectute* by W. Worcester, 1481 [B.N.]; by R. Whytinton, 1535; by T. Newton, 1577 *De Officiis* by R. Whytinton, 1533; by N. Grimald, 1553 *Pro Marcello* by R. Sherry, 1555 *Paradoxa* by R. Whytinton, 1540; by T. Newton, 1569 *Tusculanae Disputationes* by J. Dolman, 1561 *Somnium Scipionis* by T. Newton, 1569; by T. Orwin, 1597 *Pro Archia* by T. Drant, 1571 *Epistolae* (Cordier's selection) by T. W., 1575; (another selection) by A. Fleming, 1576	*De Amicitia* by L. Premierfait, *a.* 1418; by J. Colin, 1537 [B.N.]; by B. de Vigenère, 1579 [B.N.] *De Senectute* by L. Premierfait, *a.* 1418; by J. Colin, 1537 *De Officiis* by D. Missant, 1502 [B.N.] *Paradoxa* anon., 1512 [B.N.] *Pro Marcello* by A. Macault, 1534 [B.N.]; by F. Joulet, 1597 [B.N.] *Somnium Scipionis* anon., 1538 [B.N.]; by P. Saliat, 1542 *Epistola* (*ad Octavium*) by B. Aneau, 1542 *Epistolae ad Familiares* by E. Dolet, 1542 [B.N.] *Tusculanae Disputationes* by E. Dolet, 1543 *Orationes* (ten) by A. Macault, 1541 *Epistolae* (selected) by M. Cordier, 1556

INTO THE VERNACULARS

GERMAN	ITALIAN	SPANISH
Metamorphoses by J. Sieder, 1538	*Metamorphoses* by M.M. Boiardo, 1494 (printed 1518) [A.]; by A. Firenzuola, 1548 [A.]	*Metamorphoses* by López de Cortegana, 1513 [B.N.]; by Alonso Fuentes (?) 1543 [H.]
—	—	—
De Consolatione Philosophiae by Notker Labeo, *c.* 1000; by anon., 1473; by N. von Wyle, *a.* 1478 (now lost)	*De Consolatione Philosophiae* by an unknown Pisan, early 14th cent. (Bibl. Ricciardinae Cod. 1609); by Alberto of Florence, 1332; by A. Tanzo, 1550; by B. Varchi, 1520; by L. Domenichi, 1550 [B.M.]; by C. Bartoli, 1551 [B.N.]	*De Consolatione Philosophiae* by A. Ginebreda, 14th cent. (printed 1488) [B.M.]; by A. de Aguayo, 1518 [B.M.]; by P. Saynz de Viana (MS. Bibl. Nac. Madrid); by G. Zurita (ed. P. Getino, Buenos Aires, 1946)
Bellum Gallicum by Philesius, 1507 [B.N. 1508]	*Opera* by Ortica della Porta, 1512 [A.]; by F. Baldelli, 1554 [A.]	*Opera* by López de Toledo (printed 1498) [B.M.]; anon., 1549 [H]; by Garcia de la Oliva, 1570 [R.]
—	*de Dignitate Consulari* by L. Dolce, 1562 [A.]	*Historia Ecclesiastica* by Juan de la Cruz 1554 [H.]
—	*Epithalamium* by L. Dolce, 1538 [A.]; by L. Alamanni, *c.* 1543	—
De Medicina I–VIII by J. Kuessner, 1539	—	
Paradoxa anon., 15th cent. (not printed); by J. G. Von Oderheim, 1491–7 (not printed, now lost); by J. zu Schwarzenberg, 1535 [B.N.]; by S. Schaidenreisser, 1538	*De Inventione* ch. I–XVII from Latini's *Tesoro*, 14th cent. (complete) by C. Galleotto, 1478	(*Rhetorica ad Herennium*) by Enrique de Villena, *a.* 1434 [R.]; by Alfonso de Cartagena, *a.* 1456 [R.]
De Fato anon., 15th cent. (not printed); by J. G. Von Oderheim, 1491–7 (not printed, now lost)	*Pro Marcello; Pro Ligario; Pro Deiotaro* by Brunetto Latini (?), *a.* 1290	*De Inventione* by Alfonso de Cartagena, *a.* 1456 [R.]
De Officiis anon., 1488 (*Rhetorica ad Herennium*) by v. Wyle, *a.* 1478 (part) (A paraphase) by F. Riederer, 1493	*Epistolae* (selection) by F. Filelfo, *a.* 1481 (printed 1510) [A.] (*Rhetorica ad Herennium*) anon., 1502 [B.N.]; by A. Brucioli, 1538 [B.N.]; by O. Toscanella, 1561 [A.]	*De Officiis and De Senectute* by Alfonso de Cartagena, *a.* 1456 [R.]; anon., 1501 [H.]; by F. Tamara, 1546 [B.M.]; by J. Jarava, 1549 [B.N.]
De Senectute by J. G. v. Oderheim (not printed, now lost); by J. Wimpheling, *a.* 1529 (not printed); by K. Neuber, 1522; by J. zu Schwarzenberg, 1534	*De Officiis; De Senectute; De Amicitia; Paradoxa* by F. Vendranimo, 1523 [A.] *Philippicae* II by G. Giustiniano, 1538 [B.N.]; (complete) by G. Raggazoni, 1556 [B.N.]	*De Amicitia* by F. Tamara, 1546 [B.M.]; by A. Cornejo, 1548 [B.M.]; by J. Jarava, 1549 [B.N.] *De Republica* by J. G. de Sepulveda, 1547 [R.] *Paradoxa and Somnium Scipionis* by J. Jarava, 1549 [B.M.]
Tusculanae Disputationes I, ch. 1–10 by J. Reuchlin, 1501 (not printed); (complete) by J. zu Schwarzenberg, 1534	*Somnium Scipionis* by A. Brucioli, 1539 [B.N.]; by L. Dolce, 1563 [B.N.] *Tusculanae Disputationes* by F. de Longiano, 1544 [A.]	*In Catalinam* I–IV by A. de Laguna, 1557 [B.M.]; by P. Simón Abril (not printed), *a.* 1595 [R.] *Epistolae* (selection in 3 books) by P. Simón Abril, 1572 [B.M.];

AUTHOR	ENGLISH	FRENCH
CICERO (*cont.*)		*De Oratore* by B. de Vigenère, 1575 [B.N.] *De Natura Deorum* by Lefèvre de la Boderie, 1581 [B.N.] *In Catilinam* I by F. Joulet, 1597 [B.N.] *Philippica* (complete) by A. Macault, 1541 [B.N.]; I by F. Joulet, 1597 [B.N.] *Pro Milone* by du Vair (in *De ⁻l'Eloquence Française*), 1595
CLAUDIANUS	—	—
COLUMELLA	—	*De Re Rustica* III, IV by L. Meigret, 1540; I–XII by C. Cotereau, 1551 [B.M.]
CURTIUS	*De Rebus Gestis Alexandri* by J. Brend, 1553	*De Rebus Gestis Alexandri* anon., 1503 [B.N.]
EUTROPIUS	*Breviarium* by N. Howard, 1564	—
FRONTINUS	*Strategemata* by Caxton (from Christine de Pisan), 1489; by R. Morysine, 1539	*Strategemata* by Christine de Pisan (in *Faittes des Armes*), a. 1430; by N. Wolkyr, 1536
HORATIUS	*Sermones* I, 1, 2 by L. Evans, 1564; (complete) by T. Drant, 1567 *Ars Poetica*; *Epistolae* by T. Drant, 1567	*Opera* by R. and A. d'Agneaux, 1588 (Individual works): *Ars Poetica* by J. Peletier, 1545 [B.N.] *Sermones* by F. Habert, 1549 *Odae* by J. Mondot, 1579; by L. Delaporte, 1584 *Epistolae* by G.P.P., 1584

GERMAN	ITALIAN	SPANISH
In Catilinam I by D. v. Plieningen, 1513 *De Amicitia* by J. zu Schwarzenberg, 1534 *De Finibus* by J. zu Schwarzenberg, 1536; anon., 1536 *Pro Marcello* by C. Bruno, 1542 *Epistolae* (Cordier's selection), 1556	*Orationes* (complete) ed. F. da Longiano, 1545 [A.]; by L. Dolce, 1562 [A.] *Epistolae ad Familiares* anon., 1545 [A.]; by Fausto da Longiano, 1555 [A.]; by G. Fabrini, 1561 [A.]; ed. A. Manuzio, 1573 [A.] *Partitiones Oratoriae* by R. Cataneo, 1545; O. Toscanella, 1556 [A.] *De Oratore* by L. Dolce, 1547 [A.] *De Divinatione* by G. Giustiniani, 1549 [A.] *In Verrem* by G. Tramezzino, 1554 [A.] *Pro Milone* by J. Bonsadio, 1554 [A.] *Epistolae ad Atticum* by M. Senarega, 1555 [B.N.] *Epistolae ad Brutum* by O. Maggi, 1556 [B.N.] *Topica* by S. Della Barba, 1556 [A.]	(*Ad. Fam.* book II) by G. de Aulon, 1574 [R.]; (*Ad. Fam.* complete) by P. Simón Abril, 1578 [R.] *In Verrem* by P. Simón Abril, 1574 [R.] *Pro Ligario and Pro Marcello* by Lasso de Oropesa, 1585 [P.]; by P. Simón Abril, a. 1595 [P.] *Pro Archia and Pro Lege Manilia* by P. Simón Abril, a. 1595 [R.]
—	*Raptus Proserpinae* by L. Sannuto, 1551 [A.]; by G. Bevilacqua, 1586 [A.] *Phoenix* by T. Scandianese, 1555 [A.]	*Raptus Proserpinae* by Lope de Vega, 1572 (not printed) [R.]
De Re Rustica by H. Oesterriecher (not printed), 1491; by M. Herr, 1538	*De Re Rustica* by P. Lauro, 1544 [B.N.]	—
—	*De Rebus Gestis Alexandri* by P. G. Decembrio, 1438 (printed 1478) [A.]; by T. Porcacchi, 1558 [A.]	*De Rebus Gestis Alexandri* by L. de Fennolet (printed 1481); anon., 1496 [H.]; by G. de Castaneda, 1534 [R.]
—	—	*Breviarium* by J. Cordero, 1561 [B.M.]
Strategemata anon., 1532 [B.N.]; by G. Motschidler, 1540; by M. Tatius, 1542	*Strategemata* by F. Lucio, 1536 [A.]; by M. Gandino, 1574 [B.N.]	*Strategemata* by D. Guillén de Avila, 1516 [H.]; by Arcos y Alférez (not printed) [R.]
Sermones by A. Wernher (printed 1502)	*Opera* by G. Fabrini, 1566 [A.] *Ars Poetica* by L. Dolce, 1536 [A.] *Epistolae*; *Sermones* by L. Dolce, 1549 [A.] *Odae* by G. Giorgini, 1595 [B.N.]	*Odae* (selection) by Luís de León, a. 1591 [R.]; by V. Espinel, 1591 [R.] *Ars Poetica* by V. Espinel, 1591 [R.]; by L. Zapaea, 1592 [R.]

AUTHOR	ENGLISH	FRENCH
JUSTINIANUS	—	*Institutiones* by d'Annebaut, 1485; by de l'Escut, 1547; by de la Roche, 1560
JUSTINUS (the Epitome of POMPEIUS TROGUS)	*Historia* by A. Golding, 1574; (extract) by T. Norton, 1560	*Historia* by C. de Seyssel, *a.* 1520 (printed 1559) [B.M.]; by G. Michel, 1538 [B.N.]; by N. du Mont, 1578 [B.N.]
JUVENALIS	—	*Saturae* VIII, X, XI, XIII by M. d'Amboyse, 1544 [B.N.]
LIVIUS	*Opera* by P. Holland, 1600; (extract: Hannibal and Scipio) by A. Cope, 1544	*Opera* (incomplete) by P. Bersuire, 1352 (Complete) by B. de Vigenère, J. Amelin and A. de la Faye, 1583 (Extract, speeches only) by J. Amelin, 1554
LUCANUS	*Pharsalia* book I by C. Marlowe, *a.* 1593 (ptd. 1600)	*Pharsalia* anon., *a.* 1380
MARTIALIS	Select epigrams in T. Kendall, *Flowers of Epigrams*, 1577	*Epigrammata* I. 20, 33, 34, 65, 76, 90, 98, 99; II. 67; III. 26, 69; V. 13, 20, 29, 47, 58, 60, 81; VI. 23, 25, 40; VII. 14; VIII. 54; IX. 63, 73; X. 847; XII. 65, imitated by Clément Marot, *a.* 1544 (not printed till 1596)
MELA	*de Situ Orbis* by A. Golding, 1585	—
NEPOS	—	—
OVIDIUS	*Metamorphoses* (Mansion's moralisation from the French) by Caxton, 1480; III, 344 ff. (Narcissus) by T. Howell (?), 1560; (complete) by A. Golding, 1565/7; v, 287 ff. (Hermaphroditus) by T. Peend, 1565; (Ceyx) by W. Hubbard, 1569 *Ars Amatoria* anon. 1513 by T. Heywood, 1598 *Heroides* by G. Turberville, 1567 *Ibis* by T. Underdowne, 1569 *Tristia* (3) by W. Churchyard, 1572 *Amores* (some) by C. Marlowe (in *Epigrammes and Elegies*), 1590; (complete) by C. Marlowe, 1597 *Remedium Amoris* by T. Heywood, 1598	*Ars Amatoria* four medieval versions; Le Loyer 1579 *Metamorphoses* anon., 1316/29; books I–II by C. Marot, 1530; anon. (*le grand Olympe*) 1532; book III by B. Aneau (1533) (printed 1556); book XIII (Ajax and Ulysses) by J. Colin, 1547 [B.N.]; book IX (Caunus and Biblis) by G. Bochetel, 1550 [B.N.]; (complete) by F. Habert, 1556; (selection) by C. Deffrans, 1595 [B.M.] *Heroides* by O. de Saint-Gelais, *c.* 1500 [B.N.]; I–X by Charles Fontaine, 1552 [L.]; VII by J. du Bellay, 1552 [B.N.] *Remedium Amoris* anon., 1509; book I by C. Fontaine, 1555 (*de Nuce*) by R. Le Blanc, 1554

GERMAN	ITALIAN	SPANISH
Institutiones by G. Burckhardt, 1516	—	*Institutiones* by B. Daza, 1551 [B.M.]
—	*Historia* by J. Squarciafico, 1477 [B.N.]; by T. Porcacchi, 1561 [B.N.]; by B. Zucchi, 1590 [A.]	*Historia* by J. de Bustamente, 1540 [B.M.]
Satura VI by C. Bruno	*Opera* by G. Sommariva, 1480 [B.N.]	*Saturae VI and X* by J. Fernandez de Villegas, 1519 [B.M.]
Opera by Schoefferlin and Wittig, 1505 (Revised) by L. Carbach, 1523 (Revised) by L. Carbach and Mycillus, 1533; by H. Oesterreicher (no date, not printed)	*Opera* (complete) anon., 1535 [A.]; by J. Nardi, 1540 [A.]. The 1st, 3rd and 4th Decades exist also in anonymous MS. translations dating back to the mid-15th cent.; and in a translation by R. Ferrari (1466), printed 1476 [A.]	*Opera* anon., 1552 (partial editions) by López de Ayala, *a.* 1407; by P. de la Vega, 1520 [B.M.]; by F. de Encinas, 1550 [R.]
—	*Pharsalia* by L. de Montichiello, 1492 [A.]; by G. Morige, 1579	*Pharsalia* anon., 15th cent. [R.]; by Lasso de Oropesa, 1541 [R.]
Selected epigrams by C. Bruno, 1544	*Epigrammata* by G. Mazzaciuvoli, fl. 1439 (printed 1554) [A.]	—
—	*de Situ Orbis* by T. Porcacchi, 1557 [A.]	—
—	*de Viribus Illustribus Graeciae* by Remigio Fiorentino, 1550	—
Metamorphoses by H. Oesterreicher, 15th cent. (not printed); (paraphrase) by A. v. Halberstadt, 13th cent. (printed 1551) [B.N.] (Above: revised) by J. Wickram, 1545 (Complete) by H. Boner, 1534 (Verse translation) by J. Spreng, 1571	*Metamorphoses* (complete) by Simintendi da Prato, *c.*1339; by Joanne de Bonsignore, 1370 (printed 1497) [B.N.]; (complete) by Nicolò degli Agostini, 1522 [A.]; III, 344–70 by L. Alamanni, 1533; IV, 624 *seq.* I, 755 to II, 300 by L. Alamanni (no date); XIII by B. Varchi, 1539 [A.]; XIII (extract) by A. Piccolomini, 1539 [A.]; X by Camillo Cautio, 1548 [A.]; (complete—a paraphrase) by L. Dolce, 1553 [B.N.]; I by A. Dell'Anguillara, *a.* 1554 [A.]; II, III by A. Dell'Anguillara, 1554 [A.]; (paraphrase in Epigrams) by Gabriello Simeoni, 1559 [B.N.]; (complete) by A. Dell'Anguillara, 1561 [A.]; XIII (extract) by F. Coppeta, 1581 [A.]	*Ars Amatoria* (paraphrase) by Juan Ruíz, 14th cent. [R.] *Metamorphoses* (complete) by F. Alegre (printed 1494) [B.M.]; by J. de Bustamente, 1546 [B.M.]; by L. Hurtado de Toledo, 1578 [R.]; by A. Pérez Sigler, 1581 [R.]; by P. Sanchez de Viana, 1589 [R.]; by F. Mey, 1594 [R.]; by J. Gaytan [R.]; (Polyphemus and Pyramus and Thisbe) by C. de Castillejo, *a.* 1550 [R.] *Heroides* by Diego Mejia, 1596 [P.] *Ibis* by Diego Mejia, 1596 [P.]

AUTHOR	ENGLISH	FRENCH
OVIDIUS (*cont.*)		
PALLADIUS	*de Re Rustica, c.* 1420 [B.M.]	*de Re Rustica* by J. Darces, 1554 [B.N.]
PERSIUS	—	*Saturae* by A. Foulon, 1544 [B.M.]; by G. Durand, 1575 [B.M.]
PLAUTUS†	*Amphytrio* by W. Copland, 1562/3 (adapted) *Menaechmi* by W. Warner, 1595	*Miles Gloriosus* by J. A. de Baif, 1567 *Aulularia* by J. de Cahaignes, 1580 [B.N.]
PLINIUS (THE ELDER)	*Historia Naturalis* (epitome) by I. A., 1565	*Historia Naturalis* (extracts) by P. de Chagny, 1559; (complete) by du Pinet, 1562 [B.N.]

* Argellati also mentions three anonymous prose translations which have not been printed and date from the 15th cent.

† Plautus was known more through imitations than through translations. Among the more important of these imitations were:

In Italy: Machiavelli (1469–1527), *Clizia* (*Casina*); Bibbiena (1470–1520), *La Calandria* (*Menaechmi*); Ariosto (1474–1533), *I Suppositi* (*Menaechmi*), *Casaria* (*Pseudolus*); G. Trissino (1478–1550), *Simillimi* (*Menaechmi*); Lorenzino dei Medici (1516–48), *L' Aridosia* (*Adelphi* of Terence, *Aulularia* and *Mostellaria*); A. Firenzuola (1493–1543), *I Lucidi* (*Menaechmi*); G. B. Gelli (1498–1563), *Sporta* (*Aulularia*), *Lo Errore*

GERMAN	ITALIAN	SPANISH
	Heroides (complete) by D. da Monticielli, *a.* 1367 (printed 1491) [A.]; by Filippo (?) (in *ottava rima*) (not printed), 15th cent. [A.];* (Sappho) by F. J. de Pellenegra, 1515 [A.]; (complete) ptd. heirs of N. de Sabio, 1532 [A.]; by C. Figiovani, 1548 [A.]; by Remigio Fiorentino,1555[A.];by C.Camilli, 1587[A.]; (three epistles) ptd. Discepolo, 1590 [A.] *Ars Amatoria* by A. Traversagni, 1444 (not printed) [A.]; anon. (in *terza rima*), 1481 [A.]; by L. Dolce, *a.* 1561 [A.] *Fasti* by V. Cartari, 1551 [B.N.] *Remedium Amoris* by A. Ingegneri, 1576 [B.N.] *Tristia* by G. Morigi, 1581 [A.]	
de Re Rustica by M. Herr, 1538	*de Re Rustica* by P. Marino da Fuligno, 1538 [B.N.]; by F. Sansovino, 1561 [B.N.]	—
—	*Saturae* by A. Vallone, 1576 [B.N.]	*Saturae* by B. Melgarejo (not printed) [R.]; by L. J. Sevilla (not printed) [R.]
Menaechmi by von Eyb, *a.* 1475 (printed 1511); by J. Bittner, 1570 *Bacchides* by von Eyb, *a.* 1475 (printed 1511) *Aulularia* by J. Greff, 1535 *Stichus* by Freissleben, 1539 *Captivi* by H. Hayneccius, 1582	*Menaechmi* by G. Berrardo, 1486; anon., 1530 [B.N.]; by G. Falugi, *a.* 1535 [A.] *Amphitruo* by G. Berrardo, *c.* 1487; by P. Collenuccio, 1530 [B.N.] *Casina* by G. Berrardo, *c.* 1490 (printed 1530) [A.] *Mostellaria* by G. Berrardo, *c.* 1490 (printed 1530) [A.] *Asinaria* anon., 1528 [A.] *Miles Gloriosus* by C. Calcagnini, *c.* 1520 *Poenolus* anon., 1526 [A.] *Rudens* anon., 1560 [A.]	*Amphytruo* by Lopez de Villalobos, 1517; by F. Perez d' Oliva, 1530; by anon., 1554 *Miles Gloriosus* by anon., 1555 *Menaechmi* by J. de Timoneda, 1559
Historia Naturalis VII–XI by H. von Eppendorf, 1539	*Historia Naturalis* by C. Landino, 1473 [A.]; by A. Bruccioli, 1543; by L. Domenichi, 1561	*Historia Naturalis* by F. Hernandez, *a.* 1587 [R.]; VII, VIII by Gomez de Huerta, 1599 [B.M.]

(*Casina*); A. Beolco (1502–42), *Vaccaria* (*Asinaria*); E. Bentevoglio (1506–73), *I Fantasmi* (*Mostellaria*); L. Dolce (1508–68), *Il Marito* (*Amphitruo*), *Il Capitano* (*Miles Gloriosus*), *Il Ruffiano* (*Rudens*); G. Cecchi (1518–87), *Il Martello* (*Asinaria*), *Gli Incantesimi* (*Cistellaria*), *La Stiava* (*Mercator*), *La Moglie* (*Menaechmi*); Cieco di Hadria (1541–85), *La Calisto* (*Amphitruo*); L. Domenichi, *Le due Cortegiane* (*Bacchides*).

In France: J. Grévin (1538–70), imitated Plautus in all his plays.

In England: Shakespeare's *Comedy of Errors* (1592) carried echoes of the *Menaechmi*, and Ben Jonson's *The Case is Altered* (1597) blended the *Aulularia* and the *Captivi*.

In Germany: Hans Sachs produced a *Menaechmi* (1548).

AUTHOR	ENGLISH	FRENCH
PLINIUS (THE YOUNGER)	*Epistolae* (extracts) by A. Fleming, 1576	—
QUINTILIANUS	—	—
SALLUSTIUS	*Jugurtha* by A. Barclay, 1520/3	*Opera* anon., *a.* 1380; by L. Meigret, 1547; by La Roche, 1577 *Catilina* by J. Parmentier, 1528
SENECA (THE ELDER)	—	—
SENECA* (THE YOUNGER)	(Prose works): *de Remediis Fortuitorum* by R. Whytinton, 1547 *de Beneficiis* by A. Golding, 1577 (Tragedies): *Troas* by J. Heywood, 1559 *Thyestes* by J. Heywood, 1560 *Hercules Furens* by J. Heywood, 1561 *Oedipus* by A. Nevyle, 1563 *Hippolytus; Medea; Agamemnon* by J. Studely, 1566 *Hercules Oetaeus* by J. Studely, 1571 *Thebais* by T. Newton, 1581	(Prose works): *de Brevitate Vitae* by L. Premierfait, *a.* 1408 [B.N.]; by C. Chappuis, 1585 [B.M.] *Epistolae ad Lucilium* by L. Premierfait, *a.* 1408 [B.N.]; by de Pressac, 1582 [B.N.]; by S. Goulart, 1595 [B.N.] (*de Remediis Fortuitorum*) by L. Premierfait, *a.* 1408 [B.N.]; by S. Goulart, 1595 [B.N.] *de Artibus Liberalibus;* (*de Moribus*) by L. Premierfait, *a.* 1408 [B.N.] *de Beneficiis* by S. Accaurat, 1561 [B.N.]; by S. Goulart, 1595 [B.N.] *De Clementia* by A. Cappel, 1578 [B.M.]; by S. Goulart, 1595 [B.N.] *de Providentia* by A. Cappel, 1578 [B.M.]; by S. Goulart, 1595 [B.N.]; anon., 1597 [B.N.] *de Tranquillitate Animi* by C. Chappuis, 1585 *de Vita Beata* by S. Goulart, 1595 *Consolatio ad Marciam* by A. Cappel, 1595; by S. Goulart, 1595 *de Ira* by A. Cappel, 1595; by S. Goulart, 1595 *de Constantia Sapientis; Consolatio ad Helviam; Quaestiones Naturales* by S. Goulart, 1595

* There were a large number of imitations, among which the Senecan tragedies of L. Dolce in Italian (*c.* 1550), the *Hippolytus* (1573) and the *Antigone* (1580) of R. Garnier, the *Medea* (1555) of La Pérouse, the

GERMAN	ITALIAN	SPANISH
Epistolae by D. von Plieningen, 1513 *Panegyricus* by D. von Plieningen, 1515	*Panegyricus* by P. Conone, 1506 *Epistolae* (selected) by L. Dolce, 1548 [A.]	—
—	*Institutio Oratoria* by O. Toscanella, 1566 [B.N.]	—
Opera by H. Oesterreicher, 14th cent. (not printed); by D. von Plieningen, 1515; by Vinfeld, 1530 *Catilina* by G. Schrayer, 1534	*Opera* by A. Ortica, 1518 [B.N.]; by L. Carani, 1550 [B.N.]; by P. Spinola, 1563 [A.]	*Opera* by Vidal de Noya, 1493 [B.M.]; by Vasco de Guzmán, 15th cent. [R.]
—	*Declamationes* by A. Arietto (not printed), 16th cent.	—

(Prose works):
  de quattuor virtutibus by H. Hoetzel, 1507
de Ira; *de Clementia*; *de Providentia*; *de Vita Beata*; *de Otio*; *de Brevitate Vitae*; *de Paupertate*; *ad Marciam*; *de Remediis Fortuitorum*; *de Tranquillitate Animi*; *ad Serenum*; *Proverbia* by D. von Plieningen, 1515/17 (not printed)
Moralia by M. Herr, 1536
Moralia (selection) by C. Bruno, 1546
	(Prose works):
	  Epistolae by S. Manilio, 1492 [B.N.]; by A. Doni, 1548 [A.]
	de Beneficiis by B. Varchi, 1554 [A.]
	de Ira by F. Serdonati, 1569 [A.]
	(Tragedies):
	(Complete) by Evangelista Fossa, 1497 [B.N.]
	Troades by G. Bragazzi, 1591 [A.]
		(Prose works):
		Epistolae by F. Pérez de Guzmán, *a.* 1455 (?) [R.]; by Alfonso de Cartagena, *a.* 1456 (printed 1510) [H.]; by Alfonso V of Aragon, *a.* 1481 (not printed) [R.]; by Pero Díaz, 1496 [R.]
		De Artibus Liberalibus; *de Clementia*: *de Vita Beata*; by Alfonso de Cartagena, *a.* 1456 [R.]
		de Providentia by Alfonso de Cartagena, *a.* 1456 [R.]; by A. Canals (into Valencian) 15th cent. [R.]
		Moralia (extracts) by J. M. Cordero, 1555 [R.]; (four essays) by P. de la Panda [R.]
		(Tragedies):
		  Medea; *Thyestes*; *Troades*; *Hercules Furens* by A. de Vilaragut, *c.* 1400

Agamemnon (1559) of P. Mathieu and the *Hippolytus* of J. Yeuwain (1591) most deserve notice.

AUTHOR	ENGLISH	FRENCH
SENECA (THE YOUNGER) (cont.)		(Tragedies): (Complete) by P. Grognet, 1534 [B.N.] *Agamemnon* by C. Toutain, 1557 [B.N.]; by C. Duchat, 1561; by C. Brisset, 1590 [B.N.] *Hercules Furens* by C. Brisset, 1590 [B.N.] *Thyestes* by C. Brisset, 1590 [B.N.]
SOLINUS	*Collectanea* by A. Golding, 1587	—
STATIUS	—	—
SUETONIUS	—	*Vitae* anon., a. 1381; by G. Michel, 1541; by de la Boutière 1556
TACITUS	*Agricola*; *Historiae* by H. Savile, 1591 *Germania*; *Annales* by R. Greenway, 1598	*Opera* by Fauchet and La Planche, 1582 *Annals* I–IV by La Planche, 1555 *Agricola* by A. Cappel, 1574 *Germania* by B. de Vigenère, 1576
TERENTIUS*	*Comoediae* (complete) by R. Bernard, 1598 *Andria* by J. Rastell (?), c. 1520 by M. Kyffin (for schools), 1588	*Comoediae* by G. Rippe, c. 1466; by G. Cybile, c. 1470; by J. Bourlier, 1566 [B.N.] *Andria* by C. Estienne, 1541, and again 1542; anon., 1555; anon., 1558; P. Davantés, 1560 *Eunuchus* by J. Ericius, 1552; by P. Davantés, 1560; by J. A. de Baif, c. 1565 *Heautontimorumenos* by J. Ericius, 1552; by P. Davantés, 1560; by J. A. de Baif† (lost), c. 1565
VALERIUS FLACCUS	*Argonautica* by N. Whyte, 1565/6	—
VALERIUS MAXIMUS	—	*Memorabilia* by S. de Hesdin and N. de Gonnesse, 1485 [B.M.]
VEGETIUS, F. R.	*de Re Militari* by J. Sadler, 1572	*de Re Militari* by J. de Meung, c. 1300; paraphrase by Christine de Pisan in *Faittes d'Armes*, a. 1430; by N. Wolkyr, 1536

* Like Plautus, Terence became known as much through imitations as through translations. G. Cecchi's *I Dissimilli* was based on the *Adelphi*, his *Majana* on the *Heautontimorumenos*. B. Varchi's (1502–65) *La Suocera* was all but a translation of the *Hecyra*. All the eight comedies of the Spanish playwright B. de Torres

GERMAN	ITALIAN	SPANISH
—	*Collectanea* by V. Belprato, 1557	*Collectanea* by C. de las Casas, 1573
—	*Thebais* by E. de Valvasone, 1570	*Thebais* by Juan de Arjona and G. Morillo [R.]
Vitae by J. Vielfeld, 1536	*Vita Caesaris* by Pier Candido Decembrio, 1438 *Vitae* (complete) by P. Del Rosso, 1539—a paraphrase [A.]	*Vitae* by Pedro Mejia, 1547 [R.]; by J. Bartolomé, 1596 [R.]
Annales; *Historiae*; *Agricola*; *Germania* by Micyllus, 1535	*Annales et Historiae* anon., 1544 [A.]; by G. Dati, 1563 [A.]; (Ann. 1) by B. Davanzati, 1596 [A.] *Historiae* by Zaccharia, 1544 [A.]	*Annales*; *Historiae*; *Agricola*; *Germania* by Alamos de Barrientos, 1513; by P. Simón Abril, *a.* 1595 (not printed) [R.]
Comediae (complete) by Brant and Locker (?), 1499; by V. Boltz von Ruffach, 1539; by J. Bischoff, 1566 *Hecyra* anon., 14th cent. (not printed); by J. Muschler, 1535 *Andria* by H. Ham, 1535; by J. Agricola, 1543; by C. Stephani‡ (not printed), 1554; by Bebst, 1590 *Eunuchus* by H. Nythart, 1486; by P. Sperantius, 1516; by C. Stephani‡ (not printed), 1554; by J. Poner, 1586	*Comediae* by G. de Borgofranco, 1533 [A.]; by G. Fabrini, 1556 [A.] *Andria*; *Eunuchus* by G. Giustiniano, 1544 [A.] *Adelphi* by A. Lollio, 1554 [A.]; by F. Corte, 1554 [A.] *Heautontimorumenos* by G. B. Calderari, 1588	*Comediae* (complete) by P. Simón Abril, 1577 [B.M.]
—	—	—
Memorabilia by H. von Muegeln, 1369 (printed 1489); by P. Selbet, 1533	*Memorabilia* ptd. Bernardino da Lissone, 1504 [A.]; by G. Dati, 1539 [A.]	*Memorabilia* by U. de Urries (printed 1495) [B.M.], 1467 [P.]; by A. Canals (into Valencian) 15th cent. [R.]
de Re Militari by L. von Hohenwang, 1475 or 1476	*de Re Militari* by Gaetano da Posi, 1525 [A.]; by F. Ferrosi, 1551 [A.]	—

Naharo, which were composed between 1500 and 1520, were based on Terence. In France, P. de Larivey's *Les Jaloux* imitates the *Andria* and the *Eunuchus*. In Germany Hans Sachs imitated the *Eunuchus* (1568).

† Cited by Verdier.   ‡ A translation of the French version by C. Estienne?

AUTHOR	ENGLISH	FRENCH
VEGETIUS, P.	—	—
VERGILIUS	*Aeneis* by Gawain Douglas, 1513 (printed 1553); IV by the Earl of Surrey, 1554; II by the Earl of Surrey, 1557; I–VII by Thomas Phaer, 1558; VIII, IX by Thomas Phaer, 1562; X–XII by Thomas Twyne, 1573; I–IV by R. Stanyhurst, 1582 *Eclogae* I, II by W. Webbe, 1586; I–X by A. Fleming, 1589; II by A. Fraunce, 1591 *Georgica* I–IV by A. Fleming, 1589 (*Culex*) by E. Spenser, 1591	*Aeneis* (a paraphrase) anon., a. 1483 [B.M.]; I–XII by Octovien de Saint-Gelais, 1509; I–IV by Helisenne de Crenne, 1541; I, II by L. Des Masures, 1547; IV by J. Du Bellay, 1552; III, IV by L. Des Masures, 1554; V (extract) by J. Du Bellay, 1553; V–VIII by L. Des Masures, 1557; VIII–XII by L. Des Masures, 1567; I–IV anon., 1574; IV (extract) by T. de Bèze, 1576; I, IV, VI (extracts) by J. Peletier, 1581; I–XII by R. and A. d'Agneaux, 1582 [B.M.]; I–XII (extracts) by J. de La Jessée, 1583 *Eclogae* I–X by G. Michel, 1516; I by C. Marot, 1532; II anon., 1542; V by F. de Bez, 1548; II–X by R. Le Blanc, 1555 [B.M.]; I–X by P. Trédéhan, 1580; I–X by R. and A. d'Agneaux, 1582 [B.M.] *Georgica* I–IV by G. Michel, 1519 [B.M.]; I by J. Peletier, 1547; I–IV by R. Le Blanc, 1554 [L.]; I–IV by P. Trédéhan, 1580; I–IV by R. and A. d'Agneaux, 1582 [B.M.]

GERMAN	ITALIAN	SPANISH
—	*de Arte Veterinaria* anon., 1544	—
Eclogae VIII, x by A. Wernher, 1502; 1–x by A. Muling, 1513; 1–x by S. Riccius, *c.* 1590 *Aeneis* by T. Murner, 1515	*Aeneis* (Complete versions) by Atanagoras Graecus, 1476 [A.]; ptd. B. de Vitali, 1532 [A.]; by G. Vasio, 1539 [A.]; ed. L. Domenichi, 1556 [A.]; by A. Cerretani, 1560 [A.]; by L. Dolce (paraphrase), 1568 [B.M.]; by A. Caro, 1581 [B.M.]; by A. dell' Anguillara, 1584 [B.M.]; by H. Udine, 1597 [A.] (Partial versions) II (part) by Sperone Speroni, *c.* 1520 [A.]; XII anon., 1524 [A.]; II by Ippolito de Medeci, *a.* 1535 (printed 1538) [A.]; 1–VI by Bernardino Borghese, etc., 1536 [A.]; VI by G. Pollio, 1540 [A.]; by A. Piccolomini, *c.* 1540 [A.]; IV by B. de Carli, 1540 [A.]; VI by A. Guarnello, *c.* 1540 [A.]; VIII by G. Giustiniani, 1542 [A.]; IV by L. Martelli, *a.* 1543 (printed 1548) [A.]; 1–V by G. Zoppio, 1544 [A.]; XI by B. Daniello, 1545 [A.]; VII by G. Bertussi, 1546 [A.]; VII, VIII by A. Cerretani, *c.* 1550 [A.]; I by A. Guarnello, 1554 [A.]; VII, VIII by B. Bernardini, 1555 [A.]; VIII by L. Ghini, 1556 [A.]; IX by S. Minorhetti, 1556 [A.]; XII by P. Mani, 1556 [A.]; VI by M. V. Menni, 1558 [A.]; II by G.M.V., 1560 [A.]; IV by G. B. Philippi, 1562 [A.]; I by A. dell' Anguillara, 1564 [A.]; XII by L. Castile, 1564 [A.]; VI by C. Durante, 1566 [A.]; 1–VI by V. Menzi, 1567 [A.]; IV by N. d' Angeli, 1568 [A.]; IV by A. Schiappalaria, 1568 [A.]; VI by M. Garra, 1576 [A.]; IV by H. Udine, 1587 [A.] *Eclogae* (Complete versions) by B. Pulci, 1481 [A.]; by Fossa da Cremona, 1494 [A.]; by R. Corso, 1566 [A.]; by A. Lori, 1586 [A.]	*Aeneis* by Don Enrique d'Aragon, 1428 [P.] (later books lost); 1–XII by Hernandez de Velasco, 1555 [B.M.]; I, XII by C. de Mesa, *c.* 1600 [B.N.]; (Book II) by F. de las Natas, 1528 [R.] *Eclogae* (paraphrase) by F. de Encinas, 1492/6; (two eclogues) by Hernandez de Velasco, 1557 [R.]; (the tenth eclogue) by J. de Guzmán, 1580 [R.]; (selections) by Luís de León, *a.* 1591; (complete) by Fernandez de Idiaquez, 1574 [R.]; by C. de Mesa, 1600 [B.N.] *Georgica* by J. de Guzman, 1580 [R.]; by L. de León, *a.* 1591; by C. de Mesa, *c.* 1600 [B.N.]

AUTHOR	ENGLISH	FRENCH
VERGILIUS (*cont.*)		
VITRUVIUS	—	*de Architectura* (extracts) by D. de Sagredo, 1539 [B.M.] (complete) by J. Martin, 1572 [B.M.]

GERMAN	ITALIAN	SPANISH
	(Partial versions) v by Luttareo, 1525; vi by A. Conti (not ptd.) *c.* 1540	
	Georgica (Complete versions) by A. Nigrisoli, 1543; by B. Daniello, 1545 [A.] (Partial versions) iv by G. Rucellai (paraphrase), 1524 *Moretum* by A. Lollio, 1546	
de Architectura by J. Rivius, 1548	*de architectura* by C. Cesarino, 1521 [A.]; by G. Caporali, 1536 [A.]; by D. Barbaro, 1556 [A.]; by G. Rusconi, 1590 [A.]	—

INDEX

References are given for names of persons and places, for titles of books and poems written before 1600, for certain technical terms (mostly legal and rhetorical) and for a limited number of general topics. Book-titles are listed under the names of their authors, but where they occur in the text without the author being mentioned cross-references have been provided naming the title. No references have been given, however, for the titles of such classical works as are mentioned only in the Appendices, for titles of works written since 1600, or for the cross-references in Appendix I to the authorities in the bibliography on pp. 459–61.

Where there are several references, the most important are indicated by page numbers in heavy type.

DATE DUE

MAR 1 '67		
DEC 2 '68		
DEC 10 '68		
DEC 10 '69		
MAR 16 '70		
OCT 28 '71		
MAR 23 '72		
DEC 6 '72		
SE 29 '82		
GAYLORD		PRINTED IN U.S.A.